PRIVATE LIBERAL ARTS COLLEGES IN MINNESOTA:

Their History and Contributions

By MERRILL E. JARCHOW

Minnesota Historical Society • *St. Paul* • *1973*

Copyright, 1973 © by the Minnesota Historical Society, St. Paul
ISBN 0-87351-081-X

LIBRARY OF CONGRESS CATALOGING IN PUBLICATION DATA

Jarchow, Merrill E. 1910–
    Private liberal arts colleges in Minnesota.

    (Publications of the Minnesota Historical Society)
    Includes bibliographical references.
    1. Universities and colleges — Minnesota — History.
I. Title. II. Series: Minnesota Historical Society.
Publications.
LA310.5.J37   378.776   73-14951

Publications of the

MINNESOTA HISTORICAL SOCIETY

RUSSELL W. FRIDLEY

Editor and Director

JUNE DRENNING HOLMQUIST

Managing Editor

FOR OUR DAUGHTERS

Barbara and Susan

Acknowledgments

IN RECALLING the events incident to the completion of this volume, I discover that the memories crowding in on my mind are not of solitude and elusive phrases, but of happy associations with a host of extraordinary people, all of them encouraging and eager to be of help. If I became a pest at times, and I am certain I did, these individuals never exhibited that fact by even the slightest show of impatience or of irritation. It was my great good fortune to find on every campus not only materials vital for my book, but also bonuses in the form of valued new and renewed friendships. To all of these men and women, I extend a deep and enduring thank you. Lest I be guilty of seeming to assign priorities, I shall list my benefactors alphabetically by colleges and organizations.

At AUGSBURG COLLEGE: President Oscar A. Anderson; Dr. Carl H. Chrislock, professor of history; Miss Gerda Mortensen, professor emerita and former dean of women; Mrs. Theresa G. Haynes, former director of audio-visual services; Miss Avalon Okerson, former secretary to the president.

At BETHEL COLLEGE: President Carl H. Lundquist; David Guston, archivist; Dr. Roy C. Dalton, professor of history; Mrs. Florence A. Johnson, secretary to the president.

At CARLETON COLLEGE: The board of trustees; former President John W. Nason; President Howard R. Swearer; Frank I. Wright, vice president and treasurer; Donald H. Klinefelter, former registrar; C. Yale Pfoutz, business manager; Marvis R. Williams, comptroller; Jon M. Nicholson, associate director of admissions; Mrs. Ruthmary B. Penick, college archivist.

At CONCORDIA COLLEGE in Moorhead: President Joseph L. Knutson; Paul A. Thorson, director of public relations.

At CONCORDIA COLLEGE in St. Paul: Dr. Harold W. Otte, assistant to the president; Dr. Oswald B. Overn, professor emeritus of humanities; Kenneth P. Kaden, counselor and testing director; Earl P. Breuer, financial planning manager; Mrs. Omar F. Smith, secretary to the president.

At GUSTAVUS ADOLPHUS COLLEGE: Former President Edgar M. Carlson; President Frank R. Barth; Reynold E. Anderson, vice president for public relations and development; Dr. Doniver A. Lund, professor and chairman of the department of history.

At HAMLINE UNIVERSITY: Former President Paul H. Giddens; President Richard P. Bailey; Dean G. Trampe, director of admissions; the late Dr. Clarence W. Rife, professor emeritus of history; Dr. Arthur S. Williamson, professor emeritus of history; Mrs. Helen McCann White, alumna; Mrs. Lili E. Hassler, secretary to the president.

At MACALESTER COLLEGE: Former Presidents Harvey M. Rice and Arthur S. Flemming; John M. Dozier, vice president and treasurer; Dr. Edwin Kagin, professor emeritus of religion; Dr. Hugo W. Thompson, professor emeritus of philosophy; Dr. Otto T. Walter, professor emeritus of biology; James F. Holly, former librarian; Mrs. Helen M. Reinecke, senior administrative secretary to the president.

At the COLLEGE OF ST. BENEDICT: Former President Sister Mary Grell; President Stanley J. Idzerda; Sister Firmin Escher, former academic dean now director of planning and program development; Sister Nancy Hynes, director of public information; Sister Emmanuel Renner, professor of history; Mrs. Bernie D. Silvers, former secretary to the president; Marcia Halligan and Sister Vivian Major, alumnae.

At the COLLEGE OF ST. CATHERINE: Former Presidents Sister Eucharista Galvin, Sister Antonius Kennelly, Sister Antonine O'Brien, Sister Mary William Brady, and Sister Mary Edward Healy; President Sister Alberta Huber; Sister Teresa Toomey, professor emerita of history; Dr. Dwight W. Culver, professor of sociology; Sister Marie

Inez Johnson, professor of library science; Sister Elizabeth Delmore, former reference librarian; Mrs. Irene A. Gangl, library secretary; Marilyn Savelkoul, reader's assistance librarian and former student.

At ST. JOHN'S UNIVERSITY: Former President Father Colman J. Barry; the late Father Walter H. Reger, director of alumni activities; Father Christopher Bayer, archivist; Father Vincent G. Tegeder, professor and chairman of the department of history; Father Gervase J. Soukup, director of the budget; Father Benjamin J. Stein, associate librarian; Dr. Sylvester P. Theisen, professor of sociology; Dr. John E. Lange, former dean of arts and sciences; Mrs. Elaine C. Vogel, secretary to the president.

At ST. MARY'S COLLEGE: President Brother George Pahl; Brother J. Robert Lane, professor of history; Thomas J. Ruddy, vice president for college relations; William Crozier, chairman of the department of history; Brother J. Leo Northam, registrar; Miss Marilyn Dragowick, secretary to the president; Mrs. Barbara Williams, head librarian.

At ST. OLAF COLLEGE: Former President Clemens M. Granskou; President Sidney A. Rand; Dr. Albert E. Finholt, former vice president and dean of the college; Stanley L. Ness, vice president and treasurer; Inez A. Frayseth, former registrar; Dr. Clarence A. Clausen, professor emeritus of history; Dr. Gertrude M. Hilleboe, professor emerita of Latin and dean of women; the late Dr. Theodore Jorgenson, professor emeritus of Norwegian; Carl R. Swanson, director emeritus of admissions and dean of men; Dr. Howard C. Rose, former dean of academic affairs; Miss Solveig Steendal, secretary to the president.

At the COLLEGE OF ST. SCHOLASTICA: Former Presidents Sister Ann Edward Scanlon and Sister Mary Richard Boo; Sister Cabrini Beauvais, former member of the board of trustees; Harold D. Hultberg, vice president of financial affairs; Sister Margaret James Laughlin, registrar; Dr. Philip H. Richards, professor and chairman of the department of education; Mrs. Linda Novak Vukson, alumna.

At the COLLEGE OF SAINT TERESA: President Emerita Sister M. Camille Bowe; President Sister M. Joyce Rowland; Dean Emerita Sister M. Emmanuel Collins; Sister M. David Homan, former archivist and professor of history; Sister M. Bernadette Lies, professor emerita of home economics; Sister M. Lorraine McCarthy, director of public information; Sister M. Helen Barden, professor of tutorial languages; Miss Rose Mary Curtin, administrative assistant to the president.

At the COLLEGE OF ST. THOMAS: Former President James P. Shannon; President Reverend Monsignor Terrence J. Murphy; Dr. Robert P. Fogerty, professor and chairman of the department of history; the late Dr. J. Herman Schauinger, professor of history; Leonard J. Rogge, vice president for business affairs; Mrs. Delores Fladeboe, secretary to the executive assistant to the president and former secretary to Dr. Shannon; Mrs. Kathleen Boyd, secretary to the president.

LOUIS W. AND MAUD HILL FAMILY FOUNDATION: former President A. A. Heckman; Directors Harry L. Bratnober, Jr., W. John Driscoll, and Louis W. Hill, Jr., chairman of the board; former directors Francis D. Butler, the late Charles J. Curley, and the late Curtis C. Goodson; John D. Taylor, executive director.

At the MINNESOTA HIGHER EDUCATION COORDINATING COMMISSION: George B. Risty, assistant executive director for administrative services and student aids; Dr. Oria A. Brinkmeier, former director of educational resources planning; Dr. Frank H. Smith, former research associate.

At the MINNESOTA HISTORICAL SOCIETY: Russell W. Fridley, director and editor in chief; John J. Wood, deputy director; Lucile M. Kane, curator of manuscripts; Mrs. June D. Holmquist, managing editor of publications; James Taylor Dunn, former chief librarian; Mrs. Rhoda R. Gilman, assistant supervisor of educational services; Michael Brook, former reference librarian; Larry W. Oliver, accountant; Mrs. Patricia Harpole, assistant chief librarian; Mrs. Virginia L. Rahm and the late Mrs. Christina H. Jacobsen, editorial assistants.

At the MINNESOTA PRIVATE COLLEGE COUNCIL: Dr. Edgar M. Carlson, executive director.

At the MINNESOTA PRIVATE COLLEGE FUND: Bernard J. Kemper, executive director.

Although he did not live to see this study completed, Theodore C. Blegen, former dean of the graduate school at the University of Minnesota and former superintendent of the Minnesota Historical Society, gave me valuable encouragement and counsel during the early stages of the project—the last of innumerable favors this distinguished gentleman and scholar conferred on me during a friendship which spanned nearly four decades.

Mrs. Theresa H. Basquin, as she did for an earlier volume, deciphered my holographic scrawls and with impressive speed transformed them into pages of beautifully neat and errorless typing. My files of pertinent newspaper material attest to another of her contributions—that of conducting a highly efficient clipping service.

And then there is Ralph L. Henry, professor emeritus of English at Carleton College. Twice before I have attempted to relate the nature and extent of my indebtedness to him in the preparation of other books. I was not equal to the task then; I am not equal to it now. Only the other authors who have been privileged to benefit by the products of Ralph's keen eye, patient ear, facile pen, quick mind, and warm heart—and his alter ego, Mrs. Beth Henry—can fully appreciate the measure of help, comfort, and blessing bestowed on those of us fortunate enough to work with him. With words of appreciation being so inadequate, I can only hope that Ralph understands the extent and depth of my gratitude to him.

Far more than convention impels me to say thank you to my wife Doris. There are easier types to abide, I am sure, than preoccupied researchers.

Northfield, Minnesota

Merrill E. Jarchow

Preface

DOTTING the Minnesota landscape, from Winona and St. Peter in the south to Moorhead and Duluth in the north, are the campuses of sixteen private, accredited, four-year liberal arts colleges. These strikingly productive oases share a great deal in common — a deep drive to inspire and assist young people in attaining their highest potential, spiritually and socially, as well as intellectually, and to send out graduates whose lives will have a constructive impact. Yet, reflecting the varying traditions from which they sprang, these institutions exhibit a remarkable and enriching diversity.

The largest number are Catholic — four originally for women (St. Benedict, St. Catherine, St. Scholastica, and Saint Teresa), three for men (St. John's, St. Mary, St. Thomas) — a fact, however, which led to no rigid pattern of uniformity. Two of the seven (St. Thomas and St. Mary) began life as diocesan enterprises; one of these (St. Mary) is now operated by the Brothers of the Christian Schools. Three owe their existence to Benedictine endeavor (St. John's, St. Benedict, and St. Scholastica). The remaining two were founded by the St. Paul Province of the Sisters of St. Joseph of Carondelet (St. Catherine) and by the Sisters of the Third Order Regular of St. Francis of the Congregation of Our Lady of Lourdes, Rochester (Saint Teresa).

Five of the colleges are Lutheran — three of them Norwegian (Augsburg, St. Olaf, and Concordia in Moorhead), one Swedish (Gustavus Adolphus), and one German (Concordia in St. Paul). The oldest — older than the state itself — was conceived and nurtured by the Methodists (Hamline). The Congregationalists established one of the sixteen (Carleton) but soon left it largely to its own devices. The Presbyterians became foster parents to an educational orphan (Macalester) and then permitted it to languish and nearly die from malnutrition. The youngest of the group (Bethel) grew up as a Swedish Baptist college.

As these institutions possessed divergent national and denominational characteristics, they likewise varied in such matters as age, size, strength, wealth, and special emphasis. Taken as a whole, however, the sixteen institutions — through their programs, their staffs, and their students — have contributed substance, tone, and vitality beyond measure to the life of Minnesota and to that of many faraway places on the globe.

Without attempting a catalog or getting involved in a debate over which type of institution leaves the greatest impact on its undergraduates, we may note several of the major contributions. Until about 1950 at least half of all college students in the United States were enrolled in private institutions. The proportion in Minnesota was not this high; yet for many years anywhere from a third to a fourth of all the young people in the state's colleges and universities were attending those which were privately supported. The savings thus accruing to Minnesota taxpayers were scarcely inconsequential. Of greater significance were the effects on society — locally and at a distance — of the regular injections into its ranks of scores and later thousands of well-educated men and women, many of whom would play prominent leadership roles in a wide spectrum of fields from the arts and professions to government, business, and community life.

This achievement reached a high level in part because of the inherent capabilities of the individuals who chose to attend college. One cannot deny, however, that a substantial segment of the cause rested in another contribution of the sixteen institutions — their devotion to sound scholarship. There were times, of course, especially in their early days when the colleges had to sacrifice quality performance in order to serve the immediate needs of their constituencies. But even during such periods professors and presidents constantly proclaimed the virtues of scholarly attainment and sought to instill in the breasts of the unenlightened a passion for learning. Primacy was always placed on the traditional liberal arts curriculum, the studies which free the mind of man and prepare him to live humanely and responsibly in a changing world. Curricular histories further suggest that Minnesota colleges were not afraid of innovation and flexibility; indeed these characteristics constituted significant facets of their over-all contribution to higher learning in the 1880s as well as in the 1970s.

As the products of religious zeal, all of the colleges professed a strong Christian commitment, evidences of which were apparent in such common manifestations as required courses in theology, daily chapel services, and a host of rules governing personal behavior. Certain critics were prone to find in this institutional posture too much of piety and indoctrination to the neglect of matters properly academic; to such people it was a fact "that no school has ever succeeded in imposing anything but superstitions and prejudices." [1]

Vast numbers of other scholarly, creative, and intelligent persons over the years, however, have testified to an opposing opinion. For these one of the priceless attributes of the church-related college is and has been its attention to values and ultimate meanings, to attempts to deal with an individual as a whole and not merely as a mind. These men and women see no necessary conflict between such efforts and the concomitant provision of a course of study of quality and integrity. Of late the forces of secularism have cut deep crevices on all campuses, and traditional religious practices either have been dropped or altered. Nevertheless the private college in a multitude of ways—educating future clergy, preparing teachers, training students with a sense of social service — continues to further the goals resident in a religious community.

Also notable have been the institutions' roles as way stations for immigrants making the transition to a new land, as bearers of cultural, religious, and ethnic heritages from Europe and the eastern United States, and as folk centers. In these connections one conjures up sharp images of the various components that started schools in the state — of pioneer farmers, merchants, and ministers in Red Wing; of German settlers and Benedictine priests and nuns in Stearns County; of Swedes in Carver, St. Peter, and the Twin Cities; of Norwegians in the valleys of the Cannon and the Red rivers and in Minneapolis; of Yankees in Northfield; of Irish priests and Catholic sisters in St. Paul, Winona, and Duluth; of Scottish Presbyterian ministers and businessmen; and of Missouri Synod German pastors and laity. One thinks of choirs, church services, folk dances, concerts, and picnics which helped perpetuate the heritage of each college's ethnic group. Yet none of the institutions ever harbored the notion of becoming an alien enclave among its American neighbors. Rather assimilation into the life of the new land and enrichment of that life constituted the goals.

There were, of course, many other contributions: provision of an alternative to public education, one which emphasized concern for the individual as a whole along with instruction; the lives and services of dedicated personnel; beautiful buildings open to the use of noncollege groups; entertainment through athletic contests; pleasure and edification through drama, debates, concerts, lectures, and art exhibits.

Minnesota has been fortunate — more so than many states in the union — in having a sizable number of strong private colleges. The story of how they developed — of the idealism and dedication exemplified by certain presidents, professors, trustees, and laymen in the face of discouragement and lack of public interest — is one of the most heartening and attention-holding chapters in Minnesota history. Yet it is a saga which has not been systematically recorded. One leading college, for example, has not had its history written since 1910. Details about others must be gleaned from works dealing with all facets of the life and activity of several Catholic religious orders and congregations, the latest of which was published in 1956.

This neglect is by no means confined to Minnesota. A distinguished professor at Williams College in Massachusetts wrote in the early 1960s: "For some time now the general reader and the professional historian have had greater access to the history of almost any skirmish of the Civil War than they have had to the history of education in the United States." [2] Since that statement appeared, the bibliography of the latter field has received many new titles, from diatribes and polemics to filiopietistic rhapsodies and dispassionate histories. As the example of Minnesota reveals, however, there is plenty of work remaining for the historian interested in narrating and interpreting the story of higher learning in America, and the many crises afflicting the nation's colleges and universities during the 1960s and 1970s have lent a new urgency to the challenge.

This being the case, it was with both enthusiasm and apprehension at the formidable size of the task that I accepted the opportunity to prepare this history of private higher education in Minnesota. Although a product of public elementary and secondary schools in the state and of the University of Minnesota, and a onetime teacher there and at two public colleges in other states, I had spent two decades as a faculty member and administrator at Carleton College — whose history I had also coauthored. This background had convinced me of the necessity of maintaining in the United States a dual system of public and private education, each of which would both complement and challenge the other. I therefore undertook this assignment not only because the story to be told possesses great intrinsic interest, but also in the hope that publication of a general history of Minnesota's private liberal arts colleges will lead to a greater appreciation of what these institutions have meant in the past and can continue to mean in the future.

No method of relating the saga is entirely satisfactory. A certain organic unity could be achieved by developing a general outline and then giving it flesh and blood by attaching to it examples drawn from every campus under discussion. Such an approach, however, makes it difficult to capture any particular college's distinct and very real personality. This can be accomplished only by treating each institution separately, but this plan makes it almost impossible to portray the context within which the individual organizations developed and against which their actions take on understanding. To reduce the disadvantages inherent in both types of attack, I have attempted a combination of the two. General background and intercollegiate relationships are delineated in the introductions to the three main parts into which the study seemed naturally to divide: that embracing the second half of the nineteenth century, that from the days of McKinley to Pearl Harbor, and that covering the amazing decades between 1941 and 1970. College identities and distinctive qualities occupy the main body of the manuscript.

Within the confines of a single volume — even one as large as this — it was necessary to make certain arbitrary decisions. Discussion has been limited to the sixteen private, four-year, liberal arts colleges in Minnesota which belong to the Minnesota Private College Council and are fully accredited by the North Central Association of Colleges and Secondary Schools — those which after all confer by far the largest number of baccalaureate degrees in the state's private sector. The sweep of the study has been broad; more detailed treatments will have to be left to individual institutional histories. For ease of handling the stories have been told chronologically by presidential administrations; this method should not suggest that educational trends are coterminous with executive tenures. Strong presidents while in office, however, have largely determined the course of events in many institutions and left enduring imprints thereon long after retirement. I have made no attempt to produce either a muckraking treatise or a whitewash. For titillating vignettes of college life — tales of lecherous and self-serving professors, conniving faculty wives, and sinful students — readers are referred to the plentiful bookshelves of novels set in the academic world.

The author makes no claim that dwellers in the halls of ivy are paragons of virtue or pillars of wisdom and judgment — though many of these men and women have risen far above the ordinary. He harbors no doubt, however, regarding the paramount position of the constructive and the positive in the lives and influences of all the state's institutions of higher learning. The private liberal arts college has long been and still is a potent safeguard against the erosion of a strong free society.

Many persons and organizations made this book possible, as the list of acknowledgments testifies. I owe a special debt, however, to Dr. John W. Nason, former president of Carleton College, who first offered me the opportunity to tell this story, and to Carleton College, which co-operated in many ways to make the research and writing a pleasant and rewarding enterprise. To the directors and staff of the Louis W. and Maud Hill Family Foundation, whose contributions to the private college cause are legion and who financed three-fourths of this project, I offer my sincere gratitude. The other fourth was provided by the Athwin Foundation, and to that organization I also express a heartfelt thank you. I am grateful to the Minnesota Historical Society, with which I have had a rewarding association for more than four decades, and to its director, Russell W. Fridley, for that institution's part in initiating this study, in helping to raise the funds to publish it, and for seeing it through the press. The photographs which appear in these pages are from the vast collection in the Society's audio-visual library or from the files of the colleges shown. The book's design is the work of Alan Ominsky, the Society's production supervisor.

Northfield, Minnesota

Merrill E. Jarchow

Contents

PART I

*NINETEENTH CENTURY
BEGINNINGS*

1850–1900

1

Introduction: Part I — 1850–1900

WHEN SETTLERS by the thousands pushed into Minnesota Territory in the 1850s, they found not only a legislative blueprint for a full-blown school system reaching from the lowest level to the university, but also a climate of opinion favorable to the creation of such a system. The pioneer, who had usually attended at best only a few terms in a one-room school, generally brought with him a strong faith in the value of education. It was the ladder up which his children could reach heights of eminence and wealth that he could seldom hope to attain. In less than a decade after the territory was created in 1849, some seventy-two school districts were formed and scores of elementary schools erected. Public secondary schools did not exist, but their counterparts in the form of academies and seminaries supported by churches and private corporations cropped up rather frequently. All told over thirty of them were chartered by Minnesota's territorial legislatures between 1849 and 1858. Those at Chatfield, Monticello, and Wasioja were unusual in that they were coeducational. Many academies never got beyond the paper stage. The Panic of 1857 finished off some that did, but a few (like the Baldwin School in St. Paul and St. John's Seminary at Collegeville) persisted into post-Civil War days.[1]

The state university, though chartered in 1851, did not function as an institution of higher learning for nearly two decades. That fact, however, did not discourage other Minnesota promoters of education at the collegiate level. The country was on the march, and it must go forward on all fronts. "In this land of bogus towns and mad speculation," wrote a recent arrival in the territory in 1857, "universities are built on paper, with amazing facility. Every *city* has its university square, while the truth is, that there is scarcely the visible embryo of a university in the whole North-west. It is not only a ridiculous, but a wicked and lying humbug, to name every vacant plot of ground devoted to

education, or every *scheme* for getting up a school, a university." These words were written by a man who headed a Minnesota academy which in the spirit of the period had been chartered as a university. Perhaps he was merely attempting to discourage competition.[2]

Such words, of course, had little effect. Fledgling and paper colleges moved west in the three decades before the Civil War in step with the great migrations of people. Love of learning burned in the breast of many a pioneer, but more widespread, it would seem, were other passions — denominational rivalry, townsite pride, acquisitiveness, unabating optimism, a desire to keep young people at home — and all of these combined in a reckless scramble to outdo one's competitors in transforming a wilderness into bustling communities. As a result the remains of many colleges lay alongside the animal skeletons, broken wagon wheels, and other casualties on the trails west; over seven hundred of these institutions in the country at large gave up the ghost before 1860. In Minnesota Territory a number of "universities" — Lake Clinton, Cedar Valley, Fremont City, Hastings, and Hobart — were chartered but "existed only in the dreams of their sponsors."[3]

By 1860 the state of Minnesota, a sturdy two-year-old, had pulled out of the depths of financial depression, but its population of 170,000 was only about 20,000 larger than it had been when the panic struck three years earlier. Settlement was concentrated mainly along the St. Croix, Mississippi, and Minnesota rivers. Within a decade census takers would count some 440,000 Minnesotans, but again growth was uneven. The Civil War disrupted life for almost half of the ten-year period, while the Dakota Indian outbreak of 1862 added to the disturbed conditions of the times. The actual increase during the first half of the 1860s was approximately 78,000 people; in the second five years it rose about

189,000. Despite this growth and the beginning of railroad construction in the state, the 1860s were little more congenial to the development of higher education than had been the 1850s. The Morrill Federal Land Grant Act of 1862, granting public lands for the endowment of state universities, would release forces of change which would breathe new vigor into the country's corpus of higher learning. Three present-day private colleges in Minnesota — Gustavus Adolphus, Carleton, and Augsburg — trace their beginnings, feeble though they were, to Lutheran and Congregational activity during the 1860s. The oldest of them all, Hamline University, entered a period of dormancy in 1869, while the other product of the 1850s, St. John's, continued to carry on.[4]

In the early 1870s the state could claim a dozen municipalities, each having over 2,500 inhabitants. (There had been only three in 1860.) Except Duluth, all were south of Stillwater and east of Mankato, and all but two were on navigable waterways. By then, however, railroads were beginning to alter the picture. Between the latter part of 1870 and 1872, for example, St. Paul was connected by rail with Duluth, Breckenridge, and Sioux City, Iowa. New milling methods during the 1870s made Minneapolis the flour city and greatly stimulated the production of Minnesota spring wheat. The Panic of 1873, plus serious grasshopper infestations during the next few years, halted railroad construction for a time and slowed immigration. Nevertheless the state's population between 1870 and 1875 jumped from 439,706 to 597,279, while the amount of tilled land went up 74 per cent. The population increase was even more rapid in the second half of the decade, and the settlement of the prairie regions was well under way. In the older more stable section of the state some of the Scandinavian immigrants by this time felt able to support nascent collegiate institutions. Today's St. Olaf and Bethel colleges are the result. Developments among Catholics in the Rochester area beginning in 1877 would in time produce the College of Saint Teresa in Winona.[5]

Even so, as late as 1877 only 117 young people graduated from public high schools in Minnesota. (In that year the first high school graduating class in Northfield, for example, consisted of seven members.) Perhaps less than a fifth of the graduates were adequately prepared to enter upon college work. Not until 1878 did a state high school board come into existence and state aid for high schools become available. Whatever crisis existed in Minnesota education, it was not one of excessive numbers of young people demanding admission to colleges and universities. In the field of higher education the 1870s in the main were still years of preparation.[6]

From the 1870s until the depression of 1893, the tempo picked up. By 1890 the state's population had passed the one million mark, and the actual increase in numbers since 1880 — 529,510 — was the greatest for any decennial census period in Minnesota history. The northern coniferous zone of the state was still a wilderness, and settlement was sparse in the Red River Valley. Rural population, however, overspread the entire prairie and hardwood regions. Urbanization was gaining momentum and the frontier phase of Minnesota life was coming to a close. Three normal schools — Winona (1860), Mankato (1868), and St. Cloud (1869) — were in existence in the early 1880s, and a fourth at Moorhead would come along in 1888. These were essentially secondary educational institutions, but in 1882–83 Mankato began to enroll students beyond the twelfth grade. Public high schools were becoming more and more numerous, although their big surge would not occur until after 1900. The University of Minnesota with its colleges of liberal arts and mechanical arts (engineering) was showing steady growth, and in 1887 it would add an agricultural school in St. Paul.

Though Macalester College traces its roots to the Baldwin School of the 1850s, the institution really got off the ground in 1885. So, too, did St. Thomas College. St. Benedict's Academy at St. Joseph was incorporated in March, 1887, and from it would evolve the college of the same name. Somewhat less directly would arise the College of St. Scholastica in Duluth. In St. Paul in the mid-1880s more than a hundred young women boarders were attending St. Joseph's Academy, to which the College of St. Catherine traces its linage. Concordia College at Moorhead had its inception in 1891; Concordia in St. Paul came to life two years later.[7]

"To some . . . the last ten years of the nineteenth century were the springtime of life," wrote one commentator. "The land was full of sounds no longer heard: the hissing of lamps, the moans and shrieks of locomotive whistles, the clopping of horses' hoofs. . . . The decade of the 1890's marks a dividing line between that older, isolated America and the new urban society of our own times, the era of income taxes, big government, vast technology, restless minorities, and international horrors." For some it was the "Gay Nineties"; for others less fortunate it meant depression, labor strife, forty-five-cent wheat, bank failures, sweatshops, death in Cuba, and crucifixion on a "cross of gold."[8]

Minnesota was still two-thirds rural, but its urban

trend continued. Although the presence of iron ore deposits had long been known in the state, it was not until after the memorable discovery of the Mesabi Range in 1890 that the mining and shipping of iron ore became really big business, and the population of St. Louis County, with attendant needs for education, began to mount. It was in this decade that John D. Rockefeller, Andrew Carnegie, and James J. Hill entered the scene on the iron range and waxed even wealthier as a result. Some of their money would later find its way into the coffers of a number of Minnesota's private colleges. Except for the midyears of the decade, when economic depression slowed activity, lumbering and milling still flourished, while diversified farming and dairying were winning the contest with wheat. The state had a long way to go, but signs of its coming of age were apparent. The same could scarcely be said of its private colleges. With the exception of St. Mary's in Winona, however, all of them or their progenitors were in existence in varying degrees of strength and stages of development.[9]

On the national scene dynamic change was also the order of the day. Land-grant institutions, stressing the practical and nourished by federal largess under the Morrill Act, were both threat and challenge to privately supported denominational colleges emphasizing the traditional classical curriculum. Already in 1884, a New York professor who was one of a long line of prophets of doom would write: "I confess that I am unable to divine what is to be ultimately the position of Colleges which cannot become Universities and which will not be Gymnasia. I cannot see what reason they will have to exist. It will be largely a waste of capital to maintain them, and largely a waste of time to attend them. It is so now."[10]

If the good professor's vision was myopic, it was true that much was developing throughout diverse educational institutions which was foreign to the small, self-contained, private colleges that had been the backbone of the nation's system of higher education. The changes would eventually make an impact upon more traditional schools. As early as 1861 Yale, long known as a defender of elitist, classical education, awarded the first earned Ph.D. degrees in the United States. Whether merit badge or octopus, the doctorate and all it implied was here to stay. Fifteen years later Johns Hopkins University opened as a faculty-centered, graduate institution, patterned after German models with their emphasis on scientific inquiry and pure scholarship. Professors themselves by establishing a number of learned societies were foreshadowing a future time when loyalty to a discipline would supersede that

to an institution. The American Philological Society in 1869 and the American Chemical Society in 1877 had led the way. In the 1880s came the Modern Language Association (1883), the American Historical Association (1884), the American Economic Association (1885), the American Mathematical Society (1888), and the Geological Society of America (1888).[11]

Curriculums, so long dominated by classical models, found the demands of post-Civil War America increasingly insistent. The rise of science, the work of Darwin, the new psychology with its doctrine of individual differences — all these and more were knocking at the portals of the old sectarian college. The work of Charles William Eliot at Harvard beginning in 1869, Andrew Dickson White at Cornell also in 1869, and others was injecting a flexibility into the courses of study which would have delighted the likes of George Ticknor, James Marsh, Jacob Abbott, Francis Wayland, and similar prophets before their time. In the years from 1872 to 1885 subject requirements were abolished for all students at Harvard except freshmen, and even they had considerable freedom. While the elective principle had able critics and would in time provoke a reaction, it did, in the opinion of one astute observer of the academic world, "fashion an instrument that gave vitality to the American college at a time when its remoteness from society threatened the whole structure of American higher education with disaster."[12]

Before many years were to pass, these gathering forces would have immediate relevance for Minnesota's private colleges, born of the old classical tradition but growing up in an age of accelerating change and complexity. How their leaders responded to the challenges would determine to a large extent the colleges' vigor, even as the results of the response would reflect upon the wisdom, or lack thereof, of the educational theorists. For the time being, however, the problem of survival was usually paramount, leaving little leisure or inclination for experimentation or soul-searching. Each president was too busy recruiting students and faculty and pursuing the elusive dollar to engage long in discussions with his peers on the nature and function of the private college. Relations among the institutions were likely to be competitive rather than co-operative and to be confined largely to forensics and athletics.

Interestingly enough the impetus behind these forms of intercollegiate activity was more apt to be student-inspired than to spring from faculty or administrative action. Indeed the emergence of collegiate athletic competition was viewed with something less than universal enthusiasm by professors and presidents. Forensics and oratory, on the other hand, because of their long tradition and consistency with the collegiate ideal, were more ardently defended. A glance at the history of any one of Minnesota's colleges will indicate that some form of public-speaking activity appeared on campus early in the life of the institution. At Hamline, for example, a lyceum or debating group was organized in 1856, even before that Methodist institution had a college department. Among the topics discussed was: "That dancing, as practiced at balls, is fully compatible with true morality." The fact that dancing was debated in such a context suggests that the posture of the institution was not necessarily the same as that of its students. The popularity of oratory and debate, both with honored traditions in the American body politic, also indicates that the colleges' intellectual fare was not sufficiently stimulating to satisfy undergraduate appetites. Indeed it was this condition which gradually brought about, in response to student demands, a modification of the old classical curriculum as well as the rise of the extracurriculum in most nineteenth-century colleges.[13]

Intercollegiate forensic activity had to await the establishment of more colleges and increasing enrollments. Meanwhile intramural contests were carried on among the literary societies, those everpresent, Greek-named organizations whose popularity was unparalleled during the early years of most colleges' existence. These societies "in their debates, disputations, and literary exercises," as Frederick Rudolph has written, "imparted a tremendous vitality to the intellectual life of the colleges, creating a remarkable contrast to the ordinary classroom where the recitation of memorized portions of text was regarded as the ultimate intellectual exercise." Winners of these local contests were then entered in intercollegiate competition. As early as 1881 a senior man at Carleton won an oratorical contest between students of his college and representatives of the University of Minnesota. Somewhat later he took second prize at an interstate meet at Jackson, Illinois. When the word reached Carleton, a contemporary collegian wrote that "students here today have been crazy. . . . They have the flag up and tonight they had a big bonfire with an immense noise." Such was the zeal evoked by victory in public-speaking competitions in the late nineteenth century.[14]

By the 1890s a State Oratorical Association was in existence, and its contests, too, generated tremendous enthusiasm. Typical was the one held in the Congregational Church in Northfield on April 6, 1894. To transport the five hundred students who attended from Hamline, Macalester, and the university, a special train of ten coaches was necessary. Feeding the young people required the combined efforts of two local churches. The next morning students marched around Northfield "in good order," celebrating the victory of Carleton's Charles E. Burton with his oration on "The Chinaman in Future Civilization." Four years later in the same city a Hamline freshman won the state contest. This same lad's Fourth of July oration in Ortonville sometime earlier had so impressed Hamline's president that he gave the young man a full college scholarship. As a junior the same orator, in a rented dress suit, won an interstate contest. He was Thomas D. Schall, United States senator from Minnesota from 1924 to 1935. Participants frequently trained in the manner of dedicated boxers, while their supporters well into the 1920s celebrated victories with the parades and the fervor a later generation reserved for notable triumphs on the gridiron.[15]

Toward the end of the 1890s intercollegiate debate began its long career on the Minnesota scene. So highly was the activity regarded by faculties that academic credit was awarded to team members, as it was to winners in the state oratorical contests. Competition extended beyond Minnesota to colleges in neighboring states, and each victory occasioned raptures of joy and delight from fervid fans. Intramural debates also aroused much interest and generated considerable heat. As in oratory so in debate many leaders were given the experience, the confidence, and the facility with words that added to their effectiveness and contributed to their success in later years. Critics of that day suggested that debaters, required to argue both sides of a question, would suffer a loss of intellectual conviction, that they would become bloodless relativists, but those who felt truth could be best approached by a close scrutiny of all sides of an issue carried the day for some time to come.[16]

Great as was the popularity of forensics, its impact cannot be equated with that of athletics, intramural and intercollegiate. From the late nineteenth century onward after these contests became popular, campuses would never be quite the same again. In a sense the phenomenon was not new. As early as 1787 the Princeton University faculty banned a kind of hockey as "low and unbecoming gentlemen and scholars," as well as hazardous to health. During the mid-1820s, the outdoor gymnasium flourished on many campuses, but its day was brief. Hastening its decline was the Puritan view that one who whiled away his time on swings and parallel bars was pretty much of an idler or a good-for-nothing. By the time Minnesota received a large influx of settlers in the 1850s, German immigrants had introduced their Turnverein clubs, and gymnastics enjoyed another period of popularity in the United States. Students then sought facilities where they could develop their skills with rings, bars, and Indian clubs. Pleas for gymnasiums became frequent and insistent, although they were rarely granted in Minnesota in the early days. (Gustavus Adolphus in 1886 was an exception to the rule.) More common for a time was the use of nooks and crannies of regular buildings for gym purposes. But indoor exercise was apt to be more work than fun, and again a decline in general interest occurred. Unless some special impetus, such as competition or an audience were present, students were all too inclined to neglect both gymnastics and their own physical well-being.[17]

The outdoors, of course, always held allure: boating, swimming, hikes, and picnics in warm weather; sliding, skating, tobogganing, and sleighing in winter. While their development was sporadic and unstable for many years, organized team sports early appeared on college campuses. The most popular of these at first was baseball, which seems to have had its intercollegiate baptism in 1859 in a game between Amherst and Williams. Within a decade the Cincinnati Red Stockings were organized, and baseball was on its way to popularity the country over. In Minnesota St. John's had an organized team by 1873, though the playing field a few years earlier had been likened to "an angry porcupine's back." During the 1880s and early 1890s, Carleton competed against the local high school, Pillsbury Academy of Owatonna, three schools in Faribault — Shattuck, Seabury Seminary, and the Minnesota School for the Deaf — and the University of Minnesota. When the university's team arrived to play Carleton in the fall of 1882, the big city nine was "a motley crew composed of two or three university students, several black-balled professionals, a barber, and a few Minneapolis bummers." Standards were casual in the extreme. Unknown were paid coaches, eligibility requirements, or distinctions between preparatory and collegiate players. The long and cherished rivalry between Carleton and St. Olaf colleges appears to have begun with a baseball game on May 14, 1887. Four years later a Southern Minnesota Intercollegiate Baseball League, embracing the two Northfield colleges as well as Shattuck and Pillsbury, was started. Hamline's baseball history dates back at least to 1882. At Macalester a baseball team was organized on the day the institution opened in September, 1885; the players walked to neighboring St. Thomas

and gained a victory. At Gustavus baseball was introduced in 1895.[18]

In Minnesota, as in the United States, football was slower to catch on than baseball, but when it did, the results were little short of astounding. In the late 1870s lads at the new school on the hill in Northfield organized the "St. Olaf kickers" to engage "eleven picked kickers" from Carleton. The game was a sort of soccer similar to that played in 1869 between Princeton and Rutgers, which is usually credited with beginning intercollegiate football competition in the United States. It was not until the 1880s that the running style of play, adapted from Rugby, replaced the earlier kicking style. Carleton's first organized team, as opposed to "clubs," was formed in 1891, but its season consisted of only two games with Seabury Seminary. Gustavus students played a kind of football in 1893, but, as at other colleges, interest in the sport varied from year to year. Not until after 1900 did the number of games played increase, and then they were cut off altogether for a time. After five years of futile effort Hamline finally beat Macalester in football in 1898, and for some time thereafter the former enjoyed highly successful seasons. St. John's fielded its first eleven in 1900, losing two games to St. Cloud High School. Collegiate football in Minnesota could hardly be termed a rousing success by 1900, and before its heyday arrived it would fall on some bad times early in the present century.[19]

Track and field events had long enjoyed considerable popularity. Requiring few facilities, they were relatively easy to organize. Cinder, as opposed to dirt, tracks, for example, did not make their appearance until the turn of the century. In 1872 just four years after the New York Athletic Club held what is credited with being the first amateur track and field competition in the United States, Shattuck School conducted the initial organized track meet in Minnesota. The sport then gained growing popularity in the state's developing secondary schools and colleges. The University of Minnesota's first intercollegiate meet came in October, 1882, at the state fairgrounds against opponents Hamline and Carleton. A decade later the Minnesota Field and Track Association was formed by these last two institutions and Macalester. At its first meet on a private race track in St. Paul's Midway district Hamline's 60 points took the silver trophy. Carleton accumulated 48 points, while Macalester was blanked. The hundred-yard dash was won in a time of 10¾ seconds, the mile in 4 minutes and 57 seconds. A leap of 5 feet, ¹⁄₁₀ inch was first in the high jump, while the top pole vaulter could do no better than 8 feet, 8 inches. Even though these records are unimpressive by modern standards, track was well established on Minnesota campuses by 1900.[20]

Basketball, now so universal, had to await the building of gymnasiums before its popularity could rival that of other sports. Thus its development among the state's colleges forms a twentieth-century story.

In a sense college athletics just grew with little planning or design. Their inclusion as accepted members of the educational household, like their initial introduction, was due less to administrative policy based upon careful thought and planning than to student interest, effort, and pressure, with a faculty assist here and there. Typically, with but slight attention from college authorities, undergraduates would organize an athletic association for the purpose of arranging games and stimulating participation in them. When St. Olaf purchased twenty acres of land adjoining its campus in 1889, students cleared it and converted it into an athletic field. Two years later across town the Carleton freshman class,

furnishing "evidence . . . of its loyalty to the college athletics," built elevated seating, especially for "ladies," on the ball ground. Hamline had its Gentlemen's Committee for Outdoor Sports, and Gustavus its Centennial Athletic Association with "only tangential relationship to the faculty and the Board." And so it went. Traditionalists and "old fogies" might fear an erosion of academic values or the imminence of an "institute of physical culture," but they were helpless to halt a movement whose time had come. Gradually they chose to get into the act, and eligibility requirements, supervision of schedules, and all the rest of today's controls were the result. Again, however, that story belongs to the twentieth century.[21]

But despite the size and significance of all collegiate developments — athletic and otherwise — in the present century, much of what has transpired would be unintelligible without a look back into the decades which preceded it. There lie the taproots, the determinants, the bases, and much of the strength of today's colleges. Only by studying these origins can the present be understood.

2 HAMLINE UNIVERSITY

Minnesota's Oldest College

LIKE THE VAST MAJORITY of the 182 pre-Civil War institutions of higher learning still existing in the United States, Hamline University was the creation of a religious denomination. Its parental body was the Methodists, a group that had lagged behind the Congregationalists and the Presbyterians in establishing colleges and universities. In general, education for the masses rather than collegiate experience for the few had been the Methodist position. In an age of sectarian rivalry such as the nineteenth century, however, no one group could lie back and permit others to monopolize the lists. Furthermore it became increasingly apparent that collegiate training provided not only a continuing source of talented leadership, but also an avenue of upward mobility in a fluid society. Somewhat haltingly the Methodists got into the act, founding or acquiring some thirty-four ante-bellum institutions in various parts of the country.[1]

With its circuit rider system, its episcopal form of organization, and its appeal to emotion, Methodism was well suited to frontier conditions. As a result it had been active in the Minnesota region since 1837, when two preachers established a mission at Kaposia on the Mississippi River not far from present St. Paul. By 1854 the Minnesota mission district of the Wisconsin conference included preaching places at such widely separated sites as Sandy Lake, Benton County, St. Anthony, Traverse des Sioux, Shakopee, Red Wing, Stillwater, Marine, and St. Paul. Total membership was given as 289 and 16 probationers.[2]

This weak and dispersed organization, lacking an annual conference of its own, was called upon to support an institution of higher learning. Indeed as early as 1850 three ministers of the Wisconsin jurisdiction had attempted to launch one, the Reverend Chauncey Hobart having written unsuccessfully to men in the East and in Illinois for the necessary funds. To those approached Minnesota appeared

"too cold, too near the North Pole, fit only for savages, and hardly fit for them." No doubt discouraged but certainly not daunted, the men of God clung to their dream and bided their time. Then in January, 1854, the Reverend David Brooks sought the help of a prominent Methodist layman and member of the territorial council, William Pitt Murray, in securing a charter for an academy. That task, Murray indicated, could easily be handled under a general legislative act of the previous winter, but the good pastor should set his sights higher. He, Murray, would aid in obtaining a university charter![3]

"A denominational University in a frontier Territory, with a population of less than eighty thousand people — they generally without means — and the Methodist Episcopal Church without a membership sufficient to maintain a Conference, was a pleasantry the old veteran of the cross could not appreciate," was Murray's description of Brooks's reaction. Nevertheless, after consulting with other ministers who thought a university charter a great talking point and evidence of "the growth of Methodism out West," Murray went ahead, drafted a new bill, and had it introduced in the territorial legislature by General Isaac Van Etten. The bill became law on March 3, 1854. At a meeting in St. Paul in May, presided over by Brooks, the charter was read and approved. At subsequent meetings Brooks was elected first president of the board of trustees, and the location of the school was decided upon.[4]

It being the age of water transportation, the charter had specified only that the site be "on the Mississippi between St. Paul and Lake Pepin." A number of communities bid for the privilege of harboring the seat of learning — a pattern for similar contests in the future — but the choice of the trustees was Red Wing. A thriving village of about three hundred persons at the time, it "promised to be an important

7

center of population and business activity. Here came the commerce of the river from the East and South. From this place went ox-drawn covered wagons in long trains winding their way out of the valley and onto the prairies and westward.'' As events turned out the choice of location — dictated by the personal interests of certain trustees — did not prove a wise one.[5]

On July 12, 1854, upon recommendation of its executive committee the board of trustees decided to open a preparatory department as soon as arrangements could be made and a competent teacher hired. Late in the next month at the meeting of the Wisconsin conference, it was announced that Bishop Leonidas L. Hamline, whose name the newly chartered university bore, had donated for its benefit some $25,000 worth of real estate in New York and Chicago, and that other individuals had given a total of $10,000 more. It seems likely that Murray was responsible for naming the school in honor of the bishop, whom he had met in 1852 at Wesleyan Female College in Cincinnati. In any event the Hamline gift was a fine one, and probably made the difference between life and death for the bishop's namesake. The conference congratulated friends of education in Minnesota on so auspicious a beginning and resolved to send visitors to the new venture.[6]

Early in October the trustee executive committee announced that a principal for the preparatory school had been elected at a salary of $500 a year. The young man, English-born Jabez Brooks, the son of the Reverend David Brooks, was a Phi Beta Kappa graduate of Wesleyan University in Connecticut in the class of 1850. For a year he had taught mathematics at Lawrence College in Wisconsin. He was a happy choice, probably the most influential person in the life of Hamline during its Red Wing days, the author of a Greek textbook widely used both in the United States and Germany, and later a respected professor of Greek at the University of Minnesota.[7]

On November 16, 1854, although no building had been erected as yet, the preparatory department opened on the second floor of the Smith, Hoyt and Company store in Red Wing. The first academic year consisting of three terms as was usual in that period ended on August 15, 1855. The faculty numbered three, Brooks and two women associates, while a total of seventy-four students were in attendance for varying lengths of time. The academic subjects taught mainly by the principal covered a wide spectrum — English, philosophy, chemistry, astronomy, analysis, history, rhetoric, algebra, Latin, and French. The women offered

mainly painting, drawing, music, and ornamental work. Though the conference visiting committee reported that the initial year had been conducted ''with prudence, efficiency, and success,'' all these disciplines could hardly have been explored in depth.[8]

During the next two years, Hamline University continued as a preparatory school, although the challenge implicit in the second part of its name offered no room for complacency. In 1855 a three-story brick building, 81 by 37 feet, went up in what is now the heart of Red Wing on a block donated by the townsite proprietors. In it were housed a chapel, library, reading rooms, laboratories, recitation rooms, and student dormitory facilities. Enrollment mounted somewhat, with students from Minnesota, Michigan, Iowa, and Wisconsin in attendance. The curriculum was enriched by the addition of geometry, trigonometry, surveying, navigation, German, and botany. Tuition ranged from $4.00 to $6.00 a term. Instruction in piano, melodeon, or guitar cost $14 for the same period, whereas that in modern languages came to only $2.00. Board, including room and use of furniture, was $2.50 a week. Wood for heating was available at cost.[9]

Late in July, 1857, the Minnesota conference, organized in Hamline's new building the previous year, met in Winona, and among other business listened to the report of its university. Assets amounted to $37,202 and indebtedness to $8,076. Grasshopper infestations in 1855 and 1856 had undoubtedly added to the normal difficulties of fund raising, and Principal Brooks pleading ill health brought on by overwork had resigned. There was talk of relocation, resulting in the appointment of a committee to consider the matter. Signs of the approaching panic were in evidence, but the trustees determined to push forward. They voted to organize a college department and to elect a president in the person of the Reverend Benjamin F. Crary of Indiana. He was promised a salary of $800 a year plus $200 for moving expenses. Before becoming an itinerant preacher famed for his eloquence, he had taught school and been admitted to the bar. This last fact may explain why when classes resumed in August one of the innovations was a law department — the first law school in Minnesota — headed by a Red Wing attorney. At least two classes graduated in law, but by 1863 the subject had disappeared from the curriculum. Primary courses were still available, as were junior, middle, and senior classes in the preparatory department. There was also a Biblical department for ministers and a normal course for teachers. The regular college sequence had two divisions, one traditionally classical in nature, the other a ladies' course. Every effort certainly was being made to be all things to all people.[10]

Difficulties there were aplenty — shortage of funds, faculty changes, carping at President Crary in the public press and elsewhere, personal jealousies — but Hamline carried on. In June, 1859, it graduated a college class of only two members — a first in the new state of Minnesota. Of more than passing interest was the fact that the two recipients of the bachelor of arts degree were young women, daughters of a Methodist minister. Hamline was coeducational from the beginning, a contrast to the situation in most colleges of the day. Only a half dozen or so institutions of higher learning in the United States opened their classrooms to members of both sexes before the Civil War. Hamline's class of 1860 was also composed of two women, one of whom married the recently widowed President Crary that same year. The first man to receive a bachelor's degree in Minnesota was Levi N. Countryman, one of three Hamline graduates in 1861. Largely because of wartime conditions no other male achieved this distinction until 1865.[11]

On April 13, 1861, Governor Alexander Ramsey offered the secretary of war in Washington, D.C., 1,000 Minnesota volunteers for the Union Army — the first state offer to be made. Two evenings later at a meeting in Red Wing to enroll volunteers in Company F of the First Minnesota Regiment, the second man to enlist was a Hamline junior. By April 24 Countryman noted in his diary that his fellow scholars were "becoming unmanageable, and will enlist for war." In point of fact nearly every male student and three faculty members did enlist, with the result that more than one-fifth of the 104 members of Company F were former Hamline undergraduates. So gallant was the performance of these young collegians that the *St. Paul Daily Press* of August 7, 1861, carried a highly laudatory editorial entitled "Hamline University and the First Regiment." [12]

With its masculine contingent largely depleted, the university carried on as best it could. Beset by financial and family worries as well as criticism from jealous fellow preachers, Crary resigned the presidency in 1861 to become state superintendent of public instruction. Jabez Brooks, with health regained, then succeeded Crary in a most difficult position. With enrollment down and debt mounting, Brooks did double duty in the classroom, traveled the state soliciting funds, and used his own money to support his family. He was to find, along with many of his successors, that "the history of virtually every American college and university . . . has

been one long, repeated, often desperate, search for funds." Hamline's endowment brought in little money for current expenses, while low tuition charges (sometimes paid in produce rather than cash) kept operations on the brink of insolvency. By 1866 assets, consisting of five lots in Chicago, the university physical plant, equipment, and outstanding accounts, totaled $43,000. Liabilities came to $8,700. Church congregations were asked for help, but response was poor as they had their own problems. Creditors, recognizing the futility of the situation, liberally discounted their bills to no avail. When classes convened in the fall of 1868, only twenty-three students enrolled in the college department. Early the next year Brooks sent his resignation to the trustees, and in March, 1869, the last commencement in the Red Wing phase of the university's career was conducted.[13]

The trustees gave as their reasons for closing the institution the loss of students, financial embarrassment, and lack of interest by former supporters. Critics of the decision to close suggested that it was an unwise action and that there was "a question if all the truth was exposed." To them it appeared that pressure for removal to a different location plus personal politics were the basic reasons. The trustees' excuses, though not insignificant, the critics considered mere rationalizations. No doubt all these factors played their part. The conference had appointed a commission to study the removal of Hamline in 1868, and Faribault, St. Paul, Rochester, Winona, and Minneapolis expressed interest in securing the Methodist university. When the commission met at Faribault in May, 1870, to consider offers, at least three ranging up to $50,000 came in, but no action was taken. Later in the year the group concluded it would be inexpedient to entertain propositions for a bonus to be raised by taxation — not all nineteenth-century colleges were so squeamish — and that reliance from then on should be placed on individual endowments. It would be a decade before Hamline would again have a home.[14]

When operations ceased, the indebtedness was something over $5,000. The block on which the building stood was given to the city of Red Wing, which sold it and paid off the creditors. Whether Hamline could have survived in its original location is a moot question, but certainly the problem of finances was critical. Furthermore at least one device for raising money — the sale of scholarships — proved shortsighted and unwise. According to a trustee $10,000 was raised by selling scholarships (good for ten years) at $50 each. While the practice brought in money, it begged trouble for the future when the interest on each scholarship yielded only $3.00 to $4.00 instead of $30, the annual tuition rate. The more students there were on scholarships, the less ready cash was available to meet current expenses.[15]

Despite its failure to achieve an uninterrupted existence, Hamline had accomplished much of value at Red Wing. By today's standards emphasis on piety had been too great, and few current college presidents would proclaim with pride, as President Brooks did in December, 1867, that nearly 300 conversions had been attained among students. More impressive to later generations was Hamline's contribution of almost 200 teachers for the public schools and of eight ministers active in the conference when Brooks spoke. Intellectual activity had been stimulated and the lives of many people had been touched. Labor and sacrifice had been poured into the endeavor. At the final Red Wing commencement approximately 170 former students, of the 1,500 who had been in attendance, convened for a reunion marked by both sadness and joy. The fullness of time had not yet come for Hamline, but a spark had been ignited. It flickered for more than a decade, but it did not go out.[16]

Throughout the succeeding ten years Hamline sought to find a new home and to make a new start. In 1871 Rochester almost gained the plum, but inadequate finances proved an insurmountable stumbling block. During 1872 and 1873 the university's general outlook seemed to improve. With former Governor William R. Marshall, Senator Alexander Ramsey, and others giving generously toward a $27,000 purchase fund, it appeared that an eighty-acre tract of land on Snelling Avenue between St. Paul and Minneapolis would be available as a new site. Pledges of $35,000 to construct a building added encouragement. On July 7, 1873, the board of directors of the St. Paul Chamber of Commerce subscribed more than $800 toward the purchase of the land and voted to offer Hamline a home. The following day the trustees of the university accepted the location and committed themselves to establishing the institution on it. The campus would occupy the westerly seventeen acres of the tract on Snelling Avenue, Hamline's present site. Behind these few high lights, of course, lay many details, considerable maneuvering, and much hard work, especially by the Reverend James F. Chaffee, the Methodist conference's agent for its university and something of a controversial figure.[17]

Rebirth was not easy. In September, 1873, came the failure of the Philadelphia banking firm of Jay Cooke and Company, and the country sank into economic depression. Nevertheless in March, 1874,

work began on a building on the new site. Subscriptions for Hamline evaporated, however, and construction halted at the top of the second story. Likewise cash for purchase of the land was insufficient, and title to only forty acres was secured. A bond for a deed for the remaining amount was given. Meanwhile Chaffee became involved in a church dispute, and in September, 1874, the conference appointed the Reverend J. R. Creighton as Hamline's agent. Through his able efforts, a roof was put on the building. The land was subdivided into blocks, lots, and streets, and a number of purchasers were found for home sites. In 1876 the trustees elected the Reverend David C. John, principal of Mankato Normal School, as president of Hamline, and there was some hope of reopening the university that fall.[18]

Once again that perennial problem, lack of money, delayed realization of the hope, and John continued in his post at the Mankato institution. At the conference in 1878 a committee was appointed to work out a compromise with the previous owners of the land Hamline had acquired but not fully paid for. At the same time the Reverend John W. Stafford, a student in the school's Red Wing days, was appointed agent, and a plan to pay off the indebtedness was evolved. A number of factors then combined at long last — improving business conditions, Stafford's capability, the cumulative effect of past efforts — to bring about the desired result. In July, 1880, the five-story, steam-heated building was completed and dedicated, and on September 22 classes once more resumed at Hamline. In preparation Mrs. Stafford to save expense had washed windows and floors for days. Then when the big moment arrived, she and Stafford met the students at the railroad track (there was no depot as yet), "led them across the prairie, helped carry their luggage, filled their straw beds, and wiped away the tears from the cheeks of the young girls who had never been away from mother and home before." [19]

Although it was in operation again, Hamline was an academy rather than a university. Throughout the first year the college department enrolled only eighteen students — five freshmen and thirteen unclassified — while the preparatory division attracted ninety-five others spread among three classes. To Frank A. Cone, later a distinguished Methodist pastor who matriculated that year, the lone building was "like a forlorn castle in the midst of expanding fields of snow." Three or four houses occupied lots adjoining the campus, and farmhouses were visible here and there in the distance. Along with all his peers, Cone received a copy of the thirty-six rules in force, designed among other purposes to prevent intimate association between the sexes; "gentlemen and ladies" could not take walks or drives together or "seek opportunities for private conversation." But methods of evasion were discovered, causing one president to describe the institution as his "match factory." Other rules dealt with such matters as observance of study hours and the Sabbath, attendance at daily chapel, and noisy, boisterous behavior. No one could doubt that Hamline and other colleges of the day stood *in loco parentis*.[20]

The curriculum was still largely prescribed, but less time was devoted to the classics than formerly, the required study of Greek and Latin ending with the sophomore year. Modern languages, science, and literature were beginning to compete with the traditional subjects for student attention. The trend was still weak, but it was noticeable. Of special interest was Hamline's sortie into the field of medical education, which was conducted in those days mainly under the apprentice system. For 1880–81 the St. Paul Medical College became the "Medical Department of Hamline University" with a contemplated four-year course as the graduation requirement. Local doctors constituted the faculty, and some twenty students were enrolled. During the following year the department ceased to exist, probably because of insufficient funds, but it had represented an imaginative and forward-looking experiment.[21]

In 1881–82 the college department boasted three sophomores and nine freshmen; in addition there were 93 in the preparatory division and 28 "irregulars." Ladies' Hall with rooms for 60 to 70 girls, later renamed Goheen Hall, went up in 1882. Board for women in its dining hall cost $2.25 a week; for men because they ate more it was $2.50. Tea, coffee, or milk was 25 cents extra. Early in February, 1883, the main building burned to the ground. The telegram to the St. Paul fire department succeeded in bringing help only in time to view the ruins. Although inadequately insured, Hamline survived this most recent blow by utilizing facilities in the new Ladies' Hall and those in private homes nearby. In the spring a new building was started, but President John had had enough; he resigned to take a pastorate in Winona.[22]

The trustees were faced then with what is perhaps their most important function in the operation of an educational institution (giving money notwithstanding) — finding a new president. Fortunately the Minnesota bishop, Cyrus D. Foss, while heading Wesleyan of Connecticut had heard of the success of the young principal of Genesee Wesleyan Seminary in New York. That man, Canadian-born, a graduate of Victoria College in Ontario, and a Methodist minister, was George Henry Bridgman. Upon the bishop's recommendation, the forty-two-year-old Bridgman was elected president of Hamline. It was a fortunate day for the college-called-university. Its new president would remain at the helm until 1912 and earn the title "essential creator of Hamline."[23]

When he arrived in August, 1883, the locality was a village with a post office named Hamline (it would be annexed to St. Paul in 1885). There were twenty-four college undergraduates, ninety preparatory and special students, and a faculty of nine, four of whom taught music and elocution. Ladies' Hall was surrounded by fields of corn, wheat, oats, and potatoes, and the new University Hall was under construction. Bridgman had just one rule for his students — "to be ladies and gentlemen," and he consigned the rules pamphlet to "innocuous desuetude." He taught such subjects as rhetoric, logic, and Christian evidences, and opened "new vistas in the field of fiction and poetry" for such wide-eyed learners as young Frank Cone. He emphasized excellence of scholarship and the importance of a well-trained faculty. Fortunately, like so many professors of the period, several Hamline teachers embodied qualities of refinement, integrity, and sincerity, possessed broad intellectual interests on a solid classical foundation, and gave decades of devoted service to the institution.[24]

Almost immediately Bridgman found that money raising would be a never-ending burden, one which would be time consuming and which he would have to shoulder largely alone. Handsome and dignified, an excellent speaker, he became a familiar and popular figure on many rostrums and in many pulpits as he went about telling the Hamline story and beating the bushes for students. A hard worker, who was not personally ambitious, he told his hearers: "I want the central thought of this university to be that Christianity is a life; not a creed, not a ceremony, not a profession, but a daily life." Harassed, worried, and hardly ever at home, he made headway surely if slowly. In 1886 a president's house was built which became the center for much college entertaining. The next year Science Hall, a large three-story structure, adorned the campus as symbol and substance of curricular advance.[25]

By the late 1880s and early 1890s a spirit of optimism pervaded Hamline. Its board of trustees, representing wealthy business interests especially in Minneapolis and Winona, reflected the skill and success with which President Bridgman was promoting the welfare of his institution. The aid, financial and otherwise, which board member and wealthy lumberman Matthew G. Norton of Winona bestowed on Hamline was paralleled by similar bounties showered on rival Carleton by Norton's partner, William H. Laird. By 1893 Leonidas Merritt of Duluth, one of the seven brothers of Mesabi Iron Range fame, would join the board and give promise of providing significant additions to the endowment fund (it was $232,000 in 1889). Collegiate enrollment was 75 in 1889; that in the preparatory department 120. Indeed it was considered "quite the thing" to enroll at Hamline. The faculty, despite what seem today to be low salaries, appeared to live well. Most of them had made at least one trip to Europe. When the World's Fair opened in Chicago in 1893, Hamline had an exhibit there.[26]

Truly Hamline was on the march. Students prided themselves on their advanced and liberal outlook. Women were even permitted to deliver orations in public, and Professor Henry L. Osborn began to lecture on the emotionally charged theory of evolution. Chapel attendance was no longer mandatory, and *sub rosa* dancing seems not to have been unknown. The cultural offerings and other diversions of downtown became more readily accessible in the fall of 1891 when interurban electric streetcar service became available on Snelling Avenue. Students could then ride to either St. Paul or Minneapolis for a fare of five cents. By the middle of the decade the Great Northern depot and the post office of the Hamline settlement were only memories. Other vestiges of the past, however, were very much alive. Student-run literary societies were still in their heyday, and the half-hour noontime prayer meetings in Old Main largely managed by students, where one could belt out melodic, old-time Methodist hymns, had another quarter century of popularity ahead of them. The first yearbook, the *Liner*, made its appearance in 1893. The library was closed mornings until 1895, but its collection was on the increase.[27]

Then came the Panic of 1893. Retrenchment and borrowing became necessary, the hoped-for Merritt grant of sizable proportions evaporated, and the faculty suffered salary cuts widespread in all colleges of the day. Little more was heard of European tours or fancy parties. There developed rather a heightened sense of social concern, of increased interest in such groups as the YMCA and YWCA. Students, faculty, and administration drew closer together in a common endeavor. Curriculum matters and forensics tended to supersede more frivolous pastimes. As the country pulled out of the depression, President Bridgman, by then at the peak of his popularity, almost singlehandedly raised the money necessary to pay off the institution's mortgage of $35,000. From that friend of small denominational colleges, James J. Hill, came $20,000 of the necessary amount; from others, Methodists and non-Methodists alike, the president secured the remainder. Even the Spanish-American War then in progress, in which some twenty students enlisted, failed to detract appreciably from the joy induced by Bridgman's successful campaign for funds.[28]

Despite financial stringency, the campus remained a busy and exciting place. Enrollments in the collegiate department mounted steadily to two hundred in 1900, while those in the preparatory division waned to sixty-nine that year. President Bridgman brought a constant procession of stimulating speakers to the chapel platform. When Governor William McKinley of Ohio spoke in April, 1894, Governor Knute Nelson of Minnesota and the mayor of Minneapolis also appeared on the rostrum. Curricular changes in general were not dramatic, but such innovations as sociology and the "New Psychology" were getting a foot in the classroom door. A forerunner of the future department of education could be found in the noncredit classes in "Pedagogics" given seniors. Plans were laid for starting a divinity school, but they never got off the ground. The biggest innovation came late in 1895 when the Minneapolis College of Physicians and Surgeons, founded in 1883, was acquired and renamed the Hamline College of Medicine. By 1899, when it conferred ten M.D. degrees, some 125 students, including several women, were enrolled in the medical college's four-year course. In 1908 no longer able to meet expenses through student fees as it had in the past, the college joined the University of Minnesota. While it was a part of Hamline, however, the medical school had graduated most of its 288 alumni of whom 20 were women.[29]

As the nineteenth century was ending, Hamline's regular senior class numbered 34. All told 263 individuals had completed the college course and earned their degrees by June, 1900. Typically, teaching was far and away the most frequent occupation engaged in by the alumni, but other professions, especially medicine, law, and the ministry, were also represented. Nine of the group went on to graduate schools and received Ph.D. degrees; three became college presidents; one headed a surgical clinic; one became attorney general of New York; another was elected to Congress. Others became missionaries, directors of teachers' training schools, state legislators, deans of women, homemakers, and substantial members of their communities.[30]

3
ST. JOHN'S UNIVERSITY

Benedictine Education for Men

CATHOLIC COLLEGES IN THE UNITED STATES, as Edward Wakin has pointed out, have developed as distinctive responses "to a variety of local situations," rather than as the result of official American church policy. Furthermore these institutions, most of which were founded by religious orders, have been traditionally segregated by sexes with men's colleges generally antedating those for women. In Minnesota these characteristics have been typified by the seven, existent, accredited, four-year colleges bearing the Catholic seal. Three, including the two oldest, were established for men, the others for women. Only one (St. Thomas) remains a diocesan enterprise, although two began in that manner. Separate incorporation of Minnesota's Catholic colleges has been a fairly recent development, but the relationships between the new legal entities and their parental orders have continued to be strong and close.[1]

It is fitting that St. John's University at Collegeville, the oldest Minnesota institution of higher learning with an unbroken existence, should in turn be able to trace its own roots back to a more distant past. In the world-famous Benedictine monasteries of Monte Cassino in sixth century Italy and Metten in Bavaria established in the days of the Emperor Charlemagne, St. John's finds its spiritual parentage, its strength, and much of relevance for coping with current conditions. It was from Metten that a young priest, Boniface Wimmer, led a group of students and laborers to western Pennsylvania in 1846–47 to plant a monastery to be called St. Vincent's, and to establish a school. Within less than a decade he would be appointed president of the newly created American Cassinese Congregation of Benedictines and named abbot of the monastery.[2]

By the mid-1850s a large German-born population had settled in Minnesota and were in need of spiritual guidance. As Wimmer wrote his benefactor, ex-King Ludwig of Bavaria: "Without doubt many of our Catholic countrymen [in Minnesota], as elsewhere, will succumb to the Methodist sect if they do not soon receive spiritual leaders and protectors." Others, including Bishop Joseph Cretin of the St. Paul diocese, shared this concern, and the latter, upon advice from Bavaria, appealed to St. Vincent's for aid. Needless to say the plea was warmly received by Abbot Wimmer. The various disparate developments were beginning to mesh.[3]

On April 5, 1856, Prior Demetrius di Marogna, two young clerics, and two Benedictine brothers left Pittsburgh by boat for the journey via the Ohio and Mississippi rivers to St. Paul, arriving on May 2. Despite urging to remain in the capital city, they decided to hold to their original plan and continue to St. Cloud, where their arrival brought great joy to the substantial German Catholic population. A crude monastery named St. John's was soon established, but visions of a permanent one in a suitable setting were kept ever in mind. When Wimmer visited St. John's in October, 1856, the two clerics, by then ordained, took him to view some land west of St. Cloud which they felt would be the ideal spot. The abbot agreed, and that winter three of the brothers lived in claim shanties on what is now the beautiful site of St. John's Abbey and University.[4]

In keeping with tradition schools were started by the Benedictines in St. Cloud and nearby St. Joseph, but there were bigger plans in the mind of Prior Demetrius. It was his desire "to begin at once a liberal arts seminary program for training native vocations." To this end a St. Cloud representative introduced in the territorial legislature on January 22, 1857, a petition for a charter for St. John's Seminary. Although there was considerable opposition to granting legal status to a Catholic educational venture and much maneuvering in the legislative body, the bill finally passed and gained the governor's signature on March 6, 1857. It would be another eight months, however, before a new prior (Demetrius took a pastorate in St. Paul) could start the seminary and college.[5]

The beginnings of the seminary on November 10, 1857, were so modest as to escape public attention. Five young men moved in with the monks in their simple frame monastery, submitted themselves to strict discipline, and took up studies reminiscent of the seven liberal arts of medieval times. At first the mode of living was hard to take, but the young men adjusted and even found, as one student wrote: "Such regularity and punctuality inspired us with love and awe." Though mainly a seminary, St. John's also provided from its early years a "higher education" for young men who took up secular pursuits. European in nature and background, the infant institution, like most Catholic "colleges" of the period and most non-Catholic ones for that matter, was more high school than college. That it survived and never ceased operations was a tribute to its Benedictine parents. For a time in 1858–59 because of the uncertainties of land tenure, the community moved to a log structure at St. Joseph; there would be other moves later, but finally a permanent home would be found.[6]

The early years of the 1860s were understandably trying. While the Civil War left the monks relatively untouched, the Sioux Uprising of 1862 in Minnesota posed a nearby and immediate threat. Then other problems — drawn-out land litigation, talk of removing the school to the St. Paul or Shakopee areas, status of the priory, internal frictions — kept existence precarious and the future uncertain. Thus in the spring of 1864, five years after their return from St. Joseph to the St. Cloud location, the Benedictines and students again gathered up their few worldly goods and headed for the scenic region of lakes and woods west of St. Joseph where claims had been staked in 1856. Purchase of the land had been made possible by funds sent from Bavaria. On their own land the monks erected a two-story frame building which served both as monastery and school until late 1866. Then a fourth and final move took the community to a new stone structure, the first of the monastic buildings on the present location on the shores of a beautiful lake called by the Indians and later generations Sagatagan. That same summer the priory was advanced to abbey status by Pope Pius IX.[7]

For the next several years, with increasing immigration and a shortage of priests posing an ever-present problem, the Benedictines gave top priority to the strengthening of their seminary. Encouraged by the promise of an annual stipend from Bavaria, the abbot in the spring of 1868 began

construction of an urgently needed educational building. Partially ready for occupancy in the fall, the structure of homemade bricks provided a student dining room, study halls, classrooms, and dormitory facilities. The stone building then became strictly a monastery. By the end of the 1860s enrollment had inched up to over eighty, and in spite of outstanding debts another addition to the physical plant had become necessary. Known as the middle or main building, four stories high and of local brick, it was occupied in the fall of 1871.[8]

Throughout this period St. John's College, as it was usually called, offered work on elementary and more advanced levels as well as a theological course. In the elementary division students pursued the three R's and catechism and were permitted to proceed as rapidly as they were able. The so-called collegiate or classical course consisted of six years of work in the European style, that of theology required three years. In each case the traditional curriculum was modified somewhat in response to conditions and needs in the frontier environment. For example, the need for priests resulted in 1868 in the establishment of a sequence in the seminary department for students planning to become members of the diocesan clergy rather than of the Benedictine order. The faculty consisting mainly of monks "had a cosmopolitan character quite distinctive for the West of the 1860's," and it taught a student body only about five times its own size. Recognizing the quality of the work done at St. John's, the legislature in March, 1869, authorized the institution to issue college and university degrees and academic diplomas. First use of the privilege was made on June 24, 1870, when one master of arts and five bachelor of arts degrees were conferred.[9]

Armed with authority to confer collegiate degrees (though its classical course of higher level studies was only a three-year program), St. John's continued to grow slowly throughout the 1870s. By 1875 when its abbot, Rupert Seidenbusch, became first bishop of the Vicariate of Northern Minnesota — a distinct honor for the Benedictines — enrollment had reached 130. The number of faculty stood at 22, including clerics and seminarians. A department, called in true booster style the Commercial College, was organized in 1872. Its three-year course in business and bookkeeping was designed to provide young men, some of whom were immigrants unable to read or write English, with the skills needed to take their places in the business communities of Minnesota. The course possessed strong appeal, attracting students from a wide area. In 1873 a scientific course, omitting Latin and Greek, first made its appearance, a nod to reality if not a reflection of developments in the main stream of secular education.[10]

Succeeding Father Rupert as abbot was Alexius Edelbrock, one of the five original students when the seminary opened in 1857 and its president since 1873. Inheriting a cash balance of $277.49 and a debt of $30,000 incurred from the building projects, the energetic young leader plunged into his many-fronted task with a zeal characterized by one of his favorite expressions: "Put on all steam the boiler is capable of holding." By a variety of means — traveling to the East for money, refinancing debts, economizing, begging, borrowing, and selling land — he improved the abbey's financial standing. He built an abbey church and arranged to have a post office named Collegeville established on monastery land. Indeed Abbot Alexius was sometimes carried away in his vigorous efforts. In June, 1879, for example, with permission from Rome three monks were granted doctorates in sacred theology by St. John's. This action by an institution scarcely two decades old invited considerable sarcasm and ridicule, but it was indicative of Alexius' eagerness to enhance the reputation of his college. It would not be the last time his enthusiasm outdistanced his judgment.[11]

By the early 1880s, though long referred to as St. John's College, the Benedictine school was still officially a seminary. Characteristically the abbot determined to provide his educational pride and joy with a name befitting his conception of its status. With the help of a state senator from St. Cloud, the title of "St. John's Seminary" in the original charter became in February, 1883, by action of the legislature and the governor, "St. John's University." Scorn again was directed at Alexius for his unrealistic inflation of academic nomenclature, but Abbot Wimmer wrote: "I congratulate you on the grade of University to which your College has been raised. Always go on! Must I style you now *Rector Magnificus* of St. John's University? Minnesota flourishes, but always as elsewhere through hard work."[12]

Perhaps in the hope of justifying the new name, Alexius by 1883 had added three-year programs in law and medicine to the courses already existing. Both bachelor's and master's degrees were regularly conferred and, if the catalog was correct, St. John's had "passed the days of its infancy" and was "rapidly approaching a bright and glorious future." But St. John's neither then nor now had a corner on such examples of self-delusion. These grandiose expressions seem to reflect a chronic malaise in the academic world. Presumably they are supposed to

be good for recruitment and public relations, if not for campus morale. Another of the abbot's ventures was the opening on January 1, 1885, of an industrial school for Indian boys. Housed in the original stone building, the school was bred of a noble ideal, but for a variety of reasons it was neither long-lived nor a resounding success.[13]

Still St. John's progressed under Alexius' leadership, as did most of his enterprises. He labored unceasingly to build up the school and raise the level of its performance. He urged constantly the use of English instead of German by monks and students alike; in his Americanization endeavors he went so far as to discontinue the serving of beer to Johnnies at certain school functions. By adding three wings to the four contiguous buildings, he doubled their capacity. Part of the addition was occupied in 1885. By the next year the institution's massive quadrangle "formed one of the largest continuous structures in the state." With accommodations for six hundred persons, it had at least twice as much room as was then needed, but Alexius' eye was on the future. Today the complex is still imposing. An alumni association was organized in 1882, and a student monthly paper called the *St. John's Record* appeared in 1888, its twelve pages filled with news notes, editorials, essays, current events, and book reviews. Enrollment in 1883–84 was slightly over two hundred; by 1891 it would approximate three hundred — of whom fifty were Indian boys and thirty-three were seminarians. In these years, as in every year, the Benedictines provided board, room, tuition, and even clothes for a sizable number of lads who otherwise would have been unable to attend St. John's.[14]

But some of the abbot's policies had aroused opposition in the community, while hard work and constant travel had taken their toll of his health. In November, 1889, after much soul-searching, he resigned. His successor, Father Bernard Locnikar, was far different in temperament, a man of the cloister, more interested in proper attention to liturgy and the stimulation of religious spirit than in expansive operations and building projects. Never strong, he began to fail in health in 1894. In June of that year a tornado did extensive damage to St. John's, although the gigantic main quadrangle withstood the fury of the storm. Losses amounted to between $60,000 and $70,000. The experience was a severe shock to Bernard who was certain that the destruction had been visited upon the community by God because of the dissension which had caused Alexius to resign. On November 7 at age forty-six Bernard died. During his short term of office, he "had all that he could do to keep running what his predecessor had built up" without attempting to initiate additional endeavors.[15]

The new abbot, who would serve for twenty-seven years, was Father Peter Engel whose monastic life had been spent in educational and administrative work. A student at St. John's from 1869 to 1874, he went the following year to the novitiate at St. Vincent's, where he had an opportunity to study physics and chemistry. Upon his return to St. John's in the fall of 1875, he taught some classes in addition to studying philosophy, dogmatic theology, and church history. His ordination to the priesthood occurred in August, 1879. Thereafter he "taught philosophy, physics, chemistry and, off and on, Latin, Greek, Evidences of Religion, Algebra, Geometry and Astronomy." For much of the period he was also director of studies. Well-loved, he represented a synthesis of the best that had preceded him, together with an awareness of developments in the contemporary society in which he lived.[16]

Considering his background, it was natural that Abbot Peter should take a greater interest in education than had any of his predecessors. Despite new responsibilities he continued his own studies and, like many another professor turned president, tried for a time to combine teaching (in his case physics) and administration. Moreover he was eager to have his faculty keep pace with the best current practices. No longer could a professor teach every course listed in the catalog and do an adequate, let alone an outstanding, job. Thus in 1898 Peter sent Father Anselm Ortmann to Johns Hopkins to do graduate work in physics, the first member of the community to take advanced study "at a recognized secular university." Other Benedictines soon enrolled in the graduate schools of the University of Minnesota and Columbia for work in chemistry, zoology, English, and mathematics. Two doctorates, one in English and one in theology, and a master's degree in history were earned at Catholic University of America. Five priests received doctorates at the International Benedictine College of Sant'Anselmo in Rome, and two others were sent to Conception Abbey in Mis-

souri to study the Gregorian chant. Upon their return these men raised the standards of performance in classroom, laboratory, and choir loft. They also found time to do research and to publish.[17]

As would be expected, Abbot Peter also kept a constant eye on the curriculum to ensure that it was in accord with modern developments. Thus when the first meeting of American Catholic colleges was held in Chicago in April, 1899, he sent one of the monks to represent St. John's. At the conference much thought and discussion were focused "on ways to unify and improve college courses as distinct from academy or high school curricula, which a large majority of Catholic educational institutions taught together in an indeterminate program." Subsequently in the classical course at Collegeville, the preparatory department was clearly separated from the college division and the latter's four-year sequence. About the same time the appellations freshman, sophomore, junior, and senior appear to have come into use to designate the collegians. Meanwhile the scientific and seminary programs were strengthened and the commercial department continued.[18]

As Father Colman J. Barry put it: "The pioneer days were over; the 'brick and mortar' era was slowly receding, and the labors of the first fifty years had begun to take effect." Yet regarding the university, it is well to keep in mind that most students were still registered in subcollegiate classes and that total enrollment in all courses in 1896 was only 234. From 1870 to 1892 the vast majority of alumni were men who had completed the commercial course, 366 master of accounts degrees having been conferred compared to 25 bachelor of arts and 24 bachelor of philosophy degrees. Only six bachelor of arts and 22 philosophy baccalaureates were earned in the entire decade of the 1890s. The surrounding area so far was not sufficiently developed to support a large college population, but time would alter that condition. When the change came, the Benedictines would make their own characteristic response to it.[19]

4 GUSTAVUS ADOLPHUS COLLEGE

A Swedish Lutheran Institution

IN THE YEARS following its admission to the union in 1858 Minnesota felt increasingly the effects of Scandinavian immigration. From a mere 3,178 in 1860 the number of Swedish-born settlers in the North Star State grew to 20,948 a decade later. The size of the Norwegian contingent was considerably larger. Although usually assimilated into the public schools, these newcomers understandably wished to perpetuate some of their traditional customs and practices. Among the vehicles for doing so were the Lutheran church and the part-time "Swede School," forerunner of the modern vacation Bible school. But if these two institutions were to prosper, there must be a supply of pastors and teachers, and this in turn was dependent upon the existence of seminaries, academies, and colleges.[1]

The early source of Swedish Lutheran clergymen in the Midwest was Augustana Seminary in Chicago, an institution providing both preparatory and theological training in the 1850s. Some leaders in the church opposed this location for their seminary, and so there developed a tug of war among factions, each of which had its favorite site. That selected was Paxton, Illinois, a community farther than Chicago from the center of Swedish settlement in Minnesota. Disappointed by their failure to gain the seminary and with their pride injured, certain pastors and laymen from Minnesota began in 1862 to give serious thought to the founding of a school near at hand. The leader of the group was Eric Norelius, a young Swedish-born minister who had immigrated to the United States in 1850. After studying in Ohio, teaching in Chicago, and serving churches in Indiana and Minnesota, he had settled at Red Wing in October, 1861. A year later when the eleven delegates and pastors, representing the Minnesota Conference of the Augustana Lutheran Church meeting at East Union in Carver County, asked him to start a school, Norelius did not hesitate to accept.[2]

The exact sequence of events leading up to the opening of the primitive institution of learning, the seed to which Gustavus Adolphus College owes its origin, has been obscured by time. Early in December, 1862, however, Norelius wrote in a letter from Red Wing: "Next week I intend to start holding school. Five students from Carver and one from Chisago Lake are here. . . . This school shouldn't be regarded as a permanent school here in Minnesota; but possibly it can be a beginning to that." And so it proved to be. By February Norelius was working in his one-room enterprise with "30 disciples." Eleven were older students who hoped to enter church service, and the remainder were children from the Red Wing congregation. English was used part of the time, Swedish the rest. Measured by the yardstick of the time, the work appears to have been of acceptable quality.[3]

From the first it seems that Red Wing was considered only a temporary location for Norelius' fledgling. In June, 1863, three possible permanent locations were suggested by the Minnesota conference — Vasa, St. Paul, and Carver. From these the congregations were to make the selection by ballot, a device neither pleasing nor fair in the opinion of Norelius and a few others. Nevertheless it was carried out, and Carver, a hamlet twenty-five miles southwest of St. Paul, was the winner. For the next thirteen years the school was located near the small community of the East Union congregation, where the pastor and his wife opened their house and their hearts to the students. Andrew Jackson, a young Swedish-born alumnus of Augustana Seminary, was principal and sometimes sole teacher of the institution. Burdened occasionally with as many as fifty students, Jackson preached every Sunday, and in addition traveled about in search of money. But like so many early clergymen-educators, he was buoyed up and refreshed by his deep and abiding faith in the significance of his calling.[4]

For the first three years classes were held in the old log church of the East Union group; the desklike seats were removed Friday nights and returned Monday mornings. Subjects taught included Swedish and Christianity, as well as the usual three R's. After a new church was erected, the old one was moved to another spot, where with alterations and additions it provided a crude and sometimes smoky shelter for the incipient college. Enrollment varied week by week; for the first year at Carver the total seems to have been sixty-eight. Four years later it was fifty-three, all of them Scandinavian. Known for a time simply as Jackson's School, the young institution was officially chartered on June 14, 1867, as St. Ansgar's Academy. A decade would elapse before the school would undergo another metamorphosis in a third and final location.[5]

Meanwhile the Swedes had indulged in considerable introspection regarding their role in higher education and had taken long and critical looks at their academy. Out of this cerebration two conclusions emerged: the Swedes if possible should have a college, and St. Ansgar's should be moved to a different setting. Pastor Norelius had favored a new charter and a site in Minneapolis where the school might benefit by an affiliation with the University of Minnesota. Some progress in this direction was made, but there were sufficient obstacles in the way so that the plan came to naught.[6]

At the church conference meeting in St. Peter in 1873, a committee of local citizens asked what would be required to secure the educational enterprise for their community. Following the time-tested pattern, the Lutheran body created a committee to take bids from interested towns and fixed as a price $10,000 and a suitable site. But the men of St. Peter were not to be denied. Able and representative (four of the five who approached the conference were not Swedish), they pushed their project with vigor, secured $10,000 in pledges, and early in 1874 attained their goal. With stone from the nearby Kasota quarries, a three-story building (as usual called Old Main) was erected. Like its counterparts elsewhere, it would serve a multiplicity of functions from dormitory for students to home for faculty. The cost of about $25,000 was to be met from the original pledge, plus $15,000 to be raised from conference churches. Subscriptions apparently were generous, but grasshopper infestations and other factors at times made collections difficult. Thus some borrowing was necessary. Though not quite completed, the structure was dedicated with much fanfare on October 31, 1876.[7]

In his address on that occasion, delivered first in Swedish and then in English, Norelius noted that the name chosen, Gustavus Adolphus College, was eminently fitting. It was during the era of the great Swedish monarch early in the seventeenth century that "the principal [*sic*] of freedom of thought, of conscience, of free investigation and private judgment was clearly enunciated and successfully maintained" back in the homeland.[8]

Despite flowery oratory and high hopes, the problem of finding a president proved difficult. Finally, however, Jonas P. Nyquist, a Swedish-born alumnus of Augustana Seminary, accepted the challenge at a salary of $800 a year and two rooms in Old Main. Since his ordination in 1869, he had served churches in Indiana and Illinois, edited a religious magazine, and ministered to immigrants in Michigan. He assumed the presidency in 1876 and taught languages and Christianity in addition to his numerous other duties. Associated with him was an able and experienced teacher, a Presbyterian named A. W. Williamson, who was a distinct asset to the school. Unfortunately he had to leave his position in 1880, Nyquist's protest notwithstanding, because action by the conference required all teachers to accept the Lutheran confessions.[9]

From the first it was planned to have a college department in the new institution at St. Peter, but, as was true with so many aspiring educational ventures, the unit was not realized for a number of years. In the interim Gustavus functioned as a high school under the usual three-term calendar, the middle term when farm work was light being the longest. Finances were not in a desperate condition despite a debt of $14,000, but the school was far from affluent. Swedes had not yet had time to accumulate wealth, their average yearly gift to their Lutheran church in Minnesota being $6.25 in 1880.[10]

By this time President Nyquist, lacking the drive of a Bridgman, had found the struggle of getting the embryo college off the ground somewhat less than congenial. The periodic pranks of his student co-dwellers in Old Main, especially the rolling of stone-filled cans down the stairways, which "almost frightened Mrs. Nyquist into hysterics," did nothing to calm presidential nerves or to create enthusiasm for his task. He resigned and left Gustavus at the end of the 1880–81 school year. Despite difficulties he had made a definite contribution, one part of which was maintaining coeducation in the face of much opposition in the church conference.[11]

Nyquist's successor early in 1882 was twenty-nine-year-old Swedish-born Matthias Wahlstrom, a student for three years at St. Ansgar's Academy and an 1877 graduate of Augustana College in Rock Island. Ordained in 1879, he had joined the Gustavus faculty after a year spent as an Indian missionary in Colorado. Quick-witted, resourceful, understanding, he could cope with students and still maintain their respect and affection, as well as reasonable order — an art not always present in college administrators.[12]

Gustavus was still an academy or less (there was a preacademy class into the twentieth century), and students were mainly "farmer's sons and have not had many advantages." Enrollment in the fall of 1882 was about eighty; in the spring of 1884, when work on the farms was heavy, only some sixty students were in attendance. But the young president in the face of opposition and obstacles moved the institution steadily forward. Finding it impossible to secure competent faculty among Swedish Lutheran immigrants, he followed Nyquist's lead and brought in German Lutherans from Pennsylvania. These American-born teachers made significant contributions to Gustavus, but they were resented by many of the Swedes. One trustee, for example, wrote: "Shall our college in St. Peter be filled with German professors? I for my part shall cry out, No!" Wahlstrom, however, would not be deterred from his effort to maintain as fine a faculty as he could muster.[13]

In keeping with his policy of "Americanizing" Gustavus and raising its level of performance, it followed that Wahlstrom would strive to develop a college department. Early in his administration, to the three regular academy classes was added a fourth, which in 1885–86 was identified as the freshman class in a "Collegiate Department." A sophomore group materialized the next year, but not until the fall of 1888 did a junior class of seven men come into being. With the addition of one recruit, this contingent of eight members provided in 1890 the first graduates of Gustavus Adolphus College, as opposed to the academy.[14]

These efforts to create an institution of higher learning in St. Peter did not attract unanimous support among Swedish Lutherans, many of whom felt that Augustana was sufficient for their needs. And it was true that men entering the ministry had to go to Rock Island for seminary training. Nevertheless Gustavus' proponents argued that it had a definite *raison d'être* and a function different from its older relative in Illinois. When one of the latter's faculty members in 1885 suggested that the transfer of students from the Minnesota college to Augustana would be facilitated if Gustavus aligned its curriculum with that at his school, he elicited something less than an enthusiastic response. Circumstances, wrote Wahlstrom, dictated that the school he headed had a special responsibility to prepare

teachers. Furthermore its faculty, unlike that in Illinois, aimed "to give equal attention to Sciences" — English was not easy for the immigrant — "and the languages." The elective principle, however, was scarcely visible on the far horizon.[15]

The question of coeducation was another debatable issue of the period, and here too the president made his position clear. To opponents he declared, "let men measure their mental abilities with the fair sex, there will be less match-making, less of lovemaking, a better moral atmosphere, better manners, better work." To make Gustavus more attractive to women, he built North and South halls in 1884, with living quarters for some faculty members and thirty-five to forty girls. Three years later, music, a subject attractive to women, was elevated to departmental status and housed in a new $7,000 structure later known as Commerce Hall. In it were also placed dining facilities and the recently created and popular commercial department. A gymnasium "about the size and appearance of a country railroad depot" had gone up in 1886.[16]

Median enrollment during the late 1880s approximated 270, most of it still in the academy, but the president had his college under way and he had charted its course. Gustavus was to be an institution of liberal arts, offering Swedish immigrants and others as well a broad, general education. Attendance would not be restricted to ministerial candidates and parochial schoolteachers, although these two groups predominated at first and were always welcome. A debt hovered menacingly over the campus, but financial stringency did not prove fatal. Swedish churches, struggling themselves, responded relatively generously — with produce when cash was in short supply — to the college's needs.[17]

The depression beginning in 1893 accentuated difficulties, prevented for some time expansion of the modest physical plant, and in general had a disturbing effect. Enrollment at the turn of the century, for example, was only about thirty more than it had been a decade earlier. Yet there were bright sides to the picture. Several teachers of the period remained at Gustavus for many years, building their lives into that of the college. A number were graduates of Augustana and of Gustavus itself, but each had gone elsewhere in this country or abroad for specialized and advanced training. A few distinguished professors with degrees from leading universities stayed for fairly short tours at the college, leaving an impact on it. Noticeable were increasing attention to the sciences and a gradual erosion of the prescribed curriculum. By 1902 juniors and seniors had large areas of choice in course selection and the time they spent in class weekly — fifteen to eighteen hours — was down appreciably from the earlier twenty-five.[18]

In 1892–93 not long after the state began issuing teacher's certificates, a "Normal Department" was established. Alumni in most cases, however, unless they had taken some postgraduate work, were unable to secure state certificates of the first grade. These tended to be reserved for persons who had attended the University of Minnesota or a college which required a four-year preparatory course for admission. During the administration of Governor John Lind (1899–1901), who had been a student at the academy in Carver, a meeting between Wahlstrom and the Minnesota Board of Education resulted in the removal of this differential. Thereafter Gustavus was on a par with the university and some other private colleges in the matter of teacher certification.[19]

By 1894 of the thirty-five individuals who had graduated from the collegiate department, twenty were ministers, five were teachers, and four each were lawyers and doctors. In the commercial department forty-nine had finished the course and received bachelor of accounts degrees. Most of these individuals entered some phase of business. That same year Gustavus graduates were granted by King Oscar II the privilege of studying at Swedish universities without taking entrance examinations. The welcome mat was also out at American graduate schools.[20]

As President Wahlstrom's long administration entered its final stages, the campus plant was becoming ever more inadequate, and a periodically recurring issue once more came to the fore — an attempt to relocate Gustavus. To many people it seemed unwise to erect a needed building "on that barren sandhill" in St. Peter when a move could be made to where the action was. The Twin Cities, possessed of excellent transportation facilities, a sizable Swedish population, and thirteen Swedish Lutheran churches, among other attractions, seemed the place to go. At a special meeting of the church conference in New London in the fall of 1902, two days were given over to a discussion of the matter. Weighty arguments were expounded in favor of

relocation, though some persons "feared the traps set for the young in the large cities." Wahlstrom looked at all sides of the question, but in the final analysis he thought it wisest to stay put. However, the blandishments offered by ex-Governor Lind and others — $200,000 in cash and subscriptions, and $50,000 worth of growing timber — were too compelling, and the conference voted overwhelmingly to move the college to the Twin Cities area contingent upon the fulfillment of the various promises.[21]

But generous lures proved easier to articulate than to carry out. Despite contingent pledges by James J. Hill and others, the amount of money so glibly mentioned at the recent meeting was not in view by the spring of 1903. The conference of that year then voted to postpone action for another twelve months. By that time Hill had withdrawn his offer, fund raising had bogged down, and supporters of St. Peter were working harder than ever. Consequently the conference voted 141 to 105 to keep Gustavus where it was, and somewhat sheepishly accepted $15,000 which had been raised for it in St. Peter. Overtures of support were then extended to a Lutheran high school in Minneapolis known as Minnesota College. Though it never lived up to its name and was denied conference support in the 1930s, it did detract perhaps from wholehearted and united backing of Gustavus by Swedish Lutherans.[22]

In the midst of the site controversy, Wahlstrom wrote: "The question about moving the school to the cities makes my position more querulous than it has been." When the decision to move was made, he felt his usefulness was at an end. In 1903 he announced that he planned to retire as president the following year. As many college executives before and since found, the weight of office, the cares, the need "to step on many sore toes," had left him "exhausted" and with little enthusiasm for carrying on. In February, 1904, "with bleeding heart," he resigned. In twenty-two difficult years, he had moved Gustavus well along the road toward his vision of an American college of quality serving the varied needs and interests of its predominantly Swedish Lutheran students.[23]

5 CARLETON COLLEGE

A New England College
In the Middle West

POSSESSED OF A TRADITION of college founding going back to Yale, Dartmouth, Williams, and Amherst, the Congregationalists in Minnesota as early as the mid-1850s began to talk about securing a similar institution of their own. There was a brief flirtation with a school in Excelsior, but nothing came of it. In 1860, however, the committee on education of the General Conference of Congregational Churches of Minnesota urged the early establishment in the state of a "Literary Institution like Amherst." Disordered conditions prevented action on the suggestion until the autumn of 1864 at the conference meeting in Rochester. There it was resolved "That a committee of laymen be raised to inquire what can be done toward founding a College in this State for our denomination, and to report to the Conference of next year." The fact that economic conditions were depressed and that total membership in the state's sixty-six Congregational churches scarcely exceeded two thousand were not sufficient reasons to delay longer the noble work. Charles M. Goodsell of Northfield, moderator of the conference and a founder of Beloit College in Wisconsin, who had gone to Minnesota to establish "a new Northwestern Oberlin," was chairman of the committee. No better selection could have been made.[1]

At the conference meeting of 1865 the committee had no report, but Goodsell announced that people in Northfield would pay $7,000 in cash and donate ten acres of land as a site to secure the Congregational college for their community. This challenge was followed by the organization of a new committee which circularized some of the strongest churches in the conference concerning their possible interest in and support of a college. The replies from Cottage Grove, Lake City, Mantorville, and Zum-

brota were reported to the conference meeting in Faribault in October, 1866. By then, however, Northfield's offer had been increased to pledges of $18,529 and twenty-five acres valued at $25,000, so the conference's action was a foregone conclusion.[2]

On October 12, 1866 — celebrated thereafter as the college's natal day — the Congregational gathering voted "the acceptance of the offers of the people of Northfield, and the adoption of that place as the location of the College." The next day a number of men selected by the conference to organize the institution of learning appointed five of their group, including Goodsell, to prepare articles of incorporation and bylaws. A month later twelve men signed the document and thereby became incorporating trustees of the proposed "Northfield College."[3]

For the first three years of its existence the new entity was a college in name only. Actually an academy, it did not really qualify as a preparatory school, since only eleven of the twenty-three students who gathered for the first classes in September, 1867, signed up for Latin, a basic prerequisite for college admission. Housed in a former hotel on the edge of the downtown area, the institution had to wait five years before its first building on the main campus was ready for occupancy. Meanwhile by tempering the academic environment to suit the needs and abilities of the available supply of "scholars," and by showing flexibility in the matter of attendance requirements, the infant began to put on weight and gain in strength.[4]

Principal and at first the only teacher in the school was Horace Goodhue, a strapping young graduate of Dartmouth College, who like Jabez Brooks and Prior Demetrius drove himself without stint to ensure an ongoing life for the youngster entrusted to his care. His performance proved that the trustees had made a wise and fortunate selection in the man charged with the task of bringing a New England college to the Minnesota frontier. By 1870 the condition of the young institution appeared to be sturdy enough to support a full-fledged college department, and one came into being that fall.[5]

As Principal Goodhue's duties became ever more burdensome, he hoped and undoubtedly prayed for a president to share them. After various men declined the presidency, the trustees turned to one of their own, the Reverend James W. Strong, pastor of Plymouth Congregational Church in Faribault. On October 13, 1870, he accepted the call. The best explanation of his willingness to assume the leadership of a college not yet a college with a precarious margin of subsistence was probably the obvious one — his determination to build "an enduring institution for the betterment of men and the glory of God." For thirty-three years with notable success, this sedate, dignified, morally vigorous, Christian gentleman, who was "a preacher of great power," would devote his time, thought, and energy to the attainment of his goal.[6]

Possessed of a new president and a college department, the Northfield institution gave cause for optimism. Yet the future of the Congregational neophyte was far from secure in the world of higher learning. If it were to survive and to prosper, it would have to have money. And so necessity and wisdom impelled Strong soon after assuming office to head East — similar pilgrimages by mendicant educators have been legion — where the main sources of capital were centered.

In December, 1870, he was the guest at Charlestown, Massachusetts, of the William Carletons, wealthy parents of the wife of the Reverend Abel K. Packard, president of Northfield College's board of trustees. While there he preached in the Winthrop Church and in other ways created a most favorable impression. On December 23 while visiting a friend in Hartford, Connecticut, he was involved in a tragic accident. The carriage in which the two men were riding was struck by a train and the friend was killed. For a time it was feared that Strong also would die. When he recovered, his recent host William Carleton, a devout Christian, was convinced that the life of the young president had been spared by Providence for a divine purpose. Thus in May, 1871, Carleton announced his intention of bestowing $50,000 upon the obscure institution in Minnesota. In gratitude the trustees rechristened their youthful charge Carleton College. Although President Strong enjoyed considerable success as a fund raiser over the years, his money-seeking sorties

could hardly approach the dramatic impact and human interest of his first venture East.[7]

After fitful starts and stops the building on the main campus, New Hall, a stone structure of three stories, was opened in the fall of 1872 and dedicated in December with Governor William R. Marshall as speaker. Additional cause for rejoicing came the next year when a gift of $10,000 from Susan Willis, Mrs. Carleton's niece, removed the indebtedness on the recent construction. For a second time the trustees expressed their appreciation by a change of name. New Hall became Willis Hall and so it has remained. In it were located all of the college facilities, including a dormitory for "young men" on the top floor.[8]

The renovated hotel became known as Ladies' Hall where the women on campus lived. Carleton, like Hamline, was coeducational from the first. In 1878 the old observatory housing instruments "second to none in the West" was built and began to send time signals daily to cities in Minnesota and to points beyond its boundaries. A product largely of the zeal and enthusiasm of Professor William W. Payne, one of the "greats" on the Carleton scene from 1870 to 1908, this building and its successor, Goodsell Observatory, served as headquarters for the most glamorous areas of study in the college's youthful days — mathematics and astronomy.[9]

When the three men and two women composing the first class in the college department took up their work in the fall of 1870, they encountered a curriculum still heavily weighted by the classics. The only nod to an elective principle was the permission granted "the ladies" to make substitutions for Greek. After three years of intellectual delights that embraced such subjects as ancient language and literature, mathematics, French, German, rhetoric, astronomy, and a smattering of anatomy, physiology, and chemistry, all seniors were regarded as ready to cope with a wider range of courses in the fourth year. These consisted of logic, metaphysics, English literature, international law, moral philosophy (a favorite of nineteenth-century college presidents, it frequently was an attempt to reconcile reason with the old theology), history of civilization, geology, Joseph Butler's *Analogy of Religion,* and political economy.[10]

In 1874 two students completed this course and received Carleton's first B.A. degrees. Setting a precedent for many of their successors, they married each other. No further candidates for degrees appeared until 1876, when a class of six members was graduated. From then through 1880 a score of others attained the same distinction. Carleton was still largely an academy rather than an institution of higher learning, more involved in secondary education than in work of a higher level. Less than 25 per cent of its students in 1876–77 were enrolled in any college course, and of the remainder only 40 per cent were taking sequences leading to college entrance. Yet this fact was not disturbing. While the founders wanted to establish a college level institution, they also secondarily felt an obligation to provide high school level training for students needing it.[11]

As the 1880s began evidences appeared which suggest that developments at large were making an impact on the Northfield campus. The third building, erected in 1880, was named Science Hall. Three years later the trustees officially designated "this first Hall of the Scientific School by the name of 'Williams Hall,'" in appreciation of a benefactor. In it were science laboratories and other facilities, including the library of 4,000 volumes, which, typical of the times, was open only one hour a day. Then in 1886 came Goodsell Observatory which is still performing ably. That same year the faculty debated "the wisdom and advantage of the elective system" for juniors and seniors, but no action was taken. By May, 1889, however, it was resolved "that we as a faculty are in favor of a limited increase of options." The college was moving gradually in step with the times.[12]

The impact of the past, however, was much in evidence along with the promise of the future. Emphasis was still heavy on moral controls and time in class was often used to urge rectitude and to inveigh against turpitude. Textbooks were apt to be moralistic in tone and sometimes in content. Attendance at chapel daily and at church on Sunday was required of all students. Rules regulating personal behavior were strict and generally enforced. Yet undergraduates, unaccustomed to ease and frequently possessed of considerable inner drive, had their good times and were not always docile. A writer in the college newspaper in 1883 used the terms "despots" and "subjects" in reference to faculty and students. One of his contemporaries called the grading system "the exciter of ill feeling, the means of venting spite or showing approbation, of granting favors or of inflicting punishment," and declared it "encourages dishonesty, discourages the student, and fails in the object aimed at." In their literary societies students debated issues of the day, discussed college policies, and in many ways subtle and otherwise made their influence felt.[13]

On a blizzardy cold day in December, 1879, fire gutted Willis Hall and left only the walls standing. With much of the loss covered by insurance the seeming disaster was in some ways a blessing, for it stimulated giving by both old and new supporters of the college. By the fall of 1880 a new Willis was again in use. During its restoration and the building of Science Hall, work was started on a new Ladies' Hall, though the money to complete it was not in hand. Finally ready for occupancy early in 1883, the large, impressive structure was named Gridley Hall some three years later. The late Eber Gridley of Hartford, Connecticut, a relative of President Strong, had bequeathed about $40,000 to Carleton, nearly enough to cover the cost of the dormitory's construction.[14]

The constant need for funds caused the board in this period of plant expansion to undertake the college's first major campaign for endowment, the goal set being $200,000 and the deadline April 17, 1887. On April 16 a campus holiday and "a large torchlight procession" along the principal streets of Northfield "in midst of the ringing of bells and music," followed by bonfires and fireworks, heralded the successful completion of the undertaking. Only $25,000 of the total had come from the East; by then friends of Carleton in Minnesota were growing in wealth. Of the $175,000 they subscribed in the campaign, $117,000 came from Minneapolis, $29,000 from Northfield, $15,000 from St. Paul, and $14,000 from other parts of the state. A deterioration in their financial conditions prevented some of the three hundred subscribers from fulfilling their pledges, but "a very substantial addition" was made to the college's resources nevertheless.[15]

Yet for the purpose of gaining perspective, it is well to remember that enrollment in Carleton's collegiate department grew slowly. In the fall of 1891 it stood at 110, compared with 162 in the academy. By the end of that academic year, the institution in its life so far had conferred baccalaureates on 176 individuals — 114 men and 62 women — and over a score of master's degrees had been awarded.[16]

For some time numbers of Carleton people had been bothered by the hazy line distinguishing the college division from the academy. In March, 1891, the faculty took action to correct the condition, voting that the two departments should be separate, each with its own distinct faculty. The trustees concurred, and the change took place that fall. Everyone seemed pleased. College teachers were relieved of preparatory school routine. Students at the higher levels were warmed by the glow of added prestige. Graduates felt clearly identified as collegiate alumni. To celebrate the divorce, students conducted a parade replete with floats and illuminated "by torches and pyrotechnic effulgence." On the following day the "thoughtful President" declared a holiday. Within two years after the separation enrollments of the academy and the college evened off at 123 and 122, respectively, and quickly thereafter the upper division gained a rapidly increasing advantage. The handwriting was on the wall, even if administrators were loath to face the fact. As a result the Carleton Academy was kept alive until 1906. Then after a life of thirty-nine years, during which it had enrolled some 3,300 students, it came to an end. Its obituary was best expressed in the college yearbook of 1907: "The majority of Carleton's best orators, debaters, and athletes have been graduates of the academy." [17]

The reorganization of 1891 also produced the formal establishment of ten "departments of instruction" each with a professor at its head. These ranged from philosophy and Biblical literature, through history, the classics, English, and elocution, to mathematics, the sciences, and music. Except for art and physical education which came along later, practically every course in the curriculum of the 1960s traced its history back to the ten original departments. In announcing with pride the changes made, the catalog also noted that "only about one fourth of the work is prescribed" during the junior and senior years. The elective system, which in the words of the student newspaper, "has given great satisfaction to the students," had shown definite gains. So, too, had the curriculum in general. Courses in such areas as history, Bible study, science, political science, and music were considerably more numerous than they had been twenty years earlier. Students were even allowed a number of unexcused class absences without demerits after the overhaul of 1891.[18]

Unfortunately the college's financial progress during the 1890s did not match its strides in the academic realm. Student fees had never accounted for more than 36 per cent of the cost of operating Carleton. The remainder had to be made up by gifts and income from endowment. The latter, despite Strong's success as a money raiser, amounted to only slightly over $400,000 at the turn of the century. This was a sizable sum for Minnesota, but hardly one to guarantee affluence. After the Panic of 1893 hit, many mortgages held by the college had to be foreclosed and numerous pledges to endowment became worthless. Interest earnings of $18,335 in 1891 fell to $4,103 in 1895, when book assets of $56,700 were written off as of no value.[19]

The faculty of some sixteen members, committed to their calling and their cause, voted themselves additional labor to help alleviate the pinch. When that was not enough, they made generous contributions from their meager salaries to assist in defraying current expenses. Yet as late as 1899 it was necessary to reduce President Strong's salary by $500, that of the seven full professors by $200 each, and of four other teachers by $100 each. After the cut a professor received $1,400 annually. In the face of low pay and long hours, the faculty exhibited a loyalty, a patience, and even a sort of cheerful enthusiasm, which critics of the academic world find all too rare on the campus of the 1970s.[20]

For nearly two decades after 1886, money was available to add only one building. This was Scoville Memorial Library, completed in November, 1896, and made possible through the generosity of James W. Scoville of Chicago and his widow and son. After sixty years of service, the Romanesque structure was transformed into classrooms and faculty offices.[21]

In April, 1901, President Strong resigned his position, agreeing, however, to remain in office until his successor should be appointed. Under his leadership Carleton had made notable progress. One reason undoubtedly was the freedom which the Congregational Conference of Minnesota had accorded the college. Individual Congregationalists had been generous in response to appeals for money, and a majority of the trustees had been of the Congregational persuasion, but the conference as such had shown little inclination to participate in the college's management. To some extent Carleton's progress had been fortuitous. Unfortunate as was President Strong's near-fatal accident, it probably increased the size of William Carleton's gift. Furthermore there was more wealth in the older "Yankee" element than among the newer immigrant groups. But most credit should go to the president himself, to his skill as a fund raiser, and to his ability to attract an able faculty and board.[22]

The statistics of his administration make impressive reading, The campus grew by forty acres. Six buildings were erected. Fourteen thousand library books were cataloged. Endowment rose to almost $400,000. Faculty increased from four to twenty-four. The number of college students went from none to 237; college graduates from none to 480. The campus milieu was largely provincial, didactic, and dogmatically religious, but it was also cultural, friendly, and gently stimulating. Of its graduates according to a report of 1901, ninety-six were educators, twenty-nine lawyers or law students, twenty physicians or medical students, thirty-four clergymen or in a seminary, and nine were serving as missionaries.[23]

6 AUGSBURG COLLEGE

A Norwegian Lutheran College
In Minneapolis

AUGSBURG COLLEGE, like Gustavus Adolphus, can trace its roots back to Augustana Seminary in Paxton, Illinois, in the 1860s, but for a somewhat different reason. What bothered Augsburg's progenitors was not so much the location of the seminary as the fact that it was primarily Swedish. To the Reverend August Weenaas, the one recent Norwegian addition to Augustana's faculty, and to some others, the differences in language and national characteristics found at the institution were too great to be satisfactorily bridged. The wise move would be to establish a separate school to educate pastors for Norwegian and Danish settlers. In June, 1869, the Scandinavian Augustana Synod concurred with this point of view. Less than three months later, in the building of a defunct academy in Marshall, Wisconsin, Weenaas opened a seminary as well as an American type of secondary school to fulfill stipulations imposed by sellers of the property. By midyear about twenty students, mainly young adults of varying educational backgrounds, were enrolled, and Weenaas was laboring mightily to make a success of the enterprise. It was after all the first *Presteskole* or training school for pastors established by Norwegian immigrants in the United States.[1]

In 1870 the sponsoring church organization effected an amiable division, the Swedes creating their own Augustana Synod, and most of the others forming the Norwegian-Danish Augustana Synod. Later, however, fourteen pastors and three lay delegates meeting at St. Ansgar, Iowa, organized the Conference of the Norwegian-Danish Evangelical Lutheran Church in America. To this latter body, Weenaas, who had been strongly influenced by low-church movements in Norway, gave his allegiance. One unhappy result of this fragmentation was a squabble over the assets of the parent body. Shortly after classes began for the second year the school property in Marshall was successfully claimed by the new Norwegian-Danish Synod. Weenaas and his students were quite literally out in the cold, as well as shorn of their preparatory department. Half or more of the men moved into their mentor's home; others lodged elsewhere, and classes were continued in a rented attic. Discouraging as the predicament was, the loyalty of his disciples gave Weenaas the strength to carry on. The conference, keenly aware of the need for pastors, recognized the value of the enterprise. The school must continue and a suitable home for it be found.[2]

That Minneapolis provided a home was due largely to the work of the Reverend Ole Paulson, a board member of the Marshall institution and pastor of Trinity Lutheran Church in Minnesota's flour city. Through his efforts by mid-1871, various leading Minneapolitans in the hope of attracting Augsburg to their local community had made donations of land, cash, and building materials. By late summer of 1872, despite slowed payments on pledges, "quite a formidable three story brick veneered building" (later to form the west wing of Old Main) had appeared on what became the corner of Seventh Street and Twenty-first Avenue South. Now a bustling urban area, the vicinity at that time was open prairie. Classes started on September 15, 1872. Local interest in the new venture was evidenced by the presence of the Minneapolis mayor at the dedication ceremonies in October. He not only rejoiced in his city's acquisition of a "Theological Institution," but also expressed the opinion that immigrants "can be better trusted" when accompanied by their ministers.[3]

Although enrollment was only twenty-four, the future seemed assured. Thus the conference convention of 1873 commissioned Weenaas to journey to Norway in search of a second faculty member. He was Sven Oftedal, who arrived at Augsburg as professor of theology that fall. An opponent of the established church in his homeland, a supporter of democracy with a "zest for controversy," Oftedal was a prominent figure on the Augsburg and Minneapolis scenes for nearly four decades. In a small pamphlet entitled *Aapen Erklaering* (Public Declaration) which he and Weenaas published early in 1874, the newcomer's stand on matters theological was made patently clear. Attacking the Norwegian Synod for its "high-churchly and Catholic tendencies," the tract declared that congregations should govern themselves, even "with regard to policy and doctrine." In tone and content the document was offensive to many Norwegians, including some leaders of the conference, and as a result Weenaas withdrew his endorsement of it. Relations between him and Oftedal thereafter cooled considerably.[4]

Nevertheless plans to expand the school were drawn up and given approval by the conference convention in 1874. Accordingly two new professors, Sven R. Gunnersen and Georg Sverdrup, old friends of Oftedal in Norway and also proponents of ecclesiastical reform, were added to the faculty in the fall. Gunnersen had a falling out with the other two and returned to Norway in 1883, but Sverdrup remained to become one of Augsburg's great figures. In addition to new faculty, the plans also called for expansion of the physical plant. This took the form of a three-family dwelling occupied by Gunnersen, Oftedal, and Sverdrup, and of a center section and an east wing to Old Main. A barn for the then-necessary horses and cows also graced the grounds.[5]

In the curricular realm the 1874 plans can be considered the foundation of the college. Provision was made for a one-year preparatory course to serve both preseminarians and students with secular goals (Augsburg had had no real preparatory division since 1870) and for two parallel collegiate courses of four years each. One in practical studies was never successfully launched, but the other, the Greek department, survived and in time grew strong, offering work leading to the B.A. degree. The theological program was three years in duration. Electives were nonexistent, and emphasis was on the teaching of history and religion, the best means, said Oftedal, of providing a "true spiritual education." Necessary tools were five languages — Greek (it was considered superior to Latin), Latin, German, Norwegian, and English. Conventional grading practices were not adopted until the turn of the century, probably to conform with those of other institutions. Rather a baccalaureate was earned in European style on the basis of written and oral examinations taken during the last two weeks of the course's fourth year.[6]

Enrollment that fall of 1874 reached thirty-eight — thirty in the preparatory department, six in the Greek department, and two in practical studies. A year later with the additions to Old Main providing more dormitory and classroom space, slightly over a hundred students were registered. Faculty numbered six, and their duties extended from teaching a wide range of subjects to raising money and filling pulpits. One young instructor, however, found the total abstinence code too demanding and early in 1877 he departed.[7]

Meanwhile tension between Weenaas and his faculty had mounted, and in 1875 he submitted his resignation, attributing it to a yearning for his homeland rather than the problems he faced. At the conference convention the next year, however, the developing differences between him and Sverdrup came out into the open. Neither achieved a clear-cut victory, but Sverdrup was elected the second president of Augsburg by a vote of 47 to 16 over a pastor who had Weenaas' backing. The first president, whose contributions to the school had been tremendous but not always fully appreciated, then returned to Norway to resume his ministry. The new leader would remain at Augsburg until his death in 1907 to be remembered as one of the most outstanding men in the Lutheran Church in America. A fine teacher and an effective speaker, he would be the "soul" of the institution for over three decades. Internal conference quarrels, which split the faculty and left their impact on the struggling school, would be only one of the challenges Sverdrup would face, but he did not flinch nor give up.[8]

Because the educational backgrounds of some students were inadequate, it was necessary between 1875 and 1878 to extend the preparatory course from one to two years with a resultant delay in organizing upper level collegiate work. By the fall of 1878, however, despite financial and other problems, four Greek department classes were in operation. The following May the first B.A. degrees were conferred on a class of five young men. The same number would graduate in 1880. Nevertheless collegiate enrollment remained small, while the economic insecurity of the institution had been accentuated by the general depression of the 1870s.[9]

By 1877 the salary fund showed a deficit of more than $4,000, and the debt on the physical plant, incurred largely during the expansion of 1874–75, came to $10,720. These facts scarcely elevated the spirits of convention delegates at Willmar in that year of serious grasshopper devastation. Yet it was decided to raise $16,000 to save the seminary, and

Oftedal was appointed to direct the campaign. As he told it later, "in two or three months an enthusiasm hitherto almost unknown amongst a cool-headed, conservative people like the Norwegians" was generated. By early 1878 approximately $18,000 in cash had been received from over 30,000 contributors, a great lift both materially and psychologically. But this achievement was not a permanent solution. An endowment fund was needed. Deficits again mounted and teachers threatened to resign, yet because of factional strife within the church, Oftedal failed both in 1878 and 1879 to get conference approval for an endowment drive. In desperation the Augsburg trustees initiated on their own a campaign for $50,000, which the official church body after lengthy debate approved in 1880. Two years later the goal was reached.[10]

But this success had no salving effect on the wounds of theological disputation which afflicted both Augsburg and the conference and were fully aired in the foreign-language press. The details of the struggle cannot be reported here. Suffice it to say that the climax was reached at the church convention of 1882 and that the faction known as the New School gained the ascendancy. This element, which included Oftedal and Sverdrup, defended in general the position which had been stated in Oftedal's "Public Declaration" of 1874. While the opposition was not completely silenced, its influence became that of "a hopeless minority." From 1883 to the end of the decade, both church and school were marked by calm and by progress.[11]

By 1889–90 enrollment reached 160, of whom 61 were in the preparatory department, 58 in the college, and 41 in the seminary. Improved economic conditions, population increases, and additions to the physical plant had made this growth possible. A three-story building (North Hall), containing dormitory facilities for 40 men, two classrooms, and space for a publishing company and a bookstore, had been erected in 1884. Three years later a duplex was built (Morton Hall), which housed the Sverdrup and Oftedal families for many years.[12]

A constant problem was that of recruiting faculty who were both competent and committed to Augsburg's particular brand of theology. The preparatory students, for example, were taught not only by the regular professors, but also by low-paid, temporary instructors, and part-time people, mainly seminarians. A beginning was made in the mid-1880s, however, toward providing a more permanent and better qualified teaching staff. At that time two alumni of Augsburg's three academic departments were hired as college professors on a par with the seminary faculty in everything except salary. One

of them, John H. Blegen, who taught mainly Greek, German, and Norse, remained on the faculty until 1916. For $600 a year he taught five classes a day, later recalling with understatement that there "was no time to relax." Soon three other permanent professors were employed in the preparatory and college departments bringing the total to five by 1890.[13]

The curriculum, however, was not similarly expanded. For a variety of reasons — limited resources, the waning influence of traditional Christianity on Norwegian life, the need for a strong seminary in anticipation of the impending union of several branches of the church — Augsburg's scope remained relatively limited. One goal envisioned in the plans of 1874, the provision of a broad education "for young Norwegian-Americans not headed for the ministry," would have to wait. Sverdrup recommended to the convention of 1884 that Augsburg should be "exclusively" a divinity school, and the church body concurred. Some graduates of the preparatory division entered elementary school teaching, but they were exceptions. Between 1885 and 1890, 82 per cent of the Greek (or college) department alumni went on to complete the institution's theological course. Graduates went forth to preach, to teach in parochial schools, to serve in foreign missions, and to organize congregations on the frontier from Minnesota to the Pacific Coast and into Canada. School property was worth $100,000 and prospects seemed bright.[14]

The year 1890 at first provided more cause for hope. In June at a meeting in Minneapolis, Augsburg's parental organization, the Norwegian-Danish Conference, joined with the Anti-Missourian Brotherhood and the Norwegian Augustana Synod to form the United Norwegian Lutheran Church in America. Under the articles of union Augsburg's seminary was to be the United Church's official agency for training pastors and to it were transferred three professors — two from the Anti-Missourians' seminary at St. Olaf College in Northfield and one from that of the Augustana group in South Dakota. This action was fine. It would strengthen Augsburg and add effectiveness to its work. But when in the same month of June, the united body's first annual convention designated St. Olaf as the official college of the new church, some of the luster was removed.[15]

President Sverdrup and his associates sensed a conspiracy aimed at depriving Augsburg of its preparatory and college departments, which in the opinion of these men constituted integral and necessary components of the seminary. That a conspiracy existed seems unlikely, but it was not long before conflict erupted. Early in 1891 *Skandinaven*, a Chicago newspaper, printed a letter from a man later identified as a St. Olaf professor. In it he charged, among other affronts, that "Augsburg's environment encouraged a spirit of lax anti-intellectualism." So began one of the liveliest public interchanges in Minnesota's private college history. St. Olaf was too secular and humanistic, as New School Conference adherents saw it. Augsburg was a "humbug" institution, claimed the retort, and so it went. The name calling damaged the images of both colleges, but Augsburg, portrayed as a place where piety substituted for scholarship, suffered more than its rival in Northfield.[16]

Debilitating as the debates with St. Olaf were, they were not the only problems and complications Augsburg faced as a result of the union of 1890. Because the Norwegian-Danish Conference had never been incorporated whereas the seminary's board was, the former did not own the institution. Thus the method of transferring Augsburg to the United Church posed very real technical difficulties. In addition the conviction of Sverdrup and Oftedal that a conspiracy was afoot made them more than normally reluctant to relinquish control of the seminary. Only the high lights of the tangled and complex negotiations of the period can be included here, but even this brief outline is sufficient to suggest the magnitude of worry and concern under which the two colleges labored at the time.[17]

In near desperation the United Church conference convention of 1892 sought a solution to the problem by submitting two questions to the denomination's congregations: (1) "Shall the United Church operate and support both St. Olaf and the college department of Augsburg Seminary?" (2) "If the synod is not to operate and support both of these schools, which of them should the United Church operate and support?" The results of the vote favored Augsburg, contingent upon the transfer of the institution to church control. At the 1893 convention a five-point solution to the vexing problem was presented and passed. The substance of the plan provided for the revocation of St. Olaf's earlier adoption by the United Church and the maintenance of Augsburg with certain guarantees in return for stated stipulations. Should the Augsburg board fail, however, to make the long-debated transfer of its institution by July 15, 1893, the United Church would remove its divinity school to another location.[18]

On the surface it seemed that Augsburg had won a victory, but for Sverdrup, Oftedal, and others, the fear lingered that the United Church would alter the nature of the seminary once transfer of control had been accomplished. The two thereupon "submitted their resignations as theological professors of the United Church, but not as Augsburg Seminary professors." The resignations were accepted without debate. Heartening to the Augsburg faction, however, was a meeting of sympathetic convention delegates who backed the school's board, advised against the transfer, and called for continued support of the institution. Soon the loose federation of congregations which felt as these delegates did would come to be known as "The Friends of Augsburg," and their bond with the United Church would grow increasingly tenuous. The die was cast. After three years of negotiations the Augsburg board formally rejected the convention's transfer plan on July 11, 1893. By fall the United Church's new seminary (it was moved to St. Paul in 1900) was functioning in a rented building not far from Augsburg's campus. Three of the latter's theological professors and a number of students went over to the new entity, but most of the Augsburg staff remained loyal. Thus, like St. Olaf, Augsburg found itself without organized synodical support at a time when the blight of economic depression again bore down on the nation.[19]

For the next five years the squabble continued in convention meetings, in lawyers' offices, and in courtrooms. Fortunately by 1898 legal costs and "battle fatigue" led to a compromise whereby the Oftedal board retained clear title to the Augsburg property and the United Church received the school's endowment fund of some $49,000 and part of its library. The amazing survival of Augsburg during this "fiery ordeal" can be attributed to the sacrificial loyalty and devotion of its faculty and to the financial and moral support of the Friends of Augsburg. Enrollment, which had dipped to about 113 the year after the break with the United Church, was by 1897 up to 187 — 70 in the preparatory department, 84 in the college, 33 in the seminary. In 1897, too, the Friends of Augsburg, composed of some 112 loosely related congregations, organized as the Lutheran Free Church. Thus once again the backing of a synod was obtained, and the future took on a rosier hue.[20]

With facilities becoming noticeably strained and economic conditions improving, the Free Church's annual meeting in 1899 authorized, when funds became available, the construction of a new building not to cost over $30,000. Work began that fall, but money raising failed to keep pace with inflation, and construction ground to a halt in 1900. Augsburg's struggles were far from over; optimism it appeared had been premature.[21]

Throughout the turmoil and turbulence of the 1890s, two factors — the curriculum and the style of student life — remained fairly stable. The former still bore a strong resemblance to that outlined in the plan of 1874. The latter, a wholly masculine manifestation, reflected the philosophy of Sverdrup as well as the distinctiveness of the campus community.

With students generally being "relatively mature men of immigrant origin" imbued with religious conviction, conditions were favorable for developing student autonomy and responsibility, one of Sverdrup's aims. Several services now provided and managed by college personnel — dining, heating, mail, health and sanitation, library — were then left largely to undergraduate enterprise. The Augsburg Boarding Club, for example, spanned the years from 1872 to 1924. Not until 1907 did the catalog list a member of the faculty as librarian. In 1876 students had established the *Idun* society to secure books for general reading; by 1890 its collection outnumbered that of the regular library 1,137 to 818. Music played a minor role at the time, but a student quartet dating back to 1885 toured the Midwest several times in the interest of the total abstinence movement in which Augsburg was "a mighty force." In 1895 the group gave more than fifty concerts in Norway on behalf of the abstinence cause. Most pervasive of all activities were those of a religious nature. Such events as daily chapel, prayer meetings, lectures, and discussions, plus the conflict with the United Church, heightened evangelistic spirit and kept the campus, as one close observer reported, "in the grip of perpetual revival." [22]

7 ST. OLAF COLLEGE

A Norwegian Lutheran College On the Hill

DURING THE 1860s when August Weenaas and his associates in the Scandinavian Augustana Synod were planning the school that later became Augsburg College, another group of Norwegians was also giving serious thought to educational matters. They composed the Norwegian Evangelical Lutheran Synod in America, which was organized in 1853. From this faction would emerge St. Olaf College. Its founder, Norwegian-born Bernt Julius Muus, arrived in 1859 in Goodhue County, an area rapidly filling up with his countrymen, to assume the pastorate of the Holden congregation. Thereafter he traveled a wide region preaching and organizing other local units. Like most immigrant religious leaders, he was vitally concerned with the education of his denomination's young people. Minnesota schools were not only few and far between, primitive and irregularly in session, but also lacking in instruction in the Lutheran faith. To correct this last deficiency, some parochial schools were established, but they did not amount to much.[1]

By March, 1869, a number of leaders of the Norwegian Synod meeting in Madison, Wisconsin, concluded the time was ripe for starting coeducational "higher schools" or academies. Muus then set about organizing one and announced its opening for a three-month term on January 7, 1870. Three students attended each of the two terms the aspiring academy was in operation in the basement of the Muus parsonage. The necessity for grinding out a living, however, left little time for "higher" education. Furthermore Holden's location twenty to thirty miles from rail or water transportation put it at a disadvantage which could not be overcome.[2]

But Muus was not one to give up. At the Norwegian Synod meeting at Holden in June, 1874,

he declared it "the duty of all Christians according to their strength and abilities to strive to provide Christian schools for their children." The synod being noncommittal, he then approached Pastor N. A. Quammen and a layman, Harald Thorson of Northfield, regarding the possibility of locating an academy in that city where Carleton College had recently graduated its first class. Favorably impressed, Thorson the following day offered $2,000 worth of property and his help in attracting the interest of other Northfield citizens if the synod would locate the school in his home city. Members of the Lutheran body reacted warmly but promised nothing more substantial than moral support. Muus, Thorson, and others nevertheless continued the campaign to secure an academy. Their efforts bore fruit that fall when two former Northfield public school buildings and surrounding property on the east side of town were purchased. The school "under the auspices of our Scandinavian brethren" had the "hearty support" of the townspeople.[3]

Incorporated on November 6, 1874 — subsequently celebrated as Founders' Day — "to advance the education of pupils from fifteen years of age and upwards, as a college, [and] preserve the pupils in the true Christian faith, as taught by the Evangelical Lutheran Church," the infant was christened St. Olaf's School. On a stormy January 8, 1875, thirty-six young men and women were in attendance for the opening exercises. At the helm was Pastor Thorbjørn Nelson Mohn, Norwegian-born graduate of synod-founded Luther College in Iowa and of Concordia Theological Seminary in St. Louis. Inured to adversity, forceful, patient, with a fine sense of humor and an unswerving faith in God, he like fellow townsman James W. Strong was well-suited to build a rather unpromising venture into a solid and enduring institution.[4]

From the start the founders "had in mind an educational institution unlike any then existing in the Norwegian Lutheran Church of America." Other denominational schools prepared young people for the ministry and for teaching, and St. Olaf's would do so too, but it would do more. It would provide general education for the Norwegian immigrant youth to enable him to enter fully into the life and business of America on a par with all other citizens, and it would be coeducational. At the core as a guiding light for every student no matter what his goal would be Christianity.[5]

Whether the design could be carried out seemed by no means certain when upon the opening of classes in the fall of 1875, only thirty-one students were present. But faith and continued effort gradually won out. A new twenty-acre site west of town on an elevation with a magnificent view, dubbed Manitou Heights in the 1880s, was purchased for $800, and in the face of opposition a campaign for funds was undertaken. On July 4, 1877, a crowd of about a thousand persons gathered for the celebration to lay the cornerstone for Old Main, the first structure on the new campus. It was hoped that the building would be ready for use in the fall of 1878. Toward this end, Muus as president of the board of trustees and school treasurer attempted to secure synod support, but without success. (Jabez Brooks and James Strong could have warned him.) The means to enable Old Main to begin its long and distinguished period of service on schedule in September, 1878, did not come from the synod. Rather the good people of the immediate area of Goodhue, Rice, and Dakota counties provided the money and were the source of St. Olaf's salvation in its early years.[6]

Within a year conditions in the new building were becoming encouragingly crowded. The old schoolhouses downtown were then removed, and the materials were used to build Ladies' Hall on campus. Known in student parlance as "Agony Hall," it functioned first as a women's dormitory and later until 1924 as a music hall. In its early years it was completely surrounded by dense woods and was hardly suited in winter for the frail or fainthearted. Especially venturesome were nocturnal visits to the outdoor "powder room" several rods distant, "very dismal and spooky with uncertain fumbling of the way in pitchy darkness."[7]

But if the young ladies were groping in the dark, so to some extent were St. Olaf's leaders as they sought to resolve their theological beliefs with other groups in the Norwegian Synod. Like Augsburg in the 1880s, St. Olaf found itself deeply influenced by conflict within the denominational group to which the school looked hopefully, if not too successfully, for support.

For some time before 1882 the Norwegian Synod had been joined with the Missouri Lutheran Synod, a German group, and had sent professors and students to the latter's Concordia Seminary in St. Louis. In 1882, however, as the result of a dispute over the doctrines of election and predestination, the Norwegian element withdrew from the union. But despite this action, the sons of Norway were far from united among themselves. Their own synod became split between a conservative, formalistic faction and a liberal, generally American-trained opposition known as the Anti-Missourians. In the latter camp were such men as Muus, Mohn, and a future St. Olaf president, John N. Kildahl. Unable to support the position taken at the Norwegian Synod's seminary in Madison, Wisconsin — established after the break with the German Lutherans — they determined to organize a pastoral training school of their own.[8]

After considerable preparatory discussion and activity, an agreement was drawn up under which the Anti-Missourian group would pay St. Olaf $1,200 a year if the school would initiate a freshman class of collegiate rank and provide space for the proposed seminary. With this accomplished, an unofficial gathering of all interested parties, a folk meeting, was held on the Northfield campus on September 15 and 16, 1886. Despite discomfort and inconvenience caused by drenching rains, the group ratified the arrangement and elected a board of directors for the pastoral training school. Housed in two rooms in Old Main with two of its own professors, the new Lutheran Theological Seminary attracted thirty-two students its first year. It also by stimulating St. Olaf to undertake work of college level fulfilled the hopes held a dozen years earlier by the founders of the institution on Manitou Heights.[9]

Still not all problems had been erased. Neither St. Olaf's School nor the seminary had any official synodical connection, nor was there an endowment to lend a measure of financial security. At the meeting of the Norwegian Synod in 1887, the recent actions of the Anti-Missourians were termed illegal, divisive, and intolerable. Those who had gone astray were admonished "to admit their error" and return to the true fold. In response Mohn read a statement, later signed by forty-eight members of the convention, declaring that as a "matter of conscience" his faction could not close the seminary in Northfield so long as the one in Madison continued teaching doctrines to which he and his associates stood opposed. Mohn resigned from the synod and urged others to do likewise. Known as the Anti-Missourian Brotherhood, the seceders found reason for optimism in the prospect of early union with other church bodies sharing similar beliefs. These hopes for St. Olaf, as for Augsburg, were realized in the summer of 1890 with the formation of the United Norwegian Lutheran Church in America.[10]

Meanwhile students and faculty in Northfield, somewhat removed from the heat of doctrinal disputation, went about their appointed tasks. Principal Mohn was accused of extravagance when he hired a local tinsmith to fashion a movable bathtub for school use, but the critics were silenced when five-cent tickets went on sale entitling the bearer to one lavation. Rules of the period admonished: do not brag about not studying, do not mark desks, do not throw water out the windows, do not walk on the eaves. Favorite student pranks were stringing dishpans on a thread and letting them slide downstairs at lights-out time (10:00 P.M.), and taking stoves apart during class and passing the parts around the room. On a loftier level were the activities of literary and debating societies, musical groups, and religious organizations. Especially memorable was the appearance in 1887 of the *Manitou Messenger*, the first regular school paper, which is still flourishing today.[11]

During the first twelve years of St. Olaf's existence, while it was strictly an academy, 680 students (of whom about one-fifth were women) had been in attendance. Of this total only twenty-six had received certificates of graduation, sustained schooling at the secondary level being the exception rather than the rule in those days. In 1885–86, St. Olaf's final year as an academy only, eighty-two students registered. Most were from Minnesota, but nearby states were also represented. The initial college class in the fall of 1886 mustered a mere five members, but it represented a significant start and one which would be sustained. Faculty naturally were likewise few in number. In the early years two or three people carried the assignments; by 1890 the number had grown to eight, plus two music teachers, and five part-time assistants.[12]

The curriculum typically was slanted to the preparation for business and teaching at the elementary level, but a college preparatory course was also fashioned about 1880. Rather surprisingly for the time it was four years in length, as was the academy's other offering, the more "practical," or English, course. When the college department was instituted, its curriculum was projected on classical lines with an absence of electives and the usual emphasis on Greek, Latin, and religion.[13]

Debt was ever-present, causing Mohn and others

to wear constantly the garb of mendicants, but happily support from the Anti-Missourians eased the burden and made further progress possible. On June 20, 1889, the institution's name of "St. Olaf's School" was changed by action of its board to "St. Olaf College," and Mohn's title was shifted from principal to president. Thus did terminology follow fact. Basking in its higher status, the institution in 1890 conferred its first baccalaureate degrees on a class composed of three men. One big disadvantage still lay in the fact that the college was an independent organization operated by trustees. Developments on the horizon, however, suggested that this condition might be temporary and that St. Olaf would soon gain the identity and security which a sponsoring church organization could provide.[14]

As plans which culminated in the creation of the United Norwegian Lutheran Church in 1890 were taking shape, St. Olaf's position became clear. The college was more than willing to relinquish its state of single bliss in return for membership in a church family. Leaders of the Anti-Missourian Brotherhood, a loosely related group of 268 congregations before its inclusion in the United Church, were eager to be of help in effecting the college's desired change of status. To facilitate the transition, St. Olaf trustees offered to turn over their charge to the new church organization and to select their replacements thereafter from among candidates nominated by it. In return they asked only a pledge of support which would enable St. Olaf to "continue to be a college which will meet the requirements that the times demand of an institution of this kind." At commencement exercises on June 18, 1890, the first for the collegiate department, President Mohn, just returned from the church union meeting, made the happy announcement: "The one thousand ministers and delegates of the United Norwegian Lutheran Church decided yesterday to recognize St. Olaf College as their institution." The goal desired by the founders in the 1870s, though it would prove to be short-lived, had been attained.[15]

But, as the story of Augsburg has already made clear, harmony was far from complete. The Anti-Missourian seminary, which for four years had been housed in Old Main, was transferred to the Augsburg campus to be part of the United Church's school for training pastors. After that venture failed in 1893 and Augsburg went its way alone, the former St. Olaf adjunct suffered two more moves before finding its permanent home in St. Paul in Luther Theological Seminary. St. Olaf itself after three uneasy years as the designated college of the United Church was dropped from that body's list of organizations in the hope that peace among contending church factions would thereby be restored. Once again President Mohn, whose hard work among people of limited means had kept the college going, found himself without a concrete constituency to which he could appeal for support. The rejoicing of 1890 had three years later turned into deep gloom. It seemed "that the very life of the college was at stake." [16]

Though routine was fairly normal on campus, repercussions of external events were bound to occur. Evidences of internal tension cropped out here and there, and as always there were outside critics whose voices were now somewhat harder for friends of the college to take. Student enrollment of 184 in 1892 declined steadily for the next several years. Graduates of the college department from 1891 through 1898 numbered, two, six, three, seven, six, five, seven, and six, respectively. Telephones were installed in the mid-1890s, but new construction was at a standstill. The total value of the two buildings (Old Main and Agony Hall) and the campus was estimated at $40,000, with indebtedness in 1893 of slightly over $10,000. Average annual expenditures were about $17,000. This was hardly a gigantic sum, but it was big enough when the Panic of 1893 hit on the heels of exclusion from the United Church. [17]

There were, however, some compensations, some bright spots. Although the college had lost its official connection with the United Church, it had by no means forfeited the affection and support of large numbers of individual Lutherans. Between 1893 and 1899 Professor Halvor T. Ytterboe worked nearly full time among these people collecting the small gifts they were able to spare for St. Olaf. The annual totals thus collected averaged a modest $6,500 and "saved the institution in the most critical period of its history." By his cheerful and friendly manner, his commitment, his interest in people, Ytterboe also built up for the college what Wendell L. Willkie, in another connection, would term a "reservoir of good will." [18]

During these same six years, President Mohn never lost hope of regaining official connection with the church, and his efforts received tangible backing from the citizens of Northfield and others. By 1897 the college debt had been reduced to slightly less than $4,000, a sum local residents promised to raise if St. Olaf was again adopted by the church. Anticipating the promotional tactics of a later day, Mohn invited the pastors and lay delegates at the annual meeting of the United Church in Minneapolis in 1898 to journey southward to see the college for themselves. Approximately six hundred did so and went away presumably with a favorable impression. A committee of the church was then elected to look into the matter and to report at the next annual convention. Much discussion followed, but no recommendation could be agreed upon. [19]

The turning point came at the 1899 meeting when Mohn received a telegram from a Northfield merchant informing him that $5,000 for the college had been placed in a local bank. The convention delegates then voted to embrace St. Olaf once more as their church college. Members of the convention from then on would also be members of the St. Olaf Corporation with the right to elect trustees and officials of their educational enterprise. When news of this action reached the campus, "the four sons of President Mohn — then living in the Main — who had formed their own quartette, grabbed their brass instruments, rushed out on the east porch, and played triumphant tunes out over the city — till their faces were red as beets." [20]

But soon there would be sadness too. President Mohn, still in his middle fifties, was in failing health. His twenty-five years as head of St. Olaf and as pastor of St. John's Lutheran congregation in Northfield in addition to many other activities had left their mark. He died on November 18, 1899. During his administration, more than 2,600 students — 1,992 men and 636 women — had matriculated at St. Olaf. In a male-female ratio of three to one, a total of 205 had finished the academy course and 55 had earned the B.A. degree. Two of the latter group were women, graduates in the classes of 1893 and 1894. Not surprisingly teachers and pastors predominated among the holders of baccalaureates. Though mourning and sadly missing its great leader, St. Olaf College now secure in the fold of the United Church looked with confidence to the new century. [21]

8 MACALESTER COLLEGE

Presbyterians Found a College

MACALESTER COLLEGE in St. Paul did not come into possession of its permanent home as early as some Minnesota institutions of learning, but its roots go well back into territorial days. Its founder was Edward D. Neill, a Presbyterian minister who had been appointed superintendent of common schools in Minnesota Territory by Governor Alexander Ramsey in 1851. In keeping with his vision of creating one of the finest educational systems in the country, Neill laid plans to establish a school which could later rise to college level. The result was the Baldwin School incorporated on February 26, 1853, and named for the prominent Philadelphia locomotive builder M. W. Baldwin. During its first year, twenty-eight boys and forty-three girls attended the school located in downtown St. Paul.[1]

Even as this academy was in the planning stage, Neill was looking ahead to the founding of a college for men. He was an ardent opponent of collegiate coeducation, and again he shared his dreams with Baldwin. "For the sum of $5,000 a building can be erected," he wrote the locomotive tycoon in the fall of 1853, "which would serve for the purpose of a preparatory grammar school, a chapel on Sunday and a lecture room during winter nights, to which young men may be attracted from the saloons and gambling establishments." The Baldwin School would serve as the preparatory department of the proposed institution and to it would be added a scientific or practical unit and a collegiate or classical department. The name suggested, Calvary College, grated on Puritan sensibilities, and so the more pedestrian title of College of St. Paul was substituted. All in all it was a grand design.[2]

In the spring of 1855 friends of the projected college, with Baldwin as chairman, met in Philadelphia and elected Neill president. That summer a stone building to house the preparatory department was erected in St. Paul. But a number of factors — the Panic of 1857, a division of the Presbyterians (none

too numerous at best) into New School and Old School, and public apathy — defeated Neill in his efforts to get a college beyond the planning stage during Minnesota territorial days. Nothing, however, seemed to erase his determination.[3]

During the Civil War in which Neill served as a chaplain and later as a secretary to President Abraham Lincoln, local trustees closed Baldwin School and sold its property. Not one to forsake an ambition so easily, Neill would not give up. After leaving the army he again sought the aid of Baldwin and, receiving encouragement, went ahead with the incorporation of Baldwin University in March, 1864. Its purpose would be "to afford instruction in English literature, in ancient and modern languages, in moral and mental philosophy, in history and political economy, in mathematics and the natural sciences, and in the application of science to arts, agriculture, and the professions." The sky was the limit, but again disappointment was the result. Baldwin died in 1866 while he was nurturing plans to endow his namesake, leaving no provision in his will for the institution. In 1869–70 Neill was abroad serving as American consul in Dublin, Ireland. Upon his return to Minnesota, he found that the treasurer of Baldwin University had made unwise investments and that interest in the venture was about zero. Even so Neill did not turn aside from the pursuit of his dream.[4]

This time he directed his gaze to Minneapolis. There looking out on the Falls of St. Anthony stood the Winslow House, famed resort of ante-bellum days. By the early 1870s it had become through foreclosure the property of a prominent Philadelphian named Charles Macalester. In this structure Neill in 1872 reopened the Baldwin School. In order to make a go of it, he conceived a plan whereby his institution would be affiliated with the state university. Under the name Jesus College and with Neill as provost, his brain child would consist of a preparatory school like Phillips Academy, and a school of Christian literature where university students could live and receive instruction in Christianity supplemental to their studies in the secular state institution. But when neither university president William Watts Folwell nor the public responded favorably to the idea, Neill returned to his plan of founding a college for men.[5]

In the summer of 1873 he sought the help of Macalester, who offered him the Winslow House. Neill then selected a majority of the Baldwin School trustees to serve in the same capacity for his latest educational venture and declared that two-thirds of the new board should be Presbyterians. On March 5, 1874, the Minnesota legislature changed the name of Baldwin University to Macalester College, with the stipulation that its preparatory department be called the Baldwin School.[6]

Meanwhile Macalester had died, but he had provided that as soon as $25,000 had been raised to endow an educational institution bearing his name, the Winslow House property should be conveyed to it. By early 1874 the money was in hand, but the trustees, no doubt aware of history, decided to move slowly and not to open a college department until "two professorships are fully endowed." For the next four years nothing much happened. Neill's ability to conceive plans exceeded his aptitude for executing them. He had alienated the Presbyterians by joining the Reformed Episcopal denomination and becoming rector of its Calvary Church in St. Paul. Nevertheless the followers of John Calvin, observing the educational endeavors of other Protestant groups, increasingly felt a compulsion to enter the field of higher education.[7]

The reunited Minnesota Synod in the fall of 1870 had resolved to recommend the founding of a Presbyterian college, and two years later a synodical committee had commended to the brethren the institution recently opened in the Winslow House. By the fall of 1878 numbers of ministers and laymen were of the opinion that delays could no longer be tolerated. At the synod meeting in Red Wing a motion was passed empowering a committee "to consult and co-operate" with Macalester trustees "with a view to the immediate establishment of an educational institution in connection with this synod." Both parties being receptive to mutually beneficial suggestions, the main detail to be ironed out involved the presidency. The denominational committee felt quite logically that the office should be graced by a Presbyterian. Neill agreed to resign as soon as $30,000 was raised to endow the position and a man was found to occupy it.[8]

With everyone generally satisfied, the Presbyterian Synod meeting at St. Peter on October 15, 1880, recognized Macalester as its own and recommended "it to the sympathy and support of the churches under our care." With an endowment of $25,000 and a building valued at $55,000 to $60,000, Macalester appeared to be in a healthy condition. The growing Minnesota Synod composed of five presbyteries, 112 ministers, 133 churches, and 6,968 communicants seemed sufficiently affluent to support a college. Here again, however, appearances were to prove deceiving.[9]

Part of the reason stemmed from developments dating back to 1878. When the synod decided at that time to establish a school, its location was left pretty much open. Typically various communities sought the prize, and a sizable segment in the church favored accepting the offer of Albert Lea. Yet when Macalester was adopted in 1880, delegates to the meeting wisely proclaimed that "all the resources of synod for higher education should be centered on the building of one institution." Then on the very next day with no apparent warning the same delegates decided to establish a women's college at Albert Lea. The only explanation for such a contrary action was expediency, an attempt to placate a southern Minnesota element and to restore harmony. (A dozen years later the United Norwegian Lutheran Church would make a similar gesture.) Whatever the intention, the expansive plan would do Macalester a distinct disservice. Of the $45,000 which the synod felt it "practicable" to ask its churches to raise for the two institutions, Albert Lea College was to receive $15,000.[10]

In 1881 a group of men including some Macalester trustees purchased 160 acres of land in St. Paul, bounded on two sides by Summit and Snelling avenues, and offered 40 acres of it free as a site for the Presbyterian college. By this time the Winslow House was surrounded by commercial enterprises and had lost its charm; the Macalester board sold it for $40,000, three-quarters of which was payable in installments. The other one-quarter consisted of property bringing in about $40 a month. Meanwhile the Reverend Daniel Rice, as financial agent, had been canvassing Presbyterian churches for endowment funds for the two colleges. He had pledges totaling $26,300 by mid-October, 1882, but only $3,700 had actually been received. He and others nonetheless pressed fitfully forward.[11]

Finally concrete results became evident. By early summer 1884 the wing of a new building (Old Main) was completed on the site bordering Snelling and Summit. The Reverend Thomas A. McCurdy, pastor of the First Presbyterian Church of Wooster, Ohio, and a trustee of the College of Wooster, was invited to visit the Twin Cities to consider a tentative offer to head the slowly evolving institution. What he found upon his arrival — an unfurnished, inadequate building surrounded by a cornfield and difficult of access, a small endowment, no students, little public interest — left him less than enthusiastic. The "earnest representations of the trustees," however, swayed him, and he accepted the presidency with certain stipulations. The main conditions were that the board raise an additional endowment of $100,000, hire a fiscal secretary, and after six months release the president from mendicant tasks so that he might devote full time to academic duties. The trustees agreed, and in November, 1884, President McCurdy arrived to take up his responsibilities.[12]

The target date for opening the college was set for September, 1885. To secure money for current expenses, letters of appeal were fired off to Minnesota's Presbyterian ministers. Exuding optimism, lavish in promise, and rich in phraseology, these epistles offered free tuition for ministerial candidates at Macalester. Prayers, money, and students were solicited; pulpits were opened to McCurdy, but results were far from encouraging. "Macalester is an old song and a huge joke," said some people. Others declared that "The State University, Hamline, Carleton and Shattuck are enough for the Northwest." The dollars did not come in, but McCurdy, challenging "failure to do its worst," was determined that the college should open as announced. Perhaps a functioning institution would attract support that a dormant one did not.[13]

And so on September 16, 1885, came the dedication of the building and the opening. The principal address was given by Neill more than thirty-two years after he had performed similar amenities for the Baldwin School! As expected, it was a scholarly performance. A true college, he said, will "avoid a fog line" between the preparatory and the collegiate departments — excellent advice for the time. Stressing the importance of teaching about Christ, Neill assured his listeners that the message as delivered at Macalester would not offend Baptists, Lutherans, Methodists, or Episcopalians. As a male institution, however, the college would probably be smaller than other Minnesota private institutions and the university, which then had ninety-seven students of whom thirty-one were young women. Concluding on a happy note, Neill urged the trustees to keep faith: "Friends will appear at times and places least expected, and help out of difficulties as the black-winged raven with a loaf of bread came to the prophet." [14]

During the first year, enrollment varied — a normal occurrence then — reaching a high of fifty-two, of whom six were college freshmen. The remainder were in the Baldwin School. From then on the numbers gradually increased; collegiate enrollment the following three years was 18, 25, and 45, respectively. A student newspaper, the *Macalester Echo*, appeared in the fall of 1886, and there were occasional outbursts of "boyish glee" — raids on the refectory pantry and nightshirt parades, for example. Conversely there were "plentiful evidences of sterling manhood . . . and of earnest purpose to do studious work." [15]

On the faculty, where Neill reigned as senior professor, both quality and discord shared the stage. The teaching staff was able and well paid for the period ($2,000 a year for professors, plus the use of a house), but its relationship with the administration deteriorated drastically during the McCurdy years. Part of the reason could be found in the college's mounting indebtedness, but most of it resulted from faculty dislike of the president and some of his actions. If one professor's account is valid, McCurdy was lazy, dictatorial, lacking in judgment, and too concerned with petty and inconsequential matters. The climax came in the summer of 1889 when one highly regarded teacher was told that his services would terminate on September 1. The community rose up in arms, and a colleague wrote: "How long McCurdy is yet to be here I cannot tell but it is amazing that they have not kicked him out at once. . . . My feeling is that the college is going to collapse utterly." [16]

Macalester did not do so, but one can only marvel at its powers of endurance. The four faculty houses had been built with $20,000 in borrowed money, and when a new $68,000 addition to Old Main was erected in 1887, most of its cost was met in the same way. Indebtedness on December 1, 1886, was slightly over $27,900; some two years later it was $105,000 and still increasing. Many Presbyterians, honestly or by rationalization, felt that the college was being extravagant and so shut their pocketbooks. Minneapolitans had pretty largely done the same thing after 1885 when the legislature added the area in which the campus was located to the corporate limits of St. Paul. By late 1889 salaries had not been paid for a long time, and some teachers had been forced to borrow money to live on. About half of the overdue pay did arrive shortly before Christmas, but in June, 1890, the faculty received a 25 per cent salary cut which caused further distress and bitterness.[17]

Despite discord and financial stringency, not all life at Macalester was characterized by unrelieved gloom. Almost at the height of the friction between president and professors on June 12, 1889, the first college class of ten men graduated. Six went into religious work, two became lawyers, one a physician, and one a teacher. Another bright spot on February 22, 1890, was the opening of the extension of the Grand Avenue electric streetcar line. For five cents passengers could ride from the campus to downtown St. Paul in a matter of twenty minutes. By way of celebration Governor William R. Merriam made a short speech to the students.[18]

At the conclusion of that academic year, the second college class numbering seven men received degrees. Shortly afterward Dr. McCurdy gave up the struggle and returned to a pastorate. (The board in June, 1889, had given him a year ''to seek out a new field.'') His successor, the Reverend David J. Burrell, minister of Westminster Presbyterian Church in Minneapolis, where he continued to live and serve, was able to spare little time for Macalester, and in September, 1891, he accepted a call to a church in New York City.[19]

The trustees then selected the Reverend A. W. Ringland as president. A graduate of Centre College and of McCormick Theological Seminary, he had enjoyed a highly successful pastorate at the First Presbyterian Church in Duluth since 1884. Although great hopes were held for the college when he assumed leadership in the fall of 1892, they were destined for disappointment. He did, however, effect one significant change. In his first annual report in the summer of 1893, he urged the trustees to open the college's doors to young women. The board by a vote of five to four agreed to do so on a five-year trial basis. The results were hardly cataclysmic — only three women enrolled in the college and four in the academy in the fall of 1893. The first woman graduate would receive her baccalaureate degree in 1897, but in the meantime two board members resigned in protest, and before his death in September, 1893, Neill strongly criticized the action and urged its reconsideration. The following March, 1894, a discouraged President Ringland accepted a call from a church in Ohio. Enrollment at the time was an even 100 — 58 in the academy and 42 in the college department.[20]

The burden of leadership next descended upon one of Macalester's truly great men, James Wallace, who against his wishes consented in the fall of 1894 to serve as acting president. Twelve hard, grueling years would pass before he was relieved of his arduous task. Only his complete faith in his Maker, it would appear, gave him the strength to carry on.

A graduate of the College of Wooster and later a faculty member there, with a year's study in Greece behind him, he had joined the Macalester staff in April, 1887, as professor of Greek and modern languages. In the spring of 1891 after President Burrell's departure, Wallace had accepted appointment to the new post of dean of the college. On his shoulders largely rested the survival of the institution.[21]

By the fall of 1893 with economic conditions everywhere depressed, the situation was so bad that the trustees voted to open school ''with the understanding that it be kept open only as long as funds shall be provided for its current support.'' Had this resolution been enforced, classes would have been suspended before Christmas. Debts piled up. The deadline was near for redemption of college-owned real estate which had been sold for taxes. Bondholders threatened foreclosure, and professors were either not paid or were given real estate in lieu of salaries. Had it not been for Wallace's old friend, Mrs. William Thaw of Pittsburgh, Macalester in all likelihood would have closed in 1894. In response to his urgent plea, she purchased ten acres of the campus area for $25,000, and the next year bought an additional fifteen acres. The money pulled the college out of a desperate predicament. Another benefactor of the later 1890s, because of his regard for Wallace, was James J. Hill. Finally the president's efforts, sacrifices, and inspiration began to tell. The debts were removed, and the college could face the new century with reasonable confidence.[22]

In academic matters the early years of the Wallace presidency reflected developments occurring on campuses generally. The academy course in the mid-1890s was lengthened to four years, probably in response to state teacher certification standards. Electives began to creep into the schedule of courses, and science received growing attention. New faculty members tended to be specialists and to exhibit occasionally firsthand acquaintance with graduate schools in major universities. There was understandably little progress on physical plant, although a frame structure (Edwards Hall) was completed in 1892, a gift from friends. In it were housed some thirty students who formed a boarding club. In 1895 what had been the president's home (the Wallaces had one already) was fitted out as a dormitory named The Elms for about a dozen women students. All in all the college was moving ahead; the worst days were over for the institution E. D. Neill had fostered.[23]

9
COLLEGE OF ST. THOMAS

A Catholic Diocesan Institution
In St. Paul

THE IMPETUS BEHIND THE FOUNDING of the College of St. Thomas in St. Paul was the need for priests to minister to Minnesota's growing Catholic population, especially its Irish contingent. Prime mover was the famed bishop of the St. Paul diocese, John Ireland, who in education as in other areas was known for the rapidity with which he "translated his ideas into acts." Both of his predecessors had dreamed of the time when a seminary could be established in Minnesota's capital city, but financial inadequacy had seemed an insurmountable barrier to action. By 1884, however, when Ireland succeeded to the diocese, the cumulative effects of earlier efforts had created a condition in which the persuasive new bishop was able to give substance to the dream. With characteristic speed he proposed to open in September, 1885, a seminary in which young men aspiring to the priesthood "will be enabled to pursue at least their classical studies." He soon moved beyond this idea. Though the primary purpose of the proposed seminary would be to train priests, the institution would also offer a classical education "to young men who may choose other professions." Response was encouraging.[1]

Fortunately the site was also available. Some years earlier Bishop Thomas L. Grace had purchased a tract of woodland, brooks, lakes, and meadow known as Finn's Farm (the homesite is now occupied by the college chapel) and on it built an industrial school for boys. Although the school had proved a failure, the building which had housed it — a weather-beaten, three-story, frame structure facing a small lake — remained standing. By mid-1880 the deed to the property was in Ireland's name; his seminary plan was already in his mind, and Finn cancelled the debt of $23,200 still owed him in order to further the establishment of a seminary. It was

to this site that Ireland turned when direction of diocesan affairs passed into his hands. With the addition in the spring of 1885 of a new wing and a veneer of brick, the old boys' school was made ready to welcome the bishop's nascent educational venture.[2]

The official announcement boasted that the renovated edifice was "spacious, perfectly ventilated, heated throughout with steam, lighted with gas, and possessing all arrangements conducive to comfort." Later known as the Administration Building, it offered complete, if primitive, accommodations for both faculty and students. On August 10, 1885, the *St. Paul Pioneer Press* reported that a new Catholic seminary offering the "usual theological studies . . . and also a classical course" (a commercial course would "undoubtedly be added in the future") would open on September 8. Nameless until after classes had been in session for a time, the infant was christened by Ireland as St. Thomas Aquinas Seminary "in consideration of our Holy Father having made this saint the special patron of all ecclesiastical schools." The problem of securing a rector was not an easy one, but it was solved by the appointment of Father Thomas O'Gorman, a close friend and former schoolmate of Ireland.[3]

When classes opened on September 8, desks and books were still lacking, but over three-score students of varying ages and educational backgrounds were in attendance. Twenty-four were seminarians and thirty-eight were enrolled in the classical course. Their lives were carefully circumscribed from the rising hour of 5:00 A.M. (they made their own beds) until 8:20 P.M., the hour for prayers and "lights out." Yet there was time for literary and debating activity; the first topic was "Resolved that Total Abstinence Should be Advocated," which must have pleased Ireland. There was fun as well, and the food seemed to please. "They feed us better here than at most colleges, in fact it is such board as would be obtained in a two dollar a day hotel," wrote young Thomas E. Shields, one of the first students who later became a brilliant and controversial professor at Catholic University.[4]

The faculty, including the rector who taught theology and church history, numbered six priests, three of whom had been only recently ordained. One, Father Patrick R. Heffron, would play a significant role in the life of another Minnesota private college, St. Mary's in Winona. Five days of oral examinations — two for students in the classical department and three for seminarians — presided over by Bishop Ireland terminated the first semester early in February, 1886. From the start the bishop loved to visit St. Thomas, to drop in unannounced and take over a class. His favorites were "the classics — Cicero, whose rolling periods find echoes in his orations; Virgil, whose jeweled phrases he used more than once; Horace, whose urbanity, 'simplicity,' and grace were to him a constant delight." [5]

Evidence that things were going well came in March, 1886, when to ease crowded conditions it was necessary to begin work on another wing for the "spacious" building. By the end of the academic year in June, expenses had totaled slightly over $16,200. The diocese had contributed $5,428 to pay the bills for the thirty-three seminarians who had attended all or part of the year; it must have seemed money well spent for a dozen of the young men had been ordained by the time the year was out. The classical students had paid fees amounting to $6,450. By the fall of 1886 a three-page catalog had appeared, and the $40,000 addition to the building was ready to receive the growing student body — eighty-seven classicists and thirty-three seminarians. Bishop Ireland was jubilant, and in a letter to priests and laity he proclaimed: "It is the school of the Diocese, and our heart goes out to it in warmest love." [6]

Despite the gains made, Father O'Gorman, as the second year was ending, told the bishop of his wish to be relieved of his administrative position. For the rectorship Ireland then looked to a highly regarded teacher and writer, the Reverend Edward McSweeney at Mount St. Mary's Seminary in Emmitsburg, Maryland. By mid-August, 1887, Father McSweeney was in charge of St. Thomas. When classes resumed, some 75 lads, 31 of them seminarians, enrolled; before the year was out the total reached 138. The institution was still quite isolated, although Summit Avenue had reached it, and the depot of the Chicago, Milwaukee, and St.

Paul Short Line on University Avenue was a mere fifteen-minute walk away. The rigors of Minnesota winters, however, offered considerable contrast to those the rector had known in Maryland, and for reasons of health, he received permission to return to Mount St. Mary's at the end of the academic year.[7]

Shortly after commencement on June 21, 1888 — an affair graced by three bishops, some thirty priests, and an estimated five hundred laymen — Ireland announced that St. Thomas' third rector would be thirty-year-old Father James J. Keane. Born in Illinois of a family that migrated to a farm near Rochester, Minnesota, Keane had received part of his education at St. John's in Collegeville and at a seminary in Montreal, Canada. A member of St. Thomas' faculty since 1886, former bursar, and vice-rector, he would head the institution for four years.[8]

During his administration, both St. Thomas and its environs would continue to show steady if slow progress. The slightly fewer than one hundred students in the classical department in 1888–89 represented seven states, plus Dakota Territory, Canada, and Ireland. The curriculum was typically six years in length with emphasis on Christian doctrine and the classics, but no student had yet progressed to the final year. No fundamental change in offerings would be made under Father Keane, but the catalog of 1891–92 did make a bow to the future. For the first time the program was divided into a "Preparatory Course" and a "Collegiate Course," each three years long. By association Tommies felt a glow of pride when John Ireland received the pallium of archbishop in the fall of 1888. The next year the electric streetcar reached Grand Avenue, and the college was made more easily accessible. As a result day students were admitted, thereby increasing enrollment. Other high lights of 1889 were the establishment of the Sodality of the Blessed Virgin Mary and the visits of Bishops John Shanley, James McGolrick, and Joseph B. Cotter, recently consecrated on one day by Archbishop Ireland. St. Thomas was not yet a full-fledged college, but it was very much alive and on its way.[9]

One problem, however, disturbed the archbishop. As an institution with both a seminary and a classical department, St. Thomas suffered from what in modern terminology might be called an "identity crisis," a condition Ireland was eager to correct. In his opinion the seminary ought to be a separate entity, not part of a larger whole, and as early as 1890 he announced a contemplated division of the school into two parts. That he was able to effect this change fairly soon was due to a magnificent gift of $500,000 from James J. Hill, who although not a Catholic himself was married to one. In the fall of 1894 St. Thomas' sixty-five seminarians moved across the street to the fine new structure, the St. Paul Seminary, made possible by Hill.[10]

Meanwhile on January 6, 1894, papers were filed to incorporate the old classical department as the "College of Saint Thomas." Under these articles the operation of the institution was vested in a board of five directors, but the rector and other officers as well as all professors were to be appointed by the archbishop and subject to removal by him at any time. That same month, Ireland, with certain stipulations — the college should not be turned over to a religious order was one of these — conveyed to the St. Thomas Corporation the five acres and the buildings of the newly born educational enterprise. In this document Ireland indicated that the structures had cost $71,772.93. Of this amount he had furnished $45,817.96 out of his own funds.[11]

During this transitional period, two other events of significance left their imprint on the college. One was a change in top administration, the other the onset of economic depression. Early in September, 1892, Father Keane resigned the rectorship and was replaced by thirty-four-year-old Father James C. Byrne, a native of Minnesota and a graduate of the College of the Propaganda in Rome. When St. Thomas was incorporated as a college, he became its first president. Throughout his administration of seven years he had fairly smooth sailing. The economic depression and the departure of the seminarians had created some problems — enrollment fell below a hundred, most faculty joined the move to the seminary, new building projects could not be undertaken — but these were solved. The support of the archbishop, financial and otherwise, plus a loan from one of the other directors kept the college solvent, and new faculty were found without undue effort. By 1896 conditions were so well recovered that the college purchased twenty acres

of land adjoining the five acres conveyed by Ireland, borrowing the necessary $15,000 to cover its cost from a St. Paul insurance company.[12]

Probably in the hope of attracting more students a two-year commercial course was introduced in 1894–95. Geared to a high school level, it offered work in such subjects as shorthand, typewriting, penmanship, and bookkeeping. Mainly an appendage of the central academic work of the college, the program was dropped shortly after World War I. Another curricular development came in 1897 with the introduction of an "English-Scientific" course, a four-year sequence at the secondary level. It was directed at young men "whose aim in life does not demand a knowledge of the Ancient Classics, who nevertheless aspire to the attainment of much more than merely business requirements." Attractive though this description sounds, the course was short-lived. Perhaps the priests' hearts were not in it. At least college authorities in the year it was introduced proclaimed that the classical course "was the true foundation of education. This is the course which parents, if their means and circumstances permit, should select for their boys." [13]

All the while Father Byrne worked hard to build up the college and to win it new friends, but it was slow going. The largest graduating class in the 1890s, that of 1896, contained only fourteen men, none of senior college rank. Still much was made of each commencement occasion. When the apostolic delegate presided in 1893, for example, about a hundred priests were in attendance along with a large assembly of laity. From the next year on, the usual student essays and orations attendant upon the ceremonies contained one delivered in Greek and one in Latin. By 1899, the last year of Byrne's presidency, enrollment pushed beyond one hundred, and both faculty and facilities were being noticeably taxed. Plans were then laid for expansion, a task that would be handed on to a new executive and largely tackled in the years to come.[14]

A Norwegian Lutheran College
In the Red River Valley

IN 1891 WHILE NORWEGIAN LUTHERAN supporters of Augsburg and St. Olaf were casting darts at each other and attempting to evolve satisfactory relationships with the recently formed United Church, their Lutheran compatriots opened another school in Minnesota's Red River Valley. In time it would develop into Concordia College. The site of this third Norse educational endeavor was the outskirts of Moorhead, home of a three-year-old state normal school, "one of the worst saloon towns in America" with a somewhat exaggerated reputation as "The Wickedest City in the World." Railroad construction crews and the parasitic riffraff that exploited laborers on all frontiers had given the city its unsavory reputation. The rails, however, carried into the area hundreds and thousands of settlers who wanted to make homes and strike permanent roots in the flat, fertile soil.[1]

As early as 1882 the Episcopalians had opened in Moorhead a preparatory school for boys with a faculty graced by graduates of Dartmouth College and Cambridge University in England. Housed in a fine three-story Victorian mansion built for the purpose, the enterprise had been named for Bishop Henry B. Whipple. It survived only five years, but its building would provide quarters for the Norwegians' new educational venture. Other denominations, notably the Swedish Lutherans, under the prodding of their synod president, Eric Norelius, also started schools, always with high expectations. Hope Academy, started by the Swedes in a Moorhead structure originally intended for hotel use, has a certain relevance for the Concordia story.[2]

Toward the end of the 1880s the administration of the academy had asked the Norwegian Lutheran pastors of the area to lend their support to the infant institution. After discussing the request, the Norwegians not surprisingly concluded they should have a school of their own. They represented the largest single ethnic group in the valley, and like their fellow Scandinavians in southeastern Minnesota in the 1860s and 1870s, they were disturbed by the absence of religious instruction in the public schools. By the time public high schools became fairly numerous, the Norwegians would feel differently, but that time was still in the future.[3]

At a second pastoral conference in December, 1889, the Norsemen, acting predictably and in time-honored tradition, decided to locate their school in whichever town made the best offer. A number of communities showed interest and made promises beyond their abilities to fulfill. Feeling ran high among the rivals for the coveted prize. When Grand Forks seemed to have the edge, the editor of the *Crookston Times* wrote sarcastically: "The Red River Valley College is like the Irishman's fleas. When you put your finger on it [sic] and think you have it, you find it isn't there." And then with something less than complete confidence in the decision-making ability of the church group, he quipped: "Future changes in the program will be announced from time to time in these columns and its [the school's] location at Fargo, Moorhead, Ada, Fisher, and Beltrami will be duly chronicled."[4]

Meanwhile the Episcopalians were eager to sell the Bishop Whipple School property and were willing to let it go for one-third of what it had cost them. To Pastor J. M. O. Ness of Perley and others this seemed the solution to their school problem. Thus after gaining assurance of backing, they organized on April 14, 1891, the Northwestern Lutheran College Association with Ness as president. He would hold the position for thirty-seven years, and a Fargo druggist, Lars Christianson, would serve as secretary of the school's sponsoring organization for forty-three years. The name selected for the institution — Concordia — stood for "hearts in harmony." It seemed also a suitable commemoration for the recent union of three groups into the United Norwegian Lutheran Church. In July the association voted to purchase the Episcopal property and to invite Ingebrikt F. Grose, possessor of B.A. and M.A. degrees from Luther College and a professor of English at St. Olaf College since 1886, to head the new enterprise. Promised $1,000 a year and free housing in the school building, he was directed to "exercise discipline in conformity with the commandments of God's Word . . . and since this is to be a school for both sexes, there will be need for special care." Native-born inhabitants of the region were skeptical about the ability of the Norwegians to succeed in their plan, but one of the latter predicted: "These people are going to do a work for Christ and His Church for which even the sons of New England will yet rise up and call them blessed." [5]

When Grose arrived, he found his lone building somewhat the worse for wear, its most recent dwellers having been students at Moorhead Normal. Nevertheless he moved in on September 1, 1891, and set about preparing for the opening of classes. Although known in good frontier style as a "college," Concordia began small, with three teachers and twelve students, one of whom was twelve years old. The student who was fourth to register on opening day, October 15, 1891, related that he and a friend were given only mattresses to sleep on in the corridor. Chairs being in short supply, students brought their own from their rooms to sit on in the dining hall. Such games as "Pig in the Parlor" and "The Needle's Eye" were played during the social hour between supper and study time. [6]

Before Christmas enrollment was up to sixty, and the faculty was augmented by the keeper of a general store who had attended Luther College and Valparaiso University and taught commercial courses at Willmar Seminary. He had charge of the "business education department," which was as vital to the young Norwegians of the valley as St. John's "commercial college" had been to the Germans of Stearns County. There was the usual three-term calendar, and students could come and go as their whims, finances, and the demands of work on the farm dictated. The curriculum, in reponse to regional needs, offered a veritable *smörgåsbord* — the commercial course, a practical course, classical work for college-bound students, catechetical instruction for teachers of religion in parochial schools, English for immigrants, and music. [7]

Amazingly over two hundred students registered for the winter term. Young Pastor Rasmus Bogstad, a St. Olaf alumnus, had been out drumming up business in the hinterland with considerable success. Since the school building could not accommodate this number, rooms in private homes and the second floor of a Moorhead business structure were put to dormitory use. As a result the Lutheran College Association in May, 1892, decided to erect a boys' dormitory and to make Bogstad head of the building committee. With horse and buggy he traveled from farm to farm, and despite the depressed prices of wheat, butter, and pork, he had secured $12,000 in cash and pledges by December 1. The remaining $10,000 needed was borrowed from a local bank. Early in 1893, 142 boys moved into Concordia's second building (Academy Hall); the dormitory section of the main edifice housed girls, and the overflow continued to live in private homes. At the end of that academic year nine diplomas were awarded at Concordia's first graduation ceremony. One went to a young lady who had completed the practical course, the other eight to male classmates whose work had been in the commercial department. [8]

The effects of the Panic of 1893 soon threatened to terminate Concordia's life before it was well begun. Early in October the bank declared that unless the $10,000 loan was paid on December 1, a mortgage bearing 18 per cent would be demanded. Most members of the association apparently felt that the case was hopeless. Bogstad, Grose, and the druggist Christianson thought otherwise. With a salary of only $600 a year Bogstad agreed to lend $500 by borrowing money from friends, and so did Grose. Christianson promised to put up whatever was necessary after the trio's attempt at money raising was over. With three days to go, most of the necessary amount was in sight. The hurdle was the $1,000 promised by the two professors. [9]

Providentially at this juncture "a young man whose hat and coat still bore chaff from a threshing machine" arrived to enroll in Concordia. By a strange coincidence he had on his person $1,000 for which he did not have any immediate need — Edward D. Neill's "black-winged raven with a loaf of bread" — and which he planned to deposit in a local bank. Grose and Bogstad were not slow to suggest a better use for the money. Happily the young farmer concurred, accepting two promissory notes for his rather sizable nest egg. [10]

On Monday morning, December 1, 1893, the money was turned over to a surprised "Yankee" bank president. A little over two years later when economic conditions improved, the association decided to raise $10,000 to repay the friends whose loans had saved the school from the bank's clutches.

With nearly $3,000 already promised, Bogstad in high spirits set out again with horse and buggy. Preaching in churches on Sundays and calling at farm homes during the week, he rather easily and quickly secured more than enough money to cancel Concordia's debt.[11]

Throughout the 1890s the institution remained an academy. Periodically additions were made to the curriculum. Shorthand and typing came along, followed by a "Domestic Industry Department." The latter enabled "lady students to prepare themselves for those duties which are so essential to the welfare and happiness of the family." By 1896 the classical course was four years in duration; others, including a normal course, were two or three years.[12]

Professor Grose resigned the principalship after two years, but stayed on to teach until June, 1896. After that most of his career was spent teaching at Northfield's St. Olaf College. His successor as principal was Hans H. Aaker, the storekeeper who had taken charge of the business education department late in 1891. Considering this fact, it was not surprising that he believed Concordia's survival depended upon its becoming a business college, providing practical as opposed to classical courses of study. And that is largely what it did. Two diplomas in the classical course were awarded in June, 1894, but they were exceptions. Of the eighty diplomas earned by graduation time of 1898, sixty-five had gone to students taking commercial training. This emphasis was displeasing to most ministers and to some of the faculty who looked to Bogstad to champion their point of view, while the trustees, businessmen, and farmers espoused the "practical" outlook. In the impasse which resulted Aaker served briefly as a reform mayor of Moorhead in 1900 and ran unsuccessfully for Congress in that same year. On April 23, 1902, he resigned as principal of Concordia, and soon after he established a business college in Fargo. Concordia would now shift direction and head toward attainment of the status of a true liberal arts institution.[13]

PART II

THE SURGE OF THE TWENTIETH CENTURY

1900–1940

11

Introduction: Part II — 1900–1940

IN THE YEAR 1900 the private colleges in Minnesota were in various stages of development. Some were still academies, some had included reputable collegiate departments for a goodly number of years, some were yet to be born. Some would jettison their preparatory divisions fairly soon; others would maintain neighborly relationships with their former junior associates to the present day. While the institutions exhibited certain similarities, there were wide variations, many of which do not lend themselves to accurate measurement — the intelligence or respective levels of maturity of college students, or the ability of a faculty at a well-established institution, for example, compared with that of a college just coming into being.

In Minnesota and in other sections of the United States there was no blueprint for higher education, no master plan, no system whereby the over-all needs of society were best served. Consequently colleges and universities, as Frederick T. Gates put it, were "scattered haphazard over the landscape like wind-carried seeds." It is true that some control had been exercised by the legislatures through their power to grant charters and to bestow the privilege of conferring degrees. Yet there is little indication that these governing bodies did much either to inhibit the formation or to guide the progress of the educational entities to which they gave legal status. In a period of *laissez faire*, of relative individualism, of comparatively unbridled competition, such as that under which the state's private colleges had been established, it was only natural that their governing boards had been granted wide latitude in such vital matters as fashioning curriculums and making rules.[1]

In many respects this freedom from external control, this privilege of going its own way, gave the private college its virtue and its opportunity. Except for the necessity of complying with public police regulations regarding fire, traffic, sanitation, and the like, the independent institution of higher learning could determine its own peculiar nature and mission; it could experiment and take chances which a university dependent upon taxpayers for its survival would hesitate to indulge in. At least that was the theory, and in many ways it worked out.

But there was another side to the coin. Freedom could mean many things. It could permit what in modern days has been termed "the pursuit of excellence." It could also allow a sort of dinosaurian regression, a repetition of courses and methods which were becoming increasingly irrelevant to the contemporary scene. Some have argued that the colleges, or at least their faculties and administrators, tended to follow the latter path, that left to themselves they would have gone on in perpetuity doing obeisance to a static and arid curriculum. To students in their literary societies and intercollegiate athletic endeavors, to the new land-grant colleges and western state universities, these critics would award the credit for instilling new life, vigor, and relevance into hidebound and arteriosclerotic collegiate offerings and practices.

For Minnesota colleges, hardly ready to assume leadership in national education circles, the argument is largely academic. These institutions were still followers, struggling to stay alive and to find their own identities. They could emulate whichever type of institution seemed most relevant and had the most to offer. If they decided to provide prepreparatory work or to stress commercial courses, they were free to do so. The result was a glorious diversity, which is even now one of the virtues of the American system of higher education, but which carried too far would end in chaos and an absence of standards.

Of course there had always been homogenizing influences in Minnesota and elsewhere. The tendency of new, western colleges to imitate Yale, the formulation of teacher certification requirements, student opinion forged by intercollegiate debate, oratory, and athletic contests, the impact of articulate individuals, and the example of a neighboring institution had all been present before 1900, but it had been easier to ignore them then than it would be later. Too great a divergence from accepted norms thereafter would probably mean trouble, loss of students, loss of faculty, loss of status, loss of support, even though the day of reckoning might be a long way off.

New England colleges, being older and more solidly established, took the lead in tackling the problem of standardization, creating an association for the purpose in 1885. Within a decade educators farther west followed the example. Late in March, 1895, some three dozen representatives from seven Upper Midwest states, not including Minnesota, met at Northwestern University and formed what is today the North Central Association of Colleges and Secondary Schools. At this gathering it was made clear that no decisions of the new organization which bore upon internal policies or management of an institution of learning were to be other than advisory, a principle still observed. Nevertheless the influence of the association has been and is great. At its initial annual meeting in 1896, it issued the first of a long line of policy statements: "*Resolved*, that . . . no College is considered in good standing that confers the degree of Doctor of Philosophy or Doctor of Science, except after a period of at least two years of residence and of graduate study." Institutions ignoring this dictum were to be ineligible for membership in the association, a provision given legal sanction by the courts some four decades later in the Langer case.[2]

During the early years of the organization, spirited debates at annual meetings dealt with such topics as college entrance requirements, desirable differentiation of work to be assigned to secondary schools and those of higher rank, qualifications needed by high school teachers of history, and provisions for individual differences among students of secondary and collegiate status. Few practical results ensued until after 1900, but increasingly the association then became a power in education, affecting both thought and practice. Membership became highly prized, and few colleges were about to ignore the pronouncements coming out of the annual meetings.[3]

As early as 1902 the association set up a Commission on Accredited Schools to develop standards for high schools and to compile lists of accredited secondary schools which would be helpful to colleges and universities in their admissions work. Four years later the name of the body was changed to Commission on Accredited Schools and Colleges, and it was instructed to report on the advisability of providing for the inspection and accreditation of institutions of higher learning. Needless to say many people in academic life took a dim view of this development. Nevertheless in 1909 the association approved the idea and appointed a committee of five to supervise the task of accreditation. By the next year the machinery was set in motion, and by 1912 standards for accreditation had been drawn up.[4]

To be acceptable a college had to meet twelve conditions. Its faculty members must have graduated from a reputable institution and done graduate work equal at least to that required for a master's degree. Minimum semester hours needed for graduation could not be less than 120. Fourteen high school units as defined by the association were necessary for admission. Library and laboratory equipment should be adequate, and there should be at least eight distinct liberal arts departments, each with one or more full-time professors. No teacher should carry over eighteen teaching hours per week, and classes should be limited in size to thirty. Productive endowment for private colleges should fall no lower than $200,000. The buildings must satisfy certain specifications as to location, construction, lighting, ventilation, furnishings, and the like. Finally a number of rather intangible factors — the character of the curriculum, the standard for regular degrees, the general tone of the institution, its scientific spirit — would all be taken into consideration in determining accreditation. In 1912 the first list of accredited institutions appeared. On it in Minnesota were "Carlton" [*sic*], the state university, and Winona Normal School. Two years later Hamline joined the select circle.[5]

Another group interested in standards for American colleges was the Association of American Universities (AAU) founded in 1900. Between 1914 and 1948 the AAU carried "the responsibility of being the national accrediting agency for liberal arts colleges and universities." During that period, its initial list of 119 institutions was tripled. Increasingly, however, the task of establishing standards, sending visitors to campuses, handling stacks of correspondence, and defending the association against critics became unduly burdensome. Moreover it was obvious that AAU accreditation of his college made little difference in an applicant's chance of gaining admission to a graduate shcool. Thus at its 1948 meeting the association discontinued its accreditation chore, although the work had been influential in altering the face of higher education.[6]

Admission to college had always been something of a problem, both for the preparatory school and for the admitting institution. Early in the lives of most Minnesota private colleges the main criterion demanded of candidates for admission appeared to be "a good moral character," yet some minimum intellectual attainments were mandatory as well. During the period so far covered, however, Minnesota institutions were in no position to be too choosy. A reasonably good prospect was often difficult enough to secure, and if necessary special remedial and preparatory work would be given him to provide the background needed for handling courses in the college department.

The trend nevertheless was in the direction of evaluating the quality of secondary schools and of demanding certain minimum levels of ability and knowledge from applicants. All colleges, of course, would accept without question graduates of their own preparatory departments. For others achievement tests, using homespun questions probably culled from those prepared for academy courses, were usually but not always administered. By the turn of the century, however, admission without examination was being granted to a growing number of young people — graduates of recognized academies, of the advanced courses of Minnesota normal schools, and of high schools approved by the state high school board. Soon all who finished the course in secondary schools accredited by the North Central Association or the state university received the same consideration by most colleges.

But even where accreditation had been obtained, there was wide variation in the caliber of work done in the secondary institutions, and attendance in high schools was far from universal. Of over 6,000,000 young people 14 to 17 years of age in the country in 1900, only about 700,000 were enrolled in secondary schools. To rate the college prospects among the boys and girls in this latter group, a test was needed whereby students from many different schools and states could be compared. The National Education Association (NEA) gave attention to the problem and so did some of the regional associations. The upshot was the formation of the College Entrance Examination Board (CEEB), which administered its first tests in June, 1901. It would be over four decades, however, before "college boards" were required as part of the admissions procedure of a Minnesota college.[7]

Debate over the tests, over the theory on which they are based, over their validity and reliability, and over their results has gone on hot and heavy to the present day. That they have influenced curriculum and method in the secondary schools — some would substitute "tyrannized" for "influenced" — and played a large role in college admissions practice, none would deny. Like grades in courses, achievement and aptitude tests are subject to a multitude of imperfections and misuses, but they measure something, and so far substitutes acceptable to everyone have yet to be developed.

In another sensitive area — a cynic might say *the* most sensitive — that of finance, developments were occurring which gave added impetus toward standardization. The independent college was finding that if it was to share in the wealth of certain tycoons lately metamorphosed into philanthropists, it must meet stipulations laid down by them. Of course, donations to institutions of learning by men of means were nothing new in 1900 — witness the example of James J. Hill — but in matters of degree and of impact a whole new era was soon to open. It began early in 1902 with the formation of the General Education Board having the avowed purpose of promoting "education within the United States without distinction of race, sex or creed."[8]

Largely the conception of John D. Rockefeller, Jr., the board started life with a gift of $1,000,000 from his father to be spent over a ten-year period for the improvement of educational opportunities for Negroes in the South. By early 1907 at the urging of his friend Frederick T. Gates, the founder of Standard Oil had added over $20,000,000 to his original donation and expanded the purpose of the board. Its money was to be used to bring some system out of the chaos which existed in the field of higher education in the United States, especially among the private colleges. Of the nearly seven hundred colleges and universities in the country in 1902, more than a quarter had total revenues of $25,000 a year or less, and many were no better than mediocre secondary schools. Instruction in Latin, Greek, and mathematics was good, but in general little could be said for that in modern languages, literature, history, economics, and science. During the next six decades, the board made grants that totaled $325,000,000 to improve the situation and to provide the United States with a "system [of] institutions of higher learning which shall be for the United States territorially comprehensive, harmoniously related, individually complete, and so solidly founded that it will . . . survive the vicissitudes of time." The success of the Rockefeller creation in many ways, not the least of which was in the moral support it provided college presidents across the land, was monumental. What it contributed to the building of Minnesota colleges will be seen in later chapters.[9]

Another Croesus of the period, Andrew Carnegie, also wielded influence on the nation's educational institutions. While less than that of the General Education Board, Carnegie's influence was still notable. Impressed by the sad plight of retired professors whose meager salaries had permitted little accumulation of surplus against the day when earnings ceased, the Pittsburgh philanthropist established in 1905 the Carnegie Foundation for the Advancement of Teaching. Its purpose was "to provide retiring pensions for the teachers of non-sectarian universities, colleges, and technical schools." But the Carnegie people had definite ideas regarding the nature of a college — every department chairman must be a Ph.D., a four-year liberal arts course was mandatory, and denominational control must be absent. An institution seeking inclusion in the plan therefore had to show that it met these specified conditions. Only one Minnesota private college, Carleton, was included on the Carnegie pension list, but a number of others in the state benefited from a second of the steel magnate's charitable organizations, the Carnegie Corporation, created in 1911 with assets of $151,000,000.[10]

Changes such as the Carnegie and Rockefeller organizations sought to effect were bound to encounter resistance. Old ways were disturbed, vested interests were threatened, local pride was hurt. Not surprisingly outcries were raised on campuses across the land. To these critics the author of the General Education Board's report for 1914 explained: "The states have not generally shown themselves competent to deal with higher education on a nonpartisan, impersonal, and comprehensive basis. . . . Rival religious bodies have invaded fields fully — or more than fully — occupied already; misguided individuals have founded a new college instead of strengthening an old one." Perhaps the author overstated the case, but he certainly had a point. Without the efforts of the board and similar charitable organizations, American higher education would have remained more fragmented, feeble, and chaotic than it did.[11]

In spite of these developments, dozens of small backwater institutions continued to be born, to survive, and to send out young men and women whose contributions were far above the ordinary, but higher education and society did benefit by the endeavors of the early foundations, the regional associations, and certain foresighted college presidents. To measure precisely the results of these endeavors is impossible, but one New York observer in 1909 was sufficiently impressed by the Carnegie Foundation's activity to ask: "Who anticipated that in less than five years it would effect profound changes in the constitution and management of our colleges, severing venerable denominational ties, tightening up requirements for admission, differentiating the college from the university, systematizing finances, raising salaries, and in more subtle ways modifying the life and work of thousands of educators?" [12]

The growing affluence which had permitted the creation of wealthy foundations also increased young people's chances of continuing their educations beyond the secondary level. Between 1870 and 1910 enrollment in the country's colleges and universities mounted four times as fast as the total population. While the latter went up by 130 per cent, the number of college graduates increased by 260 per cent — from 9,300 to 34,200. In Minnesota the sweep upward was particularly noticeable after 1890. Even so it is well to remember that in 1910 fewer than 5 per cent of those between 18 and 21 years old in the United States were in college at all, and that as late as 1940 only 4.2 per cent of Minnesota's population had completed four years of higher education. Furthermore, while some of the private colleges in the state would be quick to take their cues from the North Central Association and similar prophets of new ideals, other institutions because of their own special commitments and functions would be more resistant.[13]

Faculties well aware of what was happening in higher education were anxious to improve their status and to assure teachers greater dignity and security. Poorly paid, overworked, and dominated frequently by an autocratic clergyman-president, nineteenth-century professors, whatever their self-image might be, were in actuality "mere servants for hire." They could be, and were, arbitrarily fired with no recourse — a procedure given judicial sanction in at least four states between 1894 and 1905. Yet there were harbingers, however feeble, of changes to come. When Edward A. Ross was forced to resign at Stanford University in 1900, the American Economic Association investigated the case and gave evidence of what might be expected in the future. Thereafter increasing numbers of college and university teachers came to the conclusion, repugnant though it was to many of their number, that they must organize for their own protection.[14]

In the early twentieth century as the extremes of great wealth on the one hand and of dire poverty on the other became progressively more apparent, this faculty conviction grew accordingly. It would culminate in 1915 in the organization of the American Association of University Professors, familiarly referred to as AAUP. Had it not been for a number of factors — the idealism and timidity of professors, their aversion to being labeled trade unionists, lack of co-ordination among academic institutions — the action would have undoubtedly come sooner. But there was — and is today — considerable opposition to the organization. The Association of American Colleges, also founded in 1915 and composed of presidents, reminded the professors that "no way has yet been found to play the 'cello or the harp and at the same time to direct the orchestra." Yet the AAUP grew in size, especially after 1920. By January, 1922, slightly over four thousand individuals from 183 colleges and universities were members. The first chapter in Minnesota was organized in October, 1916, by representatives from the University of Minnesota and some of the smaller colleges. As the AAUP grew, the Minnesota Conference with its local chapters was formed. While it is true that trustees and administration continued to exercise almost unrestricted power for many years, it is equally certain that the efforts of the AAUP, especially after World War II, were influential in fashioning widely accepted policies regarding faculty tenure and academic freedom.[15]

The extent to which Minnesota's private colleges responded to the challenges broadcast by accrediting agencies, testing organizations, charitable foundations, and faculty associations will be apparent as each institution's story unfolds in succeeding chapters. The influence of the North Central Association took hold early and has remained potent to the present day. The same has been true of Rockefeller and Carnegie money and that of other financial geniuses. College board examinations did not become a mandatory part of the admissions procedure of any Minnesota institution before World War II, but batteries of standardized tests were introduced quite generally from the late 1920s on, both to measure performance and to predict future achievement.

Of all the external educational influences of the period, however, none exceeded the University of Minnesota in its impact on the state's private colleges. From a school of about 1,000 students in 1890, the university grew seventeenfold by 1939–40, when it enrolled over half of the 33,500 students registered in Minnesota's institutions of higher learning. The four-year liberal arts colleges then accounted for a quarter of the total, nearly twice as many as the state teachers colleges. The university was literally the capstone of Minnesota's educational structure. From it the undergraduate institutions drew faculty members, speakers, consultants, edification, advice, and inspiration; to it the private colleges sent eligible transfers, graduates, and also teachers, as well as requests for guidance and accreditation. In the Association of Minnesota Colleges, all members public and private strove harmoniously to better their performances and to provide the state with facilities sufficient to meet the evolving needs

for a many-faceted higher educational structure of first-rate quality. Relationships have been friendly and mutually beneficial.[16]

The colleges were also caught up in the forces which shaped society generally, two of which — World War I and the great depression of the 1930s — stand paramount during this period. The immediate effects of the war were apparent between 1917 and 1919 in reduced enrollments, the watering down of certain curricular offerings, the appearance of Student Army Training Corps (SATC) units, and the killing and wounding of former students. The secondary impact, except for those remembered with gold stars on campus flags, was more enduring; its superficial manifestations could be seen in bobbed hair, coonskin coats, Stutz Bearcats — or more likely Model T Fords — sports spectacles, bathtub gin, and the Charleston. But beyond these surface symptoms was something deeper and traceable in large degree to the experience of men in uniform in the camps in the United States and on the battlegrounds of Europe — a loss of innocence, the pursuit of pleasure, a growing sophistication, regrettable bigotry, more than a dash of cynicism and disillusion. No one would suggest that the average Minnesota undergraduate of the 1920s personified the caricatures of John Held, Jr., or that all collegians were soul mates of F. Scott Fitzgerald, Gertrude Stein, or Ernest Hemingway in a lost generation. No more would it be accurate, however, to suggest that the campus milieu of 1925 was not vastly different from that of 1910.

In two somewhat peripheral yet pervasive segments of higher education — forensics and intercollegiate athletics — the truth of this last assertion finds convincing support. Oratory and debate, which were so popular at the turn of the century, continued to evoke general campus enthusiasm right up to the time that World War I caused a brief cessation in intercollegiate competitions. In Northfield from 1900 to 1918, for example, the Ware oratorical contests between St. Olaf and Carleton were attended by such eruptions of passionate partisanship that one year the faculties of the two colleges appointed committees "with reference to the discontinuance of yelling" at the event. College debate for a time prior to World War I was the target of criticism from such spellbinders as Theodore Roosevelt and William Jennings Bryan, who deplored the relativism implicit in requiring participants to argue both sides of a question. "What we need," declared Roosevelt, "is to turn out of our colleges young men with ardent convictions on the side of right." But debate on Minnesota campuses was still a major activity in that period and for quite a few more years. Increasingly, however, there was a difference. Interest in debate and oratory after World War I lessened among the bulk of the student population, while the popularity of intercollegiate athletics, especially football and basketball, mounted.[17]

For a time early in the century football labored under a cloud of disfavor. When, for example, eighteen or nineteen young men died playing the game in 1905, complaints regarding the game's brutality reached clear to the White House. The introduction of the forward pass the next year reduced partially the advantage of sheer strength, such as that exemplified in the famous flying wedge, but numbers of colleges nevertheless suspended the sport for several years. At Macalester President Wallace joined in the outcry, suggesting: "The authorities of the State Fair should by all means arrange to exhibit a lot of these wonderful football giants next September in one of the barns along with the prize bulls." Macalester then gave up competition for a time. The Augustana Synod was even more extreme, declaring in 1905 that "athletics, as it is carried on at the present time, is a real evil." Thereupon Gustavus Adolphus, despite student rumblings, dropped intercollegiate football until 1917. Little interest in the sport was evinced at Concordia until 1915, and St. Olaf also put a stop to intercollegiate competition until the end of World War I. At St. John's all athletic contests with other institutions were banned by action of the faculty on December 15, 1909.[18]

Although it was played after a fashion from the mid-1890s on, basketball had to await the construction of adequate gymnasiums before it could become a major activity. Such contests as were played early in the century bore slight resemblance to those of a later period. Both St. Olaf and St. John's built gymnasiums in 1901, and while that of the former "was for some years the envy of most visiting basketball teams," its dimensions were only 50 by 80 feet and its location was in the basement of a dormitory. St. John's facility was a separate building, but it had at first an earthen floor. Concordia in 1907 took pride in its "large and commodious" basement gymnasium, yet its height of 23 feet, 10 inches, permitted the basketball to be bounced off the ceiling as well as off the floor. The modern era really dates from 1910 when Carleton and Hamline erected gymnasiums which served a multitude of purposes for many years. In basketball, as in football, however, the era of the big time did not really commence until after World War I. When the two sports gripped the fancy of Minnesota's college communities, the campuses were never the same again.[19]

Until the twentieth century organization and supervision of athletics had been left largely to student enterprise, which resulted in enthusiasm but also in a lack of system and periodic abuses. Thus faculty and administration had to get into the act. In 1901 Carleton took the lead in organizing the Minnesota Athletic Conference, which included academies as well as such colleges as St. Thomas and Hamline. The latter withdrew from the organization in 1907, but its football rivalry with Carleton and the Catholic men's college across town did not abate. In 1906 the Red River Valley Athletic Association, composed of six Minnesota and Dakota schools including Concordia, made its appearance. Another group, which for a time counted Hamline, St. Olaf, and Gustavus Adolphus on its rolls, was the Minnesota-Dakota Intercollegiate Athletic Conference. All these organizations attempted to regulate competition, to restrict it to bona fide students, and to exclude paid professionals, but rules and controls remained fairly loose. Colleges competed with teams from academies, seminaries, and the YMCA (Carleton's 1913 football team beat the Faribault State School for the Deaf 118–0) as well as with squads from institutions of higher rank. Claims to titles, as a consequence, were frequently misty, mythical, and eminently controversial in supportive evidence. The organization of Minnesota colleges into fairly permanent conferences with set schedules, observed eligibility rules, and other controls was a post-World War I phenomenon.[20]

The Minnesota Intercollegiate Athletic Conference (MIAC) came into being in 1920 with charter members Carleton, Concordia, Gustavus Adolphus, Hamline, Macalester, St. John's, St. Olaf, and St. Thomas. Augsburg was admitted in 1924. St. Mary's of Winona gained membership two years later but was dropped in November, 1927, for failure to have a representative at two conference meetings. As a result it could not claim the football championship that year even though it had won all of its games. In December, 1927, however, the college was reinstated, and the following year it shared the title with newcomer Augsburg. Then in 1929 St. Mary's again had the football championship taken away and given to St. Thomas because of the use (somewhat inadvertently perhaps) of a player who did not meet eligibility requirements. Hamline thereupon broke athletic relationships with the Winona institution. These facts should not be taken as criticism of any particular college — questionable practices regarding athletics could be uncovered on most campuses of the time — but rather as illustrations of the difficulties encountered in the fashioning of wholesome intercollegiate athletic competition. The 1930s would also have problems in this area.[21]

Another attempt to systematize and regulate sports contests grew out of a meeting in Chicago in December, 1920, and led to the formation of the Midwest Collegiate Athletic Conference. At its first event, a track meet in Cedar Rapids, Iowa, in May, 1921, six colleges from four states participated. One of the institutions was Carleton, also a member of the MIAC. Soon Hamline followed the example of the Northfield college and added membership in the Midwest Conference to that in the new Minnesota organization. By December, 1923, with the addition of Ripon and Monmouth colleges in Wisconsin and Illinois, the four-state conference consisted of ten institutions. The following year James Millikin University in Illinois withdrew from the Midwest organization, and after 1925 Carleton did not continue its membership in the MIAC. A further realignment came in June, 1930, when Hamline felt compelled for financial reasons to leave the interstate conference. Carleton thereupon became the group's only Minnesota representative. In 1939 Grinnell College of Iowa accepted membership, but during the period of World War II with travel restrictions and difficulties mounting, Carleton dropped from the Midwest Conference for five years. In 1946 it returned to the fold, and in 1952 it was joined by former MIAC stalwart St. Olaf. From the beginning the conference, by affiliating with the National Collegiate Athletic Association (NCAA), by placing control largely in faculty hands, by requiring in 1925 a two-semester residence requirement for participants in sports, and in other ways, set a high example and attempted to avoid various abuses which crept into collegiate athletics. The record has not been perfect, but it has been relatively commendable.[22]

But despite the enthusiasm and the contention generated by athletics, their impact on the colleges in the 1930s cannot be equated with that stemming from the stock market crash of October, 1929. The dream of uninterrupted prosperity came to a shattering end. For nearly a decade thereafter concern over college survival would supersede most other matters. Once again as in the 1890s faculty members would be called upon for sacrifice and devotion beyond mere duty. Presidents would literally drive themselves to exhaustion in pursuit of money to meet current expenses. Expansion of physical plant would have to be postponed. Students would grow more serious and some of them, along with a few of their professors, losing faith in the American capitalistic system, would begin a flirtation with various "isms" and ideologies at odds with democratic ideals. The majority, however, would dig in, work hard, and express alarm at the rise of the forces of fascism and communism which were stifling freedom in widespread areas of the world. As a result Minnesota's private colleges, like those elsewhere, weathered the crisis and were beginning to move ahead once more when war clouds again rolled up over the horizon.[23]

12 HAMLINE UNIVERSITY

Trials and Growth

HAMLINE UNIVERSITY, during the first years of the new century when President Bridgman was still basking in the warm glow of his long popularity, was entering a period of comparative affluence. As the result of a fund drive to which the Nortons of Winona gave $80,000 and James J. Hill gave $50,000, the president in 1903 could announce the addition of $250,000 to the institution's endowment. Two years later partly as the result of a suggestion Bridgman had made to M. G. Norton, two of whose sons had been Hamline athletes, Norton Field and grandstand became a reality. By this time students and others were pressing for a new gymnasium, but to the president's wisdom and credit, he insisted that priority be given to a library. Quite naturally he addressed an appeal to Carnegie, that friend of book repositories, who promised to give $30,000 if Hamline would raise an equal amount. At the cornerstone-laying ceremony on May 13, 1907, Governor John A. Johnson made one of the speeches. When the building was dedicated in October, only $2,600 remained to be raised.[1]

Attention then turned to the matter of the gymnasium, and this meant another drive for funds. The president now directed his gaze toward Rockefeller's General Education Board, one of whose members, Charles W. Eliot, president of Harvard, spoke at Hamline in February, 1909. That same month the board agreed to grant $75,000 to the endowment if Hamline raised an additional $225,000. Under the agreement $90,000 of the $300,000 total could be spent for buildings and equipment. Symbolic ground breaking occurred in April, when a professor guided a plow drawn by three hundred undergraduates. Dedication came on the last day of November, 1909. Fitted out with the usual running track in the gallery, punching bags, climbing poles, and flying rings, the gymnasium in 1916 would receive the gift of a swimming pool. Bridgman also hoped to build a chapel, but that was not to be.[2]

In keeping with current trends a number of significant curricular changes were instituted, and well-trained specialists were increasingly sought as faculty members. From 1904 onward modern languages were accepted in lieu of Greek and Latin as admission requirements. A beginning course in Greek was then added to the schedule of studies, but the golden age of the classics was past. The preparatory division course was lengthened from three to four years to keep pace with public high schools; but like the classics, the heyday of the private academy was waning; the preparatory department at Hamline would not survive the Bridgman era. In 1906 a new department of political, economic, and social science was established, followed the next year by that of philosophy and psychology. English courses were being renovated by Professor R. Watson Cooper, whose selection as president of Upper Iowa University in 1909 seems to have been regarded as a special recognition of Hamline's excellence. By 1908 there were nine endowed professorships. One appointee of the period would remain for half a century, another for more than four decades. Both were beloved and respected. Some of the others, though too liberal for certain of the university community, also added stature to the institution.[3]

Many of these changes created a conflict within Hamline's halls. On the one hand were the progressives who were "ready to replace emphasis on missions and athletics with accents on scholarship, contemporary art, music, and drama, political reform, and the adoption of the new vernacular in writing as well as in ordinary conversation." In opposition were those whose inclinations were traditional and pietistic. President Bridgman, who leaned toward the progressive element, found himself caught in the middle. The feeling grew, despite obvious indications of curricular and faculty advance, that a small clique ran the university, that the president sympathized with this group, and that secular influences were elbowing aside those of the church. In 1908 all but four of the fifty-eight men in the junior and senior classes signed a petition asking the trustees to investigate charges — not made clear — against Bridgman. The board did nothing beyond considering the petition, but the Rockefeller grant and the new gymnasium notwithstanding, matters failed to improve.[4]

When the Methodist conference met in St. Paul in the fall of 1910, further fuel was added to the fire, and the squabble found its way into the columns of Twin Cities newspapers. The St. Paul press noted that Hamline enrollment had fallen from 425 in 1907–08 to 290 in October, 1910. That same month after Dean Loren H. Batchelder testified that undergraduates were loyal to the president, 121 out of the 155 students in the three upper classes signed a statement denying the dean's assertion. Another petition urged Bridgman to resign. Later one of the trustees told the students in chapel that if they did not like the way the institution was being run, "our doors open outward as well as inward." Irked, a group of the dissidents assembled that evening in a nearby Masonic hall to listen to talks by two Methodist ministers, two professors, and others critical of the president and his supporters. Noting all this, a Minneapolis editorial suggested that "for the good of the souls of the students who want to run things . . . some husky young vice president" should be employed "who would twist their impudent little necks for them." [5]

In the end the activists and their allies had their victory. At commencement in 1911 President Bridgman announced that he would resign a year hence, and he kept his pledge. The honors which had been accorded him were many and his contributions to Hamline great. Three persons had graduated in his first year (1883), forty-three in his last. All but 22 of the university's total of 729 degree holders by June, 1912, had been handed their diplomas by him. He came to an institution possessed of one dormitory, one unfinished building, and a debt. He left Hamline with five buildings (University Hall, Science Hall, library, gymnasium, and Goheen Hall), an endowment of $400,000, and assets of $1,000,000. Tuition and endowment income in 1911 was a record $51,000. He had attracted a strong faculty and encouraged them to publish. It was unfortunate that his long and productive administration had to be marred by unpleasantness and contention near its end. His achievements, however, far outweighing his shortcomings, are what remain uppermost in the mind of posterity.[6]

Considering events of the recent past, it was all but inevitable that the new president would be an alumnus (1889) and a clergyman. And so he was. The Reverend Samuel F. Kerfoot after serving pastorates in Minnesota had become in 1908 president of Dakota Wesleyan University in South Dakota. There he had made an impressive record, especially as a fund raiser and builder. At Hamline spurred on by pressures from the accrediting agencies (including North Central membership in 1914) and the example of the college's old rival Carleton (which was soon to receive a chapter of Phi Beta Kappa), he did what he could to modernize and improve the curriculum and to elevate the quality of the faculty. In June, 1914, under the leadership of Professor Henry L. Osborn, the first step was taken in what was to be a long and frustrated quest for a chapter of Phi Beta Kappa. To get the necessary endorsements Hamline turned to a number of institutions already in that society's fold — the state university and Carleton in Minnesota, four Wisconsin institutions, and one in Connecticut. Only the last of these responded favorably. The absence of sequence in the curriculum and the need for more faculty seemed to be the main criticisms directed at the St. Paul school.[7]

After the United Chapters of Phi Beta Kappa in 1916 failed to grant Hamline the coveted affiliation, improvement continued on campus. Already the semester system had replaced the three-term calendar, the five-day work week had gone to five and one-half, and majors and minors had been introduced. Prerequisites appeared in the modern-looking catalog, and departmental lines were more clearly drawn. Most impressive perhaps was the addition of new faculty especially in 1917. When Kerfoot assumed office, there were twelve regular faculty members, some of whom taught in two or three departments and offered more courses than they could possibly handle well. By 1920 there were thirty-one teachers on the staff, ten of whom possessed Ph.D. degrees. The work in German, mathematics, physics, and zoology was good, and so was that in history and English, but the last two departments were understaffed. Salaries were not high — Dean Batchelder was tops at $2,300 — but they were comparable to those in other colleges, and costs by modern standards were low. One teacher, for example, paid a monthly rental of $25 for his six-room house. The faint beginnings of a pension system came in 1918, when it was decided to pay $600 annually to all faculty members who upon retirement had served Hamline for at least twenty-five years. None qualified until 1923 when the librarian retired.[8]

President Kerfoot had to devote much of his time and energy to promotional activities, money raising, modernization of physical plant, and student recruitment. Goheen Hall, the women's dormitory, received needed electricity and new plumbing in the summer of 1912, but it became increasingly inadequate to accommodate the growing number of coeds. Thus three nearby houses renamed the Cottage, the Gables, and the Lodge, were used as annexes. For the money to permit new construction and to strengthen endowment, a successful effort to raise $500,000 was inaugurated in 1916. That old stand-by, the General Education Board, provided one-fifth of the total, Trustee Chairman M. G. Norton gave $50,000, and the Board of Education of the Methodist Episcopal Church added a sizable contribution. Hill had promised another gift, but he died in 1916 before giving it. World War I postponed most building operations, but Hamline had funds which could be put to good use later.[9]

World War I had the usual impact on the life of the university in the form of martial fever, military drill in St. Thomas College's drill hall, enlistments, a SATC unit, and Red Cross workers turning out bandages and dressings. In the summer of 1917 an ambulance corps of thirty-six student volunteers was organized. Along with similar units from thirty other colleges in the country, it saw active service in France and suffered serious losses. Nine of the faculty served in the army or navy, as did approximately 350 students and alumni. Five gold stars appeared on the service flag when the fighting was over. On campus the quality of the academic performance declined, but at government expense some of the buildings were refurbished. The basement of Science Hall, for example, was transformed so that it could be used as a dining room for 300 persons. After the war boarders and students living in private homes were required to eat there at a cost of $5.00 a week.[10]

Since enrollment had been declining before his assumption of office (some claimed the reason was lack of athletic facilities), Kerfoot made a determined effort to reverse the trend. Faculty and students were enlisted as envoys to journey into the hinterlands to drum up applicants, and the activity seems to have paid off. Between 1912 and 1920 enrollment rose from 251 to 498. In ability the students showed a wide variation, but in action they were far from docile. Products mainly of public high schools, these young people tended to find social life at Hamline restricting and frequently dull.[11]

In the face of the Victorian rules of the period (no dancing, coeds restricted to their dormitory after the evening meal) President Kerfoot was faced in his early years with what Hamline's historian has called perhaps somewhat strongly "a nightmare of campus ferment." A Socialist Club was organized in 1912, while the student newspaper on May 2, 1913, put out a notorious edition produced fittingly on yellow newsprint attacking various practices and personalities in the university community. The effect of such activity is difficult to measure, but the average Hamline student was by no means a single-minded crusader for social reform. He also participated enthusiastically in traditional undergraduate folkways such as cane rushes, nightshirt parades, frog pond trysts, wiener roasts, and giant bonfires after athletic victories.[12]

Change though gradual did occur. A dramatic club, the Hamline Players, appeared in 1915 and did much to soften critical attitudes regarding the theater. Although frowned on by the authorities, local fraternities were replacing the old literary societies. Movies came to the campus, and social facilities were improved. Then there were always avenues to freedom — Goheen Hall fire escapes or a dance hall such as the Dreamland. The Christian associations and mission bands (unlike the noontime prayer meeting) were still functioning, but secularism at Hamline as in the country at large was on the march.[13]

By the end of the war the institution's once rustic, peaceful, and isolated fifteen-acre campus was feeling the pinch and encroachment of urban developments in the burgeoning Midway district. Thus plans which had been in the making for some time to move the university to a new location were announced in 1919. The city of St. Paul was willing to pay $225,000 for the current site, and the Carnegie Foundation was amenable to building a much-needed library on a new campus. Several sites were considered, including one or more which were offered free, and President Kerfoot favored removal. The trustees vacillated, but wisely or unwisely because of "accessibility, present plant and traditional associations" finally decided that Hamline should stay put. Then to provide more elbowroom and better facilities for the student body, which numbered over 500 in the spring of 1921, some $300,000 was spent. A new dormitory for women called the Manor House was opened early in 1922, and plans were announced for the construction of a building a year during the succeeding decade. Things did not work out as planned. By 1926 the purchase of several nearby blocks of land had enlarged the campus to thirty-five acres, but the hoped-for expansion of physical plant had not taken place.[14]

The main reason was financial. The budget had risen from $90,000 in 1918 to $135,000 in 1921. Little help came from the endowment ($1,115,000 in 1926) because it was heavily invested in mortgages on land in western Minnesota and the Dakotas, areas hard hit when agricultural depression struck early in the 1920s. The General Education Board tried to improve conditions by offering a conditional grant of $250,000 for the improvement of faculty salaries, but President Kerfoot, suffering ill-health, found it impossible to raise sufficient money to qualify for more than part of the total. Late in 1923 he initiated the Hamline University Advance — a campaign for $1,500,000, half for buildings, the rest for endowment. Professional fund raisers were employed and a deadline set for December 18, 1924. About $1,300,000 was pledged ($15,141 of it by the faculty) but by the middle of 1925 only about $89,400 had been paid in. Tuition in 1924 was raised from $120 to $150, small help in the face of a steady enrollment decline from 636 in 1925–26 to 402 in 1928–29.[15]

Academically Hamline had continued to make progress, recent evidence of which was its endorsement by the Association of American University Women and accreditation by the American Association of Universities. Phi Beta Kappa, however, remained elusive, although eleven of thirty-seven faculty members in 1921 were entitled to wear the society's key. The main reasons given were insufficient support of the library, allocation of money for an athletic field, and a recent sortie into the area of vocational education. (Night classes in accounting and business law had been offered in the St. Paul courthouse in 1921–22.) Although disappointed in their quest for Phi Beta Kappa, the faculty went ahead to correct weaknesses and to make improvements. Certain courses were closed to lowerclassmen; prerequisites were established; admission requirements were toughened; a placement service was created. By 1926 the Phi Beta Kappa chapter at the University of Minnesota expressed its satisfaction with conditions at Hamline and endorsed it for the long-desired unit of the prestigious honor fraternity. There seemed reason to be optimistic about the reaction of delegates to its triennial gathering of 1928.[16]

By then, however, other changes had occurred at Hamline. In March, 1927, President Kerfoot resigned. Three and a half months later he was succeeded by the Reverend Alfred Franklin Hughes, Phi Beta Kappa graduate of Ohio University and president of Evansville College in Indiana. The new chief executive had distinguished himself as a builder and fund raiser. At Hamline it would be different. By the end of his first year in office, President Hughes had already involved himself in serious difficulties.[17]

A notable example was his dismissal "with great reluctance and keen regret" in 1928 of a professor whose opinions were too liberal to please some people, but who had been a popular figure on campus since 1907. The chairman of the AAUP's national committee on academic freedom and tenure corresponded with and visited Hughes regarding the case, but no action ensued. The AAUP found "some support" for the professor's contention that his removal was based on "religious grounds," but the association "decided it could not interfere in an openly recognized denominational college." Fault, it seems, lay both with the dismissed teacher and with his critics, but Hamline suffered a real blow as a result of the episode. When Phi Beta Kappa endorsements were thereafter solicited from Carleton, Beloit, and the Universities of Minnesota, Wisconsin, and Iowa, responses in all five instances were in the negative. The quest once again ended in failure.[18]

In another matter Hughes's policy also precipitated arguments. This was a plan — by no means the president's own but one which he pushed in the face of formidable opposition — to move Hamline to a new site nearer the state university. Under his proposal the old plant would be sold and the money obtained used to erect three fine structures — an administration and classroom building, a women's dormitory, and a men's dormitory — on a new location. There he would establish a junior college and a senior division of the social sciences and humanities. Whatever the merits of the proposition, it loosed a storm of protest and resentment on the part of nostalgic alumni, students, faculty fearful of losing their jobs, and loyal St. Paulites, among whom were numbered several influential Hamline trustees. The whole affair was aired in the press with the usual charges and countercharges until finally in mid-1930 the trustee executive committee once again decided that Hamline should not be moved.[19]

But all was not unrelieved crisis at Hamline during the 1920s. Far from it. Between 1923 and 1927 the institution received branches of various honor societies, such as Pi Kappa Delta (speech), Pi Delta Epsilon (journalism), and Pi Gamma Mu (social science), all of which stressed high-quality performance. The Women's Self-Government Association dates from 1921, and a student senate of both men and women from 1924. There were five local fraternities each with its own house, and five literary societies for women, though the term "literary" had become an anachronism. The annual Winter Sports Carnival (begun at Como Park in 1923), homecoming, athletics, dates, all these and more kept life interesting. There was some chafing over Methodist views on smoking and dancing, and at a conference meeting in 1925 the clergy voiced the opinion "that Hamline should not officially approve dancing." Unofficial engagement in the pleasant pastime was largely undisturbed. All administration of necessity involves a certain amount of stuttering.[20]

Beneath the calm of student life, however, especially after the crash of 1929, events moved inexorably toward a climax. The General Conference of the Methodist Episcopal Church played a role when it decided in 1928 to survey all educational institutions affiliated with it. Hamline was first on the list, and the results of the investigation appeared in a bulky volume in 1930. The men who produced it found cause both for praise and for blame. The physical plant and fiscal methods and procedures came in for considerable censure. Special criticism was directed at the existence of a salaried treasurer of the board of trustees, an individual with authority enough to make him virtually a second president.[21]

But beyond commendation and disapproval, the report carried recommendations for future action. Success in the years ahead, suggested the investigators, depended upon Hamline's ability "to render a distinctive service," rather than to attempt to emulate a university. Considering its nature as a church college, it should emphasize the social sciences and humanities. Merger with Macalester was a possibility meriting serious consideration. Hughes, as a loyal Methodist and as a person who wanted "to be considered a leader in an educational revolution," felt it incumbent upon him to carry out the suggestions, many of which were wise if sometimes expensive. In doing so he encountered considerable opposition; conflict became heated, and rival factions lined up.[22]

All the while Hamline's financial structure was deteriorating. Whereas the annual deficit in 1923–24 had been only $1,420, it was up to $44,600 in 1927–28, and to $89,490 in 1931–32. Costly efforts to increase enrollment had not been particularly effective, only 421 students enrolling in the fall of 1930. Scholarships had been given out of current funds, and there was laxity in collecting tuition and fees. In 1930, six years after the Advance fund drive was officially closed, Hughes was able to induce the General Education Board to complete payment of its $250,000, but instead of putting the sum into endowment and a building fund, a large segment was used to pay off the deficit. At last it became impossible to meet faculty salaries. Blame was directed at the president, and in early 1932 he was asked to resign.[23]

The resignation was accepted in April, 1932, the same month in which Hughes issued a bitter twenty-page indictment of the trustees. Included were allega-

tions of misuse of funds, criticism of secretive procedures on the part of the treasurer, diatribes against residents of the St. Paul area, and many other "shocking charges." Again Hamline received widespread and unfavorable publicity. To make matters worse the university for several nonacademic reasons — inadequate sources and amount of income, lack of a president, recruitment of students by a coach — lost its North Central Association accreditation. The nadir had been reached. If Hamline were to survive, the only way it could go was up.[24]

Discouraging though conditions were, they were not hopeless. Friends, faculty, church, trustees, and alumni all turned resolutely to the task of building a strong and first-rate educational institution. A committee of trustees drew up answers to the Hughes charges, and administration of campus affairs was turned over to Dean Henry L. Osborn as acting president aided by a faculty committee. That the treasurer and some of the trustees had acted unwisely and ineptly though not illegally was evidenced by the election of replacements and the correction of some of the evils to which Hughes had pointed. From June, 1932, to June, 1933, Hamline functioned under the leadership of its faculty committee and aging acting president. The budget was slashed by 32 per cent, cutting the $100,000 deficit of the previous year to less than $25,000. The faculty accepted heavier loads, along with salary cuts of 16⅔ per cent and later of 25 per cent more.[25]

In the summer of 1932 twenty-one teachers journeyed over the region recruiting students (the coach was one of them) with excellent results. The enrollment of 503 in the fall was the largest in seven years. With alumni help a former fraternity house and two floors of the Music Building (old Goheen Hall) were refurbished as dormitories for twenty-six and thirty-three men, respectively, at a rental of $25 a year. Three-quarters of the 260 Methodist churches in the state sent quantities of food for students: 2,600 quarts of home canned goods, 500 bushels of vegetables, 1,400 cases of eggs, among other items. Twin Cities' women provided a student loan fund named for President Bridgman. And so it went.[26]

Hamline was making the grade. And since practically everyone was in financial straits in 1932, the Methodist institution seemed to outsiders in no worse shape than other colleges. Indeed on campus there was much to which one could point with pardonable pride: the winning of a Rhodes Scholarship, success in debate and basketball, enthusiasm generated by the Little Theater's work. When the survey of the thirty-five educational institutions with Methodist affiliations was published in 1933, all who had struggled to keep Hamline alive rejoiced to learn that it had been rated number one among those schools with fewer than 1,000 students.[27]

In June, 1933, the trustees chose Bishop Junius R. Magee as interim president, and within a year Hamline was back in the good graces of the North Central Association. The bishop then relinquished leadership to the Reverend Charles N. Pace, who since 1917 had served with distinction as pastor of the First Methodist Church in Duluth. A poet and a member of the board of trustees since 1926, he would give Hamline able direction for nearly a decade and a half.[28]

With students able to earn part of their expenses under federal work programs, enrollment pushed upward to slightly over 600 in the middle of the decade. Well over half of the undergraduates were Methodists and most came from Minnesota, twice as many from St. Paul as from Minneapolis. Culminating a period of study by faculty committees, curricular changes which took into account individual differences and permitted greater flexibility were introduced in 1935. Five years later in conjunction with Asbury Hospital in Minneapolis a school of nursing was established. By mid-1936 it was possible to improve the salary situation, to inaugurate another Advance campaign for $1,000,000, and to begin needed additions to the physical plant. A multipurpose field house was dedicated in January, 1937, but without the Hamline victory which had accompanied a similar festivity for Norton Field fifteen years earlier. In May came completion of a new library wing, and in 1940–41 of a new central heating plant and a student union.[29]

In contrast to predepression days when teaching and other professions recruited most alumni, growing diversity — from radio and movies to art, industry, child welfare work, and nursing — characterized the fields of endeavor which more recent graduates were entering. The record is comforting to proponents of the liberal arts, even as it is confounding to anyone who doubts their practicality. The faculty to whom Hamline's survival owed so much were gaining a new status and a growing awareness of their crucial role in the life of the institution. Past difficulties were fading from memory and a future of continued development was dawning.[30]

13
ST. JOHN'S UNIVERSITY

Halcyon Days

THE EARLY YEARS of the twentieth century like those immediately preceding them were, as Father Colman Barry has written, "the halcyon days at St. John's," a time when "peace and quiet were the prevailing norms." Contemporary prose would seem to substantiate this evaluation. Far from the rush of the city, the institution bordered "a sheet of crystal water . . . studded with beautiful islands and indented with picturesque bays teeming with fish." Most of the abbey's 2,000 acres were still covered with "the mighty giants of the primeval forest" — a setting affording "an amount of innocent sport which the most fastidious will not reasonably despise." In cleared areas the monks, lay brothers, and hired men conducted "extensive" farming operations, looked after large poultry yards, and ran their own slaughterhouse. From these enterprises the university loaded its tables with "only the choicest vegetables . . . the very choicest Minnesota creamery butter, the best in the world," and fresh meat and eggs. The bread was also made at St. John's and so was the maple syrup.[1]

Visitors could reach this sylvan community via the main line of the Great Northern Railway, detraining at Collegeville. To the "weather-beaten toolshed" serving as a depot, the university in 1901 had added a white, two-story house to function as a waiting station and a telegraph, express, and ticket office. From this frame structure a school bus drawn by two horses carried travelers free the mile and a half westward through the woods to the university. Near the end of this half-hour trip, two objects resembling medieval watch towers gave promise of journey's end. One was the 2,200-barrel-capacity tower erected in 1890, from which water from springs along the Watab River was forced even to the fourth floor of the main buildings; the other was the observatory built in 1894.[2]

At the turn of the century the visitor upon reaching

his destination would find the abbey and university little altered in exterior appearance (except for landscaping) since the days of Abbot Alexius. The giant red brick quadrangle, composed of six sections all connected, contained a multitude of facilities, including such diverse entities as the church and monastery, printing presses, barbershop, seminary, commercial department, and college. In addition to the farm buildings surrounding the main complex, there was a fish hatchery (after 1906), a large orchard, and a greenhouse, all of which added to the high degree of self-containment achieved by the amazing monks.[3]

In 1899–1900 the seminary had less than 40 men enrolled, while the rest of the university accounted for only 188 students of "divers ages, talents and nationalities" — 139 of them from Minnesota, 26 from North Dakota. Seminary enrollment did not move upward for some time, but other departments — preparatory, high school, commercial, and college — showed steady increases. By 1906–07 the total stood at 271; on the eve of America's entry into World War I at 382. "First and second generation Catholic immigrants," wrote Father Colman, "were gradually but consistently sending their sons to St. John's for training." Some of these young men sought to become priests, a larger segment had commercial careers in mind, an unknown number looked mainly for "a slice of general knowledge." A small minority only could rightly be called college students. At commencement in June, 1901, for example, four B.A. degrees were conferred as opposed to forty master of accounts diplomas handed to men who had completed the two-year commercial course. Fifteen years later the situation had not changed greatly; then five B.A.s were given out, along with five M.A.s, six certificates to men who had finished two years of college, nine high school diplomas, and thirteen commercial department diplomas. Many students, of course, never advanced to graduation. With such a heterogeneous group to help, university authorities, noted one monk, "are occasionally sorely puzzled." [4]

With the leisurely tempo and close-knit community pattern, the nearly three dozen Benedictines on the faculty scarcely lived a harried existence. In addition to their other duties, some of the priests found time to do research and publishing. Father Anselm Ortmann's *Catechism of Astronomy* appeared in 1905, as did Father Severin Gertken's *Catechism of Chemistry* and Father James Hansen's *Catechism of Botany*. Two years later Father Alexius Hoffmann's *History of St. John's University* celebrated the institution's semicentennial. Though not so closely related to the liberal arts, the work of other monks, particularly that of Father John Katzner in the field of horticulture, was far-reaching. Also notable in the light of later developments was the introduction of the Gregorian chant at St. John's, especially by Father Innocent Gertken and Wilfrid Partika, in compliance with a 1904 encyclical of Pope Pius X. These men and others not only set a scholarly example for monastery and school, but in many ways, notably in sharing their experiments in agriculture, helped their neighbors in the surrounding countryside. [5]

But if life at St. John's was unhurried and conditions relatively stable, needs still arose for which new facilities became increasingly necessary. The library, as an example, had long been located in cramped quarters on the second floor of the large quadrangle. This unsatisfactory arrangement Abbot Peter now took the lead in correcting. The result was a new building completed in 1901, the abbey's first fireproof structure and the first one to be erected by an outside contractor. Placed south of the main complex but connected to it by an iron bridge, the brick addition consisted of three stories. On the ground floor was housed the monastery's collection of more than 20,000 volumes, in those days closed to students and open to faculty by appointment. The museum of curios from the far corners of the world and of stuffed animals and reptiles frequently found in colleges of the period occupied the second floor. The third floor was given over to a photography studio and a dozen music practice rooms. It would be nearly two decades before the library itself would elbow out these interlopers in its building. [6]

During the 1890s, the construction of a gymnasium — "an indispensable adjunct to a first class educational institution" — had been contemplated but not achieved. With the advent of the twentieth century, however, it was decided that the project

could be delayed no longer, especially "in our severe northern climate." Plans for the structure were approved shortly after those for the library had been accepted, and the two buildings were completed in the same year. The new red brick gymnasium, castlelike in appearance, featured among its facilities a billiard room and bowling alleys. It was the pride of its day. But by the 1960s, despite remodeling in 1937, it had become an embarrassment to the institution it had once served so well. [7]

Until 1908 the sick were cared for in wards in the old quadrangle; in that year a new infirmary building was put into use. Of the traditional brick, with two stories, full attic, and basement, the facility was located west of the main group of buildings. Divided vertically by a solid wall, the hospital contained two sections, the smaller of which was designed for the care of patients with contagious diseases. [8]

Next, attention was turned to the science teachers, who for some time had been "hampered and cramped in their work" by lack of space and facilities. In 1909 the community decided to erect a separate building for the sciences, and by the summer of the following year preparatory construction work was well under way. Completed in 1911 at a cost of $40,000, the fireproof structure consisted of three stories and a basement. Included were rooms for mechanical and electrical engineering, laboratories for physics, biology, chemistry, and geology, a large lecture hall, and quarters for the art and "draughting" department. Like the gymnasium, the science building would be called upon to serve well beyond normal retirement age; both structures played roles in the emergence of St. John's as a first-rate liberal arts college. [9]

Except for the construction of a new laundry in 1912 and a three-story extension to the quadrangle for kitchen and classroom purposes in 1914, the physical plant had attained the form it would have for the next decade. Unlike the complex erected by Abbot Alexius, the buildings added by Abbot Peter reflected no over-all plan. "They have," Father Colman observed, "the air of the American West about them." Artistic considerations were sacrificed "to the needs of a growing Catholic community in a rapidly expanding society." [10]

The courses taught in these buildings also reflected a good deal of variety. At the lowest level was a three-year preparatory curriculum for boys eleven years of age and older who had not completed grade school. As time passed the need for such education at St. John's diminished, and the program by then greatly reduced made its last appearance in the catalog of 1919. Other special offerings included the long-popular commercial course, leading to a master of accounts diploma, a "Winter School" for farm boys begun in 1901, and work in music, telegraphy, drawing, and painting. By 1912 music and drawing and painting had been accorded departmental status. All of these programs in a sense were peripheral to the direction in which St. John's University was heading, yet they fulfilled definite needs and were in line with the long Benedictine tradition of service.[11]

The future would rest essentially with the institution's liberal arts division and the seminary, and in these areas gradual evolution rather than dramatic change would be characteristic. Indeed the two sentences which introduced a description of the classical course in the catalog of 1900 and of the collegiate department in the bulletin of 1920 are nearly identical: "The primary object is a thorough liberal education, which consists in the full and harmonious development of all the faculties of the student. Long experience teaches that no other study is so well adapted to develop these faculties as the study of the classics." Though the college provided a scientific course as well as a classical one, the latter was by far the more frequently selected. Between 1900 and 1920 St. John's awarded sixty-five bachelor of arts degrees and only six bachelor of science — none from 1910 to 1927.[12]

The requirements for both degrees had much in common: the completion of courses in the classics, religion, mathematics, history, literature, composition, modern languages, science, ethics, and philosophy, and the writing of a thesis. Until 1918 that for the B.A. had to be in Latin. The main differences between the sequences lay in emphasis, in the absence of work in Greek and Latin during the last two years of the scientific course, and in its greater attention to the study of science. For the first decade of the century, both the classical and the scientific courses were seven years in length, the last four being of collegiate level. In 1910, however, to conform to general practice the classical sequence was extended by adding a year to the academic, or high school, curriculum, thereby making a clearer distinction between secondary and college work. Two years later St. John's symbolized the break by awarding its first high school diplomas. The scientific course remained at seven years.[13]

Two other degrees, the master of arts and the bachelor of philosophy, were also conferred. Until 1920 the former could be secured by the holder of a St. John's B.A., who had "passed two years in literary or scientific pursuits" and who applied to the president of the institution at Collegeville. Thereafter the procedure changed; the graduate was required to gain admission to a proposed course of study, "finish the equivalent of a year's intensive work" at St. John's under the direction of a professor, and submit a thesis. But whatever the process the institution awarded the M.A. sparingly, only twenty of the degrees being conferred prior to 1940. The bachelor of philosophy was reserved for men who had completed the philosophy sequence in the seminary, written a thesis in Latin, and passed the requisite examination. First granted in 1881, this degree was presented to twenty-eight seminarians between 1900 and 1912, when it was discontinued because of curricular changes.[14]

St. John's was slowly emerging as a triune entity of high school, college, seminary, each part of which was achieving its own distinct nature and identity. The impact of the past was still dominant, but especially from 1910 on the influence of the present was becoming increasingly apparent. The curricular changes of that year, along with the start of work on the science building, were evidences of the institution's response to trends in the academic world. Each succeeding year would present similar testimony. New disciplines were introduced — political economy (economics) in 1912 and sociology in 1919 — and catalog terminology and course descriptions were modernized. The catalog itself included an index for the first time in 1914; four years later the collegiate department was first referred to as the College of Science, Literature and the Arts, admissions requirements were more clearly spelled out, and the grading system was based on letter rather than number evaluations. Some of these changes represented more hope than substance, yet they could scarcely be termed mere superficialities.[15]

In the realm of college rules evolution is somewhat more difficult to detect. Those of 1920 were little changed from the ones in force in 1900. School authorities reserved the right to inspect students' mail and to confiscate "objectionable matter." Daily attendance at public worship was mandatory. Silence and decorum were to characterize indoor behavior. Cigarettes, snuff, and chewing tobacco were "absolutely prohibited"; cigars and pipes were all right at certain times with parental approval. Newspaper reading was "restricted to Wednesday and Saturday afternoon study periods." Departure from "the prescribed University grounds" required specific permission; visits to one's sister at the nearby College of St. Benedict, for example, were limited to one a month. And while preference was given to appeals "to the student's sense of honor," certain offenses such as gross immorality, habitual idleness, serious contempt of authority, could lead to expulsion, not so much to humilate "the culprit" as to protect other students from "the evil influence of bad example." [16]

That the rules were more closely related to monastic expectations than to actual student behavior seems to have been borne out on more than one occasion. "We note with regret," ran an item in the *Record*, "that the year of 1911–1912, which is the banner year of St. John's in point of attendance, holds the unenviable distinction of having seen the most wholesale expulsion of her students." The occasion for this comment stemmed from a Halloween march by twenty-nine Johnnies "after previous deliberation" to St. Joseph and their return at 11:15 P. M. At breakfast the following morning the father rector rose and "announced the expulsion of the whole bunch of 29." Despite some criticism of the penalty and not without sympathy for the victims, the writer concluded: "We look upon the Rector's action as an indication that St. John's intends to uphold its reputation of a well conducted, orderly school." [17]

The strict disciplinarian — of himself as well as of others — in this episode, the Very Reverend Alcuin Deutsch, had been born in Hungary in 1877, but had grown up in the large family of a day laborer in St. Paul. At age thirteen as Henry Deutsch, he had enrolled in St. John's classical course. Like many other promising lads without money, he had been given full scholarship aid. Six years later he had entered the novitiate under the name Alcuin and studied for a year at the seminary in Collegeville. Then Abbot Peter had sent the young novice to the International Benedictine College of Sant'Anselmo in Rome, where he had finished his course for the priesthood and earned a Roman doctorate in philosophy. So armed, he had returned to St. John's in 1903 as a prefect and a teacher of philosophy. In 1917 he was appointed prior of the community, and he assumed an increasing amount of Abbot Peter's work as the latter's health declined. [18]

For some time — as the pages of the *Record* disclose — World War I would impinge on life and thought at St. John's. Because of the large number of priests, seminarians, and boys of high school age in attendance, this impact was somewhat less direct than at certain other institutions. There was no SATC unit at Collegeville, nor was German dropped from the curriculum. Enrollment of nonseminarians declined only slightly, from 378 in 1917–18 to 352 the following year. On the other hand, the country's war effort received wholehearted support. A number of older students volunteered for military service

or were drafted; one lay brother entered the army, and two Benedictine priests became chaplains. Liberty bonds and war savings stamps were purchased by the abbey community as well as by students. Food restrictions were imposed, and such events as the alumni reunion were cancelled. From the ranks of the alumni over 440 were known to have joined some branch of the fighting forces. [19]

Three years after the war's end Abbot Peter died in Rochester following an operation in November, 1921. The following month after lengthy deliberation Prior Alcuin was elected abbot-designate; his blessing ceremony took place in May, 1922. Deeply influenced by his European experience, by the "emphasis on liturgical life and Benedictine principles" which he had observed in the monasteries of the Old World, Abbot Alcuin moved quickly and resolutely to transform practices at St. John's in accordance with those he had admired abroad. The liturgical movement, the Gregorian chant, spiritual retreats for the laity, all these and more received his strong support. Since he had inherited a large and financially sound community (164 members, of whom 113 were priests) at a time when the monastery was receiving a goodly supply of novices, he was able to accomplish much. [20]

Essentially his task was to bring to maturity the work which his predecessors had so well begun. Primary emphasis had been placed on meeting certain needs of the German immigrant population for priests, for instruction in business procedures, for education of high school level or less. Now the German element had reached the stage where thought could be directed to higher education in terms of preparation for pursuits other than the priesthood. St. John's increasingly would respond to this expanded opportunity. Despite the foundation already laid, the task would not be easy. A large endowment fund with which to hire lay faculty and provide student aid was lacking. The Benedictines themselves for years to come would have to serve both as a living endowment and a reservoir of teaching talent. The drain would be appreciable. Two-thirds of the student body on the average would need some form of financial assistance. The seminary would prepare priests without monetary support from church or diocese, and the high school division would be retained. Beyond all this, the abbey would meet other commitments, both old and new. Growth would not be rapid, but it would be steady and substantial. [21]

In 1923 the catalog for the first time made it possible, by listing them separately, to identify which of the 433 students enrolled were of college rank.

The breakdown showed 99 collegians, 39 seminarians, and 295 others — mainly high school students. Two years later more detail was published; of the 139 college students then in attendance, 78 were freshmen, 35 sophomores, 13 juniors, and 13 seniors. Nearly half of the juniors and all but one of the seniors were priesthood candidates. Obviously the upper division of the collegiate department was still an infant in the St. John's household.[22]

Gradually this pattern changed. By 1930–31 college enrollment had reached 205 and that in the seminary 65; high school registrations were down to 191. The collegiate department had not only grown, it had achieved better balance. Freshman through senior enrollment was 71, 56, 38, and 40 students, respectively. Of the 78 men in the upper division, the majority were still priesthood candidates, but more than 30 juniors and seniors were headed for other callings. The economic depression no doubt was a partial explanation of the decline in the prep school, but other factors, especially the improvement of local public and parochial secondary schools, played a role. In 1939–40 St. John's high school enrollment numbered only 148; that same year there were 105 seminarians and 451 college students, more than double the 217 collegians enrolled a mere seven years earlier.[23]

Even before Abbot Peter's death in 1921, plans had been made to provide more facilities for the college segment of the university, and soon after a major addition to the physical plant furthered this aim. Known at first simply as the new college hall, the structure completed in the summer of 1922 at a cost of $150,000 was soon christened St. Benet Hall. A five-story building with a complete basement, the hall provided living quarters for 130 college men, study halls, classrooms, and a variety of recreational facilities, including bowling alleys, pool tables, and handball courts.[24]

Six years later a second major addition to the educational plant was dedicated. "Ultra modern, and in complete harmony with its adjoining neighbor, St. Benet Hall," the newcomer was an auditorium-music building. The three-story structure with its additional height for stage loft space cost $250,000 furnished. Among its features were a 760-seat auditorium, music studios and practice rooms, bookstore, tailor, barber, and shoe shops. With the clouds of depression and World War II hanging over most of the next seventeen years, the New Auditorium, as it was called, would be the last substantial university building to be erected at St. John's for over two decades.[25]

But if the regime of Abbot Alcuin was not notable for plant expansion, his administration left enduring legacies in other areas. As president of both the university and of its board of trustees, the abbot carried major and final responsibility for educational developments and policies at St. John's — matters in which despite his other duties Alcuin had a continuing interest. In 1925, therefore, the sixty-eight-year-old office of university vice president and rector was abolished and replaced by three deanships — for the seminary, for the college, and for the prep school — whose holders reported directly to the abbot. With certain additions in personnel, this administrative structure would remain basically unchanged for more than thirty years.[26]

A man of unusually strong convictions and a firm believer in autonomy for private education, Abbot Alcuin regarded agencies such as the North Central Association as highly repugnant and a threat to the general welfare. Action by such leaders as Sister Antonia at St. Catherine and Dr. Mary Molloy at Saint Teresa in gaining regional accreditation for their colleges he considered inimical to the development of a "distinctive Catholic educational system in the United States." Sister Antonia for her part saw the abbot's policy as "sheer suicide" for St. John's. It did not prove to be fatal, but it created problems. In his last years Alcuin relented grudgingly under pressure from the community and permitted application for membership to be made to North Central.[27]

While it would be inaccurate to attach either full credit or entire blame to Abbot Alcuin for collegiate developments at St. John's in this period, his influence by virtue of his position and the force of his personality was considerable. For him the classical-philosophical education he had received in Rome was still the best for St. John's. The challenge was not to depart from that type, but to improve on it. Understandably he held as anathema "educational fads, premature specialization, the elective system or 'progressive' educational theories in any form." In line with his own experience and in accord with the example of Abbot Peter, Alcuin sent monks for graduate training to Sant'Anselmo and other European institutions at Munich, Louvain, Tubingen, and Salzburg, as well as to leading American universities. All told 101 Benedictines, of whom 28 received doctorates and 37 master's degrees, pursued advanced studies in 46 different institutions of learning during Alcuin's twenty-nine-year tenure. The intellectual and spiritual impact of this far-flung quest was monumental and cumulative. By the middle 1920s, as Father Colman has written, "St. John's entered upon a period of vitality, creativity and live ideas which aroused an imaginative response on the part of the community reminiscent of the days of

Abbot Alexius' ventures of the 1870's and 1880's.'' [28]

The most dramatic, controversial, and attention-capturing aspect of this ferment was the liturgical movement, which shook the church but did not realize its hopes until the time of Vatican Council II in 1962. Leader of the movement was the brilliant dynamo, Father Virgil Michel, who reminded one historian of Bede, Rhabanus, and Gerbert. The details of the liturgical revival lie outside the limits of this study, but the work of Father Virgil and others at St. John's focused international attention on the abbey and stimulated its life, educational as well as religious. Indeed the revival was the matrix from which sprang most of the ideas that influenced developments at St. John's during much of the Alcuin era. [29]

Against this background and trends in the groves of academe generally, it was natural that the college department of St. John's would grow, though slowly, and that the traditional liberal arts curriculum, especially its classical-theological segments, would retain primacy. The physical, biological, and social sciences evoked less than wholesale enthusiasm from the abbot. Theology remained queen, but in agelong Benedictine style, stress was placed on the development of the "whole man," not merely of the intellect. Even when depression struck in the 1930s, "those endless educational experiments of specialists, social reconstructionists, pragmatists, and conformists" so common at the time were absent at St. John's. Not precipitous change, but growth in depth and in quality marked curricular history there in the 1920s and 1930s. [30]

The year 1922 witnessed not only a new catalog statement of college objectives, which included the hope "that the number of Catholic young men completing a college education may increase," but also the discontinuance of that old stand-by, the commercial department. Its final diplomas were awarded to a class of twenty men on June 7, 1923. That same year catalog space devoted to college faculty lists and curricular material consumed twenty-three pages; in 1924 the pages so used had increased to thirty-seven. Mention was first made also of the M.S. degree and of a division into junior and senior colleges. Certain of the departments — philosophy, history, the natural sciences, music, mathematics, art and architecture, languages, English and drama — had well-qualified faculty, but in insufficient numbers to provide the depth of offerings demanded of a first-rate college. As monks returned from graduate study, however, and with help from University of Minnesota professors who came to St. John's to evaluate staff and curriculum and to

provide counsel, fairly rapid headway was made. Beginning in 1931, the departments of history, philosophy, chemistry, and psychology and education received the state university's approval; similar recognition went to other departments periodically thereafter. The trend was solid, traditional, and conservative. [31]

Reflections of the curriculum can be seen in the number and kind of degrees conferred. From 1920 through 1929 St. John's awarded 103 B.A.s, 50 of them during the three years at the end of the decade when eight B.S. degrees were also given. In the 1930s the pace stepped up; 313 men earned a B.A. and 51 a B.S. Two other types of baccalaureates also put in brief appearances. One, the bachelor of sacred theology (S.T.B.), was made possible by the affiliation of St. John's seminary with the Catholic University of America. Under this arrangement seminarians could fulfill the requirements for the degree from the Washington, D. C., institution while in residence at Collegeville. A total of 24 men earned the S.T.B. between 1924 and 1934. The other degree, the bachelor of architecture, was first conferred in 1937 when two men received it; in 1938 and 1939 it went to six men and to one man, respectively. [32]

A program like St. John's had its critics as well as its supporters. Of the latter the best known in the academic world of the 1930s were President Robert M. Hutchins and Professor Mortimer J. Adler of the University of Chicago. Both men were acidulous critics of developments in many colleges of the period, wherein great emphasis was placed on such matters as intercollegiate athletics, the extracurriculum, and vocationally oriented courses. To St. John's dean, Father Virgil, the views of these men "had the familiar ring of a traditional Benedictine educational program of the early middle ages," and in 1938 he corresponded with Professor Adler with the aim of setting up at St. John's a program patterned on Chicago lines. To start in 1939 and to be open to about twenty students a year, the four-year course would be composed of the Chicago list of "Great Books" plus other work in the liberal arts. Considerable progress in working out details had been made when Father Virgil's untimely death late in 1938 put an end to the project. Concern with the goals of developing the intellectual and moral virtues of students through study, discussion, and participation in the liturgy of worship has not, however, abated to the present day. [33]

Other developments in the period between depression and war suggest that, while maintaining its traditional stance, St. John's did not abandon either the refinement of its identity or its search for greater effectiveness. Notable were several changes in nomenclature. The department for training priests until 1938 was called the seminary or the school of divinity; then the latter was changed to the school of theology. The former department of music, while not offering a major, in 1936 was given the impressive title of "School of Music." Architecture underwent similar changes. Until 1935 that subject was listed under the college department of drawing. For one year architecture stood as a department on its own, but in 1936 it joined music as a school, retaining that lofty status for four years. In the fall of 1939 architecture became a six-year sequence, two-thirds of the time being spent in earning a B.A. and one-third in securing a bachelor of architecture. Meanwhile two other actions had been taken. In 1937 a two-year schedule of studies in forestry had been announced. The following year most college courses, including those in music, but not in drawing, shopwork, and architecture, had been organized into three divisions— humanitites, history and social science, mathematics and natural sciences.[34]

In the noncurricular area there had also been slow but perceptible change, a gradual relaxation of restrictions and the broadening of outlets. Some of this movement was reflected in college rules. In 1920 students were not permitted "the practice of visiting neighboring towns to make purchases." The next year this strict prohibition was gone. Likewise missing was censorship of mail between collegians and members of their families. Frequent correspondence with friends, however, was discouraged as "a waste of time and detrimental to concentrated academic effort." As late as 1932 all students were required to attend daily Mass; in 1933 they were "urged to be present." Cigarettes were still banned in 1920, but by the late 1920s nearly every issue of the *Record* carried large advertisements for Camels and Chester-

fields along with pipe tobacco. And so it went. Great emphasis continued to be placed on religious and moral training, and attendance at annual retreats remained obligatory. Benedictine prefects still lived in student dormitories, but their mission was to "form rather than reform character." The trend was in the direction of appealing to individual conscience rather than of demanding adherence to a formal list of specific regulations.[35]

The opportunities for recreation and self-improvement grew steadily. In 1920 a motion picture projector was purchased, and movies became a periodic campus feature. After banning intercollegiate sports for more than a decade, St. John's participated in the MIAC in 1921 and assumed its "rightful place as a full-grown college in athletics as in other activities." In 1925 the Spike and Cleat fraternity appeared, its purpose being to organize intramural competition in all manner of sports from horseshoes to football and to award trophies. The *Record*, previously a monthly, became a weekly that same year. The numerous religious and musical organizations remained active, and from time to time other special interest groups sprang up: the T Square Club for students in architecture in 1925, a prelaw club in 1938, and organizations for future teachers and premedics the next year. Even the beginnings of student government came along in 1938–39 with the formation of the student board and the student forum. Their function was largely to conduct undergraduate activities, but these bodies represented a new stage in the evolution of St. John's.[36]

Progress would soon be halted for a period by World War II. The foundation already laid, however, was both impressive and unique for Minnesota. The Benedictines in other dark ages had kept the light of learning alive; now in Collegeville the monks would help do so again.

14

GUSTAVUS ADOLPHUS COLLEGE

Changing Times

WHEN THE SWEDISH LUTHERANS met in annual conference at St. Peter in the spring of 1904, they were faced with the responsibility of selecting a new president for Gustavus. Their choice was the Reverend Peter A. Mattson, an immigrant from Sweden at age seventeen, a graduate with exceptionally high grades of the college he would head as well as of Augustana Seminary, and a successful pastor with a Ph.D. from the University of Minnesota. Apparently well-qualified for his new task, he would undergo during the seven years of his presidency experiences not unmindful of those suffered by his contemporary at Carleton, William A. Sallmon. The administrations of both men embraced periods of transition at the end of which each man might well feel that his career had been sacrificed to the demands of change. Sensitive, legalistic, deeply religious, committed to his task as he interpreted it, President Mattson, by the very nature of these characteristics, was bound to encounter difficulties.[1]

He found himself in the middle of the debate over intercollegiate athletics, a highly uncomfortable position experienced by more than a few college administrators. Even though his own faculty protested the veritable ban on such contests issued by the synod in 1905 and some of his fellow Lutheran college presidents disagreed with him, Mattson hewed to the line. "I have more than once," he wrote, "been ready to give up in the struggle against this worldly movement, intercollegiate athletics. There is dreadful pressure in this direction in our school world." Not until the synod in 1910 voted 219 to 192 to permit basketball games and track meets with other institutions did the president yield. During his last year in office, a "limited schedule" of basketball games was played, but by then it was too late for him to capture the support of those individuals whom his opposition to athletics had alienated.[2]

With his background and inclinations, it was natural that Mattson should place great emphasis on the creation of a Christian atmosphere at Gustavus. "Our creed," he declared, "should not be sacrificed for any . . . considerations." He favored elevating the standard of academic performance, but this was secondary to character development. The same view obtained at other colleges in the state at the time; it was only that Mattson seemed more inflexible than certain other men. As at Carleton under Sallmon, some faculty members were also disenchanted. Several resigned, including one who had served ably for nineteen years. And as always sides were taken both on campus and beyond its borders.[3]

One can imagine with what conviction Mattson later proclaimed that "loyalty by all concerned" is a requisite for presidential success. One faction, which included certain influential board members devoted to both church and college, felt that Gustavus was too narrowly Swedish, that it should move more rapidly into the main stream of American education. Toward the end of the year 1910–11, a series of incidents was climaxed by the circulation of a student petition suggesting that the usefulness of the president had ended. (Perhaps leaders at Gustavus had been in touch with their undergraduate counterparts at Hamline.) By early summer Mattson had resigned, thereby saving himself from possible embarrassment at the board meeting scheduled for July. A person of quality and integrity, sincerely concerned with the welfare of others, an indefatigable worker, he was elected president of the Minnesota conference of his church annually from 1913 to 1939. It was his unfortunate lot, and that of Gustavus, that the qualities which guarantee success in the ministry do not necessarily fit one to lead an educational institution.[4]

Although total enrollment fell from 390 in the fall of 1907 to 333 three years later, there were significant changes and developments during the Mattson administration. To keep pace with current trends as well as to improve the chances of its graduates for admission to other colleges, the academy lengthened its course in the fall of 1910 from three to four years. Typically, however, enrollment in that division declined while that in the college increased. Early in the century there had been 150 students in the secondary school department; by 1910–11 the number was 75, yet the academy was not closed until 1931. The commercial department was also losing its appeal; it would be discontinued in 1922.[5]

Plant expansion, so common everywhere at the time, was also apparent at Gustavus. First came the much-needed auditorium in 1904–05, providing seating for nearly a thousand people, as well as classroom space and administrative offices. Part of its cost was borne by the $15,000 raised by St. Peter supporters of the college when there was talk of relocation in the Twin Cities area. Next to appear was a girls' dormitory, Johnson Hall, named in honor of Minnesota's sixteenth governor (1905–09), John A. Johnson, a St. Peter native whose efforts were largely responsible for making the building possible.[6]

Always concerned for the welfare of the college, Johnson had visited Andrew Carnegie in 1906 to solicit money for a dormitory. While interest in the project was expressed by the philanthropist, the governor was informed that Gustavus' "plant and endowment have not reached the stage of development at which Mr. Carnegie considers it desirable to take the responsibility of giving money for a college." Two years later, however, came a promise of $32,500 in Carnegie funds if the college would raise an equal amount. Governor Johnson then attempted, mainly through Swedish Lutheran pastors, to secure the matching gift, but succeeded in coming up with only about $10,000. Happily, at Johnson's request Carnegie waived the matching requirement. At the fiftieth anniversary meeting of the church conference in St. Paul in October, 1908, the state's chief executive turned over the steel tycoon's check to the college trustees; the cause of Gustavus was given a tremendous boost. The total Carnegie gift plus that raised by the churches came to approximately $43,000, a sizable sum in those days. The only regret was that the governor did not live to see his namesake when it was occupied in the fall of 1910.[7]

The Mattson years also witnessed the beginning of an endowment fund, something new and strange to Swedish Lutheran schools at the time. Credit for its inception belongs mainly to the Reverend Louis G. Almén, pastor at Balaton and member of the Gustavus board, who in 1904 left his parish to devote full time to the task of raising $100,000 for the college. Month after month "He would preach sermons on Sunday, eat lunch counter food and walk for miles rather than increase his expense account." Under what was known as the "Coupon Note Plan," whereby donors signed promises payable through ten yearly equal coupons, he in a five-year period secured over 1,300 pledges totaling some $62,000. Though his strenuous efforts took their toll of Almén's physical well-being, the endowment idea was firmly planted, and it would go forward under a new administration.[8]

During the interim between Mattson's departure and the arrival of his successor, the acting president was Dr. Jacob P. Uhler, a man who served Gustavus in various capacities from 1882 to 1941. Adolph O. Eberhart, an 1895 Gustavus graduate, was then governor, and through his good offices Uhler obtained an interview with James J. Hill. The result was that the Empire Builder offered $50,000 if the college raised $250,000 in cash within two years, or $40,000 if the matching sum were $200,000.[9]

In the meantime the search was on for someone to succeed former President Mattson. With some persuasion and an increase in salary, the Reverend Oscar J. Johnson, the pastor of a congregation and president of Luther College in Wahoo, Nebraska, accepted the post. He would occupy it for twenty-nine years. A graduate of Augustana College and Seminary in Rock Island, Illinois, he had been a successful fund raiser in his previous position. Upon his arrival at St. Peter in July, 1913, he entered with enthusiasm upon the Gustavus endowment drive. When the campaign started, Hill had agreed that the $30,000 already in the fund, plus an equal amount outstanding on the pledges Pastor Almén had secured, could be counted toward the total the college must raise. In spite of appeals to pastors and alumni and a house-to-house canvass, pledges in hand the night before the conference meeting in February, 1914, were still some $40,000 short of the amount needed. In an emotionally charged meeting the following morning, most of this deficit was subscribed by pastors and delegates; the remainder was made up by citizens of St. Peter. At 3:30 P.M. on May 1, 1914, the college bell summoned the Gustavus family to hear the announcement that sufficient cash had been paid in to qualify for $40,000 from Hill. The campaign had been a success. The "most joyous jubilee" which followed was remindful of that on the Carleton campus back in 1887.[10]

With some $12,000 a year endowment income assured and spirits buoyed by the recent achievement, the inauguration of President Johnson in mid-1914 seemed to herald new and better days.

More flexible and democratic than Mattson, the new executive worked smoothly with his board, especially with such influential and long-time members as Henry N. Benson, chairman from 1916 to 1944. Loyal to his faculty almost to a fault, the president received in most instances loyalty, affection, and esteem in return. With the student body of 359 — 125 in the college, 71 in the academy, 92 in the school of music, and 71 in the school of commerce — Johnson also enjoyed a happy relationship. Prone whenever possible to defend undergraduates, he found they reciprocated and that their appellation for him, "Prexy," was one of endearment. Typically, to a rumor that four band members drank beer after a concert, he cautioned that at a distance "it is not easy to tell whether a boy has been drinking beer or Coca Cola." [11]

The most vexing problem inherited from the former regime was undoubtedly that of intercollegiate athletics. Early in 1914 the faculty had established eligibility requirements for players, but football was still banned and the gymnasium was referred to as an "Old Shack," whose atmosphere was "about as pure as that of a flour mill." In 1916, hoping to force approval of intercollegiate football, the students threatened to strike, but later thought better of it. The president characteristically commended the behavior of the athletes and noted that the faculty rather than the students now supervised all sports. The church governing body at long last in 1917 relented and gave its approval to football. Three years later Gustavus became a member of the new Minnesota Intercollegiate Athletic Conference in which its record would be singularly impressive. The new gym would come along soon thereafter. [12]

Life on campus exhibited the customary tension between the traditional and the novel. Rules remained essentially the same as they had been in the nineteenth century. No dancing was permitted; there was a regulation against smoking; drinking, of course, was taboo; and college approval to attend a movie could be secured only when a student presented a letter of permission from home. With men dispersed throughout the town instead of concentrated in dormitories, rule enforcement was neither easy nor all-pervasive. As late as 1920 teachers kept an eye on St. Peter poolrooms to apprehend Gustavians who yielded to the temptation to chalk a cue, but so did faculty members at other private colleges where the building of character was a primary concern. Literary and debating societies continued to dominate the social scene, but as on other Minnesota campuses, manifestations remarkably similar to the fraternity movement long popular in the East were

in evidence. Appealing to a student's desire for status, for acceptance by an exclusive group, for fun, for circumvention of official dictates, secret societies, though forbidden, cropped up. Scarcely consistent with the Christian virtues of humility and equality, these groups — at Gustavus they were the Reds and the Grays — tended to reflect values held dear by an increasingly secular age. [13]

In church and in chapel presidents and professors might inveigh against the blandishments of the world, but restless and red-blooded young collegians were not always listening. Required to attend religious services, the students, good Lutherans that they were, occasionally exhibited manners which were anything but meditative. The Gustavian who paid a German band to strike up a rollicking tavern ballad just after the president had prayed at one chapel service had plenty of counterparts at Hamline, Carleton, and elsewhere. Yet it was true, as a Gustavus historian points out, that religious services and organizations were in general deeply meaningful and important to the student generation of that day. Furthermore the intellectual side of life was sufficiently well developed to earn the college accreditation by the North Central Association in 1915. [14]

When the United States entered World War I, President Johnson and various faculty members made speeches in support of the country's effort against the Central Powers. A unit of the SATC was established, and Commerce Hall became a military barracks. Four officers were assigned to Gustavus by the federal government, which also prescribed the teaching of certain materials. All told about four hundred students and alumni saw active duty in the army and navy, and eleven lost their lives. [15]

The war over, the stage was set for a period of growth and progress. For the students, now that full competition in intercollegiate athletics had received the church conference's blessing, a new gymnasium seemed the first order of business. As early as February, 1919, Luther W. Youngdahl, a student destined to become governor of Minnesota and a federal judge, led a movement of undergraduates to agitate for such a facility. The main opposition rather understandably came from Swedish farmers, who feeling the pinch of recession in agriculture, regarded a gym as a frill and a luxury, something that could very well be sacrificed. But the proponents ultimately carried the day. When the General Education Board offered $100,000 toward the endowment, contingent upon the college's raising twice that amount, the conference in March, 1921, decided to accept the offer and to build the gymnasium as well. At this same time the church was called upon to contribute $100,000 for a seminary building at Augustana College in Rock Island. These commitments, plus other obligations, meant that over half a million dollars needed to be found. Despite this fact the athletic structure, including a swimming pool, was pushed to completion in 1922. It would serve the college in a variety of ways.[16]

The financial campaign, however, in spite of the earnest efforts of many individuals and President Johnson, would take longer to conclude. Through the characteristic leniency of the General Education Board as to deadlines, the college was enabled to press the collection of subscriptions through 1925. Finally on New Year's Day, 1926, "the most important date in the history of Gustavus College," in the opinion of a student columnist, "a tired committee rose cheerfully from their seats and rejoiced over the collection of $201,624.07. The gift of the General Education Board was won and the future of Gustavus once more assumed its rosy aspects." The new money provided nearly $150,000 for the gymnasium and raised the endowment fund to about half a million dollars, enough to satisfy the requirement of the North Central Association. The fund remained about the same throughout the Johnson administration. Invested in real estate, mortgages, and bonds, it netted varying amounts — $10,000 in 1921, $33,000 in 1929, $16,000 during the depths of the depression in the 1930s. The Greater Gustavus Endowment Corporation was created in 1927 in the hope of persuading two-thirds of the members of the conference to give $50 each over a ten-year period. While this dream was not realized, the corporation did raise considerable money.[17]

As the 1920s began college enrollment was about 200, composed mostly of Augustana Lutherans from Minnesota. Men were in the majority, but as yet they had no living quarters on campus, nor would they have until the end of the decade, when total enrollment was up to 500. Men's Dormitory — later christened Uhler Hall — with accommodation for 150 residents went up in 1929 and provided a partial answer to the need for housing. Depression then halted construction for ten years. In the fall of 1939 Rundstrom Hall, also named for a faculty member, added needed rooms for 85 women students. To meet the $265,000 cost of these structures, the church conference rather than the college issued bonds. In this way Gustavus' endowment fund was protected, a factor vital in the maintenance of North Central accreditation. Other structures of the Johnson era were the $25,000 stadium built in 1929 and the field house in 1939, both largely the result of promotions by George C. Myrum, the college's extremely suc-

cessful coach from 1925 until his tragic accidental death in the fall of 1938.[18]

Whether or not the building program placed undue emphasis on athletics depends largely on one's point of view. It can certainly be argued that for the decades of the 1920s and 1930s, Gustavus was doing what came naturally. To say this is not to condone malpractices; it is only to judge actions and policies by standards prevailing at the time rather than by later mores. That the college had a remarkable record in the Minnesota Intercollegiate Athletic Conference is a fact. To what extent this success was achieved by subsidization of players and questionable recruiting practices regarding athletes is impossible to say. Undoubtedly there was a basis for suspicion that all was not on the up and up, but it is difficult to compare the degree of Gustavus' guilt in violating the prevailing athletic code with that of other colleges in the state. The able historian of the St. Peter institution, Doniver A. Lund, wrote that "Dishonors were about even." In any event the MIAC in April, 1941, suspended Gustavus for one year. Considerable publicity surrounded the unpleasant and unfortunate episode, and feeling on both sides ran high. Perhaps the attention given the affair had a salutary effect in helping to place athletics in the colleges in proper perspective at least for a time. In 1942 by a unanimous vote, Gustavus was returned to good standing in the athletic conference.[19]

In other areas progress was paralleled by a number of inadequacies, the most basic of which was a shortage of money. The day of selective admissions had not arrived — too many poor risks had to be admitted — but requirements for graduation were those usual for the period: a "C" average, a major, a foreign language, and a base of general education courses. While a few older faculty members with Ph.D. and M.A. degrees from church colleges, persons reflective of an earlier tradition, remained on the staff, later appointments tended to go to individuals whose advanced training had been taken in the graduate schools of major universities and whose teaching was more closely related to their formal preparation than had been the case formerly. There was grumbling in some quarters when a professor became active in politics, especially if his support was given to a candidate whose views seemed to endanger the establishment, but in the classroom threats to academic freedom were absent. The "publish or perish" dictum had no relevance. The absence of adequate library and other facilities combined with a heavy class schedule generally determined faculty orientation toward teaching rather than research.[20]

Rules set forth in the catalogs remained fairly restrictive until the early 1940s, but practice frequently deviated from the letter of the law. For example, Sunday movies were officially proscribed until 1938. Athough the ban on dancing continued, it was standard practice by the late 1930s at fraternity and sorority parties off campus. As elsewhere, there were dormitory closing hours for coeds — 9:00 P.M. most weekday nights in 1931, 10:30 on weekends — and lights out at a certain hour was the rule in residence halls for both sexes. Such regimentation hardly won universal student approbation. Extracurricular activities — musical, journalistic, forensic, religious — were well supported and in a healthy condition. Upon graduation half of the students went into teaching at least for a time; the second most popular choice of profession was the ministry.[21]

When the depression hit, Gustavus endured the experiences common to all colleges of the time. Income dropped seriously and enrollment slumped to 334 in 1934. Salaries, never high even in the 1920s, were down by 25 per cent, and the very question of institutional survival became a matter of paramount concern. Delinquent student accounts mounted and continued to be a problem throughout the decade. But the crisis was endured and by 1936 the worst was over. Enrollment began once again to climb — it was almost 600 in 1939 — and it seemed that better times lay ahead.[22]

Despite postdepression gains, there were disturbing shadows on the landscape. Greater selectivity of students was mandatory if the college were to gain in respect as a first-rate institution of higher learning. The financial structure needed shoring up, and the advent of modern business practices was overdue. The library was embarrassingly inadequate. The board, with a strong clerical tinge, failed to reflect fully the diversity which had become characteristic of the church as a whole. Then there was the unpleasantness with the MIAC, and the weight of years on the firing line was beginning to catch up with President Johnson.[23]

The time for a change had arrived. It would come in the summer of 1942 with the assumption of the presidency by Dr. Walter A. Lunden, fated to experience the shortest and most turbulent administration (less than eighteen months) in Gustavus history. An honor graduate of the college in 1922, the new executive had been active in extracurricular activities in his undergraduate days, besides holding part-time jobs to help support himself. By the mid-1930s he had added the degrees of bachelor of divinity and doctor of philosophy to his credentials. From 1931 on he had been a member of the sociology department of the University of Pittsburgh and active in social welfare work.[24]

The doubts some board members entertained about his suitability for the presidency were prophetic, but these concerns were carefully shielded from the meeting of the church conference at which Lunden's election was unanimous. Having written his doctoral thesis at Harvard under Pitirim A. Sorokin on the structure and dynamics of institutions of higher learning and having consulted various leaders in the field before assuming his post, the new president had well-crystallized ideas regarding the direction Gustavus should take. That he did not succeed in carrying them out was the result of a number of factors: World War II, the conservatism of the board chairman, and his own characteristics — his impatience, his lack of finesse, his failure to understand many of the subtleties involved in successful administrative procedures.[25]

There seems little to criticize about Lunden's goals — plant renovation, campus beautification, institution of gracious student dining, improvement of financial practices, cessation of intercollegiate athletics during the war emergency, the building of a library, the securing of a military unit, among others. His methods, however, left much to be desired. Suffice it to say that in one way and another, he alienated students, faculty, and influential board members. Even the successful quest for a navy V-12 training unit, with its attendant advantages financial and otherwise, was accompanied by contention, some ineptness (not all presidential), and indecision. Certain of the president's remarks concerning the students may have had an element of truth, but his comments were hardly judicious. Retaliatory public embarrassment of him by undergraduates then did nothing to improve the situation.[26]

On one occasion Lunden's resignation was tabled by the board, and then after a delay of several months it was refused. Trustees commiserated among themselves, looked back nostalgically to the previous administration, and expressed growing doubts about the leadership abilities of the current chief executive. Matters finally culminated in October, 1943, when Lunden sought a leave of absence in order to accept an assignment with the military. When his request was refused, he resigned. This time the resignation was accepted.[27]

15 CARLETON COLLEGE

Maturing Years

DURING LATE 1901 and the early months of 1902, Carleton was looking for a new president, hopefully of the caliber of James W. Strong, who was soon to leave office but not Northfield. The trustee selection committee turned their eyes eastward in the hope of finding there a paragon among men, a consecrated Christian gentleman, young yet experienced, attractive and inspiring, with a gift for touching men's hearts and also their pocketbooks, one who would attune the college to the times. Their choice fell on the Reverend William H. Sallmon, minister of a church in Bridgeport, Connecticut. A graduate of Yale, Sallmon was recommended for the Carleton position by the president of his alma mater, Arthur T. Hadley. One of the qualifications possessed by the thirty-five-year-old pastor was the experience he had gained from two years of organizing YMCA work in educational institutions in Australasia. After listening to him preach in his home church and scrutinizing him in Northfield on a visit of several days' duration, the trustees offered Sallmon the Carleton position at a salary of $3,000 and a house. In May, 1902, he accepted the invitation, but previous commitments kept him from assuming office until January, 1903.[1]

Unfortunately Carleton's second president did not measure up to the high hopes held for him by the trustees, but considering the spot into which he stepped, his failure was not surprising. Strong had indicated that it was his wish and ambition to prove he could live in Northfield without being "a thorn" in the flesh of his successor. When President Sallmon rather arbitrarily slighted the older "stars" of the faculty, the retired executive proved incapable of carrying out his resolve. The result was controversy, petty quibbling, disunity, and discontent not only on the campus but in the local community as well. On May 1, 1906, several trustees felt compelled to reprimand Strong for his constant carping at Sallmon, but to little avail. Nearly a year later fourteen of the eighteen board members signed a statement in which they accepted responsibility for past policies, took note of the delicate task facing the new man when he took office, spoke of his "honesty and sincerity and motive," and repledged "to Carleton and its President our individual, united and hearty support, and bespeak a like support from the entire constituency of the College."[2]

By then it was too late, and on April 17, 1907, Sallmon submitted a letter of resignation, which he emphatically renewed on January 4, 1908. The trustees, seeing no alternative, accepted the resignation "to take effect July 1, 1908, but with continuance of salary until September 1st." Undoubtedly the president had some shortcomings. Regarding the use of wine and tobacco and observance of the Sabbath, he was at odds with local mores, but this was not the major issue. Hitting a more sensitive nerve was his failure to loosen purse strings of eastern philanthropists, something which it had been tacitly assumed at the time of his selection that he could do. (Endowment increased only slightly over $60,000 between 1900 and 1910.) Also he had a tendency to involve himself in situations too minor to invite presidential direction. There was a lack of long-range planning and perhaps too much emphasis on athletics. It was a difficult period — it would have been for almost everyone — but in many ways Sallmon lacked the vision Carleton needed, as well as the ability to win the loyalty and support of the faculty.[3]

Yet progress was made during his brief and stormy time in office. A long step was taken toward making Carleton a bona fide college of liberal arts, the kind of institution which would receive commendation and support from the Carnegie and Rockefeller people. It was during the Sallmon regime that the academy was discontinued (1906), fewer special students were admitted, postgraduate studies at the college were cut back, the degree of bachelor of literature was dropped, graduation requirements were stiffened, sabbatical furloughs were provided, and the beginnings of a faculty pension system were laid. The two-semester calendar replaced that based on three terms in the fall of 1904 and remained in force for six decades. The following year "to prevent an abuse of the free choice of electives," a group system was adopted, and provision was made for majors and minors. The *Carleton College Bulletin* was established in 1905. The second issue of its fourth volume offered a review of the Sallmon administration, the first published report of a Carleton president.[4]

And there were other important advances during the five-year period. The Carleton Mission, which supported religious and medical work and sent representatives to China until 1948, was organized in the fall of 1903. Six area alumni clubs were founded, Delevan L. Leonard's *History of Carleton College* was published, and one building (still standing) was erected. This structure, Laird Hall, was made possible by a magnificent gift of $100,000 in May, 1905, from Winona lumberman and Carleton trustee, William H. Laird. To the building in the fall of 1906 were moved the departments of chemistry, biology, and physics, and two administrative offices. Taken all in all, Carleton during the Sallmon administration was in a period of transition, moving from the age of the college-academy to that of mature institution of collegiate rank.[5]

What Carleton needed in 1909 was a creative, educational statesman capable of building a first-rate college on the very substantial foundations already laid. If it were to move forward, it must have its own prophet of new ideals. Fortunately this man was found in twenty-nine-year-old Donald J. Cowling, who was shortly to have more degrees from Yale (B.A., M.A., B.D., Ph.D.) than any other living person of his time. At a salary of $3,000 a year plus $25 a month for house rent, he took up his duties on July 1, 1909; he would not relinquish them for thirty-six action-filled years. Although reported by certain faculty members to be something of an autocrat, he was without question one of the great college presidents of his day. In 1917 the Carnegie Foundation asked him to serve on a commission to recommend changes in its pension plan. One year later he was president of Association of American Colleges and of the American Council on Education. His flair for public speaking, his "taking ways" as a fund raiser, his buoyant optimism, his disposition for work, his keen mind — all these marked him as a man of extraordinary capabilities.[6]

In his inaugural address Cowling laid down certain specifics: Carleton should remain relatively small;

its student body should be distinguished by the capacity to profit from a stimulating environment; it should steer clear of becoming or attaching to a graduate school; instruction should be cultural rather than technical; emphasis should be on teaching rather than on research; campus atmosphere should be Christian without being sectarian. This was basically to be Carleton's policy throughout the Cowling administration. Much of it sounds familiar even today. The new president was a man of splendid convictions. Technocracy, miracles, the income tax, church federation, centralized government, and federal aid to education all felt his dialectical barbs. Free men, he maintained, would fashion a well-ordered society if they were taught to think and to act in terms of the common good. The best instrument yet devised to do this teaching was the peculiarly American institution known as the liberal arts college, an organization therefore vital to the preservation of our free society and worthy of men's gifts and wholehearted support.[7]

The inaugural luncheon was served in the new Sayles-Hill gymnasium. Soon a central heating and lighting plant, costing $40,000 and featuring a 140-foot chimney, was completed. In 1914 came a $50,000 Music Hall, and two years later on October 8, 1916, as part of the observance of the college's fiftieth birthday the beautiful Skinner Memorial Chapel was dedicated. The shortage of rooms for students in private homes in Northfield, plus Cowling's admiration for the residential college he had known at Yale, dictated the next building priorities. In 1916 and 1917, respectively, West Hall (later Burton Hall) for men and a new dormitory for women (soon to be called Nourse Hall) were added to the campus sky line. All these projects were quite in keeping with "the tremendous expansion of the physical plant" which was characteristic of American colleges and universities during this period.[8]

As plant growth was the order of the day on the country's campuses, so too were campaigns for the funds necessary to pay for the new buildings, to meet accreditation standards, and to match the conditional gifts of foundations. Cowling almost immediately proposed that $600,000 be raised at Carleton, a stupendous sum for the time, but the trustees concurred in his daring plan. The General Education Board pledged $100,000, contingent upon the college's raising $500,000 by January 1, 1917. As early as October, 1913, half of the amount had been collected; in 1914, therefore, the goal was increased to $1,000,000, a total originally considered but rejected as an impossibility. The General Education Board then increased its offer to $200,000 and changed the date to November 1, 1916. With gifts of $60,000 from the Lairds and $50,000 each from James J. Hill, J. Hartwell Davis, and the estate of Levi M. Stewart, along with smaller donations from several thousand others, it was possible to announce at the college's fiftieth birthday celebration that the ''Million Dollar Undertaking for Carleton'' had been successfully completed.[9]

Within six months the country passed from a period of uneasy neutrality to complete involvement in World War I. A total of 289 undergraduate men at Carleton served in the armed forces, of whom 131 were enrolled in the SATC unit on campus. With male enrollment temporarily reduced, there was no football team in 1918, but in an unprecedented arrangement Carleton and St. Olaf men banded together to form a squad which played a limited schedule. Nearly three hundred alumni were also in uniform, and many served overseas. Eleven former students lost their lives in the conflict.[10]

During the decade and a half before the war, enrollment had increased steadily. Only slightly over 200 in 1902 (academy students not included), it had risen to 442 in 1916. Until 1913 women outnumbered men, but that fall saw the registration of 173 freshmen, the largest new class to date, with 98 men and 75 women. A fairly homogeneous lot, most of the students lived within fifty to one hundred miles of Northfield.[11]

Although traditional restrictions against drinking, smoking, dancing, or disregard of the Sabbath obtained, students as always found their means of evasion. They were, however, becoming increasingly restive under the ban on dancing, yet as late as 1915 the faculty remained adamant on the issue. But here, as in many other realms, World War I marked a turning point. With the coming of the SATC unit, the prohibition was lifted. Then on January 11, 1919, Sayles-Hill gymnasium was host to the first official dance on campus, ''a real punch-and-wafer'' affair ''with the jazziest of orchestra bands to keep the feet hopping.'' Debate and oratory continued to be popular, but there were evidences, though erratic, that students were questioning the worth of the old literary societies. Thanksgiving was a joyous occasion, and Washington's birthday was cause for a holiday and festivities. Athletics prospered, especially after Claude J. Hunt joined the faculty as athletic director and coach in September, 1913.[12]

Women, traditionally better than men at ordering their own affairs on campus, founded the Young Women's Student Government Association in the fall of 1911. The men would wait a few years to organize. In the academic area evidence of relative well-being came with the installation in 1914 of Carleton's chapter of Phi Beta Kappa, Beta of Minnesota. (Alpha chapter at the state university dated from 1892.) Not until 1937 would the United Chapters see fit to bestow another affiliate on a Minnesota institution, St. Catherine's.[13]

As the state moved into the 1920s, despite the emphasis some writers have placed on the dramatic and lurid aspects of that decade, there was no sudden rupture in life on area campuses. At Carleton what occurred were gradual ''deep-seated changes in the attitude and 'flavor' of the College, a shift from a period of being a rather provincial place to one of more sophistication, or pretentiousness if you will.'' In 1922 of the 842 students enrolled, 720 were from Minnesota; it was not until 1936–37 that students from the North Star State for the first time composed less than 50 per cent of the total enrollment. Thereafter their proportion would decrease further.[14]

Mainly Protestant and middle class, the Carleton student of the 1920s, if female, bobbed her hair and wore short dresses with belt lines at the hip, or if male, donned a coonskin coat and knickers. Both sexes attended required chapel services three or four times a week. If alcohol in that time of legal prohibition was not unknown, as alumni have testified, it was far more uncommon than in recent years. For most students diversions had changed little from those of an earlier day — winter sports, canoeing, picnics, walks with a member of the opposite sex, bull sessions. Movies were popular and fairly new, and so were campus dances which grew in number and variety. The Stutz Bearcat made an occasional appearance, but student cars were banned as early as 1923.[15]

The women expanded and perfected their self-governing association after 1920. In 1928 it was given the name ''Women's League.'' The men's comparable organization did quite well in 1924–25, but thereafter for a number of reasons it declined and died. An all-student council, the Alma Mater Association, existed from 1920 to 1930, but it never developed into an effective governing body. Although fraternities and sororities were not permitted, it was becoming increasingly apparent that the literary societies were far more social than intellectual. By 1937 the last of the women's societies had passed into oblivion. Two of the men's groups hung on until 1948–49, when they were put to rest by vote of the students and action of the faculty.[16]

Cowling always maintained that a college should look like a college. To that end he retained experts to lay out a plan for the campus and buildings. Attention was paid to appearance as well as to function. The beautiful Lyman Lakes were created in 1916–17 and have been constantly landscaped since. The scenic arboretum was begun in the late 1920s. The depression halted construction after 1929, but a number of buildings, reflective of the affluence of the period, had been added to the campus in the years prior to that date. First to appear was Leighton Hall of Chemistry, erected in 1920 and named for a trustee who contributed largely to its cost. Three years later South Hall, renamed in 1926 after generous donor J. Hartwell Davis, was joined to the south end of West or Burton Hall as part of the dormitory complex for men. In 1927 the third dormitory for women, most appropriately called Margaret Evans Hall after Carleton's distinguished dean and professor, was completed at a cost of some $250,000. In that same year the $198,000 Laird Stadium, paid for largely by the family of the late trustee William H. Laird, was constructed on the bank of the Cannon River.[17]

Near-fulfillment of Cowling's dream of making Carleton a completely residential college came in 1928 when Severance Hall, named for a former student and onetime president of the American Bar Association and his wife, who was also a former student at the college, was completed and furnished. Its total cost came to nearly $400,000. Its dedication was fittingly performed by Frank B. Kellogg, United States secretary of state, Severance law partner, and Carleton trustee. By this time the seven major buildings on campus when Cowling took office had increased to eighteen. There were also some cottages for students, a number of college-owned houses, and a faculty club for members of the staff. The houses, incidentally, were the cause of a legal case that was carried to the state supreme court late in 1922. Reversing an earlier decision of a district court, the high tribunal declared that the houses rented to students and staff, as well as the college farm, were not taxable. This decision rankled some Northfielders for years, but it was based on numerous precedents.[18]

After World War I Carleton, like most colleges around the country, set about strengthening its financial position. The trustees in 1919 entered upon a major effort to raise $4,000,000. It was hoped that $1,000,000 would come from the Baptist World Movement (the college had entered into a tenuous relationship with the Northern Baptist Convention in 1916), that a like sum would be provided by large givers outside Minnesota and by national foundations, and that the remaining $2,000,000 would stem from popular subscriptions. The campaign had the usual problems and tensions — efforts to meet deadlines on conditional gifts, mounting deficits in the face of grants which required that

the college be free of debt, lethargic support from expected workers, and disappointment in professional money raisers, pledges, and the value of properties given.[19]

Through it all, however, President Cowling persisted in his Herculean labors. Little came from the Baptist movement, but significant sums did come from outside the state — $525,000 from the General Education Board, $75,000 from the Carnegie Foundation, and $50,000 from philanthropist Edward S. Harkness. The college was unable to meet the deadlines originally established by the General Education Board, but typically that organization extended the time limits, and by early 1929 Carleton's debts had been satisfied and the matching terms had been met. Although the $4,000,000 had not been raised, the assets of the college had been more than doubled, and the fame of Carleton as a liberal arts institution of high quality had been vastly broadened.[20]

Unhappily the depression which followed put all colleges through an ordeal; the very life of Carleton hung in the balance. However, through patience and sacrifice on the part of personnel, hard work by the president, and the generosity of several trustees, survival was assured. In 1934 before economic conditions had fully recovered, another major campaign was undertaken, and the General Education Board was induced to offer $500,000 if the college would raise an equal amount and free itself from debt. By May, 1936, the conditions had been met and the board's check was received. It would be twenty years before another full-scale campaign was launched, although the annual routine of raising funds went on vigorously.[21]

The basic academic structure of Carleton had been pretty definitely cast even before Cowling took office, and during the years between the two world wars, there was no general overhaul of the curriculum nor were radical experiments attempted. In 1920 the last bachelor of science degrees were conferred; thereafter only the B.A. could be earned. Some new departments appeared from time to time as key people were promoted or added to the staff: public speaking in 1918, biography in 1919, art in 1920, hygiene and public health in 1927, dramatic arts in 1928, international relations in 1937. Older departments were reorganized and a divisional structure was created in 1929, but these moves were far from revolutionary. The college would retain its humanistic, liberal arts character. This meant shunning the trends towards specialization and shifting instead in harmony with the general education movement, which had its origins at Columbia University after World War I. The program, a reaction to the fragmentation which had resulted from the growth of the elective system, found its inspiration in Columbia's well-known course in contemporary civilization. Its premise was based on the assumption that "there is a certain minimum of . . . [the Western] intellectual and spiritual tradition that a man must experience and understand if he is to be called educated." [22]

To stimulate high-level performance, Carleton in 1922 became one of the early schools to adopt an honors program, the pioneering of which is generally credited to Swarthmore College. Students admitted to this plan were relieved of certain requirements so that they might have time, under close faculty direction, to delve deeply into some topic which held particular interest for them. The plan was reminiscent of the tutorial system at England's Oxford and Cambridge universities, and with variations it is still in effect. Many alumni also graduated with "Honors in Special Fields." In 1936 further flexibility was provided by the creation of a standing faculty committee on "Individualized Programs of Study." Its function was to arrange and approve such special programs for students requesting them as would "enable them to use the facilities of the college most advantageously for their intellectual development." [23]

Evidence would seem to suggest that the academic ability and performance of some Carleton students declined during the depression days of the early 1930s, when enrollment fell from just under 900 in 1931 to approximately 675 in 1935. Yet there is also reason to believe that expectations were high and that many undergraduates responded accordingly. One bit of testimony in support of this latter contention came in 1935 when the college was granted a chapter of Sigma Xi, the national honorary scientific fraternity. [24]

That high standards were maintained was due largely to the caliber of the faculty. Devotion to scholarship, loyalty to the college, lofty ideals — qualities found among faculty on every Minnesota campus of the period — all of these attributes characterized many Carleton professors during the two decades between the wars. Several had been presidents of other institutions, and a number were ordained ministers. Irreverent students were known on occasion to ridicule these credentials, but there was no denying the fact that some very able and well-trained men and women were on the staff. In 1936, for example, out of eighty-five members of the faculty including graduate assistants, twenty-three were listed in *Who's Who in America*, a higher percentage, according to the University of Chicago *Alumni Bulletin*, than was to be found in any other educational institution in the country. Although lacking certain provisions for pensions, full professors in the early 1920s were entitled to sabbatical leaves. In 1929 along with all other personnel, they had group insurance at low rates made available to them. More significant, however, was the academic climate under which they and their colleagues operated. [25]

In the wake of the notorious Scopes trial in 1925 in Dayton, Tennessee, a fundamentalist Baptist minister in Minneapolis, William B. Riley, made a vigorous attack upon Cowling, the Carleton trustees, and several of the college's professors — who were even mentioned by name — because of the teaching of the theory of evolution on the campus. Some two years later the Minnesota State Baptist Convention by a fairly close vote severed its relation with Carleton. Despite this action the college administration did not yield to the pressure. In appreciation the faculty sent a statement to Cowling declaring that "neither you nor anyone else in authority at Carleton has even suggested that a member of the faculty teach anything which his scientific training, his best insight and his conscience did not dictate." In the same vein the teaching staff unanimously supported a petition to the state legislature urging it "to maintain unimpaired the standards of American liberty threatened by the anti-evolution bill now under consideration." This emphasis on intellectual freedom, tempered by a sense of responsibility, continued to be characteristic of life on campus during the difficult period of the 1930s and onward to the present day. [26]

Cowling's aim had always been to create a liberal arts college in the Upper Midwest which would equal in quality the best of such institutions to be found in the New England area. Some of his plans for Carleton would elude him, but by 1940 he had transformed an impressive number of them into reality.

16 AUGSBURG COLLEGE

Search for Identity

AUGSBURG, with its enrollment down and work on its new building at a standstill, had slight cause to rejoice over the advent of the twentieth century. The year 1900 had not passed before another threat to the life of the institution — a serious charge of moral turpitude against one of its strong supporters — darkened future prospects. Target of the allegations was a distinguished and eloquent minister, pastor since 1881 of the Trinity Lutheran Congregation in Minneapolis, friend and ally of Sverdrup and Oftedal, and an influential community leader. The resulting shock is easy to imagine. At first the Augsburg professors supported their old friend, and his parishioners refused to accept his resignation. In the end, however, the Trinity community was split asunder; supporters of the besieged pastor seceded early in 1902 to form Bethany Lutheran Congregation. No matter what degree of truth lay in the indictment of the central figure in the unfortunate episode, his close and long-time relationship with Augsburg and its leaders was bound, in the public mind at least, to involve the institution in the affair. Hostility developed, fund raising suffered, and the Lutheran Free Church, Augsburg's main support, was subjected to severe internal strains.[1]

Despite the discouraging situation at the seminary, however, the church conference in 1901 took steps to improve conditions. Immediate completion of the building, New Main, was called for, and the congregations were asked to contribute $19,000 to remove the deficit in the building fund. Members of the faculty were requested to spend the summer soliciting money, which they did with encouraging results. In addition, with the co-operation of Augsburg people, provision was made for strengthening the bond which existed between the denominational body and the seminary. Adopted in 1902, the arrangement gave delegates to the annual meetings of the Free Church a hand in selecting both professors and Augsburg trustees, a procedure which continued

until 1963. New Main, containing classrooms, a library, a gymnasium, and a chapel, was dedicated early in 1902. Old Main was then given over entirely to dormitory and dining functions. These structures along with North Hall comprised the physical plant for the next thirty-five years.[2]

Although the completion of New Main occasioned a temporary improvement in morale, Augsburg's struggles were far from over. Except for an expansion of the preparatory course from two to three years in 1900 and to four years in 1909, little change was evidenced in curricular offerings until after World War I. By 1914 enrollment was down to 103, whereas that of its old rival, St. Olaf, had climbed to 545. While other private colleges were responding to changes supported by such powerful bodies as the General Education Board, the Carnegie Foundation, and the North Central Association, Augsburg continued to concentrate on its traditional role as a divinity school.[3]

Even the employment of several new and able faculty members made but a slight difference, since all were Augsburg products committed to Sverdrup's point of view. The weight of the past had a rather remarkable persistency. Language habits, for example, were slow to change. English seems to have been used in the majority of classes after 1900, but two of the four theological professors lectured in Norwegian until the 1920s. Minutes of the boarding club and records of the mission society were kept in Norwegian until 1912 and 1915, respectively, while the *Augsburg Echo*, the student publication started in 1898, was bilingual for the next twenty-seven years. The annual report of Augsburg's president to the Free Church made its first appearance in English as late as 1930.[4]

Although moving slowly, the forces of change were in operation. More and more students were American-born, anxious to cast off the image of immigrant, and eager to speak the language of the country. In an earlier day four-fifths or more of the graduates of the Greek department went into the ministry; by 1910 the proportion was only about one-half. Not unnaturally then a growing demand developed for Augsburg to emulate the academic patterns existing in many other private colleges. It seems evident that Sverdrup recognized the need to respond to this urging, but his sudden and unexpected death at the age of fifty-eight in May, 1907, occurred before he had recommended any specific innovations. The community, benumbed by shock and grief, would have its hands full trying to find someone to carry on the work of the deceased president without worrying about much else. Further, both financial stringency and a critical vocal element in the Free Church militated against an early modernization of the college program.[5]

For a time it appeared that an unfortunate division over the selection of a new president would add to Augsburg's already sufficient array of problems. Consequently Oftedal, no longer on the faculty but still chairman of the board, suggested a compromise which was largely approved by the 1907 conference of the church. As matters worked out, Oftedal became acting president, while two faculty members who had been mentioned as possible successors to Sverdrup were elected to new deanships — one for the seminary, the other for the college and preparatory departments. George Sverdrup, Jr., also a presidential possibility, became a "temporary" professor. The triple-headed administration was more than a little top-heavy for an institution of the size and nature of Augsburg, but thanks to the natures of the two deans it functioned reasonably well. In April, 1909, however, one of them died at the age of forty-two, thereby disrupting the uneasy balance which had been created.[6]

To some of Augsburg's directors, the time seemed ripe to consider the adoption of "a college program geared to non-ministerial students," but the majority in the conference of 1909 were not yet ready for such a step. The gathering did, however, endorse an overly ambitious campaign to raise an endowment of $100,000, authorize construction of a central heating plant which was finished that fall, and establish a new theology professorship. The same autumn the younger Sverdrup — back from a year's study in Germany — was serving as vice president as well as professor of theology at his alma mater. In actuality he functioned as its chief executive officer. It was he, for example, who prepared the annual report to the conference of 1910, which recommended some broadening of the curriculum by the addition of courses in botany, history of philosophy, and a combined offering in sociology and political economy.

With slight opposition, the recommendation was approved, "a first step in the slow evolution of the Greek department into Augsburg College, a process substantially completed by 1922." With the death of Oftedal in March, 1911, the era of George Sverdrup, Jr., soon to be president in name as well as in action, would begin.[7]

He was formally elected head of Augsburg in July, 1911. The main problem he faced was to transform Augsburg's collegiate department into a first-rate accredited college without alienating those individuals who wished to maintain the institution's traditional stance. The task called for patience and tact of a high order. Although sympathetic with the faction pushing for change, Sverdrup made no quick or dramatic moves. To do so would be foreign to his nature, even if he had the money such actions required. Furthermore, having been exposed to varied influences beyond the campus in a public high school, the graduate schools of Minnesota and Yale, Europe, and the Middle East, he needed time to win the confidence of church conservatives. To avoid courting conflict, he worked carefully and quietly to effect innovation. Progress was slow and success modest. At times the very survival of Augsburg seemed to hang in the balance. College enrollment of 53 in 1911–12 fell steadily to a low of 23 in 1918–19. Indebtedness of over $29,000 in 1915 was erased by 1919, but endowment then was only some $55,000. New buildings were, of course, out of the question.[8]

Considering these harsh facts, it was not surprising that accreditation proved elusive. As early as 1910 Sverdrup had asked the Minnesota Department of Education to evaluate the college department in order to determine the eligibility of its graduates for high school teaching positions. The examiner, a University of Minnesota professor, was inclined to be sympathetic, but he could not avoid pointing to obvious deficiencies, such as the inadequate facilities in physics, the absence of chemistry and zoology, and the anemic endowment. All he could do was offer encouragement and suggest that Augsburg graduates take the state examinations in various pedagogical subjects until the requisite courses were taught at the college itself. By 1913 chemistry and several educational courses had been added to the curriculum, and a modest annual appropriation for laboratory equipment had been made.[9]

Once again Augsburg turned with hope to the University of Minnesota, which made further investigations in 1915 and 1916. As before, however, the report was disappointing. Major criticisms were directed at the inadequate library, the limited curricular offerings, and the overworked faculty. The state institution, however, did accord recognition to the first two years of work at Augsburg and promised students studying classical languages, Norwegian, and English, provisional admission to the university graduate school. North Central accreditation remained out of reach, but one or two advances were made. Of four major faculty appointments between 1915 and 1919, only one went to an Augsburg alumnus, an indication that parochialism was gradually weakening. In 1917 an academic major, English, was established for the first time; three years later came a second such sequence in education.[10]

World War I plunged enrollment in the college department to an alarmingly low figure in 1918–19, but thereafter matters took a turn for the better. At the church meeting of 1919, Sverdrup felt the time was ripe finally to speak out regarding Augsburg's obligation to young men for whom the ministry was not a goal. Response was encouraging, and the faculty, board, and school directors were authorized to consider whether "a more practical academic program in the preparatory departments" could be developed. The outcome was by no means revolutionary, but offerings in English and chemistry were increased, and Greek was made an elective for all students not headed toward the seminary.[11]

That same fall of 1919 the commemoration of Augsburg's fiftieth birthday provided a natural occasion for taking inventory, an opportunity which the alumni association seized by appointing a committee to study the whole situation and to "recommend new departures in educational policy for both Augsburg and for the Lutheran Free Church." Results of a questionnaire distributed to graduates by the committee revealed wide variation in opinions, along with considerable confusion. To the question "Is Augsburg a divinity school?" forty-six answered yes, forty-four no, thirty-eight qualified their responses, and twenty were noncommittal. Consequently the chairman of the *ad hoc* group was convinced that it was necessary to emphasize "that henceforth there is conducted, in close harmony with a school in theology, a first class and standard college department, where young people may acquire a splendid education under Christian leadership." In order, however, not to arouse too much opposition, the committee decided to defer specific recommendations regarding Augsburg until the convening of the next church conference the following year.[12]

At that meeting in the spring of 1920 delegates were called upon to deal with two committee proposals: adoption of coeducation and removal of the campus to a new location. Both propositions evoked divergent views, but no real pyrotechnics erupted. On relocation, the trustees were authorized to seek a new site "in the neighborhood of Minneapolis." The decision on coeducation, on the other hand, was postponed a year, but as the *Lutheran Free Church Messenger* reported, it was "easy to read the signs of the times" that the change was coming.[13]

When church representatives convened in 1921, both the denomination's president and Sverdrup came out in favor of admitting women to the college, but one trustee spoke out sharply in opposition. Sverdrup then moved that the church approve coeducation but postpone final action until 1922. The motion carried 256 to 11. Thus fortified, Augsburg's president announced in August that several young women had applied for admission to the college and that they might be accepted. He did, however, acknowledge that the experiment could be terminated by the conference of 1922. At the start of classes in September, 1921, five women (one a sophomore and the rest freshmen) enrolled, and according to the *Echo* whatever stir their presence was expected to arouse did not develop. Some delegates at the church assembly the following summer resented the innovation as a *fait accompli*, but despite heated debate, coeducation was approved by a vote of 141 to 81.[14]

Meanwhile halting steps had been taken in the search for a new campus away from the cramped confines of the Cedar-Riverside area. In the summer of 1921, the president of the board, a former minister turned investor, announced enthusiastically that just the tract was available in the village of Richfield. Five months later he and several other men incorporated the Augsburg Park Association, acquired the Richfield plot, and subdivided it into lots. With the profits from this enterprise plus funds anticipated from the sale of the old campus, it was hoped that a new Augsburg would arise amidst the sylvan surroundings of a peaceful suburban location populated by members of the Free Church organization. It was a grand scheme, but it failed to materialize.[15]

The Park Association episode, while unfortunate in some respects, did tend to publicize Augsburg's imperfections and to focus attention on the need for change. As the postwar decade moved along, enrollment in the college department grew from 44 to 248 between 1922 and 1928, while that in the seminary leveled off, and the academy decreased. Pending possible removal, some alterations had to be made on the present site. The two residences which had long housed four faculty families, West and Morton halls, were converted to dormitories for women. The professors had to look elsewhere for accommodations. Plans were made to perform a major reconstruction of Old Main, the wooden four-story abode of the theological students and college men, but city building codes permitted only minor repairs. North Hall remained adequate for boys in the academy.[16]

Together the college and academy faculty numbered eight full-time and nine temporary or part-time teachers in 1921–22. Within ten years it would double in size to keep pace with the student body and curricular growth. In 1921 history was added to English and education as possible major fields. The following year the list was expanded to include ancient languages, Norse, social science (embracing philosophy also), natural science, chemistry, and religion. With the addition of music (1923), physical education (1926), French (1927), and biology (1930), Augsburg had come a long way since the days of the Greek department's single track curriculum of required courses. Full college accreditation lay in the future, and in most instances academic departments were one-man operations, but the institution no longer was the *Presteskole* of earlier times.[17]

That even modest progress was achieved seems rather remarkable in view of the external conditions influencing Augsburg's development. The Lutheran Free Church could claim only about 27,000 confirmed members, most of whom were far from affluent. The old disagreement over the role the school should play still existed. The denomination's board of education founded in 1922, for example, insisted that Augsburg's "program and Christian character as a divinity school must be maintained at all costs." Conversely others urged that the institution move rapidly ahead and gain full membership in the North Central Association. Some were highly critical of the church conference of 1923 for skirting the issue of accreditation. Sverdrup, caught in the middle, assessed the situation realistically, but he could hardly give complete satisfaction to those holding polarized views. A climax was reached at the conference of 1925 when all five members of the board of trustees resigned because of the dissension. When the smoke cleared, only two of the five were back on the board.[18]

Another complication concerned a desire on the part of some Free Church people to merge their organization with the Norwegian Lutheran Church of America, which had been created in 1917. Since the former body had been established to support Augsburg as a unique institution to train pastors and since the school had now altered its historic nature, it was argued that the Free Church no longer had cause to exist. This point of view, which Sverdrup did not accept, was expressed at the conference of 1923 and again in 1928. The spokesman for the merger proponents at the latter gathering was a prominent Augsburg faculty member, Dr. Lars P. Qualben, a graduate of all three of the institution's departments. Despite the fact that the collegiate division had ten times as many students as the seminary, another storm erupted, with Sverdrup coming out in strong opposition to the merger.[19]

Part of the opposition to Qualben stemmed from his bad timing. When he published his arguments, Augsburg was in the midst of a drive for much-needed funds, and it was feared that his writings would not only nurture a "deep disquiet" regarding the school within the church, but also that they would "cripple" the money-raising campaign. One of Qualben's points in favor of merger was the need for a larger financial base if Augsburg were to become "a modern American college." That argument, of course, did not sway antimerger people. On one contention, however, both sides could agree: the need for funds was great. As a result the conference of 1926 had approved a joint drive to aid Augsburg and a church secondary school in Fargo, North Dakota. At the same time a gesture favoring a campaign for $500,000 to finance the move to Richfield had been made, but it came to naught.[20]

Eliminating Augsburg's mounting indebtedness had seemed a sufficient task to the board of trustees. By April 30, 1928, during the Qualben controversy, the school's deficit was over $14,000, a sizable sum in its context. A year later the amount was considerably less, but the trustees, regarding the institution's financial plight as extremely serious, urged the conference "to act decisively" to solve the fiscal problem. A $200,000 "Jubilee Campaign" to free Augsburg and the North Dakota high school of debt was thereupon approved at the 1929 church meeting. It was not long until the October crash struck; still the Jubilee drive raised over $104,000, of which Augsburg received slightly more than $63,700, a definite help in offsetting the early effects of the depression.[21]

For the next several years, however, only grim determination and sacrificial loyalty kept Augsburg operating. For 1932–33 its share of the joint school drive came to less than $20,000, and indebtedness by spring had passed $74,000. The faculty, whose modest salaries had already been reduced, agreed to ask for no stated pay scale for 1933–34, but to accept what could be paid on a prorata basis. To effect another economy the trustees voted to abolish the academy, a move recommended as early as 1925. The action received the blessing of the conference in 1933. Despite some improvement in the general financial picture at the college, further salary reductions were necessary for 1934–35, while the orchestra and band fell victims to budgetary cutbacks, and athletics had to be curtailed.[22]

Added to all these woes was the old bugbear of uncertain academic status. In the spring of 1930, the University of Minnesota had certified Augsburg as a junior college and formalized an earlier agreement regarding admission to the state institution's graduate school. The agreement covered especially recommended Augsburg alumni whose major fields were "English, psychology and education, classical languages, Norse, history and chemistry." Biology received tentative approval in 1933, but the university did not accord Augsburg full accreditation as a four-year college until February, 1951, and membership in the North Central Association came only in 1954.[23]

New construction obviously was an impossibility, and in the retrenchment of course offerings, some majors — German, French, Latin, and social science — were reduced to minors. Enrollment, however, encouraged by low tuition of $75 a year and student financial aid, rose from 192 in 1929–30 to a record high of 249 in 1933–34. The quality of the faculty was maintained and even strengthened by the addition of certain key people, including in 1930 a future president, Dr. Bernhard M. Christensen, a 1922 Augsburg graduate. The college choir, formed in November, 1933, made the first of many successful tours in the spring of 1934, making Augsburg more favorably and more widely known.[24]

Finally times began to take on a brighter hue. For the fall of 1936 freshman enrollment in the college department totaled 147 as against 83 a year earlier, and on all sides a rise in optimism was manifest. A second choir and a male chorus were organized, and the orchestra reappeared. The faculty in 1937 received its first pay raise since the depression struck, albeit one of only 5 per cent. Still the downward trend had been reversed. It even became possible to think in terms of erecting a new building, in this case a dormitory. After various preliminaries, the project was presented to the 1937 church conference. Happily the plan, which called for a structure to house a hundred men and various facilities, was approved contingent upon keeping the cost down to $125,000. Thereafter matters moved along swiftly and early in 1939 Sverdrup-Oftedal Memorial Hall was occupied — Augsburg's first new building in well over three decades. That same year a local physician offered the institution his clinic building, which with its lot had cost $72,000, if the college would assume the unpaid mortgage balance of $12,500. The trustees gratefully agreed, and in the fall of 1940 a remodeled Sivertsen Hall was occupied by thirty-nine coeds.[25]

In the meantime, however, the college had suffered a sorrowful and sudden loss through the death of President Sverdrup on November 11, 1937, following a collapse brought on by a heart condition. He was fifty-eight years old, the same age at which his father had died. Although the younger Sverdrup had carried a heavy load, he had "encouraged rather than stifled the initiative of subordinates." Thus, despite gloom, life went on more smoothly than might otherwise have been the case. Appointed interim president was Professor Henrik N. Hendrickson, who had served in a variety of capacities including registrar and Latin teacher since joining the staff in August, 1900. Something of his determined and competent nature was evident in the fact that in 1931 at the age of sixty-two he completed his master's degree in history, a field to which he had turned in the 1920s.[26]

Precedent suggested that Augsburg's trustees possessed the necessary authority to select a new president, but they were loath to assume full responsibility, preferring rather to share it with the Augsburg Corporation and the Free Church annual conference. As developed by the trustees, the process would involve four steps: (1) a sort of Gallup poll within the corporation, (2) a board recommendation to the annual conference, (3) action by the latter body on the recommendation, and (4) election by the board. Under this plan nearly everyone could get into the act, but the process was cumbersome, time consuming, and as matters evolved, conducive to dissension and divisiveness. Had the board acted on its own, many of these difficulties might have been avoided.[27]

During the time the trustees wrestled with the problem, Bernhard M. Christensen and Norwegian-born Sverre Norborg, a recent faculty addition, emerged as the leading candidates for the presidency. Neither sought the position. Christensen appeared more at home in an American setting and far more disposed than his opponent to close co-operation between the Free Church and other Lutheran bodies. This was an issue of vital concern to many people interested in Augsburg, and one which generated great heat in the weeks before the meeting of the conference. As early as March, 1938, the board gave its backing to Christensen, but for various reasons — not all understood by pastors outside the Twin Cities and others — the decision was not announced until the middle of May. It was no surprise, therefore, that the conference meeting in Thief River Falls the following month was a stormy one. After heated oratory and the withdrawal of his candidacy by Norborg, dissension was still sufficient to warrant the calling of a recess for hymn singing and prayer. A vote was then taken on the Christensen nomination, with 214 ballots supporting it. However, over 100 delegates cast no ballots, 70 others opposed the nomination, 13 wrote "not voting" on their slips, and three came out for Norborg. The trustees completed the process on June 13 by electing Christensen as president.[28]

Despite the events surrounding his selection, Christensen was generally admired and respected throughout the church. A graduate of Augsburg College in 1922 and of the seminary three years later, he had studied at Princeton Theological Seminary, Columbia University, and two German universities before earning his Ph.D. at Hartford Theological Seminary in 1929. At Augsburg he had taught theology in the seminary and headed the new department of philosophy and psychology in the college, where for the first time "a full complement of philosophy courses" was available. The manner in "which he combined Christian piety with intellectual flexibility, and a profound respect for the world's great cultural traditions" was not congenial to all Free Church adherents, but it was well suited to continuing Augsburg's development as a liberal arts college.[29]

Like the younger Sverdrup, however, Christensen realized that the varied pressures converging upon him demanded a policy of gradualism, even though Augsburg's nature was undergoing a definite change. For a number of reasons — low tuition, the Minneapolis location, and better economic conditions, among others — enrollment pushed upward. In the fall of 1938, 413 students registered; 477 did so two years later. This was healthy, but a complication resulted from the growing proportion of undergraduates coming from Lutheran groups other than the Free Church. In 1935 contributions from the latter had accounted for 55.29 per cent of Augsburg's income; tuition had accounted for 41.88 per cent. In 1940 the comparable figures were 29.95 per cent and 63.61 per cent, respectively.[30]

If the college were to maintain its historic role, it was obvious that it would have to attract more young people from the Lutheran Free Church. The alternatives were to raise tuition charges and to seek financial support from new sources. The former route was in many ways distasteful, the latter exceedingly difficult. Christensen, like Augsburg, faced a dilemma for which there was no simple solution, but over the years he made steady, if frustratingly slow, progress. World War II intervened before he could effect many changes, but the beginnings of a more modern administrative structure and some easing of campus crowding were achieved.[31]

17 ST. OLAF COLLEGE

Norwegian Heritage – American Pattern

ST. OLAF IN 1899 was poised on the threshold of a new era. In the first year of President John N. Kildahl's administration, the institution was also enjoying its recently acquired status as the official college of the United Norwegian Lutheran Church. Kildahl had emigrated from Norway as a boy of nine, been confirmed by Pastor B. J. Muus, and gone on to ordination via graduation from Luther College and the seminary in Madison, Wisconsin. During his ministries in Goodhue County and in Chicago, he had established a reputation as a powerful preacher, a man who appealed to people in all walks of life. Deeply religious and an ardent Anti-Missourian, he had loved the ministry, but when he was elected president of St. Olaf, he had regarded the action as a call from God which he must obey. He would serve the college well until 1914, when he would be elected professor of theology at his denomination's seminary in St. Paul.[1]

When Kildahl arrived at St. Olaf, it was still a small institution. Classes had opened in September, 1899, with 46 college and 138 academy students in attendance. The faculty numbered nine, and the two buildings and seventy-seven acres of land looked a little down at the heels. Debt free and with church support assured, however, the institution looked ahead to a period of expansion on all fronts. Sectarianism might pose a problem, but the recent action of the church convention in creating a seminary separate and distinct from the college seemed to militate against such an eventuality. It was clear that the majority in the United Church wished St. Olaf to offer a program of general liberal education, to provide for all its young people who could go on to college, not just those preparing for full-time Christian service.[2]

Encouraged by financial backing from the largest Norwegian denominational body in the country, St. Olaf set about providing needed expansion for its physical plant. Ytterboe Hall, with rooms for 250 men, a dining facility, and a gymnasium 40 by 80 feet, was completed in 1901 at a cost of $68,200. Over 3,000 people attended the dedication in June. The school paper, caught up in the sanguine spirit, noted that the "woods reëcho with the noise and hammering of the busy workmen" and that "the present era of prosperity is unparalleled in our history." One caretaker, however, finding the push into the future too rapid for his tastes, quit his job lest he might get lost in the vastness of the new dormitory. In the fall of 1902 came the dedication of Steensland Library, made possible by a gift of $13,000 from Halle Steensland of Madison, Wisconsin, "the first substantial individual gift received by the college."[3]

The year 1905 saw a wholesale remodeling of Old Main, including the installation of radiators and electric wires in anticipation of the completion of a new power plant several months later. A joyous oyster supper celebrating the substitution of electric lights for oil lamps was delayed for two hours by the failure of the new illumination to make its debut as scheduled. The following year marked the advent of the college farm and dairy herd (farm investments were popular with colleges then) and the erection of Hoyme Memorial Chapel, a symbol and a facility long desired.[4]

By 1906 women's housing was desperately inadequate. Only 22 of the 136 young ladies enrolled (25 of them in the college department) were able to live on campus; their quarters in so-called Agony Hall dated back to the 1870s. Thus a campaign to raise funds for a new dormitory was undertaken. Its success was delayed, however, by a feeling among some groups that the cost of coeducation out-weighed its merits. At the church convention of 1908 a motion to phase out coeducation in the preparatory department failed by a vote of 335 to 215. But through the efforts of Kildahl and others, the money was secured, and the building with rooms for 108 women was completed in 1912. Destined to become the busy center of campus life, it was most suitably named Mohn Hall in memory of the first president, whose defense of general education for women as well as for men had been effective and unequivocal. Memory-laden Agony Hall then became St. Olaf's first music building.[5]

At the celebration of the college's thirty-fifth anniversary in the fall of 1909, it was decided to create an endowment fund to supplement the church's annual contribution, which that year was slightly over $20,000. The alumni became involved, and one of them secured a pledge of $50,000 from James J. Hill contingent upon the raising of $200,000 more before January 1, 1913. After the money for Mohn Hall was in hand, the United Church initiated a jubilee fund drive, part of the proceeds of which went to the college. By September 1, 1913 — Hill had extended his deadline — the task was completed and St. Olaf had an endowment. All told the net worth of the college during the Kildahl years grew from slightly over $44,000 to nearly $497,000.[6]

Meanwhile the nature of the institution was being transformed to bring it into line with current developments in leading colleges and universities. Though both the college and the academy shared the same administration and faculty, differences between the two components of St. Olaf were sharpened. In 1900, despite the strong opposition from the classicists, a new scientific course leading to a B.S. degree was approved by the church convention. The man selected to organize and direct it had a doctorate from a leading state university. Soon other university-trained men would add stature to the faculty. The transference in 1900 of the college department from the United Church Seminary in St. Paul to St. Olaf brought the latter four faculty members, sixty-one students, and books and equipment. President Kildahl had the ability to attract good faculty people; by 1914 they would number thirty-three.[7]

A whole new era had dawned with the arrival in 1903 of F. Melius Christiansen as music director. Three years later he took the college band on a trip to Norway, "the first time an organization from an American institution" had visited that country. Increasingly, however, "Christy" had become involved with other phases of music, and it was

his famed St. Olaf choir, dating from 1911, which is usually associated with his name. In 1913 the group made an overwhelmingly successful trip to Norway, which included the placing of a wreath on the grave of one of the institution's founders, B. J. Muus. Perennially Professor Christiansen and his choir brought fame and recognition to the little-known college on the hill in Northfield.[8]

Three years after making the Christiansen appointment, Kildahl added Ole E. Rölvaag to the staff at St. Olaf. Just returned from a year of study in Norway following his graduation from the college, Professor Rölvaag would remain on the faculty until his death in 1931. Although he published his first book in 1912 and became chairman of the department of Norwegian language and literature in 1916, it was not until the publication of his novel, *Giants in the Earth*, in the mid-1920s that his fame spread beyond the campus on Manitou Heights. Since that time, however, he has become internationally known.[9]

The curriculum continued to be enriched and experiments undertaken. New courses were added: economics (1903), sociology (1909), political science (1910), a department of home economics (1912). The catalog of 1899 had listed 30 courses; that of 1914 carried a total of 114. In 1909 a program designed specifically to prepare secondary teachers came into being. Experiments with subacademy work, the preparation of parochial schoolteachers, and the training of deaf persons proved to be temporary, but these innovations helped St. Olaf "find itself" and establish its identity as a college of liberal arts. The two-semester system replaced the three-term calendar in 1909, and the elective principle was adopted several years later. To keep the latter in bounds, a group system with distribution requirements was then approved. Formerly graduation had depended upon passing a certain number of courses; henceforth it would rest upon the accumulation of 130 credit hours. During the first decade and a half of the new century, St. Olaf moved into the main stream of American higher education. As a denominational institution, the college could not qualify for Carnegie pensions, but it would gain North Central accreditation in 1915.[10]

When President Kildahl left office in 1914, enrollment in the collegiate department was 330 and in the academy 90. During his administration, men outnumbered women two to one. Only six women graduated from the college division before 1906, but the succeeding eight years found eighty-five coeds receiving baccalaureate degrees. The class of 1906 made quite a stir when seven girls completed the course along with twenty-eight men. Of the 515 graduates by the end of the Kildahl era, 212 became teachers and 101 ministers; 50 others were either missionaries or theological students. Most were Norwegians from Minnesota and contiguous states. None was as yet wealthy.[11]

For undergraduates, rules were still strict. An Ibsen play at the town auditorium, for example, was off limits. But efforts were made by Kildahl to substitute co-operation for coercion, responsibility by the individual for policing by the administration. When free hours (5:00 to 7:00 P.M.) were extended by an hour in 1911, a writer in the school paper rejoiced, declaring "it is a well-known fact that too much confinement and too close application to books shatters the nervous system and destroys the red corpuscles of the blood." The seeds of student government were planted in 1910, and an honor system went into effect early the following year. Intercollegiate football was still banned, but Ole baseball teams gave their adherents plenty of cause for pride. The literary societies were in their heyday — 386 of the 428 students in 1912 belonged to them — and their activities and those of other groups were sufficient to keep life busy and exciting, rules or no rules.[12]

In the summer of 1914 the church convention elected the Reverend Lauritz A. Vigness to succeed President Kildahl. A native Minnesotan who had graduated from Augustana College in South Dakota and from a seminary in Iowa, Vigness for the two decades prior to his arrival at St. Olaf had been president of a Lutheran college in Ottawa, Illinois. Events in far-off Sarajevo would soon plunge Europe into war, but there seemed little reason for concern in America. The new administration on Manitou Heights got under way amid high hopes for continued growth and improvement. In his inaugural address President Vigness characterized the ideal alumnus of St. Olaf as one "who consecrates all his talents and labors to his Redeemer's service, be he in the Gospel ministry or any other legitimate calling." His remarks being favorably received, the new executive had reason to feel that he would have a successful administration ahead of him.[13]

Despite the expansion under Kildahl, however, there was much to be done if the upward trend were to be maintained. Among the needs were a science building, enlargement of the library, separate facilities for the music department, additional dormitories, an administration building, a gymnasium, higher salaries, and more faculty. Since teams from other institutions sometimes refused to compete in Ytterboe Hall's obsolete gym, a new and modern athletic plant held top priority in the minds of many students and alumni. Money for such a purpose was hard to come by, but the new gymnasium became a reality in 1919 at a cost of about $147,000. Although subjected to severe sonic strains during hotly contested basketball games with archrival Carleton, the structure served many purposes admirably for years to come. Other construction plans had to be shelved until more settled times for a number of reasons, including the war, rising costs, and uncertainty over the future.[14]

Projected estimates of faculty needs to bring student-teacher ratios in line with recommendations of the North Central Association were also thrown off by falling wartime enrollments. In 1918 the teaching staff for the first time was classified by ranks, and maximum salaries were raised from $1,500 to $2,000. Another change occurred in 1917 when the United Norwegian Lutheran Church joined with the Hauge and the Norwegian synods to form the Norwegian Lutheran Church of America. The academy at St. Olaf was then transferred to Red Wing Seminary, and the latter's senior college department was combined with that of St. Olaf. Henceforth the institution in Northfield would be strictly college level.[15]

That fall of 1917 almost five hundred men and women enrolled, but with the country at war, it was expected that a military unit would soon be activated on campus. By the time that happened, however, a new administration would be directing St. Olaf's affairs. Relationships between Vigness and portions of the student body had become increasingly strained, and major groups in the whole college family were losing confidence in his administrative actions. Like Mattson at Gustavus, Vigness "open-minded, sympathetic, friendly, humane — democratic and unassuming in his social relations . . . devoted to the welfare and success of his students and faculty" was better suited for work in the church than for running a college. The situation was resolved by the appointment of Vigness as executive secretary of the board of education of the newly united church and the election in June, 1918, of the Reverend Lars Wilhelm Boe as fourth president of the college.[16]

The new executive was to provide St. Olaf with strong leadership for a quarter of a century. A member of the class of 1898, a graduate of the United Church's seminary in Minneapolis, and an ordained minister, Pastor Boe had served with notable success for a decade as the first president of Waldorf College in Forest City, Iowa. He had also been elected to both houses of the Iowa legislature and urged to try for the state's gubernatorial chair, an honor he declined, and he had held an executive position in the Norwegian Lutheran Church of America. That his predilection was not narrowly parochial was made clear in his inaugural address when he said: "While I hope the day will never come when we do not truly appreciate everything that is worth while in our Norwegian heritage, there is no room for little Norways in America." [17]

During the first year of his administration, Boe had to grapple with wartime problems, a student body of 327 undergraduates, and 228 members of the Student Army Training Corps. Life on the hill assumed many of the aspects of a military installation until the corps was terminated in December. Meanwhile the "flu" epidemic of 1918 struck the campus and resulted in the death of four trainees. By the start of the second semester something like normal conditions had been restored, and enrollment was up to 630, including 109 men who had been in the SATC. [18]

The future looked bright, and like many other colleges of the day St. Olaf laid plans to improve its financial picture. Much was needed: $100,000 to complete the gymnasium, plus funds to provide other buildings and to pay adequate salaries if St. Olaf were to keep in step with advances in higher education generally. An encouraging stimulus came early in 1919, when Harald Thorson, who had played a primary role in bringing the institution to Northfield, offered to give $100,000 for a classroom or science building if the college would raise an equal amount for the purpose. With church approval, a St. Olaf Corporation similar to that organized at Carleton was created in 1919 to increase the endowment fund and in other ways aid the development of the college. A setback occurred early in 1920 with the death of Thorson and resulting complications over the settlement of his estate; optimism, however, remained high and a financial secretary went to work the following autumn with the stated hope of raising $10,000,000 in ten years. [19]

Not all went as planned. The financial secretary received far more kind words than substantial gifts. The consulting architectural firm made so many suggestions — including the adoption of Norman Gothic style — that more time was needed for further study. The picture was changed and priorities altered by a fire in the old power plant and the decision of the alumni association to conduct a drive for funds to erect an addition to the library. It was then decided that a new powerhouse and well should be constructed, but once again fate stepped in to interfere with the plans. Fire destroyed Hoyme Memorial Chapel in the fall of 1923. The shortage

of funds fortunately was corrected by the sale of bonds guaranteed by the properties of the St. Olaf Corporation, but there were even bigger problems to be faced. [20]

The need for better educational facilities for the growing student body had become acute. The physics department had been housed in the basement of the chapel, a frame shack was home to the chemistry department, and certain administrative offices were located in the gymnasium. To correct this condition a science and administration building was constructed. Its cost was met by money in hand, the insurance on the chapel, a grant of $80,000 from the General Education Board, and a successful special fund drive. Dedication of the $310,000 structure (later christened Holland Hall) took place in June, 1925, as part of the fiftieth anniversary celebration of the college. By then old Agony Hall had been condemned as a fire hazard, so new quarters for the music department were mandatory. Since a fund of some $50,000 had been accumulated by the choir and other musical groups, it was decided to go ahead with the erection of a building for their use. Completed in 1926 at a cost of $120,000, the new music hall was dedicated in connection with Founders' Day festivities in that year. One feature of the program was a concert by the Minneapolis Symphony Orchestra, an event which began a tradition of annual appearances at St. Olaf. [21]

Except for the construction of the new athletic field, first used in 1930, building operations virtually ceased until the country began to pull out of the depression. By the mid-1930s, however, a new women's dormitory had become imperative; of the 425 women enrolled in the college, about 300 had to live in private homes in town. Built by the St. Olaf Corporation, which had been authorized to borrow money from the college's endowment fund, Agnes Mellby Hall with quarters for 170 coeds was occupied in the fall of 1938. Its name honored the first woman to receive a St. Olaf B.A. degree in 1893. Fittingly the building's name was suggested by the college's distinguished dean of women, Miss Gertrude M. Hilleboe, herself destined to receive a similar and much-deserved honor. [22]

Final major project of the Boe era was a desperately needed and long-sought new library to replace the one built in 1902, a year when students numbered 225 and books 4,100. By 1940 comparable figures were 1,200 and 48,000. Under constant urging from the alumni who had made the library their special project, Boe repeatedly brought the question to the attention of the trustees, but for one reason and another contracts were not let until 1941. Opening of the new structure, later christened Rölvaag

Memorial Library, came in March of the following year.[23]

Despite the shortage of space, enrollment increased steadily from just under 800 at the beginning of the 1920s to 1,046 in 1930. Well over 90 per cent of these students were Lutheran; a somewhat smaller proportion were of Norwegian ancestry. Practically all were from Minnesota and adjacent states, and most were representative of the substantial middle class which populated the region. The faculty likewise was a homogeneous body, chosen because of its loyalty to the ideals for which the college stood. Only Lutherans could aspire to permanent professorships. Out of a teaching staff of seventy members in the middle 1920s, thirteen possessed a Ph.D., and twenty-seven had an earned M.A. Approximately half were graduates of St. Olaf.[24]

Boe made it clear that "the Christian character of the student" was still the principal by-product of the educational program. The pluralism and fragmentation characteristic of many campuses today was certainly missing, yet there was a definite effort to modify the offerings and practices of the institution in order to align them with those recommended by the accrediting agencies. All courses leading to a master's degree were discontinued in 1922; thereafter concern would be concentrated on improving the undergraduate program. A presentation of *The Merchant of Venice* in 1921 marked the beginning of all-college dramatic performances, not for the training of professionals, but as an aid to the appreciation of worth-while cultural activities. Eight years later a decision to set up an art department was made. In 1932 the first unit of an art studio was ready for use by students of Professor Arnold Flaten, recently returned from study in Europe. A major in physical education and athletics was established in 1930. All told, by the time World War II broke out, twenty-three departments offered majors.[25]

To pay for these developments, St. Olaf like other church colleges had three regular sources of revenue: student fees, endowment income, and annual grants from the church. Typically the first paid for less than half the cost of instruction, a necessary fact of life if tuition were to be kept within the reach of most potential applicants for admission. By 1925 the endowment was slightly over $300,000, considerably below the minimum standard set by the North Central Association for institutions of St. Olaf's size. Thus loss of accreditation became an alarming possibility. Luckily, in spite of some complications a joint endowment fund campaign undertaken with another of the church's colleges — Luther of Decorah, Iowa — in 1926 proved a great success, not only financially, but in stimulating interest in the cause of Christian education as well. In this effort as in others both students and faculty gave generously of what were frequently meager resources.[26]

By 1930 the endowment fund had reached nearly $800,000. That same year the church's contribution to St. Olaf was $60,000. All in all the college's net value of $875,000 in 1920 had risen to over $2,700,000 in 1930. Although there was a deficit of $4,358.85 in the budget of slightly over $312,000, the financial situation seemed fairly stable. President Boe's report to the church convention spoke of the year as "one of the best in the history of the college." [27]

Then came the dark days of the depression. Income on endowment fell drastically, and annual contributions from the church went down by 40 per cent. In 1933 it was necessary to tell faculty members "that no definite salary schedule could be promised"; the college would pay what it could. Enrollment the following year was down almost three hundred from the peak of 1930 with resultant loss in tuition. Institutional introspection and self-study became the order of the day. Of the eighteen educational institutions of the Norwegian Lutheran Church, five were merged or closed. Red Wing Seminary, a junior college since 1917, was merged with St. Olaf in 1932. There was even talk of combining Luther College and St. Olaf, but in the end — through sacrifice, the elimination of non-essential courses, and governmental help from the National Youth Administration program — such a merger was avoided.[28]

Enrollment by 1936 had again passed the 1,000 mark; it would go to 1,186 before the onset of World War II halted the progress of colleges everywhere. Symbolic of the spirit of good will which existed on Manitou Heights during the few years between depression and war was a student-sponsored program in November, 1937, to honor the faculty, over a dozen of whom had served St. Olaf for twenty-five years or more and eight of whom had been presidents of other colleges or academies.[29]

Throughout the 1920s and 1930s, life on campus remained rich in opportunity for student growth. Although the literary societies were not as meaningful as they had been in an earlier day, there were seventeen of them, each with some thirty-five members, in existence in the postwar years. Special interest clubs appeared periodically, and there were a number of honor societies. The annual musical programs given early in the century were revived in 1920 and held thereafter on the week end nearest Norway's Independence Day on May 17. The concert band and the St. Olaf choir made regular tours of the

Upper Midwest, and the latter won uniformly high praise on its European sortie in 1930. Indeed the terms "St. Olaf" and "musical excellence" both on campus and farther afield became practically synonymous.[30]

Interest in religion remained high, and religious organizations were active and healthy. Relationships between faculty and students were warm and often close. Boards representative of both groups dealt with matters pertaining to such areas of campus interest as music, religion, athletics, the library, and the radio station. The latter enterprise, carrying the call letters WCAL, began operations in 1922 as the only college station in Minnesota. It remains vigorous and cherished in its own building at the present time. Founders' Day, November 6, was the high light of the fall season with festivities ranging from the pep fest on Friday evening, the home-coming football game and other activities on Saturday, to a worship service and a concert on Sunday.[31]

But despite the flourishing nature of the extracurriculum, the classroom was the main focus of attention for most students. Many undergraduates developed interests which caused them to devote their lives to scholarly pursuits. In 1930 more than 80 alumni were doing graduate work in various universities, and another 141 graduates were teaching in institutions of collegiate level. By 1938, 126 holders of a bachelor's degree from St. Olaf had the right to add a Ph.D. after their names. All told nearly 50 per cent of those who graduated between 1911 (when the department of education was

organized) and the end of World War II were prepared for secondary school teaching. Many of them remained in the profession for years. During the two decades ending in 1947, more than 1,700 students did their stint of practice teaching in 458 cities located in 16 states. Religious work was second to education in attracting alumni, followed by medicine, law, journalism, and science.[32]

Soon many of these graduates as well as students and younger teachers at St. Olaf were called upon to lay down peacetime pursuits and take up arms against totalitarian aggressors in Europe and the Far East. It had been President Boe's responsibility at the start of his long and productive term of office to guide the affairs of the college through the final days of World War I. Now during the waning months of his administration, he would find campus life again upset by military conflict in the world. Though his own strength was being undermined by illness, he left no doubt where he stood. At commencement in 1941, disturbed by the apathetic tone of the latest issue of the *Manitou Messenger* regarding the menace posed by Germany and Japan, he withheld the paper from distribution. To him "democracy, liberty, and freedom" were worth fighting for. Unfortunately he had to take a medical leave of absence in April, 1942; the following December on his sixty-seventh birthday, he died. Without question he was a strong, Christian educational administrator, a man clearly attuned to his time, and eminently fitted to preside over St. Olaf's growth in the years between two world wars.[33]

18 MACALESTER COLLEGE

The Golden Key

AT MACALESTER the dawn of the new century brought promises of better times ahead. Ten college classes had been graduated, alumni numbered nearly a hundred, and the debt which stood at $180,000 in June, 1898, had finally been liquidated two years later after much effort by President Wallace and others. In the fall of 1902 Wallace suggested to the Presbyterian Synod that the time was ripe for raising an endowment, that the college had lived from hand to mouth long enough. George D. Dayton, a generous and valuable member of the board since 1894, offered to give $100,000 if an additional $400,000 was raised, or $250,000 if three times that amount was secured from other sources. The synod gave lip service, but much to the annoyance and discouragement of the president and the faculty, little else was forthcoming. Finally in June, 1904, forty trustees and friends of Macalester disclosed a plan at a dinner for Wallace to raise an endowment of $500,000; Dayton also repeated his offer. Although announced with considerable fanfare, the drive bogged down; by February, 1907, pledges had reached only $175,000, and Wallace longed to shed the responsibility he and his family had carried so long.[1]

In addition to an endowment, other urgent needs were a science building and a women's dormitory. Synod response was disappointing, and had not Mrs. Thaw and her son in the spring of 1905 returned to the college the twenty-five acres of land they had purchased earlier, the president would have found little cause for any elevation of his waning spirits. A trip East at that time to try to secure funds for the needed science building from Andrew Carnegie failed in its purpose, but the visit brought Wallace an offer of a position at a seminary in New York. One can guess his mood in the fall of 1905 by the depressing fact that, although Dayton's generous challenge for Macalester had stimulated relatively few gifts, the St. Paul YMCA had raised $250,000 in the space of a month.[2]

By commencement time in 1906, word had arrived that the Carnegie Foundation would after all make a contingent grant for a science hall, but Wallace had had enough; he asked for a year's leave of absence to teach at the seminary in New York. "It was high time," wrote Edwin Kagin, "that Dr. and Mrs. Wallace had a change of clime, both weatherwise and spirit-wise. . . . There had been 'too much cold house and irregular salary' for both of them." The board accepted Wallace's resignation as president on January 16, 1907, but arranged for him to return after his leave as head of the Greek department. The search for another president began.[3]

It ended with the selection of Dr. Thomas M. Hodgman, son of a Presbyterian minister, a graduate of Rochester University in New York, and for twenty-two years a member of the faculty of the University of Nebraska. At the latter institution his roles had been many: teacher of Latin, science, and mathematics, founder and editor of the *University Journal*, principal of the preparatory school, director of the summer school, and inspector of state high schools. Declaring his support for "the traditional classical courses and the characteristic principles of the Christian college," he took up his Macalester duties in February, 1907. His inauguration, the first formal one in the institution's history, occurred at the following commencement. In an address firmly supporting the Calvinist ethos, his eloquence reached its peak as he beseeched the trustees to complete soon the half-million-dollar endowment. In "a country of wondrous scenic beauty . . . at the heart of a lusty dominant Presbyterianism, in a soil rich with the blood of the martyr heroes," Hodgman declaimed, "Macalester stands waiting for the golden key that shall unlock the door to a larger life and usefulness."[4]

The key proved elusive, but for a decade the college's new president — the first one to devote full time to administrative duties — pursued it with considerable success. At first two matters were particularly upsetting to him. The sad state of the endowment was one, and his relationship with his popular predecessor, Wallace, the other. Through the intercession of his wife, Wallace secured a second year of leave to continue his pleasant life at the eastern seminary. While there, he was surprised to have a friend offer $10,000 for the creation of a Bible department at Macalester, contingent upon two stipulations: Wallace would head the unit and an additional $15,000 would be raised.[5]

To Hodgman it appeared that his money-raising chores would not only be increased, but that he would also be laboring under the shadow of a past president. Somewhat understandably therefore, he vented his spleen in an intemperate letter to Wallace. Trustees were incensed, and several of them urged the former president, no matter how Hodgman felt, to resume work at Macalester. The situation was unpleasant and the decision was not easy, but in the end Wallace acquiesced to the urgings of his old associates. In September, 1909, he returned to Macalester, where with the help of three other professors, he headed both the Bible department (endowed by Frederick Weyerhaeuser with $50,000) and the Bible-training department. By staying in the background and concentrating on his work, he gradually won "the respect and confidence of the president." [6]

If Hodgman had his problems, he also had his satisfactions. Not long before his arrival work had begun on a dormitory for women. With accommodations for approximately ninety students, Wallace Hall was dedicated and opened early in December, 1907. Its cost furnished came to $85,000. The year before it went into use, enrollment of women was 94, of whom 48 were in the college department; two years afterward the total was 164. In the fall of 1910 the four-story Carnegie Science Hall was dedicated; its total cost without furniture and equipment was only slightly over the $50,000 given by the steel tycoon. Proud Macalester supporters claimed the structure offered facilities second only to those of the state university. After the lean days the college had known, the addition of two major buildings in the space of three years was cause for rejoicing.[7]

Also encouraging was mounting success in fund raising, stimulated by a $50,000 gift from James J. Hill and an offer of $75,000 in 1908 from the General Education Board contingent upon the raising of an additional $375,000. By July 1, 1911, the trustees were able to certify that the task had been accomplished, that at last Macalester had an endowment fund. Of the $467,000 which had been raised, $159,000 had gone for new buildings, and $308,000 had been invested in income-producing securities. Even so, if Macalester were not to slip backward in the private college race, Hodgman and the trustees could not rest on their oars. With promises of $50,000 more from Hill and an additional $50,000 from the Rockefeller board, another campaign to add $250,000 to the endowment was launched. When the deadline of July 1, 1913, arrived, however, success had not been achieved. Principal subscribers to the drive agreed to extend the terminal date by one year, but Hodgman was far from optimistic. "I confronted the summer campaign [for students] with much trepidation," he wrote the trustees on September 29, 1913. Pointing to a number of factors — Carleton's successful $600,000 campaign, its new gymnasium, Hamline's gymnasium, and the work of "six drummers in the field," plus the "non-completion" of the Macalester endowment drive — the president concluded that he was operating at a tremendous disadvantage in the competition for new students.[8]

That the college succeeded in securing a freshman class of 145 Hodgman regarded as a "special mark of favor" from a beneficent Providence. But during the remainder of his administration, the president would be frustrated by his inability to build a gymnasium and another dormitory. Even the old Elms, where men lived between 1907 and 1913, deteriorated to such an extent that it was sold for $400 and then wrecked.

Another problem concerned the academy, still known as the Baldwin School. As late as the spring of 1907 its enrollment stood at 125 and that of Macalester's college department at 75. After that, however, a rather sudden reversal took place. By the fall of 1912 the freshman class in the college numbered 118; newcomers in the academy totaled only 17. All told college attendance was 230, that in the preparatory unit was 95. Moreover for several years the Baldwin School had operated at an annual deficit of from $3,000 to $5,000, a loss Hodgman found hard to justify in view of Macalester's financial shakiness. So in October, 1911, he appointed a faculty committee to make recommendations regarding the academy's future.[9]

In reaching a decision the group had two opposing examples to examine. Some institutions similar to Macalester — Carleton, Hamline, Lawrence, Ripon, Beloit — had already jettisoned their preparatory schools. Others — Gustavus Adolphus, St. Olaf, St. Thomas, Carroll, Coe — so far had not done so. As the committee saw it, the crucial factor in deciding the fate of an academy was not external environment, but a college's state of development. They felt that only when its college department alone demanded all of its time and energy should an institution dispense with its academy. Macalester, in the opinion of the faculty members consulted, had not yet reached that stage.[10]

Hodgman for various reasons — not the least of which was the reluctance of the North Central Association "to accredit colleges maintaining preparatory departments" — found himself in complete disagreement with the committee's conclusion. He therefore recommended to the trustees on March 1, 1913, that no beginning academy class be enrolled in September. Such an action would wind up that operation three years later, when the current first-year group would graduate. Wisely the board put the presidential recommendation into effect. Macalester had taken an important step toward full collegiate status.[11]

Other progressive steps involved increasing the size of the faculty and broadening the curriculum. Of the eighteen members of the teaching staff in 1910, more than half antedated the Hodgman regime. This older core group consisted of distinct individuals who knew what they were about; most of them still had many years of service at Macalester ahead of them. When Glenn Clark began his career as an English teacher in 1912, cows still performed the function of lawnmowers, and a barbed wire fence surrounded the campus. Besides coaching track, sponsoring the Quill Club, and serving as adviser to the *Gateway* magazine, Clark started the *Mac Weekly* in 1914. He also left delightful glimpses of the senior professors.[12]

"Looming like a flashing Elijah, invoking fire from heaven upon all the evils of society, was our dear old Dr. James Wallace," wrote Clark. Richard Uriah Jones, chemist and future dean, "spoke like Jeremiah, the pessimist" in chapel, but "laughed with his whole soul over a good joke" in the laboratory. Julia M. Johnson, dean of women and professor of English literature, who retained the advanced courses for herself and left the more pedestrian chore of teaching composition to Clark, was affectionately known as "Mother Jay." With deft phrases, Clark immortalized and made human these stalwarts and their associates of an earlier day.

Although the faculty by 1919 was larger than it had been a decade earlier, it was not until the 1920s that younger teachers of outstanding caliber came along to invest their lives in Macalester. As the teaching staff mirrored the past and forecast the future, so too did the curriculum. Its traditional orientation was reflected both in content and in the voca-

tions of alumni. In 1910 all students were required to take courses in Bible, and nearly half of the 231 graduates were either ministers or missionaries. Forty others were public schoolteachers. Foreshadowing the future, work in the sciences was expanding, and electives were becoming more numerous. The catalog made special suggestions for students intending to go into law, medicine, and teaching, as well as for those whose goal was the Christian ministry. The school of music was also an important segment of the institution, enrolling 92 of the total of 366 students in 1914–15.[13]

For individuals disturbed by these secular trends, a college bulletin of 1918 carried the comforting statement: "Macalester has not become less pronounced in its Christian influence." But by then the college had also been shaken by the struggle going on in Europe. With the rupture in diplomatic relations between the United States and Germany in February, 1917, the campus split into two factions. One group of eighty-seven students publicly commended those Minnesota members of Congress "who were resisting the pressures to force the country into war." This action so incensed a congressman from Duluth that he denounced the undergraduates "as cowards and un-American." Thereupon all of the faculty but three signed a telegram to President Woodrow Wilson urging active participation in the conflict. Hodgman, who had not been shown the message, joined in the debate by telling reporters that "any man, or group of men, who, on insufficient knowledge of the intimate facts, urges war at this stage are a hindrance rather than a help to President Wilson." [14]

Most dissension ended when the United States entered World War I on April 6, 1917. Like other colleges, Macalester made its contribution to the war effort and suffered its share of dislocations. In the fall of 1918, for example, fifty-eight upperclasswomen enrolled and only twelve junior and senior men. On October 1 a group of 120 recruits began to prepare in the SATC for subsequent transfer to officers' training camps, but with the signing of the Armistice on November 11, 1918, the unit was short-lived. The following March a Reserve Officers Training Corps (ROTC) was organized at the college, but its life was also brief. Word reached Macalester late in September, 1919, that its ROTC would be discontinued. "Physical training and athletics," announced the *Mac Weekly* of October 8, 1919, "will probably take its place." [15]

Responsibility for charting Macalester's course during these uncertain times no longer rested with Hodgman. At the end of the academic year in 1917, he had resigned to become manager of a teachers' agency. In January, 1918, the Reverend Elmer A. Bess, who for the preceding six years had been a successful student pastor at the University of Iowa, took over the presidency. Because of the war his official inauguration was postponed until October, 1919. Sharing similar favorable views concerning the cause of the Allies in the conflict, he and Wallace became close friends. Bess was not destined to have a long administration, but he would make an impact in the areas of curriculum and finance.[16]

In the fall of 1918 he introduced a new department of vocation with himself and his wife as its staff. Two courses treated a variety of subjects relating to the wise selection of a career. One of them called "Vocational Fundamentals" was required of all freshmen. Another innovation was a major in social service initiated in the fall of 1919. Dealing with such subjects as child welfare, immigration, Americanization, and social work, the new sequence, like vocation, reflected concerns with problems and developments in society generally. Both Macalester and the freshmen in Vocational Fundamentals, it would seem, were striving to find themselves in the postwar world.[17]

To aid them in the search, a third endowment campaign was undertaken in 1918 in an effort to raise $750,000. The General Education Board offered $150,000 contingent upon the raising of the total goal. By the fall of 1919 about $85,000 had been subscribed, but state-wide efforts the following year secured pledges of nearly $600,000, three-fourths of which came from the Twin Cities. The General Education Board then raised its contribution to $200,000. The Carnegie Foundation gave $75,000 and the Presbyterian Board of Education allocated $25,000. More than $915,000 was subscribed (and most of it was paid in) raising the endowment to about $1,500,000.[18]

Thus strengthened Macalester entered the "Roaring Twenties" in a sanguine mood. Some 400 college students (fairly evenly divided by sex and overwhelmingly Minnesotans) were enrolled in 1921–22. Another 220 or so, most of them from St. Paul, took work in the conservatory of music. The faculty numbered twenty-eight, two of whom divided their time between the college and the conservatory. Twelve other individuals composed the instructional staff in music. By the end of the decade, regular faculty totaled forty, that of the music affiliate nineteen, some of whom also taught in the collegiate department. Margaret M. Doty, a 1914 graduate and long-time dean of women, was hired by President Bess in 1920. Two years later he lured Otto T. Walter from the University of Iowa to build up

Macalester's work in biology. He would remain for forty years.[19]

According to the *Mac Weekly* of November 17, 1920, undergraduates complained that "if there is anything the student body of Macalester lacks badly, it is some form of student council representative of the four classes." Such a body could handle a number of momentous matters — "the all-important question of cheer leader," plans for "Big Home Coming Days," or a " 'Special Train' to Carleton." Tuition was $60 a semester and board about $6.00 a week. Women paid another $3.00 weekly for rent in Wallace Hall, but men were charged only $1.75 in their old frame dormitory.[20]

Early in 1923 President Bess resigned. Not all the events leading up to his departure are known, but it seems clear that some of his speeches had been offensive to certain Twin Cities labor leaders, who therefore set out to discredit him. The episode was not only a misfortune for Bess, but temporarily for Macalester as well. To the students, according to the *Mac Weekly*, he had been "a father and counsellor; all were free to ask his advice. . . . Through his influence many have been led to higher planes of ambition." Until a replacement could be found, the Reverend Henry C. Swearingen, a trustee and prominent St. Paul minister, served as president pro tempore.[21]

Meanwhile a gymnasium, Macalester's first new building in a decade, was becoming a reality. Erected at a cost of $150,000, the structure, it was hoped, would be the first step in an ambitious million-dollar expansion program calling for the addition of more than a dozen buildings to the physical plant. Though it was to be many years before the dream would be realized, several significant facilities were secured by the time the stock market crash on October 29, 1929, made survival rather than progress the first order of business everywhere.[22]

On May 5, 1924, President-elect John C. Acheson gave the principal address at the ceremony laying the cornerstone of the gymnasium. The new executive, an eloquent speaker with a fund of stories for every occasion, had graduated from Centre College in Kentucky in 1898. Behind him lay successful terms as president of the Pennsylvania College for Women in Pittsburgh and the Kentucky College for Women in Danville. He seemed just the man to lead a "Forward Movement" at Macalester, where he began his administration in July, 1925. Soon he was engrossed in the "great Million Dollar Endowment Fund drive," which began officially on January 21, 1926. This task was so consuming that his inaugural ceremony, an elaborate affair designed to assist the promotional campaign, was postponed until the fall of 1926. The results of his efforts quickly became apparent.[23]

When classes resumed in September, 1927, students found a number of improvements: the library of 18,000 volumes enjoyed enlarged quarters in the "commodious rooms that formerly served as a gymnasium and engine room," a new quarter-mile cinder track enhanced Shaw Field, and two new buildings were virtually completed. Kirk Hall, named in honor of a former trustee and generous contributor and financed largely by his family, was a badly needed residence with a dining hall and living space for 142 men. The other addition, an attractive home of colonial design for the president, was the product of George D. Dayton's generosity.[24]

Pledges to the endowment fund had reached $816,500 early in 1927, and hopes for attaining the million-dollar goal seemed realistic. Regular college enrollment since the fall of 1923 had remained over five hundred, while that of the conservatory, counting everyone who took a tuba lesson, pushed well above three hundred by 1927. Under a point system adopted in the fall of 1927 students were required to participate in extracurricular activities, but a limit was placed on the degree of participation. The student body in the spring of 1926 finally adopted a constitution for the governing association, which, in the opinion of a vocal minority, was a vital necessity. Once achieved, however, student government fell short of expectations. The era of its effective operation apparently lay well beyond the horizon.[25]

Curricular changes were moderate and consisted mainly in updating terminology and in clearer differentiation of disciplines. A reference to physical education made its first appearance in the catalog of 1924, when the new gymnasium made a graduation requirement in the subject feasible. Vocation did not long survive President Bess's departure, and by 1926 mental science had been replaced by psychology. Sociology, which had been grouped with political science and economics, received separate departmental status in 1929; so did psychology which had been paired with philosophy. Political science and economics remained in tandem until 1940. A subdepartment of business was established in 1929, but in general the college offerings stressed the liberal arts, and graduates were awarded B.A. degrees.[26]

With the onset of economic depression, the advances of the preceding several years came to a halt. By 1930–31 conditions were so serious that a committee of eight faculty members was assigned to find some solution. In the end, it was decided

that everyone should keep his position and accept a one-third salary cut straight across the board. Some teachers had to resort to borrowing on their life insurance, but happily except for one delay of three weeks checks were received on time. In 1932–33 after a raise in tuition of $25 a year, there was a noticeable drop in enrollment to 465. Of the 184 freshmen, only 11 came from outside Minnesota. The following year room and board charges were lowered, and tuition was returned to its previous level of $175 a year. These actions helped account for a significant increase in the size of the freshman class to 312 in the fall of 1933.[27]

Leading the fight for survival was President Acheson, who drove himself continuously to find money to increase meager faculty salaries. Giving him invaluable aid were the trustees, especially Charles H. and Fred R. Bigelow and DeWitt Wallace, who began at this time his record of magnificent giving to Macalester. The gifts of these men plus gradually improving economic conditions made possible a restoration of salary scales, but the threat of secularism continued to disturb James Wallace — still a very sharp octogenarian. Others shared his concern. So long as Acheson was at the helm, these men felt secure, but the president's strong leadership was soon to be lost. Acheson, who was diabetic, had undoubtedly undermined his health in his constant efforts to keep the college alive. After a trip in 1937 on which he had forgotten to carry his insulin, he returned home completely exhausted. On the morning of November 24, Mrs. Acheson found him in a coma from which he never rallied. It would be nearly two years before a new president assumed direction of Macalester's development. Meanwhile Dean Clarence E. Ficken served as acting head of the institution.[28]

Ninth president of the college was Dr. Charles J. Turck, a native of New Orleans, who was a graduate of Tulane University and of the law school of Columbia University. He had taught at Tulane and Vanderbilt universities before becoming law school dean in 1924 and president in 1927 of Centre College in Kentucky. For the three years before his arrival at Macalester on September 1, 1939, he had been associated with the Board of Christian Education of the Presbyterian Church in the United States. Turck's administration of nearly two decades would be the longest in the college's history thus far. He came to an institution which had undergone hardship but had witnessed little change in over a decade. Value of campus and buildings early in 1931 was slightly over $1,200,000; nine years later the figure was only $38,000 higher. Endowment figures for the same two years were $1,574,000 and $1,990,000, respectively. Enrollment at the time of Acheson's death totaled 627; it was slightly over 700 when Turck took over. There were a few foreign students and a growing number of out-of-staters, but most undergraduates hailed from the Twin Cities and Minnesota's smaller towns.[29]

Paralleling the growth of the student body had been that of the faculty, which in the fall of 1939 was composed of sixty-six members. Evolution of the curriculum had been gradual and undramatic; requirements for graduation remained much the same as they had been nine years earlier. The most notable modifications had been increased emphasis on foreign languages, history, and the social sciences, the creation of a new history of art department in the fall of 1933, and the establishment of a speech department a year later. A total of 126 credit hours had long been required for graduation, and it would continue to be for some time to come.[30]

During his first two years in office, Turck gave a foretaste of the policies that would characterize his administration. Noticeable almost immediately was an increased emphasis on such matters as public relations, admissions, alumni participation, guidance, placement, and vocational training. In the catalog of 1940 a new section printed in eye-catching type and entitled "Specific Objectives," included such concepts as "self-realization," "art of thinking," and "philosophy of life." After a lapse of thirteen years, a page once more was given over to information concerning the alumni association, groups of which were found in several of the nation's large cities. Totally, including the class of 1939, 2,152 individuals — 978 men and 1,174 women — had earned a Macalester baccalaureate since 1889.[31]

In the hope of swelling this total as well as strengthening the college, curricular innovations began to be introduced. A department of fine arts put in a brief appearance in 1939. Two years later the catalog carried a new section entitled "The Citizenship Sequence," which was "strongly urged upon" all undergraduates although it was not compulsory. Increasing attention was directed toward preparation for vocations in addition to the traditional ones of law, medicine, teaching, and the ministry. A course in social work dated back to 1928, and one in medical technology in co-operation with Charles T. Miller Hospital to 1937. Now other courses with specific contemporary relevance appeared in short order: business administration, secretarial studies, prenursing, pre-engineering, and prehome economics. Liberal arts purists were critical of these developments, but their proponents argued that financial considerations, the needs of society, and the liberal manner in which the subjects were taught amply justified their inclusion in the schedule.[32]

When Turck took office, he found a physical plant which had not been graced by a new building in over a decade. He also found a million-dollar endowment campaign, begun early in 1936, not yet fully subscribed. The recently established Byram Foundation of New York (backed by DeWitt Wallace) had given $100,000 for the enrichment of the college's educational program in 1939, and had promised a like amount toward the endowment drive if the goal set was attained by June of that year. Actually it was 1941 before the million dollars was raised. Plant improvement, however, was undertaken right away, when part of the basement of Old Main was transformed into a student community center. More significant was the construction of a badly needed library. Although World War II intervened, the building with space for 110,000 volumes was nearing completion in September, 1942. The college's book collection then numbered about 35,500 volumes, up from 28,000 in 1939.[33]

By 1942 endowment stood at $2,324,000 and value of the campus and buildings at $1,450,000. Both figures would remain fixed until after World War II. As early as autumn of 1940, Macalester had instituted a flight training program under the supervision of the Civil Aeronautics Authority. After Pearl Harbor in 1941 many other adjustments were made to serve the war effort. A catalog statement gave curricular advice to young men facing almost certain military induction. Content and emphasis in existing courses were altered, and new short-term courses were arranged. Mathematics and the sciences, by then in the ascendancy everywhere, received added teaching personnel. Civilian enrollment held up for a time, but by 1943 Kirk Hall was in use as an army barracks, and most able-bodied males were in some branch of the armed forces. Projected plans would have to yield to a changed time schedule.[34]

19

COLLEGE OF ST. THOMAS

Decades of Transformation

FATHER JOHN DOLPHIN, St. Thomas' fifth chief executive and its second to bear the title of president since the institution acquired college status in 1894, began what proved to be a brief administration in 1899. Born in Massachusetts and educated in the East, he had mainly been engaged in pastoral duties since arriving in Minnesota in 1886. Although the enrollment of 162 in 1899 was the largest in St. Thomas' history and the faculty had been increased by 50 per cent, there were the usual college problems, many of which the thirty-eight-year-old president had not faced previously. Most serious perhaps were those of a financial nature, $11,000 in students' past due accounts, for example. After four years as head of the college, Dolphin, who was never robust physically, asked for a leave to regain his health. Thereafter he returned to parish work.[1]

Dolphin's short term, however, reflected progress in the direction of transforming St. Thomas from a traditional European Catholic type of school into an American college. In 1901 the classical course was divided into the academic or high school department of four years and the collegiate department of two years, really a junior college. Despite the continued existence of the commercial sequence and some work of grade school level, the identity of the institution was coming into sharper focus. The physical plant was also expanded. In 1900 a much-needed building, Science Hall, was constructed at a cost of $50,000, a large part of which was borrowed. Then late in 1902 the twenty-five-acre campus was nearly doubled by the purchase of an adjacent twenty acres for $25,000. This money was part of a sum raised by a "Jubilee Donation," a campaign conducted in connection with the celebration of the fiftieth birthday of the St. Paul diocese. About $69,000 was collected, but when debts were paid, little was left over.[2]

Succeeding to the presidency in May, 1903, was Father Humphrey Moynihan, one of the first faculty members appointed to the new St. Paul Seminary nearly a decade earlier. His tenure would last until August, 1921, the longest in St. Thomas presidential history thus far. Born in Ireland and educated there and in Rome, he had gone to St. Paul in 1892 to serve as secretary to Archbishop Ireland. With the latter's constant friendship and support, Moynihan would move St. Thomas from a small, local institution of learning, serving approximately 250 students, to one with over 1,000 men from twenty-four states and five foreign countries.[3]

Progress would not be dramatically rapid, but it would be steady and persistent. By the time the United States entered World War I, five new buildings would grace the campus. The first one, Class Building (later Academy Building), made possible by borrowing funds, was ready in the fall of 1903, just in time to ease pressures created by an enrollment of 356. The new, three-story $50,000 structure permitted the other two edifices to be used solely for administrative offices and dormitories. The second of the additions was the infirmary, possessed of "every convenience of a modern hospital" and completed in 1905 at a cost of $25,000. A number of years were to pass before another construction project could be undertaken.[4]

All the while enrollment continued to mount; in the fall of 1906 it was 480, half boarders and half day students, and five years later it was 683. Financial support had to be attracted. In February, 1909, came the announcement that the General Education Board would grant St. Thomas $75,000 for endowment if the college would raise three times that amount. Part of the total secured under the agreement could be used for buildings. Archbishop Ireland, who gave $10,000 himself, collected nearly $258,000 mostly from wealthy friends — $50,000 from Thomas Ryan, $50,000 from the United States

Steel Company, $25,000 from Andrew Carnegie, among others — while President Moynihan raised over $42,000.[5]

By the spring of 1911 with the success of the fund campaign practically assured, the trustees decided to go ahead with the construction of a badly needed dormitory. Fittingly named Ireland Hall, the 176-room building costing about $127,000 was completed in April, 1912. The basement was equipped for the college library, which had previously been quartered in a room in the administration building. Two year laters plans for an armory were approved. When completed in May, 1915, this $84,000 addition to the plant greatly expanded the possibilities for a more varied and exciting extracurricular life. The following April the archbishop announced that ''a kind providence had provided a benefactor,'' who would furnish the money to build the foundation of a chapel. Soon the rest of the funds were in sight, and the project moved rapidly forward. Toward the end of October, 1917, it was finished — a beautiful, modern adaptation of the Byzantine basilicas found in northern Italy.[6]

Beyond bricks and mortar, other developments of the Moynihan years left their imprint on the college. One of the most distinctive, and one close to the heart of Archbishop Ireland, was initiated in the fall of 1903 — compulsory military drill in uniform. Progress was swift and by September, 1905, St. Thomas was on the rolls of the United States war department as an official military school. Pending the arrival of the first regular army officer on campus, students were organized into two battalions by personnel from Fort Snelling. Enthusiasm ran high and competition between companies was keen. Soon a band and a crack drill squad made their appearance.[7]

By the time of the first government inspection on June 5, 1906, the cadets in their familiar gray uniforms had become a major feature of the institution. A year later morale rose when it was announced that St. Thomas had become a ''Class A military school, one of only eighteen out of a hundred inspected by the war department.'' In the spring of 1908 came further recognition in the form of inclusion on the war department's honor list of military academies. Henceforth St. Thomas could nominate graduates to the regular army as second lieutenants ''without further training or examination beyond that of a physical.'' By 1911 the war department proclaimed that the St. Paul school was ''the largest private military academy in the United States.'' And all the while every effort was being made to keep the regiment among the top ten honor schools, a rank it was accorded several times.[8]

With the outbreak of World War I in Europe, the excellence of this training became all the more significant. In November, 1916, the war department named St. Thomas as one of six collegiate institutions ''qualified to send graduates to the Reserve Officers Training Corps.'' It would not be long until applications for admission to the program poured in from alumni from all over the country. Scores of the documents were favorably acted upon. Early in 1918 a senior division of the corps was established at the college itself. In all, sixteen faculty members and well over one thousand alumni, of whom the impressive number of about three hundred served as commissioned officers, saw military service in World War I. Nineteen were killed, and many others were decorated for bravery.[9]

While fashioning a distinguished military tradition, St. Thomas was also moving toward becoming an accredited, four-year college. Until 1911 the institution had not been in a position to confer the baccalaureate degree. In that year, however, two faculty members seem to have been given bachelor of arts degrees in a somewhat unusual practice. By 1913 the catalog contained a schedule of courses leading to the B.A. in the arts, science, and philosophy, as well as that suggested for students planning to go on in law or medicine. And then on June 11, 1915, in the brand new auditorium came a historic commencement. In addition to awarding the usual diplomas to underclass groups, St. Thomas for the first time conferred genuine bachelor's degrees on a class of four young men.[10]

In that year the catalog took on an even more modern appearance, listing for the first time standing committees of the faculty and spelling out exact requirements for graduation: 120 semester hours, a major, a minor, and distribution subjects. Seventeen collegiate departments advertised their offerings. That St. Thomas was ready to enter the ranks of full-fledged institutions of higher learning was verified in March, 1916, when the North Central Association admitted the college to membership, the first Catholic college for men to receive such recognition from the regional accrediting body. By September enrollment was up to 830, and a department of education headed by a lay professor had been added to the collegiate division.[11]

The year 1918, marked in September by the death of St. Thomas' great good friend and benefactor, Archbishop Ireland, terminated an era in the college's history. For thirty-three years the eminent churchman had provided the institution with much of its substance and its soul, nurturing it to a position of strength sufficient to weather his passing while mourning his loss. On October 1, three hundred men were sworn into the SATC unit, but the Armistice soon put an end to that group's usefulness. In December it was demobilized. After the war the ROTC was re-established, and the annual government inspection took place in May, 1919. Interest in the military by then, however, had dropped precipitously all over the country. Reluctantly President Moynihan yielded to the pressures of the time and permitted military training in 1921 to become optional for St. Thomas' senior college men. A quarter of a century would pass before preparation for soldiering again entered the collegiate curriculum.[12]

Another change in the fall of 1918 was the permanent discontinuance of the preparatory (grade school) department, in order to make additional room available for more advanced students and those in the SATC. The action was regretted by some, but it was hardly a blow to St. Thomas' standing as a collegiate institution. The expected enrollment increase materialized that autumn, when over nine hundred students — a record number to date — registered; the total for the year including those in SATC was 1,162. College revenue for the same period was $240,158; expenses amounted to $242,000.[13]

Late in January, 1919, the name of Archbishop Ireland's successor was made public. New ordinary of the diocese was Austin Dowling, a native of New York City and for the preceding seven years bishop of Des Moines, Iowa. The following June he would hand out diplomas for the first time at a St. Thomas commencement ceremony. Receiving these symbols of achievement were more than a hundred graduates of the high school course, sixteen men whose work had been in the commercial department, an equal number who had completed the first two years of college, and only six who qualified for bachelor's degrees. When classes resumed in the fall, a new department of engineering offering a two-year program had been added to the schedule, and a large enrollment was again overtaxing facilities.[14]

Toward the end of the academic year 1919–20 about two hundred alumni gathered in a Minneapolis restaurant to listen to an address by Archbishop Dowling. Part of his remarks concerned his hopes and plans for the improvement of the college; they also included an appeal for support in a forthcoming financial campaign. At graduation exercises several days later, eight men, all headed for the priesthood, received the B.A. degree, and twenty-six others were awarded junior college diplomas. Those who had completed the commercial and high school courses numbered 20 and 105, respectively. At the time not a single lay professor with a doctorate was on the staff. Equipment in the biology department was vir-

tually nil, and college indebtedness was causing concern. Total bills payable amounted to over $128,000, of which approximately $84,000 was owed to Twin Cities merchants.[15]

There were other problems, too, particularly growing friction between faculty members and President Moynihan. Just what went on behind the scenes is not known, but in August, 1921, the *Catholic Bulletin* printed a routine announcement of the promotion of St. Thomas' long-time head to the rectorship of the St. Paul Seminary and of the appointment of Father Thomas C. Cullen as fourth president of the college. At the same time Father John Dunphy, who had been at St. Thomas since 1900, mainly as director of athletics and dean of discipline — a figure "revered by all" — was transferred to a St. Paul parish. The impact of these changes proved shattering, especially to those not familiar with the inner life of the institution. The new president, while an able preacher and a well-known public figure in the Twin Cities, had no training or experience in education. Alumni of his day speak of his kindness to and concern for students, yet he could scarcely be called an educator. Indeed he did not claim to be one, and his six-year term as president did not enhance, in educational circles at least, the reputation of the college.[16]

Meanwhile Archbishop Dowling's fund drive, named in honor of his predecessor, was going well; its goal of $5,000,000 seemed to be in sight early in 1921. The total raised was not made public, but disappointingly St. Thomas did not receive the buildings (a dormitory, a science hall, a dining hall, and a power plant) it had hoped for as a result of the campaign. The institution was allocated sizable sums, however, to pay off some of its indebtedness and for other purposes. A total of $600,000 went to the College of St. Catherine and two Catholic high schools, and over $1,000,000 was used in carrying out the archbishop's proposal to erect a new preparatory seminary, Nazareth Hall, on the shores of Lake Johanna in what is now suburban Arden Hills. When it opened in September, 1923, it meant a loss of more than a hundred students to St. Thomas, plus scholarship money which had been given to aid seminarians. Whatever virtues St. Thomas had when Father Cullen became president, a sound financial condition certainly was not one of them.[17]

Enrollment that fall of 1921 totaled 806; only 288, however, were college men. The remainder were in the high school and commercial departments. Day students outnumbered boarders 537 to 269. Two years later came a more clear-cut separation of the high school and college departments. Henceforth the former, soon to be named the St. Thomas Military

Academy, would run its own operation, though sharing the campus and some of the buildings with the college. The next fall, 1924, men in the college for the first time outnumbered those in the academy 423 to 360.[18]

Facing the loss of its seminarians and becoming increasingly independent of its secondary school division, the college once again faced an identity crisis. What direction should it take? Whom should it serve? The answers to these questions can be found in large part in the curricular developments of the Cullen era.

In September, 1921, a four-year course in journalism (the last half of which was mainly vocational) was added to the curriculum. Two years later, partly in the hope of retaining its prelaw students, a law school was started. With local lawyers and judges serving as faculty, classes were held from 4:30 to 6:30 P.M. five days a week. Attendance the first year was twenty-eight and for the second thirty-five, considerably less than expected. That autumn of 1923 two other innovations — a school of education and a night school of commerce — were adopted in the hope of strengthening the college and of following what seemed to Cullen to be its own peculiar destiny. It was clear that St. Thomas was groping, that it was far from certain what its main function should be, and that answers were being anxiously sought. Furthermore money was not available for adequate maintenance either of faculty or of physical plant.[19]

Though it was not obvious to the average observer that all was not well, that fact would soon become public knowledge. By then, however, a new president would be in office. In October, 1927, it was announced that Father Cullen would become pastor of a Minneapolis church and that Father John P. Foley would become acting president of St. Thomas. A graduate of St. Paul Seminary, the popular Father Foley had been at the college for twenty years in various capacities from teacher of Latin to director of athletics, dean, and vice-rector.[20]

Hardly was he settled in his new position before he was informed by University of Minnesota authorities that St. Thomas was likely to lose its accreditation by the state institution — acceptance of transfer credits — unless corrective measures were undertaken in the immediate future. Among the criticisms were the "tangled situation" regarding accreditation of Nazareth Hall and the evening commercial school, inadequate library and laboratory facilities, easy grading, and weaknesses in the faculty. Similar warnings had been issued previously, but they seemingly had gone unheeded or had been impossible to follow up. This time the

university acted. In May, 1928, its senate dropped St. Thomas' accreditation. When the action was reported in the newspapers, the shock was great and the publicity unfavorable. At the college's request, another investigation was conducted by the university and a promise of reconsideration was given "as soon as matters were corrected next fall." Certain departments such as biology, history, mathematics, and physics, according to the investigators, "were in the main satisfactory." [21]

To Archbishop Dowling the solution was to turn St. Thomas over to a religious body capable of operating it well and to do so quickly in order to offset the bad publicity already received. The organization he had in mind, and one he may have approached as early as April, 1928, was the Congregation of the Holy Cross of Notre Dame, Indiana. On July 7, 1928, the St. Thomas board voted to transfer control and administration of the college to the Indiana order for a period of five years. A week later the public was given the surprising news.[22]

On August 28, 1928, approximately four thousand alumni and friends welcomed the Holy Cross group at a public reception in the St. Thomas armory. Father Foley had been assigned a church in Faribault, where he would serve for thirty-six years. The new president of the college was Father Matthew A. Schumacher, a graduate of the University of Notre Dame and the holder of a Catholic University Ph.D., an able educator with both teaching and administrative experience. Four other Holy Cross priests arrived with him to serve, respectively, as vice president and treasurer, dean of studies, director of religion, and director of student life. All were well qualified, and hopes were high that the new regime would build in St. Paul an institution comparable to Notre Dame. When classes convened in September, 1928, there were 296 students in the academy and 343 in the college. The faculty was composed of about forty members, only two of whom held Ph.D. degrees. Five other men taught in the law school. A number of fundamental alterations were in the minds of the new administration; many would be effected during the coming five years.[23]

Steps to help St. Thomas establish its identity and define its organizational nature for years to come were being taken by the order. As the result of intensive faculty discussions that first fall, "wide reaching academic reforms" were instituted: an organizational chart was drawn up, academic divisions were clearly delineated, standards and expectations were raised, and the faculty for the first time was differentiated by rank. What it all meant was that St. Thomas was emerging as a modern American college. On

December 20, 1928, the state university senate once more granted full recognition to the academy and to the work of the first two years in the college.[24]

At President Schumacher's first commencement on June 2, 1929, there were six graduates from the law school, ten in commerce, and twenty-two from the college. Prospects seemed bright, and few if any individuals foresaw the stock market crash of October. But despite economic depression, collegiate enrollment during the Holy Cross period rose from 482 in the fall of 1929 to 695 three years later. At the final commencement under the order in 1933, there were sixty graduates, thirteen of them representing the largest as well as the last class in the law school's history. A total of sixty-seven law degrees were conferred during the school's life.[25]

As there were gains in numbers, so there were other improvements and modifications. These included a four-year course in physical education, a new division of fine arts, more specific science majors, stiffer requirements for admission to the senior college, and comprehensive examinations. Constant effort was made to upgrade the faculty and to modernize the physical plant which had benefited by no new construction in ten years. A fine, modern cafeteria was opened in the basement of Ireland Hall in the fall of 1929; a new administration building, hopefully the first unit of a million-dollar expansion program, was dedicated in March, 1932. Since accrediting agencies had long been critical of college and academy sharing the same facilities, the old arts building was then transferred completely to high school use.[26]

But what of St. Thomas' future after the five-year contract with the Congregation of the Holy Cross expired? With the death of Archbishop Dowling in November, 1930, it began to be clear that the college would not remain permanently in the hands of the religious order. On the one hand, many priests in the archdiocese resented outside control of their institution; on the other hand, some Holy Cross fathers were wary of taking on any more responsibilities. In November, 1929, St. Thomas' debt had approximated $247,000, and the board had authorized Schumacher to borrow a total of $350,000. The operating deficit for the year 1929–30 had been $70,000; although financial conditions had improved thereafter, the absence of a substantial endowment fund continued to be a major problem. After Dowling's death, however, nothing definite could be done until his successor was appointed.[27]

In November, 1931, John Gregory Murray, bishop of Portland, Maine, succeeded to the archdiocese. His first meeting with the St. Thomas board occurred in July, 1932. A year later, after numerous

and sometimes strained discussions and interchanges of opinion and fact, the archbishop informed the provincial of the Holy Cross Congregation that St. Thomas would remain a diocesan institution. In making this decision, Archbishop Murray was influenced greatly by the stipulations laid down in Archbishop Ireland's conveyance of the St. Thomas deed to the college board, a document unknown to Murray when he first came to St. Paul. Schumacher, who had fought hard to retain the college, was understandably bitter. He had understood that Holy Cross would not have come to St. Thomas in the first place if there had been any indication that the arrangement would not be permanent. Holy Cross had acted in good faith and done much for St. Thomas, but all things considered, Archbishop Murray's decision made sense.[28]

The Very Reverend James H. Moynihan, younger brother of the college's sixth chief executive, assumed office as the tenth president of St. Thomas in July, 1933. Born in Ireland, James had attended St. Paul Seminary for two years before completing his study for the priesthood in Rome. In 1907 he had joined the staff of St. Thomas Academy. He had also taught Greek in the college, where in 1920 he had been appointed to the English department. Modest and reserved, he was held in high respect by all who knew him; coupled with the archbishop's wise and generous support, this boded well for St. Thomas' future.[29]

When classes resumed in the fall of 1933, enrollment in the academy was 220, in the college 626. A $250,000 mortgage still hung over the institution, as did a loan of $125,000 from the Ireland Educational Fund and other liabilities of approximately $194,000. Fortunately Archbishop Murray cheerfully assumed responsibility for debts accumulated before his arrival, as well as for future deficits and necessary capital funds. In turn, the new president was expected to "give attention to the scholastic standard of the institution," and this he did. In faculty appointments, emphasis for the first time was placed on securing individuals with doctorates; all five new department heads had Ph.Ds. Consequently it was not surprising that reports of state university investigators in the spring of 1935 were generally flattering to St. Thomas and that full accreditation of the four-year college course was again conferred by the state institution. "The faculty have confidence in the college, in the president, and in the archbishop," wrote one of the investigating professors. "There is no reason why the College of St. Thomas should not, in a few years, take its place beside St. Catherine's."[30]

That fall the golden jubilee of St. Thomas was

successfully celebrated with religious observances and speeches. Encouraged by this show of interest, Archbishop Murray established a Golden Jubilee Fund to clear the college of debt. Within five years, 292 clergy, none rich, gave $158,000, and various other groups and individuals contributed substantial sums. Soon thereafter the total reached more than $555,000, but the debt was still just under $130,000.[31]

Throughout the first four decades of the present century, the college's extracurricular life reflected a full program of religious, social, forensic, athletic, and literary activity. The first student publication, the *St. Thomas Collegian*, began its five-year existence in January, 1905. In 1912 it was succeeded by the *Purple and Gray*, whose staff in 1916 produced a quasi yearbook. The first real example of this common college genus, however, was the *Kaydet 1918*, a three-hundred-page volume of pictures and miscellany dedicated to Archbishop Ireland. It was put out by Epsilon Pi Kappa, an upper class organization of more than a hundred students with a triple function — literary, social, and athletic. Father Dunphy's Temperance Society had been particularly active early in the century, but by 1914 the Commercial Club, possessed of its own athletic teams, orchestra, and glee club, was the largest of the student groups. And beyond organized activity there was ample opportunity for private interchanges with peers and prefects, with priests and professors, as one sought to "find himself" in the growing, but largely self-contained and homogeneous, campus community.[32]

Student life during the 1920s exhibited the parochial concerns and lack of sophistication characteristic of most midwestern campuses of the period. Even the 1928 presidential campaign with Catholic Alfred E. Smith as one of the major contenders received little play in the college paper. Events on campus were of paramount interest. A student council appeared in 1920–21, but its activities would be regarded as trivial by a later generation. Special interest clubs had varying periods of popularity. One of them, the Players, after a dormant period in the middle 1920s, was revived in 1926. Shortly thereafter the group was given new zest by the inclusion of girls from St. Catherine's in its production casts, starting with that of *The Fool* in February, 1929.

Also popular were "campus nights" with movies and other types of entertainment inaugurated for dormitory dwellers in 1928.[33]

After the depression struck, students became more serious. Even the student paper in keeping with the spirit of the times adopted in the fall of 1933 a new name, the *Aquin*, a title "suggestive of something more than a sweater or a pennant." The yearbook, the *Kaydet*, from 1930 on became a mirror for academy life exclusively. The next year the *Aquinas*, the first annual restricted to collegiate doings, was born, but it did not make another appearance until 1937 when its cost was included in the student fee. Early in 1931 the "Mr. Tommy" contest to elect the most representative student was begun. Clubs emphasized social concerns and academic achievement. The Social Reform Society, for example, concentrated on combating the challenges posed by the rise of fascism and communism. In May, 1936, this organization helped bring about two hundred delegates to the college for a Catholic Youth Conference. For escape, Gilbert and Sullivan operettas, combining the talents of Tommies and members of St. Catherine's choral club, were particularly popular. In April, 1938, an all-college council replaced the former student council and a recently formed interclub body in an attempt to provide students with an effective voice, to integrate their activities, and to help St. Thomas in any way possible.[34]

In this same period, with the worst days of the depression over, Ignatius A. O'Shaughnessy was elected to board membership and his gift of $300,000 to build a health center was accepted. Named for its donor, the Gothic, sandstone structure containing a gymnasium and other facilities was completed in 1939 as the Nazi grip was tightening on Europe. Two more fairly normal years were left to St. Thomas before World War II disrupted activities. By the fall of 1941 the faculty numbered fifty-eight, of whom twenty held earned doctorates. The graduation class of the previous June had consisted of seventy members, including James P. Shannon, destined to become a future president of the institution and also a bishop. With its degree holders welcome in the graduate and professional schools of major universities, St. Thomas had clearly joined the ranks of first-rate liberal arts colleges.[35]

20 CONCORDIA COLLEGE IN MOORHEAD

From Academy to Accredited College

IN MOORHEAD, after Principal Aaker's resignation in 1902, Concordia's discouraged board of directors suggested to its number one fund raiser, Rasmus Bogstad, that he operate the institution as a private venture. Shocked at the suggestion, he agreed nevertheless to serve as principal if the directors would promise him moral support. Despite the presence of Aaker's business school just across the Red River in Fargo, North Dakota, enrollment at Concordia was up in the fall of 1902, and the new executive had hopes that the day when his educational charge would be a real college was not far off. Finding it a disadvantage to live off campus, he built a nine-room house on the schoolgrounds to which he and his family moved in the summer of 1903. Remodeled, it would become the conservatory of music in 1920.[1]

Overcrowded conditions with as many as six girls occupying some rooms and several classes meeting in the basement of Main convinced Bogstad that a large new building was a necessity. Members of the Northwestern Lutheran College Association agreed with him about the need, but the price of $50,000 left them aghast. They intimated that perhaps they would go along on a structure costing half that amount, but the principal would not settle for such a short-sighted plan. He suggested that the block east of the campus could be quietly purchased as a building site for $500. When this proposal was turned down, he bought it himself. Then in the spring of 1904, after securing on his own nearly $20,000 in cash and pledges toward his building, he and his family left for a European trip. The passage of time, he felt, would make it obvious that a $50,000 structure was imperative and enhance his chances of converting his conservative associates to his way of thinking.[2]

During the following academic year, Bogstad's overture to Andrew Carnegie for aid brought a promise of $12,500 when Concordia had raised $37,500. The college association thereupon saw the light and at its meeting in June, 1905, approved the $50,000 building. The principal's salary at the same time was raised to $1,000 a year, hardly an exorbitant amount for a man now charged with directing a construction project as well as a school. Only one detail remained — a site for the building. Now Bogstad's foresight paid off again; the members of the association were delighted to take the block east of the campus off of his hands at cost plus 6 per cent. Some doubters still thought the building would be too large, but its cornerstone was laid at commencement time in 1906, and the construction was completed the following January. Containing a "commodious gymnasium," classrooms which would accommodate five hundred students, and an auditorium with seats for eight hundred people, it was an impressive addition to the modest surroundings. As a local newspaper writer exclaimed, it was "one of the *big* things in Moorhead." [3]

Several days after the cornerstone laying, the trustees changed Bogstad's title from principal to president and created the office of vice president. Some members of the board, however, were not ready for too great a leap into the future. When the president ordered 10,000 folders at a cost of $150 to advertise Concordia, these gentlemen were appalled. But Bogstad's efforts and faith were producing results. In the fall of 1907, with the offering of courses on a junior college level, Concordia took a definite step toward becoming a full-fledged collegiate institution. By January, 1908, some five hundred students were enrolled. Concordians took note of the fact that their Norwegian rival in Northfield, St. Olaf, was much smaller at that time.[4]

That fall of 1908, Miss Emma Norbryhn, the holder of a St. Olaf B.A. and a graduate of Concordia's normal course in 1903 and its classical sequence two years later, joined the faculty. She would remain at Concordia as a teacher of languages (Norwegian, German, Latin, Greek, French) for forty years. Norwegian-born herself, she could sympathize with an immigrant struggling with the tongue of his adopted land when, in one of her classes, he declared: "I cannot English yet, but I hope I teacher by time." [5]

Like many another harried administrator, Bogstad was beginning to feel the strain, and at the recommendation of his physician the board in May, 1909, granted him a year's leave with pay. The Reverend Henry O. Shurson, financial secretary, teacher of religion, and fieldman since 1906, was made acting president. At the conclusion of Bogstad's year away, during which his efforts in the East to secure funds for a library and for an endowment failed, he urged the board to appoint a dean of instruction. When his recommendation was not approved, he resigned rather than risk overburdening his strength again.[6]

Shurson, "a modest and reserved man" who was popular with the students, accepted the presidency on an interim basis. His initial year witnessed the appearance of the first student publication, the *Crescent*, as well as the maiden concert tour of the Concordia band to Lutheran churches in the vicinity of Moorhead. At the time, according to a 1910 census, Protestants constituted three-fourths of the population of the Red River Valley, of which Lutherans made up 74 per cent — 69 per cent of them Norwegian. Most of the school's supporters were more fluent in Norwegian than in English. In the winter term of 1911, for example, seventy young persons, whose avidity for learning made them object to school holidays, were taking the class in "Special English." Norwegian was still used in some of the literary and debating societies.[7]

Meanwhile Shurson kept urging the association to elect a permanent president, a man qualified to lead Concordia to a position of greater distinction than he felt capable of doing. The man chosen in 1911 was thirty-two-year-old Johan Arnt Aasgaard, a graduate of both St. Olaf College and of the church seminary in St. Paul, who had also earned a bachelor of divinity degree from Princeton Theological Seminary. Born of Norwegian immigrant parents in Albert Lea, Minnesota, the new leader of Concordia was widely known as a preacher and editor of church periodicals; later he was destined to serve for three decades as president of the Norwegian Lutheran Church of America. From the outset Aasgaard

exhibited constant concern for the morals and spiritual welfare of the students. Attendance at Sunday morning services became mandatory, and such evils as cigarette smoking and card playing were "absolutely forbidden." When Clay County voted dry in 1915 (the wets lost Moorhead by a slim seventy-one votes), both students and president celebrated.[8]

Another cause for rejoicing came in April, 1915, when the association decided to build a gymnasium. When it was completed, Concordia had adequate facilities for basketball, but the most successful event of the first year in the new facility seems to have been the concert given early in 1916 by the world-famous singer, Madame Olive Fremstad. A literary society restricted to students in the collegiate department also appeared at this time, and there was talk of some sort of student government. But if the extracurriculum exerted an attraction away from study, a counterpoise offered a bonus for regular attention to concerns of classroom and laboratory: any student who received a "grade of 93 in three-fourths of the subjects carried" was excused from semester examinations in those subjects.[9]

Concordia was starting to come of age. The fall of 1916 witnessed two related, if in some ways contradictory, occurrences: an inglorious entry into intercollegiate football and the organization of the first college senior class ten years after work of junior college level had been initiated and twenty-five years after the founding of the institution. By then also the merger of the three Norwegian Lutheran synods — United, Hauge, and Norwegian — was assured, an important move which meant that changes would take place in the schools under synod jurisdiction. At Fergus Falls, Minnesota, only fifty miles away was Park Region Luther College, which had opened in 1892 under Lutheran leadership. Utilizing rented quarters until it was able to build a structure of its own in 1901, it offered an academy course accredited by the University of Minnesota and a college department which had been added in 1909. From 1912 through 1917 Park Region had awarded college degrees to twenty-seven individuals. Peak enrollment in 1914 had been 258. With a gymnasium, athletic teams, literary societies, a school of music, and student publications, it was hardly a fly-by-night operation.[10]

To the joint education committee representing the three Norwegian Lutheran synods which were soon to merge, it seemed obvious that two institutions as similar as Concordia and Park Region could not continue to function so near each other. What was to be done? Fearful of losing Concordia, Moorhead businessmen made pledges toward a fund to clear the college of its $30,000 debt, and the Commercial Club authorized President Aasgaard to assure the joint committee that the city would support the school. After visiting both campuses, the committee in April, 1917, decided that three of the offerings at Concordia — the normal course, the parochial course, and the special English course — should be moved to Park Region, while the latter's college department should be transferred to the Moorhead institution.[11]

When classes resumed in September, the Concordia faculty was augmented by six professors from Park Region. Meanwhile in May, 1917, Concordia had graduated its first college class of six members, one young woman and five young men. The United States had also entered World War I, and collegiate enrollment had suffered as a result. Twenty-two stars were on the service flag hung in the chapel in March, 1918. An application had been made for a SATC unit, but authorization for it did not come until fall. Consequently about sixty Concordia students had transferred to institutions that did have units. Men left on campus drilled with the Moorhead Home Guard, while the women knitted and made bandages for the Red Cross. Both sexes bought Thrift Stamps and ate sugarless meals.[12]

Plans had been made to move the academy department to Park Region whenever the number of students in the collegiate division reached two hundred, but as that time was slow in coming, the last class was not graduated from the academy in Moorhead until 1927. In the fall of 1919 total enrollment was 500 — 131 in the collegiate department. College accreditation by the North Central Association was still several years away, but Concordia was moving toward it.[13]

Although its ties with the church had been close, the college was still legally a private corporation. Gradually, however, steps were taken which integrated it more fully into the official Lutheran family. The name of the original sponsoring organization, the Northwestern Lutheran College Association, was changed in 1921 to the Concordia College Corporation. At the same time, representation in the governing body was accorded to congregations in the college's area which had belonged to the Hauge and the Norwegian synods before their merger with the United Synod in 1917. Reports were made to the annual convention of the church body, and financial help was received from it; $30,000 was appropriated to Concordia in 1923, when its annual operating budget was about $75,000. The college plant that year consisted of eight buildings and seventy-five acres of land. Finally early in 1925 the corporation formally transferred Concordia —

by then worth half a million dollars — to the complete control of the Norwegian Lutheran Church of America.[14]

In that same year of 1925 President Aasgaard was elected head of the church organization and resigned his position at the college. Chosen to succeed him in Moorhead was the Reverend John N. Brown, a graduate of St. Olaf in 1906 and of Luther Seminary three years later. His career had embraced pastoral work, a war chaplaincy, the presidency of the International Young People's Luther League, and the principalship of a normal school in Canton, South Dakota. He would remain in his new post until 1951.[15]

The years between World War I and the middle 1920s were in many ways difficult. Facilities were taxed, college accreditation had not yet been achieved, and enrollment dipped two hundred or so below the previous peak. In 1919 only ten bachelor's degrees were awarded in contrast to sixty-nine lesser diplomas and certificates. Yet the days of the academy were definitely numbered, and the ascendancy of the college was clearly on the horizon. Efforts to improve both plant and academic performance were constant. In the summer of 1919 a frame structure, built a quarter of a century earlier as the first hospital in Clay County, was acquired and adapted as North Hall, a second dormitory for women. Its former operating room became the home of the domestic science department.[16]

Shortly thereafter through the generosity of that friend of Norwegian institutions, Harald Thorson, a four-year-old stuccoed residence was purchased as a home for the president. The Bogstad House then became a music conservatory, dubbed "Agony Hall" perhaps in imitation of a similar structure at St. Olaf. The Bogstad garage was transformed into a bookstore, a snack bar, and a student post office. With $25,000 left to the college by Thorson at his death in 1920, a much needed three-story addition for a library was joined to Ladies' Hall (Whipple) and put in use early in 1922. Tables in its reading room were fashioned by students in the institution's manual training classes. The serious deficiency in the book collection was offset somewhat by new purchases made with a fund of $8,000 which Aasgaard borrowed and the church later repaid.[17]

Early in 1923 a tract of sixty-five acres adjacent to the campus was bought, and part of it was converted into the college's athletic field. Meanwhile changes in the nature of the institution went steadily onward. In 1919 the minimum level of performance for degree candidates was raised by the introduction of the honor point system; 130 honor points as well as 130 semester credits were needed for graduation.

At commencement in 1923 bachelor's degrees were awarded to 41 young people, academy diplomas to only 23. When classes opened in 1925, President Brown's first autumn in office, out of a total enrollment of 404 students, 364 were in the college department.[18]

Yet many things needed to be done. The physical plant was still far from adequate, and lack of accreditation was a serious handicap. This was especially true since Midwest high schools were requiring that at least three-quarters of their faculties must be graduates of institutions approved by the North Central Association. As an important step toward gaining this seal of approval, the church convention in 1925 authorized Concordia to launch a major endowment fund campaign. Neighboring counties in Minnesota and North Dakota were declared off limits for solicitors from any other educational institution of the Norwegian Lutheran church. Two professional money raisers were hired and a slogan, "Tell the people and ask God," was adopted. There was careful advance planning and extensive organization. Sermons in which the Norwegian Lutherans of the area were likened "to the Children of Israel gone out from Egypt to take possession of the Promised Land" helped create a receptive climate of opinion. Finally, during a week in May, 1926, over 2,500 solicitors for Concordia went out to present their cases.[19]

The response was heartening; it took the form of cash, pledges, real estate, bonds, and even an automobile. By the end of May Brown announced that the goal of $500,000 had been attained although all fronts had yet to be heard from. By fall the total was up to $750,000. The president had been able to hire new faculty, including the first full-time librarian, with the result that the curriculum was strengthened and accreditation largely assured. In March, 1927, after an inspection of the institution by one of its representatives, the North Central Association voted unanimously to admit Concordia to membership. Several weeks later, when B.A.s were conferred on forty women and twenty-eight men, the final class of eleven members received its diplomas from the academy. Since the commercial department no longer existed, Concordia had achieved full-fledged college status at last.[20]

During the relatively brief period remaining before economic depression bore down on the country in the 1930s, continued progress was made. A farm was purchased near Moorhead which supplied food for the college boarding department for the next twenty years. A total of thirty-eight other farms, each with a salaried manager, were owned by Concordia over the years until they were sold in the 1940s. In the summer of 1929 the college took over a music conservatory in Fargo, which operated as a branch of Concordia until 1937. Hopes were high that a new gymnasium would soon become a reality, but such optimism was dashed by the onset of economic chaos in the 1930s.[21]

As everywhere, enrollment declined. At Concordia it hovered around 410, and graduating classes averaged less than 80 members. Faculty salaries fell to a level, which, Brown commented, "could not be justified before God or man." The nadir was reached in 1933 when the college placement service was able to find positions for only 60 per cent of the graduating class (a respectable figure for the period) at salaries as low as $40 a month. Whereas a quarter of the student body held part-time jobs as the decade began, the proportion had risen to one-half by 1936. All expenses for a year at Concordia during this time came to only about $400. But payrolls, low though they were, were met and the college survived.[22]

Throughout the period between World Wars I and II, Concordia students and staff continued to be overwhelmingly Norwegian and Lutheran. The visit of Crown Prince Olav and Crown Princess Martha of Norway at commencement time in 1939 was certainly the high light of the era. Attendance at chapel services was a daily requirement, and the Luther League, founded on campus in 1894, would exceed in longevity that of any other college organization. For years its weekly devotional program attracted over half the student body.[23]

Yet Concordia increasingly reflected the general American collegiate pattern. English had replaced Norwegian in the chapel exercises and elsewhere, and even the celebration of Norway's independence day on May 17 had become "somewhat perfunctory." The first yearbook, the *Scout* (renamed the *Cobber* from 1932 on), appeared in 1920. It was soon followed by a new student paper, the *Concordian*, which replaced an earlier monthly publication. Boards composed of faculty and undergraduates consulted on a variety of matters. The office of dean of men came into being, as did a multitude of other manifestations of academic life — the big sister movement, Cap and Gown Day, green beanies, home-coming queens, and the freshman-sophomore tug of war. Literary societies not only remained popular, but new ones were also organized periodically. A chapter of Pi Kappa Delta, a national forensic society, was accorded the college in 1934, testifying to the high level of activity in debate and public speaking. There were also departmental and special interest clubs.[24]

Music and musical groups enjoyed tremendous

popularity. Especially successful were the band and the choir. Director of the former for more than two decades after 1926 was a man who had played under F. Melius Christiansen at St. Olaf and had been a member of that college's band when it toured Norway in 1906. He was Professor Johan A. Holvik, known to students as "The Duke." He led the Concordia band, traveling by bus over sometimes all-but-bottomless muddy roads and living in tents on its memorable annual jaunts over the Upper Midwest. In 1933 the organization performed for Norway Day at Chicago's Century of Progress Exposition. In 1935, after a month of concerts in the United States, the band toured Norway. Credit for developing the *a cappella* choir belongs to Professor Herman W. Monson, who taught at Concordia from the early 1920s until 1937. Like the band, the choir traveled in buses to bring audiences an experience described by one listener as similar to that of "breathing fine, high mountain air." Succeeding Monson was Paul J. Christiansen, son and brother of successive directors of the St. Olaf choir, a man also destined to achieve distinction in the world of choral music.[25]

When the darkest days of the depression passed, thought could once again be given to the future. In the spring of 1937 the board approved construction of a dormitory for women. Financed by a bond issue of $100,000, the modified Gothic structure offering accommodations for 250 women was named Fjelstad Hall in honor of Miss Helga Fjelstad, matron of the college and friend and confidante of students for thirty-three years. Although she was present at the cornerstone laying that fall, she died before the building was completed in March, 1938. The new residence hall eased pressures considerably, but the total plant was still inadequate. Freshmen, for example, were not permitted to use the overcrowded library during evening hours. Classroom space was at a premium, and the gymnasium as well as the auditorium was obsolete. Although steps were taken even after the bombing of Pearl Harbor to correct these conditions, further construction had to await the end of World War II.[26]

As memories of economic depression receded, consideration could also be given to the matter of curriculum expansion. A few bachelor of music degrees were awarded, and major sequences leading to a B.A. degree had been offered during most of the 1930s by fifteen departments and the conservatory of music. Six of these — English and public speaking, French, Greek, German, Latin, and Norse — were in the linguistic area. Three — biology, chemistry, physics — embraced scientific fields. Two — home economics and psychology and education — had a definite vocational orientation. The others were economics, history, mathematics, and philosophy. In the middle of the decade, Greek was dropped from the list, and art was added. Then with Pearl Harbor only three months away two new sequences were established: a five-year program in nursing education leading to a Concordia baccalaureate and a diploma from Fairview Hospital in Minneapolis; and business education providing courses for students who intended to graduate as well as for those desiring only one or two years of stenographic and secretarial training. The college also publicized its preparatory work for individuals going on into the fields of law, medicine, dentistry, engineering, and the ministry. Not until several years after World War II would there be any significant modification of this schedule of studies.[27]

21 COLLEGE OF ST. CATHERINE

Educating Catholic Women in St. Paul

IN ST. PAUL on August 20, 1902, Archbishop John Ireland preached a memorable sermon. Speaking on the occasion of the fiftieth anniversary celebration of the arrival in Minnesota of the Sisters of St. Joseph, he forecast the establishment of a promising new educational institution in the state. "I offer my congratulations to the Sisters of St. Joseph," he said, "for their promise soon to endow the Northwest with a college for the higher education of young women; and I take pleasure in pointing to this college as the chief contribution of their community to religion during the half century to come." [1]

Behind the archbishop's prophetic words lay fifty years of Catholic educational activity in Minnesota. In November, 1851, four nuns of the Congregation of the Sisters of St. Joseph of Carondelet had boarded a paddle-wheel steamboat at St. Louis and journeyed up the Mississippi River to St. Paul, their avowed purpose being to minister to "savages, infidels, and heretics." In their new frontier mission station during the 1850s, these enterprising religious founded three institutions in St. Paul — St. Joseph's Academy, St. Joseph's Hospital, and a free school for girls — as well as St. Mary's School in St. Anthony. From the efforts of these devoted and courageous women, as Archbishop Ireland proudly predicted, the College of St. Catherine would find its beginnings. [2]

The leader of the Sisters of St. Joseph in the Province of St. Paul at the turn of the century was Mother Seraphine Ireland, sister of the archbishop. A positive figure in her own right, she had held the position since 1882 and been responsible in large measure for the growth of her congregation in Minnesota and the Dakotas. There had been problems and disappointments, but there had also been notable achievements; by 1900 sisters in the Province of St. Paul numbered 428, and they staffed a hospital as well as two dozen parochial schools enrolling over 5,000 students. But this record was only a challenge for Mother Seraphine, whose watchword had been "Progress, build, increase in number, spread out." She and some of her associates looked to the day when they could erect the capstone of their educational endeavors in Minnesota — a Catholic college for women. In 1900 the archbishop turned over to the sisters rights to an edition of his book, *The Church and Modern Society*, sales of which through "weary days of peddling," yielded some $60,000 toward a fund to start the college. [3]

Later in 1902 good fortune appeared in the person of Hugh Derham, the owner of a large farm in Rosemount who had served briefly as a state legislator. Upon learning from the archbishop of the dreams and hopes of the Sisters of St. Joseph for a college, Derham gave them $20,000 for a building and $5,000 for scholarships. In December, 1904, the building named Derham Hall was completed on a scenic site lying south of Randolph Avenue, not far from the Midway district in St. Paul. On the snowy day after Christmas, several sisters left their quarters in St. Joseph's Academy for their new home. Early on the morning of December 27, the archbishop and Mother Seraphine arrived by carriage for the celebration of the first Mass at the College of St. Catherine. Archbishop Ireland selected Saint Catherine of Alexandria as the patron saint of the institution. [4]

But the nascent venture was not yet a college, nor would it spring into full bloom at once. Like other Minnesota private institutions of higher learning, it had to undergo a period of preparation and development. To the foresight of the archbishop must go credit for the fact that the sisters were ready to assume collegiate responsibilities. Before 1900 relatively few members of the Catholic hierarchy in the United States had given much thought to higher education for women, and even among the Sisters of St. Joseph some maintained that possession of an academic degree would detract from the feeling of humility which should characterize members of the congregation. Yet from the early 1890s onward, with Ireland's urging and blessing, preparations were made at St. Joseph's Academy for the day when the college for women should materialize. University of Minnesota summer sessions came to be graced by women in religious garb, and soon other sisters began summer work at the young and exciting University of Chicago. Later several of them attended Chicago during the regular academic year. One of their number, Sister Antonia McHugh, earned three Chicago degrees and became well acquainted with the dean of the faculties, George E. Vincent, later president of the University of Minnesota and thereafter head of the Rockefeller Foundation. This friendship and example did much to color her thinking and ultimately to make St. Catherine's outstanding among colleges for women.[5]

St. Catherine's officially opened in January, 1905, with an enrollment of some seventy students, mostly of secondary school level, plus "a handful of young ladies of uncertain age" who were classified as specials. The academic or high school department offered two four-year courses, the classical and the English-scientific. A collegiate course was announced, but it did not get under way until the fall of 1905, when a class of seven freshmen was organized. Despite this modest beginning, school officials aimed high — "at being the foremost girls' college in America." To quiet possible parental fears, assurance was given that a prime consideration in the construction of Derham Hall had been the "comfort and safety of its inmates" and that "the drainage and plumbing is as nearly perfect as can be found anywhere." Tuition was $40 for the two-semester year, board and laundry came to $160, and private rooms were listed at $50 and up.[6]

For some time students in the college department normally completed two years at St. Catherine's and then either transferred to the state university or terminated their formal education. It was not surprising, therefore, that as late as 1911 various individuals still thought of the institution as a high school. Nevertheless, constant development had taken place, both in enrollment and in curricular offerings. The collegiate course included religion, philosophy, classical languages, history, English, German, French, mathematics, chemistry, physics, botany, physiology, geology, and geography. Art and music

were available, and great care was given "to the cultivation of the graces and amenities of social intercourse." Stated requirements for the B.A. degree in 1910 embraced 126 credits, elocution, physical culture, a major, and four minors. Finally in the fall of 1911 two students who had completed their sophomore year returned as juniors; in June, 1913, they became the first graduates of the College of St. Catherine. Mother Seraphine's prayers had been answered.[7]

The year 1914 witnessed the appearance of Whitby Hall (known for a time simply as College Hall), the first strictly college building. It was named for Saint Hilda of Whitby Abbey, a patron of learning. A large structure costing some $300,000, it was paid for entirely by the Sisters of St. Joseph. Included in its wide variety of facilities were the Jeanne d'Arc auditorium seating 600 persons, a gymnasium, space for the music and science departments, art studios, and dormitory quarters for 250 students. More significantly the year also saw, at Archbishop Ireland's insistence, the appointment by Mother Seraphine, official head of the school as well as of the congregation, of Sister Antonia McHugh as dean, St. Catherine's "first distinct college official." In the opinion of faculty and student body alike, a better choice could not have been made. Though sometimes "regarded as aggressive and domineering," a teacher who demanded that students rise above complacency and self-pity, and who constantly condemned bad manners, she was uniformly admired, occasionally feared, and often sought out as a confidante and a guide. At St. Catherine's everyone who knew her speaks of Sister Antonia in tones of reverence, respect, and pride.[8]

With characteristic momentum and thoroughness, the new dean moved toward her goal of making the college first rate in every way. Even the catalog for 1916–17 took on a more modern appearance; in it a dozen academic majors, plus music, art, and domestic science, were advertised. The faculty roster included fourteen sisters, seven priests from neighboring St. Thomas College and St. Paul Seminary who taught part time, and fourteen lay teachers. Over the years Sister Antonia would work unceasingly to raise the level of faculty competence as high as possible. Securing a Ph.D. degree before reaching the age of thirty-five became the rule. As time went on older sisters might find the new order too heady, but the younger religious would grasp the intellectual challenge and the pleasure which Sister Antonia's vigorous educational philosophy brought them.[9]

Discouraging, of course, were the difficulties involved not only in recruiting students at the college level, but also in retaining to graduation those who did enroll. Part of the explanation lay in the newness of St. Catherine's, but there were other reasons. For one thing, the sisters usually had to interrupt their own education for a number of years in order to help relieve the great need for parochial school-teachers. Then in the junior and senior years curricular offerings were limited compared to courses available at the state university. There was also another obstacle to growing enrollment which Sister Antonia, unlike some Catholic educators, felt was particularly serious — the lack of recognized standing in the academic world.

In the dean's opinion, if St. Catherine's were to continue moving forward, accreditation by the North Central Association must be earned. With help from Archbishop Ireland, she secured permission from her superiors in the congregation to seek it. A major stumbling block was the college's failure to possess the requisite endowment fund. Along with certain other educators of her faith, however, and with the assistance of one of her old professors at the University of Chicago, Sister Antonia was able to persuade members of the association that the contributed services of the religious in Catholic colleges should be considered the equivalent of such a fund. Membership in the important accrediting organization came in March, 1916 — the first time a Catholic college for women gained such recognition. The way would now be easier for others to follow.[10]

Later that year an enlarged catalog announced the outline for a four-year course in home economics and domestic art, and a two-year program in public school music, ''the strongest course . . . in the West.'' Whatever doubts may have been harbored privately, the college was putting on an increasingly confident public front.

By then time was running out for St. Catherine's great friend, John Ireland, but so long as he was able, he continued to give the institution his wholehearted support and to make his regular and eagerly anticipated visits to the campus. When he died in September, 1918, he had the satisfaction of knowing that the college was well launched, for by then he had handed diplomas signifying completion of the collegiate course to a total of nineteen young women. The value of St. Catherine's physical plant in the year of his death was approximately $750,000, and annual income came to about $84,500. Collegiate enrollment, as distinguished from that in the high school boarding department, had been only 18 in 1911; by 1914 it was up to 61, and in the fall of 1918 to 178.[11]

That same autumn St. Catherine's planted the seed of its future library school by offering nine credits of work in the field — all that school librarians needed at the time. A start was also made on the establishment of an endowment. ''With great courage and no lack of confidence,'' Sister Antonia went to New York to seek help from the General Education Board of the Rockefeller Foundation, then headed by George Vincent, her old friend of Chicago and Minnesota days. Her persuasiveness and the board's investigation resulted in a grant of $100,000, contingent upon the raising of an additional $200,000 by the college. Archbishop Ireland did not live to participate in this endeavor, but in 1920 his successor, the Most Reverend Austin Dowling, initiated a $5,000,000 educational fund campaign named in honor of the late great churchman. On June 1, 1921, the sum necessary to qualify for the Rockefeller gift was transferred from this memorial fund to St. Catherine's.[12]

The year 1921 was an important milestone for another reason. It marked the end of an era, for Mother Seraphine Ireland after thirty-nine years relinquished her position as superior of the Sisters of St. Joseph in the Province of St. Paul. While all phases of the congregation's work had received her interest, attention, and concern, the college had been ''first in her thoughts and prayers.'' Several new buildings and other examples of progress would grace the campus before death in 1930 overtook this commanding but lovable religious leader at the age of eighty-eight.[13]

At the time of Mother Seraphine's retirement, Mary Ellen Chase, another remarkable woman and well-known writer, got her first glimpse of St. Catherine's and began a lifetime bond of affection with the college and its staff of sisters. ''I have never seen happier people, or funnier for that matter, than the nuns at St. Catherine's,'' wrote Miss Chase. Sister Antonia, president of the institution in all but name, was then at the height of her powers. She reminded Miss Chase of Saint Teresa of Avila; had ''Sister Antonia lived in the sixteenth century, she could have forded any number of streams in the Pyrenees and planted any number of religious houses.'' [14]

In 1920 Sister Antonia called the initial meeting of St. Catherine's board of trustees, a body composed largely of lay people. Marion L. Burton, president of the University of Minnesota, served as chairman until the arrival of Archbishop Dowling. Melvin E. Haggerty of the university's department of education served a long and valuable tenure on the board. Periodically other state university faculty members such as Richard E. Burton, Charles Bird, and Martin B. Ruud would sojourn at the college, lending their talents and keeping it in touch with developments in public and secular education.[15]

But major reliance, of course, was placed on the sisters themselves, and Sister Antonia pressed constantly to improve their background and training. By 1920 a dozen sisters had earned the degree of master of arts, but that was not good enough. Between 1926 and 1936, often under considerable pressure, ten sisters received doctorates from five American and two foreign universities. Making this achievement possible was money from the Ireland Educational Fund and other gifts. By 1931 twenty-seven of the sisters would have traveled abroad to study, returning to open new vistas for the girls they taught. By that time forty-one M.A.s and eleven Ph.D.s were represented on the faculty of fifty-seven members.[16]

Paralleling these efforts to elevate teaching quality went those to expand the physical plant and strengthen the curriculum. A third building was much needed, and with an endowment fund soon to be realized, construction on Caecilian Hall (honoring the patron saint of music) was begun. Dedicated to retiring Mother Seraphine, it was formally opened in October, 1921. Possessed of "exceptional facilities," the new addition was intended solely for music, but enrollment had risen so much that the two upper stories had to be utilized for dormitory rooms.[17]

Next in the realization of a "greater St. Catherine's" was the construction in 1923 of new tennis, volleyball, and basketball courts — the nucleus of a future athletic field. These improvements had been made possible by gifts from the student association. That same year the long-desired "air of privacy and selective culture" was achieved by the completion of an iron fence and two massive but attractive gates, left "hospitably open." [18]

Meanwhile, as Mary Ellen Chase wrote, Sister Antonia had been "planning and praying into being a chapel." Dedicated on October 7, 1924, Our Lady of Victory Chapel — French Romanesque in style, with stone and brick exterior, a main doorway copied from that of St. Trophime's at Arles, and a steeple tower stretching 116 feet heavenward — provided seating for some 750 worshipers and was fittingly designed as the most impressive structure on campus. The library, offering study space for 180 girls, was transferred from its former overflowing quarters on the first floor of Derham Hall to the ground floor of the new chapel. The collection of 20,000 books and 85 different periodicals would soon receive important accessions through two grants from the

Carnegie Corporation, one of $25,000 in 1925, another of $15,000 in 1930.[19]

In 1926 Sister Antonia made a cogent appeal to the General Education Board for help in housing the growing science departments. The result was a grant of $100,000 and a fifth major building, Mendel Hall, which was ready for use in January, 1928. Named in honor of the Austrian geneticist, Gregor J. Mendel, the five-story newcomer contained classrooms, art studios, laboratories, darkrooms, a ballroom, and offices for the teachers of science, mathematics, art, and psychology.[20]

At this time Derham Hall was home to high school students, some of the sisters, the bookstore, and the infirmary. Whitby contained living quarters for about 150 girls, classrooms, the post office, tearooms, the auditorium, and the gymnasium. The country's growing demand for physical education instruction and the increasing emphasis on personal fitness, however, were already exerting insistent pressures for additional facilities in the form of a health and physical education building. Ground was broken for this structure on May 4, 1931, and it was completed the following December. The $185,000 health center was soon named Fontbonne Hall in memory of the French mother superior who sent the first Sisters of St. Joseph to America in 1836. With its "spacious gymnasium," solarium, health clinic, swimming pool, and bowling alleys, it became a mecca for recreation seekers on campus. With the erection of a service building in 1937, major construction would cease for a time, but the beautification of the campus was a process dear to Sister Antonia and seldom abated.[21]

Until the fall of 1920 the college calendar followed the semester system; then, probably to conform to state university practice, the three-quarter calendar was adopted. In the same year the college community was organized along junior and senior college lines; the last two years were given over largely to major and minor sequences and electives. Less than a dozen majors were available. Five of them were in ancient and modern languages; the others were in English and rhetoric, economics and sociology, history, mathematics, biology, and chemistry. Some 70 per cent of the alumnae had gone into teaching, and the department of psychology and education, while not offering a major, did a brisk business. Religion and philosophy were mandatory for all Catholic students, which meant the great majority of those attending; in these areas the course in ethics taken by juniors seemed to be the best liked.[22]

Major emphasis rested on the humanities; from 40 to 50 per cent of all courses offered before World

War II were in that area. Where possible the curriculum reflected responses to a changing society, especially to conditions of special interest to women. In the early 1920s, for example, evidence of the college's desire to perform needed social service could be found in courses in Americanization, immigrant adjustments, racial backgrounds, and Girl Scout leadership. In 1926 the work in library science was expanded into a major sequence leading to a B.S. degree. By 1932 the department of library service had become the library school fully accredited by the American Library Association. In 1926 a major sequence in home economics was made available for the first time. The following year a department of secretarial studies, which offered a secondary sequence, was established. Then in 1929 a major in physical education appeared. Between 1928 and 1930 a training course for preschool and kindergarten work was taught by a laywoman who held a master's degree in that field.[23]

Meanwhile, as the sciences were gaining in strength in new Mendel Hall, girls were taking an increasing interest in becoming dietitians, laboratory technicians, and nurses. With these considerations in mind, Mother Antonia (her college title was officially changed to president in 1929) again approached the General Education Board and was rewarded that year with an endowment grant of $300,000 to aid in the development of a health program, particularly the training in basic sciences for nurses. Since the Sisters of St. Joseph operated two local hospitals, St. Mary's in Minneapolis and St. Joseph's in St. Paul, the board's action made sense. The school of nursing became a reality in 1930–31. Its curriculum consisted of two years' work at St. Catherine's, followed by twenty-seven months at one of the hospitals, and a final year on campus. Enrollment at first was small, and uncertainty surrounded the nature and direction the program should take, but a good start had been made.[24]

After the health center became available in January, 1932, the new offerings in physical education, nursing, and library science were greatly facilitated. In the class of 1937, for example, library science with eighteen majors was second only in popularity to English, long the strongest department. Despite the deepening depression of the 1930s, other changes were instituted. A major and a minor in speech and dramatic arts were scheduled for the first time in 1930–31. Once more a special certificate was awarded to girls who completed a two-year prescribed sequence of courses in kindergarten work. In 1931 twelve girls received such diplomas; in 1939 the number was seventeen. With poverty rampant in the land, demand mounted for trained workers

in social service, and the college reacted accordingly. Starting in the fall of 1931, a school of social service came into being with three students enrolled in its senior college courses. The beginning was small, but Mother Antonia's hopes were high. In June, 1933, four women with majors in social service (then joined with sociology) were graduated — the first in the college's history. Within the next four years emphasis would shift to preparation for specialized training after graduation, but interest in the general area of social service would remain strong.[25]

In 1934–35, again in response to a growing interest, the English department offered for the first time a two-quarter course in journalism. Conducted as an experiment and with no intention of developing a school of journalism, the venture resulted in March, 1935, in the appearance of the *Catherine Wheel*, the college newspaper begun as a project of the class.[26]

The rising demand for vocational courses caused Dean Ste Hélène Guthrie considerable concern. She felt that "an increasing watchfulness in respect to scholastic aims and standards" would be necessary "if the traditions of scholarliness and the even tenor of academic ways are to be maintained." A strong liberal and cultural emphasis was maintained even in the more vocationally oriented sequences, and the wisdom of this philosophy soon became apparent. As early as the mid-1920s, Mother Antonia had set her heart on obtaining a chapter of Phi Beta Kappa. An application in the early 1930s had been rejected in part at least because of weaknesses in St. Catherine's philosophy offerings. Disappointment led to renewed effort. In the fall of 1935 a comprehensive report was sent to the society's committee on qualifications, and early in 1937 Professor Martin Ruud visited the college on behalf of the United Chapters. This time success was to be achieved. In September, 1937, St. Catherine's became the only Catholic women's college in the United States and the third institution in Minnesota to be awarded a local affiliate of the old and honored academic fraternity. On May 17, 1938, formal installation occurred with the initiation of nine members, one of them Mother Antonia. St. Catherine's had earned an enviable place of distinction in the academic world.[27]

By then illness was plaguing the sixty-four-year-old president, forcing her to retire in 1937. As a result of her foresight, however, the matter of succession posed no great problem. A number of sisters were qualified to step into the breach. The first of these to be appointed was Sister Eucharista Galvin, a native of Waverly who had entered the novitiate in 1915. She had received her baccalaureate from St. Catherine's nine years later, and her M.A. and Ph.D. degrees from the University of Chicago in 1925 and 1929, respectively. Excellently trained and well suited by personality for the responsibilities of leadership, she served the normal six-year term as president. In 1945 she was chosen superior of the Province of St. Paul, and in 1954 and 1960 as superior general of the whole Congregation of the Sisters of St. Joseph of Carondelet. With the warm-hearted support and co-operation of her associates, she readily adjusted to her new role and kept the college moving forward.[28]

Despite the fine reputation St. Catherine's enjoyed, there were still problems. Finances, for example, were disordered. A modern budgetary system was lacking, and for special needs reliance had been placed on short-term borrowing. Early in 1938 therefore the trustees authorized a long-term loan from an insurance company. Actual endowment totaled only about $580,000, but the value of the sisters' contributed services was carried on the books as equal to about $2,200,000 in investments. There was a sound basis for this practice so long as the number of religious remained adequate, but money was still a constant concern.[29]

The teaching staff of fifty-seven members — fifteen of whom had earned doctorates — was composed of thirty-two sisters, five priests, and twenty lay persons. Many were able and committed individuals, but faculty growth had not kept pace with enrollment. Matters of tenure and rank also needed upgrading. True to the tradition established by Mother Antonia, however, opportunities for improvement were eagerly sought. When an invitation to take part in a study to test the efficiency of teaching freshmen and sophomores was received from the American Council on Education, St. Catherine's joined twenty-one other institutions in the enterprise. Supported by a grant from the General Education Board, the study was to run from 1938 to 1941, but it proved so valuable and stimulating that the board provided additional funds for another three years. As a result of its participation in this joint venture, the entire college community reflected a new intellectual vibrancy. In the fall of 1939 St. Catherine's also entered another project of the American Council, a valuable three-year study in teacher education involving thirty-four other colleges and public school systems.[30]

While administrators and teachers wrestled with matters of substance and procedure, students as always responded in myriad ways to the opportunities afforded them. One of the college's weaknesses admitted in the 1935 report to Phi Beta Kappa was the failure of many undergraduates to develop scholarly interests. Yet in the same era one senior won first prize in a national poetry contest conducted by *Forum* magazine, and another young woman took top honors in a similar competition sponsored by the *Atlantic Monthly*. Two members of the 1936 class were awarded scholarships by the Institute of International Education for a year of study in France. Although honors and awards were not absent, there were always students who failed to "catch fire," and they were the ones about whom the sisters felt regret.[31]

In the 1920s and 1930s St. Catherine's continued to be a primarily local institution. Of the forty-one lay members of the class of 1924, thirty-three called Minnesota home; six others came from the Dakotas and Missouri, one from Canada, and one from France. By the fall of 1939 although eighteen states, Canada, and the Philippines were represented among the 642 girls enrolled, Minnesota contributed 459 of whom 235 were from St. Paul. Most of the rest came from the Dakotas (58), Wisconsin (39), Montana (31), and Iowa (28). Students of Irish and German Catholic background predominated, but Protestants numbered thirty-one in the fall of 1931 and thirty-nine eight years later.[32]

The college remained small and intimate during the 1920s, not exceeding three hundred students until 1928–29. Up to this time junior college enrollment was larger than that in the two upper classes. From 1920 to June, 1930, about 1,300 freshmen matriculated, but only slightly over 400 survived to the senior year. The number of degrees awarded ranged from a low of twenty-nine in 1922–23 to a high of seventy-seven in 1925–26. In the 1930s enrollment mounted rather steadily from a base of 403 in 1930–31. Fifty-nine degrees were awarded that year; the number in 1939 was 106. By then the college had conferred baccalaureates upon 1,343 young women. The largest segment of this group had entered the teaching profession, but increasingly other occupations had captured alumnae interest. A 1935 survey found graduates engaged in fourteen different fields from nursing and dietetics, library work, and social service to journalism and commercial art.[33]

As new opportunities for women developed in society generally, so to some extent did life on campus mirror trends beyond St. Catherine's iron fence and massive gates. Change was not rapid, but a growing sophistication, complexity, and opportunity for choice was evident. Throughout the 1920s dress was prescribed for lay students. By 1930 white collars and cuffs were no longer mandatory, and the term "uniform" soon disappeared completely from the catalog. Bobbed hair, however, was acceptable even when sleeves had to reach below the elbow and no portion of the anatomy below the base of the throat could be exposed.[34]

Religion quite naturally permeated many phases of the student's life. Daily Mass attracted a major portion of the dormitory dwellers, while attendance at the monthly First Friday Holy Hour was expected of all Catholic undergraduates. The same was true for Sunday services in the chapel, for which caps and gowns were required apparel. Special devotions were conducted during October, Lent, and May, and there was an annual three-day retreat in February or March, a time of silence and prayer led by a visiting priest. The Sodality of the Blessed Virgin played a prominent role among student organizations. The stirrings in Catholicism — the new church art, the Gregorian chant, prayer arising from greater consciousness of social conditions and problems, the liturgical movement spreading out from St. John's Abbey — made little impact on the college. But echoes of these developments were heard below the surface; after 1940 the reverberations would become more audible.[35]

Early in the 1920s when the student body was small, everyone knew everyone else. A family atmosphere obtained. The faculty put on entertainments for students on Saturday evenings. Cultural events in the Twin Cities were popular, and tickets were provided so that girls could attend them. Music held a special attraction; the Choral Club boasted from 75 to 100 members and the orchestra 30, at a time when enrollment was less than 250. Mother Antonia felt that her girls should be versed in parliamentary law and in correct social usage. Thus even though they dreaded the experience, the students were exposed annually to courses in these subjects taught by visiting laywomen. On Wednesdays at assembly Mother Antonia exhorted her charges on character formation and life building or presented visiting dignitaries, both local and foreign.[36]

There was a College Association, but no real student government. Athletics were popular, especially against Hamline, and so were annual field days on other campuses. Plays under the supervision of the Campus Cast (with men from St. Thomas participating in the 1930s) were other outlets and diversions much enjoyed. Mother Antonia also encouraged outdoor pageants, such as *The Hope of the World* in 1923 and *The Fire Bringers* in 1936. Publications flourished — the early literary journal *Ariston*, the yearbook *La Concha*, and the *Catherine Wheel*. There were dances for which St. Thomas provided escorts, movies, late "spreads" in the dormitory, snacks in the college store, and just plain girl talk. Together these activities helped the college play a positive role in the development of cultured, Catholic women, able to support themselves, "and to do their share of the world's work in a gracious, beneficent spirit." [37]

As the 1930s ended, armed conflict in Europe and the Orient presaged a rupture in this rather idyllic existence but no letup in St. Catherine's continuing endeavor to provide young women of drive and ability with the best possible liberal arts education.

22 COLLEGE OF SAINT TERESA

Educating Catholic Women in Winona

THE COLLEGE OF SAINT TERESA in Winona owes its origin and development to the Sisters of St. Francis. The first members of this order reached Minnesota in the mid-1870s, when Mother M. Alfred Moes, recent head of the Franciscan Sisters in Joliet, Illinois, responded to a request and journeyed to Waseca to establish a school for girls. Her initial plans failing to materialize, the intrepid religious leader changed the location to Owatonna, where she opened an academy in October, 1877. Soon she planned and completed the construction of a convent and another school in Rochester known as the Academy of Our Lady of Lourdes, which opened in a new, three-story brick building on December 3, 1877. About 210 pupils were enrolled.[1]

Mother Alfred's difficulties were far from over. A woman of vision, initiative, and ability, she was also strong-willed and aggressive. She had offended some of her associates as well as the bishop in Illinois. As a result the latter in a letter of December 23, 1877 — considered the founding date for the Sisters of the Third Order Regular of St. Francis of the Congregation of Our Lady of Lourdes, Rochester, Minnesota — cut off Mother Alfred from "all intercourse and correspondence" with the mother house in Joliet. Any of the religious who wished to unite with the group in Minnesota were free to do so; some two dozen chose that option and became the original members in the new foundation, electing Sister Alfred as their mother general. By 1889 the congregation numbered 111, and its members were staffing 24 schools in Minnesota, Ohio, and Kentucky.[2]

In the summer of that year, Mother Alfred was succeeded by Sister M. Matilda Wagner, whose apostolate had been devoted to teaching in parish schools. It was only natural, therefore, that she would take a special interest in the educational activities of her community. In a circular letter of 1893, she outlined certain plans for the future. Part of her program called for removal of the Academy of Our Lady of Lourdes, because of crowded conditions, to a new location. The site suggested was one in which Mother Alfred had earlier shown an interest, a hospital property in the city of Winona. Title to the building and land had been transferred in 1890 by Archbishop Ireland to the recently consecrated ordinary of the new diocese of Winona, Bishop Joseph B. Cotter. From him the Rochester Franciscans acquired the property in 1894 for $1,000 in cash and a mortgage of $29,000. In March of that year Sister Leo Tracy — one of the great women in Saint Teresa's history — accompanied by one sister, both short on cash but long on dreams, arrived to take charge. Other sisters destined to teach followed in July. The building, named St. Mary's Hall, was extensively remodeled during a two-year period at a cost of $45,000. In the fall of 1894 the school, then called Winona Seminary for Ladies, was opened. By the second year it enrolled forty-three students in the literary department and thirty-eight in music. It was not yet a college, but it was on the move.[3]

By 1905 the $29,000 mortgage had been paid off; the grounds had been landscaped, and a wing containing a chapel, gymnasium, and dormitory rooms had been added to St. Mary's Hall at a cost of $17,500. Total enrollment stood at 166, of whom 64 were in music and 46 in the secondary or high school department. The directress, Sister M. Celestine Noonan, whose dignified personality and lessons in deportment made indelible impressions on the students, was joined on the faculty by sixteen sisters and half a dozen lay teachers. Rules typically were strict, but they tended to be forgotten in the full schedule of studies, "elocution programs, rhetorical exercises, music recitals . . . Shakespearean dramatizations, May pole dances, May crowning." [4]

Sister Leo, who had opened the school in 1894 but then had been reassigned elsewhere, returned to succeed Sister Celestine as directress in 1906. Having studied at Trinity College in Washington, D.C., and attended four summer sessions at the University of Minnesota, she was well aware of current developments in higher education for women. She directed her efforts not only to improving the quality of work done at Winona Seminary, but also to extending its offerings to the college level. She found that several of the sisters through summer work at universities, correspondence courses, and week-end study, had made substantial progress toward earning a bachelor's degree. To further prepare these religious to teach in the contemplated college department, she then sought the services of a well-educated Catholic woman. That her quest could have had a more felicitous outcome seems unlikely in the extreme. [5]

At the time, Mary A. Molloy, the only child of Irish immigrants, was visiting her parents in Sandusky, Ohio, while pondering her future. The possessor of an Ohio State University master's degree, she had recently completed the work for her doctorate at Cornell University — the first woman to do so at that institution. Through a teachers' agency, one of Sister Leo's letters of inquiry reached this unusual young Ohioan. Since Miss Molloy had alway felt an attraction for the life of a religious and had developed a deep interest in the field of Catholic education for women, the prospect of teaching in Winona Seminary was highly pleasing to her. Her parents were reluctant to see their only child leave, but they agreed to a trial period extending from September until Christmas, 1907. As matters worked out, it would stretch far longer. Sixty years later eyes brightened and voices were vibrant with respect when Sisters of St. Francis retold the story of Mother Leo and Dr. Mary Molloy in the burgeoning early days of their college. [6]

When the new educator arrived at the seminary on September 17, 1907, four sisters were fairly well advanced toward completion of a bachelor's degree, and it was with them that she initiated college work. Holding forth in a room on the second floor of St. Mary's Hall, Miss Molloy exhibited her scope, versatility, and endurance by teaching no less than eight subjects (mathematics, the classics, French, German, Italian, social science, history, and philosophy) during sessions which stretched from 8:30 A.M.

until 9:00 P.M. with interruptions only for meals. The next year she was given the title of assistant principal, and another year of college work was added to the seminary curriculum. [7]

By then crowded conditions necessitated the building of an extension to the west wing of St. Mary's Hall at a cost of more than $27,000. Completed in 1908, it included a power plant, a laundry, and dormitory facilities known as St. Clare Corridor. During the summer of the following year, the sisters suffered a heavy loss in the death of Bishop Cotter, but his successor, the Most Reverend Patrick R. Heffron, also proved to be a strong supporter of the members of the congregation in their endeavors. Like his predecessor, the new ordinary was a product of St. John's University at Collegeville, and he had been on the faculty of St. Thomas College in St. Paul. The encouragement he gave Sister Leo and Miss Molloy is reminiscent of the inspiration and aid provided the Sisters of St. Joseph at St. Catherine's by Archbishop Ireland. Such backing was invaluable at a time when higher education for women had numerous detractors. [8]

In the fall of 1909 the seminary took a number of significant steps: a third year of college-level courses was added, the American class recitation plan was adopted in place of tutorials, and the college courses were opened for the first time to lay students. Once again increased enrollment meant overcrowding. So the former residence of Bishop Cotter across the street from St. Mary's Hall was purchased. Remodeled and renamed Assisi Hall, it reopened in the fall of 1910 as a residence for forty-seven girls, two sister-prefects, and Miss Molloy. In 1911 to accord with generally accepted practice as well as to reflect recent developments in the seminary itself, Sister Leo's title was changed to president and that of Miss Molloy to dean. On June 6, 1911, the first bachelor's degree was awarded to Sister M. Adelaide Sandusky, who thereupon was granted admission, without condition, to the graduate school at Columbia University. There she earned her master's degree during four successive summer sessions. [9]

With one college graduate successfully launched and prospects bright but facilities still inadequate, Sister Leo — urged on by Bishop Heffron and supported by the general superior Mother M. Matilda — decided with characteristic confidence and vision that a major building project was a must. Planned was "an imposing four-story-and-basement structure, with frontage on both Broadway and Wabasha Streets, featuring handsome entrances of classic detail" — the present St. Teresa and St. Cecilia halls. Sod was turned at a ceremony on October

24, 1911. At the cornerstone laying on May 30, 1912, Bishop Heffron expressed his admiration for the work of the sisters and thanked "them for this splendid manifestation which they are giving of their abiding faith in the value of the higher education of women." The fine new facility was ready for use in the fall of 1913, providing classrooms, beautiful auditorium, little theater, study hall, library, chemistry laboratory, and domestic science kitchen. More than half a century later it remains as substantial and impressive as ever.[10]

Early in 1912 changes in institutional names recognized the metamorphosis which had been taking place in the seminary. Henceforth the institution would be known as the College of Saint Teresa. Its secondary department would be called St. Clare Seminary and the music department, the Conservatory of St. Cecilia. The elementary division, located in one of the residences owned by the sisters, was named St. Agnes Grammar School. It covered the fifth grade to high school. In August, 1913, the second bachelor's degree, a B.S., was conferred on Sister M. Blandina Schmit. By June, 1914, the college was in a position to hold a public graduation exercise in its new auditorium for a class of three members garbed for the first time in caps and gowns. Two of these graduates, Florence Dady and Anastasia Norton, later entered the congregation and earned doctorates at Catholic University. Starting a tradition, all three received a "Teacher's Codex," part of which admonished: "Do not demonstrate fads in hair-dressing. What is inside your head is of vastly more concern to your Superintendent, your pupils, and their parents than what is on the outside of your head." [11]

Meanwhile, despite harassment by an anti-Catholic group known as the Guardians of Liberty, the college continued to grow and change. In the summer of 1915 Bishop Heffron, who was deeply interested in the development of higher education, took it upon himself to appoint Sister Leo as superior general of the Rochester Congregation. Her administrative ability, as well as the high standards she demanded of her staff, undoubtedly influenced the bishop to take this action. Although the congregation had financed Saint Teresa's capital developments, Sister Leo had been mainly responsible for developing the institution into a standard college of liberal arts. The soundness of the bishop's judgment was amply borne out by Mother Leo's performance in her enlarged sphere. All segments of the work of the Sisters of St. Francis, including the college, moved forward under her leadership. At the time of her appointment, enrollment in the collegiate department stood at 70, that in the St. Clare Seminary at 180. The days of the latter, however, were numbered.[12]

In the years before Sister Leo's appointment as superior general, one of the problems which had plagued the congregation had been providing adequate educational preparation for sisters who would be designated to teach in parochial schools. At first an apprentice system had been used, but it had become increasingly obsolete. So a normal school had been established at the mother house in Rochester, and the Academy of Our Lady of Lourdes (it had not been moved as originally planned) had been designated as the school where sisters would do their practice teaching. Although progress had been made, a difference of opinion developed over the proper location for the congregation's school for training sister-teachers. Sister Leo favored Winona as the site, and Bishop Heffron threw his support to her.[13]

And so it turned out that in 1914 normal courses were organized at Saint Theresa's to train teachers, lay and religious, for both elementary and secondary schools. The two-year program was open to any young woman who had completed four years of high school or their equivalent. At its first summer session that year, approximately 150 members of the congregation were in attendance, and five lay instructors supplemented the religious who formed most of the faculty. After Sister Leo became general superior, "she established the custom of sending the postulants to the College for study, and thus Saint Teresa's rapidly superseded the Normal School at the Motherhouse." [14]

As laws in Minnesota and elsewhere concerning certification of schools and of teachers became more rigorous, Mother Leo was eager to have her teaching sisters comply as quickly as possible with the changing regulations. Curriculum planning was done with an eye to mandates issued by state departments of education, and permission was obtained for the writing of Minnesota certification examinations on the Saint Teresa campus. In 1919 Minnesota law required that elementary teachers qualifying for certification must have completed high school and two years of normal work; secondary teachers must have "a degree from a university or college endorsed by a certificate from the State Department of Education." At this point Bishop Heffron announced his "Winona Plan." It provided that each teacher in diocesan schools should "earn the certification required for the work in which she was engaged." [15]

As an outgrowth of the summer sessions held at Saint Teresa's and as a means of enabling sisters to meet certification requirements in various states, the St. Clare School of Education was organized at the college in 1920. So that no one could accuse it of competing with the state normal school in Winona, attendance at St. Clare was restricted to women religious. In order to make certain that holders of its diplomas could take professional examinations in other states, the new unit was registered by Miss Molloy with that old and powerful licensing body, the New York Board of Regents. In its first summer nearly two hundred sisters were enrolled at St. Clare; in August it awarded its first diplomas entitling recipients to certification for elementary school teaching.[16]

When Sister Leo was appointed general superior in 1915, she assigned Sister Adelaide, the college's first alumna, as directress of Saint Teresa's. The following year, however, Sister Adelaide was appointed a provincial superior in Ohio, and Mother Leo resumed her duties as president of the college in addition to those as head of the congregation. By then the students, many of whom held scholarships, represented eleven states, Canada, and Mexico. Growth thereafter continued steadily. In 1917 the institution was accredited by the North Central Association, and Miss Molloy was appointed to that body's Commission on Institutions of Higher Learning, a position she held for twenty-five years. In the next year came accreditation by the Association of American Universities.[17]

Probably unique at the time as a lay administrator in a college operated by religious, Miss Molloy in 1918 represented Saint Teresa's at the fifteenth meeting of the National Catholic Educational Association. In her address to that group, she stressed the need for work of high quality in all levels of education, and "lamented that a great number of Catholic young women were satisfied with a normal course as a preparation for teaching." She was critical of the tendency of Catholic women's "colleges" of low quality to proliferate and of obsolete "finishing schools" to hang on. Her remarks met rather violent objections from some members of the association, but they were pleasing to Mother Leo. More than any others, these two women stamped their marks on the rising young college and transformed it from "a small institution for preparation of teachers to a fully accredited college of liberal arts enjoying high scholastic rating and wide recognition for its methods of education."[18]

World War I, naturally enough, had less impact on Saint Teresa's than it did on institutions for men. The sisters and students, however, did what they could to support the Allied cause, buying bonds, making dressings and hospital supplies, and canceling various extracurricular activities. Responding to Herbert Hoover's requests as food commissioner, the college added three special courses: food and the war, fundamentals of food and nutrition, and a laboratory course in food and nutrition. To keep pace with inflation, Mother Leo on her own volition gave unannounced and unexpected salary increases to the lay faculty. Despite the war graduation ceremonies in 1918 were memorable in several ways: Dr. Charles H. Mayo gave the baccalaureate address, the apostolic delegate spoke at the commencement exercises, Miss Molloy received a papal decoration, and the alumnae association was incorporated. When finally news of the Armistice reached the college after lights out on November 11, "everyone dressed and went outdoors shouting, singing, rejoicing." After a Mass of thanksgiving on November 12 classes were suspended for the day. When the second semester opened early in 1919, enrollment was up to three hundred and prospects for continued development were bright.[19]

At commencement in 1920 the college conferred baccalaureate degrees on fourteen young women, nine lay and five religious. The number was small, but the freshman class that year had more than ninety members, and total enrollment was increasing. It would pass the three hundred mark that fall, and despite the recent opening of two new houses (Avila Hall and Whitby Hall), existing facilities could not accommodate all the students. By the autumn of 1921 school officials found it necessary to limit registration in St. Clare Academy to thirty juniors and seniors; the following June that branch of Saint Teresa's went the way of many other fading private secondary schools in the state. St. Agnes Grammar School had already been discontinued. Henceforth attention would focus increasingly on higher education. Indeed Bishop Heffron became so enthusiastic that he announced early in 1922 that a school of science similar to the Sheffield School at Yale, to be known as the Roger Bacon School of Science, would be added to Saint Teresa's, which thereafter would be christened Teresan University.[20]

It was a fine dream — the establishment on the three hundredth anniversary of the canonization of Saint Teresa of the sole Catholic university for women only — but it did not materialize. The bishop's plans for a new chapel did, however, come to pass. On Saint Teresa's Day, October 15, 1923, he broke the sod not only for that building, but also for a residence for the sisters — the two to be joined by a cloister. Built in basilica style, utilizing marble from abroad, the Chapel of Saint Mary of the Angels was completed by the opening of classes in the fall of 1925. With a seating capacity of six hundred, this lovely example of Italian Romanesque architecture has moved many a Teresan to echo the sentiment of one of their number who wrote: "And most precious of memories is that of a visit to the chapel just at twilight, before the lights are lit, but while the campanile cross above sends forth its shining beams. . . . Beauty visible and invisible." The convent, Alverna Hall, also in the Italian Romanesque style, had been opened the previous June. Reflecting much of the artistic sensitivity and imagination of Mother Leo and Dr. Molloy, both structures added immeasurably to the life and beauty of the campus.[21]

Early in 1927 a sixty-seven-acre tract, formerly a golf course, was purchased for use as an athletic field and christened in honor of Saint Michael. Enrollment was pushing four hundred, and a new dormitory was rapidly becoming a necessity. In November stakes were set out to mark the base of the building, a four-story structure in the familiar Italian style with rooms for five hundred students plus a swimming pool. Located on two city blocks across the street to the southwest of Alverna Hall, Lourdes Hall was ready for occupancy in late 1928. Although rejoicing over the addition of this new, monumental dormitory, the girls were sad at leaving their houses, where something of the joy and intimacy of family life had been so pervasive. Before their final "spread" in front of the fireplace in Loretto Hall, fifteen students marched through the college buildings and across campus singing, "Loretto is best, girls / Loretto is best." When classwork resumed at Saint Teresa's in the autumn of 1929, only Assisi Hall of the old houses was occupied; it became the home of student sisters from other communities.[22]

Commenting on the college's course of study, one of Saint Teresa's historians has written: "Its curriculum, permeated by the influence of religion, met the test of time, and, with minor changes, has endured until the present [1956] very much in original form." A study of the catalogs of the 1920s and 1930s bears out this judgment for the years between World Wars I and II. At the start of the period, the schedule of courses leading to the bachelor's degree encompassed the fields of religion, philosophy, ancient and modern languages, English, history, education, economics and sociology, mathematics, physics, chemistry, botany, zoology, and astronomy. By the end of the 1930s, except for the introduction of a combined course in nursing and liberal arts (1927), work in foods and nutrition (1931), and a major in business administration (1932), the schedule remained much the same. Actu-

ally a major in foods and nutrition was not offered until 1939, when Sister Bernadette Lies with a University of Minnesota doctorate became chairman of the department.[23]

For graduation, 120 semester hours were required. One-half of these were prescribed, the remainder were "advisedly elective." The first bachelor of science in nursing was conferred in June, 1928, but the bachelor of arts continued to be most numerous. Of the total 1,043 degrees earned through 1940, 786 were in arts, 178 in science, and 79 in the combined arts and nursing curriculums. Although women had won the vote in 1920, obstacles to equality with men remained, and occupations open to Teresans were accordingly limited. Of those who had graduated by the end of the 1920s, 60 per cent were teachers, 26 per cent had entered other professional or vocational work, and 14 per cent were homemakers. In 1937, 1938, and 1939 the number of graduates was 63, 77, and 79, respectively. Of these approximately 53 per cent took up teaching, nearly 14 per cent entered hospital service as administrators, supervisors, or teachers, and about 10 per cent became dietitians. The remainder were in social work, homemaking, medical technology, and library positions. By 1940 alumnae of the three most recent years were employed in twenty-two states, Ireland, Canada, Denmark, and the District of Columbia.[24]

To modern collegians the daily routine at Saint Teresa's between the wars would undoubtedly seem sedately mid-Victorian and not a little ludicrous. Should seniors desire to take an unchaperoned morning stroll, they must do so in groups of at least five. Shoeshining parlors were off limits, as was downtown Winona on Sunday. Required convocation was held at 8:50 each school morning. Dormitory rooms were forbidden to visitors other than the occupants' mothers or sisters. The whole tone was set by such oft-repeated maxims as: "SILENCE is essential for Concentration"; "AND THE LOUD LAUGH THAT SPOKE THE VACANT MIND." Each hall and house had sister-prefects, whose disciplinary role brought grumblings, but who "saved many a broken heart and kept many a girl from being campused." Groups and activities, as on all campuses, abounded.[25]

In 1924 came the birth of the Gregorian Choir, soon to be directed by Fred J. King, a colorful Englishman who had been organist to George V. Three years later Shakespearean plays were revived after a lapse of a decade and continued annually until 1944. The presentation of *Antigone* in the language of Sophocles on St. Michael's Field testified to the large enrollment in Greek classes. Gilbert and Sullivan operettas were extremely popular starting in 1929 and continuing each year until 1944. Visitors, famous and near famous — John Philip Sousa, Percy Grainger, Eva Le Gallienne — came to lecture and perform. Certainly no one made a greater hit than Alfred E. Smith, who stopped during his presidential campaign of 1928. Traditions, such as Pledge Day when juniors wore gold gowns, May Fete, the Sophomore Ode, and Play Day, offered pleasant and meaningful breaks in routine, while maintaining the special identity, spirit, and continuity of the Teresan community. There were also occasional trips to events in the Twin Cities. It was an environment in which a young woman could develop to the limits of her ability, discover goals, and form friendships which would stand the test of time.[26]

Continuing to provide inspiration and leadership was Mother Leo, who finished her third term as general superior in 1933. For the next six years she served as local superior of the religious community at Saint Teresa's, and for five years thereafter she lived in retirement in Alverna Hall. When she died at the age of nearly ninety-one in 1951, she had spent sixty-nine years as a religious, most of them related in some way to the college. She was a stalwart figure, one of Minnesota's great women.[27]

Mother Leo's good right arm, Miss Molloy, after the death of her father in 1922, had been able to follow her inclination to become a nun. She had entered the postulancy the next year and had returned to Saint Teresa's in the summer of 1924 as Sister M. Aloysius. Four years later she became president of the college, a position well deserved and one to which she lent distinction. Not until 1946, after nearly forty years of leadership, would she retire with the title of president emerita. In retirement she worked with love and kindness among the patients at St. Mary's Hospital, where in the fall of 1954 she died suddenly of a heart attack. She had "had the fortitude to speak out and represent the needs of women's colleges in that dark era when religious women had much to say, but no encouragement to say it." She had also maintained a scholarly point of view. She still remains much alive in the hearts of the sisters who knew her.[28]

The faculty had grown from about twenty-five in 1920 to more than forty by the outbreak of World War II. By that time over a dozen held doctorates. Despite the need for parochial schoolteachers, Bishop Heffron in 1923 had suggested that at least ten sisters study annually in the St. Clare School of Education and in the college department of Saint Teresa's sisters preparing for teaching at the college level were sent on to graduate school as soon as they were ready and could be spared. There were fifteen sisters on the faculty by 1927, and Mother Leo encouraged them to travel and to attend meetings of learned societies. Supplementing the sisters were priests and lay teachers, several of whom gave long and memorable service. Dr. Rose Smith, for example, would stay forty years after joining the faculty in 1915. A few, such as the Reverend (later Monsignor) John K. Ryan who became chaplain in 1925, and Dr. (later Monsignor) John Tracy Ellis who joined the history department in 1932, left the college after a time and went on to national prominence. During the depression of the 1930s, lay faculty suffered severe salary cuts to a scale ranging from $1,000 to $1,800, but raises were given as soon as possible thereafter. By the end of the decade lay teachers numbered about a dozen and a half, representing a variety of undergraduate and graduate institutions. Most of the sisters on the faculty were alumnae of Saint Teresa's, but that fact carries no implication of mediocrity. They, too, had done extensive graduate work, often at leading secular universities. Sister Aloysius had seen to that.[29]

23 COLLEGE OF ST. BENEDICT

Educating Catholic Women in St. Joseph

THE SEEDS OF THE FUTURE College of St. Benedict were first planted in Minnesota in June, 1857, when a small party of four Benedictine sisters and two candidates from Pennsylvania arrived unannounced and unexpected in St. Paul. Finding temporary lodging in the primitive convent of the Sisters of St. Joseph, the newcomers, through arrangements made by the prior of St. John's Abbey, proceeded north to the frontier town of St. Cloud. After living there for a time in an unplastered and unfurnished garret, they were able to rent a converted "entertainment hall." In that unlikely structure, they started convent life, opened a school, and endured — in the face of such obstacles as Indian scares, a Spartan daily regime, and great physical discomfort.[1]

In the summer of 1863 a home was offered the St. Cloud band by the parish of Clinton, later St. Joseph, a few miles to the west. Five sisters and two novices accepted the invitation and took up residence in a former schoolhouse and a parsonage in the new location. Two years later the prior of St. John's erected a new convent building for them. Gradually their numbers increased, the recruits coming mainly from the rural Catholic families of central Minnesota, but the struggle was not easy. The convent buried thirty sisters, most of them under the age of thirty, during its first thirty-one years of existence. The foundation so painfully erected, however, was permanent, and from it would develop the College of St. Benedict.[2]

The forces which were to culminate in the founding of this institution were similar to those leading to the establishment of St. Catherine and Saint Teresa: the growth of the Catholic population in Minnesota, the increasing number of parochial schools, and the need to train women religious as teachers for these local educational centers. Specifically St. Benedict's traces it lineage to an academy of the same name founded in the early 1880s in St. Joseph by the young and dynamic prioress, Mother Scholastica Kerst. At the time teacher training was still in its infancy — 40 per cent of all teachers in the state had less than a common school education — but the Benedictines in the last two decades of the nineteenth century would make a substantial contribution in this important field.[3]

By 1901, when Sister Cecilia Kapsner was elected to lead the community, the Benedictines were administering various social welfare institutions, plus thirty-one schools in the four states of Minnesota, North Dakota, Wisconsin, and Washington. Enrollment in the academy at St. Joseph was showing a steady increase, and annual admissions to the order numbered thirty or more. With such a flourishing organization behind them and with the example of other sisterhoods before them, it was not surprising that certain of the religious as early as 1905 should propose the creation of a college at the mother house. It took some persuasion to convince Mother Cecilia and her council of the wisdom of such a move, but the feat was accomplished and a period of planning ensued. Sisters designated to teach in the proposed college were sent for graduate work to University of Minnesota summer sessions, and from 1912 on to Catholic University.[4]

Meanwhile, as facilities at the convent and academy at St. Joseph were becoming increasingly overcrowded, plans for plant expansion were drawn up. In the fall of 1911 contracts were let for the construction of a chapel and a college building, each to cost an estimated $50,000. Although the outlay totaled far more than that amount — $335,400 entirely financed by the sisters — the results amply justified the efforts. At an impressive ceremony in March, 1914, the beautiful Sacred Heart Chapel, in Romanesque style with a capacity for about 550 worshipers, was officially opened. By its central location, its symbolism, and its towering dome, this edifice added a significant spiritual dimension to school and convent, and gave visual evidence that here in a picturesque, pastoral setting the glorification of God took primacy. St. Teresa's Hall — the college building completed in 1913 — was a four-story brick structure containing a gymnasium, library, classrooms, assembly hall, and residence sections. These major projects reduced congestion and permitted a more orderly existence for sisters, novices, and students.[5]

Although a "Post Graduate Course," mainly of directed independent study, had been mentioned in the academy's catalog as early as 1899, the collegiate department of St. Benedict did not open until the fall of 1913. Enrolled were "sisters, candidates for the order, and a few lay students." The faculty was composed of five sisters and one Benedictine priest from St. John's Abbey. Until 1919 Mother Cecilia carried the title of president as well as prioress, but the main responsibility for the young educational enterprise was vested in the dean, Sister Dominica Borgerding, one of the members who had first proposed the establishment of a college. For more than four decades, the succeeding prioresses would also be listed as presidents, but the deans would really direct the order's collegiate subsidiary.[6]

Financially matters went well during the second decade of the century, but academic development was slow and arduous. Enrollment remained small, and the academy was a much hardier organism than the collegiate associate with whom it shared facilities and some faculty. Even the addition of junior and senior years of college work in 1915 did not attract a sizable student body. It did, however, bring accreditation by Catholic University. Of the total college enrollment of thirteen women in 1916–17, ten were freshmen. The expanded curriculum provided courses leading either to a B.A. or a B.S. degree, but it would be some time before St. Benedict received general recognition as a four-year collegiate institution. In June, 1917, however, a transfer student, who had done three years of work elsewhere, became the first graduate to earn a bachelor's degree. Her major area was mathematics. Another step toward maturity occurred the following year, when after an inspection requested by St. Benedict, the institution was accredited as a junior college by the University of Minnesota.[7]

Among the handicaps under which the sisters felt they labored were anti-Catholicism and bigotry. These were sensationally brought up at the college's first formal commencement exercises in 1918. The candidate for governor in that wartime year was Congressman Charles A. Lindbergh of Little Falls. Two years earlier while in Congress, Lindbergh had called for a congressional investigation into charges made by an organization known as the Free Press Defense League, which had stated that the Catholic church sought to bring the United States under papal domination. Lindbergh asked for an investigation "so that the issue might be determined." Portions of his speech in Congress on July 5, 1916, were interpreted to suggest an anticlerical, if not anti-Catholic, bias. Against this background, Bishop Joseph F. Busch of the diocese of St. Cloud became indignant when he arrived at St. Benedict to deliver the commencement address and saw in front of the college building a parked car with the slogan "Lindbergh for Governor." He tore it down, and when he "rose to give the Commencement address . . . he produced a great placard . . . which many recognized as one they had seen earlier . . . on an automobile parked before the Academy. With righteous indignation, the Bishop . . . begged the good Sisters of the Academy . . . to throw their whole souls into the prayer: 'Lindbergh shall not be governor.' " Reporting the incident, the college's historian noted, "There was a moment of consternation, but quiet was soon resumed and the degrees were conferred with due solemnity." [8]

This episode, however, was only one of many in Minnesota in which charges of anti-Catholic sentiment were made. As early as 1904 the state attorney general had ruled that the wearing of religious garb by teachers was illegal in the public schools. Despite this declaration, district schools staffed by sisters (or by Lutheran teachers for that matter) continued to function with no changes in the teachers' attire. The institutions did, however, reserve time for prayers and religious instruction after regular class hours. Nearly a decade later the matter emerged again, and on March 31, 1915, the attorney general ruled as his predecessor had done in 1904. A few of the district schools then converted to parochial control, but no wholesale change occurred. In that year St. Benedict opened its own normal school. Its diploma, however, like that of all private institutions, enabled its possessor to be certified only for rural or semigraded schoolteaching. Thus the school was bucking the future, and in 1924 it closed.[9]

After World War I, when religious and political bigotry were at a peak, an act was approved by the state legislature on April 21, 1919, which many Catholics considered a threat, the "opening wedge in the program of state control of all Catholic schools.'' The law required that compulsory education statutes could be satisfied only by attendance at a school in which all the usual disciplines were taught in the English language. In many district and parochial schools German or Norwegian was still the predominant language. It was also true that many sincere, public-minded educators were behind this measure as one means of raising the state standard of instruction in the schools — a need which existed in both public and private sectors and a goal with which the Benedictines had long been in full sympathy. The sisters teaching in district grade schools regularly took the examinations on the basis of which local superintendents issued certificates. Teachers on the staffs of parochial schools, where certification regulations did not obtain, did the same. Tests for secondary school certification were administered in the state capital, and groups of Benedictines journeyed to St. Paul annually to take these examinations. To prepare these women, leaders of the order in St. Joseph provided special summer sessions and assigned relevant readings. As late as 1920, despite the fact that about one-half of the Benedictine elementary schools (by far the most numerous type) had required less than eight teachers each, the sisters were instructing over 12,000 students in Minnesota and elsewhere — a significant contribution to society.[10]

For centuries social concern had been a Benedictine tradition. Intellectual development had never been regarded by the order as ''the sole nor the adequate object of education.'' While by no means discounting the importance of training the mind, the published aims of the college had stressed the significance of spiritual, moral, and physical development — of the production of ''ideal Catholic women.'' Attendance at Mass, Communion, and vespers, as well as membership in Sodality and other religious groups, had been meaningful to students, especially in the early period when a large proportion of the undergraduates were sisters or novices. A familylike atmosphere was the ideal presented to both faculty and students, and discipline, typical of the times, was strict.[11]

In the absence of urban diversions, such activities as all-school parties, plays, picnics, lectures, debates, and musicals kept life interesting. In March, 1916, academy girls and their college counterparts debated the proposition: ''Resolved, That woman should have equal suffrage with man.'' The degree of enthusiasm mustered by the negative team has not been recorded. The atmosphere was still largely that of a secondary school rather than of a college — even a joint catalog was issued — but while

the fog line between the two entities was clearly visible, there were indications that it was in the process of dissipating.[12]

By 1919 Mother Cecilia had completed her third term as prioress and president. Her administration had been marked by expansion; two dozen new parochial schools, a hospital, a chapel, and the college had been established. Now Mother Cecilia was ready to turn over the responsibility to someone else. Her successor was Sister Louisa Walz, a German-born religious who had entered the convent at St. Joseph in 1886. As ''a woman with a motherly heart and prayerful disposition,'' the new prioress was well prepared for her assignment in which she would serve ably until 1937. During her administration, however, circumstances dictated that St. Benedict would respond somewhat slowly to the winds of change blowing across the national collegiate landscape in part because of lack of resources and students.[13]

On the other hand, it was the Benedictine way to plan in terms of the long view rather than react quickly to what might be merely transitory fads and fashions. Unlike most other Minnesota colleges, St. Benedict did not exhibit any urgency about seeking accreditation from the North Central Association. Indeed this body was viewed with considerable suspicion at the mother house, although accreditation was sought and secured before Mother Louisa's administration was over. Other trappings of academic life would also be adopted in the fullness of time when it was certain that they were consistent with St. Benedict's special mission and unique heritage.

Like her predecessor, Mother Louisa is remembered for continuing the expansion of St. Benedict's physical plant. Early in her administration as additional space for classrooms became a necessity, plans for new construction and a shifting of personnel and facilities were drawn up. The result was St. Walburga's Hall, a four-story brick building completed in 1922 to serve as both workshop and dormitory. To it was then transferred the sisters' needle art department — long known for the excellence of its design and the creation of church vestments — which had been occupying rooms in the college building. ''To this department of rare and fine work,'' noted an item in the *College Bulletin*, ''the regular art students have the privilege of access.'' Soon thereafter another four-story structure, the Scholasticate, was erected to provide quarters for the nearly one hundred candidates for admission to the order, who had also lived in the college.[14]

With more room in which to operate, St. Benedict's faculty and administration turned their attention to matters of calendar and curriculum. Previously the college had operated on the familiar two-semester system. In 1922 the three-quarter calendar was adopted. At the same time a revised curriculum was introduced. From then on the work of the four years would be divided into junior and senior college courses. Students would declare a major field at the end of their sophomore year. Majors included nearly a dozen disciplines from botany and chemistry through history and home economics to music and philosophy.[15]

From time to time new departments appeared — political science, psychology, sociology — but they did not at first provide major sequences. Care was taken not to sacrifice quality for quantity. By 1924 the University of Minnesota was admitting students from the principal departments of the senior college at St. Benedict to its graduate school. Such recognition was given only after the faculty at the state university had investigated the quality of work done at a particular college.[16]

Despite these developments, St. Benedict's remained small. By 1926 its collegiate enrollment was only slightly over one hundred, making it the least populous of the four-year colleges in the state. Of its students that year, more than 83 per cent came from Minnesota and over 50 per cent from the environs of St. Cloud. For the next forty years the number of Minnesotans in the undergraduate body would hold at approximately 80 per cent. About one-third of the students were freshmen, but 40 per cent were in the senior college, providing a much better balance than had existed a decade or so earlier.[17]

Full-time faculty numbered seventeen, giving the rather amazing faculty-student ratio of one to six, a considerable contrast to the one to twenty-two or twenty-three at Augsburg and Gustavus Adolphus at the time. Library holdings, including some valuable books printed as early as the sixteenth century, approximated 15,800 bound volumes and compared favorably with the collections of some of the other private colleges in the state. Annual expenditures for books, on the other hand, were considerably less than those at a number of institutions. Methods courses were being offered for the first time, and the college had gained accreditation by the Minnesota Department of Education for the training of secondary school teachers. Organizations and societies were quite naturally oriented toward religious and artistic concerns. In 1927 such groups as Sodality, League of the Sacred Heart, Mission Crusade, Caedmon Literary Club, and musical ensembles flourished. No building program was at the moment contemplated, but the order was in a healthy state.[18]

The crash of 1929 had its repercussions at the mother house in St. Joseph, but the Benedictines had faced many crises in their long history, and they accepted this latest one with typical serenity. Enrollment dipped slightly in 1930–31, and there was no plant construction. Otherwise life at St. Benedict's went on much as usual. Indeed notable progress was achieved, due in large measure to the work and influence of one of the college's great figures, Sister Claire Lynch. A native of Minnesota, she had entered St. Benedict in January, 1915; in 1932 she was appointed dean of the college. For the next nine years this friendly, charming woman injected new vitality into the institution and brought it closer to the main stream of American higher education. As one of her associates put it: "A hundred things needed to be done at once for the college and with astounding vigor she grappled with each one."[19]

A high light of the first year of Sister Claire's administration was the securing, with Mother Louisa's support, of a temporary membership in the North Central Association. When asked how she accomplished this feat for St. Benedict, Sister Claire replied: "By telling the truth." While admitting the college's frailties, she "offered a clear blue-print for remedying the faulty situation." There was no endowment in the technical sense, but a signed affidavit from the mother general pledging the support of the entire order to the college, plus the contributed services of the sisters, made a convincing substitute. The association's examiner was favorably impressed by the caliber of the faculty and administration, of whom six held Ph.D. degrees. He was likewise pleased with the "striking general architectural environment," noting that the chapel was "magnificent" and "unrivaled."[20]

The association's report also revealed that the college had a high ratio of one teacher for every four students. Of the teaching and administrative staff, thirty-six were sisters (all but ten of them graduates of St. Benedict), six were laywomen, and two were priests. Their methods were modern, their relationships congenial, and their aims similar. About one-third of the students were members of the sisterhood. The college was conservative in conferring only two degrees, the B.A. and the B.S. in education. In the opinion of the North Central examiner, St. Benedict's weaknesses were minor; the main ones were an absence of certain administrative mechanisms within the faculty, listing in the catalog many courses not regularly taught, and some deficiencies in planning students' programs.[21]

Sister Claire moved as rapidly as possible to correct the weaknesses. Monthly faculty meetings were instituted and six faculty committees were appointed.

Teachers were stimulated to make outside appearances, to attend national meetings, and to work for higher degrees. Before long some of the sisters began publishing articles and books. New equipment was purchased and course prerequisites were clarified. Freshmen were offered a better orientation program, and their individual strengths and weaknesses were ascertained by means of a battery of widely used tests. Though the effects of these actions were not all immediately apparent, the North Central Association's examiner in 1933 noted several improvements in a single year.[22]

For one thing the catalog was much better. Then there was less overlapping of students from different years in the same classes. The definition of junior and senior colleges was clearer. The faculty was playing a bigger role in the discussion of institutional educational problems. As a result the examiner recommended that the college be fully accredited. At its 1934 meeting the association admitted St. Benedict to full membership, subject to another examination in 1935. When that examination took place the following year, the investigator was pleased with what he found. He especially noted "a high degree of educational idealism and competent administrative practice." Particularly interesting was his inclusion of "a report of the evaluation of the college faculty by the students." [23]

Accreditation by the North Central Association was not the only achievement of Sister Claire and her associates. When the dean took office in 1932, college enrollment stood at a modest 114 students. One of her early acts was to hire taxis to bring day students from St. Cloud. In 1935 she purchased the first "Benny bus" for the same purpose. As a consequence sixty-seven young women from St. Cloud were commuting to St. Benedict in 1940–41; none had done so nine years earlier. Likewise attention was turned to increasing the number of boarders. Benedictine mission schools, alumnae, and current undergraduates were asked to submit names of prospects. As a result by the fall of 1936 four or five students had to be refused admittance because of the lack of dormitory space. Three years later residents numbered 198, day students 80, and facilities were taxed to the limit. At least 70 per cent of these enrollees came from rural districts, towns, and small cities.[24]

Because of the rather provincial background of the student body, Sister Claire was eager to expose her charges to as many cultural and intellectual stimuli as possible. She therefore set up a program of convocations and imported a galaxy of well-known speakers. To both stimulate and reward academic achievement, she aided in founding the national Catholic scholastic honor society, Delta Epsilon Sigma, and she established its Omega chapter at St. Benedict. She was responsible for the creation of a teacher placement bureau on campus, which by 1940 was locating positions for 84 per cent of the institution's graduates. Of interest in this connection was an occupational survey of alumnae who had completed their work between 1933 and 1938. About 60 per cent had entered teaching; 7 per cent each had gone into social work, dietetics, and business; 8 per cent had married and 4 per cent had entered the religious community. Nearly one-third had engaged in further academic work, many during the summers, and one-fifth of these graduate students had earned advanced degrees.[25]

To build up the college Sister Claire turned for help to numerous people and groups outside the campus. In 1934 partly as the result of promptings by the Benedictines' creditors, she established a board of lay advisers composed of St. Cloud and Twin Cities business and professional men, plus the current and past presidents of the alumnae association. The purpose of the new body, which is still a vital and important part of the college's life today, was to give financial advice, provide continuity in business policy and be helpful in matters of "public relations, publicity, and the rendering of public service." Somewhat later the initiative for another building program came from this board. Sister Claire also showed interest in the alumnae association, and it reciprocated by supporting the college. As early as 1926 the organization established the Sister Rita Marshall Scholarship, which was followed by three others before World War II.[26]

Sister Claire's manifold activities were to leave a deep imprint on St. Benedict's. Her associates, with admiration and affection mixed with occasional exasperation, might call her a slave driver, but "she drove herself harder than anyone else." Christian race relations, Christian social principles, the liturgical movement — all of these received her strong support. In the face of some protests she admitted Negroes, Indians, and Orientals as boarding students. In doing so she and the college were well ahead of the times. She also gave her approval to the inauguration in 1934 of the pageant, *So Let Your Light Shine*, in which for more than thirty years freshmen would be inducted into St. Benedict's. This colorful and impressive ceremony portrayed "the contribution to culture made by the Benedictines during the fourteen centuries of their existence." At its conclusion fourteen symbolic saints passed torches to the freshmen, who then pledged their loyalty to the college and its magnificent tradition.[27]

In the final years of Sister Claire's deanship, as

war clouds in Europe again churned into bloody conflict, change intermingled with stability on the St. Benedict campus. In 1937 Mother Louisa completed her third term as prioress and was succeeded by Sister Rosamond Pratschner, who also bore the title of president of the college. She would make significant headway in gaining for St. Benedict's Convent the status of papal institute. In 1938 the first layman joined the faculty. Two years later senior comprehensive examinations were introduced, and the college returned to the two-semester calendar.[28]

But these changes did not basically alter the life pattern of the campus. Attendance at daily Mass, while not required, was good. There, as at services on special feast days, Mother Louisa's great interest in the liturgical movement continued to be manifest in the introduction of the *Missa Recitata* and the restoration of the Gregorian chant, sung by the students. Sodality was still "the main student organization." Sodality Day in May, beginning with breakfast at the college's lodge in the woods and ending with the pledge of loyalty to the heavenly Mother, was a high light of the year. Though circumscribed and sentimental by present-day standards, life at St. Benedict's in the days immediately preceding World War II had much to commend it.[29]

24 ST. MARY'S COLLEGE

Beginnings on Terrace Heights

LESS THAN SIX MONTHS after Patrick R. Heffron's installation on May 24, 1910, as the second bishop of the Winona diocese, the *Winona Courier*, the official monthly newspaper of the diocese, reported that there was "a well defined movement on foot to have a boy's college in Southern Minnesota." Accompanying the story were illustrations of several buildings, reflecting "the ideas of the promoters," who remained unnamed, as well as the assurance that the proposed school "will adopt the standard, up-to-date curriculum of our most modern institutions of this class." That the new bishop was the chief promoter there is no doubt, but many other individuals were eager to assist him in the project. Aside from its intellectual and cultural value, an institution of learning would bring business to a community as well as a certain amount of prestige. Consequently leaders in Rochester, Owatonna, Mankato, and Lake City made overtures to the head of the diocese.[1]

Evidence would suggest that Bishop Heffron's mind was perhaps already made up, for he declared that "The college is not on a bargain counter." He seems to have looked favorably upon the table-land at the foot of Gilmore Valley overlooking Winona on the west, a fact which had not escaped the attention of residents of that city. On the property, most of which was farm land, stood "a palatial residence, modern in construction and in a good state of repair"; it would become the bishop's home. Seeing their opportunity, members of the Winona Board of Trade took an option on the 105-acre site, and in a letter of January 7, 1911, agreed to raise money for its purchase if the bishop would locate his college there. Heffron, though rather restrained until the money was in hand, replied that "the site which your committee offers is entirely acceptable to me." He added that he would build his college there if the property was conveyed to him. Thereupon he set off on his first visit to Rome, where he outlined his plans to Pope Pius X, who gave him his apostolic blessing. Meanwhile the Winona group went ahead, purchased the farm for $25,000, and deeded it to the bishop, who in turn transferred it to the diocese. This action, wrote a prophetic contemporary, "marks the beginning of a work, that, with God's blessing, will be fraught with immense and lasting results."[2]

In June, 1911, an Italian architect, Chevalier A. Leonori, was a guest at the bishop's new home on Terrace Heights to consult "on the building plans for the boys' college and the new Seminary." Just where the money would come from worried many of Heffron's colleagues, but he had implicit faith in "the good will and generosity of the people of the diocese," and he was not to be deterred or disappointed. By September it was reported that work on the building, to be known later as St. Mary's Hall, was "progressing rapidly" and that it was hoped to commence classes a year hence. In January another report revealed that all of the work done so far had been paid for, but that funds were low. The desired goal was construction on a pay-as-you-go basis, and Catholics in the diocese were asked to contribute and to heed the motto: "1912 and the Boys' College!"[3]

The name of the institution, St. Mary's College of Winona, was made public in May, 1912, and the cornerstone was laid on May 30. It was not until June, 1913, however, that the building "was rapidly nearing completion." Thus the start of instruction had to be delayed a year beyond the original target date. The nature and organization of the school were outlined in a prospectus issued in June, 1913. There would be four departments: a preparatory division corresponding to the seventh and eighth grades, an academy or high school, a commercial division, and a collegiate department. Throughout the period of construction, lists of donors — parishes, priests, laity, and confirmation classes — were printed periodically in the *Winona Courier*, which also kept its readers informed regarding progress on the building.[4]

It was announced in August, 1913, that "St. Mary's is starting with a splendid faculty and with all the courses in each department thoroughly organized." Very little was said about the college curriculum, probably because it would include only two years. Delays in securing materials pushed back the opening of the school, but by mid-September the structure of Ohio mottled pressed brick with Bedford stone trim was practically completed. It was an impressive creation with a frontage of 220 feet and two wings, each 105 by 40 feet. It contained a variety of facilities from dormitory rooms to a bowling alley.[5]

Classes actually began on September 18, 1913, the day following the formal opening ceremony. Enrolled were young boys and men in all divisions from the seventh grade into the first year of college. The first president was Father William E. F. Griffin, who also taught Latin, English, and religion. On the faculty of the high school and college departments were Father Francis M. Kelly, future bishop of the diocese, and Father John H. Peschges, destined for a long career at St. Mary's and elevation to the hierarchy. Laymen directed the work in business, commerce, science, the elementary school classes, athletics, and part of mathematics. Father Patrick F. O'Brien, a master of arts, seems to have been the only teacher with an advanced degree. These devoted men at first "veritably labored in 'brick and mortar.'" [6]

By November all was "running smoothly." Among early developments were the installation of a science laboratory for the high school and college classes and completion of the task of grading the grounds. "An Attractive Winter Course" of four months was instituted to offer "a splendid opportunity for boys who for one reason or another cannot attend during the entire year." Details of the first year are sketchy. A story in the *Courier*, announcing the close of school on June 6, 1914, called the beginnings — probably with pardonable boosterism — "eminently successful." For St. Mary's "to have raised its scholastic standard of excellence to that of any similar institution, and to have entered athletic teams in interscholastic sports is unparalleled," wrote the reporter.[7]

That enrollment had exceeded one hundred also seemed remarkable. Tuition, board, room, and laundry came to only $100, but still St. Mary's was not overcrowded. So partly in the hope of attracting more students, the four-month winter course was continued for several years, and a course in agriculture on the high school level was introduced in the

fall of 1915. Although designed to be "as practical as possible," and in tune with developments which led Congress in 1917 to pass the Smith-Hughes Act, the agricultural program did not catch on. It was last listed in the catalog of 1918.[8]

The trend, while slow, was clear. The future lay with the development of a college of liberal arts. Indeed, although only junior college work was offered, the paradigm of a four-year collegiate course heavily classical in content was printed in the catalog for 1914–15 and repeated thereafter. In the 1917 edition college admissions requirements were included for the first time, specifying graduation from an accredited high school, passage of prescribed examinations, or transfer. By 1919 the preparatory department was limited to the eighth grade; the next year even that vestige had been discontinued. The academy, the junior college, and the commercial course remained.[9]

Meanwhile Bishop Heffron missed no opportunity to emphasize the significance of his collegiate brain child. "It is to St. Mary's College," he wrote in the *Courier* of August, 1917, "that the people of the diocese must look for their future priests. This college is to become the hope and may it be the glory of the Church of God in our midst." A contemporary revealed that twenty-one young men had already gone to seminary from the college and that one had been ordained a priest. Efforts to raise money went on constantly and with considerable success. Of particular interest was the establishment in 1916 of a $6,000 scholarship fund by Sister Mary Aquinas, future general superior of the Sisters of St. Francis, who two years earlier had been one of the first three collegiate graduates of neighboring Saint Teresa's.[10]

When the country entered World War I, some students and faculty volunteered for military service, but many boys at the school were too young to be called. By May, 1918, the service flag in St. Mary's Hall displayed fifty-three stars, one of them gold. That autumn undergraduates in government-supplied uniforms engaged in voluntary daily drill under the direction of one of their number who had spent the summer at the Students' Army Training Camp at Fort Sheridan, Illinois. With the signing of the Armistice, however, the military activity soon ceased, and a contemplated SATC unit failed to materialize.[11]

Once more wholehearted attention could be given to building up the college. In September, 1918, Father Peschges had been named rector, a position he would hold until July, 1933. His administration would be called "a friendly one," marked by "harmony within the faculty, which means so much to a school of higher education." For his service in the cause of Catholic education, he was appointed a domestic prelate by Pope Pius XI in 1925. Thirteen years later he was consecrated bishop of Crookston by his former faculty colleague at St. Mary's, the Most Reverend Francis M. Kelly.[12]

The institution Father Peschges was called upon to head was still small by comparison with some of the other private colleges in the state. It had never been St. Mary's policy "to comb the country for students," noted the *Courier* of September, 1919, perhaps a bit apologetically, but because of the "cordial and loyal support" of the clergy and laity, there had been "steady and healthy growth." The hundred-plus acres of the site were valued at $50,000. The buildings, power plant, and water system were listed at $600,000, and would be even more expensive to replace. About $150,000 had been paid in by parishes and applied to building costs, and priests had contributed over $16,000 for furnishings. Still there was an indebtedness of $160,000 with an annual interest charge of 5½ per cent. The college so far had been able to meet current expenses for maintenance and operation, but if it were to gain in strength and stature, greater financial resources were imperative. At least $1,000,000 was needed to put the institution on a sound footing. Proposed as the most important facilities to be financed were a gymnasium, laboratories, and a dormitory at a cost of some $340,000. Also included were an endowment of $500,000 and a fund of $160,000 for debt retirement.[13]

To meet these pressing needs, a $1,000,000 campaign was launched on April 8, 1919, at a luncheon in the college dining hall, attended by a "notable gathering" of three hundred clergy and laity representing nearly every parish in the Winona diocese. Every Catholic family was asked to help no matter how small its contribution might seem. By August one parish of 125 families had pledged over $50,000, and the *Courier* editor assured his readers that there was "no doubt at all about the success of the campaign." Although not yet a full-fledged college, St. Mary's, thanks largely to the vision and hard work of Bishop Heffron and the sacrificial example of dozens of priests, was firmly established and possessed of reason to view the future with optimism.[14]

The sanguine mood of the postwar period proved overblown, but the high hopes did have some basis in fact. Able and committed men, especially the dean of studies, the Reverend Julius W. Haun, were doing their best to make the educational enterprise a success. The modest enrollment of some 140 students in 1918–19 jumped to about 200 the following year. The fund drive was going well, and in April,

1920, work was begun on the new $300,000 dormitory and gymnasium. Connected by a corridor to the main building, the large four-story structure was ready for use in the summer of 1922. Its dedication in August — presided over by a pleased Bishop Heffron — was attended by a crowd of nearly six hundred clergy and laity, who were treated to a luncheon, a band concert, and a baseball game. Past crowding was then relieved for some time to come. In 1929 the dormitory was fittingly christened Heffron Hall in honor of the college's founder.[15]

Certain realities, however, suggested that St. Mary's was still a very slender reed whose hold on life was highly tenuous at best. At its seventh annual commencement in June, 1920, only twenty-nine men received certificates or diplomas — five each from the junior college and the commercial department and nineteen from the high school. Funds were always in short supply, and the economic recession of the early 1920s soon reduced enrollment. It was only 133 in 1921–22. Accreditation had not been secured, and among the faculty, devotion was considerably more prevalent than advanced academic experience. Discipline was increasingly relaxed, but as late as 1923 mail was subject to inspection by college authorities and correspondence by Marians with "the city, the Girls' College, or dismissed students" was forbidden. Attendance at daily Mass, evening prayers, and reception of the Holy Eucharist at least once a month were expected of all Catholics. "The moral well-being of the students" was "carefully watched," and expulsion was occasionally invoked, not as a punishment of an offender, but for the good of the undergraduate body.[16]

No thought of failure seems to have been entertained, however, and with the completion of the building project late in 1922, the curve of progress began to swing upward. This resulted partly from improved economic conditions, but mainly it seems to have been due to the aggressive campaign on behalf of St. Mary's conducted by Bishop Heffron and Father Peschges. In the summer of 1923 four field secretaries were combing eastern North Dakota, central Wisconsin, northern Minnesota, and northern Wisconsin for students. Publicity in the diocese was pervasive and continuous. The school band was sent on a concert tour with such carefully laid plans that one priest was moved to observe, "It somewhat staggers me." [17]

Although the *Alumni Bulletin* of December 20, 1923 proclaimed that the college's "dominating trend will be towards cultural results," little was said in public announcements of this goal or of the simple joy of intellectual achievement. The lures were rather "leadership, success, and a comfortable living.'' Taking note of the ''practical condition that young men of the Northwest'' could not afford to spend four years in college before professional training, much attention was called to St. Mary's one- and two-year courses in prelaw, medicine, dentistry, engineering, and business. The college's Catholic atmosphere was emphasized, but Protestants were reminded that they did not have to attend religious services or instruction. The institution emphasized its masculine character. ''Why not request a copy of our catalogue,'' asked the college secretary, Father John J. Wagner, ''and allow us to show you what a real college for real men is like?'' St. Mary's athletic prowess in this period was no accident.[18]

The alumni association, whose first officers were chosen late in 1922, seems to have been created partly at least for recruiting purposes. Until its temporary decline in the mid-1920s, the association spared no effort to attract students. Scores of ''enthusiasm letters'' went out on its stationery singing the praises of St. Mary's and stressing the low cost of $350 a year. County chairmen were appointed and many meetings were held. Get one prospect, urged Father John Wagner in 1925, and ''keep after him until you see him sign an application blank and board the train for St. Mary's.'' The enrollment figure aimed at in 1923 was 250, and, while it was not attained, Father Peschges was not discouraged. ''To be able to boast, as we can do,'' he wrote, ''of a 50 per cent increase in our College Department . . . is an achievement worthy of recognition.'' For the next few years enrollment picked up appreciably.[19]

This increase was closely related to the evolution of St. Mary's as a four-year college, the goal desired by faculty and students alike. By late 1923 Bishop Heffron was able to announce that beginning the next fall, the institution would offer a junior year of college work and the senior year would be initiated in September, 1925. Such a move involved considerable planning and effort. The preprofessional courses and those in mathematics and chemistry for the time being would remain unchanged, but advanced work would be given in English, history, and economics, as well as philosophy, the major field of men planning to enter the priesthood. Because of the growing interest in teaching, the philosophy department would also offer ''the specialized courses in pedagogy with the assistance of a specialist in education.'' Observation and practice teaching would be done in St. Mary's own high school department.[20]

Other contemplated developments involved the addition of more work in biology and the creation of a four-year course in commerce and finance. The supply of qualified priests being limited, it was necessary to employ additional lay teachers. Since salaries were low, faculty recruitment was not easy and turnover was high. Several men, however, stayed for long periods and made major contributions. Notable were John J. Hoffman who came in 1920 and John Gruber who followed six years later. Hoffman formed the chemistry department and was instrumental in developing those of biology and mathematics. After nearly forty years ''of devoted service to Catholic education,'' he was made a Knight of St. Gregory. Gruber left St. Thomas College to direct the work in history and economics at St. Mary's and remained there for twenty years.[21]

Important changes were mirrored in the catalog. In 1922 in the college section for the first time courses were arranged by subject matter rather than by requirements in a given year. Not counting religion courses taken by all students, thirty-one junior college offerings were listed. Two years later when the expanded curriculum was instituted, sixty-one college courses were described if not all taught. By 1927 the number was up to eighty-four. Particularly noticeable was expansion in areas possessing distinct vocational application — economics, accounting, education, the sciences. On June 2, 1926, a landmark was reached when degrees were awarded to the first men to complete the four-year sequence. Ten seniors comprised this historic class, nine of whom received a B.A. and one a B.S. At the same time ten high school diplomas were given out. ''The new policy'' of granting degrees, wrote an enthusiast, ''will doubtless make the institution even more popular than it has been.''[22]

Following a familiar pattern, the waxing of St. Mary's collegiate department was paralleled by the waning of the high school division. As early as September 20, 1923, the *Alumni Bulletin* carried this forecast: ''Perhaps in five years the growth of Minnesota's youngest college will warrant the abandonment of our high school department. All indications certainly point that way.'' The prophecy was not far off the mark. By 1928–29 only six high school courses, all of them for the senior year, were listed in the catalog. At the commencement in June, 1929, with the awarding of diplomas to eight young men, St. Mary's academy passed from the scene.[23]

In 1926–27 St. Mary's total capital, including value of the physical plant, was only $915,000, while that of the nearby College of Saint Teresa exceeded $3,100,000. The comparable figure for St. Olaf, St. Catherine, and Macalester was over $2,300,000 each. The Marian faculty of a dozen and a half members could boast only two or three doctorates and three master of arts degrees. Several of the older private colleges in Minnesota had forty to seventy teachers on their staffs with ten or more Ph.Ds. St. Mary's library of some 8,000 bound volumes was relatively small, and its four-year program had been accredited by the University of Minnesota as recently as 1928. The college had made gains, but it still had a long way to go.[24]

It was during this period in November, 1927, that the institution suffered a severe loss through the death of its founder and faithful friend, Bishop Heffron. Named to succeed him was the Reverend Francis M. Kelly, who had joined St. Mary's faculty in 1913. In addition to teaching, he had managed the financial campaign of 1919, served as vice-rector since 1918, and been dean of men in 1925–26. Possessed of a milder temperament than his predecessor, Bishop Kelly after the onset of economic depression would find the college one of his increasing diocesan burdens. Particularly worrisome were the problems of student and faculty recruitment and retention and difficulties related to finances.[25]

The latter were most pressing. Pledges to the college went unpaid, student accounts became delinquent, and indebtedness mounted. No leak was too small to be noted. Faculty in the fall of 1930 were asked to notify the domestic department when they would be absent from meals, "especially on Sundays." Doing so would *effect a real saving for the College*." Despite its funding problems, St. Mary's meant much to the diocese. Twenty-five per cent of its priests in 1929 were graduates of the institution, and another seventeen were studying for the priesthood, but the task of keeping the college going began to seem almost overwhelming. In this difficult time the stage was set for the next phase of development.[26]

Moving into the spotlight were the Brothers of the Christian Schools, a religious order which traces its origin to Saint Jean Baptiste de la Salle and his schools for boys in France in the late seventeenth and early eighteenth centuries. Coming to the St. Louis area in the middle of the nineteenth century, the Christian Brothers thereafter spread throughout the Mississippi Valley from their mother house at Glencoe, Missouri. Even before St. Mary's was in existence, they had taught in Winona's Cotter High School when it was founded. Until 1916, when it was destroyed by fire, they had operated Christian Brothers College in St. Louis. Then for the next decade and a half they had instituted various programs for the education of their young scholastics. Each arrangement, however, had left something to be desired.[27]

What was needed was a college of their own, and as certification standards for high school teachers were raised, the need became more acute. Thus it was in the summer of 1932 during the brothers' annual retreat at St. Mary's that Brother Assistant Abban Philip, head of the order in the United States, asked Father Peschges if wanting an institution like St. Mary's would constitute a sin of covetousness. No direct reply was given, but Brother Philip gained an impression that the answer was no. For several months the matter rested, though considerable thought and conversation went on behind the scenes. Then word was relayed to Brother Leopold Julian Dodd, provincial of the St. Louis district of the order, that Bishop Kelly would be glad to see him. In December, 1932, the two men met at Terrace Heights.[28]

After pleasantries had been exchanged and the small talk had died down, Brother Leopold came to the point. The order had no funds for the purchase of a college, he explained, but it would assume an indebtedness of $300,000 or so to take over St. Mary's. Bishop Kelly indicated that he would expect at least $400,000, the amount he owed to the banks of Winona. As the agreement was finally concluded and approved by the superior general in Belgium, the Christian Brothers would accept a $350,000 debt with interest at 5½ per cent. At the end of five years another $50,000 would be assumed if the college was making expenses. In order to decide the latter question, an arbitration body was provided for. Although some of the younger diocesan priests, unaware of the heavy debt burdening Bishop Kelly, were unhappy over the transfer, the Winona ordinary and the older priests felt differently. In April, 1933, the public announcement was made that the Christian Brothers would take over the college at the conclusion of the current academic year.[29]

The arrangement seemed simple enough. By September, 1933, fourteen brothers, including the director of the scholasticate in Chicago, had moved to the college to assume administrative and faculty posts. The first president was Brother Leopold whose term as visitor or head of the St. Louis district had expired. A native of Chicago who had received the habit of the Christian Brothers in 1901, a man known for his sound judgment and administrative ability, Brother Leopold had enjoyed great success during his nine years as provincial before assuming the role of a college president. His performance at St. Mary's would likewise be of high caliber.[30]

One hitch that was not anticipated involved transfer of the title to the college. In Rome St. Mary's was listed as a seminary, and as such under church law it could not be alienated from hierarchical control. This fact was not known to the brothers when they contracted to buy the college, and considerable time elapsed before they actually acquired the deed to the property. A visitation by a papal representative confirmed the fact that the institution was a college and not a seminary, but illness then incapacitated Bishop Kelly before transfer of title could be consummated. That business was left to the Most Reverend Leo W. Binz who was made apostolic administrator of the Winona diocese in November, 1942. Although the original agreement of 1933 gave the brothers twenty years in which to pay off the indebtedness on St. Mary's, the final installment was met much sooner on March 31, 1943.[31]

The brothers had made it quite clear that they would be happy to have prospective priests attend the college. But the two main reasons for its take over were somewhat different in emphasis: to afford accreditation to the work done by the scholastics and to provide inspiration to all members of the order. Some brothers were timid in the face of the undertaking, but most were optimistic. After all, the entire St. Louis district, stretching from Illinois to Texas with hundreds of students in its schools, was behind the enterprise. Except for football and hockey, St. Mary's had been little known outside the Winona diocese. From now on its students would be more numerous and would be drawn from a far broader geographical range.[32]

In 1934 the scholasticate in Chicago was discontinued, and the future brothers studying there were sent to Winona. Later in the same year the scholastics at Glencoe, Missouri, were also transferred to St. Mary's. For a time they all lived in cramped quarters in a farmhouse dubbed "Heifer Hall." In 1935, however, the bishop's residence became available, and the visitor of the district advanced $25,000 to purchase it as a home for the scholastics, which was named La Salle Hall. Since these young men attended regular college classes (little change had been made in the curriculum) they were able to study more diverse courses than had been open to them previously. The move proved to be a good one. By 1947 over 180 brothers had been trained at St. Mary's.[33]

For the first several years after 1933, however, the going was far from easy. It was 1939 before the college showed its first profit. Until then only borrowing and help from the mother house at Glencoe kept the enterprise in operation. When the brothers took charge of St. Mary's, its academic reputation left something to be desired. The College of Saint Teresa was not alone in its low opinion of the quality of work done at its diocesan neighbor. Some students and alumni exhibited pique at the transfer, and careful handling was needed if their loyalty were to be retained. The faculty required upgrading. The physical plant badly needed repairs and improvements,

and an increase in enrollment was an absolute necessity. Finally recognition by an outside accrediting body had to be secured with all possible haste. The challenges were imposing, but not overwhelming.[34]

A number of the faculty who were retained, both lay and clerical, helped greatly in restoring loyalty and building up the support of graduates. By 1937 the alumni association, which had had its ups and downs, was once again "rapidly organizing into a unified body," and soon new chapters would spring up in such centers as Rochester and Chicago. Among the brothers there developed a kind of pride in St. Mary's welfare, and as a consequence growing numbers of graduates, some with financial aid already provided, were directed to Winona from the order's secondary schools.[35]

By 1938 enrollment passed the 300 mark, an increase causing "every available room" to be occupied. Freshmen comprised a record 146. Of the total in all classes, 45 per cent came from Minnesota, 42 per cent from Illinois. Several brothers, as they could be spared, were sent to Catholic University, DePaul University in Chicago, or abroad for advanced study, and a beginning was made in raising the low salaries of lay teachers. Late in 1938 the faculty roster was up to thirty. The curriculum received constant attention and a considerable array of majors such as biology, economics, and physical education, came into being. Preprofessional programs were still advertised, but with a noticeable shift in emphasis. Four years of college preparation for medicine, dentistry, pharmacy, and law were recommended in preference to the earlier two-year periods. Less was being said about training for an occupation, more about such matters as intellectual growth and personal development. All in all St. Mary's was acquiring a more sophisticated collegiate concept of itself.[36]

Both cause and effect of this growing self-confidence was the outside recognition so earnestly sought. In March, 1934, the North Central Association had accorded accreditation to St. Mary's junior college division. The small size of the two upper classes, however, had ruled out similar approval of the entire four-year program, but not for long. Full membership in the North Central organization — evidence that significant improvements had been made — came in 1937; admission to the Association of American Colleges followed a year later. Henceforth Marian graduates would suffer no disadvantage as they went out to teach, study, or engage in other pursuits. Their number was still small, but it was appreciably larger than it had been in the late 1920s. In 1935 B.A.s were conferred on seventeen men, B.S.s in natural science on five, and B.S.s in social science on twelve. Of the thirty-four graduates, fifteen were scholastics. Four years later the senior class of thirty-five members contained nineteen brothers.[37]

Just at the time then when relations among the countries of the world were again rapidly deteriorating, St. Mary's could feel it had attained its majority. Nearly a score of organizations — religious, academic, musical, and social — were flourishing. Those of a religious nature, Holy Name, Mission, and Sanctuary, occupied positions of prominence. The scholastics had their own La Salle choir, but all students were eligible to try out for the *a cappella* choir of fifty members. Daily Mass continued to attract a sizable portion of the college family, as did all the other less frequent services and celebrations of the Catholic church.[38]

During the 1920s, all St. Mary's students had been members of the College Men's Club, later to become a strictly social organization known as the Cardinals. By the 1930s a student council was also in existence. A required convocation on Wednesday mornings gave exposure to local and visiting talent and helped maintain a cohesive atmosphere. Even the absence of coeds did not render the mode of living too distinctive. Teresans lived only a mile away, and both scheduled and spontaneous joint college functions gave a coeducational dimension to the extracurriculum of the two Catholic institutions in Winona.[39]

Though World War II loomed, Marians could concur with the sentiments expressed by the school's first president, Father Griffin, in December, 1938, at the banquet celebrating St. Mary's silver jubilee. "There lurks an invisible something," he said, "that creates a change in all who breathe her air; an influence that grasps her students, inspires lofty ideals, enkindling ambition, shaping character of Christian gentlemen. This is her heritage, and the depth of her spirit." [40]

25

Benedictines in Duluth

MINNESOTA'S FOURTH CATHOLIC COLLEGE for women, St. Scholastica, derived basically from the conjunction of two forces — Benedictine missionary zeal and the mushrooming settlement of Duluth. That northern Minnesota city, touched by "the magic of iron," had seen its population of three thousand in 1880 explode tenfold within a decade. Many of the newcomers were Catholic, and the need for priests and nuns was both urgent and immediate.[1]

That the Benedictines responded quickly to this challenge was not surprising, but several factors made the response especially forceful. Bishop of the vicariate of northern Minnesota at the time was a former abbot of St. John's at Collegeville; the current abbot was the aggressive and expansionist-minded Alexius Edelbrock. Heading the convent at St. Joseph was another strong figure eager to spread Benedictine influence, Mother Scholastica Kerst. By 1883 Duluth had two Catholic parishes; when the need for a third one quickly arose, the bishop urged the monks at St. John's to establish it. Typically Alexius then came up with a project far grander than the bishop had suggested. The abbot proposed not only to establish a parish but also to build a monastery, a college, a convent, and a hospital. All but the monastery became realities.[2]

As the 1880s drew to a close two nearly concurrent events helped speed the establishment in Duluth of a Benedictine mother house and ultimately the order's college. In August, 1889, Mother Scholastica's term as superior at St. Joseph ended, and for reasons beyond the scope of this account she had not been permitted to stand for re-election. This fact aroused indignation in the minds of certain Benedictine sisters staffing parochial schools and St. Mary's Hospital, which Alexius had built in the port city. Convinced that Mother Scholastica had been unjustly deposed, these women wished to establish an independent priory in Duluth under her leadership. The Most Reverend James McGolrick, bishop of the new

diocese of Duluth established in 1889, was receptive to their wishes. Early in 1892 he secured the consent of the bishop of St. Cloud (in whose jurisdiction St. Joseph was located) for the creation of a new Benedictine foundation with Mother Scholastica as its superior. In July she and two dozen or so sisters arrived in Duluth to open a mother house and an academy. In the face of such obstacles as religious bigotry but with the constant support of Bishop McGolrick, Mother Scholastica achieved notable success.[3]

For a time both convent and school were quartered in Munger Terrace, a four-story, former apartment house in one of Duluth's more exclusive areas, but that facility soon became inadequate. So a new brick structure was erected and occupied in the fall of 1895. Known as Sacred Heart Institute, the high school grew rapidly in size and prestige. Additions to accommodate this growth were necessary in 1899 and in 1901. A school paper, the *Institute Echoes*, appeared in 1902. All of this had been pleasing to Mother Scholastica, but it had not been enough. As early as the summer of 1895, she had sent four sisters to study at the University of Minnesota. She had been one of the first religious superiors to take such a step, and she never ceased emphasizing quality in education and seeking ways of achieving it. Even then, she was contemplating the creation of a more ambitious institution, located away from the heart of rapidly growing Duluth. The new setting in the Benedictine tradition should be on a hill, commanding a view of sylvan grandeur such as "might inspire to ideals of beauty and peace." Yet to be of the greatest service the locale should be easily accessible.[4]

In 1900 the ideal spot was found and part of it purchased. Rising some 680 feet above the magnificent vista of Lake Superior, the site called the "Daisy Farm" was then three miles outside the city limits. Possessed of a stream, Chester Creek, groves of graceful conifers and numerous varieties of their deciduous cousins, rock outcroppings, and verdant glades, the future campus area played host to long-remembered picnics before its development for more serious pursuits. By 1908 the Duluth Benedictines had acquired 160 acres; part of the land would soon be transformed into a busy center of learning.[5]

Planning, preparation, and construction had gone on for some time, but at last in the fall of 1909 the first section of a building on the Daisy Farm was ready for occupancy. Of late Gothic Tudor style, its massive stone walls seeming almost a part of the natural environment, the structure's most distinctive feature was a tower stretching six stories skyward. Renamed the Villa Sancta Scholastica, the school opened its doors on September 7, 1909, with resident students from the Sacred Heart Institute in attendance. The latter institution continued as a day school for another year, when it was converted to other uses and its students transferred to a local parochial high school. About sixty girls had graduated from the academic department of the institute before it was merged with the Villa.[6]

Less than two years after the move to the new location, Mother Scholastica died on June 11, 1911. She did not live to witness the culmination of much of her work, but she left a legacy which even today is remembered and honored both in the Benedictine community and in the Duluth area generally. She helped establish St. Mary's Hospital in 1888; twenty years later she founded its school of nursing. In 1909 she undertook the operation of St. James Orphanage in Duluth, and the following year she played a prominent role in starting St. Ann's Home for the Aged in that city. She had been instrumental in the establishment of other Minnesota hospitals and numerous parochial schools. At Sacred Heart Institute and the Villa she had taken great interest in students, frequenting classrooms and taking part in many school activities. Sisters still respond to the high level of performance expected by Mother Scholastica, even as they feel a vicarious pride in her example and accomplishments. Her sister, Sister M. Alexia Kerst, succeeded to the leadership of the mother house at the Villa.[7]

By then some of the faculty at the school announced their belief that the time had come to open a junior college. Not all of the sisters agreed, so each side was invited to present its arguments to the mother superior and her council. The proponents of a college were more convincing, and they were assigned the task of formulating the details involved in setting up such an institution. Two main reasons apparently lay behind the decision to add a college department: "to accommodate . . . the desires of high school graduates wishing to pursue more advanced studies and, more especially, to supply ready means of higher education for postulants and novices of the community." High costs precluded the publishing of a catalog the first year, but the *Villa Quarterly*, successor to the *Institute Echoes*, listed fifty-two college courses to be offered in eight departments — religion, philosophy, English, history, mathematics, natural sciences, ancient and modern languages, and fine arts.[8]

To sample this menu two girls and four sisters enrolled on September 10, 1912, the formal opening date of the College of St. Scholastica. Though it was a modest beginning, no effort seems to have been spared to maintain commendable standards of performance. As one of the six later remarked, "Study was our major sport." There was, however, a rigid requirement that the academy and college girls exercise outdoors for an hour before the evening meal. Croquet and tennis were popular in warm weather, and tobogganing and skating on the campus' tiny lagoon were favorite winter pastimes. Skating provided bonuses beyond those of physical well being: at least three students of these first years found future spouses among Duluth's young men, some of whom were not slow in discovering the lagoon's special attractions. These young people could scarcely argue with a statement in the Villa catalog that "The advantages of out-of-door exercise leave nothing to be desired."[9]

If the college were to grow and prosper, it needed to attain recognized standing in the academic world. Yet to do so required at least the promise of a sizable enrollment. For this reason each "new registrant was looked upon as a gift from God." By the fall of 1914 only eighteen students, five of them religious, were registered in the collegiate department. Since several of the lay undergraduates planned to transfer to the state university, the matter of accreditation was crucial. Happily in 1914 — the year St. Scholastica was incorporated and "empowered to grant all College Degrees" — the freshman course of the collegiate department was approved by the University of Minnesota; sophomore offerings won tentative acceptance the following year. That same autumn Catholic University granted advanced standing to two sisters from St. Scholastica — another bit of welcome recognition.[10]

Despite these gains and the somewhat inflated catalog content, hopes far exceeded realization. The college was still a junior member in a household containing the four-year Villa Sancta Scholastica Academy, intermediate and primary grades, an art department, a conservatory of music, a domestic science department, and a one-year commercial course for high school graduates. For a time during World War I, when a teacher shortage existed, a normal department to train teachers for ungraded and semigraded schools was set up at the suggestion of the Minnesota Department of Education. Only ten or twelve students seem to have taken the courses in methods, practice teaching, and child psychology offered by the new unit, which was dropped after the war.[11]

In 1913–14 senior college courses were first listed in the catalog; they were, however, open to sisters only. Two years later B.A. degrees were conferred on five Benedictines, but it is doubtful that these baccalaureates were comparable to later ones. Lay collegians had their own separate class instruction, prefect, and social room; otherwise "they walked the same corridors, ate in the same dining-halls, followed the same pattern and were subject to the same direction" as the far more numerous girls in the academy. Much of the earlier "finishing school" atmosphere still obtained, and life was carefully circumscribed. But though small in numbers, the collegians were cherished. They represented hopes for the future, harbingers of what St. Scholastica yearned to become. And to identify limitations is not to scoff. Many of these junior college products transferred successfully to first-rate institutions of higher learning. One girl who entered the University of Minnesota in 1918 reported later: "All my credits were accepted. There were no handicaps. The work at St. Scholastica's was a great help to me." [12]

As funds became available, improvements to the physical plant were made. A small wooden addition to the main building to serve primarily as a science hall was erected in 1911–12, but it was gutted by fire on April 23, 1913. Luckily the main building suffered only some smoke damage, and by the fall of 1913 the burned-out area had been restored. The following year a stone building was erected with a wing connecting it to the main edifice. Containing a chapel with seats for about 260 people, classrooms, and laboratories, this unit was completed in 1919. World War I had necessitated postponement of plans to erect a gymnasium-auditorium, but work on the combination unit got under way in 1920. Located west of the Villa and featuring the latter's blue trap walls, arched windows, and horizontal lines, this addition to school facilities was formally opened in April, 1921. Some landscaping had been done, but by later standards the campus still presented a somewhat barren appearance.[13]

Meanwhile Mother Alexia, with constant support from Bishop McGolrick, had spared no effort to further the education of the sisters and enhance the quality of the faculty. As early as June, 1914, Sisters Mary Katherine and Mary Paul had received their Ph.D. and M.A. degrees, respectively, from Catholic University. The doctorate would remain in short supply for quite some time, but master's degrees became increasingly common. Sadly, in May, 1916, Mother Alexia died, as did Bishop McGolrick less than two years later. An impressive conversationalist, generous, and revered by both sisters and students, he had been a familiar figure in St. Scholastica's classrooms and school events — much in the fashion of John Ireland at St. Catherine and St. Thomas. The new ordinary of the Duluth diocese, the Right Reverend John T. McNicholas, paid fewer visits to the college, but he supported it in many other ways. The new superior of the sisterhood was Mother M. Celestine Sullivan, who served for only two years. Her successor, Mother Chrysostom Doran, during her six-year term would oversee St. Scholastica's continued progress toward the status of a full-fledged, four-year college of liberal arts.[14]

During the early 1920s, growth was encouragingly steady, though most of it was in the high school department. With the occupancy of the auditorium-gymnasium in 1921, music and dramatics, long popular subjects, at last received the facilities and elbowroom needed for upgrading their offerings. Two lay teachers were then added to the staff, and the catalog was swelled by a twelve-page supplement entitled "Conservatory of Music." Life took on a new tempo, although collegiate enrollment did not pick up appreciably. It was 84 in 1923–24. Nevertheless the idea of expanding the college curriculum was gaining acceptance. After all, the record so far called for no apology. Between the fall of 1912 and June, 1924, 160 students — 44 of them sisters — had completed the junior college course. Practically all of the religious had gone on to earn bachelor's degrees. Several attained doctorates. Of the 116 lay students, 34 had obtained baccalaureates elsewhere.[15]

If the college were to be capable of even greater service and if it were to attract more students, it would have to take the next logical step. Rather than remaining a mere adjunct to an academy, it would have to become a regular four-year institution. Amidst much enthusiasm in the summer of 1924, the step was taken. Starting with the approaching fall term, St. Scholastica's would come of age. It would have its own dean and a separate section of the building for its exclusive use. One of the collegians ecstatically expressed the general delight when she said, "Everything is wonderful; we are a college in the true sense of the word." [16]

Although Mother Chrysostom was still serving

as superior, her health for the past year had deteriorated, and direction of the college had been mainly
in the hands of Sister Agnes Somers, a woman of
vision and common sense who was one of St.
Scholastica's great figures. Born into a family of
twelve children on a farm in Ontario, Canada, she
had arrived in Duluth to enter the Benedictine Order
in 1901. As a religious she had earned her master's
degree at Catholic University. Now in 1924 just
as the four-year collegiate program was instituted,
she succeeded to the headship of the community
and the college. For the next eighteen years she
endeared herself to sisters and students alike, earning
the title "The Builder." In 1926 the Right Reverend
Thomas A. Welch, former chancellor of the archdiocese of St. Paul, succeeded to the diocese of Duluth.
His tenure would extend over more than three
decades. A friendly and democratic leader, Bishop
Welch made frequent visits to the college, where
his personal interest in students made him a great
favorite.[17]

So far the college had only ten departments: religion
and philosophy; psychology; classical languages and
literature; romance languages and literature; English
literature, rhetoric, and public speaking; social science, economics, and business; biological sciences;
mathematics; home economics; and music. The
faculty numbered less than thirty, of whom twenty
were sisters and four were priests. Only one sister
had completed her doctorate. Enrollment in the collegiate department in 1925–26 stood at ninety-two.
As yet the work of the junior and senior years lacked
accreditation, and additions to the physical plant
would soon be necessary.[18]

Several of these handicaps were eliminated in
fairly short order. In 1925 major sequences were
fashioned in five of the departments: English, history, Latin, biology, and psychology and education.
The curriculum was then given approval by the
University of Minnesota. On June 12, 1926, at the
college's first graduation ceremony, two young
women received the B.A. degree. Early the next
year came happy news from Minneapolis: "Students
who take major sequences in departments in which
majors are offered" at St. Scholastica "will be
admitted to the graduate school of the University
of Minnesota." Shortly another favorable report
arrived from the Minnesota Department of Education
in St. Paul: all graduates of the college with fifteen
semester hours of education and at least thirty hours
of observation and practice teaching in high school
would receive a Minnesota high school teaching certificate. "We are now fully approved," exulted a
writer in the *Villa Quarterly* for March, 1927.[19]

Such achievements only pointed the way to other

tasks. The sisters, with encouragement from Bishop
Welch, went ahead with completion of the administration building, known today as Tower Hall. A
central façade and right wing which gave the finished
structure a frontage of 375 feet were added in 1927–
28. With its three previously completed lateral
wings, its twin Tudor towers, end turrets, recessed
windows, and stone terrace, the complex is an awe-
inspiring sight. The interior, featuring long, wide
corridors, high ceilings, tile floors, paneling, *objets
d'art*, and Florentine glass doors, holds much of
interest for the sensitive observer. The building also
provided new dormitory facilities, classrooms, and
offices, as well as a welcome psychological lift.[20]

With the addition of sequences in German,
French, Spanish, business administration and
economics, sociology, chemistry, and home
economics, majors in twelve fields were offered by
1929. That year, through recent affiliation with St.
Mary's school of nursing, St. Scholastica began to
award a B.S. degree in nursing education. In 1936
the college's nursing department was approved by
the National Association of Collegiate Schools of
Nursing — one of the first units in the country to
be so recognized. A department of secretarial
studies, offering a two-year course leading to a diploma, was set up in 1928. Two years later a new
department of library science advertised its own
major sequence. As depression deepened, interest
in social welfare mounted, and the sociology department was expanded as a result. All the while sisters,
as they could be spared, were sent off for work
on advanced degrees. Consequently the number of
master's and doctor's degrees represented on the
faculty rose rather sharply in the late 1920s and early
1930s.[21]

Mother Agnes now felt that the time was ripe
to seek accreditation from the North Central Association. After applications had been filed for both college and academy, an on-the-scene investigation was
conducted by St. Louis University's graduate dean.
He found room for improvement, especially in the
matter of endowment, but his report was generally
laudatory. With this endorsement in hand as well
as a favorable evaluation of the academy program
by a state university dean, the North Central Association in March, 1931, admitted the "College of St.
Scholastica with her attached high school" to membership. A follow-up examination made for the
association some months later also proved complimentary. North Central accreditation plus St.
Scholastica's admission to the Association of Minnesota Colleges and to the Association of American
Colleges in these depression years did wonders for
morale among Duluth Benedictines.[22]

With accreditation a reality, Mother Agnes turned her attention to other matters. Enrollment by the spring of 1931 had reached 135; in 1933–34 — if sisters and summer school students are counted — it totaled 295. By the autumn of 1937 crowding had become such a problem that it was necessary to rent a large house in Duluth where some of the sisters could sleep at night. So, despite the uncertainty of the times, Mother Agnes launched a new building program, which drew some criticism. In 1936 she retained architects to draw plans for several campus additions — a residence hall, an auditorium, a chapel-library, and two cloisters. On July 1 contracts were let and construction was shortly under way.[23]

By the middle of December, 1937, Rockhurst Auditorium — its name suggested by features of the surrounding landscape — was completed, as was Stanbrook Hall, which was christened in honor of an English Benedictine abbey. Set at a distance to the south of Tower Hall, Stanbrook early in 1938 became home to the high school students. Several months later the chapel of Our Lady, Queen of Peace, located between Tower and Stanbrook halls, was finished. Of early Christian Romanesque style, the chapel derived its name from the hopes and pleas for peace which were being expressed in the face of Hitler's destructive course in Europe. In the Benedictine tradition, the building's first tier was utilized as the college library. The total cost of Stanbrook and the chapel amounting to $1,000,000 as well as the cost of Rockhurst was financed by the Benedictine community of Duluth. With these additions and the two new cloisters, St. Scholastica on the eve of World War II possessed an integrated complex — functional, handsome, and rich in symbolism. Off campus a fire in 1933 had damaged the old Sacred Heart Institute, then used as a nurses' home. Repairs and the construction of a five-story wing thereafter provided excellent quarters in the renamed St. Mary's Hall for the 120 or so student nurses attending the college.[24]

New buildings were only external evidences of St. Scholastica's growing maturity, strength, and confidence. As physical plant expanded so did the curriculum. Before 1932 the college program had been fashioned with homemakers and lay and religious teachers in mind. Then during the depths of the depression, openings for teachers became scarcer, and student interests shifted as a consequence. Among the innovations were a course in radio techniques and broadcasting started in 1932, sequences for hospital technicians introduced in 1935, and adult education offerings two years later. Also attracting interest were courses in dietetics, medical technology, and medical record librarianship, the last pioneered at the degree level by St. Scholastica's and St. Mary's Hospital. This thrust toward vocationalism aroused considerable opposition, and as a result substantial amounts of liberal arts work were required in all sequences.[25]

The mid-1930s also saw the introduction of majors in public school music, art, business administration, and mathematics; at the end of the decade a teaching minor in physical education was added. At the same time a demonstration house for child training was built, thus improving instruction in home economics. Soon after the college won approval by the Minnesota Board of Vocational Education for training teachers under the Smith-Hughes Act. No matter what their major field, many students were potential parochial schoolteachers or leaders in parish music activities. Hence special attention was directed toward preparing these young women in the fields of church music and liturgy.[26]

From 1929 onward all freshmen were given a variety of tests, including psychological, English placement, and silent reading, so that weaknesses and strengths could be identified and properly dealt with. In 1932 participation in the American Council on Education's sophomore testing program began. The next year a personnel office with its own director was established, its purpose being to provide student guidance and to integrate the social and scholastic life of undergraduates.[27]

In this same period St. Scholastica's took the lead in securing removal of the handicap under which all Catholic sisters seeking elementary teacher certification labored. In 1920 and 1921 before the college had an education department, numbers of Benedictines attended the state normal school in Duluth in order to earn a Minnesota teacher's certificate. Soon, however, Minnesota attorney general's rulings declaring illegal the wearing of religious garb even by practice teachers in public normal schools put an end to the arrangement. The sisters, despite the inconvenience involved, then began to attend the teachers' college in Superior, Wisconsin, where no garb restriction obtained. In 1934 it was discovered that certain other opinions of Minnesota's attorney general "seemed to circumvent the anti-garb" barrier. The supervisor of parish schools in the diocese thereupon turned for help to the state teachers' college in Duluth. At last the problem was solved. Sister students would be permitted to receive credit at the public institution for practice teaching done in parochial schools under the supervision of St. Scholastica's department of education. Nearly 120 sisters by 1950 had done some of their work in education at the teachers' colleges in Duluth and Superior and been certified by them. Most of these women also earned their baccalaureates at their own Benedictine college.[28]

Going hand in hand with developments in the areas of physical plant and academic program was expansion of the extracurriculum. Indeed Mother Agnes dubbed 1932 the *annus mirabilis*. In addition to final North Central recognition, that year saw a remarkable number of innovations, such as a student council, a college newspaper, *Scriptorium*, a chapter of Kappa Gamma Pi (an honor society for Catholic women), the start of the athletic association, and the founding of the St. Agnes Honor Society. In 1935 the college was authorized to open its own post office. The next year *Towers*, the college annual, made its appearance, as did two customs which were long cherished at St. Scholastica — the *Weaving of the Standards*, a commencement week pageant and the formulation of characteristics constituting the "Scholastican Ideal." Each spring thereafter faculty and students by secret ballot selected nine seniors who exemplified the ideals and were cited at the honors convocation. Life on campus was assuming definition and creating lasting traditions.[29]

In 1941 St. Scholastica was chosen by the North Central Association as one of twenty-eight colleges to participate in a co-operative study of the preparation of high school teachers in liberal arts institutions. As an aspect of the project the college decided to evaluate its offerings by polling its alumnae. With great care the faculty devised a questionnaire of 684 items which was mailed early in 1942 to each of the 443 graduates. An amazing 74 per cent responded, throwing valuable light on the work of the institution between the mid-1920s and World War II. In addition the information proved most helpful in the redefinition of objectives and the modification of curricular and extracurricular schedules.[30]

The poll revealed that slightly over one-third of the respondents lived in Duluth, and another 30 per cent were located elsewhere in northern Minnesota, Wisconsin, and Michigan. At least 50 were members of some religious community. Most of those replying were Catholic (242), but a sizable number were Protestant (51). Seventy-nine per cent had spent four years in college; 170 had earned the B.A. and 130 the B.S. They were engaged in twelve different kinds of work in 1941. Thirty-six per cent were teachers, mostly in secondary schools; English, history, and languages were the major fields of more than three-quarters of this segment. The second largest group of alumnae, 19 per cent, were homemakers. The remainder were in such callings as nursing, social work, medical technology, medicine, and graduate study.[31]

One assumption underlying the study had been that a college education should bring about desirable changes in the lives of alumnae. Here the results were not entirely encouraging. Since the philosophy undergirding the college's program was religious and Catholic, it was desirable that the graduate "thoroughly understands her religion, lives in accordance with its principles, and assumes responsibility for religious leadership." Church attendance and giving by alumnae was generally good, but it was obvious that the college had missed the mark in certain related areas. Graduates should have learned the importance of regular spiritual reading and of making voluntary sacrifices. However, these practices were all too rare. It also appeared that more instruction on ethical principles was called for. Many alumnae apparently had wrapped up their college "experiences as memories to be taken out and aired in nostalgic moments, but not to be utilized in the building of their lives." [32]

As a young institution attended largely by girls of precollege age, St. Scholastica's had felt only indirectly the impact of World War I. Now with another global conflict already raging, even a sheltered women's college in the Midwest could not escape the backwash of war. By 1940, however, with enrollment rising steadily, the institution was a secure and distinct entity ready to meet the challenges that lay ahead.

PART III

WAR AND
INTERCOLLEGE CO-OPERATION

1940–1970

26

Introduction: Part III — 1940–1970

"WE NOW REALIZE that World War II marked the end of one era and the beginning of another," wrote Dr. John W. Nason in 1970 in his final report as president of Carleton College. Few observers would disagree with this conclusion, whether it is applied to general historical trends or whether it is limited, as it is here, to the field of higher education. While differences of opinion arise over the major impacts of the world conflict on American colleges and universities, the war's short-term consequence in the form of a drastic decline in civilian enrollments was patently evident.[1]

Just before Pearl Harbor in 1941 approximately 1,254,000 students (756,000 men and 498,000 women) were attending the nation's institutions of higher learning. By the fall of 1943 the total was down to about 738,000, of whom only 274,000 were men. A similar pattern existed in Minnesota; in 1943–44 some 20,000 civilian students were registered in public and private institutions of collegiate rank, only 58 per cent of the 34,600 in attendance in 1940–41. The presence of 300,000 military students on the country's campuses in 1943–44 helped many colleges and universities maintain solvency, but those which lacked army and navy installations, especially if they were all-male institutions, frequently had tough going. Yet no four-year, accredited, liberal arts college in Minnesota or elsewhere had to suspend operations during the war years. In the autumn of 1945 nation-wide enrollments of 926,000 were up by 25 per cent over those of 1943; the 1945 figure, however, was still 27 per cent below that of 1941.[2]

A decline in enrollments was, of course, only one of the handicaps under which the country's institutions of higher learning labored during World War II. Every phase of operation was affected. Expansion of permanent physical plant came to a standstill. Curricular adjustments were undertaken, often at the expense of departments whose offerings seemed to bear slight relationship to the prosecution of the war. The number of full- and part-time faculty did not decrease seriously (114,000 in 1941 to 106,000 in 1945), but some of the ablest teachers entered military service or other war-related activities. Accrediting procedures were suspended, as were annual meetings of learned societies and college and university associations. The extracurriculum was curtailed, and a year-round calendar frequently replaced the traditional one extending from September to June. Surrounding society as a whole and hovering over each campus like a cloud were understandable melancholy, anxiety, and uncertainty, but also a sense of unity. Casualty reports containing the name of a friend, a classmate, or a loved one periodically deepened the gloom.[3]

The fact remains, however, that the war affected the routine more than it did the fundamental nature of America's collegiate institutions. Certain developments of the period at home and abroad, on campus and beyond it, however, proved to be powerful determinants of the nature, methods, and concerns of higher education in the days following the surrender of the Germans and the Japanese in 1945. Most obvious of these influences was the bomb, which to the horror and amazement of a public unaware of its existence rained wholesale death and destruction on Hiroshima and Nagasaki. This dreadful weapon raised before man the specter of his own annihilation, but it also elevated science to a position of pre-eminence in the halls of learning and seemed to promise a wonderful new age of control over the forces of nature. The war also greatly expanded the average American's geographical horizons and convinced him of the necessity of learning more about, and getting along with, his neighbors in parts of the world other than Europe. This lesson would later be reflected in broadened college curriculums and in a multitude of other ways. And the civilian classroom would adopt to a degree, though not to the extent sometimes predicted, the methods of the military school in the generous use of visual aids, emphasis on conversation in teaching foreign languages, objective examinations, and numerical grading.[4]

Another significant influence of the war years — widespread examination of the curriculum — was stimulated by the travel restrictions then in effect. Unable to attend national meetings or to get away for research, faculty members turned to local concerns such as the content of courses of study. These investigations led to the preparation of reports and ultimately to curricular changes. The best known and most influential of these documents was that produced in 1945 by Harvard University under the title *General Education in a Free Society*, although there were numerous others. The Harvard title indicates the burden of the argument in many of these summations: the necessity of requiring a core of general education in college curriculums in order to implant "common standards and common purposes" in the minds of educated men and women. Such action would strengthen a free society, serve as a needed balance to specialized training, and help guard against the misuse of atomic energy. People active in college work in the 1940s remember clearly the prevalence of articles and speeches on these subjects, many of which still retain their pertinence.[5]

The lack of a sufficient supply of well-qualified secondary schoolteachers, both secular and religious, was a matter which also occupied the attention of educators and set in motion developments of considerable consequence to Minnesota's private colleges. The story goes back to 1940, when a subcommittee of the North Central Association surveyed teacher training programs in twelve institutions, including St. Catherine and St. Olaf. The following year the project was expanded to embrace twenty-eight colleges, all of which set out to discover the best way of preparing teachers and encouraging experimentation and improvement. In 1945 the scope of the enterprise was broadened, as the new name of the North Central sponsoring group — subcommittee on liberal arts education — testified. Seventy-four colleges, over one-third of the total in the North Central's twenty-state area, then joined the endeavor, which was assisted by a Carnegie Corporation grant. Three years later a larger gift from the same source made possible the hiring of a nearly full-time director and six co-ordinators. The liberal arts study had its problems, but these were outweighed by its accomplishments. A monthly *News Bulletin* disseminated information from the central office in Chicago, and workshops and conferences stimulated member institutions to examine and revise

their academic programs. On local campuses self-studies dealing with a variety of matters led to modifications and improvements. By the early 1950s the co-operative study was hailed by some educators as "the most extensive and penetrating program for strengthening liberal arts education to be found anywhere in America today." It has continued to make valuable contributions since that time.[6]

In addition to pursuing its wartime studies of teacher preparation, the North Central Association and various other agencies and groups also undertook the task of planning the course educational institutions would be called upon to follow when peace again returned. Little help was provided by the example of World War I, since only 375,000 of the 4,000,000 Americans in uniform in that conflict resumed full-time schooling once the fighting was over. It became increasingly clear that the situation this time would be vastly different. In 1943 Congress enacted a bill to benefit disabled veterans, and the following year as an expression of the nation's gratitude, the Servicemen's Readjustment Act, better known as the "GI Bill," was passed. Under this legislation all honorably discharged personnel would be eligible for at least one year of education at society's expense. Depending on the length of their service stint and the degree of their disability, others would be entitled to longer periods of training. For the great majority the time would be four years; during this span a single veteran in school would receive a monthly subsistence payment of $65, a married ex-GI one of $90. In addition the government would pay annual tuition of up to $500. Responsibility for carrying out the huge program was vested in the Veterans Administration.[7]

As the war moved toward its conclusion, planners grappled with a host of perplexing questions. How many veterans would enroll in institutions of higher learning? What type of training would they seek? Should colleges and universities grant credit for service in the armed forces and for courses taken under military aegis? Where would the necessary faculty come from? Would educational plants be equal to the demand?[8]

Some of the answers missed the target. Few seers forecast either the magnitude of postwar enrollments or the excellence of the veteran's general adjustment and academic performance. Some colleges were slow to develop policies concerning the treatment of former service personnel, but over-all, educational institutions did an amazing job of making the transition to peacetime operation. Of great help was the work of such bodies as the North Central Association and the American Council on Education in publishing guides to courses offered in various military pro-

Hamline University

HAMLINE'S FIRST permanent home, built in Red Wing in 1855 and occupied until 1869, when the school was temporarily closed.

LADIES' HALL, later renamed Goheen Hall (left), and Old Main (right) loom above the prairie at Hamline's new St. Paul location in the 1880s.

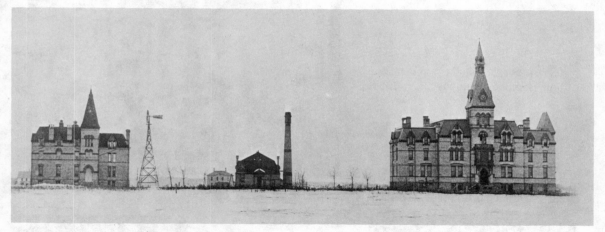

THREE former presidents of Hamline, left to right, Samuel F. Kerfoot, Alfred F. Hughes, and George H. Bridgman.

Hamline coeds photographed in 1923.

Students' "Strike against War" on Hamline's campus about 1939.

Bush Memorial Library, dedicated in the fall of 1971 and named for A. G. Bush.

St. John's University

THE MODEST beginnings of St. John's monastery near St. Cloud in 1856.

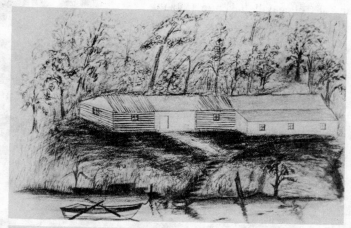

ST. JOHN'S ABBEY and St. John's College on the shores of Lake Sagatagan, 1867. Sketch by Father Vincent Schiffrer.

ST. JOHN'S CAMPUS in 1880, shortly before the name was legally changed to St. John's University.

AN AERIAL view of St. John's University at Collegeville taken in 1924.

St. John's distinctive bell tower and church designed by Marcel Breuer and consecrated in 1961.

ALEXIUS EDELBROCK (near right), abbot from 1873 to 1889.

ALCUIN DEUTSCH (far right), abbot from 1922 to 1951.

Gustavus Adolphus College

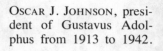

Oscar J. Johnson, president of Gustavus Adolphus from 1913 to 1942.

Eric Norelius, founder and first president of Gustavus Adolphus College.

Old Main and the Auditorium at Gustavus Adolphus College in 1927.

Nobel laureates present at the dedication of Alfred Nobel Hall in 1963.

Christ Chapel, dedicated in 1962 as a part of Gustavus' centennial observance.

THE MEN and women of
Carleton's faculty, 1888–90.

WILLIS HALL, Carleton College's first
building, completed in 1872.

CARLETON COLLEGE's baseball team in a
photograph taken about 1900.

JAMES W. STRONG, first president of Carleton, 1870–1903.

DONALD J. COWLING, president of Carleton from 1914 to 1937.

SCOVILLE Memorial Library, completed in 1896 and converted to classrooms and faculty offices in 1956.

CARLETON students in the 1920s with Willis Hall at left and Sayles-Hill gymnasium in the background.

OLIN HALL, the science center constructed in 1961 with a financial gift from the Olin Foundation.

Augsburg College

NEW MAIN, under construction for over three years, was dedicated early in 1902. It housed classrooms, gymnasium, library, and chapel.

AUGSBURG in a winter scene in the late 1920s with Morton Hall at center, Main at left, and North Hall to the right.

AUGSBURG STUDENTS at an entrance to Science Hall, which was constructed in 1949.

AUGUST WEENAAS, Augsburg's first president, 1869–76.

GEORG SVERDRUP, president from 1876 to 1907.

SVEN OFTEDAL, acting president from 1907 to 1911.

St. Olaf College

OLD MAIN, St. Olaf's first building on Manitou Heights, as it looked about 1900.

THORBJØRN N. MOHN, first president of St. Olaf.

LARS W. BOE, St. Olaf's fourth president, 1918–42.

THE LIBRARY, dedicated in 1902 and named for Halle Steensland.

STUDENTS broadcasting over WCAL, the first college radio station in Minnesota which went on the air in 1922.

AGNES LARSON Tower Hall for Women, one of two high-rise residences built in the 1960s.

A RECENT view of the St. Olaf College campus in Northfield.

THE ST. OLAF CHOIR, pictured here in 1937, gained international fame under the direction of F. Melius Christiansen, shown in the center.

NORWAY'S CROWN PRINCE OLAV (in uniform) and Crown Princess Martha at the head of the graduation procession in 1939 when they were honored guests.

Macalester College

STUDENTS at the Baldwin School in 1890, when it was located on Summit Avenue in St. Paul.

THE WINSLOW HOUSE in Minneapolis where the Baldwin School opened in 1874 as the preparatory department of Macalester College.

JAMES WALLACE, president of Macalester, 1894–1906.

CHARLES J. TURCK, Macalester's president, 1939–58.

MACALESTER COLLEGE consisted of Old Main (at left) and four faculty houses in 1890, the year the Grand Avenue electric streetcar line was extended to the campus.

HENRY A. WALLACE, second from right in front, at Macalester during the 1948 presidential race.

A GAME of pushball (far left) occupied Mac men in 1924.

THE SPECTACULAR bonfire, shown in 1946, an annual home coming event at Macalester College.

THE JANET WALLACE Fine Arts Center, a five-structure complex given by the DeWitt Wallaces and dedicated in October, 1965.

College of St. Thomas

THE CAMPUS OF ST. THOMAS is shown about 1902 with the Science Hall at left, the original building that had been a boys' school at center, and the small, frame chapel at right. The pond in the foreground, long since gone, was known as Lake Mennith.

THE CHAPEL at St. Thomas is located on the homesite of Finn Farm, the original tract of land acquired for the college in 1880.

ST. THOMAS CADETS in front of Ireland Hall, the dormitory named in 1912 for the college's founder.

John Ireland, founder in 1885 of the seminary that became St. Thomas College.

Vincent J. Flynn, eleventh president of the College of St. Thomas, 1944–56.

The five-level O'Shaughnessy Education Center, completed in 1971 and named for the college's generous benefactor, I. A. O'Shaughnessy.

A modern view of the College of St. Thomas taken in 1971.

Concordia College in Moorhead

Bishop Whipple Hall, at right, and the "gentlemen's dormitory," left, pictured about 1897.

Concordia's modern Science Hall, completed in 1967 with facilities for four departments.

Johan A. Aasgaard, president of Concordia, 1911–25.

John N. Brown, Concordia's president from 1925 to 1951.

An artist's sketch of Concordia College in Moorhead, with the original campus in the foreground and new campus at top.

College of St. Catherine

MOTHER Seraphine Ireland, founder of the College of St. Catherine in 1905.

MOTHER Antonia McHugh, first dean of St. Catherine's from 1914 to 1937.

OUR LADY OF VICTORY CHAPEL, completed in 1924, reflected in the pond called the "Dew Drop."

THE VISUAL ARTS BUILDING, part of the multiunit Fine Arts Center completed in 1970 and named in honor of Mother Antonia McHugh.

THE NEW AUDITORIUM, now a cultural center for the Twin Cities, was named in 1970 for I. A. O'Shaughnessy. Mendel Hall is shown in the background.

THE MASSIVE iron gates, built in 1923 to give St. Catherine's an air of privacy, stand hospitably open.

College of Saint Teresa

St. Mary's Hall, the first building at the Winona Seminary for Ladies, now the College of Saint Teresa.

The Collegiate Chapel of St. Mary of the Angels, left, and Alverna Hall, the convent, both completed in 1925.

Mother Leo Tracy, near right, and Sister Aloysius (the former Mary A. Molloy), the guiding figures at Saint Teresa's for over half a century.

THE ROGER BACON CENTER for Sciences and Professions, completed in 1960, fulfills the plan Bishop Patrick R. Heffron initiated in the 1920s.

NINE STUDENTS at Saint Teresa's combine their voices in the "Teresan Triple Trio" in 1972.

College of St. Benedict

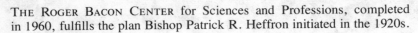

SACRED HEART CHAPEL, completed in 1914, a familiar landmark at the College of St. Benedict at St. Joseph.

ST. BENEDICT COLLEGE and Academy as it appeared in a photograph published in the yearbook for 1912–13.

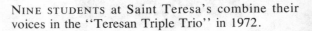

THE ANNUAL FALL PAGEANT portraying for incoming freshmen the dominance of Christianity over barbarism and stressing the centuries-old Benedictine ideals of prayer and work.

MOTHER RICHARDA PETERS, president of St. Benedict's from 1949 to 1957.

BENEDICTA ARTS CENTER, under construction from 1962 to 1965, was named for Sister Benedicta Riepp, leader of the first Benedictine nuns to come to the United States in 1852.

St. Mary's College

IN THIS IMPRESSIVE STRUCTURE on Terrace Heights, St. Mary's College of Winona opened to students in September, 1913, under the presidency of Father William E. F. Griffin.

PATRICK R. HEFFRON, bishop of the Winona diocese and founder of St. Mary's.

BROTHER LEOPOLD J. DODD, president of St. Mary's College from 1933 to 1942.

THE FOOTBALL TEAM of St. Mary's College in 1934, the year after the Christian Brothers took over the school.

A MODERN VIEW of St. Mary's College campus at Winona shows the results of an extensive building program carried out during the 1950s and 1960s.

A YOUNG PRINT MAKER takes advantage of the excellent facilities at St. Mary's College.

College of St. Scholastica

THE CAMPUS of the College of St. Scholastica in a recent view of its site high above the city of Duluth and Lake Superior. Opened as a girls' school in 1912, the college became coeducational in 1969.

MOTHER Scholastica Kerst laid the academic foundations for the College of St. Scholastica.

MOTHER AGNES SOMERS, president of the college, 1924–42, earned the title "The Builder."

ST. SCHOLASTICA's coed musical group, "The Mod Minstrels," performing in 1971.

SOMERS RESIDENCE HALL opened in 1964 with the Commons Lounge on the second floor and a dining room seating five hundred students on the level below.

STUDENTS chatting in St. Scholastica's modern Science Hall, completed in 1969.

Concordia College in St. Paul

THEODORE H. C. BUENGER, first head of Concordia College in St. Paul.

WILLIAM A. POEHLER, Concordia's third president.

TOP: One of the four buildings formerly used as the state training school for boys and purchased in 1894 as the first permanent home of Concordia on Syndicate Avenue in St. Paul.

BELOW: A statue of Martin Luther with Luther Hall, built in 1925 as a dormitory, in the background.

ONE OF the newer buildings on Concordia's campus, the Edward L. Arndt Science Hall.

Bethel College

JOHN A. EDGREN, founder in 1884 of the seminary that became Bethel College.

THE SECOND building constructed at Bethel's campus on Snelling Avenue, St. Paul, completed in 1915.

BETHEL COLLEGE choir members embarking on a European tour in 1971.

FIRST PRESIDENT of Bethel, G. Arvid Hagstrom, who served from 1914 to 1941.

CAMPUS PASTOR Maurice Lawson speaking at chapel service in the old field house in St. Paul in 1970.

SHOWN UNDER CONSTRUCTION in 1972, Bethel's new suburban campus includes college and seminary complexes and housing for seminarians.

grams, especially those of the United States Armed Forces Institute in which 1,700,000 persons enrolled during the war years. Very little blanket college credit was granted to students who had merely donned a uniform, as had been the practice after World War I.[9]

The vanguard of discharged servicemen and women reached the nation's campuses in the latter part of 1945, but the movement attained almost overwhelming proportions in the autumn of 1946 and for two years thereafter. The apex for enrollments under the GI bills came in 1947, when over 1,120,000 veterans were attending American colleges and universities. By 1949 total enrollments in the country's institutions of higher learning exceeded 2,456,000 (1,728,000 men and 728,000 women), twice the number in attendance in 1940. Altogether nearly 3,000,000 persons, the last as late as 1959, received educational benefits under the two laws passed in 1943 and 1944. In Minnesota the situation was comparable to that for the United States as a whole. More than 48,500 students were registered in the state's accredited institutions of collegiate rank in the fall of 1946; nearly 26,000 of them were veterans, two-thirds of whom were enrolled in the University of Minnesota. The private colleges also attracted many former servicemen, as well as young people just out of high school. The sixteen institutions included in this volume had a combined enrollment of over 15,160 in the fall term of 1948; their highest prewar total had been about 8,970.[10]

To arrange for this expansion, to hire adequate staff, and in the face of inflation and a scarcity of building materials, to provide necessary physical plant were challenges of unprecedented proportions. They were met in what one university president called the ''greatest project in the history of higher education'' in this country. The federal government in 1946 made army and navy equipment available to colleges and universities on a no-cost lease basis as temporary housing for 300,000 veterans; concurrently priority allocations for emergency construction were issued, and materials, including textbooks, were given out. In September President Harry S Truman signed the Mead Bill, and Congress appropriated $75,000,000 to implement it. The Federal Works Agency was thereupon authorized to provide educational institutions having shortages for handling veterans with temporary facilities other than housing. With help such as this and by their own efforts, imagination, and simply overcrowding, the nation's colleges were able to meet the demand. Big enrollments did not ease financial pressures, however, since tuition payments covered only part of educational expenses, which between 1941 and 1947 had risen by as much as 52 per cent. Faculty salaries in the same interval had gone up only a little over 40 per cent. Yet teachers, administrators, and students, too, remember the late 1940s as an exciting, stimulating, and satisfying time to have labored in the field of higher education.[11]

An indication of the concerns common to the state's private institutions in this period can be gained by reading the minutes of the meetings of their joint association, the Minnesota Private College Council, now more active than in prewar days. The subjects discussed ranged from athletics through finances to teacher training. There was a definite feeling that the colleges should become more aggressive in their public relations approach — a recognition that their contributions and advantages were not sufficiently known and appreciated. Considerable worry was voiced over the authorization given Minnesota state teachers' colleges in 1946 to expand their offerings beyond those designed for future pedagogues and to award the B.A. degree. It was suggested that the council's member institutions enter the field of training elementary schoolteachers, a proposal that had merit in view of the serious shortage of such people in the country at a time when enrollments in elementary schools were on the rise. In 1949 the state legislature and the Minnesota Board of Education made provision for the addition of elementary education sequences in the liberal arts colleges, an action of importance to those institutions as their individual histories will disclose. That same year the council discussed a proposal to create a foundation for joint fund raising, an idea that would blossom into a major endeavor in a few short years.[12]

By 1950 the country's colleges again stood on the threshold of another crisis period. Enrollment of the war veterans, which in 1947 had brought $172,000,000 to the private institutions alone, was a mere shadow of its former self. The low birth rates of the 1930s were reducing the potential student reservoir. Costs in ten years had risen nearly 70 per cent; frogs used in biology laboratories had gone from $.72 to $2.25 a dozen, to use one minor example. And then in June, 1950, came conflict in Korea, and with it increased student attention to the Selective Service Acts of 1948 and 1951. Most eligible men, on the basis of class standing or a test score, were able to stay in college under deferment classification 2-S (created by presidential order in the spring of 1951), but the uncertainty of their future still exercised a disturbing effect. Enrollments in higher education nosed downward. In Minnesota in the fall of 1951 there was a 12 per cent decrease from the previous year, from 45,500 students to 39,660. Of the latter, the state's private colleges contributed about 12,700, or a little over one-third. A year later trends began to reverse; national enrollments reached 3,068,000 in the autumn of 1957, a 45 per cent rise in six years.[13]

Mid-century, however, witnessed the appearance or the coming of age of several organizations whose interest and support would be of great assistance to institutions of higher learning in Minnesota and elsewhere. Among these catalysts were the National Science Foundation (NSF), the Louis W. and Maud Hill Family Foundation, the Ford Foundation and its satellites, the Fund for the Advancement of Education and the Fund for Adult Education, both established in 1951. An independent agency of the federal government, NSF was created by an act of Congress on May 10, 1950, but its roots lay in the tremendous scientific developments of World War II and in the report by Vannevar Bush entitled *Science: The Endless Frontier*, which was published by the United States office of scientific research and development in 1945. Among NSF's many contributions to science have been the financing of summer institutes on college campuses, the awarding of fellowships, and support of faculty and student research projects — all of which greatly benefited individual Minnesota colleges. Between 1952 and 1967 the agency's budget grew from $1,500,000 to $121,000,000. The Hill philanthropic organization was begun in 1934 as the Lexington Foundation, Inc., by Louis W. Hill, Sr., son of the famous Empire Builder, James J. Hill; it was enlarged and given its present name in 1950 two years after its founder's death. Of particular significance to Minnesota's private colleges was the Hill Foundation's early encouragement of interinstitutional co-operation and its financing of curricular expansion and experimentation.[14]

In 1953 the Hill Foundation made a three-year grant of $150,000 to five Minnesota institutions — Carleton, Gustavus Adolphus, Hamline, Macalester, and St. Olaf — for a co-operative educational experiment. Under the program distinguished scholars visited the various campuses to lecture and work with the five faculties separately and in joint gatherings on solutions to common problems. The project met with such enthusiasm that it was continued for a second three-year period by a terminal Hill gift of $164,500. The foundation in 1953 also appropriated $113,800 to help four of the St. Paul colleges — Hamline, Macalester, St. Catherine, and St. Thomas — and the capital city's James Jerome Hill Reference Library develop an undergraduate joint area studies program and conduct experiments in interlibrary co-operation. Two faculty members from each college participated and received grants for summer study to prepare for their teaching assignments in the areas

of Russia, the Near East, and the Far East. This program proved so successful and attracted such wide attention that the foundation in 1956 and 1959 made supplemental grants for its continuance. Starting in 1957, the area sequences were presented over the Twin Cities educational television station KTCA-TV, also with Hill support. Early in the 1960s the cycle of offerings was expanded by the addition of African and Latin American studies. By 1970 the co-operative course was in its eighteenth year.[15]

Though educationally significant and forward-looking, these co-operative ventures only indirectly helped the colleges' financial difficulties. For some people the answer to that problem lay in government aid; for others, including many prominent businessmen, bankers, industrialists, and educators, such a solution posed the unpalatable threat of government control. They saw in the country's private liberal arts institutions a bulwark of freedom which must be preserved at all costs. Since gifts from individuals were no longer adequately supporting these colleges, the logical move was to seek help from business corporations. Despite its stake in the system of free enterprise, business had contributed little to higher education's current budgets. Taking the initiative in changing this situation was President Frank H. Sparks of Wabash College in Indiana, where several colleges by 1950 teamed together to solicit corporate money. The following year when a stockholder challenged the right of the A. P. Smith Manufacturing Company to make an unrestricted gift to Princeton University, the courts in New Jersey upheld the company's action, and the United States Supreme Court in 1953 dismissed an appeal in the case. The legality of corporate support of private education was firmly established.[16]

In Minnesota a favorable climate for the adoption of the Indiana plan was provided by a 1949 act of the legislature, which legalized corporate contributions to educational and charitable institutions. The Private College Council and various business leaders then set in motion activities which in 1951 resulted in the creation of the Minnesota College Fund Association, called since 1957 the Minnesota Private College Fund. Membership was restricted to the institutions comprising the council. The purpose of the association was to solicit funds for current, rather than capital, use; 60 per cent of undesignated gifts would be divided equally among the colleges, 40 per cent on the basis of enrollment. A donor could, of course, designate the institution to which his money would go. The combined operating budget of the association's fourteen members in 1951–52 was about $14,000,000. In that year twenty-one contributors gave slightly over $53,000 to the joint solicitation. By 1955–56 the total was more than $277,000 and the number of business donors nearly 240. The fund in 1969 secured approximately $851,300 from 742 separate sources. Up to that time, each of the original members had received sums ranging from a low of almost $415,000 to a high of $725,000. But beyond the monetary benefits, the fund had helped the colleges in other ways, drawing them into a close and friendly relationship and building a bridge of interest and understanding between them and the Minnesota business community.[17]

By the middle of the 1950s the publicity given to the plight of the private colleges and universities was showing dividends nationally and in Minnesota. The Eighty-third Congress authorized the release of $50,000,000 in new college housing loans for fiscal 1954 and withdrew the defense relationship previously needed for such transactions, thereby making many more institutions eligible. In 1955, with Carnegie and Ford foundation support and using examinations of the Educational Testing Service, the National Merit Scholarship program was launched. Its first group of 555 winners, over 60 per cent of whom had graduated in the top one-tenth of their high school classes, entered college in the fall of 1956. Less than a year earlier the Ford Foundation had announced its magnificent gift of $640,000,000 to the endowments of the country's private institutions of higher learning. Minnesota's accredited colleges each received grants ranging in size from $105,500 to $647,500. The money was to be kept intact for ten years, and its income used for the improvement of faculty salaries, most of which were disgracefully low. Gifts from businesses were mounting, and many companies were setting up their own scholarship programs. Increasingly courted by their alma maters, alumni too were assuming growing responsibility for the welfare of the institutions they had attended. Minnesota's then fourteen private, four-year, liberal arts colleges, for example, during the seven years ending in 1956 had seen alumni annual giving go from $48,000 to $360,000. In the country at large there were 352 alumni funds in existence in 1954.[18]

But with enrollments rising and even greater increases in attendance looming, colleges were scarcely in a strong position. Again they faced a shortage of funds, facilities, and teachers. According to the 1954 *Economic Report of the President*, the nation's institutions of higher learning were $6,000,000,000 behind in their building programs; as much additional floor space would be needed in the succeeding fifteen years as had been constructed in the previous three hundred. The President's Committee on Education Beyond the High School,

appointed in the spring of 1956, painted the same dismal picture. The resources of colleges and universities, declared the committee, "are already strained, their quality standards are even now in jeopardy, and their projected plans fall far short of the indicated need."[19]

The early overcoming of these weaknesses would have constituted a monumental achievement under favorable circumstances, but such an environment hardly obtained in the mid-1950s. By then Americans had suffered a series of stunning blows — the closing of the Iron Curtain in Eastern Europe, the rise of communist China, the costly and frustrating war in Korea, and the excesses and divisiveness of McCarthyism. Such developments as urbanization, the spread of television, and jet transportation had altered old patterns and presented new questions. Meanwhile the whole educational system, especially the secondary schools, had come under growing attack. Part of the assault emanated from McCarthyites and self-appointed guardians of public morality; the remainder derived from individuals and groups seriously concerned about the lack of intellectual content in school curriculums and the resultant waste of national brain power. The crowning blow came in October, 1957, when the Russians launched the satellite Sputnik. Old doubts and fears then took on added urgency. Was the American system really best? Would the Russians bury us as Khrushchev predicted? Such questions provoked many a long look and a great deal of introspection.[20]

In addition to seeking new faculty, processing more and more applications for admission, and erecting buildings, institutions of higher learning now had also to place new emphasis on the pursuit of excellence — a phrase much in use at the time. Howard Mumford Jones sounded the alarm for the future, declaring that "we must begin to put away our pretty toys and insist that literature, art, science, and philosophy are not the mere subject of lessons dutifully to be got, but weapons to master for survival in this great critical period of human history." All along the line from grade school to college the attack on low standards of scholarship was waged. High grades and test scores became the *summum bonum*, the study of mathematics and science almost a patriotic duty. In time a reaction would set in, but that lay in the future.[21]

Out of these events and others, such as the knowledge and population explosions, arose a whole new era in the history of higher education in the United States. Among its prominent characteristics were burgeoning enrollments, vast expansion of physical plants, a golden age of fund raising, growing government support of the learning enterprise, curricular and calendar modifications, continued financial squeezes, the creation of new patterns on Catholic campuses, greater intercollege co-operation, the erosion of traditional practices and rules, the rise of the student activist, and a broadened base of institutional governance. Periodically during this flux the perennial question, "Will the college of arts and sciences survive?" kept cropping up. Indeed this query formed the theme of the 1960 meeting of the Association of American Colleges. A decade later the final vote was still out, and the fight for survival went on.[22]

Total enrollments in higher education in the United States rose by almost 35 per cent between 1955 and 1960, reaching 3,610,000 (2,271,000 men, 1,339,000 women) or 22 per cent of the country's 18- to 24-year-olds. Slightly over two-fifths were attending private institutions (one-half had done so in 1950). From this base collegiate population moved steadily upward throughout the 1960s to a figure of nearly 8,000,000 in 1970. By then only slightly over one-fourth of these students were to be found in privately controlled colleges and universities. The Minnesota picture in general reflected that of the country as a whole. Full-time enrollments in higher education in the state in 1954 were 37,784; the number in 1970 was 124,752. In the former year the University of Minnesota on all its campuses accounted for 15,804 full-time students, the state colleges for 6,315, the junior colleges for 1,428, and the four-year private colleges for 13,935. By 1970 the university enrolled 44,700 on all its campuses; the state colleges 36,805, the junior colleges 17,426, and the sixteen accredited private colleges 24,533. All types of institutions had shown marked growth, but that of the publicly supported schools had been most impressive. The reasons for this differential were many and complex. One was the establishment of additional public institutions scattered through the state, making colleges more accessible. Another was the higher tuition charges at private colleges.[23]

Although serving a decreasing proportion of Minnesota's collegians, the private liberal arts institutions in 1970 were educating 10,000 more students than they had enrolled a decade and a half earlier. To care for this great increase the colleges since 1950 had greatly expanded their physical plants, frequently with structures which were not only functional but also exciting aesthetically. The magnitude of this construction is high lighted by one study, which, though embracing several schools not included in this volume, tells the story in its essentials. Of all the buildings on the state's private campuses in 1970, slightly over 46 per cent had been erected within the preceding twenty years, 29 per cent of them since 1960. The largest amount of new space had gone into dormitories, the second greatest into classroom facilities. In 1960–61 the average cost per square foot had been $15.57; the figure in 1969–70 was $30.37. Of the funds needed to pay for the additions of the 1960s, 58 per cent had come from private sources — churches, foundations, alumni, business concerns, friends — and the rest from federal grants and loans.[24]

This rather amazing ratio clearly underscored the growing dependence of private colleges on support from the national government — a circumstance, among others, which has caused the line dividing them from public institutions to become increasingly indistinct. Federal involvement in education, of course, was not new — witness the GI bills — but the size and form of the contribution was different. The government in Washington, D.C., by 1965 was the largest single source of funds for higher education. What this phenomenon will mean to the nation's colleges and universities or how long it will continue cannot as yet be fully assessed. Some commentators equate its impact in the 1960s with that of the Morrill Land Grant Act of 1862 and government-supported research during World War II. Certainly the climate in academe has changed. Where once educators feared that federal aid would lead to the loss of their freedom, they now are afraid that the absence of such assistance in massive doses will presage their demise.[25]

In the mid-1950s the private colleges were only modestly affected by the federal government. Then Congress enacted the now famous National Defense Education Act (NDEA) of 1958, the first time that legislative body had endorsed the principle of federal contributions toward general education. Originally limited to four years, the act has thus far been continuously extended. Under its provisions government dollars were granted to colleges and universities for long-term loans to students, the maximum for undergraduates being $1,000 a year and a total of $5,000. The federal contribution to the lending funds was eight-ninths of the whole, that of the educational institutions one-ninth. For years students had been reluctant to borrow money for college expenses. Henceforth it became increasingly routine for institutions to insist that financial aid packages be split three ways — loans, scholarships, and work. Some inequities resulted, but by 1963 over 1,500 of the country's colleges and universities had negotiated about $360,000,000 of loans to 400,000 students. In Minnesota federal loans to private college undergraduates rose from $740,400 in 1960–61 to $2,170,000 in 1969–70.[26]

The next major piece of national legislation was the Higher Education Facilities Act of December, 1963; it authorized the appropriation of $1,950,000,000 over the first three years of a five-year program of grants and loans to public and private institutions for the construction of academic facilities. The money would be allocated to the states, which in turn would channel it through commissions to its final destination. The grants were not to exceed one-third of the cost of the projects financed, and the latter were to provide for increased enrollments. Under the loan section of the law, at least 25 per cent of a project helped had to be financed from nonfederal funds. Between December, 1964, and August, 1969 (when the federal funding was not renewed) more than $10,500,000 was allocated to help finance 25 projects in Minnesota's four-year private colleges; this represented almost 40 per cent of all the money allowed the state's four-year institutions under the Facilities Act. In 1964 Congress passed the Economic Opportunity Act, which allotted money to the states to stimulate the part-time employment of students, particularly those from low-income families. The work assigned could be either for the educational institution or for a public or private nonprofit organization. Between 1966 and 1968 over $367,000,000 was appropriated by Congress for this work-study program.[27]

The Higher Education Act of 1965 embraced and modified many of the provisions of the earlier laws and added a few touches of its own. It was the first federal statute to incorporate the design for student aid — the combination of grant, loan, and work — which had become usual in high tuition private colleges; it also extended the 1958 loan system to 1971. In addition the 1965 act started the first large-scale, federal undergraduate scholarship program — the "educational opportunity grants" — expanded work-study support, established a plan of federally guaranteed loans to students, aided developing institutions to set up co-operative arrangements, provided loans for the construction of academic facilities, and made money available for the purchase of equipment and the training of teachers in the use of audio-visual aids. Other laws have followed, including a 1966 GI bill, the Veterans' Readjustment Benefits Act, but the emphasis thereafter shifted noticeably at the federal level from helping institutions to assisting individuals.[28]

At the state level government support of the private colleges in the form of tax exemption dates back to the 1850s, but such aid as legislative grants and loans has encountered both philosophic and constitutional barriers. Even so many individuals and groups in Minnesota, recognizing the contributions of these institutions, have sought ways of strengthening them through governmental action. One example was provided by the governor's committee of 1956, chaired by Samuel C. Gale. Among its recommendations were the establishment of a state scholarship program and the creation of a Minnesota revolving fund to lend money to private colleges for plant additions. Nothing came of the latter proposal, but a scholarship bill was introduced in the 1959 legislature, where it died in committee. Groundwork had been laid for later action, however, and college people had gained experience in dealing with legislators. Actions in other states, growing public awareness of the need for similar programs locally, and the efforts of countless persons, induced the legislature in 1967 to appropriate the small sum of $250,000 for scholarships to be used in Minnesota higher educational institutions. Any high school senior in the state who ranked in the top quarter of his class was eligible to apply for these awards, which ranged from $200 to $800 according to the recipient's need. For 1969–70 the legislature provided $575,000 for continuance of the scholarship program and added $200,000 to be used for grants-in-aid to worthy young Minnesotans. In 1971 the Minnesota Higher Education Coordinating Commission was designated by the Minnesota legislature as the agency through which payments of up to $500 per student were channeled to private colleges for educating Minnesota residents.[29]

Neither state nor federal action by 1970, however, had given the country's private colleges a solid financial base on which to operate. Symptoms of their malaise in the form of annual deficits, swelling long-term indebtedness, and belt tightening gained almost as much attention in the popular press as campus disturbances. Institutional incomes had risen appreciably, but they had been outdistanced by expenditures. One study covering Minnesota's private four-year colleges listed their educational and general funds revenues in 1960–61 at $19,086,000; the total for 1968–69 was $47,356,000, a gain of 148 per cent in eight years. Concurrently their incomes from food services rose by nearly 90 per cent and from housing by 132 per cent. The largest share of current income derived from student tuition and fee charges; the former averaged $578 in 1960–61 (one institution charged $1,060) and $1,317 in 1969–70 (the highest then was $1,975). The average fee charge had risen from $44 to $89. Throughout the period, these two student payments provided approximately 62 per cent of the colleges' educational revenue; auxiliary enterprises contributed slightly over 26 per cent.[30]

Gifts constituted another significant source of income, and methods of attracting them took on all the accouterments of a specialized discipline. In many ways the new era of fund raising dated from the initiation in 1957 of Harvard College's campaign to secure $82,500,000 in three years. Thereafter one institution after another mounted its own special drive, which a writer in the *Saturday Review* characterized as "an epic creation tangible to the touch, glorious to the eye, compelling to the will." College development offices were paneled and enlarged, and the services of outside consultants were employed. No possibilities for tapping pocketbooks, from life-income plans to provisions in wills, were overlooked. In September, 1960, the whole movement, including that in Minnesota, received a powerful stimulant when the Ford Foundation committed $252,000,000 to a dozen universities and fifty-seven colleges if they would raise $654,000,000 from nongovernment sources; nearly a billion dollars went into higher education from this one program. By 1967, however, charitable organizations were shifting their attention to the problems of poverty at home and to those of underdeveloped countries abroad. McGeorge Bundy then wrote: "There is no solution to the problems of the private colleges and universities in simply giving away the Ford Foundation." In his opinion the average alumnus and the nation's rich should give far more money to education than they had been contributing.[31]

Statistics would seem to bear out this contention. One study showed that, whereas alumni donated $68,000,000 to their colleges in 1954 and $266,000,000 in 1965–66, over 75 per cent of the former students who were solicited gave nothing. The average corporation gift in 1966 was only 0.37 per cent of net income before taxes, and the $1,500,000,000 total given to higher education in the United States by all nongovernment sources that year represented only one-fourth of one per cent of the $630,000,000,000 earned in personal income. Obviously the potential was great; the problem was to convince people of the need and the worth of the cause. In Minnesota the fifteen colleges which were members of the Private College Fund in 1968–69 received $18,800,000 in total gifts, $10,800,000 of it for capital purposes. These were sizable sums, but they averaged only a little over $1,254,000 per institution. Much more was needed.[32]

The story of expenditures measures the magnitude of that need; all categories of outlay grew absolutely and also at an increasing rate. In 1960–61 Minnesota's private four-year colleges and universities had current fund expenditures of $27,860,000; by 1968–69 the amount was up to almost $69,000,000, an increase of more than 147 per cent. In the former year these institutions administered $2,320,000 in student loans, grants, and scholarships; in 1969–70 the total was almost $11,000,000. Over $4,500,000 of the latter amount came from the colleges themselves; the state of Minnesota provided about $313,000 and the federal government in excess of $3,800,000. Private noncollege sources accounted for over $2,000,000. When all these expenditures plus those for capital purposes are taken into consideration, it comes as no surprise that the number of institutions showing annual deficits was increasing and that long-term indebtedness was mounting. One study found that long-term indebtedness in 1960–61 was equal to more than 12 per cent of the total assets of the state's private colleges and universities; in 1968–69 the proportion was more than 18 per cent. There is great variation in the financial resources of these institutions, and in general they are not so hard pressed for support as some of their private counterparts in other states. Yet clouds on the horizon are in evidence. Unless Minnesota's independent and church-related colleges — large and small — receive more help, they appear to be on a collision course with financial crisis.[33]

One can only hope that such a costly eventuality can be prevented in good season, for the arguments in support of maintaining a healthy private sector in higher education — greater flexibility for innovation and experimentation, a stimulating diversity, decreased pressure to respond to a low common denominator — still retain validity. There have been times in the past when their own slowness to accept change and their lack of originality rendered many small colleges increasingly unresponsive to the needs of society, but the dozen years between Sputnik and 1970 scarcely constituted such an era.[34]

No decade in the history of higher learning has been so analyzed, dissected, and described as that of the 1960s. Carleton's Dr. Nason saw it in retrospect as "a disturbing, dangerous, exciting and potentially creative period," an assessment not difficult to defend. Nor has so much controversy ever centered around higher education and the college community. There was some tendency, at least in the popular media, to focus on the students, often in an unflattering way. They were called by many names, but they have not been castigated as "silent," as the students of the 1950s often were. They were described as irresponsible, unruly, egocentric, unclean, glib, and immoral, among other adjectives. They were also described as socially concerned, sensitive, creative, ruthlessly honest, and searching for their own truths, paths, and life styles. In either view they posed a challenge — some would say a threat — to an older generation's established traditions, mores, and codes.[35]

But if the popular media tended to emphasize the more newsworthy, bizarre, and destructive behavior of some elements of the student population on such campuses as Berkeley, Columbia, and Wisconsin between 1964 and 1970, other observers were also taking a look at what the students were protesting. Joseph Katz and Nevitt Sanford of the Institute for the Study of Human Problems at Stanford University wrote in 1965: "In the Berkeley events we are dealing with an entirely new phenomenon: students asking a voice and a vote in the determination of their own education. It is fair to say that we have here not a revolt, but a revolution." They suggest some of the causes of this revolution were: adolescence itself — "a time when we can expect major attacks upon the established order"; higher birth rates which resulted in increased pressure for admission to colleges and thus greater selectivity in enrolling students; and greater specialization in higher education, "mostly untied to anything in the student's experience" and to him "meaningless labor." As Louis T. Benezet pointed out in 1961, if the post-Sputnik era sent colleges in search of excellence, there was a reverse side to that coin: the emphasis on excellence made it easier for a professor to "create students in his own image." [36]

Depersonalization on campuses was another cause for the upheavals. So was the decline of *in loco parentis*. While the positive and nurturing attention to student needs was largely neglected, the constraint and punishment functions remained. With such support gone, students began to demand their rights, and in the midst of change it is often hard to separate cause from effect. A good example is the civil rights movement of the 1950s and 1960s — the most dramatic early student movement and one often cited as the beginning of student activism. Campus tutorial programs in which students assisted underprivileged children not only gave the undergraduate insight into another aspect of the world in which he lived, but forced him to devise new approaches to teaching that had not been part of his own learning experience. So did the Peace Corps in the 1960s.[37]

Later in the 1960s the Vietnam War became a major issue in American society as well as on college campuses, and the ecology movement also attracted great awareness and activity. The voting age was lowered by Congress to eighteen in 1971, allowing vast numbers of young people to take part in the political process. In short, a whole realm of relevant social action was opened. All "these non-college activities . . . unwittingly" helped students "develop a sense of their own usefulness," said Katz and Sanford. "Far from presenting a threat, these students actually represent to college authorities a unique opportunity." Students have become interested in the process of education, they "are *asking* to be educated. . . . our generation has the opportunity of discovering and bringing to fruition a system of education that is based upon the consent of the educated." [38]

Although the larger colleges and "multiversities," as they have been labeled, dominated the headlines and came under the greatest scrutiny and attack in this period, probably none of the smaller private colleges totally escaped the effects of societal and student pressures for change in the 1960s. In some of Minnesota's smaller private and Christian-oriented colleges, the degree of change has varied. Yet challenged by the demands of better prepared students coming to them from the secondary schools and stung by criticism directed their way, all of the colleges throughout the 1960s restlessly searched for improvement, engaged in penetrating institutional introspection, and adopted new patterns which the college community of administration, faculty, students, and alumni hoped would combine the best of the past with the advantages of more modern programs. A rethinking of institutional aims and objectives was reflected in annual reports, college catalogs, and the proliferation of self-studies. Considerable diversity existed in Minnesota's colleges, but many common threads were also observable. Each institution struggled to define its identity, and to learn how best to turn out students prepared to live wisely and well in the years ahead. In the process courses were added and others were dropped, calendars were revised and experimental programs put into effect. Nonetheless in 1970 each college offered about the same number of major sequences that had been taught in 1960. Many occupationally oriented majors — elementary education, health and physical education, speech and theater — were adopted, but always with the insistence that they include a strong core of liberal arts work. Indeed a reaffirmation of faith in the liberal arts and increased concentration on the awarding of only the B.A. degree have been marked tendencies from 1960 onward.[39]

Though maintaining their distinctive identities and following no single formula, the colleges in their quest for greater effectiveness also reflected certain similarities. One involved a reconsideration of the strengths and weaknesses of the traditional two-semester and three-quarter calendars. As early as the fall of 1959, the University of Pittsburgh adopted a trimester system based on three fifteen-week terms. A year or two later considerable publicity surrounded Kalamazoo and Antioch colleges' experimental plans, both of which attempted to solve problems posed by rising costs and mounting enrollments. Kalamazoo provided four, eleven-week quarters in each of which a student took three courses. Antioch adopted a similar system in 1961, combined with an existing alternate work-study program. All of these schedules permitted more students to be served without the addition of new dormitory or classroom space, thereby silencing critics who pointed to the long periods in each year when many academic plants lay virtually idle. In 1961 Carleton forsook the two-semester system for one based on three terms, in each of which three courses constituted a normal student load. Two years later Macalester and Gustavus Adolphus became two of the first institutions in the country to choose the four-one-four system, two semesters separated by a January interim term. Four courses were normally carried during the semesters and one during the interim. Other Minnesota colleges altered their calendars; the most frequent change by 1970 was the shift to four-one-four.[40]

Among other academic developments of recent years, at least three call for special mention. One has been increased student travel and study abroad, either as individuals or as part of a college program. At least 120 foreign study programs were being sponsored by four-year accredited American colleges by 1964. Some persons may have had doubts about the virtues of these projects, but contacts with different cultures have given students the opportunity to develop their own resources to cope with these differences. Vast numbers of students from the United States have been gaining firsthand acquaintance with far-flung areas of the world. Conversely foreign students were flocking to institutions in this country; about 75,000 did so in 1963–64 alone. A second perhaps partly concomitant development was the growing attention to non-Western studies, fields of interest traditionally neglected by American colleges and universities. Only thirty Ph.D.s specializing in the Middle East, for example, were trained in the United States in the decade following 1952. One report suggested that of all undergraduates in the country in 1962, no more than 10 per cent were taking courses with an international dimension. Minnesota colleges have striven mightily to correct this imbalance.[41]

A third development, reflecting conditions in society at large as well as throughout higher education, was the search for programs possessing the values denoted by that overworked term, relevance. Thus, growing numbers of colleges added Black studies, urban studies, ecology courses, and interdisciplinary courses in minority cultures. While these efforts also attracted their critics, they represented sincere efforts to keep the colleges flexible, alive, responsive, and of service to mankind.[42]

In the rethinking of the aims, objectives, methods, and techniques of the entire higher educational system, it began to occur to some that exposure to the educational pressure cooker did not always serve the best interests either of individuals who were not planning to enter a profession or of society at large. Moreover, the nation's minority groups had long been largely excluded from the ivied walls of most colleges and universities. In Minnesota in the mid-1960s, where almost 98 per cent of the population of 3,524,000 was white, 35,000 were Negro, and 38,000 Indian, the race problem may have seemed relatively remote from the ivory tower, but in actuality it was perched at the college gates. With their religious concern and sense of social service, the state's private colleges could scarcely remain aloof from the growing efforts to help the disadvantaged and to make equal opportunities for all Americans more than an empty phrase — nor did the institutions wish to do so.[43]

The movement had its share of setbacks but progress was made in numbers enrolled, in adjustments, and in understanding. In the fall of 1967 Carleton and Gustavus Adolphus each had nearly 40 American Black students, Macalester had 25 to 30, St. Thomas and Augsburg about 18 each, and the other private colleges somewhat fewer. Two years later over 500 Blacks, 38 American Indians, 36 Americans with Spanish surnames, and a sizable number of other economically disadvantaged young people were attending these institutions. But despite the fact that 40 per cent of the country's eighteen- to twenty-one-year-olds were in college in 1969, the proportion for Blacks was half that of whites, and the ratio for Indians and other minorities was even lower.[44]

To broaden opportunities in other directions, the private colleges expanded co-operative programs begun earlier and felt their way into the relatively uncharted area of joint endeavor with public institutions. Across state borders, Carleton, St. Olaf, and later Macalester combined with eight similar colleges in 1958 to form the Associated Colleges of the Midwest (ACM) through which to conduct an array of research and study programs. In the fall of 1965 the Central States College Association came into being; Gustavus Adolphus and St. John's became members of this organization. How far such developments will go, only the future can disclose. Certainly joints efforts offer advantages, but they also have shortcomings in a certain loss of local institutional identity, control, and initiative, new demands on the resources of members, and additional paper work, among others.[45]

Major responsibility for the success of any program or technique or of a college itself resides in the faculty. Since types in this protean group usually range from the devoted and self-effacing Mr. Chips to the brash and opinionated critic, the teacher defies description except in the most general and statistical terms. Throughout the greater part of the period after Sputnik, he was in short supply, especially if he possessed a Ph.D. About 10,000 of these degrees were granted in the country in 1960, and the number was up to 15,500 five years later; not all of the recipients entered teaching, of course, and even if they had, many more could have been used. The process of attaining a Ph.D. had been described by four graduate school deans in 1957 as "tortuously slow and riddled with needless uncertainties." Relatively few changes have since been effected. Consequently many small colleges with limited funds in the 1960s found themselves at a great disadvantage in the bidding for new faculty members with doctorates. And when such instructors were secured, they frequently needed in-service training in teaching and in appreciation of the traditions and problems of small colleges — subjects neglected in the majority of graduate programs.[46]

One study covering more than 75 per cent of Minnesota's private colleges and universities mustered a quantity of material concerning their faculties between 1960 and 1970. The number of full-time teachers rose from 963 to 1,347, that of part-time instructors from 120 to 238. Since enrollments showed a greater proportional increase, the institutions varied considerably in their student-faculty ratios; the median in 1969 was 15.1 to one. All told, Minnesota's faculty members produced 118 books — 87 of them by teachers in only three of the institutions, all of which had relatively low student-faculty ratios. About one teacher out of nine had published an article in his field in 1968–69.[47]

The great majority of faculty members had received their highest degrees from institutions in the central states, with Minnesota leading by a large margin. Average salaries for a full professor had gone from $7,500 to $13,470 in ten years, but the range in 1969 was from $8,585 to $20,730, a far greater spread than had existed nine years earlier. The average for instructors had risen from $5,300 to $8,250. Fringe benefits approximated 10 per cent for the three highest ranks in 1969–70. Great variation also existed among institutions in their leave of absence programs and in the amount of money

allowed staff to attend professional meetings. About 10 per cent of the full-time faculty left their colleges for other positions or pursuits each year. The greatest impediment to retention and to hiring had been relatively low salaries and fringe benefits. All colleges, however, had tried valiantly to improve their competitive positions in these matters.[48]

For Minnesota's seven Catholic colleges — beset by problems peculiar to themselves plus those of a general nature — the effort had been far from easy. Enrollments in the denomination's institutions of higher learning in the United States had swelled between 1940 and 1968 from 103,000 to 433,690, representing a gain of 60 per cent in just ten years. A similar rise, however, had not taken place in vocations for the priesthood or in the memberships of religious orders and congregations. Since clergy and religious had constituted the traditional source of faculties for Catholic colleges and universities, a shortage of these men and women made it necessary for the institutions to employ growing numbers of lay teachers. The larger the lay staff became, the greater was the chance for loss of the distinctive campus atmosphere which provided Catholic colleges with their main *raison d'être*. Furthermore, these institutions had relied heavily for their financial well-being on the contributed services of religious teachers and administrators and upon help from their controlling organizations. Now as time passed, increasing amounts of money — which could be used for other purposes — had to be channeled into salaries for lay faculty. And beyond monetary effects lay the potentials for morale problems whenever the religious were in a minority but still in control of the top administrative offices.[49]

Catholic colleges also suffered other disadvantages. Founded to train future clergy and religious and to help immigrant minorities adjust to American life, especially to its economic aspects, these institutions had tended to be insulated and to suffer from inferiority complexes. A combination of their own modesty and ineptness in public relations, along with external bigotry and the caustic comments of their critics, had prevented the colleges from making generally known their very real contributions to American society and to the world of learning. When these obstacles had been largely overcome, the institutions in the late 1960s were caught up in the incipient revolution which followed Vatican Council II. Many reforms in the church, in liturgy, parish life, and the role of the laity resulted from actions taken at that memorable meeting in 1962. They also had a tremendously upsetting impact on thousands of Catholic priests, religious, and laymen, and this effect in turn was clearly manifested in the colleges.

Their sponsoring religious orders suffered internal strains and their teaching members personal identity crises. Laymen began to dominate collegiate boards of trustees formerly composed solely or mainly of religious and to be appointed for the first time to presidencies and deanships. This trend toward laicization and a concomitant one toward professionalization had virtues, but often at the expense of traditional practices of fond memory. Denominational educators hope that out of current travail something better will emerge, that these colleges can continue to be intellectually first rate and still "distinctively Catholic." Should they become indistinguishable from purely secular institutions, society and the academic world will be diminished.[50]

Among all Minnesota institutions, only part of the revolution was in calendar and curriculum modification. Other evidences of a break with the past were to be found in the discontinuance of traditional rules concerning student living patterns and the relationships between the sexes, in de-emphasis of the college's position *in loco parentis*, and in greater freedom for students in regulating their lives. "A revolution in defining and institutionalizing the civil liberties of college students seems to have come about quietly in the last twenty years, and significant extensions of these freedoms are being explored not so quietly today," wrote educational consultant and author Gene R. Hawes in 1966. Two major, respected organizations issued official declarations on the subject. In the spring of 1966 the American Civil Liberties Union (ACLU) released a pamphlet of recommended principles on "Academic Freedom and Civil Liberties of Students in Colleges and Universities." The winter issue of the quarterly *AAUP Bulletin* presented that organization's "Statement on the Academic Freedom of Students." In large measure the same viewpoints differently phrased and organized were expressed in both declarations. Both statements stressed that each student right entailed a corresponding obligation for its responsible exercise, and both offered many further detailed explanations.[51]

In the ACLU's judgment, two basic beliefs underlie the freedoms it advocated. One was that students were most likely to mature as citizens if they had the same rights and responsibilities as adults while in college. The second was that "a college that wants respect for practicing open-minded inquiry in its teaching and research defeats this purpose if it denies free inquiry outside the classroom." Similarly, the AAUP reasoned that "free inquiry and expression are essential attributes of the community of scholars" and that "the responsibility to secure and to respect general conditions conducive to the freedom to learn is shared by all members of the academic community." Hawes concluded his article with the opinion that college presidents and deans had before them a difficult task: "to win the respect of — to educate, in the best sense — activist students who are shaken and searching; and to lead what the ACLU sees as the 'truly independent college,' one which will meet public criticism 'not by modifying its policy, but by redoubling its efforts to persuade its constituencies that freedom is an important means toward its educational goals.'"[52]

Minnesota's colleges, with their variety of traditions, backgrounds, and collective experiences, have reacted diversely to such recommendations. Some small, highly conservative colleges which tended to attract conservative young people seemed to effect few changes. Others adopted more dramatic and radical changes that were unsettling to conservative and skeptical faculty members, administrators, and community members outside the gates. In varying degrees, institutions more clearly delineated undergraduate rights and gave greater concern to the guarantees of due process of law in the handling of disciplinary cases. Finally came more formal inclusion of students in the process of college policy making and of administration, ranging from placing them on most campus committees to admitting them to regular meetings of the faculty and of the board of trustees. The effects of this recent metamorphosis in institutional governance and traditions have evoked a variety of responses.[53]

The controversy goes far beyond the scope of this history. There is, in any case, a plenitude of information and opinion in various magazines, journals, and books by observers, critics, educators, and other authorities, whose views run the gamut from staunch conservatives who firmly believe that the downfall of higher education began with coeducation, to those who firmly believe that there has been more rhetoric than real change, to those who have already adopted a new and unstructured (sometimes communal) approach to learning, to those for whom ignorance is bliss.

No one, of course, can predict what curricular, calendar, course, and structural modifications will take place in the future, nor is it possible to predict the precise reforms, attitudes, behavior, and activities of coming generations. About all that can be predicted with certainty is continued change in a continuously changing society. The pages of this history of Minnesota's private colleges sketch the broad outlines of these institutions' responses to events of the past and give reason for hope in the future. If difficulties, disorders, and uncertainties have taken their toll — and they have — there have also been many optimistic signs. On various campuses many people are attempting to make learning more exciting, more meaningful, more related to students' known and anticipated experiences, to listen to divergent voices — even the unpopular ones — to humanize impersonal relationships and procedures, to safeguard the dignity and rights and develop the potential of all individuals. If greater stress is placed on these positive aspects of higher education, if all concerned with the college communities will think more in terms of the true meaning and purpose of higher education, there is every reason to see a brighter day ahead. The private colleges in Minnesota and in other states, with all of their imperfections, have made a vast and special contribution to society. That society will be neither so strong nor so rich in texture if a robust system of private higher education no longer exists to stimulate and to supplement publicly controlled and supported colleges and universities.

Rededication to The Liberal Arts

EXCEPT FOR THE DRAMATIC REDUCTION in the number of civilian male students and the establishment of a summer session in 1942, World War II made no really fundamental changes at Hamline. Many students and alumni served in the armed forces and thirty-one lost their lives, but the government did not take over buildings on the campus as it had during World War I. No startling curricular changes were made during this period, although Hamline offered such special courses vital to the war effort as civilian pilot training, basic training for engineers, occupational therapy, and X-ray technology. In 1942–43 a school of fine arts incorporating art, music, speech, dramatics, and the Little Theater was set up with the distinguished Austrian conductor and composer, Ernst Krenek, as dean. Admittedly an anomaly, the school did not survive Krenek's departure in 1948, when the traditional departmental organization was resumed. Both during and after the school's existence, however, the arts received increased attention on the campus.[1]

Indeed on all fronts preparations were under way for continued improvement. Nearly a year before World War II ended in 1945, a campaign was started to raise $900,000, $10,000 for each year of Hamline's life. A few months later Charles M. Drew of Minneapolis, a benefactor since the early 1930s, died and left over $3,000,000 to the institution, the largest single gift in its history. By early 1946 some 660 alumni had given over $87,000 to the fund drive. Thus it became possible to carry out parts of the building program, which had been announced as early as the 1920s, and provide facilities for the swelling postwar enrollment. Manor House acquired a new wing in 1947 and thereby provided quarters for 175 women. That much-converted and faithful friend, Goheen Hall, again was called into play as a residence for forty-nine freshman coeds.[2]

With male enrollment mounting as men returned from war, still more living space was needed. The familiar veterans' village appeared and former fraternity houses bulged with ex-servicemen. A long-overdue men's dormitory could be delayed no longer. Happily the college was now in a position to undertake construction. Drew Residence was finished in mid-1947 with space for 175 men and a fine, modern cafeteria. That autumn the Little Theater, after struggling along for seventeen years on the top floor of Science Hall, moved into a quonset that would form the first unit of a fine arts building. Completion of the other units followed in 1950. Rounding out the physical plant as Hamline approached its centennial was the $800,000 Drew Science Hall, dedicated in October, 1952. Its furnishings were purchased with a fund of $150,000 given by alumni.[3]

Accompanying the postwar flurry of activity in construction were curricular modifications. The foreign language requirement was made more flexible; courses were added in business administration; a series of commercial art courses was introduced; and the Mounds-Midway school of nursing dating back to 1906 was merged with the Hamline-Asbury School to form the Hamline University school of nursing, a three-year sequence. Although these actions attracted some fine students to the campus, they also reflected a trend toward vocationalism which was not uncommon at the time but which would cause some trouble later.[4]

While this process was under way, President Pace resigned in 1948 after fourteen years of capable service. His successor was Hurst R. Anderson, an Ohio Wesleyan graduate who had taught during the 1930s and 1940s at Allegheny College in Pennsylvania and served as president of Centenary Junior College in New Jersey. Youthful, confident, and energetic, he would stay at Hamline for only four years — a time filled with promise and with disappointment. Once more an attempt was made to secure a chapter of Phi Beta Kappa; once again it failed. The recent tendency toward vocationalism and the weakness of enrollment in foreign language study were the shoals upon which the petition foundered. Another problem stemmed from President Anderson's overestimation of the impact which the Korean conflict would have on male enrollment and his hasty decision to curtail faculty for the fall of 1951. When the expected decline in male registration did not materialize, the main legacy was a deterioration in Anderson's relations with the faculty.[5]

Still there were gains. Hamline co-operated in the Student Project for Amity Among Nations (SPAN) under which students received credit for supervised independent study abroad, and in the Washington Semester plan which gave them credit for courses taken at American University in Washington, D.C. In 1952 the institution was also among the Minnesota colleges benefiting from the two significant projects funded that year by the Louis W. and Maud Hill Family Foundation — the area studies program and the visiting scholar-lecturer arrangement with Carleton, Gustavus Adolphus, Macalester, and St. Olaf. Another valuable undertaking, initiated at Hamline in 1952 with support from the Maurice and Laura Falk Foundation of Pittsburgh, gave students an opportunity to participate in and observe political campaigns. On campus, through the efforts of the faculty educational policy committee, a new general curriculum in which electives and required courses were spread over five academic divisions was inaugurated in 1950. That same year the education department offered a sequence leading to the master of education degree. Shortly thereafter work to prepare students for elementary schoolteaching was introduced.[6]

During the interim between Anderson's departure in 1952 and the selection of his successor in 1953, Dr. Walter C. Coffey, chief executive of the University of Minnesota from 1941 to 1945, served as Hamline's acting president. A former dean and director of the state university's college of agriculture, Coffey was also president of Hamline's board of trustees. Under his temporary care was an institution whose plant was worth $4,000,000 and whose endowment had a market value of approximately $5,200,000.[7]

Dr. Paul H. Giddens, the twelfth president of Hamline, began his duties in March, 1953. A graduate of Simpson College in Iowa with a Ph.D. from that state's university, he had been on the faculty of Allegheny College since 1931; he was well known and highly regarded for his writings on the history of the American petroleum industry. His future tenure of a decade and a half at Hamline would see many interesting developments, but much of his attention at first was directed toward the past in preparation for celebrating Hamline's centennial. If David and Jabez Brooks, William Murray, and the other pioneers who had been responsible for the birth of the feeble academy at Red Wing could have been present a century later in 1954 to commemorate the event, they would have been both amazed and delighted. The educational centenarian had graduated over 4,500 students; its current undergraduate body topped the 1,200 mark, full- and part-time faculty totaled four score, and its annual budget was in excess of $1,500,000.[8]

Dr. Giddens later said that one reason he accepted the presidency was his belief "that Hamline had a potential that could be more fully developed." When he arrived on campus, the physical plant was in fairly good condition, but most other areas needed improvement. Hamline had no full-time admissions counselors to visit high schools and no events on campus to which potential students were invited. Faculty salaries were low, the top being $5,900. A system of sabbatical leaves was in effect, but money to make it operable was nonexistent. There were no funds for faculty travel and research projects. The curriculum with its emphasis on vocationalism still smacked of expediency at the expense of principle. Although sizable gifts had come to Hamline and operating deficits had not occurred since 1945, the institution had no development officer, no file on donations or wills, and no list for mailings. An alumni board existed, but it was small and inactive; there was as yet no full-time director of alumni activities and no alumni fund. Two-thirds of the students were commuters, and the image of the institution was too often that of a seminary, a basketball college, or a poor man's refuge. Many of these shortcomings were more the product of the times and historical development than of former administrative ineptness, but a change of direction was mandatory if Hamline were to realize the potential Giddens discerned.[9]

After assessing the over-all picture, President Giddens, with strong support from faculty and trustees, settled on four goals: (1) to do a few things and to do them well, (2) to emphasize the academic program, (3) to restore the balance in favor of the liberal arts, and (4) to enhance Hamline's academic reputation. The task was not easy, nor was reorientation accomplished without opposition. Illustrating the problems, two episodes stand out.[10]

During the second year of the new administration, Hamline's basketball team finished second in the MIAC, a situation some alumni regarded as intolerable for an institution that had dominated the sport for two decades. Demands for more zealous recruitment and greater financial assistance for athletes were insistent. Because of his refusal to accede, Giddens in 1955 was hung and burned in effigy in front of his home. The president, who was a former second string football player himself, did not favor the abolition of intercollegiate athletics. He did argue, however, for a broad and balanced program in which all sports received fair treatment and in which athletes were accorded financial aid in proportion to their need — the same as all other students. Out of the unpleasant affair emerged policies which subjected athletics to faculty control and which undoubtedly strengthened Hamline as a whole.[11]

The second episode occurred nearly a decade later and involved Hamline's relationship to the Minnesota Methodist Conference. Under the 1854 charter there were fifteeen trustees, four of whom were members of the church conference in whose borders the educational institution was located. In 1871 the size of the board was enlarged to twenty-one, but by the 1960s this number seemed to various people, including Giddens, to be too small. At the time he wrote: "In these crucial days a private college needs the skills, abilities, resources, and support of as many trustees as it can possibly command." Agreeing with this view, the Hamline trustees at a special meeting on May 23, 1963, voted to increase their number to thirty-two. Unfortunately this action was interpreted in the press and elsewhere as an attempt to eliminate the educational institution's relationship to the church, which it was not. Actually the latter never did own, operate, or directly control Hamline, though the conference did elect four trustees and seven "Conference Visitors." [12]

On June 13, 1963, when the proposal to enlarge the board was submitted to the annual conference meeting, the recommendation was referred without debate to a special committee for study and report a year hence. President Giddens, who had led the movement for enlargement and thereby incurred the opposition of some conference members, was defeated for re-election as a Hamline trustee. Fortunately, after study the plan to increase the number of trustees to twenty-eight was approved by the conference in 1964 with the stipulation that eleven trustees be conference members, four of whom were

ministers, and that the president and the Methodist bishop be members of the board ex officio. The conference approved further increases of four trustees in both 1965 and 1966, making a total of thirty-six trustees in all.[13]

Although Methodists occasionally assumed an undue proprietary role in relation to Hamline, they were also helpful. Throughout the institution's life, the largest group of its students have been followers of John Wesley, and the conference has been a steady provider of financial support. In 1953 about $23,000 was given by the church, but in 1959–60 when a fund drive for Hamline was under way, the amount rose to some $310,000. It remained more than $100,000 annually for a time after that, but as other demands on the conference increased, its total Hamline support declined to $80,000 in 1968. This is not a large proportion of a budget of almost $3,340,000. From 1897 to 1964 nearly one-third of all ministers admitted to the Minnesota Methodist Conference had attended Hamline which suggests the donation could have been larger. In addition, over a hundred graduates became pastors outside the state. Many other alumni, of course, no matter what their occupations, have been active in local congregations.[14]

During his fifteen years as president, Giddens achieved great success in realizing the goals he had outlined. As a former professor, he understandably regarded the faculty as the most important element in an educational institution, and in retrospect he liked to feel that his greatest contribution to Hamline was in upgrading its teaching staff. Every year salaries were given top priority in the budget, with the result that the mean annual faculty pay rose from $4,500 in 1954 to $10,990 in 1968. Fringe benefits were also made more attractive. The dormant sabbatical leave plan became operable; fourteen teachers received such leaves between 1955 and 1967. Funds were also set aside to pay travel expenses to professional meetings. In 1957 Hamline assumed payment of the total 10 per cent of faculty-staff salaries contributed to the Teachers Insurance and Annuity Association (TIAA) pension fund to which employees had previously paid 5 per cent and Hamline an equal amount.[15]

With quality a matter of primary concern, efforts were made in filling vacancies to secure people with earned doctorates; current faculty members without a Ph.D. were encouraged to complete it. The "publish or perish" syndrome did not obtain, but interest in research was commended and funds to facilitate projects were sought. In 1952–53 Hamline received $15,000 for educational research and equipment in the form of two grants. By 1965–66 the institution secured 22 separate grants providing a total of $225,000 — the largest amount received in a single year. Altogether between 1952 and 1966 Hamline received $629,140 in grants for research and equipment. Foundations provided $303,300 of this amount, the federal government $272,476, research organizations $31,720, corporations $21,013, and the church board $500. Of this, the largest amount of $324,000 went to the sciences, social studies were second with $240,340, and humanities and fine arts a poor third at $21,725. The remainder went to the library and miscellaneous projects. In the 1960s a faculty research seminar was formed in which researchers could report their findings. A faculty institutional relations committee helped avoid major internal dissension, and a faculty personnel committee assisted in maintaining a high level of teaching competence. Admittedly the hiring of professors was not always easy in the then increasingly competitive market, but during the Giddens years the number of full-time teachers grew from forty-one to seventy, and the proportion with earned doctorates rose from 39 per cent to over 48 per cent.[16]

Accompanying these developments was a gradual change in direction in curricular matters, a shift which involved considerable risk. The gamble was to drop many vocationally oriented courses and to concentrate mainly on those traditionally regarded as liberal arts. The school of nursing, for example, had been a popular and successful operation, which overshadowed other departments and attracted many good students. Of Hamline's 1,180 enrollees in 1953–54, for example, 413 were in nurses' training. Furthermore certain other programs such as secretarial studies tended to draw undergraduates for only two instead of four years. After much agonizing over the decision, nursing was discontinued in 1959 and secretarial studies in 1962, though the courses in both fields were continued long enough to permit those currently enrolled to complete their work. In another action students who sought to gain certification in elementary education were henceforth required to major in one of the regular academic departments. Foreign language study received increased emphasis, and such new majors as international relations (1958), American studies (1967), and an interdisciplinary sequence with anthropology as its core (1967) were approved.[17]

In the fall of 1963 the three-term calendar was adopted with three courses each term; four years later it was decided to award only the bachelor of arts degree. Giddens, remembering his own youth in isolationist-minded mid-America, felt strongly that Hamline should be as cosmopolitan as possible, a feeling shared by faculty and trustees. Programs already in existence which furthered this aim were supported and new ones were added. Between 1953 and 1966 fifty-seven Hamline undergraduates studied in twenty-six different countries under SPAN, and seventy-one other students from 1948 to 1967 were in the nation's capital as part of the Washington Semester program at American University. In 1962 Hamline became a participant in the United Nations Semester at Drew University in New Jersey, and in 1965 along with Macalester, Carleton, St. Thomas, and St. Catherine it took part in a faculty exchange with Black colleges in the South made possible by a Hill Foundation grant. Members of the teaching staff were encouraged to travel and study abroad, and 67 per cent of them did so between 1953 and 1966.[18]

Stimulated by the emphasis on an international dimension, the intercollege co-operative area study program for undergraduates prospered. The institution's doors also welcomed students from other lands. From 1956 when the drive to attract them was begun in earnest to 1968, more than a hundred foreign students from forty-four different countries were enrolled. In 1964 with support from the Hill Foundation, summer institutes in non-Western studies were inaugurated for faculty members from other institutions. During their first three summers, the institutes enrolled teachers from twenty-seven states and fifty-five institutions, including seven Black colleges. Considering these activities, it was understandable why the United States department of state selected Hamline's *a cappella* choir of forty members to tour Latin America as good will ambassadors in the spring of 1967.[19]

The push away from parochialism and the effort to elevate the quality of Hamline's intellectual life necessitated the recruiting of able young people from a wider geographical base. In 1954 the first full-time admissions director was employed, and an annual High School Day was scheduled to which potential applicants were invited. In 1957 Hamline was the first Midwest college to establish its own local competitive scholarship examinations. Within the first seven years of the program over 2,500 high school students had written the one-day test on campus and some $300,000 had been awarded the winners. Recruitment was extended to the eastern seaboard in 1960, and by 1966–67 Hamline was becoming better known nationally, although three-quarters of the student body still came from Minnesota. To offset rising costs, the amount awarded in student aid was increased from about $39,000 in current funds in 1953 to $183,300 in 1967 (or $305,000 if federal funds are included). Enrollment did not rise dramatically, going from 1,152 in 1952–53 to 1,205 in 1967.

In the former year, however, only 815 were regular liberal arts enrollees; most of the remainder were in nursing, which had not yet been discontinued.[20]

As the over-all scholastic aptitude of undergraduates increased, more stimulating intellectual programs — advanced placement, credit by examination, honors work, and independent study — were adopted to challenge the interest and curiosity of the students. Meanwhile notable progress was made in transforming the student body from a commuting to a residential group with a distinct and enriching community life. In 1958 Sorin Hall, named for Hamline's and the state's first two college graduates, was built at a cost of $747,800 to provide quarters for 116 students. At the same time $471,000 was spent on an addition to Drew Residence. Three years later a $50,000 remodeling job was done on the Manor House. With these new facilities and modifications plus the use of two score neighborhood houses, it was possible in 1962 to raise the number of resident students from 360 in 1953 to 843, or 70 per cent of the enrollment. On-campus living and the elimination of vocational courses also helped reduce attrition. Of freshmen enrolling from 1953 to 1956, 42 per cent graduated; the comparable figure for 1959 to 1962 was 49 per cent.[21]

A concomitant of this trend was growing student interest in graduate and professional study, heightened by the draft laws and the unpopularity of the Vietnam War as well as by economic and professional realities. Whereas only slightly over 15 per cent of the 1958 class went on to such advanced study, nearly 37 per cent of the 1967 class did so. Like others of their generation, these Hamline undergraduates were not backward in asserting what they regarded as their rights, but they staged no sit-ins and created no major campus blowups. Their relative conservatism, as well as the opportunity to sit with faculty and administration on committees, may have explained the absence of uprisings like those on the Berkeley campus in California. Students were admitted to faculty meetings in 1965 and to trustee meetings in 1969. Another factor was pride in the fact that Hamline was on the move. Strengthening this feeling was the addition of two buildings: the $1,350,000 A. G. Bush Student Center in 1963 and the Edyth Bush Theatre two years later. Both structures bear the names of a family which had been one of Hamline's chief benefactors.[22]

Near the end of his administration in 1967, President Giddens declared that "Getting money to run a college is the greatest problem of colleges today." In many ways it was always so, only of late the sums involved are larger. Hamline's 1953–54 budget ran to only ten typed pages; that of 1956–57, the first detailed and comprehensive one produced, consisted of sixty-seven pages. Current operating expense in 1953 was $986,000; in 1967 it was $3,400,000. Net book value of total resources in these two years was $8,700,000 and $17,340,000, respectively. Indebtedness early in 1968 stood at approximately $1,900,000, consisting of federal loans of $750,000 on Drew Residence and Sorin Hall, a $500,000 loan on the swimming pool in the student center, and a $650,000 loan to purchase property adjoining the campus.[23]

In the face of these and other statistics, the president found little surcease from financial concerns. To make Hamline better known and thereby to assist in fund raising, a public relations program was started in 1953 and a full-time director of the recently established news bureau was employed the following year. Except for alumni, only seventeen persons donated to the current and endowed funds in 1952–53, giving about $23,800. The campaign inaugurated in connection with the Hamline centennial in 1954 — the first broadly based appeal for money Hamline had conducted in thirty years — brought in over $1,000,000 by the summer of 1956. Of this amount, 809 alumni contributed roughly $122,000.[24]

An ongoing system of donations was required, and the Ford Foundation gift of $237,500 for the improvement of faculty salaries in December, 1955, provided Giddens with an excellent and appealing opportunity to challenge potential givers. Approaching the alumni association board of directors, he suggested that its members establish a fund to be used for the same purpose which would take as its initial goal the raising of a sum equal to the income from the Ford grant. The board approved the plan, thereby inaugurating "a new and significant development" in Hamline history. For the first year of 1956–57, $11,200 came in (more than the goal set) with 14 per cent of the alumni participating; ten years later the amount was up to $59,200, and the percentage to 29. By then gifts to the fund totaled $523,700.[25]

An added inducement to alumni giving came in 1958 when Trustee A. G. Bush offered an annual challenge gift, a gesture which brought $341,500 of alumni money to Hamline by 1968. All these fund-raising efforts increased annual gifts from an average of $329,600 between 1953 and 1956 to $726,000 between 1962 and 1966. Foundations and business firms, as well as the federal government, accounted for major segments of the largess, but individuals who were not former students also joined in the endeavor.[26]

When he retired in June, 1968, Giddens had reason to feel that through his efforts and those of his associates, Hamline had become "a first-class, private, residential, four-year liberal arts college," the main goal he had pointed to fifteen years earlier. The Giddens era will not be remembered as one of great "bricks and mortar" expansion, but rather as a time when emphasis was placed on making the academic program one of quality, exciting to teacher and student alike. In addition, however, attention had been paid to the old problem of site, to the possibility of moving to a less congested area. But early in 1966 it was decided once again to stay put. Expansion could be accommodated on the fifty-two properties adjoining the campus which had been purchased since 1953.[27]

Elected thirteenth president of Hamline was Richard P. Bailey, who had held a similar post from 1961 to 1968 at Northland College in Ashland, Wisconsin. At the latter institution, enrollment had doubled and ten buildings had gone up during Bailey's administration, achievements which gained the president a reputation as a builder and no doubt influenced his appointment to Hamline. His task, for the foreseeable future at least, would be to direct the largest development program in the institution's history, which had been in the planning stage for five years. Announced in December, 1968, the ambitious ten-year project included constructing thirteen buildings and more than doubling the current $10,000,000 endowment — a $26,500,000 undertaking. The construction phase called for seven residence units to house over six hundred students ($3,600,000), a library ($2,750,000), a learning center for social studies and humanities ($1,800,000), a central dining facility ($1,150,000), a new classroom building ($1,000,000), and a women's recreational and physical education unit ($650,000). Three faithful veterans — Goheen Hall, Social Science Hall, and the old Women's Gym — would be sacrificed to this progress.[28]

Construction activity was not long in getting under way. On a wintery January 7, 1969, approximately three hundred students and faculty pulling a hand plow in a ceremony reminiscent of that for the gymnasium sixty years earlier broke ground for the first three units of the residence complex. Financing had been arranged by means of a loan of $1,665,000 from the federal department of housing and urban development. Each unit would house ninety-six students and provide facilities for study as well as for recreation. The first of the segments was occupied in September, 1969; the other two were finished soon after.[29]

Ground-breaking rites for the library were held on May 5, 1970. The ceremonies were shortened in deference to the feelings engendered by the tragic deaths of four students in an antiwar rally at Kent State University in Ohio and by the entry of American forces into Cambodia. Within a short time, Hamline's landscape reminded President Bailey of a World War II "no-man's land complete with trenches, shell holes, piled earth breastworks and wire fences." From this scarred area rose the Bush Memorial Library completed in 1971. The money to meet its cost of $3,400,000 — larger than first planned — came mainly from four sources: a loan of $1,108,000 from the federal department of health, education, and welfare, a grant of $890,000 from the Minnesota Higher Education Coordinating Commission, a gift $517,000 from Mrs. A. G. Bush, and an award of $600,000 from the Bush Foundation. With space for seven hundred readers and shelving for 240,000 volumes, the handsome structure added a stimulating dimension to Hamline life.[30]

Even while the library was taking form, preliminary drawings for the third construction project in the ten-year plan, a $2,500,000 learning center, were approved by the trustees. Containing classrooms, laboratories, lounges, study areas, and the departments of sociology and anthropology, psychology, economics, modern languages, and education, the center was completed in 1972.[31]

By the end of 1971, despite inflation and the slowdown in the country's economy, prospects suggested that the multimillion-dollar development program would reach its "halfway mark in gifts, pledges and federal funding." But the completion of the campaign, if past history serves as a guide, will only be prologue to a continuing search for money. Hamline's budget was in the red by $12,000 in 1968–69 and under $50,000 in 1969–70 — when the operating budget was $3,225,000, plus $967,700 for auxiliary enterprises. During the same time span, 2,500 alumni, the largest number in the college's history, gave over $75,000 for educational expenses, and the Bush Foundation continued and increased the matching support which Mr. Bush had begun in 1958. Yet these sources combined accounted for only 4.6 per cent of Hamline's educational revenues. (The Minnesota United Methodist Conference's grant to Hamline in 1969–70 amounted to only 1.7 per cent.) Tuition and fees provided 57.4 per cent, but loans and scholarships notwithstanding, there seems a limit to how much can be charged before students are priced out of the market. In 1972 Hamline's tuition charge was $2,250. On the expense side, the largest sums went for instruction (45.9 per cent), upkeep of physical plant (13 per cent), and scholarships and grants (11.4 per cent). Hamline's predicament was "not desperate," wrote President Bailey in 1970, but "the road ahead grows narrow, rocky and unmapped." [32]

Although the readily apparent features of the new president's first months in office concerned fund raising and plant expansion, these endeavors were purely a means to the end of providing society with a leaven of humane, involved, and effective individuals. The basic and unending quest was for the most efficacious ways by which Hamline could develop such people. To discover methods suitable for the 1970s, the college community in the last years of Gidden's administration and continuing into the new president's administration had embarked on a period of intensive study and planning. The outcome was the inauguration in the fall of 1970 of a new curriculum and a four-one-four term calendar (two regular semesters separated by a month-long interim), which represented one of the most complete changes in the institution's history. The new arrangement retained a core of courses for all undergraduates, but in keeping with newer insights into the learning process, the revision exhibited increased attention to such concepts as flexibility, relevancy, and a student-centered academic life. Included were four basic elements: (1) in-depth study in a major field, (2) an interdisciplinary experience in a cultural area or issue study program, (3) proficiency in written English, in understanding another language, and in a leisure-time physical activity, such as tennis, and (4) free electives in other academic areas. In all of these segments, the student possesses great freedom of choice, a situation designed to increase his interest and therefore, administrators hoped, the degree of his effort. In the cultural area or issue study — probably the most innovative part of the new program — a student takes eight related courses from various disciplines, develops an independent project, and writes an essay. Taken as a whole, the modified curriculum has been described by Hamline's Dean Charles U. Walker as "a bold step . . . to identify a new framework for undergraduate education, and to provide students with the opportunity to design a program suited to their own needs" in the changing twentieth century. [33]

That the new course of study is student centered is not only timely, but also in line with President Bailey's philosophy. "My administration," he declared in his inaugural address, "will be keyed to the students who are on our campus." Since he made this promise, he has learned a great deal about Hamline undergraduates. They have disrupted his sleep, taken the door off his home in a peaceful confrontation regarding parietal rules (he did not yield), and looked to him for support and leadership during the Cambodian crisis of May, 1970. A few of them no doubt embarrassed him by heckling Hubert H. Humphrey, when the former vice president of the United States was addressing the 260 graduating seniors in the class of 1970 while anti-Vietnam War feelings were very high. Nevertheless, Bailey has not lost faith, nor has he "been threatened, pillaged, derided, or molested." Pointing to the many achievements of current collegians in traditional student activities as well as in more recent programs, such as tutoring youngsters in city schools, he remains optimistic. These contemporary students are, he wrote in June, 1970, "exactly the people who should inherit leadership in our sick sad world." [34]

28 ST. JOHN'S UNIVERSITY

Vibrancy after 1,400 Years

ON JUNE 1, 1941, St. John's University awarded bachelor's degrees to a class of 56 members. Concern over world conditions was general, but college classes opened in that portentous fall with slightly over 460 young men in attendance (68 of them seniors and 187 freshmen), and life went on normally in the relatively isolated and largely self-sufficient Benedictine community at Collegeville. Then came the Japanese attack on Hawaii in December, 1941.[1]

The monks, though eager to assist in the war effort, were somewhat unclear as to how to proceed. They were pleased therefore when in December, 1942, a letter from Washington, D.C., requesting information on their facilities gave promise of an opportunity to serve. Abbot Alcuin replied that physics laboratory equipment was in short supply, but that 350 military students could be taken care of and 15 teachers supplied in half a dozen relevant subjects. On March 1, 1943, the Eighty-seventh Army Air Force College Training Detachment was activated at St. John's. By the end of the month 300 future aviation crewmen were in residence and embarked on a five-month course covering 700 hours of academic and military work. The last two or three weeks were devoted to flying and ground-school training at Whitney Memorial Airport near St. Cloud. When the detachment was deactivated in July, 1944, about 1,500 men (among them Jack Webb of later television fame) had gone through the program and developed an affection for St. John's and its friendly monks. The latter had not solicited the military unit, but they had welcomed it warmly and felt a sense of loss at its departure.[2]

When Japan surrendered in 1945, St. John's stood on the threshold of a period of unprecedented growth. Enrollment in the college division during the preceding year had been 183 (23 seniors, 18 juniors, 47 sophomores, 94 freshmen, and one special student). Within three years the total would jump to 935, of whom 340 were sophomores and 327 freshmen.

Seminary registrations remained in the neighborhood of 100, but there were about three times that number in the high school by 1947, adding to the strain on facilities and personnel. A similar upswing, of course, occurred in the size of graduation classes. Only 19 men, mostly priests, had received B.A.s in June 1945; in June, 1948, 80 degrees were conferred — 68 B.A.s and 12 B.S.s.[3]

No academic or dormitory buildings had been constructed in nearly two decades. The overcrowding and improvisation characteristic of other campuses in the late 1940s were also present at St. John's. Five former army barracks provided by the federal public housing authority sheltered some of the veterans enrolled, but did not solve the whole problem. Other barracks were obtained in 1947 and converted into a classroom structure known as St. Thomas More Hall. The following year additional war surplus material was fashioned into St. Thomas Aquinas Hall, a study and recreational facility for day students. As late as 1949, 174 students constituting nearly one-fifth of the college population were living in rooms off campus, some as far away as ten miles. Such a condition ran counter to the Benedictine ideal of a close-knit, familylike atmosphere.[4]

Faculty were still recruited mainly from the priests of the abbey. Though meetings of the teaching staff presided over by the dean were held monthly, many problems were discussed and solved informally in the monastery. Most classroom personnel were alumni of St. John's Seminary who had been carefully screened before being designated for a teaching career. Many had then been sent to graduate schools for work on advanced degrees. There were, however, nine laymen among the seventy faculty members in 1949. Until 1946 their employment had been considered temporary, but in that year a system of tenure had been adopted along with a policy of according them the customary faculty ranks. A good group insurance plan covered all employees, and raises were granted lay teachers in 1946 and 1948, bringing the scale for full professors to between $3,800 and $4,300 a year. Married men received higher pay than bachelors. There still was no regular sabbatical leave policy, however, no fixed retirement age, and no systematic provision for pensions for lay teachers.[5]

At the time of Pearl Harbor, majors had been available in only eight fields — chemistry, economics, education, English, history, Latin and Greek, mathematics, and philosophy. Biology was soon added to the list. All students took many courses in religion. Men planning to graduate from St. John's were offered little flexibility; for others there was an array of one- to three-year preprofessional courses in such areas as medicine, law, forestry, and veterinary science. In 1946–47 the faculty made a thorough study of the aims, objectives, and curriculum of the university, and numerous changes were made in the schedule of courses. Particularly notable was the establishment of a department of theology for lay students, a response to "the growing need on the part of the laity for a deeper grasp of Catholic truth." Departments were organized into five divisions, and new stress was placed on art and music appreciation. By 1948 a major in music was available for the first time, as were divisional majors in social science and natural science. Attention also turned to the integration of studies; as a consequence, the 1949 graduating class had (to them) the dubious distinction of being the initial group required to take senior comprehensive examinations in their major fields.[6]

In these postwar years St. John's college division operated in the black, an achievement made possible by the absence of major construction projects, the support of the abbey, and the raising of fees. Board, room, and tuition in 1943, for example, averaged about $460 for the year; in 1951 the total approximated $790. Student loan funds were nonexistent, but 16 per cent of the undergraduates held part-time jobs, and priesthood candidates received discounts. Forty-three students received scholarships in 1948 (the highest amount was $510), and another twenty men were accorded grants. An accounting system had been set up in 1943, but St. John's got by without preparing a budget, mainly because expenditures were under the control of economy-minded Benedictines. University outlay in 1948–49 came to $735,500, of which instruction accounted for $205,600 and auxiliary enterprises to $179,700. Income amounted to $777,200; student fees provided $200,900 of this sum, and board and room payments $236,400. Endowment earnings were a puny $1,300, but the contributed services of the religious — St. John's real endowment — were listed conservatively at $138,900.[7]

Despite its strengths, the university still lacked North Central Association accreditation. Finally, however, at the urging of the dean of the college, Father Martin E. Schirber, and others, Abbot Alcuin acquiesced, and application was made in 1948. North Central examiners visited the campus in February, 1950. They found some weaknesses: faculty were low on educational experience and on membership in learned societies, student use of the library was below average, there was no annual budget, and the board of control was not organized according to the association's recommendations. Strengths, however, outweighed shortcomings. Notable were the sound financial structure, the program in general education, the fine physical plant, and the educational integrity, family spirit, and number of doctorates held by faculty members. The examiners therefore strongly recommended that the college be accredited by North Central, an action which was taken in 1950.[8]

In the spring of 1949, while the foregoing negotiations were under way, the abbey and the diocese of St. Cloud concluded an unusual agreement. Until then St. John's divinity school, which trained men for the regular as well as the secular priesthood, had been administered and conducted by the Benedictines. Under the new arrangement suggested by Coadjutor Bishop Peter W. Bartholome, the diocese agreed to erect a seminary building on campus land leased from the university. The structure was completed in 1950. Incorporated as "St. John's Seminary of the Diocese of St. Cloud," the enterprise then became a joint operation. Its spiritual and temporal administration devolved on the St. Cloud bishop, who appointed the rector and two other officials, but responsibility for the academic program continued to rest with the university, whose president appointed the seminary dean. The students were men preparing for the secular diocesan priesthood, who lived in the new house of studies, and the regular Benedictine clerics, who resided in the monastery. In 1969 the entire administration of the seminary was delegated to the dean, who was thereafter jointly appointed by St. John's chancellor and the bishop. Students who are members of regular orders or congregations may now, with permission, live in the house of studies instead of the monastery.[9]

The events of the late 1940s had made heavy demands on Abbot Alcuin, and in the fall of 1950 he felt it necessary to petition Rome for a coadjutor. The reply authorized the election of such an official with immediate power to rule the community at St.

John's and with the right of succession. In December the monks elected Father Baldwin Dworschak to the position; his formal blessing ceremony occurred on March 29, 1951. Less than two months later Abbot Alcuin was dead of a heart attack. During his twenty-nine-year administration, St. John's had become the largest Benedictine monastery in the world and the center of significant educational and missionary apostolates. Particularly memorable had been Abbot Alcuin's interest in new ideas, his respect for scholarship, and his talents in integrating and balancing liturgical, educational, and missionary activities.[10]

Born in Wisconsin, Abbot Baldwin had enrolled in St. John's preparatory department in 1920 at the age of fourteen, entered the novitiate seven years later, and been ordained a priest in June, 1933. Thereafter, he had done graduate work in English at the University of Minnesota and taught at his alma mater. For the four years preceding his election as coadjutor, he had gained valuable experience serving as prior of the monastic community. A clue to his nature was evidenced by his selection for his coat of arms Saint Benedict's dictum to abbots — to serve their brethren rather than preside over them.[11]

Even before Abbot Baldwin's election, the post-war peak in enrollment had passed, but the physical plant was still taxed to care for both the student and monastic families. With the old army barracks "slowly but surely falling apart," one of the most urgent needs was more residential space, so a $700,000 dormitory for 222 men was planned. To pay for it, a fund-raising firm was hired, and the "first all-out drive in the 93 year history of St. John's" was mounted under the able direction of Father Walter H. Reger. (Abbot Alcuin had been opposed to soliciting the public.) Within twenty months after the effort began in the summer of 1950, over 3,500 alumni and friends had given $330,000. The building known as St. Mary's Hall was completed in the fall of 1951, permitting the university to house 600 students on campus.[12]

The new hall, which also contained a cafeteria, eased pressures but did not remove them. Furthermore, its location was displeasing to some members of the community. As a result, in August, 1951, Abbot Baldwin appointed a building committee, which met regularly for eighteen months to study St. John's needs. The group concluded that a professionally conceived, over-all plan for future development was essential. In March, 1953, the abbot wrote to twelve leading European and American architects asking each if he would be interested in drawing

up a hundred-year plan for St. John's. All but two of the dozen men sought the challenging task. The choice of the community — partly because of his "straightforward, sincere, and rather humble" manner — proved to be Marcel L. Breuer, the Hungarian-born designer of the UNESCO building in Paris and onetime research professor at Harvard University. In January, 1954, he presented drawings and models to the Benedictines, and the proposed building plan was made public the following spring. It called for the eventual replacement of three-quarters of the current plant and for the construction of nineteen new buildings around a central quadrangle. The first of these, a monastic wing stretching eastward from the old complex, was completed in 1955 at a cost (furnished) of $1,225,000.[13]

Meanwhile other changes were taking place with less fanfare. Although Abbot Alcuin had been interested in the possibility of making St. John's a center for the study of sacred art, he had never gotten around to creating a department for that purpose. In the early 1950s an art department offering a major sequence — a rarity in Catholic men's colleges — was created. Modern languages and political science gained similar status, and a three-three course was established in engineering (three years at St. John's and three at the University of Minnesota). An army ROTC program, one of two at the college level in Minnesota, was set up at St. John's in May, 1952. The wooden barracks known as the "Snack Shack" in World War II became the unit's classroom facility. The first two years of training were required of most freshmen and sophomores except divinity students, but the advanced course leading to a reserve commission was voluntary. A faculty committee whose function was to initiate curricular change began life in 1954. The same period witnessed the setting up of a testing and counseling department to help students select courses suited to their interests and aptitudes.[14]

As St. John's University grew larger and more complex, it was obvious that some change in its administrative organization would be necessary. Accordingly two monks in the summer of 1954 were sent to the North Central Association's liberal arts workshop at the University of Minnesota to study the structure of Benedictine colleges. Upon their return, they recommended that the abbot divest himself of the title of president, as several abbots had recently done elsewhere, and that St. John's appoint a director of development. As a result, Abbot Baldwin in 1958 assumed the title of chancellor of St. John's University and appointed Father Arno A. Gustin as its president. After entering the novitiate at Collegeville in 1926, the new executive had completed college in 1929 and seminary work there and been ordained a priest in 1933. He had earned his M.A. at Catholic University in 1934 and his Ph.D. in education at the University of Minnesota in 1945. In the late 1930s he had been principal of the preparatory school at St. John's, and since 1944 he had served successively as registrar and as dean of the college.[15]

During Father Arno's initial year in office, college enrollment totaled 1,077, of whom a typical proportion (742) were from Minnesota; the contiguous states, especially North Dakota and Wisconsin, also provided a sizable number of students, and fifteen foreign countries were represented. Again, overcrowded and outmoded facilities created problems. These were partially solved in 1959 by the completion of a new dormitory — the second Breuer-designed building in the hundred-year plan. Named St. Thomas Aquinas Hall and featuring the glass, concrete, and sharp lines characteristic of its architect's work, the residence provided rooms for over 400 college men. Furnished, its cost came to more than $1,470,000.[16]

The abbey's building program now moved into high gear. As originally conceived, the focal point of the plan would be a church, which, in Abbot Baldwin's words, would "be truly an architectural monument in the service of God." When it was consecrated in August, 1961, the structure, fronted by a distinctive concrete banner bell tower, fulfilled these hopes. With 36 private chapels on its lower level and accommodations for 1,800 worshipers and a choir of 264, the abbey and university church has been called by *Architectural Forum* "one of Breuer's most famous buildings, and one of the finest religious structures of modern times." Equipped, it represented an outlay of $3,015,000.[17]

The month following the consecration of the church, Abbot Baldwin broke ground for a new preparatory school. This addition would permit the clear-cut separation of high school and college operations long advocated by accrediting agencies and release needed space in the old quadrangle. Chosen as the site was the hill looking south on Lake Sagatagan, scene of many toboggan runs, an ancient ski jump, and the sixty-seven-year-old observatory. Four buildings to serve 480 boys were planned — a classroom-study hall, a dormitory, a gymnasium, and a multipurpose structure. Priorities have allowed construction of only two of the units so far — St. Bede Hall, the classroom building, and St. Michael Hall, the dormitory. Designed by Val Michaelson, an associate of Breuer, these units were finished in 1964 at a cost of $2,210,000 equipped. Phase

one of the hundred-year plan was now completed.[18]

In this post-Sputnik period, the faculty study committee took the lead in removing considerable rigidity from the curriculum and in providing special opportunities for superior students. All departments developed independent study programs, and in 1958 honors work was introduced, involving the writing and defending of a thesis. The next year sociology was advanced to major status, and the theology department was upgraded both in personnel and in course content and emphasis. After the teacher education sequence at St. John's was denied accreditation in 1960 by the National Council for the Accreditation of Teacher Education (NCATE), the course was revised and strengthened. Television teaching for credit began in 1957; five years later a language laboratory went into use, and an interdepartmental major in the humanities became available. Beyond the campus, co-operative ventures with the College of St. Benedict and St. Cloud State College were breaking down old barriers, opening up new opportunities, and expanding horizons. These joint efforts, dating back to an adult education program in 1955, led to significant modifications in St. John's academic organization and offerings.[19]

In 1957 forty Benedictine religious superiors asked Abbot Baldwin to organize a school of theology on the graduate level for sisters. He complied, and the five-year cycle of summer courses, known as the Benedictine Institute of Sacred Theology, was inititated on the campus of the College of St. Benedict in 1958. Pressure soon arose to have the sequence fully accredited and capped by a master's degree, a goal sanctioned by abbey administrators in the spring of 1959. That fall the faculty approved an M.A. program by a vote of sixty to seven, and the following January a graduate committee was appointed to work out the details. By 1963 with the hearty support of the seminary, the graduate curriculum had come to embrace (with the summer work which was located at St. Benedict's until 1965) a year-round program open to both laity and religious on St. John's campus. In April, 1964, preliminary North Central accreditation was accorded; in May the graduate school conferred its first M.A.s in sacred studies. By 1970 the degree had been earned by 124 men and women, who as a result had greatly improved their competence as high school and college teachers of religion.[20]

As part of its quest for accreditation of the graduate program, St. John's faculty committee conducted a self-study in the summer of 1962. Questions were asked and trends were noted — the considerable growth in the number of lay teachers in just a few years, for example. There were fifty-two Benedictines and thirty-four lay persons on the teaching staff in 1962. Divergent views were expressed, and the study provoked serious thought, but the data assembled and plans laid were destined to become outmoded within a few years.[21]

Finances, of course, came in for serious attention. In a period of accelerating inflation, university expenditures had climbed to $2,036,000 in 1961–62. To meet rising costs, student charges had been raised periodically; tuition was up to $650 a year, board to $450, and room to between $150 and $260. These fees, though not high relatively, were more than many Johnnies could afford. Hence, St. John's had paid out $169,500 in student aid in 1961–62, in addition to student loans from money provided mainly by the federal government. Nevertheless, the university's budget was balanced only because of outside gifts. Those from alumni had grown since the early 1950s (to $103,400 in 1962), but less than 30 per cent of the graduates made a cash donation to their alma mater in the latter year. Chief reliance still had to be placed on the monastery to make up the university's annual deficit. In 1959–60 this figure reached nearly $180,000; the following year it was $167,600. Beyond this assistance, the abbey also paid a sizable segment of St. John's capital expenditures.[22]

In 1964 Father Arno's term as president ended and Father Colman J. Barry, a graduate of the class of 1942, was appointed to the position. A distinguished church historian and editor of the *American Benedictine Review*, Father Colman had earned both his M.A. and Ph.D. at Catholic University, which in 1950 had awarded him a fellowship for historical research in Europe. Among his many writings had been *Worship and Work*, a history of St. John's Abbey and University published in 1956 to commemorate the centennial of the Benedictines' arrival in Minnesota. Well grounded in the tradition of his order and possessed of a broad historical perspective, Father Colman was a wise choice to guide St. John's through the unsettled and disturbing days following Vatican Council II. For if events moved swiftly before 1964, they accelerated both in quantity and perplexity thereafter.[23]

Within four years the self-study of 1962 became obsolete. For one thing, the face of the campus had gained several Breuer-designed buildings. Late in 1963 the members of the monastic community had voted to proceed as quickly as possible with the construction of a library to replace the one erected in 1901. Ground was broken in the summer of 1964. In the Benedictine tradition, Alcuin Library completed in 1966 was located near the church but deferring to it. Simple and unadorned on the outside, the large interior space of the $2,000,000 structure takes on a dramatic quality through the presence of two giant concrete "trees" which support the "waffle-grid" ceiling and roof.[24]

In September, 1966, when about 900 students were enrolled in various courses in the scientific field, a new Science Center went into use. Its predecessor had been erected in 1911 at a time when only a few of the 300 students took any work whatsoever in science. Similar in external appearance to the neighboring library, but featuring a granite-sheathed wing to house a lecture-hall auditorium, the three-story center is a "marvel of functionalism." This $2,630,000 complex was dedicated in a series of events extending from May 7 to November 4, 1967.[25]

In the meantime, enrollment had mounted to 1,265 in the autumn of 1964, placing a great strain on existing residence facilities. On May 9, 1966, therefore, work began on Breuer's second dormitory, a complex situated on the shore of Lake Watab and designed to serve as part of a future quadrangle. Exhibiting the bold, sculptured façades which are a Breuer trademark, the structure consists of three sections — St. Benedict, St. Boniface, and St. Patrick halls — with living quarters for 372 men. Completed early in 1968, it represented an outlay of $2,400,000.[26]

In addition to plant expansion, the profile of that year also chronicled an array of other achievements associated with Father Colman's early presidency. Most of them represented the culmination of previous efforts, and some were peripheral to the university, but *in toto* they influenced the climate under which students and faculty labored. These endeavors likewise reflected attempts to provide Benedictine-oriented leadership to the solution of problems in the world of Vatican II.

Long leaders in the crusade to increase lay involvement in and understanding of the liturgy, the Benedictine monks in the United States and elsewhere were in the vanguard of the ecumenical movement. As early as the summer of 1954, St. John's, with support from the Hamm Foundation of St. Paul, had set up summer workshops on mental health for clergy of all faiths. By 1962, 220 of the 1,052 participants had been Protestant ministers and Jewish rabbis. Formal dialogue between Benedictines and students of the Lutheran theological seminaries in the Twin Cities dated back to 1958. The Scriptural Institute, a week-long workshop at St. John's for clergy of all denominations, was begun in 1959. The next year Father Colman had been the moving force behind a historic discussion among ten prominent Catholic and Protestant theologians at Collegeville — the first such theological colloquy in the United States to be officially sanctioned by Rome. Other "firsts" soon followed: in 1961 an abbey monk spoke to the ministers of the Augustana Lutheran Synod in St. Paul; in 1962 he lectured before four hundred Protestant pastors in Minneapolis, and soon thereafter Father Colman gave the baccalaureate address at Concordia College in Moorhead; in 1965 he became the first Catholic priest to speak before the southern synod of the American Lutheran Church. These activities helped eliminate walls of inherited misconceptions, dispel ignorance, and stimulate ecumenicity at St. John's and elsewhere.[27]

Back in 1960 after a discussion of curricular revision, the faculty had voted to offer work in Protestant theology in the seminary, and Father Kilian W. McDonnell had been appointed to teach it. In preparation he had studied for two years under Protestant theologians in Europe. Upon his return, ecumenicity had made continued headway at St. John's. With promised support from the Aimee Mott Butler Trust for Charity of St. Paul and the Hill Foundation, it was proposed to the monastic community that an Institute for Ecumenical and Cultural Research be established; the response was enthusiastic. The buildings for the unique institute, designed by Breuer, were dedicated with impressive interfaith ceremonies late in May, 1968. Included are apartments for ten visiting fellows of Protestant, Eastern Orthodox, and Jewish persuasions and their families. During a stay of six months to a year, these scholars engage in research and dialogue with each other and with Benedictines as they seek to understand their differences and find ways of coming more closely together.[28]

Of inestimable value to the institute is its proximity to the Alcuin Library and the latter's magnificent monastic manuscript microfilm collection. The result of an exciting project to place on film handwritten documents antedating 1600 A.D. which have been preserved in European monasteries and libraries, the collection had its inception in 1964 with an initial grant of $40,000 from the Hill Foundation. Funds were also derived from St. Vincent's Archabbey in Pennsylvania and other sources. Actual work began fittingly at Monte Cassino, the famed home of the Benedictines in Italy, in April, 1965, and then proceeded to other European repositories. By late 1968, when the Hill Foundation made a second grant of $230,820 for the work, over 3,000,000 black and white and 31,000 color exposures had been made. The documents photographed bring together major segments of the Greek and Roman classics, the work of the early church fathers, and Scripture.

The microfilm library and the Institute for Ecumenical and Cultural Research, in the words of Abbot Baldwin, "may prove to be . . . the most valuable and unique contribution we have made to scholarship in this country." [29]

On a more circumscribed level, St. John's continued to grow and reach beyond the borders of the old Indian Bush. Historically the institution had co-operated with the sisters at the nearby College of St. Benedict, and this co-ordination now became even closer. In the fall of 1964 the faculties of both institutions for the first time held a joint workshop session. This event was followed by a modest exchange of students in 1964, which gained yearly in volume thereafter. In the summer of 1965 curriculums were studied by a committee composed of personnel from both colleges. These meetings led to new co-operative ventures and interchanges that set the stage for a really thorough investigation of ways in which St. John's and St. Benedict's could avoid duplication, provide a richer curriculum, and generally strengthen their operations. This study in depth, financed by a grant of $40,200 from the Hill Foundation in 1967, recommended that the colleges should merge as quickly as possible and hire a co-ordinator to assist in achieving that goal. In a joint meeting in July, 1968, the trustees of the two institutions agreed that merger should be considered, and they decided to employ a co-ordinator.[30]

To function smoothly co-operation required synchronization of schedules and co-ordination of course offerings, matters which received both joint and separate attention at the two colleges for a number of years. At St. John's this activity culminated on February 22, 1967, when the faculty voted sixty-six to twenty-one to adopt major curriculum and schedule changes to take effect the ensuing fall term. The traditional two-semester system was replaced by the relatively new four-one-four calendar — two four-month terms separated by a January interim during which students could pursue a variety of study possibilities. Specific course requirements in a number of areas were abandoned in favor of electives to be chosen in at least four broad academic divisions. The emphasis was to be on flexibility and depth, on relating course programs to student needs and interests. St. Benedict's also adopted the four-one-four calendar, and the two institutions published a joint catalog for 1967–68.[31]

By 1970 St. John's and St. Benedict's were in many ways enjoying the best of two worlds, the advantages of both segregated education and coeducation. Utopia had not arrived, but the common Catholic Benedictine tradition shared by the colleges had helped in smoothing over rough spots. Several positions — registrar, head librarian, director of public information — had been combined. An expanded number of majors had been provided. Women could major in economics, physics, and psychology, for example, by taking courses at St. John's, and men could prepare for elementary schoolteaching or a career in the theater through work at St. Benedict's. Several departments (foreign languages, physics, history, sociology, theology, education, communications, and theater) had unified or merged, and the others were functioning in close co-operation. Each college still maintained its separate identity but they moved ahead in tandem.[32]

The two had also shared in ventures with other Minnesota private colleges, such as offering courses on KTCA-TV from 1957 on. With St. Cloud State College, a limited degree of academic co-operation had begun in the fall of 1958 with the introduction of a jointly sponsored Tri-College Program on Great Issues, supported by money from the Hill Foundation. The first course offered was "Problems of Free Men." Eight years later the three institutions, with the help of a federal grant, created a new and unusual community leadership educational program. Its director was Edward L. Henry, a gradute of the 1943 class, professor of government at St. John's, and at the time mayor of St. Cloud. In 1968 the Hill Foundation again provided the means to further this experiment in public-private co-operation by allocating $52,000 for the establishment of a joint East Asian area studies program. Then in May, 1969, the federal office of education awarded the three St. Cloud area colleges $60,000 to stimulate continued collaboration.[33]

On a wider stage, St. John's in 1966 joined the Central States College Association, which had been organized the previous fall. Composed of a dozen Protestant (including Gustavus Adolphus) and Catholic institutions in Illinois, Indiana, Iowa, Michigan, Minnesota, and Wisconsin, the association provides its members with greater advantages than each could obtain separately. Among these are student and faculty exchanges; a monk and a professor from Luther College initiated this program at St. John's by trading positions in 1967–68. Also enjoyed jointly were concerts, exhibits, and opportunities for study at the Argonne National Laboratory in Illinois and abroad. Although it is too early to assess the long-range impact of the association, the relationship suits the spirit of the times, and so far it has been mutually beneficial.[34]

While striving to define its relationships to other institutions in the late 1960s, St. John's also continued to nourish its independent structure and protect its own unique identity. With almost cataclysmic transformations disrupting both church and school, guidelines were often obsolete, if not entirely nonexistent. Certain facts, however, remained clear. St. John's kept on growing and changing. Collegiate enrollment in the fall of 1969 approximated 1,550, of whom 427 were freshmen. Adding diversity to the total group were 75 foreign students (triple the number of nine years earlier), 43 Black undergraduates, and 50 non-Catholics, a big increase in only two years. On the faculty roster were 122 names. The college budget reached almost $5,000,000, to which the abbey gave $656,200 to offset a deficit; endowment was only a little over $1,100,000. Annual charges for board, room, and tuition averaged only about $2,300, but assistance provided to students in the form of scholarships, grants, loans, waivers, and work contracts amounted to roughly $1,000,000 in 1969–70 including federal funds.[35]

Behind these statistics stood an institution which was working to preserve its Benedictine nature while increasingly adopting many of the trappings of its surrounding society. Of its 122 teachers, 68 were lay members. One of these, Dr. John E. Lange, a 1952 graduate, became St. John's first lay academic dean in August, 1969; soon he and two other men, only one of them a monk, would be elevated to vice presidencies. At the same time, a physics professor was elected chairman of the faculty with the responsibility for calling faculty meetings and determining their agenda. The associate board of trustees by 1970 embraced more than two dozen lay persons, and the new advisory council established by the office of development to help chart future paths included parents, faculty, students, and alumni.[36]

Campus life was also in a state of flux. About a third of the monastic faculty still lived in college dormitories, but as advisers and friends, not as prefects. Whereas student attendance at Sunday Mass had once been 100 per cent, it now ran closer to 40 per cent. Since 1967 the Mass itself had been celebrated on dormitory floors as well as in the church. Many men deserted campus altogether on week ends. As at other colleges, voices were raised in favor of liquor in residence halls and of coed dormitories — the pleas have not yet been granted — and of greater student involvement in curriculum framing. Some members of the Organization of Afro-American Students in 1970 staged a sit-in in Father Colman's office to press their demands. Similar manifestations were occurring on campuses across the nation, but they were especially upsetting to the Benedictines who have a cherished reputation for racial pluralism and a familylike ideal.[37]

In general, however, the monks and their associates

pushed ahead in the work of building a greater St. John's. A capital fund drive to raise $3,400,000 was launched in the fall of 1968, $1,500,000 of it for a new physical education center, and $1,000,000 to be placed in endowment for faculty salaries. Pledges in encouraging amounts were received, and in June, 1970, the federal department of health, education, and welfare granted $306,500 for the center. Its construction is scheduled for completion in 1973.[38]

Other notable recent developments have allowed St. John's to serve its church in new ways, to extend its ecumenical thrust, and to offer its students a tutorial studies program. In the summer of 1969 the institution became the first center in the United States for the training of permanent deacons, members of a rank restored to the Catholic hierarchy by Vatican Council II. When ordained, these men, many of whom are married, will be able to perform most priestly functions except the celebration of Mass or the hearing of confessions. In August, 1969, the Jay Phillips Chair of Jewish Studies was established in St. John's department of theology by a grant of $500,000 from the Phillips Foundation of Minneapolis. Within a year about a hundred students were enrolled in courses on Jewish history and modern Jewish thought taught by the rabbi who occupies the chair. Another "ecumenical first" among educational ventures in the United States initiated by St. John's was designed to provide continuing education for Minnesota clergy of all faiths. Governed by an interdenominational board of advisers, the Archibald and Edyth Bush Interdenominational Continuing Education Program received a grant of $150,000 from the Bush Foundation in November, 1969. At the first of a series of five projected conferences, held in 1970, over four hundred Minnesota clergy were in attendance. The conferences were planned to treat developments in economics, psychology, sociology, and the sciences as "they bear upon the work of religious leaders in their communities." The grant can also be used to finance regular academic study at St. John's by pastors and rabbis. Finally, the Hill Foundation in 1970 made a two-year grant of $142,500 to the Collegeville university for a learning experiment under which selected students assisted by tutors and freed from many traditional requirements worked at their own pace toward the baccalaureate degree. This project began in February, 1971.[39]

St. John's has no intention of becoming functionally obsolete in this time of momentous and fast-moving change. By combining boldness of thought and the use of twentieth-century materials and techniques with idealism and the long view, the institution continues to honor its centuries-old tradition. Today St. John's is listed as one of the eight outstanding American Catholic colleges and universities by noted sociologist and author Father Andrew M. Greeley. Like the others, it faces a multitude of problems stemming from inadequate finances, changing social mores, and upheavals in the church. A historian, however, finds the outlook encouraging. Benedictines have faced adversity time and time again and triumphed. So long as these monks are numerous enough to exert their unique influence in the old Indian Bush, St. John's will endure and continue to enrich the family of man.[40]

29

GUSTAVUS ADOLPHUS COLLEGE

Building A Greater Gustavus

WHEN CONTROVERSIAL President Walter A. Lunden left Gustavus for World War II military service in December, 1943, less than 200 civilian students — over 160 of them women — were enrolled. A navy V-12 unit, however, had been in residence since July 1; its complement consisted of almost 390 trainees and a half dozen lieutenants and specialists. Johnson and Uhler dormitories had been relinquished for the use of these men, and the two-semester calendar had been replaced by one based on trimesters which began on the first of March, July, and November. Though it caused some grumbling and inconvenience, the naval installation permitted the college to retain its faculty, keep the physical plant in good condition, and acquire valuable equipment especially in the field of science. The trainees proved to be fine students as well as versatile additions to the extracurricular life of that uncertain period.[1]

In January, 1944, the trustees made Dr. Oscar A. Winfield, a respected philosophy professor, acting president. But already they had their eyes on another man, Edgar M. Carlson, a 1930 Gustavus graduate who was soon to be the recipient of a doctorate from the University of Chicago's divinity school. From 1933 to 1937 he had combined part-time graduate study at the University of Minnesota with ministerial duties at Mount Olivet Lutheran Church in Minneapolis; for the next five years he had taught in the department of Christianity at Gustavus and continued his graduate work in Chicago in the summers. Since 1942 he had been teaching at Augustana Seminary in Rock Island, Illinois, where he had earlier completed his pastoral training. By September, 1944, he was directing affairs at his alma mater, a task he would perform ably for almost a quarter of a century.[2]

At first conditions at Gustavus were far from encouraging. There were still nearly 390 V-12 trainees on campus, but the contingent arriving on November 1 totaled only 217 men. Johnson Hall

was returned to the college, and it was known that the days of the navy in St. Peter were numbered. Civilian enrollment during the term from July through October, 1944, had reached a nadir of two dozen men and 70 women. The faculty, though overstaffed, were told that their contracts would be honored. Yet there seemed a serious doubt that the institution would be able to survive.[3]

This worry was voiced by Gustavus' board chairman at the church convention in April, 1945, when it appeared that the V-12 unit would be decommissioned at the end of June. If the teaching staff were to be kept intact and the college to be run successfully, at least 450 civilian students would be required in the fall. Bonded indebtedness on Uhler and Rundstrom halls still totaled nearly $100,000, and the current financial situation was anything but strong. The modest endowment had increased by only $17,000 since 1939. There was no doubt that the conference's 80,000 members faced a sizable challenge.[4]

Fortunately the picture did not prove to be so dark as it seemed. The navy stayed on until October 27, 1945; the final group of 145 men brought to over 1,000 the total number of trainees who attended Gustavus. For six weeks in the fall, therefore, the college ran both the V-12 operation and a regular semester for the 385 civilian students enrolled. By March 1, 1946, veterans were filtering back to the nation's campuses and Gustavus' registration was up to 543, almost evenly divided between men and women. Freshmen totaled 305, and over 170 of the students were veterans. Rundstrom Hall was bursting with three girls in each room. No longer was there a question of survival; the problem was how to provide quality education in a Christian context to the large group of young people seeking admission.[5]

The needs were almost staggering. No classroom had been built since 1905. The library on the second floor of Commerce Hall was embarrassingly inadequate; its reading room seated 60 persons. There was no book-purchasing fund, and no full-time librarian. Old Main served as an unsatisfactory science hall. The new dean of the college had his office in a remodeled cloak room. Even in a prewar year only freshmen and sophomores among the men had been housed in campus living quarters. Now the shortage of dormitory space was far more critical. Even the chapel in the auditorium, which seated 800 persons, would soon be too small. And so it was in every area of Gustavus' life.[6]

As early as 1944 some long-range planning had been undertaken, and considerable land near the campus had been purchased. Architects for a new library had been appointed before World War II was over, and a committee to investigate the possibility of raising funds for a chapel had been established. The church convention of 1945 had looked favorably upon these projects, and had in addition authorized the college trustees to erect a $200,000 dormitory to house 150 women. A year later the library plans were being drawn, and the architects were asked to do sketches for both a chapel and a science hall. The need for living quarters for veterans had enabled Gustavus to secure building priorities for the dormitory on which work began in April, 1946. The plan of this five-story structure was altered to provide space for 200 women. Originally it had been hoped that the facility would be ready in the fall of 1946, but when it became evident that this could not be done, trustees and administrators had to act with dispatch and imagination.[7]

Part of the problem was solved by unusual utilization of existing spaces. The interior of the stadium was converted into housing for 40 ex-GIs. Women remained in Rundstrom Hall, but they relinquished Johnson Hall to men and moved to Uhler. Numerous trailers were secured from the federal government and made ready for occupancy. A kind of barracks ranch house for 128 men was built at a cost of $40,000. The cafeteria in Uhler Hall was remodeled to serve a total of 2,000 meals a day to 250 instead of 150 diners at a time. Nearly a score of new faculty members were added, and housing was found for them. Classes were scheduled from early morning to late afternoon.[8]

When classes opened in the fall of 1946, the challenge was met. Nearly 980 students from 23 states, Canada, and China were enrolled, almost double the number in any prewar year. There were 473 veterans, 80 of them married, and 346 women; more than 700 lived on campus. A majority were of full or partial Swedish descent; four-fifths were Lutheran. Once again the extracurriculum flourished. That autumn the Gusties won their third straight MIAC foot-

ball championship. Fireside gatherings on Wednesday evenings and prayer circles on Saturdays continued to attract many students. The Missionary Society was one of the largest and most active campus organizations. More than fifty undergraduates were headed for the ministry, and three dozen others had indicated an interest in foreign missionary work. When the music festival was revived in May, 1947, forty-two visiting choirs provided a massed group of 1,178 voices. The observance of Saint Lucia Day on December 13, debate, theater, band programs, and publications — these and more activities made life memorable at Gustavus in that busy, active era.[9]

Upon his retirement in 1947 after forty-three years on the faculty, Gustavus' versatile English professor, E. C. Carlton, felt that the college was "on the threshold of a new era." A sense of vitality and growth seemed almost real enough to touch, and new buildings were going up everywhere. In March, 1947, Wahlstrom Hall, the new dormitory, welcomed its first 200 veterans; in the fall twice that number moved in. The spring of 1947 also witnessed excavations for the new library and the start of work on a classroom annex constructed with war surplus materials. Attached to this building was a little theater. Later in the year Myrum Memorial Field House was converted for year-round use as an auditorium for large gatherings and as a site for basketball games. By utilizing two more army surplus structures, a building for the departments of art and music was erected soon after. With the dedication of the four additions — the annex, the dormitory, the fine arts facility, and the library during home-coming in the fall of 1948, the first phase of Gustavus' expansion program had been completed. Plans for the future consisted of a science hall, a chapel, a student union, and a heating plant.[10]

The value of capital additions made between September 1, 1945, and the fall of 1948, including property given by the government, amounted to about $1,100,000. The financing of this expansion program was handled in various ways. The $400,000 dormitory was to be paid for by means of a bond issue amortized by rentals. The $55,000 needed to convert the field house was also secured by borrowing. When work on the $413,000 library began, the college had about $185,000 on hand from previous appeals and offerings; the remainder was raised by the church and by individuals. The conference had not conducted a major fund drive for Gustavus in twenty-five years; now a goal of $600,000 was approved by the convention of 1946. Within two and a half years $320,000 in cash had come in; the final total was $470,000.[11]

The outcome suggests that the college's clientele

was scarcely wealthy. In the late 1920s the conference had given Gustavus about $40,000 a year; from 1937 to 1947 the grants had averaged $32,000. Income from the modest endowment ($601,000 in early 1948) and that from the church had dropped from $85 per student to $63 during the decade following 1937. Conversely the college budget between 1946 and 1949 had risen from $300,000 to $926,000. Obligations by May 31 of the latter year totaled $907,300— $375,000 in dormitory bonds, $167,200 to the conference, $194,200 owed to banks and individuals, and $170,900 to trade creditors and contractors. Since a large segment of the debt would be paid out of earnings and $165,000 was due Gustavus in unpaid pledges, the situation was not serious. Yet if progress were to continue, there would have to be an upswing in gift income.[12]

In the midst of this postwar period of rapid physical expansion, an alumnus suggested that more attention be given to the academic side of the college, to building up the library, providing money for scholarships, and enabling the faculty to do more research. No one questioned the wisdom of these proposals, but only so much could be accomplished in a given time and with limited resources. Priorities had to be established in the face of the great pressures for admission. Dormitories and classrooms in such a period were more urgent than student aid and professorial publications, significant as these might be.[13]

Actually the curricular side of the college had not been neglected. Music had become a regular academic department in 1943, and courses in social work had grown in number and popularity in the same wartime period. A new department of home economics, located on the first floor of Old Main, was introduced in September, 1945. That same month Gustavus began participating in a North Central Association study of course offerings. New emphasis was accorded the humanities, and more attention was given to student guidance. The library was upgraded, and both students and faculty exhibited a healthy willingness to listen and to experiment. Though not so obvious as a trailer village or a new dormitory, the college's main business of teaching and learning was nevertheless alive and flourishing.[14]

By April, 1949, President Carlson was able to report that at least some aspects of the "emergency" had passed and that no construction was then going on. In a little over a year, however, conflict in Korea, declining enrollment, and inflation would create another era of deep concern. In the autumn of 1953 students numbered only 897 (480 men, 417 women). Tuition between 1950 and 1954 was raised from $300 to $450, but that increase lagged behind the rise in operation costs. Fortunately both church and alumni gifts more than offset this differential. The conference in 1950 had given $54,000 toward the college's current budget; in 1954 the amount was $95,000. The denomination had also undertaken the "Advance for Christ" appeal for Gustavus and Augustana Seminary, which by early 1956 had brought in a total of $434,000. Meanwhile the alumni organization had adopted a growing plan of annual giving. All of this help plus the effecting of economies enabled Gustavus to reduce its bonded indebtedness, whittle down past deficits, and for several years starting in 1951 balance its yearly budgets.[15]

In this same period the college gained wide recognition and new support by paying honor to Count Folke Bernadotte, the Swedish mediator for the United Nations who had been assassinated in Palestine in 1948. At graduation exercises on June 4, 1950, a crowd of 7,000 persons heard Ralph J. Bunche deliver the commencement address and saw the Count's widow and son participate in the dedication of the Folke Bernadotte Memorial Library. On the same occasion the formation of the Bernadotte Foundation at Gustavus, whose international committee of sponsors was headed by Gustaf VI of Sweden, was announced. Its purpose was "to promote the cause of education" and support the ideals of service and brotherhood exemplified by the life of Count Bernadotte. By sponsoring institutes, arranging tours abroad, bringing foreign students to the campus, and securing funds, the organization has "stimulated a new growth of internationalism" at the college and strengthened it in numerous other ways.[16]

With the passing of the era of the World War II veteran, Gustavus introduced certain sequences which were especially attractive to women. It was hoped that among other benefits these offerings would shore up sagging enrollments. A four-year program in elementary education and a two-year course in secretarial work were initiated in the fall of 1949. One term for nursing students from Bethesda Hospital in St. Paul was already in the schedule, and efforts were now made to develop a full degree course in nursing education. These attempts did not succeed until the autumn of 1956, when twenty-five freshman women became Gustavus' first contingent in the degree program for nurses. By then the sequence in elementary education, which had received the approval of the Minnesota Department of Education in 1953, could boast of graduates in six classes.[17]

Paralleling the college's attempts to refine its role

and sharpen its identity in the academic sphere were notable developments in the areas of jurisdiction and of organization. At the church convention in April, 1951, Gustavus' trustees and administration expressed the hope that the Red River Valley Conference — which had given the institution $1,000 the previous year — would become a full partner in operating the college. The Red River body continued to make annual gifts, but in 1956 it voted down the proposal for co-ownership. The convention of 1951 also provided for a commission to study the place of Gustavus in the life of the church. The resulting report, completed in 1954, was inconclusive, but it provided some guidelines for both the conference and the college. More significant was a study of Gustavus' administrative organization requested by the trustees in the spring of 1951. Conducted by a committee composed of faculty members, administrators, and trustees, the investigation led to the systemization of procedures on campus, the freeing of the president from many routine and petty chores, and the creation of the positions of chaplain and dean of students. In August, 1950, the first full-time alumni director had been employed; the following June an alumni advisory council held its initial meeting.[18]

By the mid-1950s worry over a shortage of students was yielding to fear that facilities were seriously inadequate for the task ahead. In the fall of 1955 enrollment, as it had from 1946 through 1950, again passed the thousand mark; more Minnesota high school graduates that year chose Gustavus than any other private college in the state. By 1962 when the college celebrated its centennial, students would number more than 1,200. In the late 1950s, however, the institution was better equipped to cope with a burgeoning undergraduate population than it had been a decade earlier. Growing support from alumni and church, help from the Bernadotte Foundation, the foresight of the president and trustees, all accounted for the readiness to meet changing conditions.[19]

After 1954 the campus would seldom be free from the sounds of excavation and construction. In that year Gustavus secured a $600,000 forty-year federal loan to build a dormitory for two hundred men. When the new structure, as yet unnamed, was occupied in the fall of 1955, the crowding in Uhler Hall was reduced, Johnson Hall was returned to the women, and the Ranch House was remodeled for classroom use. At commencement in 1960 the five-year-old building was christened Sorensen Hall in honor of Mr. and Mrs. Charles Sorensen, a couple from Minnesota Lake. Neither was Swedish nor Lutheran, but they had given Gustavus $225,000 under

a life annuity plan out of admiration for what the college was doing.[20]

For a long time Gustavians had dreamed of having a student union, but by 1952 it was evident that such a facility could not be financed in the foreseeable future. An alternative plan would have to be developed. The alumni board then approached the college trustees with the suggestion that the old gymnasium be remodeled as a student center. Plans were drawn in 1953, and the renovation was begun two years later. When completed in 1956 as the central section of a contemplated union complex, the building provided a setting which undergraduates took to "like ducks to water." The $95,000 cost of the transformation was paid by the Greater Gustavus Association — a portion immediately, the remainder in annual installments. Organized in 1944 to replace the old alumni organization, the efforts of the Greater Gustavus Association on behalf of the college have been of monumental proportions.[21]

A new chapel had also long been desired, but again lack of money had been a stumbling block. The church convention in 1955, however, approved a three-year appeal to its congregations to raise a chapel fund of $450,000. Two years later the college trustees were authorized to borrow up to $150,000 to add to that collected in the conference appeal and instructed to begin building operations no later than the spring of 1958. Revisions in the plans necessitated by financial considerations omitted an annex and a cloister wall and delayed ground breaking until March 2, 1959, when the ceremony was graced by the presence of Lord Clement R. Attlee, former British prime minister. Placed appropriately in the center of Gustavus' eighty-eight-acre campus, crownlike in appearance, and featuring a 187-foot spire, Christ Chapel was completed in 1961 at a cost of $700,000. Its dedication in January, 1962, was the first major event in a yearlong series commemorating the college's centenary.[22]

While work on the chapel was progressing, the second section of the union was constructed. Containing a bookstore, post office, and a dining area capable of serving 450 people at a time, the new food service facility was opened on January 4, 1960. Its cost came to about $325,000. The carpeting, drapes, and certain other accessories were purchased by the Greater Gustavus Association, but most of the money needed for the project was obtained through a federal loan.[23]

In the early 1950s one of the goals of the Bernadotte Foundation had been the construction of a science building which would include a gallery honoring the memory of Alfred Nobel, Swedish inventor and philanthropist. But once again money was lacking. In the spring of 1958, however, President Carlson announced to the conference that a Swedish industrialist in Minneapolis had made a conditional offer of $50,000 for the badly needed science hall. With the warm support of the Nobel Foundation in Stockholm, the entire structure would be dedicated to the man whose name was perpetuated in the world-famous prizes given to those who ''have conferred the greatest benefit on mankind.'' A dinner in Minneapolis on December 8, 1958, launched a campaign to raise money for the building — the first time Gustavus had sought substantial financial help outside its own church family.[24]

Work on the Alfred Nobel Memorial Hall of Science began in the fall of 1961, and the building was occupied after Christmas vacation in January, 1963. Its dedication — perhaps ''the most impressive event'' in Gustavus' history — took place on May 4, 1963. In attendance were twenty-six Nobel winners, the second largest gathering of these distinguished men ever held in the United States, a fact which focused world attention on the college at St. Peter. The hall had cost $1,550,000, nearly one-third of which had been given by the Minnesota Synod and its members. A debt of $713,000 remained, which would be paid off in time. A special lecture-study program envisioned in 1958 with the proposed Nobel memorial became a reality in January, 1965, when the first annual Nobel Symposium was conducted at the college with a grant from the Hill Family Foundation. Four Nobel prize winners participated.[25]

Meanwhile three other buildings had risen on the Gustavus landscape. In the summer of 1960 ground was broken for the Edwin J. Vickner Language Hall, which would contain classrooms, offices, and a language laboratory vitally needed by the growing institution. Most of its $240,000 cost was provided by two gifts: $30,000 from the estate of a Mankato publisher and $163,300 in securities from Dr. Vickner's widow. The hall went into use in the fall of 1961.[26]

The remaining two structures were dormitories made necessary by expanding enrollments and resultant crowding. In 1959–60, for example, the college housed 525 women in its residence halls and homes, 116 above their normal capacity. The conference, therefore, authorized Gustavus to apply for a federal loan of $1,200,000 to finance the construction of dormitories for 192 women and 200 men. That for the women was finished first and occupied in February, 1962. Known initially simply as South Hall, it was renamed Sohre Hall in October, 1965, in honor of Mr. and Mrs. Charles Sohre of Good Thunder whose four children had made life income agree-

ments with the college. By July, 1962, when the men's dormitory (North Residence) was completed, Gustavus for a time was totally residential. Dedication of the two buildings and of Vickner Hall, like that of Christ Chapel, constituted major events of the college's centennial year.[27]

That milestone provides a convenient occasion for a brief look backward. Gustavus' academic calendar had not changed since the fall of 1945, nor to any appreciable extent had the requirements for graduation. A three-two program in engineering with the University of Minnesota, involving a few students annually, had been added in 1953. A variety of degrees were still conferred. Of the 216 members of the 1960 class, for example, 92 had received B.A.s and 29 B.S.s; four had earned a bachelor of music education, and a considerable number had gained a B.S. in certain specialties — elementary education (32), business administration (27), nursing (19), physical education (12). There was one graduate in home economics, an offering discontinued in 1961. That same year the college's education and nursing programs were accredited by national agencies. By 1960 Gustavus could count about 4,500 graduates, plus some 3,000 other former students; over half of the two groups were living in Minnesota. Teaching had attracted the largest proportion of alumni, with business and the ministry following. Three Gustavians had served as governor of the North Star State, and a fourth would be elected to the position in 1966. These men and others had exhibited great affection for and loyalty to their alma mater, only one evidence of which had been generosity. The annual alumni fund had raised $32,300 in its first year of 1954 and $87,000 in 1960. These achievements had tied Gustavus with Hamline in alumni giving, according to the American Alumni Council, an organization made up of nearly two hundred coeducational colleges.[28]

Faculty at the end of World War II had numbered forty-five; by 1960 the total had more than doubled to nearly one hundred full- and part-time teachers distributed over two dozen academic departments. About 25 per cent of the instructional staff at the latter date held earned doctorates; seventeen individuals were full professors. They and many of their associates had served Gustavus with a devotion entirely unrelated to what the college could offer them in return. Despite inflation, no raises in salaries had been possible between 1948 and 1952; the highest professorial pay in 1954 had been $5,000. The next year the trustees had adopted a higher scale for the faculty, but funds had been insufficient to implement it fully for some time thereafter. By 1957 the Ford Foundation grant of $278,500 elevated spirits, although its income permitted only small salary increases at first. Gradually, however, conditions improved; in 1959–60 a few senior professors received over $8,000 each. Also helpful were growing fringe benefits and an increasing number of grants for research.[29]

The college's educational budget for 1949–50 had been about $506,000; ten years later with a slightly lower enrollment, the budget had risen to $1,230,000. In spite of soaring costs there had been only one deficit year (1958–59) during the decade. A number of factors had made this achievement possible: increased tuition charges, more gift income, larger church allocations, and the modest salary scale. Tuition between 1950 and 1960 had gone from $150 to $375 a semester. Total gifts, including those from the church, had risen from $105,000 in the late 1940s to $514,300 in 1958–59. The church's contribution for current operations in 1959–60 reached $252,000 — the largest amount given by any denominational body in the country to one of its colleges. Forty per cent or so of the conference's annual donation was used to support student scholarships. With an endowment of only slightly over $1,000,000, Gustavus could not rest on its financial oars. So once again the church mounted a special appeal called "Our Christian College Advance" in the hope of raising $1,000,000 for endowment and capital improvements at Gustavus. Although the goal was not attained, the conference collected $835,500, more than it had ever before raised for any single cause.[30]

Like colleges elsewhere, Gustavus was caught up in the growing concern over directions and procedures. A long-range planning commission was established in 1958 to advise President Carlson; a president's council composed of about forty Minnesota and South Dakota business and professional men held its initial meeting on campus that same year. In 1959 at Dr. Carlson's request the board approved a management survey, which resulted in changes relieving the trustees of many administrative duties so that greater attention could be given to policy matters. Meanwhile a revision of the college's constitution and bylaws was being framed; the new document approved in 1961 increased the number of board members from twelve to eighteen and made changes in the method of nominating them. All these changes merely emphasized the fact that Gustavus like other colleges increasingly required stronger organizational structures and procedures.[31]

After the planning commission had defined Gustavus' needs and goals, a long-range curriculum study committee of the faculty went to work in 1960 to update the college's course offerings and calendar. Early in the centennial year of 1962 the group submitted its report, which was later approved by both the full faculty and the board. The report recommended a rather dramatic break with the past. Starting in the fall of 1963, Gustavus would be one of the first institutions in the nation to adopt the four-one-four calendar, two semesters separated by a January interim term. Instead of 132 credits for graduation, 32 courses and four interim terms of work would be required. To reaffirm a liberal arts stance, a reading course for all students was introduced, greater weight was given to core subjects, and only the B.A. degree would be conferred. With refinements, the calendar and curriculum in the early 1970s remain essentially the same as when they were introduced in 1963.[32]

With fresh academic garb and membership in the newly formed Lutheran Church in America created by the Augustana synod's merger with other Lutheran groups, Gustavus entered its second century. Fall enrollment in 1962 stood at 1,262, including almost 700 women. By 1968 the total exceeded 1,800, of whom 626 were freshmen and 356 seniors. Most undergraduates were still natives of Minnesota and Lutherans, but in 1969–70 slightly over 80 minority students were also in attendance. By then the annual comprehensive fee was up to nearly $3,000. As a consequence, Gustavus administered over $1,500,000 in student aid. Of this sum, $555,000 went to 1,004 men and women in the form of college grants and scholarships; another $112,300 in similar aid was derived from noncollege sources. All types of student loans amounted to $817,800; in addition $125,000 was earned by undergraduates in various types of campus employment. It may be noted that until 1954 Gustavus had no regular budget for scholarships; the first such budget was for $19,400.[33]

Five buildings had been dedicated between January, 1962, and May, 1963, but continued enrollment increases necessitated still further plant expansion. Valley View Hall, a dormitory for 200 women was dedicated on May 3, 1964. A federal loan had provided the $700,000 necessary for construction. In September, 1965, the $250,000 Link Hall for 88 men was occupied. Built without resort to government borrowing, the residence gained its name by virtue of joining North and Sorensen halls. A year later a $715,000 federally financed two-story unit was added to the food center, a project made necessary by the adoption of a comprehensive student fee which included payment for board. Finally with the help of another government loan a dormitory complex known as Coed Center was constructed to house 192 men and an equal number of women.

With its opening in 1967, on-campus living quarters were available for more than 1,730 students.[34]

Among academic facilities the wooden fine arts building had done yeoman service, but it had become obsolete; the library so proudly dedicated in 1950 now was no longer adequate. Included therefore in a ten-year $18,000,000 Second Century Development Program announced in May, 1964, were a new fine arts center and a library addition. The center received impetus when Mrs. Jussi Björling, widow of the renowned Swedish tenor, suggested that a memorial to her husband be erected at Gustavus and a campaign to bring this about was undertaken. The outcome was a beautifully modern $3,300,000 complex consisting of an art building, theater, the Jussi Björling Recital Hall, and a building for music, speech, and drama. Ready for use in the late fall of 1970, it had been made possible by a grant of $986,000 from the Minnesota Liaison and Facilities Commission for Higher Education and a federal loan of $1,180,000.[35]

The library would come along somewhat later. After a careful study of future needs, it was decided to build a new structure rather than an addition and convert the old library to classroom use. Inflation and tight money slowed progress, but in February, 1970, the trustees approved contracts for the building. Two and a half stories high with space for 300,000 volumes, the $2,700,000 library was dedicated on October 25, 1972, in the presence of Princess Christina of Sweden. A large share of its cost was met by a federal grant of $821,700 and a forty-year government loan of $1,000,000 at 3 per cent interest. The remaining sum would be raised by the college.[36]

The pressure to secure funds, ever present in the past, promises to be even more strenuous in the future. In 1963–64, for example, of the college's budget of almost $2,000,000, the Red River Valley Synod contributed $22,100 and the Minnesota Synod $392,000. To do so, however, the latter had to dip into its contingency fund. The following year the church found it impossible to pay Gustavus all that had been allocated — a new experience. Even so the denominational body, though its gifts have declined in relation to the college's growing budgets, has remained the institution's largest single contributor. Yet of the $1,273,600 received by Gustavus in donations in 1967–68, the church gave only about one-third. It seems probable that to keep its momentum the college must increasingly look for support to individuals and organizations outside its traditional constituency. To do so without sacrificing features vital to the institution's heritage would be no mean task.[37]

In the spring of 1968 President Carlson resigned effective the following September 1 to devote his talents to the cause of the state's private liberal arts institutions as first executive director of the Minnesota Private College Council. The changes wrought and the progress made at Gustavus during the twenty-four years of his administration can only excite admiration. Also impressive were the quiet modesty and the unyielding devotion to his church and to Christian principles displayed by the man himself. For the academic year 1968–69 Dr. Albert G. Swanson served as acting president. He joined the staff in 1947 as chairman of the mathematics department; since 1955 he had been dean of the college.[38]

Frank R. Barth, a Chicago businessman and active Lutheran, was nominated to the trustees as tenth president of Gustavus by a search committee on which both faculty and students were represented. Elected to the position in June, 1969, by the executive board of the Minnesota Synod of the Lutheran Church in America, President Barth became the first layman in its 107-year history to head the college on a permanent basis. A graduate of Luther College in Decorah, Iowa, he had returned there for a temporary assignment after service as a naval officer in World War II. He had remained for six years, however, as chairman of the economics department during which time he earned an M.B.A. from Northwestern University in 1947. He had joined a public accounting firm in Chicago in 1953. More recently he had been financial vice president of a firm manufacturing heavy construction equipment.[39]

The task to which President Barth now turned called for his combination of business acumen, academic experience, and executive skills. With gross assets in excess of $18,000,000, Gustavus in 1969–70 had an operational budget of $5,500,000, of which $4,500,000 was paid by the students. Gifts and grants during the year totaled $2,220,000, the first time they had been so large, but the fourth consecutive year they had exceeded $1,000,000. The largest portion of the record donation came in the form of government grants, a sizable $672,600. Foundations contributed $505,300 and the church, $493,200. Also notable was the $229,000 given by the large number of alumni who continued to set a fast pace for former students at most other colleges in the country. Gustavus' indebtedness had reached $6,970,000, but $5,530,000 of it was amortized out of the institution's housing and food operations.[40]

During his initial months in office, President Barth found over 600 other novices on campus — the largest freshman class in the college's history and one of its ablest academically. Total enrollment for the year would be slightly under 1,800. The faculty numbered 121 full- and ten part-time teachers. The four-one-four calendar had been well tested, as had membership in the Central States College Association. Several faculty members would exchange posts briefly with teachers at other association institutions, and over a hundred undergraduates would participate in a variety of January interim programs. A recent self-study at Gustavus would provide the president with an overview of the current situation and a basis for future action. "Creativity and Learning" would be the theme for the academic program. Except for the fire on January 8, 1970, which destroyed the sixty-five-year-old auditorium and valuable college records, President Barth's first year would be busy, exciting, and in the main satisfying.[41]

On the undergraduate scene, one observer noted that students were replacing an interest in traditional social and recreational activities with a concern over broader civic and political conditions. Well attended "teach-ins," as they came to be called, in October and April, 1970, focused on the unpopular Vietnam War and on environmental problems. Then came the crisis days in May, brought on by the sending of United States troops into Cambodia and the shooting of four students at Kent State University in Ohio. But despite emotionally charged demonstrations, lectures, meetings, and discussions, no disruptions developed at Gustavus. Most students conducted themselves in a responsible manner and emerged from the experience wiser and better informed. On campus throughout the year, voluntary attendance at the daily and Sunday religious services was good. The issues of curricular reform, coed housing, and interresidence visitation aroused growing interest and led in the autumn of 1970 to a liberalization of open dormitory rules by the trustees. On May 31, 1970, a class of 327 members received B.A. degrees. Their most frequently selected majors were biology (40), economics (37), nursing (36), and history and elementary education (29 each). Thirty-two per cent of these young people entered the teaching field and another 28 per cent went on to graduate or professional schools.[42]

After a year in office President Barth looked back on his early experiences at Gustavus and expressed optimism for the future. He found the men and women in the 1970 class lovable, concerned with the welfare of others, and able exponents of the college tradition. "Gustavus," he wrote, "will continue to strive for excellence as a church-related educational institution in an atmosphere conducive to global understanding and social consciousness."[43]

30 CARLETON COLLEGE

The Pursuit of Excellence

As THE 1930s pushed to a conclusion, enrollment at Carleton was approaching the 850 mark. War in Europe gave new cause for concern, but there was still hope that full involvement in that conflict by the United States could be avoided. Even the Selective Service Act of September, 1940, did not erase that hope or disturb life on the campus to any appreciable extent. The Japanese attack on Pearl Harbor in 1941, however, put an end to dreaming and left students, like everyone else, in a state of shock and disbelief. In an atmosphere charged with anger, fear, and confusion, the question for young men was whether to enlist or not to enlist. For the college, it was how best to serve.[1]

For the time being it seemed wisest to continue operations as normally as possible. In the fall of 1942 male enrollment was still 455, but the "draft complex" was clearly noticeable, studies suffered accordingly, and drop outs grew in number. By autumn, 1943, only 92 civilian men were in attendance with 510 women. Fortunately the college received detachments of the Army Air Force Technical Training Command and of the Army Specialized Training Program, thereby utilizing faculty and physical plant and maintaining financial solvency. Coeds did their best "to preserve the spirit of Carleton while molding its activities to the exigencies" of the time. Slightly over 1,500 former students served in the armed forces during World War II, and 55 men representing every class but one between 1931 and 1947 lost their lives.[2]

The surrender of the Japanese and the sixty-fifth birthday of Carleton's president of thirty-six years fell in the same month, August, 1945. Cowling thereupon resigned and moved to St. Paul. After living and breathing the college for more than a third of a century, he could not have found complete detachment easy. Yet he firmly believed that he should give his successor an entirely free hand. There would be no repetition of the meddling of an earlier day. Statistics of the Cowling administration are impressive: gifts to the college of nearly $7,000,000; total assets up sixfold to $5,500,000; endowment and other funds increased more than sevenfold to almost $3,500,000; campus area expanded from 65 to 905 acres; annual expenditures grown from $49,684 to $511,954; ten major buildings erected; enrollment of less than 300 raised to over 800 with wider geographical distribution. Carleton moved from a position of bucolic isolation to one of national prominence, and all the while the stature of Cowling grew. Even after leaving Carleton, he devoted his time gratis to promoting worthy causes and organizations, a score or more at a time.[3]

Laurence McKinley Gould, holder of three earned degrees from the University of Michigan, second in command of the first Byrd Antarctic Expedition of 1928–30, and the college's popular professor of geology, was elected fourth president of Carleton. Members of the board and staff had first met this dashing academician-explorer in 1930, when he delighted a campus audience with tales of his exploits by dog sled on the ice sheets of Antarctica. Two years later a chair of geology and geography had been created at Carleton, and he had been induced to accept it. For the next three decades he served the college widely and brilliantly. His luster beyond Northfield included membership on the boards of the Ford Foundation and the National Science Foundation, his prominence during the International Geophysical Year of 1957, and his presidency of the United Chapters of Phi Beta Kappa. After leaving Carleton, he was elected president of the American Association for the Advancement of Science.[4]

Early in 1946 men began to trickle back to the campus, somewhat to the consternation of certain "Townies" who had been dating Carleton girls. Immediately plans had to be made to provide for

177

the influx expected in the fall. When September arrived, 260 freshman men enrolled, giving a total male registration of 529; comparable figures a year earlier had been 49 and 95. Ranging as they did from lads fresh out of high school to veterans of four or five years of military service, the men were scarcely a homogeneous lot, yet problems were not serious. Enthusiasm ran high. The strain of the war years was over. One new feature was the presence of a married veterans' community called Pine Hill Village, housing some fifty couples on the periphery of the campus. Since Carleton traditionally, however, had restricted enrollment to unmarried students, this community was a transitory manifestation. In 1946–47 returning servicemen constituted about 70 per cent of the male contingent; two years later the percentage was 40, and it dwindled rapidly thereafter.[5]

Depression and war having halted building operations for more than a decade and a half, Carleton's physical plant was hard pressed to serve the needs of the largest student body in the college's history — over 1,100 in 1947. In his inaugural address President Gould had stressed the paramount need for a new library and listed other essentials: an art building, a women's gymnasium (Cowling had cited this need in 1909), an auditorium with several classrooms, a student union, a warehouse, and a shop. Not until 1949, however, did the first of these structures — Boliou Hall, an art and classroom building — become a reality. Costing about $325,000, it was made possible by an unexpected donation of $150,000 and a conditional, anonymous matching gift of $75,000. The college provided the remainder. Less substantial in appearance than the Tudor Gothic buildings of the Cowling era, Boliou's functional quality and the manner in which it blended into the surrounding landscape set an example for future construction. The shop and warehouse came along in 1951.[6]

Meanwhile a faculty committee labored diligently to plan a new and modern library to replace Scoville, which despite the erection of a postwar, temporary, wooden annex was bulging at the sides by 1947. Spurred on by an anonymous "angel's" conditional gift of $1,000,000 in securities to endow a library (securities which had increased in value by one-third when they were turned over to the college) President Gould and his associates by the fall of 1954 had raised in excess of $1,500,000. Two years later the new structure, as yet unnamed, was completed, and in a carefully planned operation on May 22, 1956, students and faculty in a matter of hours transferred the contents of Scoville to its successor. In the task force was the former governor

of Minnesota, J. A. A. Burnquist, a graduate in the class of 1902, who as an academy student sixty years earlier had carried books from the old observatory to the then proudly new Scoville Memorial Library.[7]

The student union was not built, but between 1952 and 1954 the interior of Willis Hall was adapted to that purpose as a memorial to men who had lost their lives in World War II. In 1957–58 two new dormitories — Richard Drew Musser Hall for men and Reine Myers Hall for women partly financed by a forty-year loan of $800,000 from the federal Housing and Home Finance Agency — were erected in the hope of making Carleton completely residential. This hope had to be deferred when new plans in 1958 called for gradually increasing enrollment to 1,300.[8]

Final structures erected during the Gould years were the Olin Hall of Science, dedicated in the fall of 1961, and a men's dormitory and adjoining air-conditioned dining facility, Horace Goodhue Hall, completed in 1962. Both were designed by Minoru Yamasaki of Michigan, who had been appointed college architect in 1958. The former was made possible by a gift from the Olin Foundation in the amount of $1,510,000 — up to that time the largest single donation in Carleton's history; the latter structure, costing $1,490,000, was built by borrowing $1,295,000 from the federal government.[9]

Bricks and mortar, necessary as they are, were not of top priority in President Gould's vision of the Carleton he hoped to see. Of first importance was what went on in the brains and hearts of the men and women, faculty and students, who met together in the buildings. Frequently the president proclaimed the necessity for keeping in mind an eternal "vision of greatness," to use Alfred N. Whitehead's phrase. He suggested that a first-rate liberal arts college was known by the courses it did *not* teach, and that it could not be, nor indeed should it try to become, all things to all people. Frills and side shows would be eschewed. Effort would be concentrated on doing one job well — on advancing with vigor each of the conventional liberal fronts in science, literature, social science, art, and music.[10]

To accomplish this goal demanded the retention and recruitment of able and stimulating teachers and the admission of talented and motivated students. By 1960 President Gould had hired 90 per cent of the faculty of 110 members. The average age was forty-one years. Fifty-nine undergraduate colleges and fifty-two graduate schools were represented, providing a healthy diversity among the teachers. The Ph.D. degree was held by 59 per cent of the faculty, and most of the remainder were working toward its attainment. The mean salary of the teaching staff in 1957–58 was $6,116; five years later it was $9,216. In 1946 a college pension plan, added to the group insurance provision in effect since 1929, gave the president new leverage in attracting and holding good faculty members. Also helpful were such other fringe benefits as partial payment toward the higher education of faculty children, assistance in the purchase of homes, travel and study grants, reasonable teaching loads, a growing voice in policy making, wide latitude in the matter of academic freedom, and a generous policy on sabbatical leaves. The over-all level of the faculty was high.[11]

Early in the Gould administration, as part of the policy of raising the intellectual ability of the student body, a major change was instituted in the admissions procedure. Starting in the fall of 1947, all applicants were required to take the scholastic aptitude, the English composition, and two other achievement tests of the College Entrance Examination Board. Carleton was the first college in the Middle West to insist on college boards, and prophets of doom forecast all manner of dire consequences — declining enrollment, friction with high schools resentful and fearful of having their graduates show up badly on the tests, financial setbacks, and erosion of athletics and general campus well-being. The college's annual "Junior Show" had a field day satirizing the sad fate awaiting Carleton.[12]

Admittedly the college board tests are controversial and they do not measure except very indirectly traits of character, yet no dreadful results ensued from their adoption. They are still required at Carleton, and they have had a number of important uses beyond those relating to admission. Test scores have assisted students in taking stock of their own abilities, in gaining exemption from certain college requirements, and in receiving advanced standing and course credits. Enrollment dipped to about 850 during the early years of the 1950s, but this change was a response to conditions in the country at large not to test requirements.[13]

The scholastic aptitude of entering Carleton students as measured by board scores steadily increased. Freshmen in the fall of 1948 had an average verbal score of 538 as against 650 in September, 1964. This kind of statistical evidence has caused pre-1950 alumni to remark: "It's a good thing I went to Carleton when I did; I couldn't get in now." In fairness to the generation of the late 1940s, it is well to note that those Carleton students who took the medical college admission test in 1948–49

achieved a mean score in chemistry, physics, and biology which placed them among the top 6 per cent of comparable student groups from 356 colleges and universities. Despite this fine showing by students who entered Carleton before college boards were mandatory, it seems that the gamble taken in admissions procedure in the fall of 1947 paid off.[14]

Accompanying the attention given to improvement in the quality of faculty, students, and physical plant was constant concern for curricular matters. There had been a faculty standing committee on curriculum as early as 1921, but it was not until after World War II that this committee undertook a continuous, comprehensive study of the whole subject of graduation requirements in relation to the ideal of a liberally educated person. Even then, however, as a reflection of the college's tendency toward a conservative educational philosophy, no wholesale overhaul of the course of study took place.[15]

Improvement and refinement rather than experimentation were the order of the day. Notable was the introduction in 1948 of written and oral comprehensive examinations for seniors in their major fields. Although the prospect of "comps" and the attendant intellectual endeavor it engendered were rarely joyous experiences, the feeling of achievement which resulted from a successful encounter with the tests usually offset the trauma. But the examinations made no substantive change in the curriculum. With truth President Gould could write that during his twenty-eight years at Carleton, "the requirements for the bachelor's degree have changed but little." These consisted of English, some foreign language, literature, laboratory science, philosophy, a major, and "supporting hours."[16]

By 1957, however, with public interest in education intensified by such Russian scientific developments as Sputnik and with campus morale high, many people felt that it was time for some rather dramatic alteration of academic schedules and methods. Others contended that slowly but surely change had occurred, that innovations had been made while the best of the past had been conserved. Against this background of diverse feelings, the curriculum committee in 1958 recommended the adoption of a three-term calendar in which a student would take three courses a term instead of the five or six under the semester plan. After considerable debate and further investigation, the faculty gave its approval to the three-three proposal in 1960 and 1961. It went into effect the succeeding fall.[17]

No longer could one speak in traditional terms of semester hours and course credits; now it was term courses. With minor variations a student carried three courses each of three terms during a year in order to acquire the thirty-five term courses needed for graduation. In the final term of his senior year, when he was facing his comprehensives, he could carry two courses. Class periods were extended from fifty to seventy minutes, but faculty enjoyed flexibility in the matter of classroom demands. Emphasis was placed upon values to be derived from independent work, experimentation, and the search for the most effective method of instruction in each discipline.[18]

Reaction to three-three was varied. In general students favored the reduction in the number of courses taken at one time, and they seemed pleased that their Christmas holiday was no longer marred by worry over approaching final examinations. (The student who had fallen behind in his work was an exception.) On the other hand, three-three did not achieve one of its aims to ease the pressure felt by students, nor did its ten-week terms provide sufficient time for reflection and the assimilation of materials in certain courses. Within seven years after a thorough review by faculty and students, three-three would be modified in the light of its past imperfections. Truly the quest for the most effective curriculum and calendar is never-ending; it must go eternally on if colleges are to respond to the needs of changing times.[19]

Although neither by experience nor inclination a fund raiser, President Gould typically found mendicancy a perennial demand on his talents and energy. No major financial campaign was conducted during the first decade after the war, but an office of vice president in charge of public relations and promotional work was created in 1948 and efforts to strengthen the college's economic condition were continuous. As a result, when the Ford Foundation in 1955 made its famous gift to American colleges and universities for faculty salary endowment, Carleton not only received $399,500, but was also accorded an "accomplishment grant" of $248,000 in recognition of its leadership in improving the status and compensation of faculty in its geographic region.[20]

By the end of June, 1957, total assets of the college were $12,000,000, of which some $8,000,000 were in the form of endowment and special funds. Despite this impressive vitality, the challenge of a changing and rapidly expanding society rendered insistent a new thrust forward. Carleton could not remain static. After the report of a New York fund-raising firm indicated that the college's position and prospects were encouraging, the trustees in the fall of 1957 decided that a thorough self-examination of the institution's effectiveness and future needs by board, faculty, and students was imperative to the success of a contemplated financial campaign. On the basis of these studies, a goal of $12,000,000 was set, to be raised by June, 1962, the time of President Gould's intended retirement.[21]

This successful development program had as its theme the pursuit of excellence. President, trustees, alumni, and parents all helped with generosity and enthusiasm, and in contrast to earlier experiences, the employment of professional fund-raising assistance was found to be worth while. The Olin Foundation's gift of $1,500,000 for a science hall was both heartening and sizable. Then in October, 1961, came another timely offer of encouragement and support: the Ford Foundation would make a contingency grant of $2,000,000 to expand and improve Carleton's academic program if the college would match Ford dollars three for one in cash and securities by June 30, 1964. Spurred by this challenge, numbers of individuals who had already contributed gave again, with the result that on June 15, 1962 — the day President Gould presided over his last Carleton commencement — the chairman of the board of trustees could happily report that $12,004,864.60 had been raised.[22]

It was a fitting capstone to an administration whose records bristle with tangible evidences of progress. Between 1945 and 1962 endowment funds multiplied from $3,422,900 to $15,134,500; total assets rose from $5,487,400 to $22,121,900. Annual expenditures mounted from slightly over $500,000 to more than $3,100,000. The number of faculty went from 58 to 122 and the yearly budget for teaching from $197,500 to $977,000. During these seventeen years of Dr. Gould's presidency, enrollment more than doubled and sums awarded in scholarships and loans expanded tenfold. Four Carleton undergraduates won Rhodes Scholarships, and dozens of other students were awarded fellowships for advanced study both in the United States and abroad.[23]

Other evidence of achievement could be found in a 1953 national study measuring the production of scholars among college alumni in which Carleton placed fifth in social studies, seventh in humanities, and eleventh in science, to achieve a composite seventh place nationally in proportion to the number of men graduates. A 1958 report, covering the period 1920 to 1949, ranked Carleton in a tie for eleventh place among 302 colleges and universities in proportional representation of male graduates listed in *Who's Who in America*. Not surprisingly

Carleton found itself on many lists of the nation's best colleges. In response to such recognition, President Gould was fond of remarking that the college was not as good as people said it was, yet he was obviously proud of its accomplishments and jealous of its good name.[24]

The Gould administration has been called a time of realization, a period when the planning and organization of the Cowling years came to fruition. By contrast with the climate on many of the nation's campuses in the 1960s, most of the Gould presidency could also be labeled an era of good feeling. Immediately after World War II two-thirds of the student body came from Minnesota, Illinois, and Wisconsin. By 1957 those states contributed only 57 per cent of the undergraduates, but no matter where their origin, Carleton men and women in general were white, middle class, and Protestant. As such they possessed a homogeneity and consensus in goals, outlooks, and values which tended to minimize differences and militate against serious conflict. The majority of the faculty, enthusiastic over the pursuit of excellence, also shared the feeling of unity and did not seriously rock the boat. Expectations were clear and largely supported; fragmentation and pluralism, except in academic discussion, were strangers within the gate. For college administrators it was a relatively quiet and happy time.[25]

There were, of course, periodic squalls to disturb the general equanimity, but about the only issue on which there was a long-standing difference of opinion between the students and the administration was required attendance at religious services. In the period following the war these consisted of a Tuesday morning chapel service and a Sunday evening vesper service with seating segregated by sexes. There was considerable griping about the compulsory attendance, but no concerted effort to oppose it. One big cause for complaint was removed in the spring of 1951 when segregated seating was abolished. By the late 1950s, however, students had become more aggressive in their struggle against the traditional chapel and vesper requirement. As a consequence, a new program was inaugurated in the fall of 1959. Chapel attendance then became voluntary, and Sunday evening vespers were replaced by a morning service. For students opposed to attending religious observances various types of Sunday evening programs were held in Severance's Great Hall. Each student was expected on his honor to attend so many Sunday services or programs every term. This system proved unworkable, and in June, 1964, the trustees removed all requirements

for attendance at religious services. That the virtual demise of chapel and vespers made a change in the pattern of life at Carleton none could deny; whether the difference was basic or superficial is a question still debated.[26]

Dr. John W. Nason, the only alumnus to hold the position, became the fifth president of the college on July 1, 1962. Coming from a family with numerous Carleton connections, he had earned a Phi Beta Kappa key and distinguished himself as a debater during his undergraduate days. Following two years of further study after his graduation in 1926 — one of theology at Yale, the other of philosophy at Harvard — he had spent the period between 1928 and 1931 as a Rhodes Scholar at Oriel College at Oxford. In the latter year he had joined the department of philosophy at Swarthmore College, where he served as president between 1940 and 1953. Thereafter he had been president of the Foreign Policy Association, a trustee of Phillips Exeter Academy, Vassar College, and the Hazen and Danforth foundations among numerous other responsibilities. Although his administration would last only eight years (like his two immediate predecessors he retired at the age of sixty-five) it covered most of the explosive decade of the 1960s which witnessed rapid and dramatic changes.[27]

As the previous administration had been one of realization, at least the early part of the Nason presidency was a time of consolidation, a period during which enterprises already under way were brought to conclusions. The recently completed Development Program had injected great momentum into the college's inflow of dollars; gifts, grants, and bequests to Carleton in 1962–63 totaled $2,670,000 — the fifth straight year they had been in excess of $2,000,000. For 1963–64 the figure came to $2,630,000; that same year $40,000 was given to the Parents' Fund by the largest number of donors in its history, and 40.6 per cent of the alumni body gave a record $192,000. Such generous support reflected credit on both college and contributors; it was heart warming to everyone on campus. But it also posed a challenge to the new administration. Of the $5,300,000 given to Carleton between 1962 and 1964, $3,500,000 represented pledges made during the Development Program. By the end of that drive $562,000 of the $2,000,000 Ford grant remained unredeemed. It thus became the task of President Nason and his associates to fulfill this commitment and attempt to maintain the momentum in giving without the fanfare which accompanies a major campaign. In 1964–65 the last of the Ford money was matched, but total contributions reached only $1,500,000 — the first time in seven years that the $2,000,000 level was not attained. Student fees and the college's endowment funds were rising, but so were costs. The overcast on the financial horizon showed no sign of clearing.[28]

In the area of physical plant President Nason also found himself committed to carrying out previously conceived plans. When he took office, two buildings were already under construction and the number, nature, and sequence of appearance of several others had been largely agreed on. The first to be completed was the men's gymnasium designed by architect Yamasaki and dedicated in May, 1964, with ceremonies which included a concert by the Minneapolis Symphony Orchestra. The $1,100,000 cost of this aesthetic and functional structure was paid for with money raised during the Development Program drive. A year later the Elizabeth Stehman Cowling Recreation Center for Women also designed by Yamasaki was dedicated. The occasion was rendered especially poignant by the last visit to the college of Cowling for whose wife the long-desired building was named. Friends and alumni had provided the $700,000 to cover the center's cost.[29]

Since plans for the future of the campus called for the razing of once-regal Gridley Hall, a new dormitory for women became an immediate concern. Designed by Yamasaki, the residence would be the college's first high rise structure, an edifice of seven stories to house 156 students. Construction began late in 1965 on a site southwest of Cowling Center, and late in the academic year 1966–67 the novel addition to the physical plant was occupied. Named in honor of a woman who had graduated from Carleton in 1885 and then taught there for thirty-nine years, Isabella Watson Dormitory cost $1,350,000, of which $1,000,000 was borrowed from the federal government. Wreckers then moved in to demolish Gridley. Meanwhile the college had acquired the local Methodist parish house and remodeled it as a foreign language home for forty-five men. This substantial, brick structure was occupied toward the end of the 1966–67 school year. Carleton had achieved its earlier goal to accommodate 1,300 students in college residence halls, but three new buildings were still needed: a music and drama center, a science laboratory, and a student union. In June, 1968, even though the problem of financing was not entirely solved, the trustees voted to go ahead with construction of the center. Work began in the spring of 1969 and completion followed late in 1970. The $2,500,000 facility was paid for without resort to borrowing thanks largely to foundation gifts.[30]

In a third area, that of curricular affairs, the new administration likewise inherited ongoing developments. The three-three program was only one year old, and the latest of several long-range planning committees of the faculty was wrestling with its definition of a liberal education. Indeed every facet of Carleton life was being scrutinized by this group separately and in conjunction with similar committees of students and the board of trustees. Progress was slow and differences of opinion manifest, but most people seemed to agree that the college could not be content with the status quo.[31]

One major decision was reached in 1963–64 to initiate a program of Asian studies. A separate department would not be created but relevant material would be added to existing courses in a number of departments, such as history, sociology, art, and religion. There would also be a variety of activities and special events such as recitals, lectures, symposiums to supplement the work of the classroom. With financial support from the Hill Family Foundation and the McGregor Fund of Detroit, the program was inaugurated in the fall of 1964. The following summer seventeen students studied in Japan under the direction of a Carleton faculty member. Since that time, the summer trip has been a regular feature of Asian studies, which have become a significant part of the college's intellectual program.[32]

Paralleling this expansion of the curriculum was the growing number of opportunities open to Carleton students through the programs of the Associated Colleges of the Midwest (ACM), which Carleton had helped to organize in 1958. These included study in Costa Rica, scientific work at the Argonne National Laboratory in Illinois, research at the Newberry Library and urban studies in Chicago, and scientific projects at the Wilderness Field Station in northern Minnesota, to name a few. A modification in the grading system was introduced in the fall of 1965 by which a student after five terms could elect to take a grade of pass or fail instead of the traditional letter grades in one course a term. This change was based on the premise that the student, feeling less pressure, would perhaps be inclined to broaden his schedule to include courses he had previously avoided for fear of getting a low grade. Although pass-fail has its critics, it has since been extended to include freshmen, and it appears to be firmly entrenched in the college's teaching methods.[33]

During the year 1966–67 in a carefully planned and wide-reaching series of commemorative events that included concerts, symposiums, creation of a sculptured fountain, and publication of its history, Carleton celebrated the completion of its first century. Although it was an occasion for looking backward and rejoicing over past achievements, the centennial also served as an impetus to the continued search for improvement. In the words of President Nason, "the College was wide open to change." [34]

Characteristically, however, evolution rather than revolution in curriculum resulted. Three-three was retained, but it was modified in 1967–68 by the introduction of five- and fifteen-week courses with variable credits to parallel the regular ten-week offerings. The requirement for graduation was reduced from thirty-five to thirty-four term courses. In an attempt to make the freshman year more intellectually stimulating, experimental seminars were introduced in the fall of 1968 and a first-year humanities course was approved. With more and more students interrupting their campus residence for study abroad, an office of international studies to facilitate such endeavors was established that same fall. New programs emphasizing the fine arts were instituted and increasingly classroom and laboratory looked to the college's computer system to solve their problems and improve their efforts. Flexibility, innovation, relevancy — these became the watchwords in the quest for up-to-date curricular content and the latest pedagogical methods. The search might be hectic and wearing, but it certainly was not dull. [35]

Similar adjectives with equal validity could be applied to Carleton students of the Nason era, or at least to their leaders and image makers. Products of their time, pluralistic, bright, and informed, these undergraduates recognized no sacred cows, constantly questioned the college's traditional regulations and mores, and kept up a continual campaign to effect changes. Their success was little short of amazing. Throughout 1965–66, they sat with trustees and faculty on a joint social-policy committee. The result of this endeavor in 1967 was further liberalization of already liberal dormitory hours for women and the legalization of the drinking of liquor by twenty-one-year-olds in the college residence halls. A standing committee on social policy composed of faculty and students as well as administrators was another outcome. Early in 1968 students were accorded voice and vote on a number of other college committees. By 1970 many critics on the dark side of the generation gap would feel that acceptance by the administration of the new mores had gone far enough. No longer were all dormitories segregated by sexes; men and women now lived on the same floors in certain halls. Much has been written regarding these innovations but what impact — if any — they have upon college and students remains to be seen. [36]

But if the Carleton student was aggressive and demanding, he also shared his generation's concern for social justice. Of the 278 members of the class of 1964, for example, 23 entered the Peace Corps — a higher percentage than in any other college or university in the country. Increasingly the voice of the undergraduate was raised in support of minority groups, especially Blacks. Aiding this cause was a Rockefeller Foundation grant of $275,000 to the college in 1964 to provide financial aid for underprivileged students. By the fall of 1967 there were 38 Negroes in attendance; a few years previously a Black student at Carleton had been a rarity. In 1968 a Negro was appointed assistant director of admissions and special counselor to Black students, who that fall numbered 52. It is the college's intention that as soon as possible minority group undergraduates will constitute 10 per cent of the student body. [37]

To a large degree finances will determine whether Carleton will succeed in this program, even as they will influence greatly the college's ability in every respect to remain a first-rate institution. Consequently the trustees early in 1968 endorsed an ambitious development program which President Nason had outlined in his report of the previous year. Emphasizing the need for continuous support, the project was forecast for a decade rather than for a shorter period typical of most fund drives. The amount aimed at was $44,000,000, or slightly over $4,000,000 a year. Of the total, about $12,860,000 would go for current expenses, $9,000,000 for plant improvement, and $22,000,000 for augmenting the endowment. With this money the college could continue its efforts toward faculty and curricular improvement, provide the financial and other help students would need, and carry out the plans for plant development already begun with the construction of the music and drama center. As the 1970s began the $4,000,000 a year schedule had not been maintained, but it is too early to predict the outcome of the ten-year enterprise. [38]

Toward the end of his administration, President Nason responded to a query regarding his problems and achievements as president of Carleton. First among the former, he said, was the perennial task of getting enough money to run the college and to move it forward. Second, with pressures on administrators constantly proliferating was the problem of time, of finding enough hours to do all that needed to be done. Third, especially during the early 1960s was the difficulty of recruiting able faculty people who understood what a small college was all about. Fourth, was the personal challenge of learning "to adjust to modern times," of discovering how to get decisions made "in the mélange of conflicting views and demands." Finally, was the matter of timing; it was easier and less nerve-racking to be a college president in earlier periods.[39]

Achievements are somewhat more difficult to pin-point until they are high lighted by the passage of time, yet President Nason liked to think that he made contributions in three areas. Most important was his role in helping to ease the transition from an "old authoritarian stance to one in which everybody has a piece of the action" — in which each person in the college enjoys a say in the decision-making process. Although he had to change his own prej-udices, he recognized that changes in academe gen-erally necessitated the modification of traditional governance and administration at Carleton. Second, he detected a greater tendency on the part of the faculty to view the college as a whole and a healthy breakdown in the semiautonomy which formerly characterized most academic departments. Third, Dr. Nason missed no opportunity to encourage co-operation between Carleton and St. Olaf, a develop-ment he regarded as absolutely vital to the welfare of both institutions.[40]

Taking office as sixth president of Carleton on July 1, 1970, was Dr. Howard R. Swearer, a thirty-seven-year-old graduate of Princeton University, with M.A. and Ph.D. degrees from Harvard University. His major academic field is political sci-ence. From 1960 to 1967 he had been on the faculty of the University of California at Los Angeles, where he had served as director of certain Peace Corps training programs and headed the university's Russian and East European Studies Center. For the three years before coming to Carleton, he had been program officer in charge of the Ford Foundation's office of European and international affairs. In his Carleton post he presides over the fortunes of an institution with assets of over $41,000,000 and an annual income in excess of $7,000,000. Recogniz-ing that the task facing him will not be easy, Presi-dent Swearer nevertheless welcomes the challenge. He possesses the characteristics needed to succeed in his demanding position.[41]

31 AUGSBURG COLLEGE

Coming of Age in the City

As AUGSBURG moved into the war years of the 1940s, its seminary department, though strong, remained small. Its collegiate division, however, was growing in size and attracting students from a broadening base. For twenty years or more people had spoken of "Augsburg College," although the institution's official name had always been "Augsburg Seminary." Now the trustees with approval by the church conference of 1942 gave legal endorsement to what had become common practice. Under a revision of the articles of incorporation, name and purpose were both updated. Henceforth the title would be "Augsburg College and Theological Seminary." The *raison d'être* of the institution would continue to be "the training of young men in the ministry of the Lutheran Church," but in addition it would "aim to offer both young men and women an education in general Christian culture as well as a training for Christian service in lay vocations." Corporation, board, and administration would be the same for the two bodies, but now college would be peer to seminary rather than a subordinate.[1]

President Christensen had already turned over many financial responsibilities, including fund raising and supervision of plant, to a business manager. The next major step in the evolution of modern administration came in 1942 with the appointment of a college dean in the person of Martin Quanbeck, graduate of the class of 1929, registrar, education department head, and director of teacher placement. Except for the period between 1946 and 1950, he would serve as dean until 1965 and define the office's duties in accordance with generally accepted collegiate practices. Happily for the college the climate of opinion in the Free Church had become clearly favorable to the development of a good liberal arts institution. The denomination's committee on educational policies, created in 1941, for example, commended Augsburg in 1943 for having

"adjusted its plans and expanded its work to meet the demand and need of young people for college education," and urged the trustees to "make every effort to secure accreditation of the College by the North Central Association." All of this was quite in contrast to the attitude of the church's board of education in the 1920s. Encouraged by this support, the faculty began planning curricular revisions to meet postwar demands, and President Christensen felt free to declare: "The colonial period of our existence is practically past." Church and college had captured a larger vision of the latter's scope and role.[2]

For a time World War II slowed developments. Early in the conflict, even after Hitler's take over of Denmark and Norway in the spring of 1940, sentiment on campus remained largely neutralist and antiwar. For his part Christensen recognized the necessity of defending the "human ideals of justice and freedom," but he warned the church in 1942 that Christian colleges "must never become the instruments of un-Christian or anti-Christian attitude and propaganda." In the aftermath of Pearl Harbor enrollment dropped somewhat in 1941–42, but the big decline came in 1943–44 when approximately 225 students failed to resume their college careers. Faculty members likewise departed for military service or to take different positions.[3]

Somewhat paradoxically, however, the college's financial picture took on a rosier hue. It was true that declining enrollment meant lowered tuition payments, but offsetting this loss was an accompanying reduction in the cost of the curtailed academic program. The specter of idle plant was removed in 1943–44 by renting Memorial Hall to the University of Minnesota to house one of its military training units. Free Church congregations, more prosperous as a result of wartime economic activity, stepped up their giving to an extent which permitted Augsburg to pay off all its indebtedness in 1944. Once again administration and trustees could think in terms of plant expansion to care for the anticipated postwar enrollment bulge. A library-classroom building was badly needed; so it was proposed to the conference in 1944 that money to erect such a facility be secured through a campaign conducted in connection with Augsburg's seventy-fifth birthday celebration. The outcome was the authorization of a drive for $200,000, plus a lesser amount for Oak Grove Academy in Fargo. By 1946 the drive had gone over the top, raising more than $260,000, but inflation and the scarcity of building materials delayed the start of construction for nearly two years.[4]

Meanwhile in the spring of 1945 with victory over the Nazis in Europe seeming ever closer, steps were taken to carry out the 1943 recommendation of the church committee that "every effort" be made to win North Central accreditation. A University of Minnesota professor of educational administration was engaged to determine what needed to be done, and in July he submitted his findings. Unfortunately, in his opinion four areas were not up to the standards set by the accrediting association: the library collection, physical facilities, business administration, and such matters of faculty concern as salary, appointment, tenure, and retirement. Some progress had been achieved in correcting these weaknesses when the college was suddenly faced with another major challenge — the end of the war and the influx of male students.[5]

In the fall of 1945 enrollment totaled 244; by the second semester it had jumped to 464. Then in 1946–47, 400 ex-GI's helped swell the student body to an unheard-of 794. The high point, however, was not reached until 1949–50 when 966 men and women enrolled — more than twice as many as were in attendance in 1940. Crowding and improvisation became necessities. A former church was transformed into a music building, and nearby residences were purchased for dormitory use and faculty housing. Two barracks and a recreation hall (the college's physical education center for more than ten years) were secured from the War Surplus Administration, space for classes was rented in Riverside Chapel, and regular buildings were called upon for double duty.[6]

The faculty roster was also expanded by the return of former teachers and the employment of new people, and efforts were made to improve their working conditions. In 1945 retirement age was set at sixty-eight, and small pension benefits were provided. A year later the hiring of permanent faculty members, except seminary professors, was left to the board of trustees without the conference

approval previously required. The traditional categories of permanent professor and temporary instructor, neither of which guaranteed tenure, were abolished in 1947 in favor of the four ranks recognized in most college teaching staffs, tenure being given after five years to all above the rank of instructor.[7]

Curricular changes and additions were also made. Economics in 1946 was separated from sociology and political science, its partners in the old department of social science, and joined with business administration and secretarial studies in a new academic unit. Thereupon history welcomed political science, and sociology moved in the direction of separate departmental status. Home economics by 1949 provided both a teaching and a regular major, while courses in speech were numerous enough by 1953 to fulfill requirements for a major. Older departments, too, added courses from time to time, and in 1947 the curricular structure of the college was brought closer to general practice by the creation of three academic divisions of humanities, social science, and natural science. But typically departmentalism still remained a potent force.[8]

By 1948 the trustees decided to go ahead with building plans, but not according to the schedule outlined during the war. Construction of the library was postponed; on a site created by tearing down West Hall and Old Main, Science Hall with classroom and administrative offices was erected instead. Completed in 1949 at a cost of $575,000 fully equipped, it left Augsburg with a debt of about $100,000. The time now seemed right for seeking accreditation; an application was submitted to the North Central Association in the fall of the same year. Early in 1950 an inspection team visited the campus and local hopes were high. Some two months later, however, the association acted unfavorably, citing "the need for improvement" in a number of areas, including faculty competence and conditions of service, the program of advanced education, the library, business administration, and financial support. President Christensen admitted to great disappointment, but he detected a silver lining in the challenge thus provided to move ahead more rapidly than might otherwise have been done.[9]

Hardly had the shock of North Central's rejection been absorbed, however, when a new worry in the form of the Korean conflict broke on the scene. As it developed, few male students were drafted, but wartime inflation did occur, and enrollment and tuition income once again began to decline. The 1950–51 student body of 877 was about 90 below that of the preceding year. To offset Augsburg's first operating deficit in some time, the trustees and administration increased tuition from $150 to $165 a semester and cut back the teaching staff by about 18 per cent. In addition the church was asked to raise its contribution by $25,000 to a total of $80,000. This was done, but with needed salary increases and a continued drop in enrollment, deficits were also incurred in the following two years.[10]

In 1954 tuition went to $200 a term, and the church was called upon for $110,000. The relatively new Minnesota College Fund and the Augsburg endowment then contributed a total of about 2 per cent of the institution's income, not a very substantial proportion. In the face of this shaky situation, however, the administration did not falter in its determination to move Augsburg forward. The board in 1952 had secured conference approval for a drive to raise $400,000 to build a library wing and remove the debt on Science Hall. Within two years more than $220,000 had been subscribed, and it was decided to go ahead with the badly needed library.[11]

During this same difficult period of the early 1950s, the effort to meet the standards of the North Central Association persisted. Part of it involved the usual self-study project, which accomplished much by way of building *esprit de corps* and familiarizing teachers with the problems and possibilities facing the institution. Great credit was due Dean Quanbeck, on whom a major share of the responsibility rested, for the success he achieved in "broadening the faculty's role in the direction of academic affairs" — something that had needed doing. Other accomplishments involved larger appropriations for library purchases, a reorganization of student personnel services, including the health service, and more up-to-date practices and procedures in business management. Thus strengthened the administration in the fall of 1953 submitted another application for membership in the North Central Association. This time the outcome gave cause for rejoicing. After another investigation, the long-sought goal of association membership was attained on March 26, 1954. Augsburg could now hold its head up in select academic company and look forward to a brighter future. Characteristically President Christensen warned against complacency, and pointed to accreditation as "a true 'commencement' affording both new responsibilities and many new opportunities for our college."[12]

In the remaining eight years of Dr. Christensen's administration, a great deal was accomplished. Enrollment nearly doubled from 765 to 1,402, while full- and part-time faculty rose from 64 to 102. In 1955 Augsburg was notified that its share of the Ford Foundation grants to private institutions would amount to $165,500. Although one of the smallest Ford gifts to Minnesota's private liberal arts colleges, it permitted needed increases in faculty salaries and more than doubled Augsburg's meager endowment funds. Expansion of the cramped campus area under a hoped-for federal urban renewal program did not materialize, but the physical plant was augmented significantly. Gerda Mortensen Hall, a dormitory for women built with assistance from a federal loan, became a reality in 1955. That same year the George Sverdrup Library, containing shelving for 100,000 volumes, was also completed. Within a decade after 1957 the library budget would increase nearly fivefold to about $100,000, and book holdings would pass 90,000.[13]

The fall of 1959 saw the conversion of a former church into a building for speech and dramatics, heretofore stepchildren housed in the Music Hall. Finally in the spring of 1960 ground was broken for the $1,000,000 Si Melby Hall, an auditorium-gymnasium planned as the first step in a twenty-year $8,000,000 development program. A year later the structure was ready to provide the setting for the Spring Antiphony. This event "blending art, music and the spoken word," like the well-established Creative Arts Week, thereafter became a regular spring attraction. Many other college functions, including chapel services, could now be scheduled in the new facility; no longer would home basketball games have to be played in the Minneapolis Armory. A sizable debt had been incurred in this physical expansion, but investment in plant had grown from $1,500,000 in 1954 to $3,700,000 eight years later. In the same period the operations budget had tripled.[14]

Lack of sufficient funds was a handicap, however, as the college sought to attract permanent faculty personnel and to improve and expand curricular offerings. As a result, progress in achieving these goals was spotty and frequently slower than desired. Yet changes in the curriculum as in the more intangible, but significant, climate of opinion did occur. Augsburg now responded to general trends in educational developments, becoming less a closed, parochial enclave and more a part of America's main stream. The sociology department, for example, which had the largest number of majors, high lighted the advantages of Augsburg's urban location. Henceforth, catalogs need not apologize for the campus' city setting; rather they could boast that "students prepare for careers in our increasingly urban society."[15]

Courses in religion further illustrated this subtle transition. Traditionally the emphasis in teaching had been more on "encouragement of Christian commitment" than on "exposure to theological scholarship," but by the late 1950s a shift toward the latter was evident. If this change was disturbing to various segments of the college community, it was liberating and in line with developments in leading institutions of higher learning. Science courses were also strengthened. Biology had long offered a respectable program, but chemistry had been plagued by frequent turnovers in its staff. Physics had suffered a similar fate, as well as inadequacies in equipment and in the number of its courses. Key appointments during the late 1950s corrected many of these weaknesses and led in April, 1962, to Augsburg's being placed on the approved list of the American Chemical Society. Mathematics responded somewhat more slowly to change, but the advent of a new teacher in 1961 set the stage for expansion and revision there.[16]

Business administration and economics formed a single department within the division of social sciences, but the former enjoyed greater popularity. Even the establishment of a major in economics in 1960 failed to redress the enrollment imbalance. The history department, which was down to two faculty members in the early 1950s, soon received additional staff and gave increasing attention to the study of non-Western areas. Its associate, political science, had yet to achieve full status. In 1961 psychology was separated from education and accorded departmental status on its own. Since teaching was the professional goal of many students, the education department was strong and its relations with other departments generally cordial. In the spring of 1962 its program for training secondary school personnel won full accreditation by the National Council for the Accreditation of Teacher Education. The following year the college graduated the first students prepared for elementary schoolteaching under a sequence approved by the trustees in 1959.[17]

Revived interest in other cultures, together with faculty commitment to the liberal arts ideal, led in 1959 to an increase in the amount of work required in foreign languages. Art and drama began to take on new importance, and music moved forward on the strong foundation already created. An art department offering a minor was established in 1960 and moved to new and better quarters a few years later. The band and choir, whose tours had been confined to the Midwest, soon traveled to points as far away as Alaska and Europe, adding to the standard classics of earlier concerts selections as contemporary as the latest composers could conceive.[18]

The student body, drawn increasingly from the Twin Cities and still mainly Lutheran, was less docile in accepting traditional rules and practices than in the past. An attempt by the administration in 1958 to tighten up a ban on drinking, for example, was reversed by the faculty. Social dancing on campus was approved in 1965. Religious activities, including daily chapel, continued to receive strong support, but emphasis tended to shift from a search for personal salvation to social concern and action. Efforts were made by student leaders to gain representation on faculty committees; though only modest gains were made, future trends were visible.[19]

The faculty labored long and hard to define its role in the determination of college policy. As the size of the staff increased, it became progressively more difficult to recruit teachers who were both competent in their fields and committed to Augsburg's Christian heritage. This task was never accomplished to everyone's satisfaction, but it was obvious that professional competence carried more weight than piety in hiring and promotion in the 1960s than it had a decade or so earlier. Happily tolerance and freedom were cherished legacies of the college's intellectual tradition, and adherence to a special creed was not a condition of employment. President Christensen might be too conservative in social matters to suit liberals, but his support of "honest intellectual inquiry" was a potent factor in Augsburg's successful effort to advance into the ranks of first-rate educational institutions. By the early 1960s the effort had achieved notable success.[20]

The college by that time was also on the threshold of a new relationship with other groups in the Lutheran family. Attempts in the 1920s to merge Augsburg's parent body, the Free Church, with another synod had failed, but the idea of union had never died. It had gained strength in 1950, when President Christensen stated his belief that the college's sponsoring organization of 100,000 members "might well . . . begin to explore the possibilities of union with other Lutheran bodies closely related to it in spirit and background." Opposition of one sort and another delayed consummation of a merger for more than a dozen years. In February, 1963, however, all but a few Free Church congregations became part of the recently formed American Lutheran Church (ALC), a denomination with over 2,400,000 baptized members. As part of the agreement Augsburg's theological seminary was merged with Luther Seminary in St. Paul, a move which relieved trustees of the Minneapolis institution of considerable financial and educational responsibility. Henceforth Augsburg would be strictly a college of liberal arts — one of eleven four-year colleges and universities of the American Lutheran Church.[21]

Perhaps it is too early even yet to measure fully the effects of merger on Augsburg. Certainly there were advantages. With a greatly enlarged constituency, the college now appeared to possess an expanded potential for student recruitment. The services of the church's board and department of college education were at Augsburg's disposal, as was accessibility to loan funds not previously available. By association the college would benefit from the fine reputations of other ALC institutions of higher learning and be strengthened through a competitive, but friendly, relationship with them. With the headquarters of the denomination located in Minneapolis, Augsburg was well situated close to Mecca, as it were.[22]

It would not be accurate, however, to suggest that only sunshine followed in the wake of merger. Augsburg had possessed in the Free Church a cohesive, dedicated body of supporters. Dispersed in the new church family, they were not so easily identifiable. In 1961 the Free Church had contributed $136,250 to the college; two years later the ALC allocated $126,750 for current operations and $13,250 for capital funds. By 1967–68 the church grant to Augsburg for the operating budget was up to $161,700, plus $31,800 to the building fund; $61,500 for capital purposes also came from a special church drive. Nevertheless the cost of maintaining the college went up even faster, causing the president to note in 1969 that "the merger of 1963 marked no miracle in terms of greater tangible assistance to the institution." Such a situation was bound to give pause not only to authorities at Augsburg, but also to those of the ALC.[23]

Despite his leadership in the campaign for merger, President Christensen was not directly involved in the actual transfer of the college and the seminary to the American Lutheran Church. Factors, not all of which are clear, led him late in 1961 to announce unexpectedly his resignation to take effect in September, 1962. Augsburg's vice president in charge of development also left his job rather precipitously. These sudden departures, which seem to have been related to the trustees' hiring of an outside firm to chart future development, understandably shocked many faculty members and "created an atmosphere of crisis" on campus. A successor to Dr. Christensen was not agreed upon until early in 1963. Thus for a year, while details of the church merger were being carried out and the report of the consulting firm was being considered, Leif S. Harbo, a public school administrator and Augsburg alumnus, presided over his alma mater.[24]

The direction to be followed by an incoming president was largely laid down in October, 1962, when the trustees adopted a new development plan. It proposed expansion of the physical plant, but placed greater emphasis upon improvement of the educational program than upon buildings. The man selected to lead the college in accordance with these guidelines was the Reverend Oscar A. Anderson, who assumed his duties on July 1, 1963. Born in Minneapolis, he had spent part of his undergraduate career at Augsburg but had earned his baccalaureate degree *magna cum laude* at St. Olaf in 1938. A parish minister for six years following his graduation from Luther Theological Seminary in 1942, he had been executive director of the International Young People's Luther League of the Evangelical Lutheran Church for another half dozen years. Thereafter he had served as pastor of the Trinity Lutheran Church in Moorhead, where he had observed at close range educational developments in the two colleges in that western Minnesota city. Friendly, confident, and energetic, he would succeed in continuing Augsburg along the path already laid out and in establishing rapport with elements outside of the college's traditional ethnic community.[25]

His honeymoon year, the initial one under the church merger, saw the start of work on the "bold, new 10-year master plan of development," the essentials of which had earlier been formulated by the consulting firm. As refined by the college's administrative committee and approved early in 1964 by the faculty and board of regents (the term favored in place of trustees by the ALC), the plan was divided into five-year segments. The first of these, called appropriately the "Centennial phase," would end in 1969, when the institution would celebrate the one-hundredth anniversary of its founding in Marshall, Wisconsin. Among the proposed goals to be reached by that time were: an enrollment of 1,600, a full-time faculty of 82 members with a salary average of $10,000 annually, an educational budget of $2,000,000, and the construction of an art building, a dormitory, and a student center.[26]

Though formidable, these goals were not beyond reach; enthusiasm on campus ran high and an air of expectancy was everywhere apparent. The students, ''the brightest spot in the Augsburg picture'' that first year, totaled 1,175 full- and part-time undergraduates, plus 220 registrants from the Minneapolis nursing schools of Fairview, Lutheran Deaconess, Swedish Lutheran, and Methodist hospitals who took some course work at the college. More than 87 per cent of the regular students were Lutheran. Men were in the majority, and commuters were about equal in number to students residing on campus. Classroom and housing facilities were ''sorely pressed.'' The two dormitories, Sverdrup-Oftedal Memorial Hall and Gerda Mortensen Hall, were completely filled — mainly with freshmen — and the overflow lived either in nearby private homes or in college-owned houses. The faculty of relatively young teachers numbered sixty-eight, of whom twenty-four held earned doctorates. Total college assets amounted to $5,000,000, but there was an accumulated deficit of $110,000 to which operations in 1963–64 added $89,700 more.[27]

During the next five years, notable progress was achieved in bringing to reality the goals set for the ''Centennial phase'' of the college's development program. Counting special and part-time students, enrollment by 1968–69 was slightly above the 1,600 target figure. Of this total 503 were freshmen and 303 seniors. In addition about 225 nursing students were registered. The following year with Swedish Hospital out of the program their number was down to 144. It would be further reduced in 1971, when Methodist Hospital also withdrew. The loss of these students was offset, however, by an increasing retention of regular undergraduates. In 1961, for example, only 31 per cent of the student body had been enrolled in the junior and senior classes; in 1969 the proportion was up to 40 per cent. Numerous factors accounted for this gain, among them growing financial assistance, new curriculum developments, and better housing.[28]

As they had earlier, the students in the centennial year came mainly from Minnesota, but there had been some changes in their characteristics and points of origin over the preceding decade. In 1960 students from out of state had constituted 15 per cent of the undergraduate population; in 1969 the percentage was down to 12. The seven-county metropolitan area surrounding the Twin Cities had contributed 51 per cent of Augsburg's students in 1960; nine years later the proportion was up to 60 per cent. Men composed 59 per cent of the student body in the early 1960s, only 49 per cent in 1969. Blacks accounted for 3½ per cent of the undergraduates in the latter year — married students for 9 per cent — the highest proportion in any of Minnesota's private colleges. Only 10 per cent of the enrollees

had been non-Lutheran in 1961; eight years later this element constituted 24 per cent of the total. Meanwhile the students' intellectual aptitude (as measured by college board tests) had been slowly rising, a trend which the faculty hoped to quicken and to facilitate.[29]

In order to care for this growing student body in an area ''where concrete, curbs, cars and congestion'' were typical, Augsburg authorities had to cope with a number of vexing problems, all of them more or less interrelated. Among these were a shortage of campus space, a deteriorating neighborhood environment, an inadequate physical plant, and limited financial resources. Since it was decided in 1946 that the college would remain in its urban location, it had been essential that more land be acquired near at hand. Thus Augsburg had quietly bought up adjacent properties, a highly expensive process especially in the mid-1960s. Between 1962 and 1966, for example, 46 parcels of land containing 111 structures and embracing 6.2 acres had been purchased at a total cost of $1,090,000. Despite the sizable debt thus incurred, the college by late 1967 possessed the land needed to carry out its plan for future expansion.[30]

Concurrently far-reaching developments had been taking place in the Cedar-Riverside district of Minneapolis, which would influence the type and quality of the college's surroundings. Among them were the construction of a freeway south of the campus, the erection of new hospital facilities, the state university's expansion to the Mississippi's nearby west bank, and agitation for urban renewal. There had been an attempt at renewal planning as early as 1960, but because of strong opposition from certain quarters the Minneapolis city council had not acted at that time. Gradually, however, the movement had taken on new life spurred by events in other cities; in October, 1968, after an all-night session the council adopted an urban renewal plan. What it meant in essence for Augsburg was an orderly development and beautification of its neighborhood area, and the guaranteeing of campus boundaries against encroachment. Although a cutback in federal funding slowed renewal efforts, impressive progress was achieved by 1970, benefiting both city and college.[31]

In determining building priorities, some of these external forces played roles along with the more powerful factors of college needs and available financing. The first structure erected during the Anderson years was an art building called ''The Studio'' opened in the fall of 1964 and dedicated the following February. Its cost of $100,000 had been provided largely by accumulated student gifts and a legacy of $40,000. For a time the new facility served as a badly needed student center, but in 1967, when the University of Minnesota's west bank development forced Augsburg's art department to vacate its quarters north of Riverside Avenue, The Studio was given over to the purpose for which it had originally been designed.[32]

Although a welcome and valuable addition, the art building did not fulfill Augsburg's pressing plant requirements. With the two regular dormitories providing rooms for only slightly over 185 women and about 125 men, the need for new living quarters was obvious. The acquisition of neighborhood properties helped, since houses on them could be transformed into student residences. In 1965–66 nearly 230 women lived in 18 of these college-owned houses, and 111 men occupied another 27. Nevertheless new dormitories as well as a modern student union were needed.[33]

Three new buildings were planned: a high rise residence for women, a college center, and a men's dormitory. The latter building was postponed because of lack of finances. The other two buildings, Urness Tower (which became coeducational in 1972) and the Augsburg College Center were opened for use in 1967. With rooms for 324 students, the eleven-story tower cost $1,600,000, the center about $2,000,000. A federal loan of $2,600,000 and a capital gifts campaign financed their construction. In the fall of 1973, the delayed fifteen-story Mortensen Apartment Tower, also coeducational, was opened to 312 students. Its $1,747,350 cost was financed through the Minnesota Higher Educational Facilities Authority and a housing and urban development grant. "No greater physical leap forward," declared President Anderson, "had ever before been taken by the college." The great contribution these facilities have made to the life of the college can be readily appreciated merely by visiting them.[34]

Not so obvious to the casual observer, but of paramount importance, was the continued striving to improve the academic program. "We are trying hard to be a good college," wrote President Anderson in his first annual report. The effort involved both curricular and calendar modifications, as well as concern for faculty quality. New emphasis on foreign languages in 1960 was soon reflected in expansion of offerings in that area. Majors became available in French, German, and Spanish in 1963 and in Norwegian in 1965. A similar opportunity in art appeared in 1963 and interest in that field mounted rapidly. Only 59 students had been enrolled in six art courses in 1959–60, but seven years later 393 undergraduates were registered in the four-

teen courses the department then offered. Because of its high cost, the major in home economics was phased out in this period, but that loss was offset by the addition in the fall of 1966 of a separate department and a major in political science.[35]

Among the 243 members of the 1966 class, 25 different majors were represented, but the most frequently selected were elementary education (44), sociology (23), English (19), and history (19). Reflecting general trends in higher education, about 45 per cent of the class went on for further schooling, a considerable gain over the 33 per cent of the 1957 class who had done so. All told 551 of the 1,533 Augsburg graduates of the decade from 1957 to 1966 attended an advanced school; education attracted the largest number by far, followed by theology and social work. Most of the remaining degree holders of the period entered teaching (507), social work (84), and the armed services (52).[36]

Along with most colleges in these years, Augsburg introduced a new calendar and revised graduation requirements. Beginning in the fall of 1966 after a study initiated by Dean Quanbeck and refined by the faculty, the two-semester system was replaced by a three-term calendar. A student's normal load consisted of three, or perhaps four, courses a term instead of the six or more subjects he had carried previously. In addition, the whole curriculum was overhauled and the general education requirements revamped. But more fundamental than these changes — important though they proved to be — was, in the words of Dean Kenneth C. Bailey, "the adoption of a new educational philosophy, which provides freedom for understanding valid educational experiences in a much broader, and at the same time deeper, sense than has been possible in the past."[37]

Manifestations of this new task — a phase of what Augsburg's historian has called the nation's "second academic revolution" — assumed a variety of forms as the institution restlessly searched for greater effectiveness, leaving few stones unturned in exploring ways of transforming a crowded, metropolitan location into an educational asset. One, the "Crisis Colony," took students away from the campus for a term to live, study, and work in a north Minneapolis neighborhood. Another permitted undergraduates to take courses at state penal and mental institutions in company with inmates. A third offered work in Afro-American culture taught by Blacks at a local community center. Other programs arranged for study in Europe and for research into Twin Cities urban problems.[38]

More rapid progress would undoubtedly have been achieved had Augsburg's financial standing been different. On the one hand, total income and assets had shown impressive upward movement. The former in 1963–64 had been $1,760,000; five years later it had climbed to $3,550,000. Assets for the two years were $5,728,000 and $12,698,000, respectively. In the absence of a sizable endowment, chief sources of income had been student fees, auxiliary enterprises, and gifts. These, too, had increased. Fees, which provided anywhere from 73 to 87 per cent of educational and general income during the 1960s, rose from $1,000,000 in President Anderson's first year to $2,130,000 in 1968–69. Auxiliary enterprises contributed $433,800 and $1,100,000 in the same two years, and gifts went from $462,100 to $993,800. Particularly encouraging were the near doubling of alumni giving, a large increase in corporate donations, growing government support, and the backing of the American Lutheran Church.[39]

But there was a darker side to the picture. Inflation, for example, caused building construction costs to go up by 20 per cent between 1967 and 1969. As student charges rose, it became necessary to increase scholarships, loans, and student work contracts; the amount expended for such assistance in 1964–65 had been $488,200 compared to $942,100 in 1968–69. Some of these funds came from outside sources, but a sizable amount had to be furnished by the college. Salary increases, debt retirement, and carrying charges imposed additional strains on each annual budget. Consequently total annual expenditures mounted between 1963 and 1969 from $1,849,900 to $3,557,100.[40]

Although the college hoped for substantial capital gifts from two fund drives in 1965 and 1967, the results were somewhat disappointing. In the former year Augsburg initiated a centennial building fund drive (its theme was "Excellence Beyond Scholarship") for $1,050,000 and sought contributions from many sources, Lutheran and non-Lutheran. In 1967 the ALC inaugurated a three-year $20,000,000 campaign called the Lutheran Ingathering for Education (LIFE) for the benefit of all its colleges and seminaries. Actually, the capital needs of these institutions were at least twice that amount. Unfortunately while Augsburg received considerable sums from these two solicitations, neither drive attained its goal, and several of the college's hoped-for additions to and renovations of the physical plant had to be delayed to an uncertain future time. These facts plus such realities as an accumulated operating deficit of $400,000 on June 30, 1970, and liabilities equal to more than 50 per cent of assets — mainly the result of land purchases and building projects — cannot fail to worry and

concern friends of higher education in general and of Augsburg in particular. It is understandable that the institution's authorities should wonder whether the church, the alumni, and the surrounding community really want the college to survive.[41]

Neither the never-ending financial worries nor the many other problems and conflicts besetting institutions of higher learning, however, have caused the Augsburg community seriously to despair. On the contrary, having successfully weathered changes of its location, its educational character, its curriculum, and its constituencies during a hundred years — and gained strength thereby — the college confidently laid plans for its second century of existence. While preparation for celebrating the centennial were under way in the fall of 1966, Augsburg's regents asked the faculty senate to study academic needs and goals for the 1970s. Between that autumn and February 5, 1970, when it was adopted by the whole faculty, a blueprint or agenda was fashioned with teachers, students, and administration participating in the process. What was envisioned was not so much new as it was the consummation of goals already set and the improvement of programs currently in progress. With a strong Christian commitment, an urban setting, a world view, and a deep concern for the problems confronting man, Augsburg would continue its endeavor to be the best liberal arts college possible.[42]

As Augsburg embarked on what it called "Decade I: Century II," there were encouraging omens. Its position as the only private four-year liberal arts college in populous Hennepin County gave the institution an excellent opportunity to bolster its image and attract a growing, loyal, and interested new body of supporters. In these efforts at least two circumstances should prove salutary: (1) half of Augsburg's alumni settle in the Twin Cities; (2) starting in 1970, membership on the college's board of regents was no longer restricted to Lutherans. In addition, salary levels of the 125 full- and part-time teachers had been raised and their fringe benefits expanded. A students' bill of rights gained faculty approval in May, 1970, and undergraduates were represented on the the the charter commission charged with devising an up-to-date system of college governance. Several co-operative ventures were being conducted, and ways of achieving closer relationships with other colleges were being studied. Augsburg's future connection with the ALC seems somewhat tenuous, but a conviction exists at the college that its type of education can be successfully sold "in a very busy and overcrowded academic market." Those familiar with Augsburg's history agree.[43]

32 ST. OLAF COLLEGE

Quality Education and
Christian Commitment

IN THE SPRING OF 1942 when it became necessary for Lars W. Boe to take a leave of absence, the acting presidency of St. Olaf became the responsibility of the dean of men, J. Jørgen Thompson. To him fell the task of supervising the adjustments necessitated by the country's active entry into World War II. Like all college administrators in that frightening and uncertain period, he suffered many anxious moments. The college was fortunate, however, in being selected as one of a score of institutions at which a Navy Pre-Flight Preparatory School would be established. On January 7, 1943, the first contingent of cadets took up residence on the hill and turned Old Main, Steensland, Ytterboe, and Mohn halls into military installations. By the time the unit was phased out three years later, some 3,500 potential navy pilots had been given training.[1]

Meanwhile in April, 1943, the trustees had elected Clemens M. Granskou as the new president of the college. He took up his duties three months later. A 1917 graduate steeped in St. Olaf tradition, President Granskou had had a wide and varied experience. Following service in naval aviation in World War I, he had completed his studies at Luther Theological Seminary and, with his bride, gone as a missionary to China, where he was also principal of an American school until 1927. From 1929 to 1932 he was president of Waldorf College at Forest City, Iowa. Then for eleven years prior to accepting the St. Olaf position, he served as head of Augustana College at Sioux Falls, South Dakota. During twenty years "as an able administrator . . . an outspoken advocate of Christian higher education which is . . . academically sound," and a defender of academic freedom, he won affection and respect for the manner in which he led St. Olaf through challenging and complex days. Because of wartime

conditions President Granskou's inaugural ceremony was delayed until home-coming on October 14, 1944. In his address he paid homage to the past contributions of liberal arts colleges and reaffirmed his faith in their unexpendable relevance then and for the future. "The function of liberal education," he declared, "is to give moral and spiritual direction to a highly specialized civilization."[2]

The college President Granskou was called upon to lead possessed assets of some $4,000,000, half of which was in endowment and other funds and the remainder in campus and buildings. The annual educational budget came to roughly $400,000, that for auxiliary activities to $300,000. About twenty-five alumni clubs were active, and the gymnasium, athletic fields, and library stood as testimony to the interest and generosity of former students. The Norwegian Lutheran Church of America had recently approved a campaign to raise funds for a new chapel, but some time would elapse before that addition to the campus would become a reality. Behind the measurable assets were intangible moral and spiritual values, less subject to quantitative analysis yet fundamental and real. In the words of President Granskou: "St. Olaf may be looked upon as the avenue by which an immigrant people were able to give expression to their cultural and spiritual heritage and thus enlarge the areas of their service to the country of their adoption."[3]

More than a year passed after the new president's investiture before his faith in the future of liberal education was really tested. Would veterans returning from the war seek narrow specialization and training in specific skills, or would they pursue liberal learning in a Christian context? By the second semester of 1945–46 the question had been answered: about 260 former GIs were registered at

St. Olaf and total enrollment had climbed to 1,106. A year and a half later it would be up to a booming 1,738, of whom 1,013 were men — 617 of them veterans. Both faculty and facilities were strained to the utmost, but morale was high and inconveniences paled. Temporary buildings secured from the federal government were transformed at a cost of slightly over $100,000 into a married veterans' village, classroom and office space, a dining hall, and a bakery. "The most critical urgent need," however, was for more dormitories. This was partially relieved in March, 1948, with the completion of imposing Harald Thorson Hall, which had rooms for 270 men and had been made possible by utilizing $700,000 from Thorson's estate.[4]

Late in 1949 contracts were let for a much-needed women's dormitory. Dedicated at home-coming in 1951, the $540,000 structure was christened Hilleboe Hall in honor of the college's gracious and long-time dean of women. It would be home to over one hundred senior coeds. There were several other concurrent projects: a $50,000 addition to the fine arts building and one of $115,000 to radio station WCAL, a faculty housing development on Lincoln Lane near the campus, and a 260-seat drama studio in the old auditorium of Ytterboe Hall. Despite all this construction the physical plant was still inadequate, and well over four hundred students had to live off campus.[5]

Faculty salaries were low; the average for full professors in 1943, for example, was $2,779. There was no pension fund, no written faculty personnel policy, and no tenure plan. Furthermore some of the older teachers who had given years of devoted and inspirational service to St. Olaf were reaching the stage when provision would have to be made for their retirement. Fortunately a retirement insurance plan on which a trustee committee had been laboring for several years was implemented in 1948–49. At the end of that year Carl A. Mellby, who came to teach at St. Olaf in 1901, and Julius Boraas, who arrived in 1910, retired. In the following year others of like stature ended their careers, retirements that truly marked the passing of an era.[6]

To replace such devoted teachers was not easy, but it was a task to which President Granskou assigned high priority. In addition he worked continually to create a climate in which free inquiry could flourish. At times progress seemed slow and occasionally a teacher "died at the top," but there were causes for rejoicing over academic developments. In 1947 the chemistry department was placed on the approved list of the American Chemical Society, a recognition well merited. In October, 1947, the report of the President's Scientific Research Board to President Harry S Truman on science and public policy noted the contributions of St. Olaf and other liberal arts colleges to scientific research and study.[7]

There was soon another honor for the institution. In December, 1948, a letter arrived indicating that the senate of Phi Beta Kappa had voted to invite members of that honor fraternity at St. Olaf to submit a formal application for the establishment of an affiliated unit at the Manitou Heights college. Needless to say the papers were filed without delay, and in September, 1949, "the twenty-second Council authorized the granting of a charter to . . . St. Olaf for the establishment of a chapter of the Society." Installation of the Delta Chapter of Minnesota occurred on November 5, 1949, in connection with the college's seventy-fifth birthday celebration. The shades of Muus, Mohn, and other founders must have rejoiced as they contemplated the status their school had attained at the time of its diamond jubilee.[8]

The class graduating in 1949 totaled 289, nearly evenly divided between men and women. It was the largest class in the college's history thus far, and 44 of its members were headed for a seminary thus continuing the St. Olaf tradition of service to the church. Of the 6,045 alumni who graduated between 1890 and 1948 and whose occupations were surveyed in preparation for the jubilee observance, 20 per cent (including wives) were "directly dependent upon the church for their livelihood" as pastors, missionaries, and social workers. Another 20 per cent in education, medicine, and social service not related to the church were aiding "the welfare of their fellow citizens." The college was affiliated with Fairview Hospital in Minneapolis in a nursing education program, but it was not until 1952–53 that St. Olaf instituted a regular four-year nursing course leading to a B.S. degree.[9]

Following the jubilee year of 1948, enrollment began the downward trend typical of the period generally, dipping to a postwar low of 1,499 in 1952. College administrators on Manitou Heights faced another time of uncertainty. One measure of security seemed to be offered by an air force ROTC unit, and so St. Olaf along with 450 other institutions of higher education in the country put in its application for a military training operation on campus. In April, 1951, the college was one of sixty-two institutions selected to train air force reservists. In the long run the survival of the liberal arts college did not depend upon the possession of a military organization, but that belief did little to offset the money shortages and declining enrollments of the early 1950s. St. Olaf, therefore, felt fortunate when its ROTC unit was activated in September, 1951.[10]

In due time, of course, enrollment again pushed upward. By the fall of 1957 the number of students reached 1,858. As had been traditional, over one-half of them were residents of Minnesota and nine out of ten were Lutherans, factors which combined to create a high degree of homogeneity and a result-ant consensus foreign to many campuses of the 1960s. A large portion of the student body partici-pated regularly in chapel and other religious activities. In 1951 the St. Olaf Student Congrega-tion was established, the first of its kind in the Evan-gelical Lutheran Church (the name adopted in June, 1946, by the former Norwegian Lutheran Church of America). With the completion two years later of the beautiful and long-desired Boe Memorial Chapel, the student church had an edifice in keeping with its aspirations. Centrally located for both sym-bolic and practical reasons, the chapel, costing some $677,000 fully equipped, was made possible by the gifts of more than 60,000 persons.[11]

While postwar development at St. Olaf gave cause for satisfaction, certain areas of the organiza-tional structure, designed for a different day, needed overhauling to meet the demands of the 1950s. With this in mind the trustees employed a Chicago con-sulting firm to take a long look at the college's oper-ation and make recommendations for improvement. The resulting report, dated March 26, 1951, and the steps taken to implement it had important results. Generally speaking, the recommendations clarified lines of authority and responsibility and outlined ways by which the academic and business areas of the college could be streamlined. It was recommended that the office of dean of the college be established with authority over the entire academic program. The president was urged to delegate more authority, but to hold on to the major responsibilities of leadership.[12]

The outside consultants made clear their view that St. Olaf's future success would lie with its faculty, its academic program, and the elevation of its educa-tional standards. As always in such times of self-analysis, some people were hurt, but the major pro-posals of the report were effectuated to St. Olaf's benefit. There was a strong desire on campus for improvement. Much help came from the board, which was composed of strong, active, concerned individuals rather than "beefeaters," as President Granskou termed trustees who did little other than consume free meals. Considerable attention was given to curriculum matters, and a fine arts require-ment was adopted. No startling changes were introduced, but due largely to the urging of Profes-sor Howard V. Hong a faculty committee of six

members was appointed and charged with analyzing the college's academic program and seeking ways of making it more integrated and effective. The result of the group's labors, entitled *Integration in the Christian Liberal Arts College*, was published in 1956. This informative and provocative study favored a capstone course for integrative purposes in the senior year. Although it received wide and favorable attention and thorough discussion, the report had no immediate impact in reshaping the St. Olaf curriculum. The time apparently was not yet ripe.[13]

But the tempo was accelerating. In June, 1957, St. Olaf received its second installment of the important Ford Foundation gift, making a total of $442,500 from that source earmarked for the endowment fund to improve faculty salaries. This largess stimulated greater giving by the church, as well as by sources beyond the college's immediate constituency, and permitted overdue salary increases in both 1956 and 1957. Concurrently the alumni association approved a Development Fund appeal for $1,500,000 to be used for salaries, scholarships, a student center, and a pipe organ for the chapel. Gifts to the college, which had averaged about $316,000 annually from 1952 to 1955, rose to approximately $726,000 a year between 1957 and 1960. Faculty and administration pledged $78,000 to the appeal, an amazing average of over $750 per subscriber. The mean salary of a full professor in 1952 had been $4,600; in 1963 it was $11,500 with much greater fringe benefits and a definite system of tenure and leaves.[14]

Further changes in the face of the campus accom-panied these vital advances. At a cost of $300,000 East (now Flaten) Hall in 1956 received added class-rooms, the education and art departments, and housing for 80 sophomore women. In a departure from past fiscal policies the college that same year applied for and received a forty-year $1,000,000 federal loan to construct two more dormitories. By the summer of 1957 Agnes Kittelsby Hall for 164 women and Kildahl Hall for 180 men were com-pleted and named for a teacher of the pre-1914 era and the former president. The college then had on-campus living quarters for over 1,400 students, but even so additional dormitories were needed. A more pressing demand, however, was for additional dining facilities, since the existing ones had expanded but little since the 1920s.[15]

With the means of financing available, the final years of the Granskou administration witnessed a veritable flurry of new construction. In the fall of 1960 occurred the dedications of the chapel organ, the $1,850,000 St. Olaf Center, and the $425,000 administration building. Featuring "striking façades of glass and stone," the center contains a wide range of facilities: a cafeteria seating 800 to 1,000 people, a bookstore, faculty club, lounges, and eight bowling lanes. As the dedications were taking place, two new dormitories, costing over $1,900,000 and financed by a federal loan, were taking shape: Hoyme Memorial Hall for two hundred women (named for the first president of the United Church in 1890), and Ellingson Hall (named for a long-time chemistry professor) housing an equal number of men. These structures were dedicated at the 1961 home-coming.[16]

Plans had also been completed to start construction of two high-rise residence halls, one of twelve stories to house 290 women, the other of ten stories for nearly 300 men. Named in honor of Agnes M. Larson, popular history professor, and the late President Mohn, the $3,000,000 vertical structures gave a new look to the sky line and conserved the dwindling open space of the campus. Between 1946 and 1962 an impressive total of over $10,000,000 was spent on new buildings and remodeling.[17]

As St. Olaf was experiencing this notable physical growth, it was also undergoing changes in its relationship to the church and to other educational institutions. By late 1956 three denominational bodies — the United Evangelical Lutheran Church, the American Lutheran Church, and the Evangelical Lutheran Church — had committed themselves "to full organic union with each other." Combined, the three religious organizations controlled nine senior colleges, five of which, including St. Olaf and Concordia at Moorhead, were affiliated with the Evangelical Lutheran Church, the name adopted by the Norwegian Lutheran Church of America in 1946. Each denomination had a different formula for dispensing money to its educational institutions and varying notions regarding their management. The American Lutheran Church exercised rigid centralized control, and its three colleges were not separately incorporated. Those of the Evangelical Lutheran Church, on the other hand, were granted a large measure of autonomy with control vested in their own boards of trustees, a gesture of faith which seemed to work to the advantage of both college and church. The federal loans that had been negotiated by the Evangelical Lutheran institutions caused concern in some quarters. All conflicting issues, however, were referred to a Joint Union Committee of twenty-seven members created to resolve matters standing in the way of merger. Throughout the negotiations President Granskou argued in defense of distinguishing between church and college, and his point of view carried the day.

When finally in October, 1962, the merged body known as the American Lutheran Church held its first convention, St. Olaf retained its separate corporate structure under the new constitution. Its integrity as an academic institution had been preserved.[18]

A number of factors in the late 1950s combined to create a climate receptive to academic change at St. Olaf. Among them were world events, the pending church merger, and the college's affiliation in 1958 with the newly formed Associated Colleges of the Midwest. The introduction of a course in the Russian language in 1958 was only one example of the impact of world events on the post-Sputnik curriculum. Starting that same year, summer institutes in science and mathematics for selected high school students and graduates reflected the same influence, as well as an urgency to identify and educate talented young people. Beginning in the fall of 1960, the college board scholastic aptitude tests were made mandatory for St. Olaf applicants. None of these developments represented a radical departure from the past, but each was prelude to what followed.[19]

The trustees in the spring of 1962 made funds available to permit four faculty members to spend the summer studying the college calendar and making recommendations for its revision. In November the summer group's report was approved by the faculty curriculum and educational policies committee. With subsequent refinements a substantially new calendar and a revised curriculum resulted. Beginning in the fall of 1964, St. Olaf would adopt the four-one-four plan under which a student would carry four courses for each of two semesters and the equivalent of one course during a month's interim term in January. New emphasis was placed on independent study, and freshmen were made eligible for honors work. Interdisciplinary courses, comprehensive examinations, optional senior theses, and possible acceleration toward graduation were included in this break with tradition. The program remained in effect throughout the rest of the 1960s, and despite some discontent on the part of scientists and foreign language people, the consensus has been that its merits far outweigh its shortcomings.[20]

In preparation for commencement in 1963, the faculty in a secret meeting voted to recommend President Granskou for the Doctor of Humanities degree. At the time no one could foresee that after addressing the class of 1963 and speaking characteristically of "minds brave" and "faith strong," the president would surprise the graduation audience by announcing his retirement. During his tenure at

St. Olaf, the "outward emblems of growth" had been little short of monumental. Diplomas had been conferred on 5,500 young people, more than half of all the college's graduates. A plant of fourteen buildings worth approximately $2,200,000 had grown to one of twenty-nine buildings valued in the neighborhood of $13,300,000. A college budget of $700,000 in the first Granskou year had reached $5,500,000 for 1963. Faculty salaries had tripled and enrollment nearly doubled to just under 2,000. But it was in the realm of the intellectual and the intangible that the president found his greatest satisfactions and made his greatest contributions. A warm and humble individual, he was unyielding in his insistence that the church-related college must be free and unafraid in its pursuit of truth. As one of his colleagues said at a farewell dinner honoring President Granskou, he had proved himself a "senior statesman in the field of Christian education." [21]

Dr. Sidney A. Rand, a native Minnesotan and a 1938 graduate of Concordia College in Moorhead, was elected to succeed President Granskou in July, 1963. After completing his studies at Luther Theological Seminary in St. Paul and being ordained, he had spent two years as a pastor before returning in 1945 to join the faculty at Concordia. In 1951 as president of Waldorf College in Iowa he had begun the same administrative apprenticeship served earlier by Lars W. Boe and Clemens M. Granskou. From 1956 until his election to the St. Olaf post, he had gained further experience and invaluable perspective as executive director of the Board of Christian Education of the American Lutheran Church. [22]

The Rand years have so far witnessed a continuation of the growth which characterized the previous administration. Three months before the occupation of the new high-rise dormitories in mid-1964 the Ford Foundation offered St. Olaf $2,200,000, provided the college raised $5,500,000 from other sources by July 1, 1967. Encouraged as well as challenged by the commendation implicit in the grant, college authorities embarked on a "Forward Fund" drive to secure $10,450,000, a sum arrived at by totaling the costs of St. Olaf's most pressing needs: additional endowment, an athletic center, a science building, a music and drama facility, and support of current operations. With assistance from a money-raising firm and unceasing efforts by college personnel — especially President Rand who spoke at fifty-five area dinners — the campaign was a resounding success. A total of over $11,500,000 was obtained before the Ford deadline. [23]

In mid-1964 early impetus had been given to the fund drive when Trustee Chairman Howell P. E. Skoglund, a 1925 graduate, and his wife made a magnificent pledge to finance the cost of the proposed athletic center. Tangible evidences of growing affluence soon dotted the campus, which was itself increased by one-third with the purchase in 1965 of 110 contiguous acres of land. In September, 1966, the Ole G. Felland Wing of the Rölvaag Memorial Library was completed at a cost of about $890,000 — an addition which gave St. Olaf one of the three largest liberal arts college libraries in the Upper Midwest. With shelving sufficient for 400,000 volumes, the building has 1,000 study spaces, more than one-third of which are in the form of individual carrels. In November, 1967, the dedication was held of the $2,750,000 Skoglund Athletic Center, an impressive complex containing a gymnasium-auditorium seating 4,000, a field house, a swimming pool, and offices. Only a little over a year later in January, 1969, St. Olaf dedicated its $3,500,000 Science Center, a four-story structure housing the latest in facilities for the study of biology, chemistry, physics, and mathematics. [24]

By this time the assets of St. Olaf had reached the formidable total of approximately $37,000,000 — an increase of more than $15,500,000 since 1964. The budget for 1969–70 came to $8,878,000, of which $6,500,000 was for the educational programs, three-fourths of it paid by student fees. Including those for room and board, student charges by 1970 had reached a worrisome average of about $2,900 a year. Since college costs were pushing upward at the rate of at least 8 per cent annually, however, St. Olaf despite its many assets was feeling the financial squeeze common to all liberal arts institutions. For one thing, more than $1,310,000 was paid out in the form of scholarships, college-administered loans, and student work contracts in 1969–70; for another, the endowment of $3,560,000 was unable to produce a sizable portion of the college's yearly income. Consquently a deficit of $261,400 occurred in 1969–70, and another was projected for 1971 at a much lower level. [25]

Fortunately tangible evidences of confidence in the form of gifts and grants have been forthcoming; for the nine years preceding June 30, 1970, they added up to a total of $20,500,000. In 1969–70 alone more than $2,226,000 was given to St. Olaf, of which about $475,000 was earmarked for plant. The remainder was distributed as follows: $480,000 was unrestricted and available to help pay normal operating expenses, $300,000 was awarded for research projects, approximately $150,000 went for student aid, and a little over $800,000 was placed in endowment funds. The contribution of the American Lutheran Church was $306,700 — $183,100 to meet the current budget, the rest for equipment and construction. The college anticipates the help of its concerned and generous body of supporters, but with inflation and various capital and other needs in view, there is no foreseeable end to wrestling with forces financial.[26]

Obviously there will be no cessation either in the continuing effort to make St. Olaf's academic life more exciting and more effective. Through its membership in the Associated Colleges of the Midwest, St. Olaf's students and faculty have been eligible to participate in ACM programs, which have grown in number and popularity. In the mid-1960s, as an example, the Ford Foundation granted $500,000 to these associated midwestern institutions to improve their programs in non-Western studies. Increasingly St. Olaf undergraduates combined on-campus pursuits with those in distant lands. In addition to such long-established outlets as SPAN and the University of Oslo summer session in Norway, a whole array of new possibilities tempted students to broaden their experiences and their horizons in a fast-shrinking world. Among these new programs were study terms in such diverse places as England, France, Israel, Ethiopia, India, Thailand, and Japan. With other Minnesota colleges on the four-one-four schedule, St. Olaf joined in co-operative projects which permitted study for credit during the interim term in Malta, Mexico, and the Soviet Union. In 1964–65 six St. Olaf students studied abroad; three years later the number had jumped to 162. By 1970 more than half the members of the graduating class "had participated in some aspect of foreign study."[27]

All of these changes in student life had their effects in breaking the much-maligned lock step of an earlier day. The two Northfield colleges were beginning to look at each other as co-workers in higher education rather than as bitter rivals. In 1967 the governing boards of Carleton and St. Olaf expressed their support for active co-operation between the institutions, and a joint faculty committee began discussions leading to mutual academic endeavors. The modest start was limited to certain courses in classical languages in 1968–69, but already joint majors in classics and Russian are available, and a high degree of co-ordination exists between the two libraries and the two computer centers.[28]

Another imaginative curriculum departure was the establishment in the fall of 1969 of an experimental "paracollege" at St. Olaf. With an initial enrollment of about seventy-five freshmen, the new entity operated out of existing facilities but not under traditional procedures. The emphasis was on independent, individual learning. Students were given great latitude: they might take or audit regular courses, work independently, or study under the direction of a faculty tutor. Progression was dependent upon the successful completion of examinations. The object of the experiment was to test "academic innovations without threat to the stability and tradition" of the institution. The paracollege demonstrates that St. Olaf has retained the "adaptable attitude of mind" of which Carl A. Mellby wrote on the occasion of its fiftieth anniversary.[29]

With its one-hundredth birthday just over the horizon in 1974, the college still possesses many marks of its Norwegian heritage, a birthright of which it is justifiably proud. A major event of 1968, for example, was the visit of Olav V, King of Norway. As Crown Prince Olav, with Crown Princess Martha, he had spent a memorable two days on campus in 1939 and had received an honorary doctorate of laws. As late as 1966 nearly 80 per cent of the students were Lutherans, and approximately 300 were taking courses in Norwegian — more than at any other college in the country. By the fall of 1970, 65 per cent were Lutherans and 203 were taking courses in Norwegian. St. Olaf's radio station WCAL still broadcasts church services in the Norwegian language, a practice stretching back to 1924.[30]

Though obviously strengthened by its Norwegian and Lutheran bonds, St. Olaf has long been in the main current of American collegiate life. The Manitou Heights faculty, for example, exhibits wide experience and good preparation; nearly 50 per cent of its 183 members in 1970 held earned doctorates, and a sizable proportion had traveled and studied abroad. The instructional staff enjoyed the fringe benefits usual in first-rate colleges of the period and possessed a strong voice in the formulation of institutional policy. In addition opportunities for faculty growth and scholarly activity have been provided increasingly by outside, as well as by college-funded, grants. Such gifts have supported research and teaching in the natural sciences for a goodly number of years, but of late substantial assistance also went to other divisions of the college. In 1967 the Hill Foundation made a grant (later renewed) for St. Olaf's first summer humanities institute for high school juniors and seniors. Its teaching staff consisted of members of the college's departments of art, English, music, and philosophy. Two years later the National Science Foundation awarded $271,900, half of the amount needed for a three-year improvement program in the behavioral sciences of economics, political science, psychology, and sociology. A considerable portion of the money was used to improve faculty competence in research methods in these fields, which have grown significantly at the college in the past ten years.[31]

By the fall of 1967 St. Olaf's student body had passed the 2,500 mark — larger than any of the other Minnesota private colleges. Size, however, does not worry President Rand, in whose mind numbers and quality are not equated. If undergraduates are to receive an education suitable for living in the modern world, he feels they must have access to a faculty and facilities greater than most colleges with enrollments of four hundred to five hundred can afford. What the ultimate size of St. Olaf will be, no one can predict. Plans were laid in 1964 for a college of 3,000 students by 1974, and that total remains a goal. Inflation, the growth of publicly controlled institutions, and shifting attitudes toward higher education in general, however, may cause the arrow to fall short of the target.[32]

As St. Olaf students became more numerous, they also like their peers elsewhere became more demanding. "Gone," wrote President Rand, "is the decade of the quiet fifties." In its place in the 1960s were highly individualistic attitudes toward life accompanied by pressures for the easing of already relaxed parietal rules. Individualism was nothing new to Norwegians in America; it was part of their tradition, and they knew how to cope with it. Violence has been avoided on Manitou Heights and so in general have physical demonstrations. An exception occurred during the tense spring of 1970, when anti-Vietnam War feeling ran high in the nation's colleges and universities. Following a three-year campaign against the continuance of the air force ROTC at St. Olaf, about sixty students (a few of them from Carleton) occupied the college's administration building on April 16 and 17. The sit-in protesting ROTC lasted twenty-four hours and was attended by plenty of dialogue but no damage other than work stoppage. Some results, however, did ensue. The faculty recommended in a close vote and the college regents approved the continuance of the ROTC program at St. Olaf, but in a modified form.[33]

Along with antimilitarism and a strong desire to order their lives free of external restraints, St. Olaf students have also shown a desire for involvement in the administration of the institution and a heightened sense of social concern. In 1966 undergraduates were placed on regular faculty committees as discussing, voting members; four years later selected students began attending faculty meetings. Proponents credit the moves with developing a more responsible student body and better channels of communication. Other evidences of the fact that St. Olaf men and women were in tune with times could be found in their establishment of a free university with noncredit courses on campus in 1967, in their fasting to create a scholarship fund for Blacks in 1968, and in their founding of a tutoring program for disadvantaged students in 1969. More traditional activities also attracted supporters. In Midwest Conference athletic competition, for example, the Oles won the football title in 1969 and 1970, the basketball crown in 1969, and three successive baseball championships between 1968 and 1970. In the summer of the latter year the St. Olaf choir and band, with a total of 145 members, performed for three weeks in seven European countries.[34]

As St. Olaf looks to the future wondering what changes it should make and what traditions must endure, its leaders face a multitude of tasks and a host of questions. In the financial area "the critical need . . . continues to be funds supporting current operation." For the physical plant, the most pressing demand is the long-awaited music and theater building. No longer — except legally — is the college's relationship to the church so direct and so simple as it once was. With a declining proportion of its students professing the Lutheran faith and with a decreasing percentage of its income deriving from its denominational sponsor, St. Olaf has something of an identity problem. The college's loyalties have become more pluralistic and its system of governance more complex. Although those responsible for directing the institution admit to some worries and frustrations, they also evidence an abiding faith and confidence. Their aim is clear: the continuing merger of quality education with "a serious understanding of and commitment to the Gospel of Jesus Christ." This combination has successfully guided the institution through nearly a century; it will, as President Rand has written, give St. Olaf "balance and a sense of direction" in the years to come.[35]

33

MACALESTER COLLEGE

Metamorphosis

THE YEARS FOLLOWING World War II brought Macalester not only the prospect of a new day but also the problems common to most colleges in that transition period. The graduating class of June, 1946, reflecting wartime conditions, numbered only 78 members. Total enrollment that spring, however, approximated 900, about 200 above the pre-Pearl Harbor average. Despite the high incidence of students from the Twin Cities, housing became a problem since the campus had not added a dormitory in two decades. Macville, a veterans' village, accommodated 64 married and single GIs, but the college needed more substantial residence facilities. A new dormitory and a drive for funds to pay for it were begun, with the result that Bigelow Hall was partly occupied early in 1947 and ready to receive its full complement of 110 women by the following September. It had been necessary, however, to borrow $143,000 from a St. Paul bank in order to cover the deficit in the building fund.[1]

Another 1947 addition to the campus was a wartime structure worth $85,000 which the federal government donated to the college. Known as the Little Theater Building, it provided an auditorium, student lounge, offices, classrooms, and space for the art and drama departments. But expansion of facilities, important as that was, represented only part of the demands on the college's resources. Operating costs between 1940 and 1947 increased from $375,400 to $1,000,000, while annual tuition charges went from $175 to only $350. Faculty salaries, pensions, and insurance protection urgently needed attention.[2]

In the face of the slow growth of endowment, which had a book value of $1,346,000 in January, 1947, more money somehow had to be found. A sharp look at investment income suggested the wisdom of selling some of the college-owned farms. As a result, fourteen of them were disposed of in 1947 at a total price of $94,000. DeWitt Wallace continued to help, and the Presbyterian Board of

Christian Education contributed $25,000 to the Bigelow Hall building fund. By the end of 1947, however, Mr. Wallace, though still interested in the college, was "convinced that the time has come for Macalester to stand more fully on its own feet financially." So it was decided to undertake a campaign for $500,000 to begin in December, 1948, about $350,000 of which was to be used to build a new infirmary and a student union and cafeteria. By the fall of 1949 slightly over $336,000 had been subscribed, but the campaign itself had cost almost $63,000.[3]

Among course offerings, the trend toward vocationalism begun before the war seemed to gain momentum. The catalog of 1946 publicized the planning of careers in dentistry, the foreign service, library science, homemaking, journalism, and recreational leadership, in addition to the more traditional areas of law, medicine, teaching, and the ministry. In June, 1948, the trustees authorized Macalester's affiliation with Miss Wood's Kindergarten-Primary Training School, Inc., formerly located in Minneapolis. Recognizing that his policies were provoking criticism, President Turck told his board in 1947: "There are risks when an educational institution dedicates itself to the achievement of a world better than the one that now is. Its methods may sometimes be misunderstood and an occasional word from staff or faculty may be criticised. But I would rather see Macalester a living organism, have a vital, constructive part to play in the throbbing life of this region with the world view controlling us, than to see it become a safe and sane repository of dead learning."[4]

When members of Phi Beta Kappa on the faculty attempted in 1948 to secure a chapter at the college, the considerations weighing most heavily against the acquisition related to the curriculum. Singled out for criticism were "the degree of vocational emphasis permitted," and the "serious unbalance between departments as to the number of courses offered, the systematic coverage of the fields, and the apparent emphasis or point of view of the instruction." The offerings in economics, history, sociology, political science, and religion were classified as good by Phi Beta Kappa investigators, those in science as adequate. In literature and the foreign languages, however, the courses were described as "weak." Though the college was commended for retaining a foreign language requirement, increasing salary scales since 1940, and granting pensions, the unfavorable decision of the academic honor fraternity came as a great disappointment. Later in 1948 Macalester's application for an air force ROTC unit was also turned down.[5]

In spite of criticism, the college continued its efforts to improve its physical plant. To provide quarters for Miss Wood's School (which added 150 students to the roster late in 1949) a house on Summit Avenue was purchased for $38,000. The next year shortly before the Korean conflict erupted ground breaking for a $500,000 student center took place; work on it was completed in 1951 with $400,000 borrowed from a Minnesota insurance company. By this time the low birth rates of the early 1930s were beginning to be reflected in declining enrollments and a resultant lowering of college income. The freshman class of 1949–50 had numbered 524; that of 1951–52 was down to 333.[6]

Deficits developed despite efforts to pare budgets and the adoption of various remedies, including membership in the Minnesota Private College Fund and the initiation of an alumni fund and a gift annuity plan. Even so the year 1952–53 showed a deficit of nearly $60,000. Although smaller than in 1949, the number of students still exceeded 1,300, and further additions to the physical plant became necessary. Luckily some help was forthcoming. Trustee David J. Winton, his brother, and his sister, gave a modern health center in memory of their parents, and the Wilkie Brothers Foundation provided money for an observatory. Both structures were in use by 1953. Two years later three friends offered $100,000 toward a field house if Macalester would raise an equal amount. The trustees accepted the challenge, a campaign was undertaken, and the athletic plant was occupied in 1956.[7]

To finance vitally needed dormitory facilities a fifty-year federal government loan of $800,000 with interest at 2¾ per cent was negotiated in 1955, raising college building indebtedness to over $1,000,000. Turck Hall for 152 women and Dayton Hall for 132 men were completed in 1957. Macalester could then house 696 of its 1,275 students in college dormitories. To enable professors to buy

homes at reasonable rates and to handle real estate operations adjacent to the campus, DeWitt Wallace created a High Winds Fund. In mid-1957 it totaled $322,000. By that year campus and plant were worth more than $4,700,000, and the endowment bolstered by the recent Ford Foundation grant totaling $379,000 had a market value in excess of $4,500,000.[8]

During these years of plant expansion, a number of interesting curriculum developments occurred. Before the college acquired Miss Wood's School, Macalester students desiring to teach in elementary grades had to transfer after two years in order to secure the requisite work in education. In 1949, however, a four-year sequence in both kindergarten and primary teacher training was drawn up and sent to the Minnesota Department of Education for approval. That same year courses leading to a master of education degree were approved by the college faculty and the University of Minnesota. Of these changes President Turck declared: "We are really embarked on a program that will save the liberal arts colleges if they comply with the . . . requirements . . . and many other liberal arts colleges including Hamline and St. Thomas are following our lead."[9]

Early in 1951 an agreement to help train nurses was entered into with three Minneapolis hospitals — Abbott, Northwestern, and St. Barnabas. With a grant of $40,500 from the Hill Family Foundation to assist in financing its initial costs, the three-year, nondegree course in nursing education began on an experimental basis that fall with 139 young women enrolled. Two years later a program leading to a B.S. degree with a major in nursing was instituted; in 1957 arrangements were made for student nurses from St. Paul's Ancker Hospital to take certain courses at Macalester.[10]

In 1951 also a combined engineering program was approved in co-operation with Lafayette College in Pennsylvania (and later with the Illinois Institute of Technology) in which the student spent three years at Macalester and two at the engineering school. This was followed a year later by a major in business administration capped by a B.S. degree. These innovations attracted students and involved the college "in the throbbing life of this region," but they did not bring a chapter of Phi Beta Kappa to the campus. In a letter dated January 28, 1953, the secretary of the United Chapters again criticized "the vocational overtones permitted in programs leading to the A.B. degree," and informed the college that representatives of the national organization would not make another visit to Macalester at that time.[11]

Faculty leaders in the Phi Beta Kappa crusade did not give up hope. They took encouragement from two successful intercollege projects being supported by the Hill Family Foundation in the mid-1950s. The first was the four-college area studies program initiated in the fall of 1953 by Macalester, Hamline, St. Catherine, and St. Thomas. The second was the college co-operative project under which the five participating Minnesota institutions brought visiting scholars to their campuses. The trustees in 1953 also approved a co-operative program between Macalester and the Minneapolis School of Art (now the Minneapolis College of Art and Design), and three years later abolished the home economics department, in which only four students were enrolled.[12]

With these developments and others plus the improvements in physical plant to bolster their petition, Macalester again made overtures to Phi Beta Kappa in 1956, and again was rebuffed. The secretary of the United Chapters commended the college's recent progress in improving teaching loads, library purchases, and student financial aid, but noted that faculty salary scales were too low and so was the ratio of faculty members with doctorates (about one in four). Furthermore, he said, the fact remained "that the number of A.B. candidates in each graduating class is nearly equalled by the number of senior candidates for special degrees in business administration, education and other professional fields." The "relative prominence of these special programs" was the rub as far as Phi Beta Kappa was concerned. It would be over a decade before the coveted chapter was won.[13]

In various ways the year 1956 marked a sort of watershed for Macalester. The repeated rejections by Phi Beta Kappa served to convince certain faculty members and trustees that curricular changes were mandatory. Paul H. Davis, who had had a successful career in planning and development at Stanford and Columbia universities, was hired as a consultant in a ten-year development program for Macalester. DeWitt Wallace agreed to pay half of his salary and expenses. In the same year the size of the board of trustees was increased, and a development council was organized. Both trustees and faculty served on its committees, which were concerned with nearly a dozen matters from alumni giving to special occasions.[14]

A year later President Turck indicated that he wished to resign as of June, 1958; the board thereupon appointed a committee to find a successor. Although his educational policies and political leanings had been controversial, President Turck had worked hard during difficult times to make Macales-

ter one of the best Presbyterian colleges in the country. On all fronts he left the institution stronger than he had found it.[15]

Chosen early in 1958 to succeed him was Dr. Harvey M. Rice, for the preceding seven years president of the New York State University College in Buffalo. A native of West Virginia and a graduate of Concord College there, with a Ph.D. from Ohio State University, the new executive had been a history teacher and a navy lieutenant in World War II. He had begun his career as a college president at the New York State University College at Oswego in 1947. The ten years he would spend at Macalester were to be a time of almost fabulous growth for the St. Paul college.[16]

With something of a mandate from the trustees to reorient the direction in which Macalester had been moving and make it essentially an undergraduate liberal arts college of high quality, President Rice took office on August 1, 1958. A good start had been made on the ten-year development program begun two years earlier. Gifts from over 1,800 contributors during the first twelve months of the project had totaled $1,100,000. By November, 1961, with half of the drive's time yet to run nearly 5,000 donors had given over $11,000,000 — more than had been raised in all of the college's previous history.[17]

This heartening display of support permitted concurrent advances on many fronts, academic as well as bricks and mortar. Within a few short years graduates of the 1950s would scarcely recognize their alma mater. The blueprint for this transformation was fashioned by a long-range planning commission of thirty-four members drawn from faculty, students, trustees, and others appointed by the president of the board early in 1961. The ten-year blueprint officially approved in September, 1961, carried a price tag of more than $30,000,000, of which $12,280,000 would be for new facilities. It was intended that most of the rest would go to increase the endowment. Although approximately $12,000,000 was already in hand, the magnitude of the undertaking was formidable. The board in September, 1963, however, authorized the immediate launching of a drive for $32,000,000 in capital funds.[18]

The following month the cause received a tremendous thrust when Mr. and Mrs. DeWitt Wallace offered a ten-year challenge gift of $10,000,000, thereby also providing the enterprise with a name, the "Macalester Challenge Campaign." Shortly thereafter former Minnesota Governor Elmer L. Andersen accepted chairmanship of the drive for a two-year term and inaugurated what became one of the nation's most successful achievements in small college money-raising efforts. What would have happened without the Wallace stimulus — a largess of about $30,000,000 by 1968 — makes for interesting speculation, but approximately $14,000,000 was secured from other sources during the Rice administration. The statistics tell an exciting story. In the mid-1950s the annual budget was roughly $1,250,000 and total college assets were $5,918,000; the respective amounts in 1965–66 were $4,688,000 and $43,300,000. Total student aid in 1953–54 came to just under $46,500; a decade later it was $353,770 from college funds alone, or twice that amount if outside funds are included.[19]

Accompanying this dramatic upswing on the financial charts and accounting for part of it was a truly amazing expansion of the physical plant. Thanks to the generosity of the Weyerhaeuser family a needed addition to the library costing $375,000 was completed in the fall of 1960. By then the college's collection numbered over 80,000 volumes, but within six years it would total more than 138,000; again a new library seemed a necessity. In the autumn of 1961, when so many developments were coming into focus, the board approved the hiring of an architect to design a whole array of new buildings: a science hall, an arts center, a dormitory for 150 to 200 women and one for 250 men, a dining commons, and a stadium. Also given a green light was the rehabilitation of Carnegie Hall, Old Main, and the power plant. Thereafter the campus became a maze of construction activity with nine projects going on simultaneously in 1962–63.[20]

The following year Shaw Athletic Field was relocated and the new stadium built. In the fall of 1964 the dining hall and the two dormitories were ready for use. One of the latter was named for long-time dean of women, Margaret M. Doty, the other for J. Huntley Dupre, former dean of the college and biographer of its founder, Edward D. Neill. Dedication of the Olin Hall of Science, for which the Olin Foundation gave $1,600,000, occurred in May, 1965. The following October the beautiful, five-structure, $3,500,000 Janet Wallace Fine Arts Center, a gift of the DeWitt Wallaces in memory of his mother, was also dedicated. All told, the value of campus and buildings during the decade following 1955 mounted from $2,360,000 to about $17,000,000.[21]

But plant and endowment are, of course, secondary in importance to the people using them. Macalester now renewed its efforts to attract faculty of ability and excellent preparation, to recruit students whose motivations and previous records held promise of continued growth, and to provide both groups with a curriculum reflecting the best thinking in the country's leading colleges of the liberal arts.

Here again developments that were foreshadowed in the late 1950s culminated in 1961. Beginning in 1955 when the Presbyterian Board of Christian Education undertook to upgrade faculty salaries in the colleges of its denomination, efforts were made to improve the lot of Macalester professors and to add distinguished teachers and scholars to the staff. In this endeavor the role of Mr. and Mrs. DeWitt Wallace was again immense: $25,000 for general salary increases and funds to endow three professorships honoring James Wallace in 1956–57; $34,000 the following year for salary raises, plus $1,000 to each of twelve younger faculty members to enable them to spend the summer studying for their doctorates; money for eighty further salary advances in 1958–59; and a gift in 1963 to make possible the new pension plan under which faculty for the first time could look forward to dignified and secure retirement.[22]

At its important meeting in September, 1961, the board adopted, among other proposals, a statement of purposes and goals regarding faculty drawn up by the long-range planning commission. Dealing with such matters as salary, work load, sabbaticals, retirement benefits, and opportunities for growth, the document articulated past policy and set targets for the future. The results achieved were substantial. In 1955 it had been hoped that within three years the range of professors' annual salaries would reach $5,000 to $6,000; the median pay for faculty members of that rank in 1965 was $14,000 and going higher. This trend, accompanied by increased perquisites, made recruitment easier even in the growing sellers' market of that day. As a consequence the percentage of full-time teaching staff with doctoral degrees rose from twenty-six in 1955 to fifty-five a decade later. In view of these advances, it is not surprising that a visiting committee of the North Central Association in 1966 remarked on the "recent dramatic upgrading of many departmental staffs" at Macalester.[23]

A somewhat similar statement could have been made regarding the students. Under the policy adopted in 1961, admissions people were charged with attracting able undergraduates of varied financial and social backgrounds, at least 20 per cent of whom should come from outside the Upper Midwest. Lack of money was not to be a deterrent to enrollment, the sex ratio was to be about equal, and three-quarters of the students ultimately were to live on campus. The average verbal score of entering freshmen on the required college board examinations rose from 541 in 1961 to 601 in 1966.

An increase in the number of full-time students from about 1,425 in September, 1962, to over 1,800 in the fall of 1965 was also registered.[24]

Meanwhile the Macalester curriculum also underwent a major transformation in the course of which certain individuals whose positions were phased out suffered considerable trauma. As early as March, 1960, the trustees decided that the nursing program should be discontinued in accordance with the decision "that the future of the College lies in the direction of a true liberal arts college." At the momentous September, 1961, meeting, the board ruled that Macalester would henceforth confer only two degrees, the B.A. and the master of education. Current students in sequences leading to a B.S. degree or to one in medical technology would be allowed to finish their courses; the same rule applied to undergraduates majoring in journalism and those in the two-three engineering program. The three-two engineering arrangement would be retained, but the nursing curriculum, the evening sessions, and the secretarial courses for college credit would become only memories.[25]

That same autumn the faculty curriculum review committee under the leadership of an able new dean, Lucius Garvin, began its work of implementing the policy recommendations of the planning commission as adopted by the board. After two days of deliberations, the faculty in June, 1962, approved the review committee's report abolishing majors and minors (to be replaced by fields of concentration), five degree programs, credit hours, and — after departmental adjustments to the change — 119 former courses. The two-semester plan was retained, but a student would take only four courses of equal weight each term instead of five to seven as previously. For graduation 32 courses (11 of them required) would replace the 126 credit hours formerly needed.[26]

A special faculty committee had studied the wisdom of adopting an interim term in January, during which a student on campus or elsewhere, in class or independently, would pursue intensively the work of one course. When the new calendar and program were put into effect in the fall of 1963, the interim term was part of the parcel, and Macalester was among the first three institutions in the country to adopt it. With constant review and modification, the curriculum as refashioned between 1961 and 1963 remains in operation to the present.[27]

In reporting on these curriculum developments, Dean Garvin declared that the outstanding college of the future "must not only exploit, but should deliberately create and nurture within itself areas of strength — things which it does superlatively well. It must erect 'steeples of strength' . . . so impressively high that they will stand out as the badge, the mark, the special gift or gifts of this college to its students and to the world." Two such steeples at Macalester, said Garvin, were its science division and its international programs.[28]

President Turck had been widely known for his interest in world affairs, and Macalester's Canadian-American Conference had originated in November, 1941, but it was not until about 1960 that money was available to permit a "deliberate effort to increase our foreign student programs." Thereafter a distinctly international atmosphere permeated the campus. Not only were fifty or more foreign students regularly enrolled at the college, but a growing number of native-born Macalester undergraduates were traveling and studying in far-flung places on the globe. In 1966–67 over two hundred members of the student body worked, toured, or studied in two dozen foreign countries.[29]

But it was not only in science and world affairs that the college attempted to push on to new frontiers. "We should certainly be short on wisdom," noted Dean Garvin, "if we were to reject proposals for . . . the whole train of new intellectual tools that crowd in for places in our academic enterprise." Early in the 1960s, for example, a trustee subcommittee was created on new developments in the improvement of instruction, and in 1966 Mrs. DeWitt Wallace agreed to support a program of institutional research and experimental innovation, having as one of its aims "to play a substantial role in nurturing and supporting a climate of innovative thinking and experimentation among the faculty and academic officers." By this time officials of Phi Beta Kappa were ready to stamp the institution with their seal of approval. In August, 1967, Macalester became the fourth private college in the state to be awarded a charter for a chapter of the honor society, and a goal long sought was at last attained.[30]

To delineate in broad outline only the exciting growth of Macalester in the 1960s is not to suggest that tensions did not exist or that counteracting pressures were not present during the metamorphosis. Forces of the past are always in contention with those of the future, and the conflict is most severe during times of rapid change. Although the trustees in 1961 reaffirmed "their devotion to the cause of Christian education" and pledged to continue the "historic relationship of the College to the Presbyterian Church," they could not stem the tide of secularism sweeping across the land and the campus. Indeed their pronouncement was itself partly a response to their own recent action loosening the bond between church and college by deleting from the latter's articles of incorporation the seventy-five-year-old provision that two-thirds of the trustees must be Presbyterians — a sectarian tie that had become uncomfortably constraining to an institution seeking national prominence. By the fall of 1966 another vestige of the past — required attendance at chapel and convocation — also disappeared.[31]

The administration, to its surprise, found itself occasionally portrayed as both despot and bulwark of the status quo. Faculty members, aware of their privileges and growing prestige, took periodic pot shots. In 1960, for example, about thirty members of the Macalester chapter of the AAUP censured the administration for merely considering ways in which students in a class where the proportion of failures had seemed unreasonably high could receive passing grades, even though none of the proposals considered had been put into effect. Four years later the faculty expressed its concern over the great growth of administrative costs and over losing some of its powers of decision making. But such squabbles are after all par for the academic course.[32]

Although Macalester, as President Rice pointed out, was no Berkeley, students in the style of the 1960s were increasingly seeking and receiving more involvement in administrative affairs. Now and then writers in the student newspaper, the *Mac Weekly*, skidded over the line of good taste, but undergraduates did not insist on "taking over" the college. Indeed on the curriculum committee, where they were voting members, the students exhibited a distinct sense of responsibility.[33]

In the autumn of 1967 President Rice announced that he would leave his Macalester post as of June 30, 1968. "Many college presidents across the country," he declared, "have found that their first 10 years have been the most productive, have seen the greatest achievements and have meant the most to the institution." Certainly President Rice's decade of service had recorded memorable achievements: the erection of twelve new buildings worth $13,000,000, the complete revision of the curriculum, the increase of the endowment from $3,600,000 to $26,800,000, the doubling of the faculty, and the enlargement of the student body from 1,300 to 1,800. Prospects for the future were bright. Although the faculty was "shocked and surprised" by the announcement, to the president the timing seemed right.[34]

In March, 1968, Dr. Arthur S. Flemming, a member of Macalester's board of trustees, was elected eleventh president of the college. A onetime head of Ohio Wesleyan University, he had served as secretary of health, education, and welfare in President Dwight D. Eisenhower's cabinet; since 1961 he had been president of the University of Oregon. At the time of his Macalester appointment, he noted the attractions of the college — a strong faculty and student body, exceptional financial support, co-operative relationships with other colleges and the University of Minnesota — and expressed his concept of academic life. "A campus," he said, "should provide the maximum opportunity for the expression of views on all issues, and student leaders should have the opportunity to participate in the decision-making process of the school." His presidency in St. Paul was destined to span only three years and to be handicapped by mounting financial problems, but his brief tenure coincided with imaginative and controversial attempts to find solutions to a number of society's dilemmas.[35]

Other major developments in the spring of 1968 were a grant from the Olin Foundation to construct and equip a science building for the departments of biology, geology, and psychology, and the receipt of pledges in excess of $500,000 to establish a Hubert H. Humphrey endowed professorship of international affairs. The former vice president of the United States had taught political science at Macalester in 1940–41. Now he would become the first occupant of the chair named in his honor. In February, 1969, he resumed his association with the college by keynoting the annual political emphasis week symposium, which took as its theme the nation's urban crisis. Less than two years later he returned to the United States Senate, and the chair was filled by visiting lecturers in 1971–72.[36]

Meanwhile in the summer of 1968 President Flemming had taken up his executive duties in St. Paul. Greeting him that fall was a student body of 1,971 men and women and a faculty of 136 full-time teachers. Three score of the undergraduates had come from 36 foreign countries, but 55 per cent of the student population were Minnesotans — 30 per cent of the total hailing from metropolitan Ramsey and Hennepin counties which include the Twin Cities. Sixty-seven per cent of the instructional staff possessed earned doctorates; by the autumn of 1970 the proportion would be up to 81 per cent. At his first Macalester commencement, President Flemming handed baccalaureate degrees to a record-sized class of 428 members, 136 of whom had been promised admission to 52 different graduate schools.[37]

The new president would not find it necessary to initiate large construction projects. The recent expansion of the physical plant had in general obviated the need for more major buildings, and the increasingly tight money market rendered further expansion costly and unwise. Yet the college's facilities were augmented during President Flemming's brief tenure. In May, 1969, the glass-walled Weyerhaeuser Memorial Chapel was dedicated. It had been given to Macalester by the family of Frederick Weyerhaeuser, a trustee from 1957 until his death in 1961. Ground breaking for the science building which had been made possible by the second Olin Foundation grant followed in March, 1969. Dedicated in November, 1970, the $2,400,000 addition was christened the Harvey M. Rice Hall of Science in ceremonies attended by the institution's immediate past president. Off campus a biology field station was constructed along the Mississippi River on the nearly 280 acres of the Katharine Ordway Natural History Study Area, a gift to the college in 1967. Two years later 35 acres of desert ranch land near Tucson, Arizona, was donated by an alumnus and his wife. Known as Macalester's Southwest Center, it was first used during the 1970 interim term by biology and geology faculty and students.[38]

Although not memorable for its contributions to campus architecture, the Flemming administration gained distinction by its efforts to foster "the development of individual human potential." On the curricular front in 1969 and 1970 this endeavor took the form of abolishing certain graduation requirements — freshman English, physical education, religion, foreign language, and speech, and of injecting flexibility into the courses of study. Interdepartmental programs were also encouraged. The continuing quest for improvement was helped in 1969 by a National Science Foundation grant of $224,000 to be used over a three-year period for the benefit of the departments of the sciences, mathematics, and psychology; Macalester added $76,000 of its own money for the same purpose. On other fronts concern for the individual was shown in a multitude of ways: by greater involvement of both students and faculty in community governance, by guarantees of undergraduates' rights and freedoms, by increased salary scales and fringe benefits, and by summer Upward Bound precollege courses for fifty underprivileged youths.[39]

But Macalester's most daring break with the past was charted in December, 1968, when the Expanded Educational Opportunities (EEO) program received student, faculty, administration, and trustee approval. Seven years earlier the board had decided that the undergraduate body should reflect greater social, economic, and cultural diversity, but progress in implementing the policy had been rather modest. Now in a major and dramatic move, the college would show observers how people could learn to live together in a pluralistic society. Mac-

alester would commit $900,000 of its money and a maximum of its imagination, energy, and patience to the endeavor. Total financial aid and all possible academic and personal assistance would be given each year to 75 new students, at least 60 of whom came from minority ethnic groups. The first contingent arrived for summer orientation in June, 1969; by the fall of 1970 the EEO group from twenty-seven states and the District of Columbia consisted of 112 Blacks, 18 Indians, 14 Spanish-surnamed Americans, and six whites. By then an individual learning center to help all students had been established, and a grant of $142,000 had been received from the federal office of education to provide special services for disadvantaged students. All had not gone smoothly, but to President Flemming EEO was "a demonstration project of national significance."[40]

Another facet of Macalester's recent history which evoked both interest and concern on campus and beyond its borders was the college's financial operations. Part of the story's fascination lies in the sheer magnitude of the sums involved. By August, 1970, the institution's total assets approximated $57,500,000, of which property, plant, and equipment accounted for $24,300,000. Endowment was roughly $30,000,000. General and educational income in 1969–70 was slightly over $9,100,000. But against these staggering totals must be placed the countervailing figures of soaring costs. The college's expenditures in 1969–70 came to almost $11,800,000. Scholarships, grants, loans, and student work amounted to $2,778,000; over 65 per cent of all undergraduates received some form of financial aid. The deficit for the year was an unusual $2,500,000. And despite cutbacks, the deficit for 1970–71, the third year in a row, dropped only to $2,400,000. Total liabilities in mid-1970 exceeded $5,300,000, and the trustees found it necessary to borrow from endowment. To make matters worse, it was announced in 1971 that DeWitt Wallace, who had been contributing over $1,000,000 a year to current operations, was going to cease his donations.[41]

Macalester once again — as in its early days — faced a crisis. Some commentators laid the blame on extravagance and an overly ambitious academic and construction program. Dr. Flemming could scarcely be held responsible for the 1961 blueprint which had led to the great outlays of money, but as president he was in a vulnerable position. Rumor suggested that the EEO project and permissiveness on campus had disenchanted DeWitt Wallace and other friends of the institution. Be that as it may, in January, 1971, President Flemming — despite strong student support on his behalf — submitted his resignation to take effect no later than the end of the academic year. A deeply religious man, sensitive "to the agonies of students" and "outraged by racial injustice," he left a distinct imprint on the college in a brief time.[42]

As the uncertain 1970s got under way, Macalester appeared to be facing an era of relative austerity. At its helm as a "thorough reappraisal of the College's commitments" began was the youngest man ever to serve as its president. James A. Robinson, thirty-nine years old when he was appointed, former provost and vice president for academic affairs at Ohio State University, became Macalester's twelfth president on August 1, 1971. Despite problems, President Robinson was able to report that "Macalester achieved a balanced budget at the end of the [1971–72] fiscal year." The total budget of over $9,500,000 was 14 per cent below that of the previous year, some expenditures were cut, others delayed, alumni giving was substantially increased, and with other measures, for the first time in four years Macalester's expenses equaled its income. As the college looks toward the celebration of its charter centennial year in 1974, Macalester's 1971–72 report to the Presbyterian Synod commented that the school "faces the future in the throes of apparent dilemmas: a traditional academic liberal arts orientation versus relationships with and involvement in the surrounding community and the ever present tension between tradition and change."[43]

To this, President Robinson remarked, "For my part, there is no dilemma. Macalester cannot justify its academic distinction without dedicating the knowledge and capabilities of its faculty and students to mankind. Macalester cannot serve mankind unless its teachers offer and its students acquire the best in education.

"The viability of Macalester depends both upon its admiration and respect for tradition and its willingness to meet the developing opportunities of each new area. Macalester aims for a spirit of humaneness. The college is not a temple of expertise but a laboratory of human diversity, committed to maintaining the best that men have historically brought to the questions of living, coming to terms with things as they are, and welding a realistic base from which to examine the fundamental questions of the future." Thus the institution looking toward its second century seeks to fulfill its objectives and to continue its role as one of the leading liberal arts colleges in the country.

34 COLLEGE OF ST. THOMAS

Faith, Piety, and Discipline

FOR A TIME AFTER PEARL HARBOR, no matter what fears were uppermost in people's minds, life at St. Thomas went on in a fairly normal manner. At the June commencement in 1942, degrees were conferred on 66 graduates, and thanks to the presence of several military reserve units, collegiate enrollment held at about 750 that fall. The academy had a record 640 students. By the second term, however, the college was down to 250, a figure that fell by another 120 when the reserve corps was called out in March, 1943. One bright spot offset the gloom. When 75 seniors received their degrees at commencement in 1943, the public got its first look at the giant wall murals, the stained glass windows, the new altar, and other features of the redecorated chapel — one more of I. A. O'Shaughnessy's gifts to St. Thomas. On July 1 came the navy V-12 training program and a new three-semester calendar. To the 96 civilian students were now added some 260 naval trainees.[1]

For the Reverend James H. Moynihan, president of the college since 1933, this period of tension and uncertainty was rendered even sadder by the death on Christmas eve in 1943 of his brother, Father Humphrey Moynihan, pastor of the Church of the Incarnation in Minneapolis. Shortly thereafter St. Thomas' president was relieved of his heavy responsiblities and appointed to fill his brother's post in the Incarnation parish. Despite Father James Moynihan's feeling of unsuitability for the task of college president, his administration had meant much to St. Thomas in material ways and in the more intangible areas of atmosphere and standards. He was especially proud of the faculty he had been able to attract; thirty-eight graduates had gone on to earn Ph.D. degrees during his term of office. He had always received the help and support of Archbishop Murray, through whose efforts the mortgage and much of the college's indebtedness had been removed. Father Moynihan had generously extended financial aid as needed to many young men of the diocese; it is not surprising that students of the era hold their president in high respect and affection.[2]

In January, 1944, Archbishop Murray appointed Father Vincent J. Flynn, chairman of the college's English department, as the eleventh president of St. Thomas. A native of Minnesota, the eldest of eleven children, the new executive had excellent preparation for his post. A graduate of St. Thomas Academy and a former student at St. Paul Seminary, he held bachelor degrees from St. Thomas and Catholic University, a master of arts from the University of Minnesota, and a University of Chicago Ph.D. He had also studied in Europe. Considering his background, his attractive personality, his ready wit, and his unusual success as a teacher, it followed that distinction marked his performance in his new role. At his inauguration in April, uniformed young men far outnumbered civilian college students, and the end of wartime restrictions seemed nowhere in sight.[3]

Under such conditions President Flynn set himself to the work of making "St. Thomas well and favorably known wherever I could," a task he pursued often at the expense of his own physical well-being. As his name became better known, so too did that of the college. In January, 1949, he was elected to the presidency of the Association of American Colleges, an organization composed of more than six hundred institutions of higher learning. His presidential address to the group in 1950 received favorable comment the country over.[4]

The welcome return of peace in 1945 ushered in the period of precipitous increases in enrollment which posed problems for colleges everywhere. Registration at St. Thomas in the spring of 1946 was about 990; the following year it reached 1,890, and in 1948 it climbed to a peak of 2,273. Of the 1946 students 81 per cent were veterans, including

175 who were married. The proportion of veterans in the 1946 student body at St. Thomas was the highest in any Minnesota college. A total of twenty-five men received diplomas during 1944; eleven of them were in service and received their diplomas by mail. The number rose to a record ninety-eight four years later, placing considerable strain on faculty and facilities.[5]

With much effort and care, utilizing such leading agencies as the National Catholic Welfare Conference, Father Flynn increased the faculty from 43 in 1944 to 146 (106 full time) in 1948. One addition in the sociology department was Eugene J. McCarthy, a graduate of St. John's University at Collegeville, who would soon embark on a political career climaxed by a Pied Piperlike campaign for the presidential nomination in 1968. Accompanying faculty expansion was the delegation to committees of such vital responsibilities as curriculum revision and the conduct of faculty meetings.[6]

Even before fighting ceased, the president concluded that his predecessor's expansion program, which included a new science building, should be implemented to handle the anticipated enrollment flood. As the initial step in raising the necessary money, a campaign was launched at a dinner in July, 1945, at which an anonymous gift of $100,000 was announced. In December ground-breaking ceremonies were held for what would become the modern, four-story science building, Albertus Magnus Hall. Completed in 1948 after delays due to scarcities of labor and materials, the facility cost over $1,300,000. Its dedication was followed by a day-long symposium on "Science in the Modern World." Meanwhile, beginning in the summer of 1946 twenty-six war surplus structures valued at nearly $500,000 were acquired for approximately $50,000. They included three temporary units for 194 students, twenty two-family units for married couples, and three two-story buildings to provide a cafeteria, classrooms, and a student union. The clergy contributed $87,000 to the fund drive to help pay off the debt incurred in all this physical expansion.[7]

College life now began to resume a certain normality, as Tommies took up where they had left off before the call to arms. Music gained a new importance and dramatics was revived. The "Mr. Tommy" contest was renewed in 1947; new clubs were organized, and the yearbook, the *Aquinas*, again put in its appearance after a four-year lapse. The All-College Council was delegated increasing responsibility, and relationships between it and Father Flynn were friendly and close. In 1948 St. Thomas joined both the National Student Associa-

tion and the National Federation of Catholic College Students. That fall the air force ROTC program, required of all freshmen and sophomores, was inaugurated with a registration of 585 men. The college for the first time participated in the SPAN project, and the memory of Archbishop Ireland was refreshed through the first Founder's Day observance. In this period, too, the old breach between St. Thomas and Notre Dame dating from 1933 was closed. Father John J. Cavanaugh, president of the South Bend institution, gave the June, 1949, commencement address at St. Thomas and received an honorary degree. Father Flynn delivered the baccalaureate address at Notre Dame the following January and was similarly honored.[8]

By the fall of 1949 the era of the World War II veteran was waning, and St. Thomas faced a difficult interlude of declining enrollments. Registration in September, 1949, was 1,949; by 1955 it was 1,383. Accompanying this trend was a loss of college income, making it impossible to continue raising faculty salaries. As a consequence some able teachers were lost. Reluctantly made increases in tuition necessitated increases in student aid. Certain capital outlays such as a new boiler and conversion of the heating plant to gas were mandatory; in the absence of a substantial endowment they had to be paid for out of current funds.[9]

Fortunately the generosity of friends kept the college in business, but mendicancy meant hard work for Father Flynn. St. Thomas' share of the amount collected by the Minnesota Private College Fund solicitation helped increasingly from 1952 on, but that, of course, was a minor part of the annual budget. The Ford Foundation grant in December, 1955, of $348,500 to be used for endowment to underwrite faculty salaries provided both a psychological and practical lift. In Father Flynn's last year as president in 1955–56, total college income was slightly over $1,260,000, and expenditures were close to $1,285,000. For the academy the comparable sums were $389,000 and $400,000.[10]

In the academic sphere the faculty curriculum committee kept a constant watch on trends and on ways of improving class offerings. In the fall of 1949 credit was allowed for night school courses which the college had offered from 1946 on. A program leading to a master of education degree was instituted in the summer of 1950. Before the Flynn administration ended about four hundred students pursued this course, seventy-three of them to its conclusion. In 1956 the program was expanded by the addition of work leading to an M.A. in secondary school administration. Two other variations in the traditional curriculum were also introduced about this time: the combined liberal arts-engineering, three-two course, and the area studies sequence. The former began in September, 1952, in conjunction with the University of Notre Dame. The latter, financed by the Hill Family Foundation and enjoying the co-operation of the Hill Reference Library in St. Paul, was started in the fall of 1953 in association with St. Catherine's, Hamline, and Macalester. Both programs proved successful and remained a part of the St. Thomas curriculum. With other developments they testify to the wisdom, vitality, and willingness to change that were characteristic of the Flynn presidency. Sadly, the weight of his burdens had taken a heavy toll of Father Flynn's health. On July 6, 1956, he died of a heart attack. His death was a great loss, not only to St. Thomas but to the whole world of education as well.[11]

Twelfth president of the college was Father James P. Shannon, another native Minnesotan, honor graduate, and member of the faculty since 1954. A onetime assistant pastor and parochial school-teacher, he had earned his master's degree at the University of Minnesota in 1951 and his doctorate in history at Yale in 1955. Though his appointment to the presidency of his alma mater in 1956 by ailing Archbishop Murray came as a surprise to the thirty-five-year-old priest, Father Shannon proved during his decade-long administration that it had been eminently wise. At the outset as he viewed the task before him, he concluded that St. Thomas' most pressing needs were plant improvement and increased staff salaries. To these ends he directed his attention.[12]

The first major step toward plant expansion was announced at the president's formal inaugural ceremony in May, 1957, by the newly appointed Archbishop William O. Brady. Mr. and Mrs. I. A. O'Shaughnessy would give St. Thomas a new library. Such a key facility had been badly needed for a long time. The library's quarters in the basement of the administration building had become woefully inadequate, and books were stored all over the campus. After much careful planning, ground breaking followed the June, 1958, graduation exercises. By the end of September, 1959, the four-story, semi-Gothic, O'Shaughnessy Library was in full operation. Built at a total cost of over $1,500,000, the handsome modern library provides space for 150,000 volumes, an auditorium, a visual aids center, a browsing room, and study carrels.[13]

Meanwhile with enrollment mounting from 1,333 in 1957 to 1,559 in 1958, housing had become an ever-more-critical problem. In 1957 about 450 students were living in off-campus rooms. So, like most of his fellow college presidents, Father Shannon filed an application with the federal housing and home finance agency for a loan to erect a dormitory. Approval came in March, 1958, and the building, Dowling Hall, was opened in September, 1959. Costing more than $1,240,000, it contained rooms for 300 men. Even so, as enrollment pushed upward, over 400 students still had to start the year in off-campus quarters. The third major construction project at this time was the union building (Murray Hall) put into use in September, 1960, with dining facilities capable of serving 1,400 people at one meal. Partially financed by a federal loan of $1,300,000, the remainder of its $1,900,000 cost was contributed by such friends as Mr. O'Shaughnessy, Patrick Butler, and Thomas P. Coughlan. Altogether approximately $5,000,000 of new plant facilities were built during Father Shannon's first five-year term.[14]

This is not to suggest, however, that the president had an "edifice complex." A warm-hearted, friendly man, he was much more interested in the people using the buildings. Always generous in testifying to the debt he owed his own teachers at St. Thomas, he wanted similar teaching excellence and stimulation for the students attending during his presidency. He was particularly pleased by certain key departmental chairmen he was able to appoint. One advantage he enjoyed in recruiting faculty was the presence of some five hundred priests in the archdiocese on whom he could draw. Although the twenty-eight to thirty-two priests constituted a minority of St. Thomas' teaching staff, they provided a central core, and Father Shannon, with the archbishop's help, constantly encouraged them to continue self-improvement. In 1956 only two teaching priests had earned doctorates; five years later eight more had joined the faculty, and others were soon to be added. Relations between ordained and lay teachers were cordial; each group served as a healthy challenge to the other to keep performance at a high level.[15]

President Flynn had taken steps leading to the adoption of a retirement and pension plan for the faculty, but he did not live to see it realized. Father Shannon, as part of his program for the college, asked the faculty service committee to study plans in effect elsewhere and to frame one for St. Thomas. This was done, and after trustee and faculty approval was obtained, the resulting proposal covering teaching and administrative personnel became operative in the fall of 1959. Rules for promotion and tenure were also brought up to date, and the collective authority of the faculty in a variety of areas was further clarified. As it was possible salaries for lay teachers were raised, payments were put on a twelve-month basis, and each faculty member received a full summer free every third year. If all this activity reduced his power, the loss was more than offset by the satisfaction President Shannon felt when he observed the growing self-confidence and strength of the teaching force.[16]

A high light of the Shannon years was the Ford Foundation announcement in June, 1962, of a $1,500,000 grant to St. Thomas if the college would raise another $3,000,000 over a three-year period. At the time the announcement was made, St. Thomas was the only Catholic men's college in the country singled out for a Ford grant, a fact which brought national attention and prestige to the St. Paul institution. St. Thomas' inclusion in the foundation program was based on its regional importance as a center "of serious study and academic excellence." Delighted by the honor and challenged by the opportunity, the St. Thomas trustees decided to aim at raising $6,000,000 to support a "Program for Great Teaching." If they were successful, $2,400,000 of the money would go into endowment for salaries; $1,600,000 would be allocated to endow four distinguished professorships; $1,200,000 would be placed in an endowed scholarship fund; and the remainder would be used to provide office space, a computer center, a botany laboratory, and library equipment.[17]

By May 2, 1965, after an intensive and carefully organized campaign, the sum of $6,300,000 had been raised, 30.5 per cent of it from more than 2,300 alumni, and 33 per cent from 14 foundations. Approximately 50 parishes had contributed about $745,000 or 11.7 per cent of the total to what was called the Murray Fund for teacher training. The drive had been a grand success in every way, not the least of which had been the forging of stronger ties between college and alumni, a distinct rise in morale, and a glow of pride in their institution.[18]

It now became possible to undertake the plant improvement called for in the Program for Great Teaching and to raise faculty salaries again. In spite of this favorable turn, the average salary of the 94 lay teachers on the faculty in 1968 was only $9,800, and the AAUP's over-all rating of St. Thomas for faculty salary scale was D on a scale of A to F. Tuition in 1956 had been $450; in 1963 it was up to $825, but it had not kept pace with rising educational costs. Student aid outlay in the former year had been $52,800; the total in 1963 was $184,200 and going higher. Over 600 students would receive half a million dollars in aid in 1966–67. The physical plant valued at $4,998,000 in 1956 would be listed at $10,500,000 in 1963; the endowment figures for the two years were $521,200 and

$1,154,800, respectively. Priests' contributed services of $127,700 in 1967–68 were nearly $20,000 less than they had been the previous year. Despite the fact that the college was better off than many of its cousins, St. Thomas seemed to be on a financial treadmill.[19]

Because of the emphasis on improvement of physical plant and financial condition, no fundamental changes in curriculum were instituted during the early years of the Shannon administration. That the college remained attuned to community needs was evident, however, in several developments of the period. St. Thomas offered summer institutes for high schoolteachers under grants from the National Science Foundation and the Hill Family Foundation. The first of these for teachers of mathematics and biology was conducted in the summer of 1958. Later institutes dealt with such subjects as communism, child care, geriatrics (for religious sisters), economic education, and computer programming.[20]

One of the most far-reaching innovations in St. Thomas' program had its inception in 1956 with the establishment of a Management Center for study, research, and teaching in this field. A separate administrative unit within the college, the center has helped make St. Thomas known from Switzerland to Thailand through its courses for private companies, governmental agencies, and other nonprofit organizations. Seminars are held on campus or "in house" at the organization's office or plant. St. Thomas' Management Center became affiliated with the Industrial Relations Center of the University of Chicago in 1959, thus adding the resources and programs of that institution to those already available. In the first four years of its existence about 750 executives representing 450 organizations participated in the center's seminars. Between September 1, 1967, and August 31, 1968, it enrolled 2,761 persons in 61 courses dealing with effective communication, motivation, job training, drug abuse, and women in management, to name only a few. By 1972 an annual average of 3,000 persons representing approximately 500 organizations were utilizing the services of the center's five full-time staff members and about forty part-time specialists.[21]

By 1961 with these programs well launched, the time seemed propitious to undertake a thorough study and analysis of the whole St. Thomas curriculum. With a grant from the Hill Family Foundation to support its work, a standing committee was appointed by President Shannon to tackle the arduous and ticklish task. After delineating the elements distinctive to a Catholic education, the committee made several recommendations in its first report:

a reduction in the number of courses carried each term; inclusion of work in fine arts, foreign languages, mathematics, and European history in every student's program; and fewer and better philosophy courses. Soon most of these proposals were given faculty approval and new ones were also adopted. In 1963 and 1964 a selected group of students engaged in a spring semester program in Cuernavaca, Mexico. In the fall of the latter year a special sequence in mathematics leading to a master of education degree for Twin Cities high schoolteachers was introduced, and a Family Institute was established. Academic rules were tightened and performance expectations raised. In 1965 a new plan, since expanded, went into operation under which a student at any of the four St. Paul colleges of Hamline, Macalester, St. Catherine, and St. Thomas could take one course a term at one of the other three institutions without a special payment. The time-honored credit-hour system was dropped at St. Thomas in 1966, and one based on courses was adopted. Henceforth 36 courses rather than 136 semester credits would be required for graduation. Emphasis would be on depth rather than superficial exposure to a broad spectrum of disciplines.[22]

In the midst of this period of curricular study and innovation, another change occurred which would have pleased former neighbor Edward D. Neill of Macalester. Years earlier he had cautioned that a good institution of higher learning avoids a fog line between itself and a secondary school. St. Thomas had long since sharpened the line, but high school students still roamed the same campus with their collegiate counterparts. In February, 1963, however, the academy was formally incorporated as a separate institution with its own board of trustees. That fall ground was broken for its new home on a suburban campus at Mendota Heights on the shores of Rogers Lake. The attractive modern complex of three buildings plus student houses was financed entirely by gifts. With approximately 550 boys in attendance, classes opened in the suburban location in 1965. After eighty years of sharing facilities with older students St. Thomas Academy was now out on its own.[23]

As the $2,500,000 academy plant was nearing completion, a new distinction came to the man who headed St. Thomas. In February, 1965, Father Shannon was named to the episcopacy to serve as auxiliary to the archbishop of St. Paul. While he remained president of the college, his new responsibilities would leave him less time for St. Thomas. Because of this fact and his belief "that there is a certain periodicity in the term of every college president," Bishop Shannon on May 2, 1966, wrote the archbishop asking to be relieved of his duties as head of St. Thomas at the end of that academic year. In his letter he listed the goals he had set for his administration: securing funds with which to increase faculty salaries and build a library, a student center, a residence hall, and a new campus for the academy, and revising the curriculum. With these aims largely realized, it seemed a suitable time to turn over the presidency to someone else. Although his resignation came as a surprise to most people, Bishop Shannon's request was granted, and he was appointed pastor of a church in Minneapolis.[24]

His choice as his successor and the man so designated was Monsignor Terrence J. Murphy. The holder of a Ph.D. in political science from Georgetown University, he had been a member of the St. Thomas family since 1954. During the last three years of the Shannon administration, Monsignor Murphy had gained valuable experience as executive vice president of the college. His formal installation as president took place on October 27, 1966. So far no dramatic break with the past has occurred in his administration; rather progress has continued along the lines already laid down. Differences, if any, have resulted from the general milieu in which institutions of higher learning found themselves in the late 1960s and early 1970s, not from any change in basic philosophy. The "goal of the committed Christian concerned with and active in society" still motivates St. Thomas' leaders as it did in the past.[25]

In his first fall as chief executive President Murphy greeted 2,150 students, of whom 525 were in the freshman class and 350 in the master of arts programs in education By September, 1968, the enrollment of 2,359 was the highest in the college's history. Housing was tight, but better conditions were in prospect. In the winter of 1966–67 construction had begun on a five-story, 246-bed dormitory located on the site of one of the recently razed academy buildings. Its cost of $1,172,000 was met mainly through a federal loan. With its dedication as Brady Hall in the fall of 1967, over 800 St. Thomas men could live on campus, creating a more cohesive collegiate environment than had been the case formerly.[26]

When students returned to the campus in September, 1966, they found a new curriculum on which the faculty had been laboring for four years. The two lower classes were required to switch to the system of thirty-six courses, but for upperclassmen the change was optional. Most of them in fact changed over and forsook the old 136 semester credit sequence. (Interestingly enough those who did so usually found their grade index rising.) The revised curriculum included new majors in journalism, speech and theater, geology, and psychology, subjects previously offered only as minors. Another innovation was a paid teaching internship program leading to an M.A. in education. In 1967 new plans for reorganizing seminary training in the archdiocese were made operative. Previously a seminarian had spent six years at suburban Nazareth Hall and an equal time at St. Paul Seminary. Henceforth, living in nearby St. John Vianney Seminary, he would take his four college years at St. Thomas. Approximately 120 men attended the college under this program during its first year.[27]

Another interesting recent development at St. Thomas has been the growing co-operation with neighboring St. Catherine. This relationship was not new; in the social realm it went back many years and in the academic area to the early 1950s. What was novel was the degree and, to some extent, the climate of opinion under which mutual endeavors were conducted. In the fall of 1966, for example, 125 St. Thomas men were taking courses at St. Catherine, and 85 women from the latter were similarly engaged at the men's college. To explore more fully the advantages and possibilities of further co-operation between St. Thomas and St. Catherine, a joint study was undertaken in 1967 with support from the Hill Family Foundation. Thirty-five teachers and administrators from both colleges participated under the direction of an outside consultant.[28]

The results of the study were issued in the spring of 1968. Although some of the premises and recommendations of the consultant evoked heated dissent from many faculty members, the report favored greater co-operation between the two institutions. Since that year a great deal has been done to implement the suggestions. An intercampus bus service has been provided, and a co-ordinated calendar has been adopted. An increased number of majors are available. St. Catherine's students can complete majors in geology, journalism, physics, and business administration, and St. Thomas men by attending classes at the women's college have access to eight new majors. In the fall of 1970, 588 Tommies were enrolled in courses at St. Catherine, and 500 Katies were attending classes at St. Thomas. Monsignor Murphy wrote in 1970 that the "co-operative program has proved itself highly workable." It also provides a partial answer to the problems of rising costs and declining enrollments that currently plague private education.[29]

By the late 1960s St. Thomas had become a big business. Total expenditures in 1949–50 had been $1,400,000; two decades later they exceeded $5,722,000. By then, for example, custodial services for the educational buildings ran to about $240 a day, and financing of the pension and retirement program consumed another $529 daily. But in spite of skyrocketing expenses, the college succeeded in balancing its budget. A major portion of its income was provided by student fees. Including those from the Management Center, fees brought in more than $2,980,000 in 1969–70, or 68.3 per cent of general educational income. The $1,550 tuition charge in 1970 was about average for Minnesota's private colleges, yet a substantial amount of student aid had to be dispensed. Scholarships and grants came to $321,500 and work contracts to $177,100. In addition loans to undergraduates totaled over $195,000; the bulk of this sum derived from federal sources, but St. Thomas loaned $49,600 of it under a program initiated by the college with a fund of $100,000 borrowed from the Catholic Aid Association.[30]

To operate in the black St. Thomas, like most private colleges, had to look for outside help. Gifts and grants to the college in 1969–70 totaled approximately $1,130,000; the federal government provided slightly over $353,000 of this amount, mainly for a variety of student assistance programs. The contributed services of the priests accounted for $175,550, and gifts from foundations, individuals, and other friends added up to $200,000. The archdiocese of St. Paul-Minneapolis granted $63,900 to be used for scholarships and aid to students from that Catholic jurisdiction. Another gift of similar size came from the alumni; this donation represented the largest sum secured through that group's annual giving program in the twenty-two years of its existence, although the 1,428 contributors constituted less than 10 per cent of St. Thomas alumni. Since 1969 when the President's Council was organized, the proportion of former students who directed gifts to the college increased to 13.5 per cent in 1972. Made up of alumni and friends of St. Thomas to provide both financial and advisory assistance to the president, the council has also been helpful in obtaining support from nonalumni.[31]

Most recent physical evidence of St. Thomas' sanguine outlook for the future is the new $3,600,000 O'Shaughnessy Educational Center. Work on the five-level structure began in the spring of 1969, and the finished result was put into full use in the fall of 1971. About one-third of the center's cost was provided by the college's great friend, I. A. O'Shaughnessy; the balance came through a federal loan of $1,346,000 and a federal grant of $951,000. Besides providing attractive modern quarters, the center relieved a great deal of congestion. Included in this largest and most complex of St. Thomas' buildings are fifty-six offices for faculty in the social sciences, foreign languages, journalism, and the Management Center; numerous classrooms, some of which are fitted for closed circuit television; a 622-seat auditorium; and the latest in audio-visual equipment. Completion of the center "brings to fruition plans formulated" twenty years earlier, when it was decided that such a facility would be needed "to accommodate an anticipated enrollment of 2,500 students." [32]

This number had not quite been reached by the fall of 1970, but the prediction was not far off the mark. A total of 2,430 young people were then attending St. Thomas — a record 418 of them in the graduate school — making the college second in size behind St. Olaf among Minnesota private four-year institutions of higher learning. These Tommies of the 1970s marched in step with their peers elsewhere. No longer did they wear green beanies or haze freshmen. Although social injustice and the Vietnam War evoked strong reactions in St. Paul as well as in New York and California, these issues did not result in sit-ins or in demonstrations protesting ROTC. Partly this lack of turbulence was due to the nature of the students and to the Catholic tradition of the college. Another reason no doubt lay in the way administrators and faculty involved undergraduates in the operation of the institution, consulting them in departmental meetings and on faculty promotions. In 1970 the teaching staff voted to make students members of its standing committees. Four years earlier they had been given much greater freedom in controlling their own lives, especially in the dormitories. [33]

The faculty, too, had changed by 1970. It then totaled 112 full-time teachers, 53 of whom held earned doctorates. Never before had so high a proportion of the instructional staff possessed that degree. On the other hand, the number of diocesan priests on the faculty had declined to 13. There were also seven secular priests serving as administrators. Through their many functions both in and out of the classroom, this traditional core of consecrated men helped "set and maintain the proper religious tone at St. Thomas." Similar influence emanated from three teaching priests who belonged to religious orders and from two groups recently arrived on campus in the fall of 1970. These consisted of Jesuit and Franciscan priests, who had relocated at St. Thomas with more than 30 of their seminarians. The seminarians of both orders were regularly enrolled students at the college. Since then the Columban fathers have also attached themselves to the college. [34]

These men found a curriculum which in general emphasized, as it had in the past, the traditional undergraduate liberal arts studies. In its attempt to serve both God and man, St. Thomas had striven to keep pace with progress in scholarship and in methods, but the college had resisted any temptation toward proliferation of departments and courses. All students were required to gain a general foundation and to pursue more deeply one of the score of major sequences offered. These ranged from business administration, history, modern languages, the natural and social sciences to music, philosophy, psychology, and theater. Two recent additions to the list had been geology, which graduated its first majors in 1967, and quantitative methods, which dealt with the uses and purposes of computers. For Catholics some work in theology was mandatory. The majors most frequently selected in the spring of 1970 were business administration (272), political science (100), sociology (99), and history (82). These choices reflected the vocational and professional interests in business, law, and education that had long motivated St. Thomas men. [35]

In its nonbaccalaureate sequences the college adopted two programs of considerable promise for the future. A post-M.A. course leading to a specialist in education degree was introduced in the graduate department in 1969. One of only two such offerings in the state to hold North Central accreditation, it enabled school superintendents and principals to meet new Minnesota requirements. Within a year thirty-one individuals had completed the program. The other innovation, named "Project Discovery," reflected the college's concern for disadvantaged people and its constant effort "to make teacher-education responsive to community needs." With money from the local archdiocese, the Hill Foundation, the federal government, and St. Thomas itself, this project was designed to make teachers in urban areas more effective and more knowledgeable concerning problems and conditions in inner city and minority communities. Nearly forty teachers were enrolled in the first course in the summer of 1970. [36]

By the late 1960s St. Thomas counted well over 15,000 living alumni, 46 per cent of them in the Twin Cities and another 19 per cent residing elsewhere in Minnesota. Between 1936 and 1966 more than 210 of them had earned Ph.D.s. Many had been awarded various other graduate and professional degrees. Early in the 1960s the federal department of health, education, and welfare ranked St. Thomas seventh among all Catholic colleges in the country in the percentage of male graduates becoming doctors of medicine. Between 1945 and 1963 St. Thomas placed in a tie for second among Catholic institutions in the number of Woodrow Wilson Fellowships won by its students. By the mid-1960s nearly 1,500 alumni were certified to teach in the public schools. Others had achieved success in business, industry, the law, and the church. Only a few had become nationally known, but a goodly host fulfilled former President Shannon's description of St. Thomas alumni as "men of deep faith, active piety, and disciplined intellect." [37]

In the difficult 1970s of private education, the leaders of St. Thomas hold fast to their faith that the college's Christian commitment and long-established goals are still valid. The institution, Monsignor Murphy declared, "is endowed with special kinds of strength which will enable it to meet the challenges of these stressful days." Past performance suggests that he is right and that St. Thomas will extend and improve upon its eighty-five-year record of service. [38]

35

CONCORDIA COLLEGE IN MOORHEAD

Service and Achievement

CONCORDIA'S GOLDEN JUBILEE YEAR OF 1941 started off auspiciously with an encouraging enrollment level and an expanded curriculum. The recent graduating class of 103 members had been the first in a decade to number over a hundred. The large home-coming turnout in October was given special luster by the presence of three former presidents — Rasmus Bogstad, the Reverend H. O. Shurson, and Dr. J. A. Aasgaard. But war soon put an end to rejoicing. By 1943 there were only 61 civilian men in attendance along with 367 women. Early that year 125 cadets of the Seventy-first Army Air Force College Training Detachment arrived to begin a course of instruction, but despite readjustments by Concordia authorities, the officer in charge of the unit declared that the college's facilities were inadequate. He thereupon moved the trainees and his staff to nearby Moorhead State Teachers College. Until 1946 coeds dominated the scene at Concordia, and did what they could to aid the war effort and keep up their own morale.[1]

Despite the world conflict, however, college and church officials agreed that the effort to strengthen Concordia and add to its limited facilities must go forward. To that end a major fund drive was undertaken, the first such campaign in more than a decade and a half. Its target was the sum of $350,000, an amount sufficient to remove the debt on Fjelstad Hall and help finance a badly needed library building and a long-desired gymnasium-auditorium. Careful preparation preceded solicitations in May, 1942, but heavy rains, impassable roads, and wartime conditions greatly reduced the success of the endeavor. For the next few years the burdens of money raising fell mainly on faculty shoulders. In 1944 three district conventions of the Norwegian Lutheran Church of America voted to assume responsibility for providing Concordia with a library and a new gymnasium. Shortly after the surrender of Japan in 1945 the drive

for funds was successfully concluded with $450,000 having been pledged.[2]

Then came the return of the veterans and with them the need to reorder priorities and stretch every available facility to the utmost. A permanent dormitory building now became urgent, and ground was broken for it in April, 1946. Not for more than a year, however, would the stone residence hall of Gothic architecture in the Tudor style be ready to ease housing pressures. Called simply Men's Dormitory until it was renamed John Nikolai Brown Hall in 1951, the handsome addition to the college plant provided rooms for over two hundred men.[3]

While this major project was under way, enrollment mushroomed. Early in 1946 it had been 635 (472 women and 163 men). By fall the total reached 940, of whom 350 had to find living quarters off campus. Two years later the postwar bulge crested at 1,277, a peak that would not be surpassed until the mid-1950s. To take care of the sudden upswing in attendance, the inevitable village for married ex-GIs appeared, as did double-decked beds for single veterans in the gymnasium, soon dubbed "Paradise Hall." Other undergraduate males found shelter in a former army barracks christened "Boe's Bunkhouse" in honor of the dean of men, Victor C. Boe. Later called Cobber Hall, this wooden facility would serve as a classroom and office building until it fell victim to progress and a wrecking crew at the end of the 1960s. Materials from the army air force base at Sioux City, Iowa, in 1947 were transformed into a science hall, which would see service for two decades. Thoughts still turned to the gymnasium and library plans, but the general shortage of building materials and a lack of capital funds forced postponement of actual construction.[4]

Makeshift arrangements and crowding did not dampen student enthusiasm. Modified by the presence of World War II veterans, college life blossomed in a myriad of forms. Choir tours were revived in 1946, and as many as four hundred students in 1948 competed spiritedly for membership in the organization directed by Professor Paul J. Christiansen, who had rigorous demands for perfection of performance. The singing groups visited virtually all parts of the United States, and in 1949 members had the thrill — tempered by seasickness — of a tour to Norway that included a concert before the crown prince and princess. A dozen societies for both men and women with mottoes, colors, and distinctive sweaters and jackets still flourished and held joint brother-sister group meetings. Student government in 1949 became more pervasive when a senate and an executive council were created representing such interests as athletics, religion, publications, and the National Student Association. Tournament debate enjoyed a new era of popularity; at the Red River Valley meet of 1950, for example, fifty-three teams from twenty-one colleges in five states competed on the Concordia campus. With all these activities as well as Cobber Capers and the annual Christmas choral concert there was slight risk that ennui would afflict the average undergraduate.[5]

By the end of the 1940s with nearly a quarter century of service and the postwar transition behind him, President Brown looked to retirement. During his administration, Concordia had not only weathered the worst economic collapse in the nation's history and the world's bloodiest conflict, but student enrollment had tripled, and the number of faculty members had almost done likewise. Fund drives to increase endowment and raise capital funds had been successfully conducted, and North Central accreditation had been earned. The physical plant was expanded by the addition of several buildings, and another major structure was begun before Brown left office. Perhaps even more appreciated by his associates in the sponsoring body now known as the Evangelical Church had been the president's qualities of leadership, vision, and spirituality. His "conservative Lutheran stand, his biblical faithfulness, his emphasis on personal Christian life on the part of faculty and students," said the Concordia board of directors in a citation of appreciation, had "given a strong impulse to a warm, evangelistic atmosphere on the campus." In April, 1951, a successor was secured. At the commencement that year where he received an honorary doctorate of laws, President Brown and a senior class of 120 men and 66 women joined the alumni body of the institution he had headed for twenty-six years.[6]

The new president was the Reverend Joseph L. Knutson, pastor of University Lutheran Church of Hope in Minneapolis. Born in North Dakota, he

had graduated from St. Olaf College in 1927 and from Luther Theological Seminary in St. Paul three years later. Before he went to Minneapolis in 1948, he had served churches elsewhere in Minnesota, Illinois, and Iowa. As a campus pastor he worked from 1943 to 1948 with students at Iowa State College at Ames and later at the University of Minnesota. Popular with undergraduates and committed to the cause of private education, he would serve Concordia into the 1970s and become the dean of the state's liberal arts college presidents.[7]

When President Knutson took office in July, 1951, the Korean War was raging, and he found a sufficiency of tasks to occupy his attention. In line with general trends enrollment had declined steadily from its 1948 peak; a low of about 900 was reached in the fall of 1951. Plant facilities were inadequate. Classroom and office space was at a premium; many teachers possessed no campus offices; a library building was still nonexistent. The chapel in Old Main could not seat the entire college family at one time, and it was necessary to repeat each daily chapel service. Ground had been broken in 1950 for the long-sought gymnasium-auditorium, but in April, 1951, the project suffered a serious setback. High winds caused the collapse of seven great beams of the superstructure weighing twelve tons apiece. Almost a year elapsed before new steel could be secured and the work resumed. Insurance litigation dragged on through 1954, but the $625,000 field house played host to its first basketball game in December, 1952. Gifts paid for three-quarters of its cost; a bank loan covered the remainder. The giant structure, able to seat 6,500 persons for such events as the annual Christmas concert, added a significant dimension not only to life at Concordia but in the surrounding area. It was much in demand by outside groups until nearby Fargo, North Dakota, built a new municipal auditorium in 1959.[8]

Enrollment and physical plant were not the only parts of the college operation calling for President Knutson's attention. Those perennial concerns, faculty matters and financial needs, raised insistent voices. Several key teachers such as the dean of instruction and the chairmen of the English, Norse, history, and economics departments had served Concordia for more than twenty-five and in some cases more than thirty-five years. Within two years all of them would be in retirement. Not only would new faculty members have to be recruited, but also efforts would have to be made to raise salaries and to increase the proportion of teachers holding doctorates (about 12 per cent in 1951). Endowment was less than $600,000, and gift income had been rather unstable. From highs of about $250,000 in both 1945 and 1946, the trend in giving (except for 1950) had been downward. The total for 1951 was less than $150,000.[9]

A glance at college charts will show that budget income, enrollment, and size of teaching staff reversed their downward trends shortly after 1951. Part of the reason for this upturn lay in such general developments as rising affluence and population growth, but credit also belongs to Concordia's administration, faculty, and board.

Progress was not always uniform. President Knutson characterized his second year in office, 1952–53, as one of both "triumph and defeat." A financial appeal in Fargo and Moorhead to raise $200,000 to complete payment on the gymnasium had brought in only $72,000 in cash and pledges. It had therefore been necessary to refinance the debt on that building, as well as the obligation still remaining on Brown Hall. Faculty salaries were considerably lower than they should have been. On the other hand, there had been a 14 per cent increase in enrollment, a balanced budget, and the completion of the gymnasium. Current income had totaled $804,000, expenditures $787,000. Student fees had contributed $365,000 to income and gain from auxiliary enterprises $304,000. In addition there was on hand a fund of about $165,000, which was earmarked for the increasingly needed library and a music hall.[10]

On the academic side a sequence in elementary education had been adopted in 1951. Concordia had not prepared grade schoolteachers for nearly thirty-five years, but during all that period, more than half of each year's graduates had entered some branch of the teaching profession. The new program at first offered a two-year course as well as one leading to a B.S. degree. The shorter sequence was phased out between 1956 and 1958, but the remaining education courses continued to attract large numbers of students. Of the 305 members of the 1960 class, for example, 190 (or more than 62 per cent) were prepared to teach, and 161 actually did so upon graduation. Kappa Beta Kappa established in 1952 by students in education was one of the largest organizations at the college with nearly 200 members in 1960. A majority of the academic departments prepared students for teaching, and several of the units periodically sponsored a variety of conferences, institutes, and workshops for people already in the profession.[11]

The introduction of the elementary education program undoubtedly attracted more public notice than any other curriculum development of the decade following World War II, but other modifications appeared from time to time. In 1953 a major in physical education was instituted, and three years later,

education and psychology were separated into two departments. Between 1955 and 1958 the faculty curriculum committee and the senate conducted a thoroughgoing study of the whole academic program. The result was a rewriting of Concordia's objectives and a strengthening of the general education requirements for graduation. However, nothing dramatic or revolutionary ensued. Indeed the curriculum of the early 1950s and that of the mid-1960s exhibited great similarities. The differences lay largely in course changes and refinements within departments and in an over-all growth in maturity and sophistication. Partly at least to bolster sagging enrollments in the earlier period, much ink was used to advertise an array of preparatory programs in over two dozen fields from physical therapy and optometry to interior decorating and pharmacy. Many of these courses were gone by the later decade, when emphasis rested principally on the traditional baccalaureate sequences.[12]

In contrast to curricular affairs, enrollment statistics showed rather dramatic changes. From the low in 1951 the number of students during the regular year rose steadily to almost 1,600 (nearly evenly divided by sex) in 1958–59. Minnesota provided slightly over 800 of the undergraduates, North Dakota 467, and Montana 112. Some of the others came from 13 foreign countries. Lutherans totaled 1,404, of whom 1,150 were adherents of Concordia's sponsor, the Evangelical Lutheran Church. Almost two-thirds of the students were freshmen and sophomores. The beginning class in 1955–56 had numbered about 540 individuals; as seniors the count was down to 267, a reflection of the attrition which plagued most colleges and universities.[13]

With enrollment rising so rapidly, needed expansion of plant could be delayed no longer. Even though less than one-fourth of the money to pay for it was in hand, construction of a library building was at last undertaken. Named in honor of Carl B. Ylvisaker, a beloved teacher of religion at Concordia during the twenty years before his death in 1945, the $400,000 structure was opened in February, 1956. Its collection of 44,000 volumes was transported by students from the basement of Fjelstad Hall in an "Operation Horsepack," which anticipated a similar activity at Carleton the following May. The previous fall the cornerstone had been laid for a women's dormitory to be known as Park Region Hall, an allusion to the Lutheran school which had existed for four decades at Fergus Falls. Financed by a federal loan of $650,000, the new residence for 228 women went into use in September, 1956. Concordia could then house most of its coeds on campus, but in other areas the physical plant was still far from adequate. The one men's dormitory could accommodate only about 300 of the 730 men enrolled. Kitchen and dining space had not increased for half a century. The excellent music department was still using two frame buildings which originally had been erected for other purposes. Classroom and laboratory facilities were overtaxed. But with money also in short supply, Concordians would have to go "limping along" for a while yet.[14]

Financial needs and faith, however, gave rise to one of the most intriguing chapters in the college's history. In 1955 when the institution's board of directors decided to go ahead with the library project, the cost seemed staggering. Two members of the board then came up with the happy thought that the sum might not seem so large if 400 persons could be recruited who would pledge $1,000 apiece. Thus was born — outside the college's official structure but heartily endorsed by President Knutson — the well-known C-400 Club. Progress was steady but scarcely rapid. It was 1957 before a quarter of the goal was reached, and 1960 when the three-quarter mark was attained. All the while, however, the gospel of private education was being broadcast, and individuals of various religious persuasions, Protestant, Catholic, and Jewish, from many parts of the country were pledging the necessary fee for membership. A special C-400 Day, on which those who belonged would seek more recruits, was instituted in November, 1958; three years later the 47 persons who joined on that occasion gave the club more than enough supporters to justify its name. By April 29, 1966, when over 950 people gathered for the annual C-400 Founders' Day Dinner, the organization had raised $1,134,000 for Concordia. Of this amount, $336,300 had been used to complete payment on the library.[15]

The years that gave birth to C-400 were memorable in the college's financial history for at least two other reasons: Concordia's budget in 1953–54 for the first time exceeded $1,000,000, and the Ford Foundation in 1955 granted $289,000 to the institution's endowment fund, the income from which was to be used for raising faculty salaries. Certain other realities, however, were not so encouraging. Current obligations were being paid (though not without difficulty), but money for new construction and for augmenting the modest student loan fund was not at hand. Tuition and fees could not be raised much higher lest Concordia price itself out of the market. As it was, only 15 per cent of all college students who belonged to the Evangelical Lutheran Church were attending its institutions, and the low charges and expanding facilities at state colleges and universities were exercising ever-

increasing attractions. The ELC gave Concordia more than $120,000 each year, but a considerably larger sum was needed, as President Knutson constantly emphasized, if the college were to meet the challenge facing it. So in 1956 Concordia halted the initiation of building projects and launched a development program with the help of Paul H. Davis, a well-known educational consultant.[16]

By 1959 the institution's financial situation had been considerably strengthened, and it was possible to begin again the expansion of the physical plant. In March ground was broken for a student union building, the college's first air-conditioned structure. Named Cobber Commons, it was finished in the winter of 1960. Its cost of $300,000 was covered by gifts and a fund to which students had contributed $5.00 a semester since 1955. At that time by a vote of 673 to 94, undergraduates had agreed to assess themselves in order to hasten the day when the union would be available. A less imposing structure but one that was unique for a college like Concordia was erected in 1959. This was a $25,000 brick building to house an ion accelerator, or "atom smasher." The device had come to Moorhead from Iowa State College largely through the efforts of four Cobbers who were doing graduate work in physics at the institution at Ames. Early in 1960 a language laboratory went into operation in Grose Hall.[17]

Not for nearly two years would construction activity again be undertaken, a state of affairs which, in President Knutson's words, "always makes us feel uneasy." During the ten years of his administration so far, however, enrollment had risen to slightly over 1,680, and the college was merely catching its breath before entering another period of rapid expansion. Plans were already drawn for two additional facilities, and with the new American Lutheran Church practically organized, Concordia could hope for increasing support from its denominational body. At the end of seven decades of existence, the college's total assets for the first time had reached $5,000,000, and its academic program had recently gained prized recognitions. Among them were membership in the American Association of University Women, approval of the teacher training sequences by the National Council for Accreditation of Teacher Education, and certification of the home economics course by the Minnesota Board of Vocational Education. Faculty numbered over 100, about 32 per cent of whom held doctorates in contrast to the 12 per cent a decade earlier. Professors' annual salaries ranged between $6,000 and $7,500, but raises were being given, and a leave of absence program had been in effect since 1958. To further strengthen the instructional staff's stature and income, a Great

Teacher Program was announced in 1960. Two years later the college received its first endowed professorship established in honor of Alma and A. Reuel Wije by members of their family.[18]

In 1961–62 work began on two vitally needed structures, a dormitory and a music building. The first, named Livedalen Hall for a North Dakota farmer who willed over $324,000 to the college, its largest single gift, included a wing for a bookstore, a post office, and dining facilities. It was financed by a $931,000 federal loan and occupied in the winter of 1962. The service wing was named the Normandy. The following year saw the completion of Hvidsten Hall of Music, christened in honor of a generous benefactor and former member of Concordia's board. Costing $650,000 paid for by cash gifts, the glass and brick addition featured a 300-seat recital room and an open court among its appointments. With about 230 residents housed in Livedalen, only 150 single men were forced to find off-campus quarters, about the number of upperclassmen who preferred to do so in any event. There were also 50 married male undergraduates for whom the college could provide no housing. More urgent, however, had become dormitory space for women; in 1961 one-third of the coeds had to find rooms on their own. And then there were the wooden barracks still serving as a science building. Concordia had progressed, but the institution was "a long way from her destination."[19]

In 1962 the C-400 Club instituted "Operation Gold Shovel," a drive to assist in providing the college with a new administration building and in converting Old Main for classrooms. Given this added instructional area, Concordia could then grant admission to 200 more students. Ground breaking for the new facility by C-400 members using gold-painted shovels took place in September, 1963. By the time the $500,000 structure, fittingly named the C-400 Administration Building, was finished a year later, the remodeling of Old Main had relieved pressures for classroom space, and work was also progressing well on a dormitory for women. At first called simply New Hall, the 230-bed residence went into operation in the autumn of 1965. The following year the building was designated Hoyum Hall in honor of the Jacob Hoyum family of Havre, Montana, who had given the college 3,660 acres of grain land under an annuity plan. But as usual, events had outrun achievements and created new problems. Between the fall of 1964 and that of 1965, enrollment had risen from 1,830 to 2,100. Because of lack of space, a few classes were being held in the evenings, and the need for a science building was becoming desperate.[20]

It became possible in May, 1966, to begin construction of this valuable facility. One-third of the $1,578,000 needed was secured through a federal grant; much of the remainder came from the American Lutheran Church's Lutheran Ingathering for Education (LIFE) campaign. In the summer of 1967 the departments of chemistry, physics, psychology, and mathematics vacated their old quarters and moved into the modern Science Center. The barracks were then remodeled and renamed the Biology Building. Meanwhile food service had been expanded by a $100,000 addition in the summer of 1966. Soon thereafter the new Jake Christiansen Stadium had hosted its first football game. More than a third of the $325,000 expended for it was given by C-400, and part had been raised by friends of the man for whom the stadium was named — Concordia's longtime athletic director and football coach, the son of F. Melius Christiansen and a brother of the college's music chairman. By the start of its diamond jubilee year the institution was a far cry from the infant enterprise begun in 1891. The 110-acre campus and buildings were valued at $7,698,000, and their replacement cost would run much higher. Total assets exceeded $11,400,000. The yearly budget came to more than $4,000,000, and annual gifts of $874,000 in 1965–66 were on the increase. Yet more students than ever were living off campus, classroom space was still limited, and indebtedness stood at $3,036,000.[21]

These developments of the first half of the 1960s and thereafter followed closely "A Blueprint for Concordia College," a report issued in November, 1962. The result of a comprehensive study made by the faculty over a period of more than two years, the document's purpose was to provide a general pathway along which the college could proceed in an intelligent and fruitful manner. Reaffirming the institution's commitment to the Christian way of life and to the liberal arts, the blueprint outlined the steps by which Concordia could serve its students in the decades ahead.[22]

Considering the faculty's devotion to liberal arts studies, it followed that the report recommended no startling curricular changes, no introduction of technical schools or programs. The door was left open for new courses, but only those relevant to the liberal tradition. As to methods and procedures, however, flexibility and experimentation were to play major roles; there should be more independent study, more use of audio-visual aids, a revision of the calendar, and more study in other countries.[23]

These then were the lines along which the academic program evolved. The usual tinkering with the curriculum resulted between 1961 and 1966 in such changes as the addition of a minor in library science and a major in international relations, the extensive redesigning of various offerings, and the adoption of a number of new courses. A revised calendar went into effect in September, 1964, under which the first semester ended before Christmas, commencement occurred about May 1, and two six-week summer sessions replaced the one of eight weeks. Students then had an advantage in gaining summer jobs or by attending every term of being able to graduate in three years. A liaison with Schiller College in Germany was established in 1964; the next year a student exchange was arranged with Virginia Union University, a coeducational Black institution in Richmond. A faculty exchange would follow later. With support from the Hill Family Foundation, the teaching of lower-division English courses over television station KFME was begun in 1965 and repeated successfully thereafter. Selected students were aided in spending a year abroad, after which they returned to Concordia as teaching assistants in a foreign language. A program in hospital administration — one of only four in undergraduate institutions in the nation — also made its appearance. In these and other ways the college sought to keep itself stimulating and effective, a difficult and never-ending process.[24]

Typically, the quest seemed to gain momentum and to engage the time of more and more people. In 1966 a permanent long-range planning group of teachers and administrators was established. Its purview embraced all matters relevant to Concordia's future; during 1967–68, for example, it took a long and systematic look at the 1962 blueprint. The following October, a Commission on Instruction (Curcom) was appointed to review the whole academic program. After nearly a year of study, including full-time work on it in the summer of 1969, Curcom issued a 176-page report, which formed the subject of faculty discussions beyond 1969–70. Ultimately, the whole curriculum was to be revamped, and graduation requirements were expressed in terms of courses rather than of credits.[25]

Meanwhile innovation, modification, and the volume of off-campus study grew. Some students did practice teaching in Europe, others gained the experience in Black schools in Virginia. May seminars abroad were initiated in French, German, and Spanish, and then were extended to cover art, drama, and religion. The Principia Plan in the fall of 1969 permitted two dozen freshmen to work at their own pace in physics, political science, philosophy, religion, English, and psychology under the close supervision of eight faculty members; at the same time about one-third of their classmates were fulfill-

ing the basic English requirement by independent study. The old classroom lecture was by no means extinct, nor were all schedules student centered, but flexibility was far more popular than rigidity, and a restless searching for improvement held primacy over any vestiges of complacency.[26]

Facilitating these changes between 1967 and 1969 had been further additions to the educational plant. The first of these was the Science Center. Next the C-400 Club in 1965 volunteered to undertake as its third major project the initial unit of a humanities and social sciences complex. Opened in the fall of 1969, this Humanities Center presented the Concordia sky line with its tallest buildings. Containing a 450-seat lecture hall-theater, a laboratory theater, a rehearsal hall, a two-story art gallery, and audio-visual resources, the versatile newcomer evoked enthusiastic reactions. A federal grant of $283,000 and a loan of $335,000 provided almost two-thirds of the cost involved. The C-400 Club raised $600,000 for this first unit. Meanwhile plans had been drawn for a four-story addition to the library, and a government grant of slightly over $280,000 had been secured for the project. The C-400 Club offered to pay the balance of the unit's $850,000 cost. When it was finished in 1971, the new section increased the library's shelf capacity from 120,000 to 370,000 volumes and reader accommodations from 450 to 850. The two top floors temporarily housed offices and classrooms.[27]

Accompanying this flurry of construction had been a continued rise in enrollment. Each year Concordia attracted the largest freshman class of any private college in the states of Minnesota, Iowa, and the Dakotas; in 1966 it was necessary to limit the size of the group to 800. Three years later the whole student body numbered 2,405 (1,149 men, 1,256 women). Just over 1,500 were from Minnesota. The need to augment campus living quarters was again acute. So after the daily chapel service on March 13, 1967, ground was broken for a $2,500,000 residence hall. Financed by a federal loan, the East Dormitory Complex was occupied in September, 1968. Popular with students, the impressive structure consisted of two main units, one for 230 men and the other for an equal number of women, connected by a one-story wing containing dining, post office, and recreational facilities. Concordia could then house over 1,700 undergraduates, but within a year dormitory space had again become tight.[28]

As the visible evidences of the college's growth increased, so had the sums of money needed to sustain the institution's operation. The annual budgets in 1950 and 1960 had been $839,000 and $2,090,000, respectively. By 1970 the figure was

$6,000,000, double that of five years earlier. As late as 1963–64 the basic cost of attending Concordia had been a relatively low $1,465 (the annual fee at Carleton was $2,400, and at St. Olaf $1,800). Tuition then accounted for only 63 per cent of total Concordia instructional expenses. By 1970–71 charges at the Moorhead institution were up to $2,500, still not high by comparative standards but too large to be paid without help by many applicants for admission. Hence multiplying amounts of money had to be found for student aid programs. In 1954–55 Concordia dispensed $164,500 to students: $43,000 in scholarships, $54,000 in loans, and $67,000 in work contracts. For 1969–70 the total was $1,989,000 of which scholarships accounted for $443,500, Educational Opportunity Grants for $178,700, National Defense Educational Act loans for $322,100, federally insured loans for $780,000, and student work for $264,700.[29]

In financial matters Concordia, like most church colleges, seemed in President Knutson's phrase "to pass from crisis to crisis." Yet through the work, generosity, and concern of many people, budgets were balanced and capital funds were raised, albeit slowly and inadequately. Major responsibility for this effort rested with the president, but after 1960 he was assisted by a staff of development personnel. In the absence of a large endowment the college depended for income mainly on students, alumni, the church, the government, and friends — individual and corporate.[30]

Both in 1960 and 1970 more than 85 per cent of the current operating budget derived from student payments for tuition, fees, board, and room. The rest, as well as funds for capital improvements, came from gifts, grants, and loans. Between 1962 and 1969 this annual giving not only grew in amount (from $587,000 to $1,742,000) but its sources also changed considerably in relative importance. In the former year the American Lutheran Church gave Concordia $180,300, and various congregations contributed another $38,000; these two sources accounted for almost 39 per cent of the college's gifts during that period. In 1969–70 the church bestowed $382,000 on Concordia, but that sum was by then only 26 per cent of the institution's gift income. An even greater differential appeared in the size of state and federal grants. Negligible in 1962, they rose to $438,000 in 1969–70, representing 30 per cent of the total. Including alumni, individuals provided over 43 per cent of all gifts in 1962–63 ($257,000), but their 1969–70 contributions ($330,000) though larger in dollars were down to 22.6 per cent in proportion to the whole. It is clear that the willingness or the ability of the church

and individual supporters to give money to Concordia has been outdistanced by the college's needs.[31]

There is no doubt that Concordia has been "developing in maturity and scope," as Dean Carl L. Bailey wrote in 1968. Plenty of evidence supports this contention. In addition to examples already cited, one can point to closer co-operation with neighboring institutions, changes in college governance, and a relaxation of traditional parietal rules. Discussions with Moorhead State College and North Dakota State University in Fargo over a period of several years began to show promising results after 1967. Dr. Albert B. Anderson of Concordia in 1969 was appointed executive provost of what was termed Tri-College University, and serious study was directed toward the initiation of joint projects. Among the early benefits derived from this effort have been faculty exchanges, library co-operation, co-ordination of health training programs, a grant to finance visits by distinguished professors of philosophy, and permission for Cobbers to enroll in ROTC at North Dakota.[32]

General developments in other colleges and universities were also clearly reflected at Concordia in the areas of rules and governance. Traditionally the college had been conservative in its social regulations, but this stance had become increasingly difficult to sustain. In the early 1960s, for example, two district conventions of the church had approved social dancing — though by small majorities; in 1968 President Knutson noted that the college had enjoyed a peaceful year despite the campus outbursts elsewhere, but that there had been growing resentment by more and more students against various rules. The bans on social dancing on campus and on smoking by coeds, practices forbidden throughout Concordia's history, were lifted by the regents in 1969 and 1970, respectively. A committee on student affairs had been established in 1968, and after many discussions the faculty voted ninety-four to fourteen to adopt a new constitution, which provided for a representative form of government and greater student involvement in the decision-making process. On several faculty committees and in the enlarged senate, students became voting members.[33]

Although noting that tensions in 1969–70 had caused "no open breaks with the institution or with segments of the college family," President Knutson admitted that it was "a difficult time in which to keep a college oriented to Christ and his Word." Several months later, faced with an obdurate editor and a student newspaper which, in the opinion of many critics, had been deteriorating in quality as well as traditional moral stance, President Knutson suspended the editor from his position and terminated publication of the *Concordian*. The episode was reported (and some of it misreported) in the public press, thereby provoking widely differing reactions. Many persons apparently appalled by the permissiveness of the academic world applauded the president's action. Others disagreed. The Minnesota Professional Chapter of Sigma Delta Chi, the honorary journalism fraternity, regarded the penalties as a violation of academic freedom and censured President Knutson. The whole incident epitomizes the problems faced by an administrator of a church-related college attempting to maintain the institution's traditional standards in an increasingly secular society.[34]

In 1964 President Knutson said wryly that in the past Concordia had "been pretty much the lonely orphan of the north. But things have changed." With ample reason neither President Knutson nor his associates are pessimistic or discouraged as they face the unknowns of the 1970s. They can point to Concordia's vast strides "in the quality of faculty, students, physical facilities, academic achievement, and public acceptance," perhaps more so in the past twenty years "than any private college in the upper middle west." With such a heritage, there is slight danger that the vicissitudes of the moment will divert the institution from the pathway of service and achievement that it has followed for eight decades with dedication and mounting success.[35]

36 COLLEGE OF ST. CATHERINE

"Behold, I Make All Things New"

THE COLLEGE OF ST. CATHERINE IN 1941 exhibited a strength and a vitality remarkable for so young an institution. Over 690 students were enrolled, about 100 more than had attended when Sister Eucharista assumed the presidency in 1937. Over 500 of the full-time undergraduates were from Minnesota (261 came from St. Paul and 102 from Minneapolis), but the Dakotas, Montana, Iowa, and Wisconsin each contributed a score or more of young women. By June more than 5,600 young women from twenty-nine states and fifteen foreign countries had attended St. Catherine's. The number of collegiate degrees conferred had exceeded 1,560 and the graduates were dispersed from Europe to Hawaii and from Panama to Alaska. Of the faculty of sixty members (thirty-two sisters, eight priests, and twenty lay persons) about one-third possessed earned doctorates.[1]

Unusual influences made the college alive and exciting. The tonic effects of both the co-operative study in general education and that in teacher education were already being felt. New courses such as "Introduction to the Humanities" and "Child Development" increased the effectiveness of the college program, and the adoption of evaluation instruments and attitude scales helped teachers and counselors take inventory of their performances. The Ninth National Eucharistic Congress held in the Twin Cities in June, 1941, had made the preceding year at St. Catherine's a memorable one. During the congress about a hundred students served as hostesses and assistants, and twice that number in caps and gowns marched in the impressive procession closing the gathering.[2]

A feeling of insecurity combined with the availability of high-paying jobs caused a decrease in enrollment in the fall of 1941. After Pearl Harbor changes, of course, became more apparent. The desire "to do something" to assist in the war effort, the tempta-

tion to take jobs in defense industries, became more insistent. As a result nearly eighty students withdrew during the academic year. But after the initial shock, life on campus settled into the serious business of study, prayer, and home-front co-operation in the world-wide struggle then going on. In January, 1942, a board of defense was created at the college to supervise and synchronize the whole gamut of war-related activities, from stamp and bond sales, blood donations, classes in first aid and nutrition, to spiritual endeavors.[3]

Through it all, however, the main objectives of the college and the long-range point of view were sustained. By 1942–43, though total enrollment was below its previous peak, that of resident students was the highest ever. That year the nursing education curriculum was reorganized. Thereafter St. Catherine's would have a new, experimental three-year program along with the five-year course leading to a B.S. degree. Twenty-three students enrolled in the latter in September, 1943, and forty-five others were admitted to the three-year sequence in the following March. Nursing was firmly established in the schedule, and the course's popularity would put a definite strain on college facilities.[4]

In the summer of 1943 Sister Eucharista's term as president was concluded. Though modestly playing down her accomplishments, she could leave office with the knowledge that St. Catherine's under her direction had lost none of its momentum. She was particularly pleased that some of her lay faculty appointments, especially in art and drama, remained at the college for long periods of time and that Black and Japanese women had become students during her regime.[5]

Succeeding to the presidency in August, 1943, was Sister Antonius Kennelly, who had enrolled as a freshman at St. Catherine's in 1918 and received her B.A. there in 1926. In the interval she had taught in a country school and taken her first vows in the Congregation of St. Joseph. From 1929 until 1933 she had studied at the University of Munich and earned a Ph.D. in chemistry. Her administration would witness unusual conditions and not a few problems.[6]

In September, 1943, the government sent more than one hundred women in the Cadet Nurse Corps to take their basic science courses at the college; eighty other cadets were added in the spring. The result was an unprecedented strain on faculty, equipment, and physical plant. The need for dining space, for example, was so great that even the librarians conceded it priority over their long-desired new building. Faculty teaching schedules were very heavy, and new and part-time professors were secured when possible. To ease shortages of office and domestic help the College Student Association organized a system of undergraduate volunteer workers. But despite the pressures students and teachers seemed to have energy for religious activities and for work related to support of the war effort. Increased enrollment meant higher college income, which coupled with inability to expand the plant because of the war, permitted the retirement of part of the college debt. Plant obligation in mid-1938 had stood at $700,000; by June, 1945, the total was down to $375,000.[7]

The end of the fighting in August, 1945, removed the emotional strain of recent years but not all of the war-related problems. Regular fall enrollment of 769 in 1945 was augmented during the first term by 140 cadet nurses, a situation taxing facilities to the limits of ingenuity and forcing faculty "to carry seemingly impossible loads." The cadet corps was soon phased out, but the influx of nurses from St. Mary's and St. Joseph's hospitals for the basic college courses in the three-year program continued to create strains. Travel was still difficult, and the faculty quite naturally tended to turn inward, devoting what little time they could to considerations of curricular revision. Late in the war period several of the departments had been grouped into a new division of community service. Then in 1945–46 because of growing interest in the field, a department of occupational therapy was added to the division.[8]

Accompanying these vocationally oriented interests was an encouraging student desire for more work in the traditional liberal arts areas. A major in humanities, including courses in literature, philosophy, music, language, art, and religion, was instituted in 1944. So was a requested course in religion for non-Catholics. The faculty undertook a systematic study of the curriculum and made pro-

posals for reshaping many sequences. A first step was inaugurated in the fall of 1947 when revisions in philosophy and theology were effected. Previously students had been required to take two years of work in each of these fields; henceforth four years in each was mandatory.[9]

In 1945 inflation had necessitated an increase of 10 per cent in the annual tuition charge of $150 — the first such raise in two decades. The following year staff additions and salary adjustments had made necessary another increase of 25 per cent to $210. So began at St. Catherine's the cost spiral which has plagued all colleges ever since. On the other hand, it became possible to reduce the indebtedness by the end of June, 1949, to $170,000.[10]

By then Sister Antonius could write that the preceding academic year had been "marked by a gradual return to what might be termed 'normal' for the college." During the trying academic year of 1946–47, 895 regular and 426 nursing students had been enrolled; the comparable figures two years later were 805 and 306, respectively, still too many for the physical plant. The students represented eighteen states, two territories, and four foreign countries, but 77 per cent were from Minnesota. Further encouragement came on the occasion of the Feast of Christ the King in October, 1949, when the alumnae association, which had become increasingly active, set in motion a fund drive to help finance some of St. Catherine's most pressing needs — a library and a cafeteria-student center.[11]

On June 2, 1949, St. Catherine's conferred certificates on 47 students who had completed the kindergarten-primary education course. Four days later when Sister Antonius presided at her last commencement as president, bachelor's degrees were awarded to a class of 152 members. Their most popular majors were English, library science, history, art, and sociology; the strong liberal arts bias was obvious. About one-third of the graduates were qualified to teach. With a feeling akin to that of a mariner who has successfully navigated a difficult voyage, Sister Antonius could now return full time to her first love of teaching and research in the field of chemistry. More than two decades of service at St. Catherine's still awaited her.[12]

Her successor was Minneapolis-born Sister Antonine O'Brien, who had entered the novitiate in 1921 and graduated from St. Catherine's in 1926, the same year as her predecessor. From 1922 until 1927 she had taught as well as studied at the college. Then she had been sent to Oxford in England for two years of study and European travel. Armed with an Oxonian M.A., she returned to her alma mater in 1929 to teach English language and literature. In 1937 with the retirement of Mother Antonia, Sister Antonine, as dean, began an administrative career which led not only to leadership of the college, but to that of the Province of St. Paul as well.[13]

In a sense Sister Antonine's administration benefited from the frustrations war and readjustment had imposed on Sister Antonius, but this fact was not immediately apparent. During 1949–50 a daily population of more than 1,200 attempted to operate in buildings planned for about half that number. When conflict erupted in Korea in 1950, some observers foresaw a drastic general decline in enrollment, but this did not occur at St. Catherine's. Consequently additions to the plant for classroom, office, and dining purposes became matters of especially urgent necessity. Fortunately what was left of the old $700,000 debt was erased completely in the spring of 1952.[14]

New construction now became feasible as well as imperative. The result was St. Joseph Hall, a four-story stone structure costing $1,500,000, officially opened with a candlelight supper in December, 1954. The hoped-for completion date typically was delayed, demanding no little ingenuity in finding housing for the forty-five girls scheduled to live on the top floor. The building, the first major addition to the campus in over two decades, did a great deal to relieve the crowding of previous years. Its timing, too, was felicitous, for it was ready to provide a setting for a number of events held in connection with the celebration of the college's golden jubilee in 1955.[15]

No other achievement of Sister Antonine's administration was quite as dramatic as the erection of St. Joseph Hall, but several noteworthy academic actions were taken during the same period. One of these — the establishment of adult evening classes — though relatively short-lived, reflected the college's concern for the Twin Cities area and a desire to meet the need for adult education among Catholic women. Starting in the fall of 1950 with an enrollment of more than eighty, this program offered courses in such fields as Catholic social thought, Christian family living, and ceramic sculpture. By the late 1950s, however, attendance at evening classes fell off, and they were discontinued. More enduring was a major modification of the two-year sequence to train teachers for kindergarten and the first three elementary grades.[16]

This action, following a tightening up of teacher-training requirements by the state, was facilitated by an opportunity to combine with the archdiocese's teachers' college in St. Paul to set up a four-year elementary education sequence. The archdiocesan superintendent of schools became head of the college's new department, and in June, 1950, St. Catherine's graduated the last of its students in the two-year course. That fall with thirty-two freshmen registered, the new program — heavily weighted in the liberal arts — got under way. In June, 1952, the first thirteen students to complete the four-year sequence received their B.S. degrees. The curriculum, commended by the Minnesota Department of Education, proved extremely helpful in attracting students.[17]

Modifications also appeared in the nursing and library science curriculums in these years. In the fall of 1951 it was decided to confine the degree program in nursing to St. Joseph's Hospital and the three-year diploma course to St. Mary's Hospital. The result was more effective work all around. Then in September, 1954 — because of a decision by the American Library Association not to recognize a bachelor's degree in library science — St. Catherine's with misgivings offered courses in that field on a graduate level. Ultimately a number of M.A.s were conferred. In 1956, however, the college reversed itself and phased out its graduate program. This change was made for a number of reasons, among them a negative reaction to the postgraduate experiment by the North Central Association and the failure of professional librarians to unite in support of the American Library Association's earlier decision. The undergraduate major remained popular, and its graduates continued to be much in demand.[18]

Other contemporary curricular developments included the college's participation with Hamline, Macalester, and St. Thomas in the library project of 1952 supported by the Hill Foundation and the area studies course which was its by-product. In addition St. Catherine's in 1954 installed a language laboratory, the first in a Minnesota college, and formulated a major in American studies to begin in the fall of 1955. With such vocationally oriented fields as nursing, occupational therapy, and elementary teaching enjoying a growing attraction, a tough battle to maintain the college's liberal arts character had to be waged, but the institution never lost sight of its basic commitment.[19]

Major guardian of this liberal arts stance was the faculty, which by 1949 was about evenly divided between sisters and lay teachers — 55 and 53, respectively. There were also eight priests on the staff. Out of a total educational income of roughly $443,000 in 1949–50, approximately $157,000 came from the contributed services of the sisters. The $650,000 endowment yielded only a little over $23,000. To keep St. Catherine's financial structure strong, more teaching religious were needed. More faculty members with advanced degrees (20 of the staff had doctorates in 1949) were also desired. Lay teachers received encouragement in 1950 through their participation in the federal social security plan, but many of their significant concerns about promotion, tenure, salary scales, rights and obligations still awaited satisfactory systemization. Considerable progress was made in 1954, however, when a faculty constitution dealing with these matters was adopted on a trial basis and continued thereafter.[20]

When Sister Antonine retired from the presidency in mid-1955, she could feel that St. Catherine's was keeping pace and serving its constituency well. Regular enrollment in her final year had been 950, nearly 150 higher than in 1949–50; the number of three-year nursing students during the same period had gone up by 50 to 366. The summer session enrollment of 1954 was twice as large as that of 1948. But there were also worries and regrets. The fall of 1955 would see annual tuition go to $360 — 38 per cent above what it had been when Sister Antonine became president. The library was scattered in three buildings. And there were more general educational questions — how to preserve quality in the face of mass education and how best to educate the gifted student for the leadership the country so desperately needed.[21]

To wrestle with these problems became the task of Sister Mary William Brady, who assumed the presidency in the summer of 1955. Born in Fall River, Massachusetts, the new president had graduated from St. Catherine in 1931 and entered the novitiate the following year. She had earned her M.A. at the University of Minnesota in 1941, her Ph.D. in English at the University of Chicago six years later. In 1937 she had joined the English department at St. Catherine, remaining there except for periods of graduate study until becoming president. Like Sister Antonius, she resumed teaching at the college when her administrative tour ended in 1961. In most respects Sister Mary William found her presidential experience a satisfying one, especially since she was able to bring to fruition some of the hopes and plans of earlier years. This was particularly true in three areas: administrative organization, physical plant, and curriculum. As a self-survey report of 1954 had indicated, the "growth in administrative personnel" had "not kept pace with the growth of the College and the increasingly heavy demands of modern life."[22]

Sister Antonine had recommended a reconsideration of the administrative pattern, and her suggestion became one of the first orders of business under the new regime. What was accomplished essentially was to draw lines of authority more clearly and to effect a division of responsibilities. The goal was to delegate work while keeping channels of communication open. The dean of studies would now be assisted by new officers: a dean of students, a dean of admissions, and a director of testing and placement. While some of the administrators were new to their tasks at St. Catherine's, they worked smoothly together to bring the college into line with modern administrative practices.[23]

In 1956–57 St. Catherine's received $253,000 as its share of the Ford Foundation gift for the improvement of faculty salaries. The institution was also awarded an accomplishment grant of $157,000 — one of only two given to Minnesota colleges for trying to keep salaries high and for operating at a superior level of efficiency. The latter grant was put into the library building fund. The college was again financially sound, but increasing costs necessitated tuition raises for the next two years. As for the library, Sister Mary William wrote in 1958, "Traffic in the reading room has become a hazard, and traffic in the stacks is well-nigh fatal." Something had to be done.[24]

Through years of saving and sacrifice by the sisters and through the efforts of parents and alumnae, a considerable sum of money had been set aside. Therefore the college in 1958 announced the start of a twenty-year $10,000,000 expansion plan, its first stage to be the erection of the long-dreamed-of library. The "serenely beautiful" building, fully paid for and Sister Mary William's greatest joy, became a reality in 1960. A feature of its dedication in October was a unique Scripture symposium, participated in by scholars of wide reputation. Meanwhile pressures for admission kept mounting, but only about 340 of the 1,100 students enrolled could be housed on campus. A dormitory — the second phase of the twenty-year plan — was another urgent necessity, and in 1961 St. Mary's Hall was completed. Financed by a forty-year federal loan of $1,000,000, the structure provided rooms for 190 undergraduates, eight prefects, and a housemother.[25]

On the academic front change and experimentation had also been occurring. In September, 1956, the two-semester calendar was adopted in place of the three-quarter system. An interdisciplinary humanities sequence for freshmen was introduced. Utilizing sixteen regular faculty members, guest speakers, and visual aids, the new course had the benefit of careful preparation made possible by a $20,000 grant from the Hill Foundation. Nevertheless some of the participating teachers found it difficult to break the shackles of thought imposed by their own special disciplines. Because of this and the pin pointing of certain curricular weaknesses by a North Central committee, the year 1957–58 was given over to an extensive study of courses. Although this endeavor revealed wide differences of opinion regarding the proper nature and province of the liberal arts, it resulted in the adoption of a revised program of general education for a trial period of two years; in April, 1960, the program was readopted on a permanent basis. Sister Mary William had some doubts regarding the wisdom of certain features of the program — too many required courses, for example — but she never wavered in her conviction that ongoing experimentation with new courses and methods is essential to the maintenance of quality education.[26]

Always concerned with the relevance of St. Catherine's program, Sister Mary William in her first annual report had urged that more attention be paid to Asia and to the Near East; in 1961 she recommended the study of Africa, India, and Latin America, areas then neglected in the college's classrooms. Her suggestions were implemented by the expansion of the area studies course conducted with Hamline, Macalester, and St. Thomas from a three- to a five-year cycle and the addition at St. Catherine of a sequence in Latin American studies. During these same years, the language laboratory was virtually revolutionizing the teaching of German and French at the college, and some of the sisters were beginning to offer courses for credit over the Twin Cities educational television station KTCA-TV. Only members of the music and drama departments, however, seemed enthusiastic about appearing before the television cameras.[27]

Significant steps were also taken in the education and nursing curriculums. In 1958 secondary and elementary education were combined into a single department, and preparations were begun for a visitation by a committee of the National Council for Accreditation of Teacher Education (NCATE). After this group came to the campus in the fall of 1960, the council granted three-year provisional approval of St. Catherine's teacher training program. In nursing, the high cost of instruction caused considerable worry. Consequently it was decided to retain only the four-year degree sequence at the college and to return the diploma course to St. Mary's Hospital. The change was little short of dramatic. In 1957–58 there had been 318 three-year student nurses at St. Catherine; by 1960–61 the program had been phased out except for a few courses.[28]

Sister Mary Edward Healy, chairman of the sociology department since 1948 and also dean of students since 1955, was named president of the college in 1961. She had attended St. Catherine for two years before transferring to the University of Minnesota, where she had received a B.S. degree in 1928. After teaching in public and parochial schools, she had joined the faculty at St. Catherine in 1938. Her master's and doctor's degrees had been earned at Catholic University in 1940 and 1948. Her presidency would be relatively short, but it would be marked by progress on several fronts. The NCATE made its approval of the teacher education program full and complete. New techniques were adopted in biology and chemistry, and interest in computers and in the social and behavioral sciences noticeably increased. The French department in 1962 conducted a summer institute at the college for high school teachers; the next year the setting was Rennes, France. A major in philosophy was begun on an experimental basis in September, 1964, and new courses in psychiatric nursing and in public health were supported by governmental grants. Students — influenced by race problems, struggles over civil rights, and changes in the Catholic church — became particularly active in volunteer social and religious work. Of the class of 1964, about one-third went into teaching, 22 per cent went on to graduate study, and 19 per cent entered nursing.[29]

Many of the old concerns, however, remained. With the adoption of an expanded college program for sisters in training, enrollment climbed to 1,354 in 1961–62. Some space was released the following year when Derham Hall High School moved to a new location, but facilities for St. Catherine's still remained inadequate. Each weekly convocation program had to be repeated, for example, because neither the chapel nor the auditorium could seat the entire student body at one time. Furthermore, there was urgent need for more religious and for more teachers with doctorates on the faculty.[30]

Since a plenitude of funds could solve most of these problems, it was with great joy that the sisters learned in 1963 of St. Catherine's selection by the Ford Foundation for a $1,000,000 grant. At the time only one other women's college in the country and no other Catholic institution was on the Ford list. Terms of the gift stipulated that St. Catherine must raise an additional $2,000,000 within three years after July 1, 1963. The first $300,000 of the grant was to be used for debt retirement on St. Joseph Hall, for curricular expansion, for faculty improvement, and for library acquisitions; the rest was unrestricted. The college had qualified for this recognition because it had taken significant steps in a number of areas, including the adoption of co-operative programs, the development of foreign area courses, and the encouragement of independent study. The award was a magnificent opportunity, the most challenging event of Sister Mary Edward's administration.[31]

The college had no previous experience with a major campaign for funds, but the sisters accomplished the task without employing a professional promotional firm. The alumnae, who were already well organized, led off the money-raising endeavor with Mass and a breakfast on campus on January 19, 1964. Details of the drive were made public the following day: instead of $2,000,000 St. Catherine would attempt to raise $3,000,000 to add to the Ford gift by June 30, 1966. Everyone pitched in with enthusiasm, and $2,500,000 had been raised by mid-1965, including a gift of $500,000 from St. Thomas benefactor I. A. O'Shaughnessy, of which $300,000 was designated as endowment for a chair in education, the college's first endowed professorship. By the time of the successful conclusion of the drive, over 5,000 donors had made contributions; an amazing 73 per cent of the alumnae had responded and accounted for $300,000.[32]

Meanwhile in 1964 a change had taken place in the administration of St. Catherine. Sister Mary Edward had been appointed superior of the Province of St. Paul to succeed Sister Antonine, whose six-year term had been concluded. The dean, Sister Fides Huber, then succeeded to the college presidency. A graduate of St. Catherine in 1939, she had made her decision in her junior year to enter the Congregation of St. Joseph. A member of the college's English department since 1940 and its chairman for a decade after 1954, Sister Fides — or Alberta, as she was now called — held a University of Minnesota M.A. and a University of Notre Dame Ph.D. Among the many problems facing her, two in particular called for persuasion, salesmanship, and cogency of a high order: the self-deprecating attitude of the sisters and the image of St. Catherine's as a contained entity divorced from the reality of life outside the massive fence. Despite recruitment efforts, only 18 per cent of over 700 high-ability women graduates of Twin Cities Catholic high schools in 1965 enrolled at St. Catherine. To make the college more attractive to young women of ability and to convince the religious that their role vis-à-vis St. Catherine's is legitimate and valuable were ends to which Sister Alberta directed her efforts with notable success.[33]

A flurry of experimentation with honors work, new courses, independent study, and teaching methods characterized the early period of Sister Alberta's presidency, but it was several years before major changes were effected. In 1967 a joint committee of faculty and students from St. Thomas and St. Catherine began a study of the merits of an interim term. When the investigation was completed, however, the participants arrived at different conclusions. The representatives of the men's institution did not feel that they could recommend the interim for their college, but those from St. Catherine took the opposite view. The latter's faculty concurred, and in November, 1968, adopted the proposal of their colleagues. Beginning in the autumn of 1969, St. Catherine's would operate on the four-one-four calendar and abandon its credit-hour system in favor of one based on completed courses. Seven to ten of these units would be required for a major, thirty-five of them for graduation.[34]

Although they have not been able to agree on a common calendar, St. Catherine and St. Thomas co-ordinate starting dates, and they have made great headway in other shared endeavors. Starting in the academic year 1965–66, free exchange of students between the two colleges was arranged, and the following autumn shuttle bus service between the campuses was provided. The results of the joint interinstitutional investigation of 1967 had been issued early in 1968. To study and apply the document's recommendations, a board of overseers had been organized composed of the presidents, academic and student deans, the development directors, and faculty and undergraduate representatives of both institutions. As the two colleges move into the 1970s, their imminent merger seems unlikely, and many areas of co-ordination remain to be explored. Their academic and social interchanges, however, continue to increase.[35]

Within St. Catherine's gates Sister Alberta found that physical facilities demanded much of her attention. With on-campus living quarters available for only 500 of the 1,350 students enrolled, additional dormitory space seemed desirable. In 1967–68 a temporary solution was found in the creation of Campus Court at a cost of $60,000; this facility consisted of nine furnished mobile homes each housing eight women. Two residences — each with rooms for 53 students and a faculty member — were in the process of construction. Financed by a loan from the sisterhood of the St. Paul Province, these small dormitories were occupied in the fall of 1968. Known for more than a year as New Dorm I and New Dorm II, they were officially christened Stanton and Crandall halls in the summer of 1969. The former honors the famous woman suffragist Elizabeth Cady Stanton, the latter Prudence Crandall, a teacher driven by public pressure from her home in Connecticut because she had admitted Black girls to her school. By utilizing space in the novitiate, the college could now house 650 students, but at least two more dormitories still were needed.[36]

The newest structure on campus, the Mother Antonia McHugh Fine Arts Center, is also the most impressive in appearance. Formally opened with a week-long series of cultural events in October, 1970, the complex appropriately memorializes the sister whose vision and work raised St. Catherine to the front ranks of the nation's colleges. Though primarily an administrator, Sister Antonia was a champion of the arts, a person convinced "that beautiful surroundings in which to work can stimulate and enhance creativity." At least five years in planning and two years under construction, the center consists of several facilities, all but one of which are joined. The latter, the Visual Arts Building — providing a variety of studios, workshops, galleries, and classrooms — was put into use in January, 1970. The other parts of the spacious and flexible edifice contain a 1,804-seat auditorium named for the distinguished Catholic layman, I. A. O'Shaughnessy; the Theatre Arts Building; and the Music Building. Total cost of this magnificent addition to St. Catherine's physical plant was over $5,350,000. This money was secured in several ways: $3,150,000 was allocated from the 1963–66 capital fund drive; $400,000 was received in gifts since that time; $1,000,000 was obtained as a grant under the federal Higher Education Act of 1963; and $800,000 was borrowed from the St. Paul Province of the Sisters of St. Joseph. The center not only adds immeasurably to the life and work of the college, but also serves as a cultural mecca for the Minnesota Symphony Orchestra and the surrounding city of St. Paul.[37]

The most immediate beneficiaries have been St. Catherine's faculty and student body. The former in 1969–70 consisted of 102 full-time teachers, 40 of them members of the sisterhood. There were also thirty part-time faculty, of whom ten belonged to the congregation. This ratio reflects the growing difficulty in recruiting religious for the instructional staff, a problem which poses financial challenges and a possible threat to the traditional character of the institution. Most of the senior professors are still sisters, and there is a core of able younger nuns ready to replace those who retire. But the time when the great majority of teachers wore the habit of St. Joseph is past. What this change will mean in the long run, no one can predict. The quality of the faculty as a whole remains high; the presence of gracious and committed sisters, however, cannot be underestimated as the factor which sets off the college from secular institutions and gives it a special and valuable dimension.[38]

The student body in 1970 numbered slightly over 1,300, of whom 664 lived on campus. These undergraduates were drawn from 34 states and 18 foreign lands, but typically the largest segment (921 young women) came from Minnesota. Something of the Katies' vocational interests is revealed by a survey of the leading major fields selected by the 277 seniors who graduated during 1969–70. The most frequently chosen sequence was that in elementary education (55), followed by nursing (45), occupational therapy (25), English (21), and sociology (20). Although the traditional liberal studies appear to lose out in this list, many of them were required as supporting courses in all majors. The new four-one-four system was meeting with favorable response and facilitating closer relationships with other colleges on the same calendar. Numbers of students from Macalester, St. Olaf, St. John's, and St. Benedict had taken interim work at St. Catherine's in January, 1970, and Katies had been similarly engaged at these colleges, as well as in Europe and elsewhere. Outside the classroom, these young women had shared the interests and concerns of their generation — war, pollution, race relations, poverty. Discussions, an all-college Mass, a prayer vigil, and the cancellation of social events rather than violence had been the campus manifestations of the Vietnam War crisis period of 1970. Over 50 per cent of the student body had been involved in social action and in volunteer work in the Twin Cities. Some women had agitated for later closing hours in their residence quarters. And still there had been time for fun.[39]

For both students and the sisters there had also been money worries. With charges for board, room, and tuition exceeding $2,500 for a year, about half the undergraduates required financial assistance. For 1969–70 aid administered by the college amounted to nearly $640,000. Scholarships and grants accounted for the largest portion of the total, but $107,750 — most of it from the federal government — was dispensed in the form of loans, and $87,000 was allocated in student work contracts. Discounts for sisters of St. Joseph and for those in attendance from other religious orders approximated $35,000. All this assistance represented a sizable sum of money, yet even more aid funds will be needed if St. Catherine's is to be kept within the reach of interested and deserving students of limited means.[40]

The financial squeeze in which private colleges find themselves has been publicized to such an extent that the message may have lost its power to persuade. The condition is nonetheless critical, and it is one which St. Catherine, despite the presence of religious on its staff and help from the Congregation of St. Joseph, has not escaped. In 1969–70 the college's income approximated $3,400,000. Of this amount, student tuition and fee payments furnished $1,598,000 and the contributed services of the sisters nearly $750,000. Total expenses came to about $3,500,000, leaving a deficit for the annual operation of nearly $100,000; the deficit for the previous year had been $176,000. Only minor income can be secured from the small endowment of about $1,460,000. What is needed, therefore, is an increase in the proportion of sisters on the faculty, continued careful operations, and additional outside support. In fiscal 1969–70 St. Catherine's received $1,013,000 in gifts and in government grants — the largest amount in a noncampaign year in its history. The government portion totaled over $408,000, that from friends of the college $453,300. Alumnae gave $43,100; parents contributed $44,000. The future seems to demand even greater achievement.[41]

Although Sister Alberta is disturbed by the financial problems facing St. Catherine's — especially as they deter the enrollment of capable and intelligent young women — she harbors no doubts regarding the ability of the institution to survive and to progress. Her earlier concern over the tendency of her religious associates to deprecate their role in higher education has been largely dispelled and so has her uneasiness over St. Catherine's image. With its numerous off-campus programs and its interchanges with St. Thomas and with other dwellers in the academic community, the college can scarcely be considered a cloistered retreat from the world, although rich opportunity abounds for meditation and for worship. The road to the future has yet to be mapped in detail, but the journey so far would suggest a continuation of certain habits and characteristics. St. Catherine's will hold to its Catholic commitment as modified since Vatican II; the traditional emphases on service to society and on integrity in scholarship will be maintained; the Sisters of St. Joseph, who earlier had sought to convert "savages, heretics, and infidels," will not shrink from the demands of an uncertain tomorrow. It cannot be otherwise with a congregation that selected as the inscription to be carved in granite on its chapel altar: "Behold I Make All Things New."

37

COLLEGE OF SAINT TERESA

Building in the Franciscan Spirit

WHILE THE COLLEGE OF SAINT TERESA did not suffer a loss of enrollment in the wake of Pearl Harbor, the war did not leave it untouched. Numbers of Teresans in one way or another contributed to the main effort of the time — teaching radio to army signalmen, for example — but those on campus carried on as normally as possible. A year after the Japanese attack in 1941, the Right Reverend Leo Binz was named coadjutor bishop of Winona to act for the ailing Bishop Kelly. The same year a major in music education was added to the curriculum.[1]

By the time fighting in the Pacific had ceased in 1945, Sister Aloysius, whose example and precepts are still very much alive on the Teresan campus, was about ready to lay down the burden of leadership she had borne with distinction for nearly forty years. In the summer of 1946 the newly elected Mother General Alcuin appointed Sister M. Rachel Dady to serve in a double capacity: as religious superior of the sisters at the college (a term limited to six years) and as the college's president. Sister Rachel had been one of three graduates in the college's first public commencement in 1914 (only two baccalaureates had been conferred up until then). A "keen and perceptive scholar, a gentle, gracious and kindly woman," Sister Rachel had earned a master's degree at Columbia University and a Ph.D. from Catholic University. In addition to teaching in the departments of English, philosophy, and religion, she had served as registrar of Saint Teresa from 1918 until 1926 and as secretary of the college during the succeeding four years. Associated with her in the new administrative team were Sister M. Camille Bowe, vice president, and Sister M. Emmanuel Collins, dean. All of these women had excellent academic training and they were well qualified to direct affairs in the postwar period.[2]

Once again student life, freed of the pervasive apprehension and the sadness of the past few years, took on its traditional buoyancy and variety. With the arrival of three Dominican priests in the fall of 1947, provision was made for students to receive spiritual guidance from members of that order, a practice still existing. Although vespers on Sunday afternoon were a thing of the past, religious feeling remained strong. To the organizations reflecting this fact on campus — the Sodality and the Third Order Secular of St. Francis — was added the Legion of Mary, whose purpose was service to the college and to the local community.[3]

Modifications and additions were effected in the academic area. The five-year nursing program, while not altered in quality, was reduced by one year in 1947. Previously the sequence had been geared to professional nurses, most of whom were nuns majoring in teaching, supervision, and administration. Henceforth the majority of enrollees would be lay students without prior training in nursing. Late in 1949, with needs of the city of Winona in mind, adult education classes — first in Russian history, elementary German and Spanish, and labor problems — were offered. Two years later a minor in library science and a training program to prepare lay students as teachers for kindergarten through grade six were introduced. Between 1958 and 1967 a total of 400 graduates were placed in elementary teaching positions — 222 in Minnesota, 216 outside the state. Comparable figures for alumnae accepting positions in secondary schools were 133 and 162.[4]

A new phase of the college's history began in the fall of 1952, when Sister Camille Bowe was appointed to the presidency, now a full-time responsibility separate from that of local religious superior. Sister Rachel had completed her term in the latter position and her health, never robust, had been impaired by long hospitalization following a back injury. She returned to her former post as professor of philosophy and chairman of the department.[5]

Sister Camille, who was born in Waseca, had become a sister of St. Francis in 1922 and had taught in various elementary and secondary schools of her congregation for a number of years thereafter. She had received her professional certificate from the St. Clare School of Education in 1927 and her B.A. from Saint Teresa in 1935. For the next four years she had studied at the Sorbonne in Paris, where she received her doctorate in literature, *très honorable* — the highest honor conferred by that French university. She had been the first American Catholic sister to complete a doctorate there. For a number of years she had been chairman of the department of modern languages at her alma mater, and even while president she would refuse to forsake classroom teaching. She would preside over the college's fortunes in a period of unprecedented growth, of more than doubled enrollment, and of impressive additions to the physical plant.[6]

Through it all, however, the basic commitment would remain unchanged; the student "is educated in the Franciscan spirit of looking on all that she has as possessed for the glory of God and the good of her neighbor." Of the constant reminders of this goal, none, except the examples of the sisters themselves, is more beautiful than the interior of the Chapel of Saint Mary of the Angels. Sister Camille, who was named chairman of the committee on decoration of the building in 1949, directed the project to a successful conclusion with funds provided by the alumnae in 1957, the year of jubilee. She counted the results as one of the major satisfactions and achievements of her term of office. All who have responded to the restrained magnificence of the stained glass windows, the extensive mosaics, the delicate gold leaf work, the figures of the angels and the Blessed Virgin and Saint Joseph agree with the importance attached to this artistic creation by Sister Camille.[7]

Although Mother Leo had built with an eye to the future and no major new buildings were erected during the first years of Sister Camille's administration, a committee began in 1957 to formulate long-range plans that included Roger Bacon Science Hall, the name chosen as early as 1913 by Bishop Heffron, Mother Leo, and Dr. Molloy. Completed in 1960 at a cost of $1,650,000, about one-third of which was contributed by various friends, the hall provided excellent, up-to-date facilities. Saint Mary's Hall, the old, original building which had been the scene of so much of the institution's history and something of a fire hazard for some time, was then razed.[8]

Once begun, new construction continued to add to the campus. For many years Lourdes Hall had been adequate for housing students, but by the second half of the 1950s this was no longer the case. Enrollment, which had been 542 in 1954, increased to 753 in 1957, and to 879 in 1961. The need for a new dormitory was critical. Consequently the four-story Loretto Hall, with accommodations for two hundred students and lounge and recreation areas, was built in 1961–62; its cost of $1,158,000 was financed largely by a federal loan. Two years later Assisi Hall, a residence for 120 student sisters, was completed at a cost of $1,178,000 borne by the Sisters of St. Francis themselves. Then in 1966 came Maria Hall, a counterpart of Loretto which cost $1,300,000 covered by a nongovernmental loan. During this same period, additions to the power plant and service facilities plus the adaptation of Cotter Hall for the art department increased the college's capital expenditures by another sizable sum of approximately $582,000.[9]

Finally with the completion and dedication of the Saint Teresa Learning Center in 1967, the long-cherished dream of a separate and adequate library building was fulfilled. For some time classroom space in Saint Teresa Hall of necessity had been devoted to library use — an improvisation at best. Thus on March 17 and 18, 1967, faculty, students, and staff enthusiastically transported over 90,000 volumes to the new air-conditioned center, located on the site formerly occupied by Saint Mary's Hall. With seating for about 500 students and shelving for 200,000 volumes, the $1,450,000 facility is modern in every respect. Not the least of its virtues is a spacious room for the college archives, a valuable resource neglected on all too many campuses. In a special ceremony on October 15, 1970 — Teresa of Avila Day — the structure was fittingly named in honor of Dr. Mary A. Molloy.[10]

The library, Maria Hall, additions to the power plant, and various renovations constituted Phase II of the long-range planning program. Slightly over $3,500,000 had been spent on these capital projects in the two years from 1965 to 1967, giving Saint Teresa total physical plant assets in the neighborhood of $13,000,000. Other structures — notably a fine arts building with auditorium — are still needed. As debts are paid off and money becomes available, these facilities will no doubt be built.[11]

In the absence of a wealthy benefactor, the college had traditionally depended for its well-being on the mother corporation and the contributed services of the sisters. The first large outside gift was the Ford Foundation grant of 1956–57 in the amount of $196,500, which has been kept intact and supplemented from other sources. The income from the grant has been helpful in raising the salaries of lay faculty, but not, of course, in paying for capital improvements. Thus rather late in the game for Minnesota private colleges generally, Saint Teresa's initiated a fund-raising campaign in 1965 — the Year of Commitment, as it was called. About $1,800,000 of the $4,770,000 goal was to go to increase endowment for faculty salaries, and the remainder was to be used for capital purposes. Happily the drive was a success, with parishes, Winona business interests, and alumnae as the biggest contributors.[12]

As everywhere, however, the campaign turned out to be merely a prelude to continuing efforts of a similar sort. Representative statistics tell the story. The sisters' contributed services had amounted to slightly over $146,300 in 1954–55; the total ten years later was $402,000, equal to the return on an endowment of $10,000,000. This was a healthy condition so long as the percentage of religious on the staff remained fairly high, but in this respect the picture was not so bright. There had been eighteen lay teachers and thirty-six religious on the faculty in 1955–56; a decade later the respective totals were sixty-four and thirty-six. College income in 1954–55 had been $693,192; in 1968–69 it was $3,387,800, but expenditures in both years had been even higher, $696,300 and $3,486,900. Costs of instruction, for example, rose from $194,700 to $1,219,000, yet the need to raise faculty salaries continued, and the end seemed nowhere in sight. Student aid in 1955–56 totaled $68,200; in 1968–69 it was $223,900. As in Alice's wonderland, the college found it necessary to run just to stand still.[13]

Until the late 1950s Saint Teresa's educational program remained largely traditional. In keeping with the Teresan purpose "to send forth Apostolic Women thoroughly trained in Secular Learning, militants to uphold the ideals of Catholicity in society," 26 of the 128 credits required for graduation were in the field of religion and philosophy. Leading sequences, as befitted the institution's heritage, were — and in many ways still are — nursing, education, and languages. In 1958, for example, of 137 recipients of bachelor's degrees, 65 were prepared to teach in elementary or secondary schools and 36 had completed the course in nursing.[14]

While maintaining its basic commitment to Catholicism and spirituality, Saint Teresa has kept pace with changing educational developments. As early as 1957 through a grant of $36,000 from the Hill Family Foundation, the college was able to establish a language laboratory on Saint Teresa's campus. With it in operation undergraduate instruction was not only greatly improved, but a number of projects and educational experiments were carried out as well. A second Hill gift of $35,000 made possible several language workshops, seminars, and summer sessions in which over eight hundred teachers received up-to-date in-service training in

their specialties between 1957 and 1960. As a result of this experience, Saint Teresa's was well prepared to conduct the four National Defense Education Act (NDEA) summer institutes for secondary teachers of French and Spanish which were held on campus from 1961 to 1964.[15]

The Hill Foundation also provided funds to allow the college to share with others some of the techniques developed in its nursing course. In 1962 four films, entitled "Meeting Patients' Needs," were produced with the co-operation of the Mayo Clinic and St. Mary's Hospital in Rochester. These helpful materials have been used on a rental basis by over 160 colleges and universities, nearly 230 hospitals, and some 160 nursing schools. In the same year fifteen half-hour films demonstrating teaching of the "new" mathematics to children in the elementary grades were produced by the mathematics and drama departments. Widely circulated as far away as Australia and Guam, these visual aids have done much to publicize the name of the college. They were responsible to some extent for the large number of applications for admission to the mathematics institutes for elementary school personnel supported by the National Science Foundation at Saint Teresa in the summers of 1963 and 1964. The drama department alone has produced over two hundred television programs in recent years; in 1966 and 1967 it conducted the only NDEA English institutes in applied theater arts in the United States.[16]

Shortly after the college had embarked on its language laboratory endeavors, a team of the North Central Association reviewed Saint Teresa's over-all operation. The general conclusion reached by the investigators was "that the program is ordered along the lines and aims of the college, is well managed, adequately staffed, in a friendly environment where improvement of the program is encouraged." One of the few weaknesses noted was the "unusually high number of required hours of work" for graduation. To correct this rigidity curricular revision was undertaken and kept up regularly thereafter. In 1960 art, speech and drama (previously available only as minors) and psychology were offered as majors. That same year an honors program was introduced. Two years later advanced placement opportunities were provided for students who had made special preparation in secondary school.[17]

By the late 1960s, 22 majors and about 470 courses were offered. Somewhat more than one-third of the credits required for graduation could be selected as electives. Instruction in ballet had become a fixed and popular part of the curriculum in 1964. By then philosophy and theology, which had constituted part of the general education core of required courses and had been a single department, had begun to move in the direction of separation. A major in philosophy had been approved that same year, and offerings in the field had been expanded. Concurrently courses in religion had been restructured, and by 1967 both disciplines had attained independent departmental organization. Preceding these changes and in keeping with Saint Teresa's liberal arts stance had been deletions of majors in business in 1958 and in medical technology in 1960.[18]

Long-time social relations with nearby St. Mary's and the joint venture in the language laboratory were merely preludes to closer academic relations between the two colleges and resultant enrichment of their curricular offerings. Various problems — schedule co-ordination, transportation, financial adjustments — had to be resolved. Committees worked them out, however, and it was agreed that each institution would admit the other's upper-class students to courses which were not offered on the students' home campus. The arrangement began in the fall of 1964 when Saint Teresa's permitted junior and senior Marians to enter classes in French literature, music history, experimental psychology, and anthropology. St. Mary's reciprocated with courses in mechanics and in money and banking. Thereafter the areas of co-operation were enlarged. Saint Teresa's supported the master's program in Spanish which St. Mary's offered from 1966 onward, and beginning in August, 1968, the two schools offered a sequence leading toward a master's degree for the teaching of Latin. In 1966 Winona State College also joined the undergraduate exchange arrangement.[19]

In the academic year 1968–69 nearly 220 men from St. Mary's studied at Saint Teresa's and 121 Teresans were enrolled in classes in the Christian Brothers' institution; the same year 30 students from Winona State took work at Saint Teresa's and five Teresans attended the public college. Co-operation was particularly close among the departments of classics, mathematics, philosophy, and theology. A further step was taken in the summer of 1969 at a joint meeting of the trustees of the two Catholic institutions. The following motion was passed: "Resolved, that the College of Saint Teresa and Saint Mary's College, while retaining their individual identities as determined by their stated philosophies, shall move toward combining operations at all levels and in all areas insofar as practicable and advisable." In pursuance of this resolution, an educational consulting firm was retained to make a joint study, which concluded that the two colleges "could develop natural areas of cooperation." How far this path will lead is yet to be determined.[20]

As in curricular matters so in other areas Saint Teresa's has modified its programs and procedures in order to maintain relevance. It has done so without serious sacrifice either to traditional and time-tested values or to its own unique heritage. The realm of administration and control, for example, has witnessed two new departures. A lay advisory board, composed of men and women from a wide spectrum of the business and professional worlds, was established in 1957 to lend counsel in the planning and decision-making process. Secondly, in accordance with usual practice in the academic world (though not without some opposition) the College of Saint Teresa was separately incorporated under the laws of Minnesota on December 14, 1963. The emotional, spiritual, and practical bonds with the mother house of the congregation in Rochester, however, remain strong and cherished, even though the college is now legally independent. As early as 1959 it had been recommended that lay members from the advisory board be included with the religious on the board of trustees. This proposal was acted upon a decade later. In January, 1969, seven laymen joined the eight sisters constituting the college board; several months later the number of lay trustees was raised to sixteen, one of whom serves as chairman.[21]

As part of the effort to raise the quality of student intellectual performance, there has been greater selectivity than in earlier years in admissions procedures. College board tests, for example, were first required of applicants in 1959. But along with this concern for the undergraduate of superior ability, a "deepening responsibility for the disadvantaged student has been keenly felt." The summer Upward Bound program for forty high school girls was conducted on the campus in 1966 and commended by the United States office of economic opportunity. Similarly in a tradition dating back to Mother Leo and in the face of high tuition costs, no effort has been spared to enable poor, but motivated, young women to attend the college. An awareness of contemporary race problems and a desire to become involved in the search for their solution resulted in a student and faculty exchange program with Spelman College in Atlanta, Georgia.[22]

Since 1918 many foreign students have studied at Saint Teresa's, and an international dimension has characterized many aspects of campus life. In recent years this world view has become increasingly pervasive in course content and in curricular innovation. It is evident in a Latin American area studies program started in 1967, a Slavic studies program initiated in 1969, in lecture series, and in opportunities for both students and faculty to study abroad. The ageless goals of personal identity, wisdom, knowledge, skill, effectiveness, and commitment to worthy causes are implemented with the help of modern techniques. On the academic side, closed circuit television, films, and audio-visual aids have been mobilized; on the personal side, psychiatric counseling and mental health workshops are among new resources utilized.[23]

By the middle of the 1960s enrollment had grown to 1,350 (1,129 full- and 221 part-time students) with a future ceiling of 1,800 contemplated. Although the majority of students have regularly come from Minnesota, Illinois, Wisconsin, and Iowa, 58 per cent in 1966 hailed from out of state, a proportion exceeded by only two other Minnesota private colleges, St. Mary's and Carleton. (The average of all the state's private colleges in that year was 37 per cent.) The retention rate at Saint Teresa has been excellent, averaging 57 per cent for the ten years ending in 1967; in that year an amazing 76 per cent of the freshmen who had enrolled four years earlier graduated. Majors such as biology, mathematics, and sociology reflect interests in society generally and have been increasingly popular; so also has graduate study. A sizable number of alumnae hold advanced degrees in the fields of education, nursing, social work, classical and modern languages, English, library science, history, and mathematics; other alumnae are doctors of medicine.[24]

Students have been accorded more responsibility for directing their own lives and have been given more voice in policy making. Starting in the spring of 1960, as a case in point, nineteen undergraduates were selected as dormitory proctors (later called resident assistants), and gradual success was achieved in freeing the sisters from their image as authoritarian figures. A student judiciary board to help handle disciplinary matters on campus was established in 1966–67; the same year a college executive council with representatives from each of the three Winona educational institutions was created to help promote and smooth out the mutual ventures among the participating colleges.[25]

Saint Teresa's faculty in the late 1960s, totaling more than 150 full- and part-time individuals, was loyal, productive, and professional. Its position in the college has been more clearly specified and its role in policy making enlarged. As a result of its efforts and through the interest and co-operation of the administration, a faculty constitution and by-laws were accepted on an experimental basis in the fall of 1968. At the same time a fifteen-member faculty council was set up. Salary scales rose from an average of $8,198 in 1964 to $10,725 in 1968, but they were still below those of some other Minnesota private colleges.[26]

At the conclusion of the academic year 1968–69 Sister Camille retired from the presidency. For nearly two decades this warm, quiet, yet gently firm woman had given Saint Teresa leadership of a high order. In 1952 she had assumed direction of a college possessing a strong academic tradition, a cosmopolitan climate, and a dedicated staff. It was an institution which differed in many respects, however, from the one she passed on to her successor. Still an integral part of the corporate structure of the Franciscan sisterhood, the Saint Teresa of the early 1950s had no development program, no long-range planning blueprint, no recent additions to the physical plant, inadequate library and science facilities; and there had been a lag in the program of sending sisters off for graduate study.[27]

In retrospect, Sister Camille would disclaim major credit for the changes and advances made during her administration, but an impartial observer would take issue with this view. Although her paramount interest was — and still is — in the intellectual and academic side of college life, she made distinct contributions to its other facets. Through her persistence, Saint Teresa had emerged in the mid-1960s as an independent legal entity, no longer a subordinate division of a religious body supported by St. Mary's Hospital and the Mayo Clinic — as many outsiders wrongly supposed. She had interpreted changes in the size and structure of the college to alumnae and to the general public, gaining understanding, support, and involvement in return. She had encouraged faculty members to be imaginative and daring, and she had increased their degree of participation in institutional governance. Students likewise had been given greater freedom and responsibility. In her person and in her career, Sister Camille had graced the tradition of capable and committed Catholic women educators whom Minnesota has been fortunate to call its own.

Succeeding to the presidency in August, 1969, was Minneapolis-born Sister M. Joyce Rowland, who had received her B.A. in English at Saint Teresa in 1949. Both before and after her graduation, she had taught in parochial schools in the Winona diocese. She had earned her M.A. degree in 1953 at the University of Minnesota and her Ph.D. in philosophy at St. Louis University nine years later. Between 1953 and 1956 she had been an instructor in education at Saint Teresa, but her current period of service had begun in 1962, when she joined the department of religion and philosophy. The following year she had been named chairman of the department. From 1967 until her appointment as president, Sister Joyce had been vice president and dean of the college.[28]

Following in the footsteps of a seasoned and successful leader at a time when all institutions of higher learning were burdened with a plethora of problems, Sister Joyce inherited no easy sinecure. In addition to the parcel of worries carried by all college presidents, she bore the concerns peculiar to the chief executives of Catholic residential colleges for women — the decline in vocations and the nation-wide trend in favor of coeducation. Both faculty composition and enrollment reflected these phenomena. The full-time teaching staff during Sister Joyce's first year in office numbered 104, about 28 per cent of whom held the Ph.D. degree; there were 67 lay instructors, but only 37 religious. Regular enrollment stood at 1,088, of whom 312 were new students; part-time undergraduates totaled approximately 100. Saint Teresa was somewhat smaller than it had been two and three years earlier, and its applications for 1969 admission had been fewer than those of the recent past. The college increased its recruitment endeavors and looked into the desirability of maintaining an admissions representative in the New York area.[29]

Another problem Sister Joyce shared with her peers in higher education was that hardy perennial, the need for more money. Current revenues for 1969–70 came to $3,368,000; student fees accounted for $1,420,000, auxiliary enterprises for $987,000, and the services of the religious for $514,000. Other gifts and grants, including those for student aid, brought in $377,800. Expenditures, however, amounted to $3,490,000, leaving a deficit of slightly over $122,000 for the year. The biggest portion of the total outlay, $1,230,000, was spent on instruction, but over $372,000 went for student loans, scholarships, and work — $127,000 of it coming from the college itself. Almost half of the women enrolled received some form of assistance, the average amount being $710. And beyond meeting its current expenses, Saint Teresa in mid-1970 carried interest-bearing indebtedness of almost $2,000,000 on past capital projects, plus another interest-free obligation of $550,000 to the mother house in Rochester.[30]

The college's financial condition in 1970 was not critical, but "the second priority" after continued improvement of the educational program was, as Sister Joyce said, "money." To facilitate raising it and to make Saint Teresa's better known, the various divisions constituting the office of college relations were forged into a more effective working unit, and new personnel were employed to head those sections concerned with public relations and alumnae affairs. Concurrently closer bonds were formed with the people of Winona. This preparation and planning led early in 1971 to the launching of a "Year of Commitment" drive to raise some $2,500,000. The specific goals sought were $850,000 for academic programs, $750,000 for faculty development, an equal amount for student aid, and $720,000 for plant renovation and campus improvement. The college's devoted band of 6,000 alumnae and the institution's past achievements bode well for the success of the campaign.[31]

This effort to secure funds, like those preceding it, is only a means to the ongoing purpose of perpetuating the college's academic goals and ideals, however the word "academic" may be interpreted. An attempt at definition occupied a curriculum committee of faculty, students, and administrators between 1967 and 1970. The results in the form of a changed calendar and a completely revised curriculum were instituted in September, 1970. Relegated to limbo were such traditional elements of campus life as the two-semester system, all general education requirements, and credit hours. Henceforth students would carry an average load of three courses in each of the three terms into which the school year was now divided. For graduation thirty-five full courses rather than a certain number of credits would be necessary. Quality, depth, and diversity, it was hoped, would replace quantity, superficiality, and conformity. Each student, instead of being forced into a general mold often with ensuing lack of interest and motivation, could now within limits fashion a schedule of studies in line with her special aptitudes and inclinations. Faculty also enjoyed greater flexibility and freedom to engage in team teaching, to vary individual methods of instruction, and to experiment in a variety of other ways.[32]

The theory behind Saint Teresa's altered calendar and curriculum was scarcely novel, but it had considerable appeal and currency during the decade of the 1960s, when the concepts of pluralism and of "doing one's own thing" had gained great popularity in colleges and universities. Indeed Sister Joyce's report of 1970 carried a section entitled "Openness to Diversity," which dealt with student affairs. Certainly the college's efforts to educate women for life in a fast-changing world and by permitting great latitude of choice to stimulate students' inner motivational drives have merit. Time alone will tell whether the high hopes and great expectations which accompanied the adoption of the new program with its desire to create an "exciting atmosphere of learning" wherein young women can realize their potential will be fulfilled.[33]

Graduation classes have varied considerably in size in the recent past, from a low of 170 in 1966 to a high of over 260 in 1967. By the end of the following year the college had conferred 4,442 baccalaureates — 2,261 in the arts and 2,181 in science. Of late, however, there has been a notable increase in the number of B.S. degrees earned from 75 in 1966 to 140 in 1969; in those same two years B.A.s awarded totaled 95 and 110. Concurrent with this trend was a change in the popularity of two of Saint Teresa's important major fields. More than a quarter of the 1966 class had majored in elementary education; the proportion of the 1970 class who did so was down to 19 per cent. Conversely nursing at the earlier date had attracted 23 per cent of the graduates, whereas in 1970 the proportion of the class with a major in nursing was 32 per cent. Looking at the needs of society and the excess of teachers over openings in 1970, this change in vocational goals would seem both encouraging and wise.[34]

As Saint Teresa looks to the future, it continues to ponder many old but still pertinent questions. What does it mean to be a Christian college today? What are the legitimate areas for a liberal arts institution to enter? Should there be an expansion of the adult education program and a sortie into the graduate field? What gains will derive from more interdepartmental courses and more team teaching? How far should independent study be carried?

No final or completely satisfying answers have been found, but that is in the nature of things and not the result of lack of time and effort. Indeed, consistent with Sister Camille's contention that the college "cannot afford to experience growth without purpose or expansion without plan," a profile of the institution to the year 1976 has been carefully prepared. Using past performance as a guide, it seems safe to predict that Saint Teresa's will remain a "vibrant institution," determined to "meet the challenges of today's society." One can only hope that the staff of gracious, committed, and scholarly sisters of St. Francis who give the college its special charisma will be continually renewed.[35]

38 COLLEGE OF ST. BENEDICT

New Independence and An Ancient Tradition

IN THE MONTHS before Pearl Harbor in 1941, curricular offerings at the College of St. Benedict were little different from what they had been a decade earlier. Only commercial or business education, designed to prepare commercial teachers for secondary schools, had been added in 1934. The size of the faculty remained stable at about forty, of whom thirty-two were sisters — twenty-three of them graduates of St. Benedict's. Administration, however, underwent an important change in 1941 when Sister Claire left the deanship to study for her doctorate at Catholic University. Her successor was Sister Incarnata Girgen who had spent the preceding three years doing graduate work at St. Louis University. (She would obtain her Ph.D. in 1945.) A native of Minnesota, she had received her high school diploma from St. Benedict in 1917 and had made her first profession two years later. After interspersing parochial schoolteaching with further study, she had earned her B.A. at the college in 1933. Her administration as dean would extend to 1947.[1]

Enrollment at St. Benedict was affected by the threat, and later the actuality, of World War II. Freshman mortality had always been higher than desirable, but for 1940–41 it reached a record 55 per cent. Full-time enrollment in 1942–43 was 191; the next year it dipped to approximately 160. But by 1944–45 registrations were on the upswing again, reaching 213 of whom 118 were freshmen. Graduates during the war years also declined. From 1943 through 1946 degrees conferred totaled 127 in all. Of these 39 were in home economics and 31 in English, by far the two most popular majors.[2]

Students remaining in school sought ways of doing their bit for the defense effort. Early in 1942 a school lunch program was instituted by the college for the more than a hundred children who stayed over the noon hour at the St. Joseph village school. Many of the customary campus activities such as the fall symposium and the spring home-coming were dropped and replaced by the sale of war bonds and stamps and the preparation of surgical dressings. Some of the faculty took a first-aid course in St. Cloud in preparation for teaching the subject at St. Benedict. But "normal" routines had to be followed, too, and some thought given to preparation for the return to peacetime conditions. In the spring of 1945 the college accepted an invitation to participate in the North Central Association Study for the Improvement of Teacher Education in Colleges of Liberal Arts. As a result three sisters attended the summer workshop held in connection with the study at the University of Minnesota.[3]

The surrender of Japan in 1945 quickly resulted in an increase in enrollment (it reached 270 in 1946–47), the return of campus life to familiar patterns, and the injection of new enthusiasm into the North Central study. Special attention was given by the faculty to the objectives of the college and how best to attain them. A visitor from Hunter College spoke to the staff on Catholic education as seen by an outsider, and Dr. Frank Earl Ward of Macalester, co-ordinator of the North Central study, discussed the problems of St. Benedict with its entire teaching staff. Thought was given to affiliation with the American Association of University Women and with the Association of American Universities, but it was decided to postpone further investigation of these matters until the fall of 1947. St. Benedict, however, joined the National Federation of Catholic College Students and sent representatives to its Chicago and Minnesota regional meetings. Once again the future seemed brighter.[4]

Sister Incarnata, having completed her term as dean in 1947, returned to teaching as professor of philosophy. Succeeding her in the administrative post was Sister Enid Smith, also a Minnesotan by birth, who had obtained her B.A. at the college in 1930. She then taught in several high schools, made her first profession in 1934, did graduate work, and was a member of the wartime teaching staff at St. Benedict. She had earned her M.A. at the University of Toronto and her Ph.D. *summa cum laude* in philosophy at Catholic University. She would guide the college from 1947 through the uncertainties of the Korean conflict to the days of Sputnik in 1957. Most of this time her superior would be Mother Richarda Peters, who became prioress and nominal president of St. Benedict in 1949.[5]

Among the problems which Sister Enid faced were declining enrollment — a common manifestation after the postwar bulge had passed — and tightening finances. By the early 1950s full-time students numbered only slightly more than 220. In 1950–51 the undergraduate body was composed of about 150 resident lay students, 38 lay commuters, 14 sisters, and 13 aspirants. The senior class totaled 28. Not until the final year of Sister Enid's administration in 1956–57 would enrollment pass the 300 mark. Attrition, especially among freshmen, remained a perennial problem. Low enrollment not only complicated course scheduling and teaching assignments, but it also meant reduced income. St. Benedict's fees for tuition, board, and room in 1951 were roughly $520, approximately $354 below the average of 111 Catholic women's colleges surveyed by Sister Enid. In spite of this fact by June 1, 1952, more than one-third of the applicants for fall admission had applied for financial aid. Under such circumstances, the importance of the Benedictine order's support of the college and the contributed services of the sisters can be readily understood as crucial elements in its financial picture.[6]

Changes in curriculum during Sister Enid's deanship were modest. The one exception was the introduction in 1950 of a four-year course in elementary education leading to a B.A. degree. Preparation for this new program involved considerable work and the expenditure of money, particularly for related books for the library. In 1953 the first eleven women to major in the new sequence received their degrees. From then on students specializing in elementary education far outnumbered those majoring in any other department. By the middle of 1970 graduates in this discipline had totaled 609.[7]

In November, 1953, a committee appointed by the Minnesota Department of Education visited St. Benedict to examine the new major. The investigators reported favorably, and the state board gave probationary approval to the college's program for a period of five years. At the end of this time in November, 1958, a second examination was conducted. By then four members of the department of education held master's degrees and one a doctorate; the chairman was especially capable and had carried out numerous state and national assignments. The examiners reported some weaknesses: the curriculum had gaps in science, mathematics, geography, and history; the aims and objectives had not recently been reviewed; the women did not live in the communities where they did their student teaching. Strengths, however, outweighed shortcomings, and the Benedictine ideal of devoted service and community spirit was everywhere in evidence. The committee recommended that the elementary education sequence be fully approved, subject to annual reviews and suggested improvements. The state board implemented the recommendation in 1959.[8]

St. Benedict's and St. John's University joined in 1955 in sponsoring a program of evening adult classes in St. Cloud. Six courses including theology, ethics, and art and music appreciation were offered the first year. Enrollment totaled 110, a figure which increased to 366 in 1959 when twelve courses were taught. After six years the St. Cloud program was discontinued, but in early 1964 St. Benedict provided evening work for adults in its new arts center on the campus at St. Joseph with about 65 persons enrolled. Similar opportunities were offered in 1965 and 1966, but then the project was dropped. Annual summer sessions at St. Benedict reached many more students. In the mid-1950s enrollment, composed mainly of sisters, averaged about 250 each year. A decade later it was up to some 300. Commencement exercises concluded each session with approximately 25 sisters receiving bachelor's degrees.[9]

College building projects for a variety of reasons including the depression, the order's attention to other matters, and low enrollment had not been undertaken for three decades as St. Benedict entered the 1950s. Although commuters did come out from St. Cloud, their number was small; the only hope for growth lay in providing more dormitory space. With this in mind Mother Richarda appointed a faculty committee to survey the situation and to plan future development. After thorough study the committee concluded in 1954 that immediate needs called for a 200-bed dormitory, a recreation center, and an auditorium. Not all of these could be financed at once, but plans were drawn for the center and for a dormitory which could be constructed in stages. Total cost for these facilities plus a necessary expansion of the power plant was estimated at over $1,500,000.[10]

Previously, the order had relied for financing mainly on its savings and the help of close friends. In October, 1954, however, Mother Richarda appointed a building fund committee of nine sisters to solicit money from a variety of sources ranging from foundations and businesses to parishes and relatives. During the first year of the endeavor about $73,000 was secured, over $18,000 of which came from raffles, the sale of turkeys raised on the order's farm, and from handiwork made by the sisters. By August, 1957, receipts reached about $223,000. The alumnae association also created its own fund committee to assist in the effort. Between May, 1957, and April, 1958, this group added over $36,000, an amount then matched by an anonymous donor.[11]

In anticipation of the increased enrollment which the new residence hall would permit, the fourth floor locker room of the main building was converted in the fall of 1954 into living quarters called Montserrat Dormitory. By crowding, this action made possible the admission of twenty-five extra students. Ground for the new building was broken the following spring; the first students moved into Mary Hall, an attractive modern structure, in the fall of 1956. The college then had rooms for eighty more undergraduates. Some unused dormitory space in the main building was now given over to classroom use. In the commons area of the new hall were lounges, a snack bar, and suitable space for parties, receptions, and other social events which previously could not have been easily arranged. St. Benedict's had substantial cause for rejoicing, but urgent needs still existed for an auditorium, a music hall, and a gymnasium.[12]

Despite these exigencies, the college had been definitely strengthened in the mid-1950s. The time seemed ripe therefore to create a collegiate administrative organization more like those generally found in academic institutions. In 1957 Mother Richarda appointed Sister Remberta Westkaemper president of the institution. A native Minnesotan who had made her first profession in 1908, Sister Remberta for a decade had combined parochial schoolteaching with the pursuit of her own education. In 1912 she had received her diploma from St. Benedict's Academy and in 1919 her B.A. from the college. She had then taught biology at her alma mater and done graduate work at the University of Minnesota, where she had obtained her Ph.D. in botany in 1929. As the first president of the college who was not also superior of the religious community, she would serve a term of four years.[13]

Considerable sensitivity in the area of state-church relations existed during this period especially on the national scene, and a great deal of study was given to the matter of further separation of college and convent. Culmination of this activity came in 1961, the year Mother Richarda's second term as prioress expired. Thereupon another change in administration occurred and with it the legal incorporation of the college. Sister Linnea Welter, a graduate of the academy in 1928 and of the college in 1932, took office as president. A member of the English department since 1944, she had been a high school teacher both before and after making her first profession in 1939. Prior to her administration, the college had been merely a subsidiary of the order. Henceforth under articles of incorporation filed in October, 1961, the educational institution would be an independent legal entity governed by a board of directors. However, the bond with the Benedictines would still be close: the first board was composed of the new head of the religious community, Mother Henrita Osendorf, and three other of its officials, plus the college's president, academic dean, and dean of students. The board of advisers, though reconstituted, continued to be valuable.[14]

In this transitional period of growing independence, which coincided quite fittingly with the beginning of the Benedictines' second century in Minnesota, the college continued to develop mainly along lines already laid down. Enrollment in 1959–60 passed the 400 mark for the first time; about 300 were resident lay students, 52 lay commuters, 47 sisters, and 30 aspirants. A sizable number of the undergraduates came from large families where parents had only an elementary education. It was necessary to award scholarships to 41 students and to provide service or work contracts to 111 young women, some of whom also had financial grants. In money terms this amounted to $9,300 in scholarships and $26,500 in work. College expenditures for 1960–61 exceeded income by about $125,000. To cover this deficit the mother house made a grant of an equal sum. The dependence on the Benedictine sisterhood thus continued to be crucial.[15]

Enrollment was rising and more facilities were needed. In 1959 the board of advisers recommended that plans for both a gymnasium and a fine arts building be drawn. When the former was completed in 1961, the space previously used as a gymnasium was given over to library use, thereby adding room for about 35,000 volumes. Meanwhile as students and faculty labored under crowded conditions — "a drain on physical and psychic energy," noted the president — efforts to secure the fine arts building and more dormitory space went forward but not without obstacles. Only after the college was separately incorporated, for example, could a federal loan be negotiated to build a new wing on Mary Hall. With legal independence accomplished, the $650,000 loan to run for 38 years with interest at 3½ per cent was approved in April, 1962.[16]

Work on the 150-bed addition, known as Regina Hall (the older part of Mary Hall was called Aurora Hall) began in August, 1962. Some three months later the site was blessed and ground broken for the beautiful Benedicta Arts Center, "the culmination of more than ten years of planning and study by the Sisters of Saint Benedict." Costing approximately $3,500,000, it was dedicated to the memory of Sister Benedicta Riepp, leader of the first group of Benedictine nuns to come to the United States in 1852.[17]

The year 1963–64 witnessed "the completion of . . . the greatest single physical expansion project in the history of the College." Regina Hall and the section of the arts center designed for the art department were sufficiently finished to permit their use in September. A second segment of the center for music, speech, and drama was ready in December, and the auditorium and forum were completed the following spring. With the removal of some operations to the new structures, extensive renovations were made in the older buildings. Dormitory rooms in St. Cecilia Hall were remodeled into an infirmary and quarters for home economics. Loretto Hall, vacated by the art department, provided new classrooms, laboratories, offices, and space for the bookstore. The second floor of St. Cecilia Hall, former home of the music department, now housed offices, a radiation laboratory, the news service, and a large classroom. Finally a language laboratory was installed in St. Gertrude Hall and made ready for use late in 1964. The college as a result of this expansion had incurred an indebtedness of about $2,000,000, but the value of the physical plant had grown to more than $6,300,000.[18]

Although the college had always been conservative in curriculum matters, the growth in enrollment and the prospect of new facilities permitted the addition of several major sequences — philosophy and art in 1960, medical technology in 1961, and speech and drama in 1963. Thorough study was given to the possible inauguration of a four-year degree program in nursing in co-operation with St. Cloud Hospital, but the board of directors in 1964 was forced to conclude that the plan was not financially feasible. When KTCA-TV started operations in St. Paul in the fall of 1957, Sister M. Inez Hilger became the first teacher to offer a televised course for credit. Entitled "Anthropology of the Americas," it was completed by thirteen St. Benedict students as well as ten others. Additional innovations of importance in the college's total program in the 1960s and early 1970s have included the employment of audio-visual aids, the use of college board test scores, the adoption of a revised mathematics sequence, the introduction of physical therapy studies and a language laboratory, the development of honors programs, individualized majors, and an associate of arts degree in liberal studies and music — a nontraditional program for adults offered by the Center for Continuing Education established in 1972.[19]

Few curricular developments of recent years, however, surpass in effect or potential the interchanges with St. John's University and St. Cloud State College. A committee representing the three institutions was formed in 1957 to study the possible benefits of a joint academic venture. From the deliberations evolved the Tri-College Great Issues Program, which had its inception in 1958 with a four-semester credit course entitled "Problems of Free Men." Supported by a grant of $25,400 from the Hill Family Foundation, faculty and students held eighteen intercollegiate meetings (as well as others restricted to members of each participating group) to consider various political, economic, scientific, and artistic aspects of each year's main theme. For six years the Hill Foundation supported this enterprise, making possible, among other benefits, travel in Europe and Asia by faculty members involved.[20]

Another joint program offered concurrently with the great issues project was a community leadership training course aimed at revitalizing local government. Made possible by a $25,000 grant under Title I of the federal Higher Education Act of 1965, it consisted of thirteen Saturday workshops rotated among the three institutions during 1966–67. Students could either audit the course or take it for credit. A combined East Indian major became available in the fall of 1968, and a tri-college service center was established. A committee representing the three institutions was created in 1968 to help plan the centennial celebration of the foundation of St. Cloud State College in 1869. The stage seemed solidly set for continuing experimentation and coordination.[21]

St. Benedict's had carried on a limited program of co-operation with St. John's University over the years. In 1956–57, for example, a priest from Collegeville had taught a course called "The Family" at the women's college, and one of the sisters offered "Creative Writing" at the men's institution. The following year two sisters taught social work and art at St. John's. In 1962–63 at the suggestion of the board of advisers co-operation began in earnest. A committee representing both colleges met periodically to investigate exchange possibilities, and the faculties were polled to learn their reactions to greater co-ordination. The responses were generally favorable, and a meeting of department chairmen of both institutions was held in March, 1963; their task was to decide which courses and instructors might be shared. Other details of scheduling, transportation, and tuition were left to administrative officers. In the fall of 1964 the two faculties for the first time met jointly for half of the annual two-day workshop preceding the opening of classes. Then followed the exchange of some teachers and the enrollment during the first term of forty-eight women at St. John's and forty-two men at St. Benedict's. That same year the two speech and drama departments fashioned the first combined major.[22]

Paralleling these intercollegiate excursions were developments at St. Benedict of a more strictly intramural nature. The presidency changed hands and the college continued to feel its way as an independent, legal entity. Because of illness, Sister Linnea relinquished her administrative position in August, 1963. Her two-year term had been too brief to permit the formulation and consummation of many projects. Yet her tenure had witnessed some landmarks beyond those of plant expansion and academic exchange. In November, 1961, the American Association of University Women had extended its approval to the college, and the following year a revision of the schedule had strengthened the sequence in education. With an eye to future recognition by the National Council for the Accreditation of Teacher Education (NCATE), the faculty in 1962–63 conducted a thorough self-evaluation of St. Benedict's program, which resulted in a preliminary report for the national agency. Having come of age and legally severed the cord binding it to the mother house, the college in its fiftieth year was restlessly testing its strength and seeking its identity.[23]

Directing the institution's progress for the next five years was Sister Mary Grell, born in Pierz, Minnesota, and a 1933 graduate of St. Benedict. For the three decades prior to assuming the presidency, she had combined the teaching of biology at the college with advanced study and travel and had earned her Ph.D. at Fordham University in 1945. The first year of her administration was a full and exciting one, marked by the completion of Regina Hall and the Benedicta Arts Center, a 12 per cent enrollment increase, the formal commemoration of the college's fiftieth birthday, and a morale-raising review of St. Benedict's teacher

education program by a representative of the Minnesota Department of Education. The remainder of her tenure would show the same record of spirited accomplishment.[24]

In 1965 at the college's invitation, Father Edward V. Stanford, O.S.A. — who four years earlier had recommended separate incorporation — again visited the campus as a consultant. Pleased with the progress achieved in the interim, he made further suggestions regarding St. Benedict's administrative organization. His report included criticisms of standing committees, courses offered, and major sequences, all of which, in his opinion, were too numerous. Instead of the twenty-two academic departments and six divisions then in existence, he suggested reorganizing into only eight departments. Such action would reduce the number of chairmen and make them a less unwieldy and more effective segment of administration.[25]

That summer a joint curriculum committee of St. Benedict's and St. John's studied the two Benedictine colleges and formulated a plan, subsequently approved by the faculties, for the regrouping of departments within a revised divisional structure. Henceforth there would be only three divisions: humanities and theology, social sciences and history, and natural sciences and mathematics. There would be thirteen instead of twenty-two departments. Meanwhile the college had re-entered the North Central Association Study on Liberal Arts. The culmination of these investigations came on March 28, 1967, when the faculty in a daylong meeting voted to adopt the four-one-four calendar and a new three-track curriculum consisting of basic, supplementary, and major fields of study. Of special interest was the basic or integrated studies program designed to provide a four-year "common academic experience for all students which will lay the 'in breadth' liberal arts foundation of the academic program," as well as to "demonstrate the interrelatedness of all knowledge."[26]

On the subject of co-operation between the two Benedictine colleges, the 1965 joint curriculum committee was firmly convinced of the value — even the "survival-value" — of the academic exchange. To this end, the *ad hoc* group recommended: regularly scheduled intercampus transportation, the co-ordination of class schedules, the adoption of identical calendars, a common public announcement of courses, and the creation of a combined committee for major convocations. In 1965–66 bus service was instituted, and the exchanges of personnel grew in number; approximately a hundred women from St. Benedict's and seventy-three men from St. John's were involved during the second term. A joint course bulletin was first published for 1967–68, when a combined curriculum on the four-one-four plan of two semesters separated by a January interim term was instituted. There were still budgetary, emotional, and psychological problems, but great progress in co-ordination had been made. It remained to be seen whether the two institutions could or should move beyond social and academic exchanges to a closer union, or even to a complete merger.[27]

By this time the visitation by representatives of the National Council for the Accreditation of Teacher Education, for which faculty committees had spent two years in preparation, had taken place in November, 1965, and the college had been granted provisional accreditation. The visitors were particularly impressed by St. Benedict's commitment "to the philosophy that the teacher is to be socially aware of the community in which the school is located" and by the arrangement for six weeks of full-time student teaching. The council's main reservations involved the curriculum; it was feared that the heavy requirements in theology, philosophy, and foreign language left insufficient room for other subjects vital to a general education. The program for elementary practice teaching was superior to that provided for prospective high school teachers. Special commendation went to its counseling and admissions practices, its well-kept records, the enriching program in music and the fine arts, the faculty, and the excellent physical plant.[28]

A survey of the academic programs of graduates in the 1960s testified to the wisdom of this careful attention to the teacher training sequence. Of the fifty-one graduates of 1961, forty-two were qualified as either elementary or secondary teachers. In the class of 1968 — composed of seventy-eight lay women and thirteen sisters — twenty-eight taught in elementary schools and twenty-two in high schools the year following their graduation; several others planned to do so later. Marriage, social work, medical technology, and graduate school accounted for most of the other alumnae. In the Benedictine tradition, these occupations generally involved service to one's fellow man. The Peace Corps and the Lay Apostolate also provided outlets for this desire to be of service.[29]

By the latter part of the 1960s some of the structure for the college's new independent identity had been erected; other parts were still in the blueprint stage. Excellence was the theme: "to develop self-educating Christian persons dedicated to the discovery of truth and the service of others." To achieve such a goal involved efforts on many fronts, not the least of which was that of finance. Support from

the Benedictine order in money and personnel had been extremely generous in the past, but could it go on indefinitely? The endowment of slightly over $200,000 in 1968 was only a drop in the bucket. In earlier years, when the lay teacher was an exception, recruitment and paying of faculty had posed fewer problems than they did in 1968 when the instructional staff of forty-six included seventeen lay persons. To operate efficiently would mean reducing the large number of classes which existed and at least doubling the enrollment; this would bring in more money, but it would require more faculty and facilities. Co-operation with other institutions would help solve the financial problem, but St. Benedict's would also have to strive harder on its own.[30]

In 1966–67 educational income amounted to roughly $777,500, but expenditures came to more than $1,000,000. The deficit was made up by a profit of some $40,000 on auxiliary enterprises and the contributed services of the sisters computed at a little over $262,000. As late as 1960–61 the annual educational cost per student had been $1,060, but by 1966–67 the amount was up to $2,052 and still rising. Under the circumstances the administration had no choice but to raise tuition and fees. In the fall of 1966 these charges were approximately $1,840 — lower than those at many institutions, yet high for numerous potential students at St. Benedict's. Consequently the sum allotted for student aid had to be increased. National Defense Education Act loans and those secured through the United States Aid Funds Loan Program alleviated but by no means solved the problem. If the college were to move into the future with survival assured, it would need additional capital.[31]

Two possible methods of securing the funds needed were a financial campaign and a government loan. Both were tried. After some investigation, a professional firm was engaged in May, 1966, to conduct a drive for money. Response was encouraging; nearly $90,000 was raised within two years, but at least $60,000 more was needed. Early in 1967 applications for a federal loan to finance construction of a new wing to Mary Hall were filed unsuccessfully. A third attempt fared better when the department of housing and urban development in June, 1968, approved a $1,085,000 loan. This money made possible the erection of Corona Hall, a 185-bed residence unit completed in November, 1969.[32]

To the leaders at St. Benedict's, however, the best long-range solution to the problems confronting the college seemed to lie in greater co-operation with St. John's. A proposal therefore was submitted to the Hill Family Foundation for money to support a thoroughgoing study of the potential such a course of action would provide. Forthcoming in September, 1967, was a grant of $40,200. To make the study a joint committee was appointed and outside consultants retained. Few if any stones were left unturned. Every phase of operations on each campus was scrutinized, reactions of students and faculty were surveyed, and colleges which had engaged in co-operative ventures in Minnesota and elsewhere were visited. After all of this was completed, a panel of well-known educators was employed to react to the recommendations of the consultants. The final outcome — the consultants' recommendation, supported by the panel and the joint committee — called for far-reaching actions. Both institutions should merge into a "new corporate entity" and do so quickly. To facilitate this development, a co-ordinator should be appointed and be given status equal to the two presidents.[33]

After studying the report separately, the boards of St. Benedict's and St. John's met jointly on July 12, 1968, to consider the recommendation. Out of this meeting came a declaration of "the desirability of a merger" and the boards' decision to hire a co-ordinator for the task. As a result, all academic departments and some administrative services were unified. The colleges received a second Hill Family Foundation grant of $19,200 in April, 1972, for the study of administrative services and the development of a model for the two schools' co-operation. By 1970, 1,000 of the 2,300 jointly enrolled students shared academic time on both campuses, and the figures were rising.[34]

Other events, too, in 1967–68 constituted significant landmarks at St. Benedict. For one thing, the board of trustees exercised its recent option by electing two laymen to its membership — the first such individuals to serve on that body in its history. Then with the resignation of Sister Mary Grell as president at the close of the academic year, another innovation followed. Beginning on July 1, 1968, the presidency would be held by Dr. Stanley J. Idzerda, the first layman and the first man to head the college since its founding. A native of New York City, the new president had earned bachelor's degrees at Notre Dame and at Baldwin-Wallace College in Ohio. His M.A. and Ph.D. had been conferred by Western Reserve University. With broad experience in teaching, administration, and consulting, he was well qualified to bring a new perspective to the campus and to direct the institution as it moved along unfamiliar paths in the search for ways of providing more effective service in an evolving and baffling world.[35]

After three busy years in office, President Idzerda, by no means blind to problems and uncertainties, could find ample cause for satisfaction. Full-time enrollment almost doubled from 1968, the year he took office, to the fall of 1971, when the college enrolled 896 students, a 25 per cent increase over the previous year and the largest increase experienced by any of the Minnesota colleges. Of the total 589 students in 1970, 523 undergraduates had come from Minnesota; its nearest rival was North Dakota which had sent 34 enrollees. In general these young women took a greater interest in the contemporary issues of war, environmental pollution, civil rights, and poverty than in traditional college organizations. There was even support for coed dormitories. Yet the campus remained quiet. There was no pressure for a cessation of classes in the turbulent May of 1970, despite strong feelings regarding the Vietnam War. The climate at St. Benedict remained one of concern and of calm. Manifestations took the form of Masses and discussions, not conflict and destruction.[36]

The full-time faculty in 1970 consisted of fifty-three teachers, thirty-six of them sisters. There were also eight part-time teachers, six of them religious. Twenty-one of the men and women, or 35 per cent, possessed earned doctorates. There was need to improve the system of academic governance, but there was plenty of evidence that members of the instructional staff were devoted to their calling, hard working, and actively engaged in improving their competence in their academic disciplines. Particularly impressive were the qualities of mind, the dedication, and the excellent preparation possessed by the sisters on the staff who gave the institution its special Benedictine character. In its turn the college was doing its best to increase salaries (the average for full professors in 1970 was $14,400) and raise the level of fringe benefits.[37]

Gains were also being made in the instructional program. The long-discussed nursing course leading to a baccalaureate degree became a reality in the fall of 1969. The sequence was not fully delineated, but twenty-four students registered in recommended classes and became the vanguard in the new venture, which will graduate its first class in 1973. A permanent chairman for the department arrived in August, 1970. Several months earlier, certain longer-established elements of the curriculum had won heartening endorsement. NCATE had reviewed St. Benedict's teacher education program in November, 1969, and had given it full accreditation; the following April the Minnesota Department of Education had approved the college's home economics department for vocational consumer-homemaking teacher certification. And to add to the general satisfaction, the North Central Association after a regular ten-year review visit in March, 1970, had accorded continued accreditation to St. Benedict's whole operation. The basic or integrated studies program completed its third year in 1970 and its first offering for junior students. Although some faculty participants viewed this interdisciplinary sequence with a lack of enthusiasm, 95 per cent of the students who had taken it all three years regarded it as worth while. During the interim term in January, twenty-three courses were taught, three of them off campus; 417 students were then in residence, 70 of whom were engaged in independent study. Another 144 undergraduates spent the month in classes or in independent work away from St. Benedict.[38]

Between August, 1969, and May, 1970, baccalaureate degrees had been conferred on 153 students. These graduates had concentrated in twenty different fields (seven women had done so in two disciplines), but elementary education with seventy-five majors had been by far the most popular selection. English with eleven majors and art with nine ran a poor second and third. Such fields as Spanish, psychology, and nutrition science had only recently contributed to St. Benedict's list of majors. At the regular May commencement exercise, ninety-nine lay students and fifteen sisters had received degrees. No report was available on the occupations of twenty-one of these graduates, but fifty-five of the group entered teaching in the fall and seventeen others planned to do so. St. Benedict and Concordia of Moorhead achieved the highest teacher placement rates in the state in this period with nearly 95 per cent of their graduates obtaining jobs.[39]

In April, 1970, President Idzerda called "time out" and a thirteen-member master planning committee composed of college administrators, a trustee, a faculty member, and a student was formed. The committee in turn established task forces that studied specific areas. The following year the committee completed its report on a five-year plan entitled *Directions for the Future*. It concluded that the college should continue to offer a liberal, Christian, Catholic and Benedictine education but one that emphasizes family, community, and the quality of human life.[40]

In many ways the most worrisome of President Idzerda's problems in 1970 was the one he shared with all of his academic peers, that of finances. For 1969–70 the college's current fund revenue had come to $2,119,000, of which student fees had provided almost $798,000 and the contributed services of the religious $422,000. Expenditures, however, had amounted to $2,190,000. The cost of instruction had been slightly over $639,000 and the expense of operating the auxiliary enterprises in excess of $494,000. So there had been a deficit for the year of about $70,000. With increased full-time enrollment rising from 786 in 1970 to 996 in 1971 and 1,197 in 1972, the college moved well into the black. Revenue for 1971–72 was about $3,500,000. To support its educational plans for the 1970s the college launched a capital "Concern for the Quality of Human Life" campaign in 1971 to raise $4,785,000 over a five-year period.[41]

As the 1970s began, the college was embarked upon ambitious long-range plans and a $2,000,000 construction program to provide student alternatives in campus living, other facilities, and a more diversified curriculum subject to continuous review. In 1973 St. Benedict's and St. John's continue to conduct a fully co-operative academic and social exchange program with each college retaining its individual identity. As the College of St. Benedict plans its course and defines its objectives for the vastly enlarged enrollment on campus in the 1970s, it will continue to draw strength from its ancient Benedictine tradition of modesty, tolerance, gratitude, patience, openness to diversity, humility, and a desire to serve others. Woven into the fabric of the college and modified and tested by the years, this strong tradition has continuing meaning and special relevance for the twentieth century.[42]

39 ST. MARY'S COLLEGE

Responsibility, Concern, And Community

REGULAR ENROLLMENT AT ST. MARY'S in the spring of 1941 approximated 325, of whom 127 were freshmen; another two dozen young men from the Civilian Conservation Corps in Winona were taking special evening classes in rhetoric, composition, and algebra. Since September, 1939, a Civilian Pilot Training program had also been in operation. Its ground courses were taught on the campus, but flight training was given at a local service operated by alumnus Max A. Conrad — later famous as the "Flying Grandfather." Expenses were borne by the federal government, and participants were selected by St. Mary's, which allowed four semester hours credit for completion of the advanced course. Life at the college still went on much as it had in past years. In May, 1941, degrees were conferred on thirty-nine graduates, twelve of whom were scholastics.[1]

The following October witnessed the first large addition to the college property since its establishment in 1913. Expansion had become imperative because the scholastics were outgrowing their quarters in La Salle Hall, the bishop's former residence. Since there were only ten people at the nearby county poor farm, the Winona County board of commissioners was willing to accept St. Mary's offer to purchase it. Acquired for about $22,000 were nearly forty acres of land, some buildings, livestock, furniture, and miscellaneous farm equipment. In December, 1941, Bishop John H. Peschges of Crookston, the school's former president, presided over the dedication of the main structure, christened St. Joseph's Hall, as a home for the scholastics.[2]

By then the country had been thrown into World War II, and the future of the college looked bleak. Enrollment held up well until May, 1942, when fifty-two men received degrees, but then change became the order of the day. The president, Brother Leopold Julian Dodd, was appointed to a second term as visitor of the St. Louis district to succeed Brother Landrick Jerome (Eugene J. Foy). The latter then became president of St. Mary's. The holder of advanced degrees from Chicago and DePaul universities, Brother Jerome guided the institution successfully through a trying period, one of his notable achievements being the acquisition in 1943 of a navy V-12 unit for the college. Unfortunately illness led to his hospitalization a year after assuming the presidency and to his death in 1944.[3]

The first contingent of potential naval officers took up residence in Heffron Hall in July, 1943. The declining number of civilian men lived on the third and fourth floors of St. Mary's Hall. Two years later in August, 1945, when a farewell dinner marked the end of the navy program, over six hundred trainees had been assigned to the college's V-12 unit. Their average stay on campus had been about eight months. To accommodate these cadets the two-semester calendar had been replaced by trimesters beginning about the first of July, November, and March. The program had added color and life to the college, and the government dollars had strengthened its shaky financial structure. According to navy sources, the V-12 unit on Terrace Heights ranked second among all such organizations in participating colleges, a credit to the ability and concern of the brothers.[4]

The task of administering the military program had devolved upon Brother Joel Stanislaus Nelson, a Ph.D. whose field was classical languages. Named acting president in October, 1943, he was given the title in his own right in March, 1944. He would serve until 1950. Despite the existence of war, considerable thought was given to the course St. Mary's would follow when peace returned. The main theme of the blueprint was expansion. Its details, divulged by Brother Joel at the farewell dinner for the V-12 unit in 1945, envisioned a student body of 1,000 men and a $1,400,000 building program comprising a dormitory, an auditorium, a dining hall, and a chapel to which the scholasticate and the brothers' home would be attached. Work would start when labor and materials became available. The ambitious undertaking would come to pass, but realization would take longer than expected.[5]

With the departure of the V-12 contingent, enrollment dropped, but the three-term schedule was maintained for several months. Students were permitted to enroll at any time and to take special classes or refresher work. In November, 1945, 195 men, including 22 veterans, were in attendance. The following June, 32 graduates, of whom 20 were brothers, received degrees. During the war, practically all degree recipients had been members of the Christian Brothers order. By the fall of 1947 enrollment reached a peak of about 490 men, over 50 per cent of them veterans. Two years later the percentage of veterans was down to 20, but total registration approximated 500. Brothers numbered slightly over 50. On the faculty were two dozen brothers, four priests, and several laymen. At commencement in 1949 degrees were awarded to 86 students; 11 received a B.A., 34 earned a B.S. in natural science, and 41 a B.S. in social science.[6]

A fund drive had been going reasonably well, but it had not been possible to undertake the announced building program. In 1947 a former officers' club had been moved from Sioux City, Iowa, and transformed into a student union. That same fall some federal housing units (named Rooney and Ditter halls for Marians killed in the war) had been relocated as residences for forty-eight students. A score of married veterans had to find quarters in Winona. A new addition to the dining hall eased some pressures, but it was not ready for use until January, 1949. Shortly thereafter ground was at last broken for the enlargement of St. Joseph's Hall outlined nearly four years earlier. Included in the new space were dormitory, study, and dining facilities and a chapel. The scholasticate, La Salle Hall, was then remodeled as a dormitory for lay students.[7]

Crowded conditions in no way dampened student enthusiasm. A veterans' club, organized in 1945, by the following spring had 140 members — or over half the student body. The *Redman*, the first yearbook in St. Mary's history, appeared a number of months later. The glee club, the band, and the choir performed periodically and combined their talents for annual Christmas concerts. When female voices were required in a production such as *The Mikado*, women from the nearby College of Saint Teresa obliged. Redmen *Revels*, a mélange of skits, solos, chorus and instrumental numbers, was a much-anticipated diversion each autumn. Intercollegiate events once more found a place in the calendar. At the student government workshop in 1950, for example, over a hundred delegates from more than forty institutions gathered on St. Mary's campus.[8]

Throughout its history the college had offered preseminary courses in Latin, Greek, and philosophy, and by mid-1948 slightly over a hundred priests had received part of their training there. St. Mary's, however, had not been canonically erected as a seminary, a condition Bishop Leo Binz, with the co-operation of the Christian Brothers, soon changed. On July 16, 1948, he established the Immaculate Heart of Mary Seminary as a diocesan institute within the framework of the college. There being an acute shortage of priests, it was hoped that the new institution would foster vocations which might otherwise be lost. The future clergy would major in philosophy and minor in education and Latin; the curriculum would embrace the last two years of a minor and the first two years of a seminary major.[9]

The twenty-four seminarians who initiated the new venture in the fall of 1948 lived on the fourth floor of St. Mary's Hall. One of them became the first seminarian to graduate from St. Mary's in May, 1949; his ordination occurred four years later. In mid-1950 Bishop Binz laid the cornerstone for Kelly Hall, a separate, three-story seminary building for about sixty students and professors, which included a chapel dedicated to the patron of parish priests, Saint John Vianney. The Winona diocese paid the total cost of $250,000. A decade later an annex was added for thirty-two seminarians and four priests named St. Leo Hall in honor of Pope Leo I, the patron of Bishop Binz. Although its enrollment had never been large (40 students in 1950 and 85 in 1961), the seminary by 1969 had graduated 130 men who later were ordained to the priesthood.[10]

In January, 1950, a change took place in the college's top administration. Brother Joel was given a different assignment out of the state, and Brother J. Ambrose Groble succeeded him at St. Mary's. A graduate of DePaul University with an M.S. from the University of Minnesota, the new executive had been on campus since 1941 as an English professor and head of the department of education; from 1944 on he had served also as college vice president. His administration would extend to mid-1956.[11]

A freshman class of 254 men, the largest up to that time, greeted Brother Ambrose in the fall of 1950. Total enrollment was about 540; lay undergraduates numbered 444 of whom 386 were dormitory dwellers and 58 commuters. There were 55 scholastics plus 40 seminarians. After 1950 St. Mary's experienced the decline in student attendance which was country-wide. In its effort to maintain enrollment levels, the college admitted students whose academic aptitudes were borderline. The result was unhappy; by the end of the second semester in 1951–52 freshman attrition had reached an eye-opening 45 per cent. As late as 1954 St. Mary's was not overwhelmed by applications, and nearly 30 per cent of that fall's freshmen had been in the lower half of their high school classes. By 1956, however, enrollment was up to 655, and the students' intellectual caliber had also improved.[12]

Even in the early 1950s the physical plant had been inadequate. The library had been overcrowded, and another dormitory, a science laboratory, and a classroom building had been needed. Consequently Brother Ambrose sought the assistance of alumni and civic leaders in Winona; in December, 1952, he announced the outcome: St. Mary's would start construction of $1,225,000 worth of new buildings. The initial project would be a $125,000 dormitory for sixty men, the first of five residence halls, and the second unit would be a $350,000 science building. The latter would be financed by a drive for funds, the dormitory by long-term loans. It was hoped that additional help would come from annual giving by alumni to what was designated as the "Christ the Teacher Living Endowment." A third project would be the library. This program, unlike the one announced in 1945, got off to a good start.[13]

Work on the one-story dormitory began in March, 1953. It soon became apparent that its cost without furnishings would be about $139,000, so the European headquarters of the Christian Brothers authorized the negotiation of a $150,000 bank loan to cover the outlay. The completed residence, occupied in the autumn of 1953, was christened Aquinas Hall after the patron saint of Catholic colleges and universities.[14]

The 1953 fund drive in Winona raised about $100,000, slightly less than one-third of expectations. Nevertheless ground breaking for the science building took place in September, 1954. Construction at first was slow, and a shortage of money made necessary the deletion of a greenhouse and a lecture auditorium from the plans. Part of the facility went into use early in 1956. Fully completed that fall the three-story $540,000 hall provided excellent quarters for the departments of chemistry, biology, and physics. For almost a decade the building was known simply as Science Hall, but in 1965 it was named in memory of Dr. John J. Hoffman, the college's long-time chemistry professor, who had died the previous year.[15]

On the academic front major sequences in 1950 had been offered in only eight departments — biology, chemistry, classical languages, economics, English, history, mathematics, and philosophy. During Brother Ambrose's first year in office, a major in physics and minors in religion, music, and speech, drama, and radio were approved. Then after much study a department of fine arts combining art and music was established in the fall of 1953. At the same time general education courses in the natural sciences, social sciences, and humanities were introduced. Toward the latter part of Brother Ambrose's term, offerings in sociology, psychology, and political science were increased, and each discipline was raised to the status of a minor department. Meanwhile, three-two programs in engineering had been fashioned with Marquette University in Milwaukee, Illinois Institute of Technology in Chicago, and Notre Dame. A similar arrangement in law was effected with DePaul University.[16]

While chairman of the education department, Brother Ambrose had developed a master's program for teachers, and in the summer of 1950 his plan was at last instituted. Calling for six courses in academic fields and four in education, the sequence led to a master's degree through summer session study. On May 29, 1955, nine brothers constituted the first group to be awarded M.A.s by St. Mary's. A year later the graduate program was accorded provisional accreditation by the North Central Association; full endorsement was given in 1960. Work leading to a master's in educational administration was introduced in 1961. But despite these offerings, St. Mary's remained essentially an undergraduate institution committed to the liberal arts.[17]

A determining factor in curriculum building is, of course, the availability of qualified faculty. The teaching staff of 1950 consisted of thirty-one brothers, three priests, and six laymen. Several of these men had been long-time professors at St. Mary's, well known in educational circles and highly capable in the classroom and the laboratory; ten held earned doctorates. The faculty as a whole, however, needed to be upgraded and professionalized. Brother Ambrose noted in 1951 that more teachers with advanced degrees were especially needed in physics, history, social science, fine arts, and library science. Two years later he pointed out that the instructional staff had not done much foreign study or tried very hard to win fellowships and grants at home. By the end of his administration the president had made progress in improving the situation; annual workshops were begun in the fall of 1952, and a comprehensive two-year self-study in preparation for a North Central visit was started a year later. Nevertheless there was still a shortage of teachers, and good lay people were difficult to recruit.[18]

Brother Ambrose was assigned to the Christian Brothers College, a high school level institution in St. Louis, in the summer of 1956, and Brother I. Basil Rothweiler, a 1938 graduate of St. Mary's, was appointed to succeed him. The possessor of a master's degree from St. Louis University, Brother Basil had been dean of men at St. Mary's between 1943 and 1947. Since 1950 he had served as director of De La Salle High School in Chicago, where enrollment had soared 40 per cent to over 1,400 during his tenure. In his new position he would preside over a period of notable expansion at the college.[19]

Enrollment his first year reached 699 — 124 seniors, 138 juniors, 165 sophomores, 261 freshmen, and 11 specials. The 1956 summer session registration totaled 256. From then on the size of the student body moved steadily upward; by the fall of 1961 it was well over a thousand — 774 lay boarders, 56 commuters, 82 scholastics, 110 seminarians, and 65 graduate students. There were also 66 young men in the new Christian Brothers novitiate on campus. Illinois continued to provide the largest proportion of students, and Minnesota was in second place. There was also a contingent of undergraduates from foreign lands.[20]

Rising enrollment necessitated further plant expansion. Early in 1957 a forty-year federal loan to finance the construction of a faculty residence and a dormitory for lay students was approved; ground for both structures was broken in August. Students moved into the new two-story dormitory after Easter vacation in 1958. Its accommodations for 120 men then permitted St. Mary's to plan for an enrollment of 850. Bishop Edward A. Fitzgerald dedicated the two buildings (as yet unnamed) in July, 1958. A year later the St. Louis provincial announced that the residence for students would be called St. Edward's Hall, that for faculty brothers De La Salle Hall. The old bishop's home of that name was redesignated Cotter Hall.[21]

When these projects were completed, contracts were let for St. Thomas More Chapel, the college's seventh building since 1950. It represented the culmination of a drive (which had begun in the 1940s and then bogged down) and the efforts of countless alumni and friends. Bishop Fitzgerald selected the chapel's name and spearheaded a new campaign by promising to underwrite the architect's fee, plus $50,000. The St. Louis headquarters of the order also pledged $50,000. Costing in all about $250,000, the attractive building with seating for 1,000 people was finished in time to provide the setting for baccalaureate services on May 31, 1959.[22]

During the preceding decade, St. Mary's had spent $2,500,000 on plant improvement, yet no letup in construction was in sight. On January 1, 1960, Brother Basil announced a ten-year $4,725,000 development program. Its salient features were a library — books were spread over five floors of St. Mary's Hall — two dormitories, a student center, and a lecture hall for the science building. The first of these projects to be initiated was one of the proposed dormitories christened Benilde Hall. With housing for 122 men, it was occupied in the fall of 1961. Its cost of $350,000 was financed through a forty-year federal loan.[23]

Bids for the new library were opened in January, 1961; the finished structure was dedicated with impressive ceremonies in February, 1962. A three-story building of reinforced concrete, faced with St. Mary's familiar Winona travertine, it contained seating for four hundred persons, shelving for 200,000 volumes, and over sixty student and faculty study carrels. Friends and alumni had contributed the $457,000 needed to pay the bills; of this total the Winona diocese had given $350,000 and local business interests had subscribed $100,000. Former book space was then transformed into five classrooms and twenty-two offices. In February, 1963, at the third annual Founder's Day convocation it was announced that the long-desired addition to the campus would be named Fitzgerald Library in honor of the bishop of the Winona diocese.[24]

Meanwhile other developments had produced further alterations in the campus landscape. The Christian Brothers St. Louis district grew rapidly after World War II, and so plans were drawn to divide it and to establish a Winona district covering Minnesota, Wisconsin, the Dakotas, Upper Michigan, and northern Iowa. In preparation for the new jurisdiction, it was decided to erect a novitiate at St. Mary's where young men would spend fourteen months before moving on to the scholasticate,

St. Joseph's Hall, and attendance at the college. Placed in operation in September, 1961, the $600,000 building paid for by the order became a combined dormitory and academic facility for St. Mary's in 1968. It was named St. Yon Hall for a martyred disciple of the first bishop of Paris in the third century. Another campus structure stemmed from permission given by Bishop Fitzgerald to the Congregation of the Sacred Hearts of Jesus and Mary to establish a minor seminary at the college. This enterprise had been initiated in the autumn of 1959, when fourteen seminarians and a priest had moved into the institution's former farmhouse. Within three years the congregation built the $275,000 modern, self-contained Damien Hall providing quarters for forty-five seminarians and six priests.[25]

One other building project, a student center, had its inception before Brother Basil left St. Mary's in 1963 to become provincial of the new Winona district of the Christian Brothers. "Sole emphasis" during the college's golden jubilee year of 1962–63, it was decided, should be on the creation of a student activities center. The project received encouraging support from the Frank J. Lewis Foundation of Chicago, which offered $50,000 if St. Mary's would raise another $150,000 by June 30, 1963. Alumni and others redeemed the gift with contributions of $180,500. Ground then was broken for a $700,000 gymnasium, the initial section of the center, which for the first time in St. Mary's history would make possible a co-ordinated, unified indoor and outdoor athletic program.[26]

Although St. Mary's had never been wealthy and had always kept student charges as low as possible, the college had generally been able to operate in the black. Major help, of course, had come from the contributed services of the brothers and priests, but as the lay staff grew, these services declined proportionately. In 1957–58 they were listed at $177,600 or 32 per cent of general college income; in 1962–63 they were $179,700 or 20 per cent of income. Annual tuition in the fall of 1957 had been $500; five years later it was $700, but costs had gone up even faster, and growing reliance therefore had to be placed on annual outside giving. In 1958 the current budget had been $465,000; in 1962 it was $1,815,000, of which $81,700 went for scholarships, $49,000 for student work contracts, and $46,700 for loans. Total college income that year exceeded $2,000,000, and gifts including contributed services amounted to $419,000.[27]

No fundamental curriculum changes occurred while Brother Basil was president, but new techniques were adopted, courses were added, con-

tent was expanded, and groundwork was laid for later developments. Brother Basil and Sister Camille of Saint Teresa as well as the deans of the two colleges met frequently to survey past co-operation and to explore possibilities for increasing it. The college also experimented with educational television, but it aroused little faculty enthusiasm. More successful was a course in solid state physics for International Business Machines (IBM) employees in Rochester in 1958, followed in 1960 by work in mathematics. These led, at the company's request, to the fashioning by St. Mary's of a short-lived master's sequence in both fields. Of the 194 students in the college's graduate program in 1961, 44 were IBM employees and 130 were Christian Brothers; the program was phased out a few years later.[28]

Despite the absence of major curriculum changes, a faculty committee between 1958 and 1961 engaged in the most thorough study of course offerings that had been made at St. Mary's in a quarter of a century. Each teacher was asked to participate in departmental discussions, and each department in turn met with the committee. In these ways it was hoped that every instructor would gain an over-all perspective and that the cause of liberal education would thereby be well served. In this same period honors programs, advanced placement, and exemption from requirements testified to the rising level of preparation of incoming students. All of them, however, still had to take at least fourteen semester hours in religion and twelve in philosophy, among other requirements. The most popular major fields in the early 1960s were biology, business administration, chemistry, English, mathematics, and philosophy. There were also divisional majors, mainly for prospective teachers.[29]

When Brother Basil assumed the presidency in 1956, St. Mary's needed more faculty in chemistry, education, and business administration; most of the current staff had been so burdened that they had no time for writing and research. About a dozen laymen were then teaching and their salary scale was low; the average for a full professor was $5,800 a year. The grant of $180,000 for endowment made by the Ford Foundation in 1956–57 had helped somewhat, but when Brother Basil left office in 1963, the average professorial pay was only $8,275. Still there had been bright spots. Even the provision of more office space in the wake of plant expansion had helped. Two brothers had been enabled to do fifteen months of graduate study in chemistry and physics at Notre Dame by winning fellowships from the National Science Foundation. The same source had provided funds for Brother Charles Severin's summer field course in biology, and Brother George Pahl's research had been supported by the American Cancer Society and the National Institutes of Health. These and other examples had a leavening influence on the entire faculty.[30]

Appointed to succeed Brother Basil was Brother Josephus Gregory Robertson, who took office in September, 1963. For three years following his graduation from St. Mary's in 1939, he had taught in a high school in Chicago, where in 1942 he had received an M.S. degree from Loyola University. For a decade thereafter he had served at St. Mary's, the latter half of the period as director of the scholasticate. Then followed ten years as director of the novitiate, first in Glencoe, Missouri, and later in Winona. In his new capacity he was head of the community of faculty brothers as well as of the college.[31]

Although enrollment leveled off during Brother Gregory's administration, he had to devote part of his time to building projects. Work on the new gymnasium began in December, 1963, and the first basketball game was played there with old rival St. Thomas on February 11, 1965. A loan from a St. Paul bank had made the structure possible. The next summer the old gymnasium was converted into dormitory space for 120 men. Named Skemp Hall, in honor of Thomas H. Skemp, the college's successful coach of the 1920s and other members of his family, the converted facility was financed by a federal loan of $360,000. Meanwhile the trustees had approved completion of the student center and the eventual renovation of St. Mary's Hall as a classroom and administration building. A federal loan of $500,000 was secured in the summer of 1968, but at least $1,000,000 more was needed and not yet in sight. Thus the first phase of a capital gifts campaign — "Reach Out For St. Mary's" — was initiated that June. Since people in the area would be permitted to use the center, an unusual drive was undertaken in Winona in conjunction with the city YMCA. It secured $703,000, of which $308,000 went toward the cost of the college center.[32]

Ground breaking for the $1,800,000 three-story complex took place in June, 1968. By the fall of 1969 the attractive twin to the gymnasium was finished and in use. Containing an array of facilities — lounges, offices, post office, a dining room with seating for 750 people, meeting areas — it immediately became "the focal point of campus activity," a perfect setting for relaxation and games or more serious pursuits, such as lectures, conferences, and concerts. It also provided southeastern Minnesota with its largest convention center, available to outside groups when the college was not in session.[33]

In academic affairs a modified calendar and a revised curriculum were introduced in 1965 as a result of a committee report and faculty action. The semester system was retained, but the first term was shortened so that it ended before the Christmas holidays. Changes were made in general education requirements, and student course loads were reduced. Emphasis henceforth would be on study in depth, on greater student independence, and on critical thinking. Shortly thereafter psychology and political science joined the circle of departments offering major sequences. Periodically new courses were initiated utilizing the computer or involving team teaching by faculty from several different disciplines. St. Mary's, however, was conservative in its approach to innovation in higher education.[34]

Early in his presidency, Brother Gregory turned his attention to strengthening co-ordination with Saint Teresa's and to increasing co-operation with Winona State College. Student exchanges between St. Mary's and Saint Teresa's began on a limited scale in the fall of 1964, as did discussions regarding similar reciprocity among faculty. By 1966 a half dozen professors from Terrace Heights were teaching at Saint Teresa's, and Winona State had joined the student exchange program. Two years later the class schedules and calendars of the two Catholic colleges were synchronized in order to facilitate the co-operative endeavor; as a result 220 Marians were enrolled in classes at Saint Teresa's, and 121 women were taking work at St. Mary's in 1968. While co-operation offered great opportunities for expanded service, it also posed problems. One of these followed a decision by Saint Teresa and Winona State early in 1970 to co-ordinate their calendars. Since St. Mary's faculty decided to retain the two-semester system, student exchanges were considerably inhibited until starting dates were altered; in the fall of 1970 they totaled only thirty-one men and ten women. The future of these inter-college programs remains an unanswered question.[35]

Having women in classes on an exchange basis became a prelude to the next stage in St. Mary's evolution. After careful thought and research, the trustees in December, 1968, voted to admit women to the college as regular undergraduates beginning in the fall of 1969. This decision stemmed largely from a belief in the intrinsic value of coeducation coupled with the harsh fact that male applications for admission had dropped in 1968. The change to coeducation, it was hoped, would enlarge the student recruitment pool, strengthen the college academically and financially, and add a valuable new dimension to campus life. Women had been admitted to St. Mary's graduate program since the early 1950s. Moreover, the shift was attuned to the trend of the times. Of all Catholic men's colleges in the country in 1958, one-third became coeducational during the succeeding decade. The third floor of Skemp Hall was prepared to receive the coeds, and a woman was employed as associate dean of students. St. Mary's did not intend, however, to decrease the exchange with Saint Teresa's or to add such special programs as nursing or elementary education which have strong appeal for women. The new era began when twenty-nine women enrolled at St. Mary's in the fall of 1969.[36]

Other trends — the increasing secularization of society and the growing impact of the federal government — were also clearly evidenced during Brother Gregory's tenure. As late as 1968 key positions at St. Mary's were still held by Christian Brothers, but they and the priests were outnumbered on the teaching staff forty-three to sixteen by lay persons. That year an *ad hoc* steering committee of teachers and students evolved a constitution and by-laws for the faculty, which formed the main business of the October workshop and later gained trustee approval. For the first time laymen were appointed to the posts of vice president for development and public relations, vice president for student personnel, and director of admissions. At the top level the trustees revised St. Mary's articles of incorporation in 1969, leaving Christian Brothers in control of at least one-third of the enlarged board's seats, but conferring broader policy-making powers to lay members. The arm of government could be observed mainly through grants supporting research and teachers' institutes; over $200,000 went to three science departments and to the English department for these purposes in 1963–64 alone. Three years later a renewable government grant of $45,000 permitted St. Mary's to employ six new teachers, one each in history and economics and two in both sociology and political science, thereby enabling these disciplines to offer major sequences.[37]

The growth of secularism was understandably disturbing to many friends of the college. Equally upsetting was the emergence in the 1960s of a new kind of student — a highly vocal, active, questioning student who challenged established mores and traditions ranging from dress codes to international policy. There was a noticeable decline in the number of religious clubs, mounting criticism of

rules, practices, and tenets, and the virtual extinction of the hall rosary. A graduate of the 1950s declared in 1967, "If the students of today possess strong ties, other than purely personal ones, they are difficult to discern." Brother Gregory, however, noted that such undergraduates were a minority and that to "encourage an environment of complaisant conformity" could lead only to intellectual sterility. St. Mary's was a lively place where the majority of students showed a deepening sense of social concern and a desire for involvement, but where some of the excesses of sex, drugs, and the drop-out subculture seemed largely absent.[38]

In the fall of 1968 Brother Gregory submitted his resignation to take effect at the end of the academic year. His successor under the college's articles of incorporation had to be a Christian Brother; a search committee which included a student and an alumnus was assigned the task of suggesting three choices to the trustees, who would make the final selection. Brother George Pahl, one of the college's most distinguished faculty members, received the appointment on June 15, 1969. A 1936 graduate of the college and a biology teacher at St. Mary's since 1942 who was well known for his cancer research and his interest in limnology, Brother George held an M.S. from DePaul and a Ph.D. from Notre Dame. Between 1962 and 1969 he had directed summer institutes at the college for high school biology teachers. A believer in "the principle of subsidiarity" and a strong supporter of co-operation with Saint Teresa's, he hoped to evolve for St. Mary's "a long range, flexible blueprint for the future . . . wherein adaptive renewal is the key word."[39]

During Brother George's initial autumn in office, full-time undergraduate enrollment, including St. Mary's first regular coeds, approximated 970. Of these 107 were seminarians — 54 diocesan, 34 Congregation of the Sacred Hearts, and 19 scholastics of the Christian Brothers. The last had declined steadily in numbers since 1961, when 93 future brothers had been in attendance. Freshmen in 1969 totaled 236, seniors 256; comparable figures a decade earlier had been 325 and 132, respectively. In the interval, therefore, despite a considerable decrease in the size of the entering class, a much better balanced student body had been attained. About one-half of the freshmen at the later date had ranked in the top 50 per cent of their high school classes; less than one-fifth had attended public, rather than private, secondary schools. In the fall of 1970 thanks to the registration of 81 freshman women, the beginning class contained slightly over

300 members, an increase of 50 per cent in two years. Total enrollment remained at about 970, but the contingent of coeds had risen to 128, suggesting that the college had been wise to alter its all-male nature. Illinois contributed 51 per cent of the student body, Minnesota 28 per cent, and Iowa and Wisconsin combined 9 per cent. Summer school enrollments composed mainly of graduate students had varied from 485 in 1965 to 238 two years later.[40]

The faculty in 1970 was composed of 62 full- and 10 part-time teachers; only 13 of the former were Christian Brothers — a distinct contrast to the pattern in 1957 when 30 brothers constituted more than 61 per cent of the instructional staff. Just over one-third of the entire faculty possessed earned doctorates. Salary scales had risen appreciably, placing the range for full professors in 1970 between $13,300 and $19,800. There had also been improvements in faculty fringe benefits.[41]

Instruction was provided in nineteen academic departments; those offering the largest number of credits included English, psychology, education, theology, and business administration. The junior member of the community was fine arts, which had its inception in the fall of 1970. Quarters for the newcomer had been created by remodeling St. Joseph's Hall, the former scholasticate. Starting with a staff of two brothers and courses in music, painting, drawing, and ceramics, hope was high for future expansion. The majors most frequently being pursued by seniors in 1970–71 were English 46, political science 35, business administration 33, psychology 32, and history 27. Other fields lagged far behind, though sizable shifts in student interests reflected in declines in economics and sociology, for example, had occurred in a relatively short period of time. On the graduate level work leading either to the master of science or to the master of arts for teachers was offered; the latter could be secured in nine fields, but biology led in popularity by a wide margin. All in all, evolution rather than

revolution had characterized recent academic developments. The main thrust had been in the direction of injecting greater flexibility into student schedules through more independent study, some pass-fail grading options, individualized majors, a freshman seminar program, and expanded counseling services.[42]

St. Mary's was subjected to the same financial pressures felt throughout all of higher education: mounting costs and constant search for revenue. Between 1966 and 1968 total expenditures per credit offered had risen from $1,350 to $1,740, and they had continued on an upward course thereafter. The college's income in 1966–67 had been $2,312,000; in 1969–70 it was $2,968,000. Of this amount gifts of the Christian Brothers accounted for $168,500, tuition and fees for $1,260,000, and auxiliary enterprises for $817,000. Thus student payments provided more than three-quarters of total income. Tuition in 1969–70 was $1,200; for 1971–72 it was $1,500. How much higher it can go is, of course, a moot question. Expenditures for 1969–70, including $247,600 in scholarships and grants, came to $3,130,000 — leaving a deficit of about $162,000.[43]

The challenges lying ahead cannot be minimized. Not the least of these relate to the declining numbers of Christian Brothers available to staff faculty and administrative posts and to the need for greater income. St. Mary's is not alone in facing these and other problems; neither will it be excluded from whatever measures society takes to perpetuate the lives of its private colleges. With an attractive and up-to-date physical plant, a beautiful setting, six decades of educating a growing body of men — and now women — and with recent broadening of its governing base, St. Mary's is possessed of the sinew necessary both to survive and to continue helping generations of young people "to better understand such terms as 'responsibility,' 'concern,' and 'community.' "[44]

40

COLLEGE OF ST. SCHOLASTICA

The Fruits of Northern Harvests

IN THE FALL OF 1941 more than 450 young women, of whom 137 were freshmen, enrolled at the College of St. Scholastica. Past efforts were coming to fruition and the future seemed to promise continued advance. Then came the sudden trauma of Pearl Harbor. Prayer, sacrifice, stamp and bond sales, and Red Cross activities replaced many traditional extracurricular endeavors. Enrollment decreased slightly at first, but it took a decided upturn in 1944. From then until 1947–48 it remained not far from five hundred. Some lay faculty went into war work, and several of the religious engaged in projects designed to assist in the successful prosecution of the conflict. Sisters Agatha Riehl and Petra Lenta, for example, while at the Institutum Divi Thomae, a graduate school of scientific research in Cincinnati, Ohio, sought new and more effective drugs for the treatment of malaria and dysentery. They returned to the college in 1945, and several months later established a cancer research unit which has done significant work in conjunction with the institutum.[1]

The three-year cadet nursing program was reinstituted in 1944 as a war measure, but St. Mary's Hall proved inadequate to house the new group as well as the regular nursing students. To alleviate this condition the first unit of Our Lady of Victory Hall, subsidized by a federal grant of $80,400, was constructed next to the hospital. Containing dormitory facilities, offices, classrooms, and lounges, the Victory Hall section was formally opened in May, 1945, as a home for the cadet nurses. When the remainder of the four-story brick structure was completed in 1950, all nursing students were transferred to it, and St. Mary's Hall became a convent for sisters working at the hospital.[2]

It was during the war also that the first fifteen-year study of alumnae was compiled, that the graduate record examination to determine the college's strengths and weaknesses was introduced, and that the annual faculty institute first convened. The intent of this last-named activity was to keep teachers and administrators informed of "current trends in higher education." Though a trying period, the war years were by no means unproductive or a time for merely treading water.[3]

With the return of peace the tempo of progress picked up under the leadership of Mother Athanasius Braegelman. A graduate of Catholic University in 1924, she had received her Ph.D. degree from the same institution in 1939. One of three girls from the same family in Richmond, Minnesota, to become Benedictines, she had served as head of the history department at St. Scholastica from 1927 until 1936, and as dean of women from 1940 to 1942. In the latter year she had been elected prioress to succeed Mother Agnes Somers. For twelve years Mother Athanasius would hold this position. Then after a six-year interval, she was reelected to a third term in 1960. Upon completing this assignment in 1966, she was elected Mother President of the whole Congregation of St. Benedict. Between her second and third terms as prioress, the position was held by the distinguished musician and composer, Sister Martina Hughes.[4]

During the early period after the war, the most striking developments on campus were in the curriculum area. There were some minor additions to the physical plant, but in general Mother Agnes' building achievements of 1937–38 had provided facilities which would be adequate for the ensuing quarter of a century. On the other hand, curriculum in a developing college never seems equal to the occasion for long. The fifteen-year study of alumnae had suggested that changes in St. Scholastica's academic offerings were in order. There followed the perennial tinkerings with the schedule which are characteristic in colleges and universities — the addition of a course here, the dropping of one there. But there were also more basic alterations and changes. A philosophy minor had appeared for the first time even before the war ended. Then in 1947 came the creation of major and minor sequences in journalism, a social service department which asked 120 hours of field work of majors, and primary sequences in differential and clinical psychology.[5]

Because of the critical shortage of teachers and the need to improve qualifications, the Minnesota legislature in 1949 authorized liberal arts colleges to initiate programs leading to the bachelor's degree in elementary education and to certification of individuals completing these sequences. St. Scholastica acted quickly. In 1951 the college became the first institution in the state to receive approval of its program under the new requirements. About a hundred lay students and sisters were enrolled in elementary education courses in 1951–52.[6]

Also new at the time were major and minor sequences in speech and drama. The nursing curriculum rather typically fluctuated all the while in length and in content. One of its most significant changes came in the early 1950s when provision was made for including public health nursing in the course of study. This innovation flourished, and in June, 1960, the National League for Nursing gave full approval to the public health section of the college's nursing program. Only the University of Minnesota also held this approval in the state at the time.[7]

The faculty, now numbering slightly over forty in the postwar period, were teaching in a score of fields including art, biology, music, nursing, sociology, and speech. Two priests handled philosophy and religion, and three or four lay people had charge of economics, physical education, and medical technology. The vast majority, however, were sisters of St. Benedict. Somewhat less than twenty of these religious held their undergraduate degrees from St. Scholastica; about an equal number were alumnae of secular institutions, especially the universities of Minnesota and Chicago. A half dozen or so had earned their baccalaureates at Catholic University. Most sisters had completed their M.A.s, and about ten had been awarded the doctorate, usually by Minnesota or by Catholic University. Over-all the faculty was of high quality, committed, and interested in its students. Most engaged in some form of creative activity along with their teaching. Sister Raymond M. McLaughlin's *A History of Legislation Affecting Private Elementary and Secondary Schools in the United States, 1870–1945*, which appeared in 1946, was the first comprehensive study to trace the development of the relationships between the state and private schools. Sister Digna Birmingham's volume analyzing the questionnaires returned by St. Scholastica alumnae for the period from 1926 to 1941, published in 1947

under the title *First Fifteen Years*, was "hailed as an initial work on the effectiveness of higher education in Catholic colleges for women."[8]

The pattern of life on campus did not change appreciably in postwar days. Students continued to come mainly from Minnesota and contiguous areas and to share the same general outlook. Traditional activities such as teas, dinners, dances, week-end outings, and sports provided fun and relief from studies. Outlets for students with special interests existed in a variety of organizations: the Athletic Association, the Playmakers' Guild, the choir, the Music Club, and the Press Club. Weekly convocations gave not only a sense of belonging, a chance to identify with the group, but also an opportunity to listen to visiting lecturers and artists.[9]

But what gave St. Scholastica its special flavor, its distinctive personality, was its religious orientation. All Catholic students belonged to the Sodality of the Blessed Virgin through which many activities of a religious character were integrated. Particularly cherished were the crowning of the Blessed Mother in May and the Rose Procession at the Feast of Christ the King. For the latter each student placed a rose before the altar, thus "symbolizing her love for Christ in the Blessed Sacrament." It was in this period also that great interest was taken in the liturgical movement fanning out from St. John's Abbey at Collegeville. On Easter Sunday in 1951, when the sung vespers were introduced, "the liturgy was an established fact at St. Scholastica's."[10]

The year 1951–52 seems to mark a closing phase in one era of St. Scholastica's development. By 1952 the Sisters of St. Benedict had spent a century in the United States. For forty of those years they had been laboring to fashion their college in Duluth. At last the institution had attained full maturity. Physical plant, including the recently completed Victory Hall, was aesthetically memorable and adequate for some time to come. Curriculum had achieved the form it would present for a number of years. Certain national agencies had taken a look at the operation and found it worthy. The prestigious American Association of University Women had granted membership to St. Scholastica in 1951, and the National League for Nursing would accredit the college's department in its field in the following year. The library, not large by some standards, nevertheless possessed 34,500 titles, an impressive gain over the 12,000 it had in 1932. The time seemed at hand once again to take stock, to evaluate what had been done since Pearl Harbor. Thus a questionnaire was distributed to the several hundred alumnae who had earned degrees in the ten years since the previous study had been made in 1941. When the results were in, Sister Digna presented them in a mimeographed volume entitled "A Second Look." [11]

A comparison with the earlier study covering the period from 1926 to 1941 revealed expected similarities between the older and younger alumnae, but it also uncovered decided differences. Whereas only three out of ten graduates among the pre-1941 respondents were married when the first analysis was made, only three out of ten were single in the 1942 to 1951 group. Very few of the married alumnae were employed outside the home in 1941; of the recent graduates one-fourth of the wives were so engaged. Both groups seem to have established happy Christian homes, but there was considerable doubt regarding the degree to which St. Scholastica had prepared its alumnae for the responsibilities of matrimony. [12]

There were marked contrasts in social outlook. Among the younger graduates there appeared to be more tolerance toward racial minorities and more political, social, and civic activity than among their predecessors; even so the later record was not outstanding. The improvement that had taken place, it was hoped, was related to the social science survey course which had been required of all freshmen since 1942. A larger proportion of recent students had lived on campus and had remained for four years than had the pre-1941 group. Here credit seemed to belong in large measure to the program of formal counseling instituted at St. Scholastica after the first study was published in 1947. Both surveys indicated that the college had made a difference not only in its graduates' professional but also in their personal lives, although some of the findings in both instances were rather discouraging. St. Scholastica, however, had made impressive attempts to measure the effectiveness of its work and to high light the difficulties of preparing women for the dual roles of homemaking and career. [13]

Another virtue of the later study is the picture it gives of the women who attended St. Scholastica in the 1940s and through them of the contribution the college was making to society. About 42 per cent of the alumnae had received financial aid from the college while they were students, and a large segment of them had secured their first employment through the efforts of faculty members or the institution's placement office, which made initial contact. Curiously, this latter fact was frequently not realized by the students. Most of the graduates went into the professions for which they had studied and remained in them until they married. Teaching and nursing had attracted the largest numbers, 32 and 28 per cent, respectively. The remainder had entered the fields of medical technology (14 per cent), medical

record librarianship (13 per cent), social work (8 per cent), and dietetics (5 per cent). One in ten had joined a religious order. It is of interest to note that over 50 per cent of the women said they had decided on their profession before going to college, and 77 per cent had made that decision by the end of their sophomore year. Their average salary in 1951 was $3,333. About 27 per cent of the alumnae had done further study after leaving St. Scholastica, but only 6 per cent had earned advanced degrees. [14]

No dramatic change in the college's educational program occurred as a result of the findings in the second study, though several curricular modifications were introduced. Answers to some of the questions had revealed considerable confusion in dealing with moral issues. Consequently ethics, previously an elective, was made a required course for all students. To emphasize the commitment to liberal arts as well as to stimulate a closer relationship between faculty members and advisees, more flexibility was introduced into major sequences by reducing requirements in them from thirty-six to twenty-four or twenty-seven credits. A number of suggestions for changing and improving administration, instruction, curriculum, and extracurriculum were made, but in general they were reminders of the institution's basic goals and appeals for more effective performance. [15]

The 1950s were in the main a time of holding the line at the college. There was some experimenting with television instruction under a Ford Foundation grant of 1958, but methods and procedures during the decade remained more traditional than innovative. Enrollment, despite the establishment of several scholarship and loan funds, tended to fluctuate between 300 and 350, hitting a low of 290 in 1957–58. Physical plant was still adequate; the only significant additions were two spacious mansions in Duluth, gifts to the priory in 1955 and 1956. Named McCabe and Sellwood halls, these homes have been used as student dormitories since that time. The faculty by the middle of the 1950s consisted of about 65 members; slightly over a dozen of them were lay people, three of them men. Nearly one-quarter of the group were in the field of nursing. Salaries, as practically everywhere, were too low, but improvement came with the important Ford Foundation gifts of 1956–57. St. Scholastica's share amounted to $184,500. [16]

Except for a relaxation in the rules concerning dating and week-end home visits, the extracurriculum like the classroom program exhibited more stability than change. One in ten of the alumnae, according to the second study, tended to favor coeducation — a fact which disturbed college officials — but 76 per cent of the respondents said they would recommend St. Scholastica to a daughter or a younger sister. Reasons given for this loyal support included the college's spiritual life, the family atmosphere which prevailed, the enduring friendships which were formed, and the social activities available. If male companionship was sometimes at a premium, there were opportunities and diversions sufficient to keep life interesting, eventful, and meaningful — the autumn picnic at Gooseberry Falls, a cabin party, a spiritual retreat, Duluth Symphony concerts, the junior-senior banquet. For home economics students there was Phi Alpha Chi, for those in nursing Alpha Tau Delta. Women interested in publications found an outlet in producing the college newspaper, *Scriptorium*, or the annual, the *Towers*, Most alumnae remembered life at the college as highly satisfying.[17]

But though stability and a large measure of self-containment characterized St. Scholastica during the 1950s, administration and faculty followed closely major developments in higher education and constantly sought ways of strengthening the college and its operation. As early as 1948 the college advisory board, which is still a very effective and helpful body, had been organized. Composed of area businessmen and women and alumnae, it began to meet periodically to discuss means of improving and assisting the institution. Eleven years later significant innovations affected both the Duluth Benedictines and their college. Through the leadership of Mother Martina Hughes, the Villa Sancta Scholastica, known since then as St. Scholastica Priory, was affiliated into the Congregation of St. Benedict, whose constitution had been accorded final approval in Rome three years earlier. By this action the Duluth priory not only benefits from closer relations with other Benedictine communities, including that at St. Joseph, but it also enjoys the status of a papal institute.[18]

Although the prioress had always carried the title of president of the college, the day-by-day direction of affairs had been the province of a sister-dean. Finally nomenclature would follow practice. In 1958 the office of president of St. Scholastica was separated from that of prioress. This was done for practical reasons, as well as for consistency with general academic custom. Sister Joselyn Baldeshwiler, a member of the class of 1942, was selected to head the college under the new form of organization. After receiving her M.A. at the University of Minnesota in 1947, she had joined the English faculty at St. Scholastica, and except for time off to do further graduate study, she had remained there until assuming the presidency. Her Ph.D. had been conferred in 1954 by Fordham University. Reasons of health limited her term of office to two years.[19]

Succeeding Sister Joselyn in 1960 was Sister Ann Edward Scanlon, who had taught history at the college beginning in 1938 and had served as academic dean since 1952. She had earned her B.A. at St. Scholastica in 1932; her M.A. and Ph.D. had been conferred by the University of Chicago in 1941 and in 1949. She would serve a seven-year term and preside over the college's destiny in another period of expansion. The institution already possessed its own separate chief executive officer. Now another significant organizational step would be taken. On February 27, 1962, articles of incorporation for St. Scholastica were filed. The evolution of the college as an independent legal entity — though one closely bound in many ways to the priory — was then complete.[20]

Enrollment had not increased appreciably for a number of years, but by the early 1960s it approximated 400; in 1965–66 it pushed well beyond 500. The physical plant at long last was no longer adequate, and early in 1962 an architectural firm was retained to design a new dormitory with dining accommodations for 500 students. Ground breaking took place in May, 1963, and the finished structure was formally opened in September of the following year. Located below and slightly northeast of the main complex of buildings, the clean-lined modern facility was named Somers Hall in honor of Mother Agnes, the former "Builder," president, and prioress. Financing was made possible by a $2,000,000 loan from the federal housing and home finance agency. Former dormitory space in Towers Hall was then converted into much-needed classrooms.[21]

In January, 1965, the college was given $45,000 for an addition to the library as a memorial to Victor F. Ridder, later publisher of the *Duluth News-Tribune* and *Duluth Herald*. Construction began the following June and dedication took place in November. As a result of this gift, the library's capacity was doubled, a periodical room added, thirty-six study carrels installed, and a technical processing department created. Another important addition to campus facilities, a language laboratory, was put into use late in 1966. Its cost was met by a federal grant of $12,250, matched equally by the college.[22]

Throughout Sister Ann Edward's administration, perennial attention would be paid to the curriculum, but no startling departures from its basic structure would appear. One rather major change had been made during her final year as dean, when in keeping with practices in liberal arts colleges of high quality, St. Scholastica's diploma nursing program had been phased out. Thereafter only the nursing sequence leading to a bachelor of science degree was retained. At that time a B.S. was also conferred on graduates in home economics. Women who majored in any one of the score of other disciplines available were awarded the B.A. Minors could be pursued in fields in which majors were offered, as well as in journalism, philosophy, library science, German, and physical education. "Literature Research Chemistry," a course similar to a regular chemistry major but including a technical library science minor, was added to the list of majors in 1964, perhaps the first course of its kind at the undergraduate level in the United States. Health and physical education were added shortly after. But majors in economics and art were dropped between 1966 and 1968, and the department of journalism and communication was discontinued.[23]

In June, 1967, Sister Ann Edward was succeeded in the presidency by Sister Mary Richard Boo, a 1951 graduate of St. Scholastica. For the eight years prior to earning her M.A. degree at St. Louis University in 1960. she had taught English on the campus at Stanbrook Hall. She joined the faculty at the college in 1961 and became chairman of its English department four years later. Her Ph.D. degree had been conferred by the University of Illinois in 1966. She would lead St. Scholastica during a time of innovation and experimentation in the late 1960s and guide the institution until 1971.[24]

During Sister Mary Richard's first autumn in office, ground was broken for a three-story science center, the culmination of a dream and one of the college's most impressive structures. It was completed two years later. In this handsome, modern addition to the physical plant are housed the departments of chemistry, biology, home economics, mathematics, psychology, and medical technology. Most of the $2,700,000 needed to construct it was secured from the federal government in the form of a grant of $733,333 under the Higher Education Facilities Act of 1963, a loan of $1,084,000, and a supplementary grant of $170,500. To these sums the United States Steel Foundation added an award of $15,000. That this building was given priority in the multimillion dollar expansion program announced early in 1965 was consistent with St. Scholastica's traditional role in higher education. Some 60 per cent of the college's graduates up to 1966 had pursued scientific studies, and of this group 85 per cent had concentrated in the health sciences.[25]

The same fall which witnessed the start of construction on the science facility also saw the introduction of a revolutionary teacher-training system

called "Project Criterion." This program was evolved in response to a request from an educational administrator in Duluth, where a pilot project of individualized instruction had recently been instituted in several of the public schools with notable success. The project's major problem had been the difficulty of finding suitably trained faculty. Because he had been favorably impressed by the high quality and dedication of St. Scholastica's education majors who did their practice teaching in the city schools, the Duluth school official turned to the college for help. He proposed that St. Scholastica's education department co-operate with the public school system in creating an innovative elementary teacher training program. The suggestion was welcomed, and a great deal of time, effort, and money went into making the transition in courses in education from teacher-centered classroom methods to individualized instruction.[26]

The endeavor, however, was eminently worth while, not only for the attention St. Scholastica received, but more importantly for the contribution to education which resulted. What the program did essentially was to train teachers to give personalized instruction to elementary school pupils. By using what came to be called "simulabs," majors in education were given an opportunity to work regularly with children during the whole period of their professional preparation, not just in the final year. Such experience enabled students fairly early in their college careers to determine whether teaching would be a congenial profession. "Project Criterion" soon brought visits, letters, and telephone calls from many parts of the United States and beyond asking for information and advice. One California educator declared that St. Scholastica was "the only college in the nation practicing what it preaches in teacher education." And at the meeting of the American Association of Colleges for Teacher Education in 1969, the annual Distinguished Achievement Award went to the institution for its "Project Criterion." The individualized method of instruction proved so successful on the elementary level that it was launched in the secondary education department of the college in 1969. The only obstacle to the program's expansion would seem to be lack of adequate funding.[27]

Another interesting and undoubtedly productive curriculum development of the late 1960s was growing co-operation with the University of Minnesota, Duluth. Partly to facilitate this interchange St. Scholastica, which had operated on the semester system since 1937–38, adopted the three-quarter calendar in the fall of 1968. Eight women from the Catholic institution then enrolled for work at their publicly supported neighbor; by the following spring term twelve students from the state university branch and thirty women from St. Scholastica were participating in the class exchange. In the fall of 1970 a total of twenty women and nineteen men were involved. This interinstitutional co-operation is reminiscent of those between private and public institutions in St. Cloud and Winona. There seems little doubt that both the Duluth branch and St. Scholastica will benefit.[28]

But perhaps the greatest hope for the future, as well as the most dramatic break with the past, was heralded in the fall of 1965. At that time a lieutenant at the Duluth air force base was permitted to attend classes at the college. Thereafter polls were taken of alumnae, students, parents, faculty, administration, and the college advisory board regarding the advisability of switching to coeducation. Except for current undergraduates who opposed the change, these groups favored coeducation; in due course the college announced in 1968 that it would go coeducational in the fall of 1969. Actually, however, nine full-time and six part-time male students were enrolled earlier during the first term of 1968–69. A year later the comparable numbers were 42 and 23, respectively; all were commuters to the campus. In June, 1970, two men earned baccalaureate degrees, the first of their sex to do so in St. Scholastica's history. That autumn found the college's contingent of men grown to 80 full-time and 37 part-time students.[29]

A student writing in the school paper, *Institute Echoes*, as early as 1903 had taken a dim view of coeducation; she had pointed out "the harm which comes to good girls from associating with bad boys, and vice versa," and cited the possibility that "daughters of refined parents may be placed alphabetically next to a boy with the manners and morals of a slum." In 1946 an undergraduate had advanced an opposing view in the college newspaper, *Scriptorium*. Attendance by men, she had suggested, would not only "solve the problem of social escorts," but also that of "stringy locks, dirty shoes, unpressed clothes, sloppy socks . . . so lamented by the faculty." The long view suggests that coeducation will also bolster enrollment, strengthen finances, and contribute to the intellectual endeavors of classroom and laboratory.[30]

In the 1960s the college received added strength in the form of new scholarship grants, both private and governmental, and federal financial assistance for educational programs and equipment. Particularly encouraging have been awards from local groups. In the fall of 1965, for example, the Ordean Foundation of Duluth gave twelve scholarships to

the nursing department, and the family of the late Max H. Lavine, former general manager of the *Superior Evening Telegram*, established one for other departments. In 1968 the John C. Dwan Educational Foundation of Duluth announced that it would provide grants for students enrolling at St. Scholastica in the fall of 1969.[31]

Like all colleges, St. Scholastica's harbors hopes and dreams — for a new library, a student union, a fine arts center, a classroom building — which must be suppressed or anticipated in a distant future because of a lack of money to fulfill them now. Yet in finances, as in other areas of the institution's operations, growth has taken place, and current budgets have usually been balanced. Comparative statistics tell the story. Total income in 1954–55, including gifts and receipts from auxiliary enterprises, came to $448,400; for 1969–70 the amount was $1,515,000. Expenditures during the same two years were $455,400 (leaving a slight deficit) and $1,488,000, respectively. Such encouraging records would not have been possible, of course, without the contributed services of the Benedictine sisters on the staff. These evidences of devotion and commitment were computed at almost $266,000 in 1954–55; they had risen to $408,000 in 1969–70.[32]

Student charges likewise had increased, though not to so high a level as those at other Minnesota private colleges. Annual tuition and board and room costs at St. Scholastica in 1969 averaged only about $1,755. Nevertheless the institution had found it necessary to administer a student aid budget of almost $425,000. Scholarships totaling about $122,600 had gone to 226 recipients of which over $58,000 had come from college funds, the remainder from endowed scholarships. Work contracts amounting to $90,000 had been assigned to 225 undergraduates, and $82,600 in federal economic opportunity and in nursing grants had been awarded to 133 students. Finally $130,000 in loan funds, provided largely by the government, had been borrowed by 191 Scholasticans. A large proportion of these people had received more than one kind of assistance. It was obvious that the college needed increasing and continuing gifts and grants and that it was functioning on a rather close margin. Yet in the absence of a wealthy benefactor, a large group of rich alumnae, and a big endowment fund, St. Scholastica had made remarkable progress.[33]

Tangible evidences of this advance in 1969–70 could be seen in the completed science building and in the presence on campus of growing numbers of male students. Just as apparent was "a spirit of fast-paced vitality," a sense of being on the move. Enrollment was increasing. By the fall of 1970 it would approximate 630; if part-time registrants in all programs were counted, the total would be almost 200 higher. These men and women no longer observed some of the old traditions, such as the Rose Procession and the crowning of the Blessed Mother; rather in the style of the day students sought both freedom and involvement. Three seniors became the first undergraduate counselors in Somers Hall. Other Scholasticans, in association with teachers and administrators in the North Central Liberal Arts Study, helped lay the foundation for greater student participation in the governance of the college. And on issues of general import — the Vietnam War, pollution, human rights — many undergraduates made their concern clearly manifest. The year 1969–70 was, Sister Mary Richard wrote, one "of progress, communication, and exploration." [34]

Full- and part-time faculty members in 1970 numbered about seventy, half of whom were Benedictine sisters. Another dozen religious were on leave for teaching or administrative assignments elsewhere or for doctoral and foreign study. This vigorous force of well-educated and capable sisters gave St. Scholastica not only its distinctive character, but also a degree of financial well-being greater than that possessed by many Catholic institutions where lay teachers held a sizable majority. Nearly a score of the college's instructional staff, including the academic dean, were men. For all of the faculty, both lay and religious, the year 1969–70 offered a full quota of work and challenge. Among the rewards and satisfactions was the National Council for Accreditation of Teacher Education approval in June, 1970, of the college's baccalaureate programs for elementary and secondary teaching for a ten-year period. [35]

By then St. Scholastica offered majors and minors in more than twenty fields; minors only were available in such subjects as library science, physical education, philosophy, and theology. In the fall of 1970 the institution set a precedent by introducing a teaching major in the humanities, a field fairly new to secondary school curriculums in the Midwest but quite common in those of the East and West coasts. St. Scholastica became the first college in Minnesota to gain certification from the Minnesota Department of Education for this course of study. The largest academic departments in 1970 so far as staff was concerned were those in the health sciences, music, education, and English — a pattern

reflected, of course, in the occupations of recent graduates. Of the 138 members of the class of 1970, for example, more than one-third entered the teaching profession. The largest number accepted positions in the general area of Duluth, but other degree recipients were located as far away as Massachusetts and Arkansas. Nursing and medical record librarianship, as well as matrimony, also claimed a goodly representation from the class. [36]

When Sister Mary Richard took over the college's presidential reins in 1967, she had set a number of goals, one of the foremost being to increase enrollment. Toward the attainment of this end, she had favored the adoption of coeducation (then in the discussion stage), expanded involvement with the University of Minnesota, Duluth, and the introduction of a unique program, which would be both attractive to applicants for admission and educationally exciting. Within three years all of these innovations had been effected: "Project Criterion" in 1967, student exchange with the state university in 1968, and official coeducation in 1969. One other suggestion favored by the president herself — that St. Scholastica's name should be changed in the hope of gaining wider appeal — did not fare so well. [37]

As St. Scholastica moved into the 1970s, the institution took another step in its evolution as an independent educational enterprise. Although the college had been incorporated since 1962, its eight-member board of directors continued to be chaired by the prioress of the Duluth Benedictines, and the only lay people on the board were those holding college administrative positions. Now that structure was changed. Under revised articles of incorporation filed on August 6, 1970, the board was enlarged to fifteen members, and its chairman was a lay person. The revision reflected a trend in Catholic higher education, as well as the expanding role of the laity since Vatican II in church life. [38]

While St. Scholastica, of course, cannot escape the problems which beset all of higher education in the 1970s, its remarkable Benedictine heritage of emphasis on worship and work provides the college with a reserve of quiet confidence and pertinacity with which to overcome the obstacles. Heartened by a balanced budget, a sound educational program, a qualified faculty, a rising enrollment, and broadening lay support, the college confidently faces the years ahead with renewed commitment and enthusiasm.

41 CONCORDIA COLLEGE IN ST. PAUL

German Lutherans Nurture A College

MINNESOTA'S SECOND COLLEGE to bear the name Concordia is located in the Midway district of St. Paul. Although it did not become a four-year institution of higher learning until the 1960s, it traces its existence back to the latter part of the nineteenth century. While it is a Lutheran college like Concordia in Moorhead, the St. Paul enterprise sprang from a different church body, the Missouri Synod, and from a German rather than a Norwegian immigrant element. Its intellectual, ethnic, and religious forebears were migrants from Saxony who settled in Missouri in 1839 seeking the freedom to worship as their consciences dictated. Since their leaders were ministers educated in German universities, it was not surprising that one of the early projects of these men was the establishment of a log cabin school in which to educate future pastors and teachers.[1]

Out of this humble beginning developed the influential and well-known Concordia Theological Seminary of St. Louis. The Missouri Synod itself grew out of conferences among various representatives of German Lutherans who had left the homeland for a better life in America. The first convention of this emerging denomination occurred in Chicago in 1847 with delegates in attendance from an area stretching from New York to Missouri. Then officially entitled the "Evangelical Lutheran Synod of Missouri, Ohio, and Other States," the body for a century was usually known simply as the "Missouri Synod," although it was never confined to one state alone. Since 1947 its official name has been "The Lutheran Church — Missouri Synod."[2]

In 1854 the synod was divided into four districts, one of which consisted of Michigan, Wisconsin, Ontario, and Minnesota Territory. Not until the

summer of 1856, however, did one of the body's missionaries visit the last-named region, and not until the following year did one come to work there on a permanent basis. By the mid-1880s, however, nearly fifty Missouri Synod pastors were laboring in the North Star State, and "a goodly number" of parish schools had been established. Growth thereafter was so rapid that an increasing number of Lutheran leaders, including Dr. Frederick Pfotenhauer, president of the Minnesota-Dakota district formed in 1881, and Dr. Francis A. O. Pieper, head of the seminary in St. Louis, became convinced that a higher school to prepare church workers should be established in the Twin Cities area.[3]

In the face of considerable opposition at the synod convention of 1893 in St. Louis, these two men won unanimous support for their point of view. They deserve to be called the "founders of Concordia College." Because of their eloquence and reasoned arguments, the synod appropriated $25,000 out of its total resources of only twice that amount to start the institution in this period of economic depression. Envisioned were the first three years of a high school composed of two courses, one of a classical nature for preministers, the other for preteachers. To get the project under way a local "board of control" was elected by convention delegates. Not everything the founders asked had been granted, but they had achieved a good beginning.[4]

The first task was to find the right person to head the venture. As was customary, the College of Electors of the General Synod met for that purpose in July, 1893. The man selected was the Reverend Theodore H. C. Buenger, pastor of Zion Lutheran Church in St. Paul, who was already a member of the board of control. Thereupon the board extended to him a call as professor and temporary director. Relinquishing his place on the local board, he accepted and assumed his new position immediately. Born to parents who had gone to Missouri in the migration of 1839, Buenger had been thoroughly immersed in German Lutheran tradition. His high school and junior college training had been received in the synod's six-year Gymnasium at Fort Wayne, Indiana, and his three-year seminary work had been taken at Concordia in St. Louis, where he graduated in 1882. He then undertook strenuous missionary endeavors in Wisconsin and held pastorates in Illinois and in St. Paul. In 1896 he accepted the permanent directorship of newly established Concordia, a position he would hold until 1927, when he resigned to become professor of Latin. Not until 1933 did he retire at the age of eighty-three after an amazing half century of service to the institution he had been called upon to initiate. A theologian, a Latin scholar, a lover of the visual arts, interested in all fields of knowledge, Buenger was a fine example of that almost extinct genus, the clergyman-president Renaissance man.[5]

Formal opening of the school was celebrated in Zion Lutheran Church on September 13, 1893. Luckily a brick building with auxiliary frame structures located near the church had been available for a rental of $60 a month, and these became the infant institution's first home. In attendance were thirty boys pursuing the first segment of the proposed three-year course. Four of these lads "eventually became pastors and six became teachers in the parish schools." Although Buenger taught an incredible twenty-seven classes a week in addition to his many other duties, he could not do the entire task alone. So two part-time teachers were hired at the acceptable salary of $200 a year each.[6]

During the first year, the board of control kept a constant watch for a permanent site for the school, and this vigilance was soon rewarded. In 1890 the state training school for boys, which had been located in St. Paul since 1868, was moved to Red Wing, leaving the old facilities vacant but still in good condition. With the help of Governor Knute Nelson about five acres of this property, including the four main buildings, were acquired from the state in September, 1894. The price was only $21,865, far less than Minnesota had invested in them. The location on a high plateau midway between St. Paul and Minneapolis was excellent. To the south and west extended woods, pastures, and frog ponds. To the north stood the fence-surrounded race track of a local millionaire, a mysterious and wonderful Shangri-La designed to stir the imagination of any impressionable schoolboy. Since St. Paul did not as yet extend west of Lexington Avenue, Concordians in fancy at least considered themselves "lords of creation for the whole territory between the College and Fort Snelling." [7]

The four buildings, solidly constructed and connected by tunnels, were readily converted to school use. One of them which became Buenger's home had three stories, a mansard roof, and a cupola. Built in 1860 at a cost of $20,000, it was razed in 1963 after also serving briefly as a women's dormitory. The largest structure — typically dubbed Old Main and possessing a lookout tower above the attic — served as administration building, chapel, dormitory, dining hall, and kitchen. Another known then as West Hall survived into the early 1970s as the Music Building; the fourth called South Hall later was named the Faculty Office Building. It was torn down in 1968. Shortly after the original acquisition three more lots and a frame house were purchased; the total outlay did not exceed by much the $25,000 granted by the synod.[8]

Concordia got off to a good start in its second year with a new full-time teacher, twenty-five sophomores, and twenty-nine freshmen. These high school students, "a motley gathering" of varying ages, came mainly "from humble homes and rural surroundings." To them Concordia opened "a new, wonderful, and somewhat perplexing world." Even though the daily regimen from the 6:00 A.M. rising bell to an early bed time was rigidly prescribed, one student at least felt: "Our whole life at that time could justly be termed an idyl." With the enrollment of twenty-four boys in the junior class in the fall of 1895, the plan of a three-year high school, or Progymnasium, was brought to fruition. Total enrollment reached sixty-eight. Twenty students finished the course at the end of the year. Eventually seven of them became pastors, and an equal number went into teaching.[9]

Upon leaving Concordia preministerial students transferred to the "college" of the same name in Milwaukee; those planning to teach went to the synod's school at Addison, Illinois. Many Minnesotans would have preferred to see these graduates continue their education at the St. Paul institution. The board of control at the church convention of 1896 sought to have the school's course expanded to six years, but without success. In 1902, however, the church body did approve a fourth year, and Concordia amidst much rejoicing became essentially a regular American high school.[10]

That fall enrollment rose from 80 to 112. Ten acres of adjacent land were acquired, giving the campus an area of approximately fifteen acres.

Finally in 1905 the synod agreed to permit Concordia's expansion to a full six years and to "call" the additional necessary teachers. The latter procedure was involved and at times lengthy. Until 1911 the General College of Electors for the synod chose permanent professors from a slate of nominees submitted by various groups in the church. Then the school's local board of control issued a "divine call" to the man selected. If he accepted, he was installed in a formal service usually conducted by the district president.[11]

After the General College of Electors was abolished in 1911, each synod school was granted its own group of electors chosen by the church convention. This procedure continued until 1947. Since that time the election of professors with tenure has been a function of a committee composed of representatives of an institution's board of control, the presidents of the synod and the district involved, and the denomination's board for higher education. The last-named body was created in 1938; six years later it was given full policymaking powers over the church's educational program, "the beginning of a new era of progress in all the colleges of the Missouri Synod."[12]

Concordia introduced its freshman college course in the fall of 1905; members of its recent high school senior class were the first enrollees. Two years later eleven of these young men became the junior college's first graduates. All of them went on to the seminary in St. Louis; with one exception all became pastors. Except for Hebrew the subjects they studied at a more advanced level in the junior college had been the same as those they pursued in high school: Greek, Latin, German, English, religion, history, mathematics, and natural science. By September, 1906, when Concordia first enrolled sophomores, the faculty numbered nine and the students 181. Crowding had become a problem, and facilities were overtaxed for some time to come, despite the discontinuance of the preparatory department for the teachers' colleges of the church the following year. As many as seven students were forced to study in a dormitory room having only one window. Some relief was provided in 1912 with the dedication of a gymnasium, whose cost of about $10,600 had been contributed by friends of the institution. The main features of the structure were a basketball floor, 50 feet by 90 feet, and a supply of gymnastic equipment.[13]

Within another two years conditions were again critical. Enrollment stood at 177; classrooms could accommodate only 150. Consequently the board of control sought approval for a new academic building to cost $100,000. The synod convention approved a structure to cost only $60,000 and agreed to pay $30,000 toward its construction. Since the cheaper building did not seem adequate to local people, the Minnesota district of the church voted to raise $70,000. While the fund drive was being successfully conducted, the board sold the ten acres acquired in 1902 and purchased a somewhat larger tract of state land lying west and south of the campus. On this new site ground was broken in July, 1917, for the much-needed structure. Dedicated the following summer as part of Concordia's twenty-fifth anniversary, the red brick and Bedford limestone administration building (then called Recitation Hall) gave those interested in the school's welfare a tremendous lift. A booklet issued at the time contained the names of all the students who had been enrolled, a total of 1,088.[14]

In a sense the first period of Concordia's history had come to a close. Although the institution would continue to be essentially a preministerial junior college for the Missouri Synod, it would increasingly conform more closely to general trends in American education. For some time certain faculty members and pastors had felt that the curriculum, with its emphasis on religion, languages, and humanities, was not sufficiently responsive to changes in society. At the synod convention of 1917 provision was made for the appointment of a committee to study the church's whole system of higher education and to make recommendations for its modification. One result of this action for Concordia in 1919 was greater emphasis on the sciences and a reduction in the number of courses required.[15]

To teach the courses in science, the first professor in Concordia's history who had no formal theological training was called the following year. Care was taken then and thereafter, however, to assure that he and succeeding appointees possessed acceptable religious beliefs. Another evidence of change was Concordia's decision to seek outside accreditation, since traditionally the synod had held that the church should be the judge of its own institutions. Buenger did not agree with this view, and he succeeded in winning over the faculty and board of control to his way of thinking. Accordingly after an inspection in 1920–21 Concordia's two-year college division was granted accreditation by the University of Minnesota. Similar recognition was given to the high school in 1934.[16]

Another example of outreach in this period following World War I was Concordia's participation in the junior college movement, which had been gaining national momentum for nearly a score of years. Its establishment in 1905 of two years of college work made Concordia one of the country's earliest private junior colleges. When the American Association of Junior Colleges was formed in Chicago in 1920, Concordia became one of twenty charter members. Buenger was present at this initial meeting and read a paper. Within two decades the association would list 183 institutions on its rolls.[17]

Many converging developments were soon reflected in a sharp enrollment increase from 173 to 222 in 1921. By the end of the decade the figure would be slightly over 280. Whereas 14 sophomores finished the course in 1923, a record 43 constituted the 1927 class. It then became necessary to divide classes into two sections for the first time, and the familiar strain on faculty and facilities again became evident. As many as 30 students, for example, had to sleep in the attic of President Buenger's residence. When delegates to the synod convention of 1923 heard of such crowding, they responded by voting $125,000 for the erection of a new dormitory. The building, dedicated in 1925, was known as East Dormitory until 1947, when it was rechristened Luther Hall. With accommodations for 100 men, plus rooms for the library, literary societies, and the music department, the structure added greatly to the enjoyment and effectiveness of campus life. Dining space remained at a premium until November, 1930, when a modern dining hall and health center, for which the church appropriated $145,000, was ready for use. Not for two decades would another new building grace the campus as the nation struggled to survive the vicissitudes of economic depression followed by a second world war.[18]

Meanwhile changes had occurred on the faculty roster, the most notable resulting from the death in 1926 of a beloved professor of German, Hebrew, and Latin. Elected to replace him was President Buenger, then traveling in Europe with his wife. The call came as something of a surprise to him upon his return, but he decided to accept it. The search for a new president (the title recently had replaced that of director) resulted in 1927 in the election and calling of the Reverend Martin A. H. Graebner. Like his predecessor a graduate of the synod's institutions in Fort Wayne and St. Louis, President Graebner had been professor of Greek and Latin at Milwaukee's Concordia College at the time of his call. He would head the St. Paul institution until 1946. An active man, an orator, and an author, Graebner was known in educational circles beyond those of the Missouri Synod.[19]

Campus life during the years following World War I was similar to that of a family, the students being the children and the faculty the parents. In the dormitories upperclassmen served much as older brothers keeping younger siblings in line. On occasion this resulted in "shagging," or using a young lad as a personal valet, but from 1925 on the high school freshmen were segregated in Old Main and conditions improved. Rules were strict, but the faculty frequently was soft of heart. Morning and evening inspections of dormitories were routine, as were twice-daily religious devotions. Study hours were enforced, and off-campus social activities were restricted to Friday and Saturday evenings. The ideal set forth for attainment was that of a Christian gentleman. Student government did not exist, but from 1908 on a student athletic association planned and conducted many activities, athletic and otherwise.[20]

By the middle 1920s nonathletes felt that student life needed a different orientation. As a result a constitution was framed and the Concordia Student Association, representing all undergraduate organizations, came into being. Yearbooks were produced periodically, the *Blue and Gold* in 1920, and the *Concordia Moccasin* in 1926 and 1927. A quarterly literary magazine, the *Concordia Comet*, made its debut in the fall of 1925. Silent movies were featured regularly on campus from 1921 on; after 1925 music on the school's own radio set accompanied them. Literary societies, until their popularity waned about 1930, provided considerable social, athletic, and forensic activity. With its traditional Lutheran emphasis on a "singing church," the synod insisted that music be included in the curriculum. Thus all students were required to take two hours of singing each week. In addition there was an orchestra, a glee club from 1927 on, and a band after 1928.[21]

The depression years of the early 1930s ushered in a grim stage in the school's history. Total enrollment in 1930 stood at 282; by 1941 it had sunk to 131. In the junior college department enrollment was 84 in the former year and 44 (of whom 15 were sophomores) in the latter. Only 17 college freshmen were enrolled in the fall of 1936. Teachers took the usual severe salary cuts, and not until 1942 did faculty pay scales return to their pre-1932 levels. The supply of ministers exceeded the number of vacant pulpits, and some people growing panicky suggested closing the church's schools for a period of two years. When Concordia in 1932 made an overture to the North Central Association looking toward accreditation, a preliminary investigation suggested that the school was not yet ready for such recognition. By 1937 South and West halls stood vacant; by 1941 so did Old Main. Every legitimate device was used to keep Concordia operating. Congregations sent produce and canned goods. Students did volunteer custodial work. Facilities on campus were rented periodically to outside groups. No additions were made to the staff, and the faculty went out scouting for prospective students during the summers. The school survived and even made some progress in the years of adversity.[22]

General Culture Tests were introduced for college sophomores in 1933, and Concordians did relatively well on them. The following year, when the University of Minnesota granted accreditation to the institution's high school division, praise was accorded the quality of its work. In order to earn this recognition, some of the Concordia faculty had recently taken the education courses required for teachers in accredited secondary schools. In 1935 high school graduation exercises were held for the first time in Concordia's history, an event which marked "the beginning of the ultimate separation" of the lower division from the college. That same year there were some nonministerial students in the sophomore class who wished to graduate but who lacked the ninety-four credits needed by men planning to go on to seminary. To meet this situation the faculty, following the practice in other junior colleges, settled on sixty semester hours as the minimum permitted for graduation.[23]

In 1937 Concordia adopted on an experimental basis a revision of its curriculum for preseminarians, the first real change since 1919. Involved were a major reduction in semester hours, the transfer of Hebrew to the seminary, elimination of mathematics, and the addition of courses in social studies and the humanities. Essentially the revision represented "a definite shift in the philosophy of ministerial education," by reducing emphasis on such matters as classical grammar and syntax and providing a broader liberal arts background. It would be years before the curriculum received another similar improvement in its offerings.[24]

Since most students at Concordia were heading for the ministry, World War II did not decimate the enrollment. Indeed, conditions on campus finally began to improve. Instead of the excess of synod ministers which had characterized the 1930s, a shortage was now developing. This situation played a role in providing a 12 per cent gain in enrollment in the fall of 1942, the first upward turn in a dozen years. Money was still in short supply, but at least Concordia's future seemed brighter. Furthermore, the institution's graduates were performing well in seminary and elsewhere, giving evidence that their preparation had been sound.[25]

As the war deepened and draft restrictions under which divinity students could remain in school became more stringent, it became necessary to operate summer sessions in 1944 and 1945. This meant additional burdens on the faculty, but the move seemed eminently reasonable in view of the sacrifices many people were making. In the midst of the war period, Concordia completed its first half century and paused at commencement time in 1943 to commemorate the event. An additional cause for observance was the retirement of Buenger, whose service to the school likewise spanned fifty years. At this historic graduation sixteen college sophomores and twenty-six high school students received their diplomas. For its part, the church's Minnesota district convention approved a drive to raise money for a much-needed library building.[26]

In March, 1946, Graebner, who was then sixty-five years of age, submitted his resignation with the understanding that he would continue as a professor once his successor took office. "A man of great charm and versatility," he had not only kept Concordia alive during a most trying period, but he had also advanced it educationally and initiated plans for a library and a memorial center. Chosen as the third president was Dr. William A. Poehler, a native Minnesotan who had graduated from Concordia in 1924 and from the seminary in St. Louis in 1929. He had held three pastorates in the state and done graduate work at the University of Minnesota, where he received his master's degree in 1945 and his doctorate in 1954. His administration at Concordia began on July 1, 1946.[27]

During President Poehler's first autumn term, total enrollment (augmented by 18 veterans) rose to 273, a number 22 per cent over that of the preceding year; about 200 of these students were in the high school division. After a drop in the late 1940s, registration of secondary students would hold around the 200 mark for the next decade or so. On the other hand, collegiate enrollment mounted steadily, going slightly past 700 in 1966, by which time the high school was down to only 100.[28]

To modernize the administrative organizations in its schools, the synod in 1944 had approved the appointment of certain new officials and the extension of more authority to the presidents. With the advent of President Poehler, a registrar and two deans were selected, and the faculty was relieved of its unpleasant task of dispensing discipline. Three new men were also brought in to augment the teaching staff of eleven members. The president directed the faculty to continue its effort to secure North Central Association accreditation of the high school division. Application was made to the regional body in 1948, and a team of investigators visited the campus early in 1949. At the following commencement, President Poehler made the happy announcement that Concordia's secondary school had been accorded the desired accreditation.[29]

Securing similar recognition for the college division was not so easy. After much study and many faculty meetings, a report was submitted to the association in June, 1954, along with a request for an inspection. On the basis of the latter, however, membership in North Central was refused. The main reasons for the denial included excessive teaching loads, an unrealistic grading system, and an inability because they were too recent to evaluate "improvements in organization, counseling, and library." As soon as possible, the weaknesses were removed, and the faculty again went through the lengthy task of preparing and submitting a new report in 1958. Then came another examination and this time success. On April 21, 1959, the junior college was admitted to North Central membership, the only Minnesota institution of its kind to be so recognized during the past two decades. President Poehler declared a day of celebration.[30]

By this time notable changes had occurred on the Concordia scene. In 1948 the campus had been enlarged by about five and a half acres. The fund drive for a library initiated in 1943 had bogged down after a good start, but the synod had come to its aid and appropriated $161,000 to help provide the $187,000 the building would cost. On November 11, 1951, the Buenger Memorial Library was dedicated; it housed some 50,000 volumes in 1966 in contrast to the 19,000 held by the college in 1943. A small prayer chapel was added to it in 1952 with money raised entirely by the students. That same year ground was broken for the Lutheran Memorial Center. The brain child of Concordia's well-known athlete and coach, Richard W. ("Dick") Siebert, the center had been approved by the district synod in 1945 as a memorial to members of the school family who had lost their lives in World War II. Hundreds of people worked in a variety of ways to raise a fund of some $362,000 to make the dream come true. Rising costs made it necessary to eliminate certain facilities, but the center was finally finished in the fall of 1953.[31]

The old gymnasium was thereupon transformed into an attractive chapel dedicated in November, 1955, to the memory of former President Graebner. The space previously used as a chapel in the administration building was converted to classroom and office use. The cost of these two operations authorized by the synod came to $150,000. Final additions to the physical plant in the 1950s were three dormitories made imperative by the steadily rising enrollment. The first of these, named Centennial Hall to mark the coming of the synod to Min-

nesota in 1856, was dedicated in December, 1957. Its cost of about $196,000 was paid by the Minnesota district. The building was designed for forty women students but sixty actually moved in. Minnesota Hall, commemorating the state's one-hundredth birthday, was ready for occupancy less than a year later. Planned for fifty women undergraduates, it housed seventy-three. The synod underwrote its cost of $205,000. The third residence hall, named in honor of Dr. C. F. W. Walther, one of the synod's pioneer leaders, was completed in 1959. With rooms for a hundred men, it cost slightly over $400,000.[32]

Undoubtedly the most dramatic development of this period was the introduction of coeducation in 1950–51. In the early 1920s the Lutheran Education Association of the Northwest had worked for this change, but the majority of the synod's leaders and members had felt that Concordia should remain solely a training ground for the seminary. Starting in 1935 the board of control and other groups had periodically and vainly urged the synodical convention to alter Concordia's nature; Buenger even composed a song supporting the move. Finally, however, when the church's board for higher education on the basis of a study showing the urgent need for women teachers in parish schools came out for coeducation, the convention of 1950 concurred.[33]

In anticipation of this action, the college administration had already drawn up a preteacher training curriculum and won approval for it from the University of Minnesota. In September, 1950, 24 young women, mostly from small midwestern towns, enrolled in the college freshman class and became pioneers in Concordia's new venture. The second year saw their number grow to 41. In June, 1952, diplomas were awarded to 20 coeds and 41 men. The high school graduating class numbered 36. Normally the women would have gone on to the synod's teachers' colleges at Seward, Nebraska, or River Forest, Illinois. Because of the demand, however, three-fourths of them did a stint in the parish schools first. By 1956 coeds graduating from the junior college would number 52 and men 59. Three years later women outnumbered men in the college, and they continued to do so thereafter.[34]

The reinauguration of a summer session in 1957 and the inauguration of a four-year curriculum in 1962 can be traced fairly directly to the presence of women on campus. After the introduction of the teacher training program in 1950, prospective pedagogues had been required to take a methods course during the summer at either Seward or River Forest. With the graduation of more than sixty trainees at Concordia in 1957, however, it seemed feasible to conduct the summer course in St. Paul as an extension department of the college at Seward. That year an eight-week session was held; additional work in education as well as language courses for preministers were included in the schedule. Concordia has continued summer sessions since that time. The first summer graduation ceremony occurred in August, 1965, when nineteen students completed their courses.[35]

The dream of a four-year college had long been in the minds of many people interested in Concordia, but it had not seemed feasible for the church to support another such school. In 1957, however, the synod "established a senior college for ministerial students at Fort Wayne, Indiana." Supporters of Concordia then directed their efforts toward securing a senior teachers' college as the first step in gaining a more complete program. The next encouragement came at the synod convention of 1959, where it was decided that starting in 1966 no new teachers would be assigned to parish schools unless they had graduated "from a recognized four-year teachers college." As part of its campaign Concordia retained the services of a consultant who reported that the institution "was in a very favorable position" to expand its offerings. Thus encouraged the faculty worked long and hard to produce a satisfactory new curriculum. With endorsements from other districts of the synod, the new program was presented to the convention of 1962, which approved Concordia's request to institute the four-year college. Enrollment in the senior division would be restricted to women, but this limitation did nothing to dampen the enthusiasm engendered at Concordia by the news.[36]

When classes resumed in September, 1962, forty-six young women constituted the college's first regular junior class. Some of them took time off to teach, but on May 30, 1964, the remaining twenty-six received their B.A.s in elementary education. The following year the convention authorized the enrollment of men in the college's senior division teacher program, and in July a vanguard of them arrived. Nearly one-fourth of the 103 graduates receiving B.A.s between the fall of 1966 and the summer of 1967 were men. Meanwhile the college was in the process of terminating its close relationship with the high school. Separate catalogs had been issued since 1958. In 1967 Concordia's lower division merged with the St. Paul Lutheran High School, although the college continued to supervise the now separate institution until 1972. The attainment of another major goal in the institution's evolution also occurred in 1967, accompanied by joy and celebration, when the North Central Association granted full accreditation to Concordia's four-year course.[37]

This satisfying new status capped not only many years of slow and laborious effort, but also a decade of mushrooming growth and expansion at Concordia. Faculty between 1957 and 1967 increased from twenty-nine to fifty-five (ten of them in the high school). Despite a strong belief in equality, the teachers in 1958 reluctantly accepted ranking in formal titles from instructor to professor. Only $6,000 had been awarded in scholarships in 1957; ten years later counting federal loans and other help the total had mounted to $120,000. Physical plant too had grown, but it had not been able to keep pace with enrollment.[38]

Buenger's former home and Old Main were razed in 1963, and a combined student union and men's dormitory was erected. Named Wollaeger Hall for a long-time German professor and librarian at Concordia, the building was so designed that its three stories could be supplemented by six more floors. The major portion of the hall's $520,000 cost was provided by the synod. Between 1960 and 1967 five apartment houses near the college were purchased and converted into residences for women students. The first two were christened Mary and Martha, but the others were given the names of esteemed former faculty members — Moenkemoeller, Schlueter, and Dobberfuhl. A sixth new apartment building was leased in the summer of 1967 and christened Berger Hall also in honor of a deceased teacher at Concordia; since 1969 the structure has housed married students. The Edward L. Arndt Science Hall, memorializing a missionary to China who had taught all the science courses offered on the campus between 1897 and 1911, was completed in 1965 at a cost of $550,000, paid largely by the synod. The new facility, so constructed that it could be enlarged, permitted the upgrading of the college's offerings in science. The final structure of the Poehler era was a wing added to the administration building. It was approved in 1968 by the synod, which also granted $425,000 from the Ebenezer Thankoffering toward the addition's cost; Concordia was authorized to use up to $70,000 from local funds for the same purpose. Ground breaking occurred in June, 1969, and dedication of the finished product took place the following year.[39]

Less than a month later in June, 1970, Poehler left office, having reached the retirement age of sixty-five set for presidents of Missouri Synod colleges. Rather remarkably Concordia had only three chief executives in its first seventy-six years, a circumstance that gave considerable continuity to its operations, but perhaps had also limited the "free sweep of innovative activity'' on the campus. Be that as it may, the retiring president had led the college in a period of notable change and growth. He oversaw a $4,300,000 expansion program which embraced the construction of eight buildings and the enlargement of the grounds from fifteen to twenty-six acres. He directed the development of the junior college into a four-year coeducational institution of liberal arts accredited by the North Central Association. He also had the satisfaction in 1969 of seeing the college's elementary education sequence gain full approval from the National Council for Accreditation of Teacher Education for a ten-year period effective in the fall of 1968. And he presided over the initiation of a bold new venture, the Metropolitan Teacher Education Program Selection begun in 1968 with twenty-five students, mainly Blacks, enrolled. The purpose of this addition to the curriculum, which would be augmented by twenty-five new undergraduates each year, was ''to provide an on-going supply of minority elementary teachers to serve the seven county area surrounding and including the Twin Cities.'' This imaginative venture was commended by the North Central Association as a fine example of one way in which a small college could help solve society's race problems. Another experimental program begun in 1969 was designed to prepare directors of Christian education for service to synod congregations in music and in youth ministry, as well as in education; twenty-two students were enrolled in the course in the fall of 1970.[40]

During Poehler's final year as president in 1969–70, enrollment in the college reached 800 — 447 of whom were from Minnesota and 107 from Wisconsin. A majority of the collegians (328 women and 244 men) were planning to become elementary schoolteachers; among the remaining 228 students, 116 expressed no specific vocational goal, 75 were headed for the ministry, 19 were studying to become deaconesses in the church, and 18 hoped to enter the field of social work. This pattern reflected several trends characteristic since the mid-1960s: a near doubling of the number of potential male teachers, an increase of about 55 in vocationally uncommitted men and women, and a decrease of approximately 45 in the size of the preministerial contingent. Attendance at the two six-week summer sessions of 1969 totaled 158. An interesting feature of the summer terms beginning in 1967 was a cooperative arrangement with Augsburg College in Minneapolis by which students could register for courses on both campuses. At commencement in May, 1970, B.A. degrees were conferred on 105 men and women; 23 junior college graduates received associate in arts diplomas. A score of other individuals would complete work for their baccalaureates at the end of the 1970 fall quarter.[41]

Some of Concordia's graduates became doctors, engineers, and businessmen, but the vast majority entered the ministry, or became counselors, teachers, and homemakers. Consequently few became wealthy except in spirit; yet they frequently have been generous in their giving both to their church and their alma mater. The college is unusual in possessing no indebtedness, even though its charges have been modest by comparison with those of many other institutions. The basic fee for resident students in 1970 covering board, room, and tuition was $615 for each of the three quarters of the academic year; undergraduates in preprofessional church work sequences paid $535. These sums were a far cry from the $100 which covered these costs in 1945. The college's total current income in 1969–70 was $1,924,000; of this amount the Missouri Synod gave $715,000 (a substantial 37.1 per cent of income), auxiliary enterprises contributed $699,000, and general and educational income $487,000. Ten years earlier total income had been $647,600, of which the church had given $294,300. Expenditures in 1969–70 were $1,870,700; of this $1,221,700 went for general and educational expenses, and $649,000 was used to operate auxiliary enterprises. The outlay for student aid came to $269,500 — $96,060 in scholarships, $102,800 in campus employment, $39,350 in student loans, and $31,300 in work-study grants. All such assistance ten years previously had added up to only slightly over $59,000. The college has turned in a very creditable financial performance. One of the questions to be answered by the future is how long will the synod be able to subsidize Concordia at the level it has in the past.[42]

Following Poehler's retirement, the board of control named Dr. Harold W. Otte, academic dean and professor of education, to serve as acting president. He had joined the faculty in 1951 and earned a doctorate in education at the University of Colorado in 1965. During the year he directed affairs at Concordia, it continued its evolution from an institution concerned mainly with the preparation of seminarians and teachers toward that of a far more general liberal arts college. Of the 810 students in 1970–71, 518 were still planning to teach, but 168 others — more than twice the number of two years earlier — had declared no definite vocational goal. Full-time faculty numbered more than sixty; relatively few held a Ph.D., but a half dozen or so others were nearing its completion. The construction of a music and classroom building, toward which a sizable number of donors had contributed, got under way to replace 104-year-old West Hall. By 1969 undergraduates had raised $25,000 for a student center, and, somewhat later, the synod's board of directors gave the college permission to apply for a $600,000 federal loan to construct it, the debt to be amortized by student fees. In the fall of 1972, the Concordia College Union was opened.[43]

Early in 1971 the Reverend Harvey A. Stegemoeller, professor of political science and history at the synod's Concordia Senior College in Fort Wayne, was elected to Concordia's presidency. A native of Texas, he had graduated from St. John's College in Winfield, Kansas, and from Concordia Seminary in St. Louis; he holds an M.A. degree from the University of Toledo, and he has done additional graduate work at three other institutions.

Along with teaching and administrative experience at several colleges and universities, he brought to his new position knowledge gained from service as an assistant in Washington, D.C., to Senator Vance Hartke of Indiana. What new mantles Concordia will don during President Stegemoeller's administration, only a prophet can tell. It seems likely that a close relationship will be maintained between the college and the parishes serving the 250,000 Missouri Synod Lutherans in Minnesota, Iowa, the Dakotas, and Wisconsin, and that a continued effort will be made "to recruit the finest of our high school graduates for the Lord's service." Beyond this traditional endeavor, Concordia will undoubtedly reach out to serve more and more students, who while desiring education in a Christian context, will find their vocations in fields not directly connected with the church.[44]

42 BETHEL COLLEGE

A Swedish Baptist Dream
Comes True

BETHEL COLLEGE AND SEMINARY of St. Paul is the only major educational institution owned and controlled by the Baptist General Conference, which in 1969 represented about 100,000 members and 650 churches in the United States. Conservative in matters of faith and morals and Bible-centered in its theology, the denomination emphasizes, among other doctrines, that of a regenerate church membership. Bethel (*beth el* meaning "house of God") College as a fully accredited, four-year institution of higher learning is relatively young. Its roots, however, stretching from Sweden to the American Midwest, are anchored deep in the soil of the nineteenth century. Another distinctive, though not unique, characteristic of Bethel is the close relationship still maintained between its collegiate and theological divisions.[1]

The spiritual forebears of the institution were the minority of Swedes both in the homeland and in the United States who forsook Lutheranism to embrace the Baptist faith. Sweden's first Baptist church was established in 1848, that in this country in August, 1852, at Rock Island, Illinois. Despite the attacks which had been directed at the cold formalism of the state church in Sweden and at the immorality and crude manners of many of its clergy, Swedish Baptists felt the sting of bigotry on both sides of the Atlantic. Nevertheless they survived and in time gradually increased in number. By 1870 they would be found rather widely dispersed in America from New York to Kansas and Nebraska, with a sizable concentration in Chicago. Minnesota welcomed its vanguard of nine individuals of the denomination at Houston in 1853; five years later, grown to five churches and 157 members, the group conducted its first conference in the North Star State. Its increase, however, would not be rapid.

By the early 1950s Minnesota could claim approximately 13,000 Swedish Baptists, the United States as a whole about 47,000.[2]

Their early pastors were all laymen, many of whom shared with most of their parishioners a prejudice against book learning. Still there were exceptions, notably John Alexis Edgren, who went to Chicago in the summer of 1870 to assume the pastorate of the First Swedish Baptist Church. With little to go on except drive and faith, he started a seminary that could muster only two students during its first year. Yet it is to this humble school that present-day Bethel traces its origin. For six years the new endeavor was housed on the south side of Chicago at the American Baptist Union Theological Seminary; in the fall of 1877 the operation was moved to Morgan Park, Illinois. By 1883 Edgren's department had thirty-two students, including some Danes and Norwegians, but its prime mover had suffered many hardships to keep the enterprise going. Even though lacking in money, Edgren resigned from Morgan Park in July, 1884, in order to establish a separate seminary for Swedish Baptists. Some of the American Baptists ridiculed his plan, but he went ahead.[3]

For the next four years Edgren's school had no permanent home. From October, 1884, to April, 1885, under the name of The Swedish-American Bible Seminary, it was located in the First Swedish Baptist Church in St. Paul. About forty students enrolled in such subjects as Bible, Hebrew, Swedish, Greek, and pastoral duties, and it appeared that the venture was off to a good start. However, a promise of forty acres of land and $10,500 for a building fund from Stromsburg, Nebraska, caused Edgren to move his school there and rename it the Central Bible Seminary. Doctrinal squabbles and

271

Edgren's departure to California for health reasons put an end to the Nebraska interlude after two years. In 1888 the perambulating enterprise was back in Morgan Park as something of a foundling in the Union Theological Seminary. There it remained until 1913, its last years disturbed by the attitudes of individuals associated with the Baptist Theological Union.[4]

Early in 1912 the trustees of the union announced that its support and management of the Swedish department would be discontinued the following October. This blow was softened somewhat by a promise to pay the dispossessed group $10,000 over a five-year period in order to facilitate the transition to a new location. A number of people now favored a return to St. Paul and merger with Bethel Academy, a Baptist high school which had been established in 1905. The church's conference of 1912, however, refused to approve the suggestion, and the Swedish Baptist school remained in Morgan Park one more year.[5]

At the annual gathering of the denomination in 1913 in Duluth, the future of the seminary was settled. A motion to merge it with Bethel Academy passed with only one negative vote cast. Officially named Bethel Academy and Theological Seminary of the Swedish Baptist General Conference of America, the combined institution would be owned by the church organization and subject to the direction of a school board of twenty-one elected members. The intellectual fare would consist of a regular high school course, capped by a three-year theological program. To serve as first president the conference elected the Reverend G. Arvid Hagstrom, then a pastor in St. Paul. Born in northern Sweden in 1867, he had been taken to Minnesota as a child, living first at Red Wing and later in Minneapolis. He entered the seminary at Morgan Park in 1889 and graduated in 1892 as one of a class of twelve members. Assuming the Bethel presidency in January, 1914, he would continue in the post for twenty-seven years.[6]

He would find money raising and providing plant facilities his immediate tasks. As a site for the newly wedded educational entities in St. Paul, two blocks were acquired on Snelling Avenue in the spring of 1914; one was donated, the other purchased for $7,500. During the summer, a two-story seminary building, including dormitory quarters, classrooms, offices and a chapel, was erected at a cost of $35,000. By fall, with a gift of $10,000 from James J. Hill, President Hagstrom could report to the conference that he had been able to raise $27,000. The following year a three-story academic building was constructed, giving Bethel a plant worth $153,000.

The debt by then was $52,000, but within five years it would be paid off.[7]

Classes opened in the fall of 1914. For the next seventeen years, while making minor changes in response to its environment, Bethel did not alter its basic nature; it remained a dual entity — a high school and a seminary. By 1916 a few courses in the latter were being taught in English rather than in Swedish, but it would be a decade and a half before the transition to English was complete. As late as 1930 most of the catalog for the pastoral training division was printed in Swedish; rules governing student behavior, however, were in English.[8]

At the conference meeting in August, 1920, the name of the school was changed to Bethel Institute, and so it would remain for the next twenty-five years. In 1921 authorization was given for the establishment of a Bible and missionary training department in connection with the seminary division. Open to men and women sixteen years old and over, the new unit began operation in the fall of 1922. A two-year sequence taught in English, the course was designed to train young people for Sunday school and other work in local churches. Under various titles, it had a rather long life. By 1929 enrollment in its courses approximated fifty, but during the depression of the 1930s the numbers dropped sharply. In 1935 the department was transferred to Bethel's young junior college and renamed the "Christian Workers' Course." Its graduates were awarded the title of associate in religious education.[9]

The largest division of the institute continued for some years to be its academy or high school. In 1928 enrollment stood at 231. Characteristically, 32 per cent of the total came from the Twin Cities, 35 per cent from other parts of Minnesota, and 33 per cent from outside the state, even from Sweden. Counting individuals taking courses in the music department, total registrants numbered 282 (159 women and 123 men). The seminary and the Bible training department each had 42 students. From 1905 to 1929 over 2,000 men and women matriculated in Bethel Academy and more than 500 of them graduated.[10]

Scores of these alumni had become ministers, but others were engaged in a variety of occupations and professions. Officials at Bethel were proud of the fact that their graduates were welcome at the University of Minnesota, Hamline, and many other institutions of higher learning. The catalog of 1930 carried a picture of the three women and thirteen men from the institute then studying at Macalester. In many ways the class schedule and the extracurriculum were similar to those in a public high school, but the differences between the two were also great.[11]

Most noticeable was the all-pervasive influence of the Swedish Baptist faith at Bethel. Church attendance on Sunday was expected of everyone. Each school day began with a 7:30 A.M. prayer service "to which all are invited." At 10:00 A.M. classes recessed for a chapel service — attendance required. Two hours later came a noonday minute of prayer and in the evening a vesper prayer meeting. The faculty, all active church workers, sought "to set a worthy example in faith and right living" in addition to teaching. Three of the most important student organizations were the Missionary Band, which conducted school religious activities, the Ministerial Students for individuals heading for the ministry, and the Student Volunteers for those planning to become foreign missionaries. Many undergraduates conducted services in local churches and missions.[12]

Rules were strict and confining by some standards, but they mirrored the beliefs of the controlling church organization. The use of tobacco "in any form" was a barrier to admission and a cause for expulsion, facts which were printed in italics in Bethel catalogs. Also forbidden were "dancing, card playing, visiting pool rooms and other dubious places . . . [and] all amusements of a questionable character." Time-wasters would not be tolerated, nor would anyone unwilling to co-operate with his teachers. Girls were required to live in the dormitory unless institute officials had approved other arrangements. Academic performance was important, but "the real purpose of education" was character development and "the acquisition of right habits of thought and action." Such an environment was "peculiarly adapted to students of the serious and earnest type," but these and all other students became increasingly difficult to recruit after economic depression swept over the land in the 1930s.[13]

The academy continued to function, but it was living on borrowed time. First the freshman and sophomore years were dropped, and by 1934 only sixty-five students were enrolled. The following year it was decided to discontinue the high school division altogether. When the current senior class of eight members graduated in 1936, one chapter of Bethel's history came to a close.[14]

Meanwhile another chapter had begun to unfold — the establishment of a college, which founder John Edgren had dreamed of back in the 1880s. Recognizing that the days of the academy were numbered and that better-educated ministers were needed, the conference of 1930 had voted to open

a junior college at Bethel. It was also decreed that two years of college work would be required for admission to the seminary.[15]

The sortie into the junior college field began in the fall of 1931. Although the first year was limited to a preseminary course and the country was in the grip of the great depression, school authorities maintained a brave front. The modest beginning, they declared, was merely "prophetic of a continued and safe advance." And so it proved to be, but not without sacrifice, devotion, and hard work.[16]

Bethel in the late 1920s was scarcely affluent. The church had gradually accumulated an endowment fund for the school totaling about $58,000 in 1924. As part of its diamond jubilee celebration three years later, the Swedish Baptist Conference conducted a financial campaign, part of the proceeds of which raised Bethel's endowment to about $175,000. From this source the institute realized some $10,000 a year. Another $2,000 was added annually by the Northern Baptist Convention, and student payments brought in approximately $12,500. But since expenses amounted to $50,000, nearly half of that sum had to be secured from local churches or other sources. None of the 300 Swedish Baptist congregations scattered over the United States or any of the 34,000 members could be called rich. Between 1921 and 1931 Illinois parishioners had given Bethel an average of ninety-five cents each annually, those in Minnesota ninety cents; members in other states had done considerably worse. Yet the institute survived the 1930s, and salary checks, low though they were, arrived on time.[17]

Junior college statistics during the first year were likewise modest. The faculty of nine members could count only one Ph.D., held by the dean of the seminary. Three were women, all young and generally lacking in collegiate teaching experience. Total enrollment was only twenty-two. Curricular offerings were limited to English, history, Greek, German, Swedish, mathematics, philosophy, and religion. Academy and college students sat side by side in some of the classes. Tuition was $50 a term — less for ministers' children — and 64 semester hours were needed for an associate of arts or science diploma. But each year saw expansion and improvement of the junior college program with an eye on the standards demanded by accrediting agencies.[18]

By the second year enrollment was up to forty-one and a preprofessional liberal arts course had been added to the curriculum. Soon the catalog was advertising a whole array of preparatory sequences for education, medicine, dentistry, engineering, and the ministry. In the spring of 1934 accreditation by the University of Minnesota was announced. The school newspaper, the *Bethel Clarion*, was reorganized in 1932, and participation in basketball and baseball in the Southern Minnesota Junior College Conference was arranged. Other familiar extracurricular activities blossomed in the form of a student council, glee club, chorus, debate, and forensics, but the school's religious program and emphasis continued to provide Bethel with its own distinctive identity.[19]

With a largely limited clientele and with the nation suffering economic depression, Bethel grew slowly. The gross budget for the institute now composed of academy, seminary, junior college, and music school in 1932–33 was only $48,700; that for junior college salaries came to $7,600. Value of endowment had fallen to $100,000 and income from it to $4,700. Total expenses in 1934 approximated $43,000, of which the church was called upon to raise just under $20,000. The next year the members of 183 churches contributed to Penny-a-Meal banks over a month-long campaign, which started a tradition. The initial Penny-a-Meal effort brought Bethel $5,400. Well over a hundred other churches failed to participate. New construction could not be undertaken, and even needed repairs had to be neglected. In 1938 a promotional secretary was employed, and little by little the institution gained in strength.[20]

That fall junior college enrollment reached 151 (74 women and 77 men). Seventy-one students were from Minnesota; Wisconsin and Michigan followed with 13 and 12, respectively. Two were from India, where Bethel missionaries had been active for years, and three came from Canada. For some time school officials had spoken of the need for a new dormitory for women; at last in 1940 one costing $40,000 was approved as soon as a cash fund of $25,000 could be obtained. By the summer of 1941 in the face of problems and difficulties of various kinds, sufficient money was in hand to permit the start of construction. The building, later named Bodien Hall, with rooms for about 50 women and a dining facility, was occupied in the fall of 1941. It had cost $62,000 furnished. Although not large, it was Bethel's first new structure since 1915.[21]

The year 1941 witnessed the graduation of the junior college's largest class so far, thirty-one students. The seminary class numbered thirteen. That same year President Hagstrom's long administration ended, but not his service to the institute, where he continued to teach. The Reverend Henry C. Wingblade, a Kansas-born son of Swedish immigrant parents, was elected the second president of

Bethel. A graduate of Washburn College, Topeka, Kansas, in 1910, he had spent the next twenty-eight years teaching in the academy and junior college of the institution he would now head. In 1931 he had received his M.A. degree at the University of Minnesota. For the three years prior to returning to Bethel, he had served as minister of the Addison Street Baptist Church in Chicago. A friendly, warm individual, he would hold the position at Bethel for thirteen years and have the satisfaction of seeing the school well launched as a four-year college in company with the seminary.[22]

For the immediate future, however, it was his burdensome task to cope with the problems created by World War II. Bethel officials left no doubt regarding their patriotism. Symbolic of their position was the cover of the July, 1942, "Victory Number" of the *Bulletin* with its colored reproduction of the Stars and Stripes and the motto "Loyal to God and Country." In 1944 the institute's service flag displayed 107 stars. The preceding December two women graduates of the 1936 class, who were missionaries in the Philippines, had been beheaded by Japanese troops. Other casualties, too, brought sadness to the school, but they did not shake the deep religious faith on which the institution depended.[23]

Except for the tragedy of war, the years from 1942 to 1946 could be considered a rather bright period in Bethel's history. In the fall of 1942 for the twelfth successive year junior college enrollment showed an increase, totaling 177. In 1943–44 the number dropped to 132 (92 women and 40 men), but it was up to 230 in 1945; there were then 61 students in the seminary. Lack of dormitory space was a real problem. Consequently a drive to raise $75,000 for a men's dormitory was launched early in 1943. Within twenty months, $65,000 in cash and pledges had been secured. Also $30,000 had been obtained to erect an annex to the women's dormitory; this $65,500 unit, containing rooms for 52 women and including a chapel, was dedicated in November, 1945. The men's residence hall, later named in honor of John Edgren, accommodated about 80 men and cost $144,800. Since it was not quite ready for occupancy in the fall of 1946, men assigned to it lived for a time in a building dubbed "Hotel El Barno" on the state fairgrounds. The year 1946, Bethel's diamond jubilee, also saw a $136,800 apartment building, christened the G. A. Hagstrom Residence, rise on campus as housing for thirty-two married couples. It was the first of four structures in a $200,000 expansion program approved by the conference of 1945.[24]

The same gathering also gave the school a new name, "Bethel College and Seminary," a title more meaningful and descriptive than "Bethel Institute." The time now seemed near for the institution to take another step in its evolution, to add the final two years to its college program. In his report of 1946 Dean Emory A. Johnson outlined the reasons why such a move was not only wise but urgent. The future of four-year colleges appeared brighter than that of two-year schools. The addition of an upper division would reduce the degree of immaturity found in the Bethel undergraduate body, where freshmen at the time were well in the majority. With enrollments bulging everywhere, graduates of the junior college division were having difficulty gaining admission to other institutions. Yet in seminaries the trend was to require four years of collegiate work for admission. Indeed Bethel's ministerial training division might very well gain full accreditation from the American Association of Theological Schools by adopting such a requirement.[25]

Supported by these arguments and with backing from the education board, President Wingblade sought approval from the conference of 1947 to expand Bethel into a four-year college. The request was granted unanimously. A third year of work was added that fall and a fourth in the autumn of 1948. In framing the new curriculum, the existing schedule of courses provided the foundation; Bethel's goal "to promote the cause of Christ by the developing of Christian personalities who will be worthy and effective representatives of the Christian faith" served as the guideline. Offerings at first were of necessity limited, but it was hoped that majors could soon be available in six fields: literature, history, sociology, philosophy, psychology and education, and religious education.[26]

Enrollment of approximately 525 in the fall of 1947 was the largest in Bethel's history to that time. In contrast to World War II days, men outnumbered women 344 to 181. Seventeen different religious faiths were represented, but 354 of the students were Baptists. In the junior college enrollment was about 440; of these 160, including three women, were veterans of military service. The freshman class was a sizable 274; the new junior year had attracted slightly over a dozen registrants. Seminary enrollment was nearly 100, of whom 32 had been in some branch of the military. Faculty numbered about 30 persons, none of whom had completed his doctorate.[27]

During the next few years, Bethel took memorable steps forward. The library previously had been dispersed in several locations. In 1948 work was begun on a new two-story building to which the book and periodical collections were moved the following year. Costing about $147,000, the new facility provided stack areas for 50,000 volumes and study space for 102 collegians and 27 seminarians. Shortly after the library was occupied, baccalaureate degrees were conferred on members of the first class of nine men to complete the course of the senior division. Also in 1949 the B.A. degree became a requirement for admission to Bethel Seminary. Three years later a field house was completed at a cost of $281,700. It seated 1,100 spectators for basketball games, or 1,800 people when used as an auditorium. With its completion Bethel had a capital indebtedness of $200,000, but it was in a position to function more effectively than in the past.[28]

At this time Bethel sought unsuccessfully to gain accreditation by the North Central Association. The required self-study was made in 1951–52; then followed a visit by an investigating team representing the regional agency. Its members found a great deal to commend, but they pointed also to weaknesses. One was the size of the debt created by the expansion of the physical plant. Another, also stemming from an insufficiency of funds, was the failure to strengthen the faculty, especially in the senior college. As a consequence accreditation was not achieved on the first try, not an unusual occurrence though a disappointing one.[29]

Efforts were begun immediately to improve performance all along the line. Other studies of various aspects of Bethel's operation followed that of 1951–52. New sequences were added to the curriculum, notably a program in secondary education for which there was strong student demand. This innovation gained the approval of the Minnesota Department of Education in 1957. That same year the college (but not the seminary) returned to the semester calendar which was then usual in other Minnesota private institutions. A concurrent change transformed the course in religious education to a regular major instead of an independent program as formerly. General education and the sciences received increasing attention. With the help of federal loans, a third addition to Bodien Hall costing $185,000 and one of $172,400 to Edgren Hall were completed in 1957, as was a $56,000 rebuilding of the power plant. Faculty improvement and salary increases gained momentum; by 1958 more than one-quarter of the regular teaching staff held doctorates. The top pay for professors went from $5,460 to $7,050 between 1953 and 1958. Fringe benefits likewise were increased, and Bethel's administrative structure was modernized. All this cost money. The budget in 1954 had been $632,950; in 1958 it was $947,300 and the debt about $725,000. But Bethel had moved impressively forward in the 1950s.[30]

Again the quest for North Central accreditation was undertaken. Another thorough self-study was made in 1957–58 and an application filed. Now the efforts of the preceding years were rewarded; Bethel was fully accredited by the association on April 24, 1959. Then followed admission to the Minnesota Private College Council and somewhat later to the Association of American Colleges and the American Council on Education. The report of the North Central examiners had been pleasantly complimentary, but Bethel's president urged his associates to regard accreditation, not with complacency, but as a springboard to greater achievement.[31]

Making this exhortation was Dr. Carl H. Lundquist, who had assumed the presidency on September 1, 1954. A student at Bethel for a time in the 1930s, he had graduated from Sioux Falls College in South Dakota in 1939 and from Bethel Seminary three years later. He had earned his master's degree at Eastern Baptist Theological Seminary. When called to the administrative post, he had completed a decade of successful ministry at Elim Baptist Church in Chicago. To prepare him for his new responsibility, the conference of 1953 had arranged for Mr. Lundquist to spend the succeeding year at Bethel in association with President Wingblade, a decision which proved to be highly fortunate. Late in October, 1953, Dean C. Emanuel Carlson was permitted to accept an important Baptist position in Washington, D.C. President-elect Lundquist thereafter combined the duties of acting dean with those of training for the even weightier responsibilities facing him.[32]

After a year as president, in which efforts were directed toward the day when accreditation would be secured, Mr. Lundquist wrote: "A spirit of eagerness pervades the campus. The breathlessness of tense anticipation can be sensed everywhere. Yesterday's dreams are coming true." On the national front, a new conference Baptist church was being organized on an average of every seventeen days, giving promise of increasing demands on Bethel. Beyond achieving North Central accreditation, the whole nature and future of the college and seminary had to be determined.[33]

To the solution of this task, a great deal of time, money, thought, and labor was spent in the next half dozen years. A standing committee on long-range planning was organized in 1955; in October of the following year a private firm was employed to counsel with the committee on campus expansion. Considerable money was devoted to purchasing property adjacent to Bethel's campus, and yet there were serious doubts regarding the wisdom of attempting to grow in this restricted location. In January, 1958, the church's board of education voted that a full-scale study be made to map the path Bethel should take. The result in the form of a 285-page mimeographed report was transmitted by the faculty group that prepared it to the board of education in August, 1959.[34]

Going on the assumptions that the conference would continue to control and support Bethel but that the latter would be free to fix policy, the planning committee addressed itself to four areas: students, academic program, campus, and finance. Valuable and pertinent information was collected and agreement was reached on a number of points: the college should remain essentially a liberal arts institution, the seminary and the college should stay together, and many students would continue to require financial aid. The committee was unable to agree, however, on a recommendation concerning a site for Bethel. A ninety-nine-acre tract in suburban Arden Hills was one location under consideration.[35]

The next step was the engaging of a retired University of Minnesota professor to chart a ten-year development program. His report was submitted in the spring of 1961. He favored retention of Bethel's site on Snelling Avenue, but in spite of missing the mark in several predictions, he was helpful in setting goals. Later in 1961 when the conference met, numerous divergent views were still held, but faculty and board of education were united on at least six recommendations. (1) College enrollment in the centennial year of 1971 should be 1,200, that of the seminary from 200 to 300. (2) Top priorities should concern balancing the budget and upgrading the faculty, curriculum, and library. (3) Most features of the professor's proposals should be followed: courses in economics, business, elementary education, prenursing, mathematics, and women's physical education should be added; salaries and scholarship funds should be increased. (4) Bethel should move to "one of three locations north of the present campus" at a cost of $12,000,000. (5) Temporary adjustments should be carried out at the old location for at least three years. (6) There should be no prolonged separation of college and seminary. In a "gigantic step of faith," the conference voted to approve this development program, which was given the name "Decade Ten."[36]

During these years of wrestling with basic policy

decisions, the college division continued its steady growth. Enrollment in the fall of 1956 reached 498; three years later, with North Central accreditation a reality, the total was 571, about 56 per cent of whom were men. In the fall of 1961 after the adoption of "Decade Ten," the figure rose to 734 — 279 freshmen, 213 sophomores, 123 juniors, 83 seniors, 17 unclassified, and 19 postgraduates. Though heartening, these statistics also high lighted problems of long standing: the strong vocational bent of large numbers of students and the high rate of attrition. Although progress had been made in reducing the rate, it remained worrisomely high. Of the 226 freshmen, nearly equally divided between men and women who had matriculated in 1956, only 85 were still enrolled as seniors; 24 were women and 61 were men.[37]

All told by June, 1960, there were nearly 4,000 living Bethel alumni; more than 960 were in pastorates and nearly 250 in foreign missions. Graduates of the senior college since 1949 numbered 440. At commencement in 1958 the seminary awarded divinity baccalaureates to 26 graduates. The college conferred degrees and diplomas on another 71 students; 54 received the B.A., 15 the associate of arts, and two the bachelor of religious education. The most popular collegiate majors in these years were philosophy, literature, history, and psychology. Between 1953 and 1957 the large majority of graduates (103 out of the total of 192) went on to a seminary, but teaching was gaining in popularity. Twenty-four alumni of the period either entered that field or enrolled in education classes after earning their baccalaureates.[38]

Despite past achievements, Bethel's challenges as it poised on the threshold of "Decade Ten" were scarcely minimal. Total endowment was less than $50,000. A gradual rise in college tuition charges from $213 in 1948 to $550 in 1960 still left Bethel's rates among the lowest in Minnesota's private colleges. Fees in the seminary, amounting to $100 per pupil in 1959, paid only 8 per cent of the cost of operation. Large sums in student aid had to be allocated to both collegians and seminarians; scholarships and grants in 1962–63 came to $85,000, work contracts to $67,000, and loans to $50,000. Believing strongly in the separation of church and state, Bethel was loath to accept governmental subsidies. Furthermore its moral stance would not permit it for a time to accept money from the Minnesota Private College Fund, one of whose benefactors derived its support from a brewery. Lacking an I. A. O'Shaughnessy or a DeWitt Wallace, Bethel had to rely largely on the Swedish Baptist churches in order to stay in the black.[39]

For three decades following the early 1930s, the institution had been in the red in only five academic years (1948 to 1951 and 1952 to 1954) because of the building program of that period. Student fees had brought in a growing proportion of the college's income, 49 per cent in 1955–56 and 62 per cent in 1959–60, but gifts also had been necessary in order to avoid deficits. Contributions in 1950–51 had totaled roughly $120,000, of which $50,000 went to the building fund; nine years later gifts had risen to $405,600, yet Bethel ended the year in the black by only $218. Two-thirds or more of the contributions regularly came from the church, but even there the record provided slight cause for complacency. Although $1,700,000 was given to Bethel by the church between 1949 and 1958, the conference during the decade prior to 1963 actually paid only about 60 per cent of the amount it had voted to give its college and seminary. In 1957 when it approved a budget of $877,600 for Bethel, the denomination asked its churches to give $370,000. They managed $201,000, but 58 per cent of them gave nothing. These figures illustrate how narrow was the margin on which President Lundquist and his associates operated.[40]

With optimism high and faith strong, however, they pushed foward on "Decade Ten." Its estimated cost over ten years would be $25,000,000; they hoped this amount would be raised as follows: $9,000,000 from donations, $7,000,000 from student fees, $5,000,000 from loans, $2,000,000 from the sale of the old campus, and $2,000,000 from LIFT — a church drive entitled Living Investment Forward Thrust. Under the timetable adopted, the seminary would be the first to move to Arden Hills. The schedule called for its buildings to be begun in 1964, and its classes opened on the new campus in the fall of 1965. It was hoped the entire institution would be located at Arden Hills by 1971, Bethel's one-hundredth birthday, but there was about a two-year lag in carrying out this plan. College classes began there in the fall of 1972, and all administrative functions will be transferred by the end of 1973.[41]

Some modifications were made in the program and there were delays, but the design in essence had taken shape. By mid-1966, $2,244,000 had been spent on the Arden Hills campus, which then totaled 214 acres and included attractive Lake Valentine. Of this amount, $250,000 had been spent for the original land purchase, $1,400,000 had gone into the academic complex of six buildings connected by glass-enclosed pavilions, and the remainder had been used to buy additional land, improve the site, and pay for furnishings. Financing had also been arranged for what was known as Phase Two of the program consisting of the construction of a chapel, a student center, and about seventy housing units. With completion of the chapel in 1969, the task was accomplished. At a cost of slightly over $3,680,000, the seminary possessed an arresting, functional, and forward-looking physical plant. Although near the city, the setting itself was scenic and uncrowded. Still, only part of "Decade Ten" had been fulfilled. The bigger challenge of transporting the college to Arden Hills lay ahead.[42]

In the 1960s, with the prospect of new and better days beyond the horizon, Bethel's collegiate division had cause for rejoicing. Enrollments continued upward from 852 in 1963–64 to slightly over a 1,000 in 1966 and thereafter, all that could be accommodated. The curriculum received constant attention, and, so far as possible, it was rendered responsive to the needs and interests of current students. A sequence appealing to a sizable number of undergraduates was a new program in elementary education to which the Minnesota Department of Education gave full five-year accreditation in 1964–65, the year its first students earned their degrees. The calendar was modified by the adoption of an interim semester in January, 1970. Total gifts to the institution rose encouragingly, reaching $1,423,000 in 1968–69. Equally heart warming was growing support and attention from sources outside Bethel's traditional community. Corporate business and foundations, which had not been historically significant contributors to either college or seminary, provided $108,600 for current operations in 1968–69; the churches that year gave $397,700 for the same purpose.[43]

A dramatic example of broadening support occurred in 1967–68 when a gift of $500,000 to build a college dormitory at Arden Hills came to Bethel "from sources altogether unknown to us." The first definite step in the removal of the collegiate division from its old site was then taken. By the fall of 1968 the initial unit of a contemplated four-dormitory complex, which would house about 960 collegians when completed, was ready for occupancy on the shore of Lake Valentine. The sixty men and sixty women who took up residence there in separate wings attended classes on the old campus five miles away. Like the other buildings on the new location, the dormitory in its structure and design attempted not only to be as convenient and functional as possible but also to delay obsolescence for as long as man could peer into the future. The inclusion of faculty office space and study carrels in the living quarters illustrates the imagination used

in planning the building. With the installation of electronic components a few years hence, students should be able to sit in carrels and by pushing buttons read pages of books stored hundreds of miles away, or to hear or see playbacks of a variety of audio-visual programs.[44]

But change and removal are seldom unaccompanied by trauma and anxiety; the usual problems are then accentuated by those associated with relocation. And so it was at Bethel. Was it a mistake to move? Should the college continue at all? Such questions kept arising. In 1962–63 for the first time in nine years there was a deficit of $31,700 out of $1,466,000 spent; the following year the amount in red ink was $75,000, even though gift income was at an all-time high and salaries were relatively low. The question naturally arose in some minds whether the capital drive to finance the Arden Hills development was not hurting the current budget. A number of faculty members, as a result, secured positions elsewhere. There were also frustrations bred of plant inadequacies and necessary improvisation. Despite the conversion of Hagstrom Apartments in 1962 into a dormitory for 125 women students, a limitation had to be placed on admissions. By the fall of 1964 seven former homes adjacent to the Snelling Avenue campus were being used for classrooms and faculty offices. And to add to the travail, the college between 1966 and 1968 had no permanent dean, thus leaving the faculty somewhat without a rudder; twenty-one teachers of short tenure left Bethel in that brief period.[45]

While not trying to avoid or minimize its problems, the Bethel family in the springtime of the 1970s exudes an air of confidence and optimism. This stems partly from a deep religious belief, from a firm conviction in the eminent significance of the task which has been faithfully carried out for a century; it also derives from the very real advances that have relatively recently been achieved from small beginnings. Collegiate enrollment in 1969–70 totaled 1,034, of whom 370 were freshmen and 172 seniors. Minnesota contributed 519 members of the student body, but sizable groups also came from other states. Illinois sent 112, Wisconsin 50, California 46, Iowa 37, and Ohio 25. There were also 36 foreign students from 13 different countries. To make possible the attendance of many of these undergraduates, Bethel administered over $344,000 in financial aid — $149,100 in scholarships and grants, $107,200 in work contracts, and $88,600 in student loans. The annual budget of the college was $2,860,000, that of the seminary $730,000.[46]

The former academy is now in every respect a

full-fledged college of liberal arts with all the trappings such status involves. Its extracurriculum offers a rich program of religious activities and compares favorably with that in older institutions; the Bethel College Student Association in 1968–69 administered a budget of $25,000 and held membership in the liberal National Student Association. One-fourth of the faculty of about sixty-five full-time teachers hold Ph.D.s and another sizable number are working toward that degree; salaries and fringe benefits are in line with those in many colleges. And true to its democratic tradition, Bethel heeds the voice of the professor in its councils of decision making. The student, the end product, continues to exhibit a strong social drive. Of the 163 members in the class of 1968, for example, 28 per cent entered the teaching field, 23 per cent enrolled in seminary, 14 per cent went to graduate school, 10 per cent took up social work, and 2 per cent became missionaries.[47]

If all goes as planned, the college will have fully joined the seminary in Arden Hills by 1973, making Bethel the only one of the state's sixteen private, accredited, liberal arts institutions to erect a campus on a new site in nearly a century. The buildings already under way for the academic complex reflect the same forward-looking and imaginative thinking that went into the construction of the 1968 dormitory unit. The estimated cost of the replanting of both seminary and college is now $18,000,000, about $7,800,000 less than predicted in 1961. Although refusing federal construction grants — a rarity in the groves of academe — Bethel can see its way clear to securing all but $2,500,000 of the total sum needed; that portion was sought on a national basis from corporations, foundations, and individuals.[48]

With parietal rules all but eroded in contemporary academic circles, one cannot help feeling a certain amazement at the college's efforts, grounded in Scripture though they may be, to maintain bans on student smoking, drinking, social dancing, gambling, and the use of drugs. It is not easy for current undergraduates to define clearly the limits of personal freedom at Bethel or elsewhere. It may be that a losing battle is being fought, but it is difficult not to commend the fighters and to admire an institution which dares to proclaim the standards it believes in — especially when those in positions of leadership recognize the pitfalls of "moralism, escapism, Pharisaism, perfectionism, and legalism." That Bethel's "emphases upon humane learning within a Christian frame of reference," as President Lundquist put it, are relevant now and in the future could be accepted on faith. Proof of the proposition's validity, however, is seen in the institution's continuing growth and its widening base of support.[49]

Bethel's "over-arching objective" in the 1970s, as in the 1870s, is "the preparation of a task force for Christian penetration of society." Success in such a venture has never been easy or complete; the challenge in recent years seems in many ways greater than ever before. On the other hand, the disrupting forces in today's society, the conflicts, the decline in traditional moral standards, the secularization, the dehumanization, make it all the more imperative that the values which Bethel espouses be preserved and extended.[50]

Reference Notes

PREFACE
Pages xi to xiii

[1] Jacques Barzun quoted by Edward D. Eddy, "What About the 'Sinful' Student?" in *Saturday Review*, 70 (March 19, 1966).
[2] Frederick Rudolph, *The American College and University: A History*, vii (New York, 1962).

1. INTRODUCTION, PART I
Pages 1 to 6

[1] Lois M. Fawcett, "Frontier Education," in *Minnesota History*, 14:144–148 (June, 1933); Theodore C. Blegen, *Minnesota: A History of the State*, 186 (Minneapolis, 1963).
[2] *New York Independent*, September 17, 1857.
[3] Fawcett, in *Minnesota History*, 14:148 (quotation); Rudolph, *American College and University*, 44–67; Donald G. Tewksbury, *The Founding of American Colleges and Universities Before the Civil War, With Particular Reference to the Religious Influences Bearing Upon the College Movement*, 27 (New York, 1932). Only in the New England states was college mortality low.
[4] R. W. Murchie and M. E. Jarchow, *Population Trends in Minnesota*, 7–9 (University of Minnesota Agricultural Experiment Station, *Bulletins*, no. 327 — [St. Paul], 1936); Rudolph, *American College and University*, 247–252; Blegen, *Minnesota*, 420.
[5] Murchie and Jarchow, *Population Trends*, 9–11; Merrill E. Jarchow, *The Earth Brought Forth: A History of Minnesota Agriculture to 1885*, 172, 178 (St. Paul, 1949); Franklyn Curtiss-Wedge, *History of Winona County, Minnesota*, 1:467 (Chicago, 1913).
[6] Blegen, *Minnesota*, 410; Northfield High School Alumni Record, Classes 1877–1938, in superintendent's files, Northfield.
[7] Murchie and Jarchow, *Population Trends*, 7, 13, 14; Minnesota Commission on Higher Education, *Higher Education in Minnesota*, 239, 320 (Minneapolis, 1950). The normal school at Duluth was opened in 1902, that at Bemidji in 1919.
[8] Oliver Jensen, ed., *The Nineties*, 5–11 (quotation), 127–129 (New York, 1967).
[9] Murchie and Jarchow, *Population Trends*, 14; Blegen, *Minnesota*, 369–372.
[10] Rudolph, *American College and University*, 250–263, 330 (quotation).
[11] Rudolph, *American College and University*, 269–286, 332–346, 406.
[12] Rudolph, *American College and University*, 118–124, 237–240, 290–306 (quotation).

[13] Hellen D. Asher, "A Frontier College in the Middle West: Hamline, 1854–1869," in *Minnesota History*, 9:373 (quotation) (December, 1928); Rudolph, *American College and University*, 136–138.
[14] Rudolph, *American College and University*, 138–144 (quotation); Leal A. Headley and Merrill E. Jarchow, *Carleton: The First Century*, 373–378 (quotation) (Northfield, 1966).
[15] Another United States senator, Ernest C. A. Lundeen, a 1901 graduate, was a leading orator and debater for Carleton while Schall was at Hamline. Headley and Jarchow, *Carleton*, 378 (quotation); Grace L. Nute, "In Hamline Halls, 1854–1954," 185, 309, an unpublished manuscript in the possession of Hamline University.
[16] Headley and Jarchow, *Carleton*, 379–381.
[17] Rudolph, *American College and University*, 150–155 (quotation); Doniver A. Lund, *Gustavus Adolphus College: A Centennial History, 1862–1962*, 70 (St. Peter, 1963); *Gustavian Weekly* (student newspaper), March 17, 1931; Ingebrikt F. Grose, *Fifty Memorable Years at St. Olaf*, 32 (Northfield, 1925). Grose writes that some St. Olaf men obtained their exercise by splitting, piling, and carrying wood in return for their board. At Gustavus in the early days students participated in calisthenics directed in Swedish; Conrad Peterson, *Remember Thy Past: A History of Gustavus Adolphus College, 1862–1952*, 54 (St. Peter, 1953).
[18] Rudolph, *American College and University*, 154; George M. Stephenson, *American History Since 1865*, 63 (New York, 1939); Alexius Hoffmann, *St. John's University, Collegeville, Minnesota: A Sketch of Its History*, 23 (Collegeville, 1907); Colman J. Barry, *Worship and Work: St. John's Abbey and University, 1856–1956*, 118 (quotation) (Collegeville, 1956); Headley and Jarchow, *Carleton*, 404 (quotation), 406; Edwin Kagin, *James Wallace of Macalester*, 86 (Garden City, N.Y., 1957); Nute, "Hamline Halls," 128; *Gustavian Weekly*, May 23, 1922.
[19] Rudolph, *American College and University*, 373; Headley and Jarchow, *Carleton*, 406; Nute, "Hamline Halls," 172, 182; William C. Benson, *High on Manitou: A History of St. Olaf College, 1874–1949*, 46 (quotation) (Northfield, 1949); Barry, *Worship and Work*, 232; Lund, *Gustavus Adolphus College*, 88. See *Minneapolis Tribune*, September 30, October 1, 1882, for accounts of a Hamline-University of Minnesota football game in which the former quit after being defeated twice in half an hour.
[20] Walter M. Ostrem, "The Beginnings of Track and Field Sports in Minnesota," in *Minnesota History*, 39:18–21 (Spring, 1964). Carleton held its first high school track meet in 1902, an annual event which has continued to the present. See Headley and Jarchow, *Carleton*, 406.
[21] Benson, *High on Manitou*, 87; Headley and Jarchow

Carleton, 405, 406 (quotation); Nute, "Hamline Halls," 205; Charles Nelson Pace, ed., *Hamline University*, 44 (quotation) (St. Paul, 1939); Lund, *Gustavus Adolphus College*, 89 (quotation); Rudolph, *American College and University*, 378.

2. HAMLINE UNIVERSITY, PART I
Pages 7 to 12

[1] Rudolph, *American College and University*, 47, 55–57, 68, 70; George P. Schmidt, *The Liberal Arts College: A Chapter in American Cultural History*, 31, 57 (New Brunswick, N. J., 1957); Sylvanus M. Duvall, *The Methodist Episcopal Church and Education up to 1869* (New York, 1928).

[2] Alfred Brunson to B. F. Hoyt, March 28, 1859, in Methodist Episcopal Church, Minnesota Annual Conference Historical Society Papers, in the Minnesota Historical Society, hereafter cited as Methodist Papers; Methodist Episcopal Church, *Minutes of the Annual Conference, 1854*, 423, 425 (New York, 1854).

[3] Talk by Winifred Murray Milne, 1, in William P. Murray Papers, in the Minnesota Historical Society.

[4] Milne talk, 2–4; Pace, *Hamline University*, 14–17 (quotation); Minnesota Territory, *Laws*, 1854, p. 105.

[5] *Laws*, 1854, p. 105 (quotation); Pace, *Hamline University*, 13 (quotation), 16; Hellen D. Asher, "The Growth of Colleges from 1850 to 1860, Particularly in the Northwest," 21, Master's thesis, University of Wisconsin, 1926; Nute, "Hamline Halls," 14–17.

[6] Asher, "Growth of Colleges," 34; Pace, *Hamline University*, 14–16; Malcolm C. Shurtleff, "The Introduction of Methodism in Minnesota," 84, Master's thesis, University of Minnesota, 1922; Methodist Episcopal Church, *Minutes of the Wisconsin Annual Conference, August 20, 1854*, 20; Nute, "Hamline Halls," 7–13; Walter C. Pahner, *Life and Letters of Leonidas L. Hamline* (New York, 1877). From the 1820s to his retirement in 1852, Hamline was one of the dynamic church leaders of his day. His wealth, most of which stemmed from his wife's family, weighed heavily on his mind.

[7] Nute, "Hamline Halls," 17; Hamline College of Liberal Arts Alumni Association, *History of the Hamline University of Minnesota When Located at Red Wing, Minnesota, 1854–1869*, 10, 40–42 ([St. Paul], 1907); Chauncey Hobart, *History of Methodism in Minnesota*, 286 (Red Wing, 1887); William McKinley, *A Story of Minnesota Methodism*, 249 (Cincinnati, 1911).

[8] Shurtleff, "Introduction of Methodism," 86; Nute, "Hamline Halls," 18–21; Alumni Association, *History of Hamline at Red Wing*, 13; *Red Wing Sentinel*, February 9, 1856; J. R. Creighton, *Hamline University Annual* (September 15, 1875). The *First Annual Catalogue of the Preparatory Department of Hamline University, Red Wing, Minnesota* (August, 1855) shows that there were four classes the first year: primary, junior, middle, and senior.

[9] Nute, "Hamline Halls," 18, 21; *Red Wing Sentinel*, January 5, 1856.

[10] Nute, "Hamline Halls," 20, 26–28, 33–35; Creighton, *Hamline University Annual* (September 15, 1857); Methodist Episcopal Church, *Minutes of the Minnesota Annual Conference, 1857*, 16; Hamline University, *Biennial Catalogue*, 17, 19 (1859–60); *Catalogue*, 6–10, 12–16 (1863); Asher, in *Minnesota History*, 9:370; Minnesota Superintendent of Public Instruction, *Annual Report, 1862*, 121 (St. Paul, 1862). Margaret Densmore, Hamline music teacher, wrote to her brother on August 12, 1858: "I have resigned my situation in the University they are too slow in paying — father thinks they do not intend to pay — so highly does he esteem the methodists."

See Benjamin Densmore Papers in the Minnesota Historical Society.

[11] Nute, "Hamline Halls," 30–56; Henry L. Osborn, ed., *Alumni Record of Hamline University*, 6–9 (St. Paul, 1924); Rudolph, *American College and University*, 310–318. Details of life at Hamline in 1861 are found in Countryman's interesting diary preserved in the Minnesota Historical Society.

[12] Nute, "Hamline Halls," 49–73 (quotation); Paul H. Giddens, "Hamline University Students Fight and Die to Save Union," in *Hamline University Alumni Bulletin* (Fall, 1961); John D. Hicks, "Raising the Army in '61," in *Minnesota History*, 2:324–368 (February, 1918) notes that three successive senior classes were broken up by enlistments. A total of 119 Hamline students served, at least 30 of them as officers.

[13] Pace, *Hamline University*, 23; Nute, "Hamline Halls," 30, 34–48, 62; Schmidt, *The Liberal Arts College*, 14 (quotation); Methodist Episcopal Church, *Minutes of the Minnesota Annual Conference, 1861*, 23, *1866*, 44, *1868*, 43; Shurtleff, "Introduction of Methodism," 94. The New York property given by Bishop Hamline was sold for something over $6,000 to help pay for the building in Red Wing. By the 1920s the property was worth $500,000.

[14] Shurtleff, "Introduction of Methodism," 94–97 (quotation); Methodist Episcopal Church, *Minutes of the Minnesota Annual Conference, 1869*, 24, *1870*, 3; *Rochester Post*, July 10, 1869, May 7, 14, October 15, 1870; *Hastings Union*, May 18, 1870; *Goodhue County Republican* (Red Wing), May 12, 1870. Miss Nute feels the real reason for the rejection of the offers from Rochester, Red Wing, and Faribault in 1870 was the fact that the chairman of the commission on removal and his supporters wished to see Hamline located in the Twin Cities. Nute, 93.

[15] Asher, "Growth of Colleges," 59; *Dakota County Union* (Hastings), July 28, 1869; James F. Chaffee, "Relations with Hamline University," 1–3, Methodist Papers. William P. Murray to Samuel S. Thorpe, May 10, 1907, Murray Papers, states: "The fact is, but for bad management and the attempt to keep its doors open during the civil war Hamline University would today be at Red Wing."

[16] *Northfield Recorder*, December 27, 1867; *Goodhue County Republican*, June 27, 1862, January 28, March 11, 1869; *Catalogue*, 26 (1866). Miss Nute regards Hamline's crusade for a fine public school system at a time when such a system was far from strong in the state and Hamline's teaching graduates as "probably her greatest regional and national contribution during her Red Wing days." See "Hamline Halls," 82.

[17] Methodist Episcopal Church, *Minutes of the Minnesota Annual Conference, 1871*, 16, *1872*, 19; *Rochester Post*, November 18, 1871; *St. Paul Daily Pioneer*, June 29, July 8, 1873; Chaffee, "Relations with Hamline University," 4, 6, Methodist Papers; Nute, "Hamline Halls," 96–102. In 1871 the legislature amended Hamline's charter permitting the conference to choose a new site anywhere it desired and adding six laymen to the board of trustees. Miss Nute has suggested that Chaffee and his supporters were responsible for the latter provision. See Minnesota, *Special Laws*, 1871, p. 105.

[18] Nute, "Hamline Halls," 103–109; Methodist Episcopal Church, *Minutes of the Minnesota Annual Conference, 1874*, 43, 47–49, *1875*, 30; *Waseca Weekly News*, October 7, 1874; Chaffee, "Relations with Hamline University," 6–8, Methodist Papers.

[19] Nute, "Hamline Halls," 109–114; Methodist Episcopal Church, *Minutes of the Minnesota Annual Conference, 1877*, 25, *1878*, 31, *1879*, 28; *St. Paul Pioneer Press*, June 26, 1878; *Rochester Post*, June 13, 1879; Hobart, *Methodism in Minnesota*, 289, 290 (quotation). According to Miss Nute, Chaffee seems to have been largely responsible for a third charter amendment approved in February, 1877, authorizing the trustees

to make nominations to the conference to fill board vacancies. See Minnesota, *General Laws*, 1877, p. 337.

²⁰ Pace, *Hamline University*, 39, 118–121 (quotations); Nute, "Hamline Halls," 116–123 (quotation).

²¹ Nute, "Hamline Halls," 114, 115 (quotation), 120–122, 128.

²² Pace, *Hamline University*, 27, 123; *St. Paul Daily Globe*, July 27, 1882, February 8, 1883; Nute, "Hamline Halls," 112, 127–138; Methodist Episcopal Church, *Minutes of the Minnesota Annual Conference, 1882*, 52; *Daily Minneapolis Tribune*, October 24, 1883. Miss Nute says that President John's strict discipline caused resentment. This fact as well as friction with some trustees and the illness of his wife played major roles in his resignation. He was, however, a hard-working, cultured, Christian gentleman.

²³ Pace, *Hamline University*, 25, 28–35, 76; *Daily Minneapolis Tribune*, October 24, 1883; Methodist Episcopal Church, *Minutes of the Minnesota Annual Conference, 1883*, 76, *1884*, 32; Nute, "Hamline Halls," 138–140.

²⁴ Dr. Henry L. Osborn arrived as professor of biology and geology while Science Hall was being constructed. For over forty years, in building up the science department and by his personal example as a scholar and gentleman, he made an immeasurable contribution to the Hamline family. Nute, "Hamline Halls," 140–144; Pace, *Hamline University*, 25, 34, 38, 124 (quotations).

²⁵ Nute, "Hamline Halls," 142; Pace, *Hamline University*, 35–39 (quotation).

²⁶ Nute, "Hamline Halls," 162–164, 170. Norton joined the board in 1878 and was its president from 1902 until his death in 1917.

²⁷ Nute, "Hamline Halls," 157, 163, 166–168.

²⁸ Nute, "Hamline Halls," 175–177, 188. In a commencement speech at Hamline in 1898, Hill declared that small liberal arts colleges were so important that they should be assisted by money from public universities.

²⁹ Nute, "Hamline Halls," 175, 177, 179, 186, 202.

³⁰ Nute, "Hamline Halls," 189. Although by 1900 it cost only about $200 to attend Hamline for one year, a majority of students worked for at least part of their expenses, a widespread condition in Minnesota colleges. See the *Oracle* (student magazine), 13 (February 1, 1901).

3. St. John's University, Part I
Pages 13 to 16

¹ Edward Wakin, *The Catholic Campus*, 3 (New York, 1963).

² Barry, *Worship and Work*, 6–16; Hoffmann, *St. John's University*, 1.

³ Barry, *Worship and Work*, 16–23.

⁴ Barry, *Worship and Work*, 23–45; Hoffmann, *St. John's University*, 2–4.

⁵ Barry, *Worship and Work*, 46–50 (quotation); Hoffmann, *St. John's University*, 5; A. C. Krey, "Monte Cassino, Metten, and Minnesota," in *Minnesota History*, 8:226–231 (September, 1927). Krey points out how St. John's helped stabilize the German Catholic population and taught it the arts of American life. The aid of the monks extended to northwestern areas of Canada and the United States. Opportunities for higher education were made available to communities which could not have afforded even elementary schools.

⁶ Barry, *Worship and Work*, 55–60, 62 (quotations); Hoffmann, *St. John's University*, 7–10; Andrew M. Greeley, *The Changing Catholic College*, 24 (Chicago, 1967). Of the 55 Catholic colleges started in the United States between 1850 and

1866, 25 were abandoned by 1866, according to Rudolph, *American College and University*, 219.

⁷ Barry, *Worship and Work*, 68–92; Hoffmann, *St. John's University*, 10–16.

⁸ Murchie and Jarchow, *Population Trends*, 24; Barry, *Worship and Work*, 93–106. By 1870 Minnesota had 48,000 immigrants from Germany and more than 21,000 from Ireland, and St. John's "was the only Catholic institution of higher education available" to them, according to Barry, 101.

⁹ Barry, *Worship and Work*, 103–105 (quotation), 109, 112, 114; Hoffmann, *St. John's University*, 27, 33. According to Barry, one of the five 1870 graduates was Joseph B. Cotter, first bishop of Winona.

¹⁰ Barry, *Worship and Work*, 109–112; Hoffmann, *St. John's University*, 35–46.

¹¹ Barry, *Worship and Work*, 131, 144 (quotation); Hoffmann, *St. John's University*, 50–61. Krey, in *Minnesota History*, 8:226, calls Alexius a man of "that iron age of strong men in Minnesota," which included James J. Hill, Archbishop John Ireland, and Bishop Henry B. Whipple, all of whom the abbot knew well.

¹² Barry, *Worship and Work*, 144, 145 (quotation).

¹³ Barry, *Worship and Work*, 145–148 (quotation); Hoffmann, *St. John's University*, 61–78; Vincent Tegeder, O.S.B., "Pioneering Monks," in *Minnesota History*, 33:53–60 (Summer, 1952). The *St. Paul Daily Globe* of August 15, 1885, commended St. John's University to its readers, stating that its location "in the healthiest part of the state . . . is removed from the distractions of city life — an advantage that secures regularity and firm but gentle discipline." The "excellent commercial department" was singled out for special mention.

¹⁴ Tegeder, in *Minnesota History*, 33:53 (quotation); *St. John's Record* (student newspaper), September, 1892; Barry, *Worship and Work*, 148–154; Hoffmann, *St. John's University*, 78–93. Music was always promoted at St. John's, and in 1885 an orchestra was formed which has survived, with new personnel, of course, to the present.

¹⁵ Barry, *Worship and Work*, 163–202, 204, 212–221 (quotation); Hoffmann, *St. John's University*, 96–109. Early in 1889 Archbishop John Ireland of St. Paul investigated St. John's for Rome. Although the monks had all received five years of classical and three years of theological training — more than secular clergy of the time received — Ireland, according to Alexius, felt that "the *intellectual* and *spiritual* training at St. John's Abbey and University was . . . too low," reported Barry. A brief outline of the episode is included in James H. Moynihan, *The Life of Archbishop John Ireland*, 16–18 (New York, 1953).

¹⁶ Barry, *Worship and Work*, 222–228 (quotation); Hoffmann, *St. John's University*, 110, 119. In 1899 with power generated in its own plant, the electric light became omnipresent throughout St. John's whole vast establishment, even in the stables.

¹⁷ Barry, *Worship and Work*, 228 (quotation), 233; Hoffmann, *St. John's University*, 114–120, 124, 127. From 1867 to 1892 a total of 106 individuals taught at St. John's.

¹⁸ Barry, *Worship and Work*, 231 (quotation); Hoffmann, *St. John's University*, 121–127.

¹⁹ Barry, *Worship and Work*, 230, 233 (quotation); Colman Barry to the author, February 23, 1968.

4. Gustavus Adolphus College, Part I
Pages 17 to 20

¹ Murchie and Jarchow, *Population Trends*, 24; Lund, *Gustavus Adolphus College*, 9.

² Lund, *Gustavus Adolphus College*, 3–13, 33; G. Everett Arden, *Augustana Heritage: A History of the Augustana Luther-*

an Church, 102, 116 (Rock Island, Ill., 1963); *St. Peter Herald*, May 28, 1937. The Paxton colony did not prosper, and Augustana was moved to Rock Island, Illinois, in 1875. The Minnesota Conference was organized in 1858 with five ministers and thirteen congregations; it became the largest component of the Augustana Synod, created two years later. See Peterson, *Remember Thy Past*, 10.

³ Lund, *Gustavus Adolphus College*, 13–17 (quotations); J. Oscar Backlund, "Gustavus Adolphus College," in *American-Swedish Monthly*, 23, 52, (December, 1953). Backlund says that Norelius' first pupil, Jonas Magnuson (later changed to Magney), was the father of Clarence R. Magney, mayor of Duluth and a Minnesota supreme court justice. Jonas paid $1.00 a month for his room and $.75 a week for his board. Tuition was free.

⁴ Lund, *Gustavus Adolphus College*, 18–25; Adolph B. Benson and Naboth Hedin, *Americans from Sweden*, 229–241 (Philadelphia, 1950).

⁵ Lund, *Gustavus Adolphus College*, 25–31; Conrad Peterson, *Gustavus Adolphus College: A History of Eighty Years, 1862–1942*, 16–29 (St. Peter, 1942); Benson and Hedin, *Americans from Sweden*, 229–232. Christianity was the main subject taught in Swedish public schools until well into the twentieth century. The educational aim was largely to train members of the Lutheran church.

⁶ Lund, *Gustavus Adolphus College*, 32–35; Peterson, *History of Eighty Years*, 30–33; *St. Peter Herald*, May 28, 1937. Edward D. Neill, the founder of Macalester College, and the leaders of Augsburg College shared Norelius' views regarding the value of affiliation with the state university. See Chapter 8, below.

⁷ Lund, *Gustavus Adolphus College*, 35–40; Peterson, *History of Eighty Years*, 33–37. In true booster fashion the *St. Peter Tribune* early in 1874 reported that the college would serve others besides Swedes and that it would develop into "the great central educational institution of the northwest." See Lund, *Gustavus Adolphus College*, 37.

⁸ Lund, *Gustavus Adolphus College*, 40 (quotation). There were 75,000 Swedes in Minnesota and adjacent areas, according to the *St. Peter Herald*, November 1, 1876.

⁹ Lund, *Gustavus Adolphus College*, 41–45; Peterson, *History of Eighty Years*, 40.

¹⁰ Lund, *Gustavus Adolphus College*, 45–48. The *St. Paul Daily Globe*, February 11, 1878, gave the current enrollment as 63 students.

¹¹ Lund, *Gustavus Adolphus College*, 48 (quotation). Nyquist was somewhat troubled by coeducation in an age when "it was considered highly improper to permit books written by male and female authors to stand side by side on the book shelf," says Backlund, in *American-Swedish Monthly*, 21 (January, 1954).

¹² Lund, *Gustavus Adolphus College*, 50–53; Peterson, *History of Eighty Years*, 44.

¹³ Lund, *Gustavus Adolphus College*, 53–63 (quotations); Peterson, *History of Eighty Years*, 51–55; *Minneapolis Tribune*, September 23, 1882. Lund notes that the organization by the "American" professors of an English Lutheran church in St. Peter to add to the German, Norwegian, and Swedish Lutheran churches already there did little to lessen ethnic friction.

¹⁴ Lund, *Gustavus Adolphus College*, 64; *Gustavian Weekly*, May 15, 1923.

¹⁵ Lund, *Gustavus Adolphus College*, 64 (quotation), 70. Before 1891 the state did not issue teachers' certificates. Local and county authorities decided who was qualified to teach and whom they would hire to do so.

¹⁶ Lund, *Gustavus Adolphus College*, 67–70 (quotations); Peterson, *History of Eighty Years*, 46–51; Henry N. Benson, "Gustavus Adolphus College: Seventy-Five Years of Service to Church and State," in Daniel Nystrom, ed., *My Church:*

An Illustrated Lutheran Manual, 23:68 (Rock Island, Ill., 1937).

¹⁷ Lund, *Gustavus Adolphus College*, 69–71.

¹⁸ Lund, *Gustavus Adolphus College*, 59–65; *St. Peter Herald*, May 28, 1937; Peterson, *History of Eighty Years*, 58–62, 64.

¹⁹ Lund, *Gustavus Adolphus College*, 70.

²⁰ Lund, *Gustavus Adolphus College*, 70.

²¹ Lund, *Gustavus Adolphus College*, 74–77 (quotations); Peterson, *History of Eighty Years*, 70.

²² Lund, *Gustavus Adolphus College*, 77–79; Peterson, *History of Eighty Years*, 72.

²³ Lund, *Gustavus Adolphus College*, 79.

5. CARLETON COLLEGE, PART I
Pages 21 to 24

¹ Headley and Jarchow, *Carleton*, 1–3 (quotations); Delavan L. Leonard, *The History of Carleton College: Its Origin and Growth, Environment and Builders*, 42–89 (Chicago, 1904); Warren Upham, ed., *Congregational Work of Minnesota, 1832–1920*, 148–156 (Minneapolis, 1921). The section on Carleton in the Upham volume was written by Walter M. Patton, who taught at the college from 1913 to 1928.

² Headley and Jarchow, *Carleton*, 3; Upham, *Congregational Work*, 156–158; Leonard, *Carleton College*, 96–103.

³ Headley and Jarchow, *Carleton*, 4 (quotation). The articles of incorporation were filed on December 17, 1866.

⁴ Headley and Jarchow, *Carleton*, 37–39, 56; Upham, *Congregational Work*, 160–162; Leonard, *Carleton College*, 118–140.

⁵ Headley and Jarchow, *Carleton*, 129–131, 143, 211; Upham, *Congregational Work*, 162. Goodhue headed the preparatory department until 1891, was dean of the faculty from then until 1906, and served thereafter as a trustee.

⁶ Headley and Jarchow, *Carleton*, 9, 18, 94–98, 112, 113 (quotation), 119, 120 (quotation), 275; Leonard, *Carleton College*, 152–173. President Strong was born in Vermont. He was a graduate of Beloit College and of Union Theological Seminary. Ill health and poor eyesight plagued him most of his life.

⁷ Headley and Jarchow, *Carleton*, 95, 268; Leonard, *Carleton College*, 178–191, 208–211; John N. Greer, *The History of Education in Minnesota*, 161–163 (U.S. Bureau of Education, *Contributions to American Education History*, no. 31 — Washington, D.C., 1902).

⁸ Headley and Jarchow, *Carleton*, 39; Greer, *Education in Minnesota*, 163; Leonard, *Carleton College*, 197.

⁹ Headley and Jarchow, *Carleton*, 39, 41 (quotation), 191; Leonard, *Carleton College*, 200–205. Along with Professor Payne, recognition should be given to Miss Margaret J. Evans, who was on the staff from 1874 to 1908 as teacher of English literature, preceptress, lady principal, and dean of women — one of the college's towering figures.

¹⁰ Headley and Jarchow, *Carleton*, 23, 213; Rudolph, *American College and University*, 140, 244. Ever alert to ways of strengthening their young college, Carleton trustees, cognizant of the influx of Scandinavians into the state, considered establishing a Scandinavian professorship in 1870. While it was not done, the college paper, the *Carletonia* of January, 1886, thought the idea a good one, as such action might "give one more of an interest in them [Scandinavians] and in mingling with them." The *Carletonian* first appeared in 1877, but came out irregularly in its early years. It was known as the *Carletonia* from 1881 until 1921, when its name was changed back to the *Carletonian*. Headley and Jarchow, *Carleton*, 387.

¹¹ Headley and Jarchow, *Carleton*, 57, 426; Carleton College, *General Directory, 1866–1926*, 41 (Northfield, 1927).

[12] Headley and Jarchow, *Carleton*, 41–43, 218 (quotations), 245; Leonard, *Carleton College*, 220–222, 233–235. James J. Hill's gift of a $5,000 meridian circle spurred the building of the new observatory.

[13] Headley and Jarchow, *Carleton*, 8, 144, 153 (quotation), 158, 230 (quotations), 236, 334–338, 373–375, 387.

[14] Headley and Jarchow, *Carleton*, 42; Leonard, *Carleton College*, 230–232, 287, 344. Gridley Hall, the pride of the campus for many years, was razed in 1967. See p. 182, below.

[15] Headley and Jarchow, *Carleton*, 276; *Minneapolis Tribune*, April 17, 1887 (quotation); Leonard, *Carleton College*, 223–228 (quotation).

[16] Headley and Jarchow, *Carleton*, 59, 214, 427. In 1893 Carleton amazingly conferred a Ph.D. degree, the first of six in astronomy and mathematics granted by 1909 when the doctoral program wisely was dropped.

[17] Headley and Jarchow, *Carleton*, 57–61 (quotations); Leonard, *Carleton College*, 257. Enrollment in the college in 1903 was 245, in the academy 69.

[18] Headley and Jarchow, *Carleton*, 161, 219 (quotations), 227–229. Methods of instruction also were changing, getting away from "perfect memorization and parrot-like recitation."

[19] Headley and Jarchow, *Carleton*, 273, 287. Even in 1901 over $84,900 in real estate, farm mortgages, and pledges to endowment were charged off as worthless.

[20] Headley and Jarchow, *Carleton*, 144. From 1870 to 1902 12 members of the faculty rendered an average service of 19 years.

[21] Headley and Jarchow, *Carleton*, 43; Leonard, *Carleton College*, 350.

[22] Headley and Jarchow, *Carleton*, 64–68.

[23] Headley and Jarchow, *Carleton*, 96, 431.

6. Augsburg College, Part I
Pages 25 to 29

[1] Carl H. Chrislock, *From Fjord to Freeway: 100 Years Augsburg College*, 3 (Minneapolis, 1969); Bernhardt J. Kleven, *The Story of Augsburg*, 9–13 (Minneapolis, [1933]); [Lars Lillehei, ed.], *Augsburg Seminary and the Lutheran Free Church*, 35 (Minneapolis, 1928). Chrislock notes that the school was named Augsburg Seminarium in October, 1869, to commemorate the city where the famed Augsburg Confession, the basis of the Lutheran creed, was presented to Emperor Charles V in 1530.

[2] Chrislock, *Fjord to Freeway*, 5–7; Lillehei, *Augsburg Seminary*, 36; Kleven, *Story of Augsburg*, 13–16.

[3] Chrislock, *Fjord to Freeway*, 7–9 (quotation); Agnes M. Larson, *John A. Johnson: An Uncommon American*, 98–100 (Northfield, 1969); Lillehei, *Augsburg Seminary*, 37. Chrislock reports that Minneapolis had a population of about 20,000 in 1870, many of them Scandinavians. It also had the state university which Weenaas hoped would serve as a preparatory school for Augsburg.

[4] Chrislock, *Fjord to Freeway*, 9–12 (quotations); Lillehei, *Augsburg Seminary*, 37, 38 (quotations), 49.

[5] Chrislock, *Fjord to Freeway*, 11; Andreas Helland, *Georg Sverdrup: The Man and His Message, 1848–1907*, 11–24, 47 (Minneapolis, 1947); Theresa G. Haynes, "Augsburg Park: A Forgotten Dream," in *Minnesota History*, 40:375 (Winter, 1967). Sverdrup came from a distinguished family, active in both church and state. Chrislock notes that his uncle rose to the position of prime minister of Norway in 1884.

[6] Chrislock, *Fjord to Freeway*, 12–27, 97; Lillehei, *Augsburg Seminary*, 39–42 (quotation). Augsburg faculty in 1874 hoped the institution would "become a major Norwegian-American culture center," writes Chrislock, but matters did not develop that way.

[7] Chrislock, *Fjord to Freeway*, 28.

[8] Chrislock, *Fjord to Freeway*, 30; Helland, *Georg Sverdrup*, 49, 53–70.

[9] Chrislock, *Fjord to Freeway*, 20; Helland, *Georg Sverdrup*, 70.

[10] Chrislock, *Fjord to Freeway*, 32, 33 (quotation); Helland, *Georg Sverdrup*, 67, 73–76, 80–84. The latter records that the church conference had only 34,239 members at the time of the fund drive of 1877.

[11] Chrislock, *Fjord to Freeway*, 31–35; Helland, *Georg Sverdrup*, 84–111; Lillehei, *Augsburg Seminary*, 42, 43 (quotation). The organ of the New School stance was the paper *Folkebladet*, started by Oftedal in 1877 to assist in the financial campaign and later revived with Sverdrup and Oftedal as its prime movers.

[12] Chrislock, *Fjord to Freeway*, 35.

[13] Chrislock, *Fjord to Freeway*, 37–39 (quotation); Helland, *Georg Sverdrup*, 118.

[14] Chrislock, *Fjord to Freeway*, 36 (quotations), 39; Kleven, *Story of Augsburg*, 21–23.

[15] Chrislock, *Fjord to Freeway*, 46–48; Helland, *Georg Sverdrup*, 140–145. A full account of the Augsburg controversy is found in E. Clifford Nelson, *The Lutheran Church Among Norwegian-Americans: A History of the Evangelical Lutheran Church*, 2:38–81 (Minneapolis, 1960). On St. Olaf, see p. 32, below.

[16] Chrislock, *Fjord to Freeway*, 48–62 (quotation). That St. Olaf was not quite so infused with "rationalism" as its opponents contended was indicated in 1890 when Thorstein Veblen's application for a position there foundered on the shoals of the economist's unorthodox religious sentiments. See Kenneth O. Bjork, ed., "Thorstein Veblen and St. Olaf College: A Group of Letters by Thorbjørn N. Mohn," in *Norwegian-American Studies and Records*, 15:122–130 (Northfield, 1949).

[17] Chrislock, *Fjord to Freeway*, 63–66. Augsburg was incorporated in 1872, but the church conventions continued to exercise control of the school. A legislative act of 1877 ratified previous convention actions and empowered the conference to choose Augsburg's trustees.

[18] Chrislock, *Fjord to Freeway*, 66–73 (quotations). Lillehei, *Augsburg Seminary*, 46, says that one old, experienced member of the conference who was a rich farmer in southern Minnesota said he would sue Oftedal for breach of trust if Augsburg's property was transferred to the United Church.

[19] Chrislock, *Fjord to Freeway*, 73–76 (quotations). It is interesting to speculate on the course of Augsburg's development if the transfer to United Church control had been made.

[20] Chrislock, *Fjord to Freeway*, 77–82 (quotation); Helland, *Georg Sverdrup*, 150–179 (quotation). Chrislock records that the state supreme court in 1898 handed down a decision favorable to the Oftedal board.

[21] Chrislock, *Fjord to Freeway*, 82.

[22] Chrislock, *Fjord to Freeway*, 97–112 (quotations). Following the quartet's concert in Marinette, Wisconsin, in 1892, the director persuaded F. Melius Christiansen to enroll at Augsburg, where he spent a student year which he regarded "as a turning point in his life." From 1893 to 1897 he served there as a part-time music instructor. His feeling for Augsburg remained warm after he joined the faculty at St. Olaf in 1903. *Idun*, a variation of the name Ithunn or Ithun, was according to Norse myth the keeper of the golden apples of youth.

7. St. Olaf College, Part I
Pages 30 to 33

[1] Benson, *High on Manitou*, 1–13. Theodore Jorgenson, professor and biographer of Ole E. Rölvaag, regards Muus as "one

of the most original thinkers the Lutheran church has had in this country. . . . [He is] also one of the two or three greatest statesmen our church has fostered." See the *Northfield Independent*, June 17, 1943.

[2] Benson, *High on Manitou*, 13–15; C. A. Mellby, *St. Olaf College Through Fifty Years, 1874–1924*, 9–22 [Northfield, 1925]; *Manitou Messenger* (St. Olaf student newspaper), September 30, 1930.

[3] Benson, *High on Manitou*, 16–21.

[4] Benson, *High on Manitou*, 21 (quotation), 24–28; *Manitou Messenger*, November 6, 1923, April 25, 1934.

[5] Benson, *High on Manitou*, 22–24 (quotation).

[6] Benson, *High on Manitou*, 30–45; *Northfield News*, January 20, 1875; *Manitou Messenger*, May 22, 1917, May 16, 1934. October 26, 1876, was a "red letter" day on which the trustees debated at length the question of building Old Main. Many regarded the school as a failure. The "unyielding pertinacity" of Muus, Thorson, and Quammen saved the day, writes Grose, in *Fifty Memorable Years at St. Olaf*, 29.

[7] Benson, *High on Manitou*, 45; Georgina Dieson-Hegland, *As It Was in the Beginning*, 32–45 (quotation) (Northfield, 1950); *Manitou Messenger*, November 17, 1950.

[8] Benson, *High on Manitou*, 48–53.

[9] Benson, *High on Manitou*, 53.

[10] Benson, *High on Manitou*, 55–58, 73. On Augsburg, see p. 27, above.

[11] Benson, *High on Manitou*, 60, 63–65; Dieson-Hegland, *As It Was in the Beginning*, 47–67, 80, 94, 128–137, 140; Eugene E. Simpson, *A History of St. Olaf Choir*, 13–56 (Minneapolis, 1921); *Manitou Messenger*, February 22, 1927, May 9, 1934, February 20, 1942. The St. Olaf student newspaper, started as a monthly, became a weekly in 1916.

[12] Benson, *High on Manitou*, 62, 66–68, 333. Two able and devoted men who served St. Olaf for many years joined the faculty in the early 1880s: the Reverend Ole G. Felland in 1881 to teach languages and Halvor T. Ytterboe in 1882 to handle commercial subjects. The former remained on the staff until 1926, the latter until his untimely death in 1904.

[13] Benson, *High on Manitou*, 69; *Manitou Messenger*, April 18, May 2, 1934.

[14] Benson, *High on Manitou*, 58, 70–72. In the mid-1880s the school's indebtedness included a $7,000 mortgage and $4,800 in personal notes held by some trustees.

[15] Benson, *High on Manitou*, 72–75 (quotations); Dieson-Hegland, *As It Was in the Beginning*, 81.

[16] Benson, *High on Manitou*, 75–84.

[17] Benson, *High on Manitou*, 84–91.

[18] Benson, *High on Manitou*, 89–91 (quotation); St. Olaf College, *Bulletin*, 110 (April, 1967); Mellby, *St. Olaf College*, 29–32; Dieson-Hegland, *As It Was in the Beginning*, 81, 87, 94–96. Mrs. Ytterboe was also much beloved; her 70th, 75th, and 80th birthdays were celebrated by the whole college family. Recollections of the Ytterboes are found in the delightful volume, *Manitou Analecta: A Collection of Narratives of Selected Events and Recollections*, 1–5 [Northfield, 1968], by St. Olaf's longtime and remarkable dean of women, Miss Gertrude M. Hilleboe, Professor Ytterboe's niece.

[19] Benson, *High on Manitou*, 92.

[20] Benson, *High on Manitou*, 93–95; Dieson-Hegland, *As It Was in the Beginning*, 82–86 (quotation).

[21] Benson, *High on Manitou*, 96–99, 107–109. Founder Muus died in Norway in May, 1900.

8. MACALESTER COLLEGE, PART I
Pages 34 to 37

[1] Henry D. Funk, *A History of Macalester College: Its Origin, Struggle and Growth*, 29–31, 146–156 ([St. Paul], 1910); Kagin, *James Wallace*, 82; Huntley Dupre, *Edward Duffield Neill: Pioneer Educator*, 3–58, 99–107 (St. Paul, 1949). Neill was born in Philadelphia in 1823 and was graduated from Amherst College in 1842. He went to St. Paul seven years later as a missionary to the white population of the region. He was the first chancellor of the University of Minnesota.

[2] Funk, *Macalester College*, 31–35 (quotation); Greer, *Education in Minnesota*, 188. Funk writes that the Puritans objected to naming institutions after localities associated with the life of Christ.

[3] Funk, *Macalester College*, 33, 35; Dupre, *Edward Duffield Neill*, 58–66.

[4] Funk, *Macalester College*, 36; Dupre, *Edward Duffield Neill*, 66–71; Minnesota, *Laws*, 1864, p. 354 (quotation) (St. Paul, 1864). Material on Baldwin University can be found in an undated notebook in the Neill Papers, in the Minnesota Historical Society.

[5] Funk, *Macalester College*, 37–42, 46; Dupre, *Edward Duffield Neill*, 75–77.

[6] Funk, *Macalester College*, 42–44; Greer, *Education in Minnesota*, 188; Dupre, *Edward Duffield Neill*, 78–80; Minnesota, *Special Laws*, 1874, p. 331.

[7] Funk, *Macalester College*, 44, 45 (quotation), 47–51; Dupre, *Edward Duffield Neill*, 80–83. "Macalester College is prospering, and has over 20 students in attendance upon its classes," reported the *Minneapolis Tribune* of October 17, 1874.

[8] Funk, *Macalester College*, 51–61.

[9] Funk, *Macalester College*, 61–63 (quotation), 65. The trustees' desire to set their sights high was stated in a circular of the period. The board intended "to adopt all reforms accepted by Amherst, Dartmouth, Princeton, and Yale, believing it safe to defer to the matured opinions of the wise men of the East." See Greer, *Education in Minnesota*, 188.

[10] Funk, *Macalester College*, 66–81.

[11] Funk, *Macalester College*, 82–87; Dupre, *Edward Duffield Neill*, 85–88.

[12] Funk, *Macalester College*, 88–90, 100–104 (quotation).

[13] Funk, *Macalester College*, 104–112.

[14] Funk, *Macalester College*, 113–128 (quotation); Dupre, *Edward Duffield Neill*, 88–92. In reporting the occasion, the *St. Paul and Minneapolis Pioneer Press* of September 17, 1885, stated that an institution like Macalester "deserves a triple welcome. It is an important element in the upbuilding of a city to which it adds both character and attractiveness."

[15] Funk, *Macalester College*, 136–140 (quotations); Dupre, *Edward Duffield Neill*, 92–94. The *Echo* was discontinued in 1898.

[16] Funk, *Macalester College*, 131–136, 140–142; Dupre, *Edward Duffield Neill*, 94–97; Kagin, *James Wallace*, 78, 81, 92–94, 122, 123 (quotation).

[17] Funk, *Macalester College*, 157–166; Kagin, *James Wallace*, 92, 125, 130. Contributing to faculty bitterness, writes Kagin, was the fact that the board of trustees contained some "men of great wealth who had given nothing to the college and yet insisted on reducing salaries."

[18] Funk, *Macalester College*, 140; Kagin, *James Wallace*, 126.

[19] Funk, *Macalester College*, 144; Kagin, *James Wallace*, 121 (quotation), 129, 133.

[20] Funk, *Macalester College*, 156, 199, 202–209, 216–226, 229; Dupre, *Edward Duffield Neill*, 107–110; Kagin, *James Wallace*, 137, 140–142, 144. In lodging his opposition to the

adoption of coeducation, Neill reminded the board that he had "expended several thousands of dollars" in establishing Macalester and that "To it, as a college for young men," he had given a library of about 1,000 volumes, as well as valuable manuscripts, and many articles for its museum. See Kagin, 140.

[21] Only a reading of Kagin's excellent biography of Wallace can convey an appreciation of what the Macalester president and his long-suffering wife endured to keep the college alive. Against this background, the time and money bestowed by their son, DeWitt Wallace, on Macalester in the twentieth century becomes readily understandable. See chapters 18 and 33, below.

[22] Funk, *Macalester College*, 144, 183 (quotation), 187–196; Kagin, *James Wallace*, 129, 133–135, 143. The Reverend David E. Platter, fiscal secretary, in a statement dated January 15, 1891, and headed, "Macalester in Peril," outlined the college's desperate financial condition: "If Macalester College is allowed to suffocate in its cradle under its present debt it will be a reproach to Presbyterians in the Northwest for all time to come." See William F. Davidson and Family Papers in the Minnesota Historical Society.

[23] Funk, *Macalester College*, 199–201, 212–214; Kagin, *James Wallace*, 157–159. Kagin says that students held Wallace in great affection. On one occasion a disgruntled instructor, who had resigned, got a court judgment against the college for $250 for salary in arrears. He then appeared on campus in Wallace's absence with the sheriff and two secondhand dealers bent on seizing furniture to sell in satisfaction of the judgment. What the intruders got, however, was a soaking from student-operated pitchers and slop jars. A college band escorted the three off the campus, where a streetcar saved them from a barrage of eggs and further assaults on their dignity.

9. College of St. Thomas, Part I
Pages 38 to 40

[1] Moynihan, *Archbishop John Ireland*, 234, 243 (quotation); Herman Schauinger, "A Page of Minnesota History: St. Thomas of St. Paul," 1–5, 7–9 (quotations), unpublished manuscript in the possession of Mrs. Schauinger. Dr. Schauinger had kindly permitted its use, as did Mrs. Schauinger after his death. Before the founding of St. Thomas, seminarians from the diocese of St. Paul studied at St. John's University in Collegeville and at other seminaries in Canada, Europe, and the United States.

[2] Schauinger, "St. Thomas," 5–8; Edward Keenan, "The Story of St. Thomas College," in *Aquin Papers*, No. 1, p. 3, [St. Paul, 1935?].

[3] Schauinger, "St. Thomas," 10–13 (quotation), 24; Keenan, in *Aquin Papers*, 4 (quotation); Sister Helen Angela Hurley, *On Good Ground: The Story of the Sisters of St. Joseph in St. Paul*, 86–89, 131–133 (Minneapolis, 1951). The fathers of O'Gorman and Ireland had gone to the same school in County Kilkenny in the old country, and both families had arrived in St. Paul in May, 1852. Young Thomas and John also attended seminary together in France. See Schauinger, "St. Thomas," 10; Moynihan, *Archbishop John Ireland*, 1.

[4] Schauinger, "St. Thomas," 13–15, 20.

[5] Schauinger, "St. Thomas," 15, 23; Moynihan, *Archbishop John Ireland*, 246 (quotation).

[6] Schauinger, "St. Thomas," 17–24 (quotation). The first St. Thomas Day celebration, a cherished tradition, occurred on March 11, 1886. Celebrations of the Mass and a festive dinner marked the occasion.

[7] Schauinger, "St. Thomas," 24, 26–28, 30; Keenan, in *Aquin Papers*, 4. Two laymen had taught music and drawing during the second year. A third layman was added in 1887 to teach mathematics, penmanship, and bookkeeping.

[8] Schauinger, "St. Thomas," 28, 31.

[9] Schauinger, "St. Thomas," 31–36, 40, 45. A simple frame chapel seems to have been erected in 1891 just north of the administration building.

[10] Schauinger, "St. Thomas," 36, 59, 61; Keenan, in *Aquin Papers*, 5; Hurley, *On Good Ground*, 90, 222; Moynihan, *Archbishop John Ireland*, 243. According to Schauinger, during the ten years the seminary had been part of St. Thomas, 63 priests had been ordained there.

[11] Schauinger, "St. Thomas," 54–57.

[12] Schauinger, "St. Thomas," 48, 50–53, 57. In 1902 Keane was consecrated a bishop and in 1911 an archbishop. Byrne died at the age of 84 in 1942 as the "grand old man" of Minnesota Catholicism. For 26 years he was pastor of St. Luke's Church in St. Paul. From 1917 until his death, he was a member of the St. Thomas board of trustees.

[13] Schauinger, "St. Thomas," 60, 64; Keenan, in *Aquin Papers*, 6 (quotation); Mothers' Club, College of St. Thomas and St. Thomas Military Academy, *Tradition of Excellence: A Tribute and a Testimonial*, 41 (quotation) (St. Paul, 1957).

[14] Schauinger, "St. Thomas," 65–69.

10. Concordia College in Moorhead, Part I
Pages 41 to 43

[1] Erling Nicolai Rolfsrud, *Cobber Chronicle: An Informal History of Concordia College*, 10–12 (Moorhead, 1966). Of Minnesota's total population of 1,310,000 in 1890, Norwegian-born residents of the state accounted for 101,000 and Swedish-born for 99,900. Far more Norwegians than Swedes settled in the Red River Valley. See Murchie and Jarchow, *Population Trends*, 7, 25, 29, 34.

[2] Rolfsrud, *Cobber Chronicle*, 10. Hope Academy students would later taunt those from Concordia by calling them "Corn Cobs," which after some thirty years was gradually transposed to "Cobbers." See Rolfsrud, 12.

[3] Rolfsrud, *Cobber Chronicle*, 13–15.

[4] Quoted in Rolfsrud, *Cobber Chronicle*, 15.

[5] Rolfsrud, *Cobber Chronicle*, 15–18; C. E. Bale, "Saga of Concordia College: An Historical Sketch," in Kermit Overby and Victor Boe, *Pioneer Paths Blazed by Builders of Concordia College*, 5–7 (n.p., [1931?]).

[6] Rolfsrud, *Cobber Chronicle*, 19–22; *Moorhead Daily News*, October 10, 1941; *Concordian* (student newspaper), October 9, 1941, January 22, 1942. In addition to problems of cramped facilities, lack of finances, and competition, the school was nearly destroyed by fire in its first year. Luckily Grose detected and smothered the blaze which had broken out in the laundry room. See *Moorhead Daily News*, October 1, 1941; Rolfsrud, *Cobber Chronicle*, 23.

[7] Rolfsrud, *Cobber Chronicle*, 20, 28.

[8] Rolfsrud, *Cobber Chronicle*, 23–28, 30.

[9] Rolfsrud, *Cobber Chronicle*, 32.

[10] Rolfsrud, *Cobber Chronicle*, 33. On Neill, see p. 36, above.

[11] Rolfsrud, *Cobber Chronicle*, 33, 38.

[12] Rolfsrud, *Cobber Chronicle*, 35 (quotation), 39.

[13] Rolfsrud, *Cobber Chronicle*, 20, 37, 40, 42; *Concordian*, October 31, 1931. Men of the faculty commonly wore cutaways. Many of the students were in their twenties and thirties. The Monday evening literary programs attracted the elite of Moorhead.

11. INTRODUCTION, PART II
Pages 47 to 53

[1] William K. Selden, *Accreditation: A Struggle Over Standards in Higher Education*, 26–28 (New York, 1960); Raymond B. Fosdick and Henry and Katharine Pringle, *Adventure in Giving: The Story of the General Education Board*, 128 (quotation) (New York, 1962). Gates, a Baptist minister, served for years as an adviser to John D. Rockefeller especially on philanthropic and educational matters. Rudolph, *American College and University*, 349; *Who Was Who in America, 1897–1942* (Chicago, 1942).

[2] Selden, *Accreditation*, 30, 43; Calvin O. Davis, *A History of the North Central Association of Colleges and Secondary Schools, 1895–1945*, 3–8, 12 (quotation), 35 (Ann Arbor, 1945). The Langer case involved the North Dakota Agricultural College whose president and senior staff members were fired summarily by the state board of administration, causing the North Central Association to drop the college from membership in 1938. Governor William Langer of North Dakota filed suit against the association, but the association was sustained by the U.S. Circuit Court of Appeals on October 19, 1938.

[3] Davis, *The North Central Association*, 14–16, 44–48.

[4] Davis, *The North Central Association*, 57–61.

[5] Davis, *The North Central Association*, 61; *A Study of the Colleges and High Schools in the North Central Association*, 5–11 (U.S. Bureau of Education, *Bulletins*, no. 6 — Washington, D.C., 1915).

[6] William K. Selden, "The AAU — Higher Education's Enigma," in *Saturday Review*, 77 (quotation) (March 19, 1966); Selden, *Accreditation*, 67–70, 74, 89, 106–108.

[7] Rudolph, *American College and University*, 436–438; Claude M. Fuess, *The College Board: Its First Fifty Years*, 3–52, 178 (New York, 1950); Frank Bowles, *The Refounding of the College Board, 1948–1963: An Informal Commentary and Selected Papers*, 1, 160 (New York, 1967). The idea of the college board originated with Charles W. Eliot; its implementation was largely the work of Nicholas M. Butler. The first examinations were written by 973 candidates; in 1945–46 the number was over 46,000. By 1966–67 more than 864,000 twelfth graders, a number equal to 60 per cent of all persons first entering colleges and universities that year, wrote the scholastic aptitude tests.

[8] Fosdick and Pringle, *Adventure in Giving*, vii, 8 (quotation). The last of the board's major grants was made in 1960.

[9] Fosdick and Pringle, *Adventure in Giving*, 1–12, 127–139 (quotation). In return for financial help, the board demanded of colleges precision in budgeting and accounting and so was influential in the improvement of business management in educational institutions. Frequently this management had been slipshod, to say the least. The board's grants were usually made on a matching basis.

[10] Rudolph, *American College and University*, 431–433; Howard J. Savage, *Fruit of an Impulse: Forty-Five Years of the Carnegie Foundation, 1905–1950*, 11 (quotation) (New York, 1953); Ernest V. Hollis, *Philanthropic Foundations and Higher Education*, 6, 31, 34–38, 50–58, 130, 136–138, 190–196, 286 (New York, 1938). The Carnegie Plan was terminated in 1915 because of actuarial errors, but professors already covered by it continued to receive pensions upon retirement thereafter. The well-known Teachers Insurance and Annuity Association of America was incorporated in 1917 and financed by the Carnegie Foundation.

[11] Rudolph, *American College and University*, 433 (quotation); Selden, *Accreditation*, 2.

[12] Rudolph, *American College and University*, 434 (quotation); General Education Board, *Annual Report, 1928–1929*, 8–10 (New York, 1929). Between 1902 and 1919, 120 colleges in 37 states including Minnesota received $15,700,000 on a conditional basis from the board, mainly for the increase of endowment funds. Between 1919 and 1924 as the value of the dollar decreased, Rockefeller gave the board $50,000,000 to help increase faculty salaries. This fund and its income provided money to 203 institutions in 40 states and to 36 Black schools in 16 states.

[13] Bowles, *Refounding of the College Board*, 142, 160; Minnesota Commission on Higher Education, *Higher Education in Minnesota*, 10. About 15 per cent of those 18 to 21 years old in the country were in college in 1940.

[14] Richard Hofstadter and Walter P. Metzger, *The Development of Academic Freedom in the United States*, 374, 437–445, 454, 460–466 (quotation) (New York, 1955).

[15] Hofstadter and Metzger, *Development of Academic Freedom*, 456, 468–506 (quotation); American Association of University Professors Minnesota Chapter, Papers, 1916–40, in the University of Minnesota Archives. As late as 1940, according to an AAUP study, the typical college and university still "had no definite system for facilitating exchange of opinion between the faculty and trustees or regents," nor did such institutions "provide a definite procedure whereby the faculty might consult the board of control in the choice of a president, a dean, or departmental chairman."

[16] Minnesota Commission, *Higher Education in Minnesota*, 59, 347. Whereas the Association of Minnesota Colleges is composed of both public and private institutions, the latter sometime in the 1920s constituted their own private college council. With Dr. Edgar M. Carlson, former president of Gustavus Adolphus College, as executive director, the council still meets regularly to discuss matters of common concern. As early as September, 1915, the presidents of the state university, Carleton, Gustavus Adolphus, Hamline, Macalester, and St. Olaf met and decided to recommend to their boards a program of joint action involving such matters as newspaper advertising and student recruiting. See Macalester, *Bulletin*, 3 (October, 1915).

[17] Headley and Jarchow, *Carleton*, 379 (quotation); Rudolph, *American College and University*, 451 (quotation). Chapters of Delta Sigma Rho, the national forensic honor society, were established on a number of Minnesota campuses. Intercollegiate debate competition for women was inaugurated in the state in the 1920s. Headley and Jarchow, 380.

[18] Rudolph, *American College and University*, 375–381; St. John's, *Catalogue*, 52 (1909–10); *St. John's Record*, November, 1910; Kagin, *James Wallace*, 169 (quotation); Funk, *Macalester College*, 138; Benson, *High on Manitou*, 170–172; Rolfsrud, *Cobber Chronicle*, 56, 65; Lund, *Gustavus Adolphus College*, 88–94 (quotation). Football had its protagonists, too, some of whom were college presidents, notes Rudolph. They heralded the game's virtues — manliness, hard work, the equivalent of the "playing fields of Eton," a means of sublimating riotous and rebellious tendencies, a stimulus to institutional unity and enthusiasm, and preparation for the hurly-burly of life. Carleton, Hamline, and St. Thomas suspended play only during World War I.

[19] Benson, *High on Manitou*, 169 (quotation); Barry, *Worship and Work*, 232; Rolfsrud, *Cobber Chronicle*, 52 (quotation), 202; Pace, *Hamline University*, 44, 101; Headley and Jarchow, *Carleton*, 44, 409. Basketball was also popular among bloomer-clad women players in the early years of the century.

[20] Benson, *High on Manitou*, 171; Headley and Jarchow, *Carleton*, 407, 410; Carleton, *Algol* (yearbook), 196, 198 (1915); Rolfsrud, *Cobber Chronicle*, 49; Nute, "Hamline Halls," 205, 249; Lund, *Gustavus Adolphus College*, 123; *St. Paul Pioneer*

Press, December 13, 1904. Around 1910 coaches began to receive faculty status. In the same period courses in "physical culture" were being added to graduation requirements.

[21] Barry, *Worship and Work*, 295; *St. John's Record*, October, 1921; Chrislock, *Fjord to Freeway*, 152; Lund, *Gustavus Adolphus College*, 123–131; *Minneapolis Tribune*, December 5, 1926, December 19, 21, 1929; *Winona Republican Herald*, November 26, 1927, November 13, 1928, December 19, 21, 31, 1929; *Minneapolis Star Journal*, April 6, 1941. During the years between 1920 and 1940, Gustavus Adolphus won nine baseball titles, while St. Olaf and St. Thomas earned five each. In football Gustavus also led with six championships, followed by St. John's, St. Olaf, and St. Thomas with four each. In basketball Hamline had a big lead with seven titles. In minor sports Macalester and St. Olaf enjoyed pre-eminence.

[22] Ralph L. Henry, *The Midwest Collegiate Athletic Conference: The Story of an Association of Liberal Arts Colleges in Four States in the Middle West, 1920–1963*, 7–14, 26–35, 57 (Mount Vernon, Ia., 1964); Headley and Jarchow, *Carleton*, 412. In addition to the colleges mentioned above, the conference included from 1921 on Beloit, Coe, Cornell, Lawrence, and Knox. From 1927–28 through 1936–37 Carleton won or tied for the Midwest Conference basketball championship every year but two.

[23] Of the total enrollment of 27,310 in 1931–32 and 34,647 in 1939–40 in Minnesota institutions of higher learning, private colleges accounted for 6,284 and 8,751 students, respectively, according to Ruth E. Eckert, "Higher Educational Opportunities in Minnesota," 3, 24 (President's Committee on Minnesota's Needs for Post-High School Education, Report no. 1 — March, 1946), a typewritten report in the University of Minnesota Archives. The University of Minnesota enrollment is given as 13,997 and 17,526 for the years in question, and the rest is accounted for by the state teachers colleges and junior colleges. The breakdown for the private colleges in 1931 and 1939 is as follows; those marked by an * more than doubled their enrollment during the 1930s.

Institution	1931–32	1939–40	% of change
*Augsburg College	219	465	+112.3
Carleton College	881	869	− 1.4
*College of St. Benedict	123	278	+126
College of St. Catherine	519	664	+ 27.9
*College of St. Scholastica	176	421	+139.2
College of Saint Teresa	404	407	+ .7
Concordia College at Moorhead	431	523	+ 21.4
Gustavus Adolphus College	412	598	+ 45.2
Hamline University	445	690	+ 55.1
Macalester College	553	706	+ 27.7
*St. John's University	196	520	+165.3
St. Mary's College	208	360	+ 73.1
St. Olaf College	904	1,144	+ 26.6
College of St. Thomas	656	866	+ 32
*Bethel Institute	77	186	+141.6
Concordia in St. Paul	80	54	− 32.5
	6,284	8,751	

12. HAMLINE UNIVERSITY, PART II
Pages 54 to 59

[1] Nute, "Hamline Halls," 190, 193–195, 203–207. Graduation exercises and other activities were held in the old Hamline Methodist Church completed in 1901. A second floor was added to the rear wing of Science Hall in 1906.

[2] Nute, "Hamline Halls," 207. Physical education was a requirement by the time the gym was built.

[3] Nute, "Hamline Halls," 192, 199–203, 211; Pace, *Hamline University*, 44, 82. Cooper started a literary magazine, the *Maga*, which continued to be a publication of quality under the guidance of Thomas P. Beyer. Beyer and James King were the two faculty members of long tenure mentioned above.

[4] Nute, "Hamline Halls," 196 (quotation), 203, 208. Prayer meetings on campus were still very well attended during this time, and many graduates became ministers and missionaries.

[5] Nute, "Hamline Halls," 209; *Minneapolis Journal*, October 6, 8, 23, 24, 25, 28, 31, 1910; *St. Paul Dispatch*, October 19, 27, 1910; *Minneapolis Tribune*, October 4, 25 (quotations), 26, 1910. Professor Beyer placed considerable blame for the affair on the alumni, whom he characterized as being "in a state of coma, quiescence or violent eruption all the time." He also laid the guilt to "faults and foibles" of the faculty. See Nute, 210.

[6] Nute, "Hamline Halls," 210–215.

[7] Nute, "Hamline Halls," 216, 226, 259–261. Kerfoot "was a tall, spare, fatherly type, slow to anger, and benevolently tolerant of youthful shortcomings. . . . He consulted the faculty freely . . . and left to them most decisions on academic matters — the curriculum, for example," wrote one of his faculty appointees; see John D. Hicks, "My Six Years at Hamline," in *Minnesota History*, 39:213–226 (Summer, 1965). Hicks, who joined the Hamline faculty in 1916 and was later Morrison Professor of History at the University of California, Berkeley, gives a delightful picture of life at the college. One of the students he remembers well was Daniel C. Gainey, later a successful businessman and a state university regent.

[8] Nute, "Hamline Halls," 223–226, 262–265; *Oracle* (May 8, 1914).

[9] Nute, "Hamline Halls," 227.

[10] Nute, "Hamline Halls," 228–232; Henry L. Osborn, *Hamline University in the World War* (St. Paul, 1920); Edward N. Voorhees (class of 1914), "Hamline in the Great War," in *Alumni Quarterly*, 14–16 (July, 1920). The problems facing faculty members during the war were recalled by Hicks, in *Minnesota History*, 39:218–220. "What can a distracted teacher do," he asked, "when an army sergeant appears at his classroom door . . . with a loud command for Private So-and-So to report to such-and-such a place p.d.q., then departs noisily, followed by the uneasy victim?"

[11] Nute, "Hamline Halls," 217, 228; Hicks, in *Minnesota History*, 39:216, 221–223; Hicks and Hamline business manager, Ivan T. Jones — "Ivan the Terrible" to students — "had the time of my life" recruiting students, traveling about Minnesota and North Dakota in a Model T Ford.

[12] Nute, "Hamline Halls," 217–223.

[13] Nute, "Hamline Halls," 219–221, 226, 228.

[14] Nute, "Hamline Halls," 237–239 (quotation), 251, 267. In 1925 the old Hamline Methodist Church burned, and Hamline University gave $25,000 toward the cost of the present stone Gothic replacement.

[15] Nute, "Hamline Halls," 235, 237–244, 251, 266. Miss Nute gives the average for professors' salaries at Hamline in 1926–27 as $3,027. At Carleton it was $3,876; at Macalester $2,850; at Gustavus Adolphus $2,500; at St. Olaf $2,400.

[16] Nute, "Hamline Halls," 240, 252, 265. The alumni by the mid-1920s had compiled an impressive record of service and achievement; see Osborn, *Alumni Record*.

[17] Nute, "Hamline Halls," 241, 245, 252–255. Alumnus Harold S. Quigley, Hamline's first Rhodes Scholar in 1910 and later a political science professor at the University of Minnesota, was critical of church conference and trustee influence at Hamline in this period, but Theodore C. Blegen, a Hamline teacher in

the mid-1920s and later dean of the University of Minnesota graduate school, retained respect for the quality of work generally done at Hamline.

[18] Nute, "Hamline Halls," 256–258 (quotations), 267. In 1954, when he was nearly 85 years of age, Gregory D. Walcott, the professor dismissed, retired from teaching as "the grand old man of Long Island University." See *St. Paul Pioneer Press*, April 12, June 6, 1954.

[19] Nute, "Hamline Halls," 255, 274, 278.

[20] Nute, "Hamline Halls," 245, 249, 253 (quotation).

[21] Nute, "Hamline Halls," 269–272, 280; Commission on Survey of Educational Institutions of the Methodist Episcopal Church, *Report of a Survey of Hamline University* (Chicago, 1930). Kerfoot and Bridgman were both members of the board of trustees, a situation the report condemned. Kerfoot died in 1930, Bridgman in 1931.

[22] Nute, "Hamline Halls," 268, 273–279. Hughes's proposals were published in Hamline, *Bulletin*, 7 (May, 1930), 8 (June, 1930).

[23] Nute, "Hamline Halls," 280–283.

[24] Nute, "Hamline Halls," 283–286, 300. Hughes was not responsible for Hamline's plight, but a more perceptive individual might have been more successful. The curricular changes he attempted to effect, for example, bewildered and irritated some of the faculty. In the fall of 1931 Milton C. Towner, an assistant professor of education at the University of Chicago, was brought in as dean to carry through a complete curricular reorganization patterned on that carried out at Chicago under Robert M. Hutchins. Much publicity was given the plan, but it and Towner departed with Hughes. See *St. Paul Pioneer Press*, September 13, 1931.

[25] Nute, "Hamline Halls," 284, 290–295, 302.

[26] Nute, "Hamline Halls," 295–298, 301.

[27] Nute, "Hamline Halls," 298–300, 302. Joseph W. Hutton, a Carleton graduate, joined the Hamline staff in 1930 as director of athletics. His basketball teams over the years achieved phenomenal records. He retired in the mid-1960s. Hamline had its first Rhodes Scholar in 1910. By then the University of Minnesota had had two such scholars, and Carleton, Macalester, and St. Olaf one each. See note 17, above.

[28] Nute, "Hamline Halls," 300, 304. President Pace edited the delightful volume, *Hamline University*, as part of the celebration of the institution's 85th birthday in 1939. By a happy coincidence, the conference that year met at Red Wing.

[29] Nute, "Hamline Halls," 303–307.

[30] Nute, "Hamline Halls," 307–321. By 1939, 24 alumni were superintendents of schools in Minnesota. William Bushnell Stout (1903 graduate), who built the first metal and the first thick-wing airplane in America and operated the first passenger air line, ranks as one of Hamline's most famous and colorful alumni. See Robert W. Marks, "Detroit Da Vinci: Inventor Bill Stout Makes His Practical Genius Pay," in *Saturday Evening Post*, 21 (December 7, 1940); and "Bill Stout," in *Fortune*, 46 (January, 1941).

13. St. John's University, Part II

Pages 60 to 66

[1] Barry, *Worship and Work*, 233 (quotation); St. John's, *Catalogue*, 3 (quotation), 7 (1900). The glowing catalog descriptions were toned down after 1905. St. John's did not dispose of its dairy herd until 1958, when the barn was transformed into a workshop for stained glass.

[2] *In and Around St. John's University, Collegeville, Minnesota*, 3–7 (quotation), 29 (n.p., 1909); *Catalogue*, 8 (1900).

[3] *In and Around St. John's*, 7, 11–19, 26, 28, 30–33; Wakin, *Catholic Campus*, 120.

[4] *In and Around St. John's*, 17, 18 (quotations); Barry, *Worship and Work*, 233 (quotation); *St. John's Record*, June 20, December, 1901, January, September, 1902, September, 1905; *Catalogue*, 52–58 (1900), 65 (1901), 76 (1916), 66–76 (1917). As late as 1913 nearly 21 pages in the annual catalog were given over to listing an array of medals, premiums, and distinctions won by students for everything from good deportment and excellence in Christian doctrine to spelling and elocution. In 1914 only two pages were allotted, listing only medal winners.

[5] Barry, *Worship and Work*, 228–230, 234–239; *In and Around St. John's*, 10; *Catalogue*, 48–51 (1900), 3–6 (1906). Father Bruno Doerfler, holder of a doctorate from Sant'Anselmo in Rome, and Father Albert Erkens, who had done graduate work in zoology at the University of Minnesota, served successively as vice president and director of the college at St. John's during the first decade of the century.

[6] Barry, *Worship and Work*, 229; *Catalogue*, 11 (1902), 14 (1922); *In and Around St. John's*, 23–25; *Record*, May, 1901, November, 1902. In the summer of 1922 the second floor was taken over for a reference library. By then it was open most of the day.

[7] *Record*, November, 1901 (quotations), November, 1908, January 14, May 27, 1937; *In and Around St. John's*, 20, 34; *Catalogue*, 16 (1908). In 1908 a new athletic field was laid out over a cranberry bog north of the campus. Heavy rains in October hampered the work, and the plans were not fully carried out at that time.

[8] *In and Around St. John's*, 22; *Catalogue*, 16 (1908); Barry, *Worship and Work*, 229; *Record*, May, 1907; *Off-Campus Record*, July, 1963. In 1904 a brick building was erected southwest of the quadrangle as a residence for the Sisters of the Presentation, who ran the institution's kitchen. In 1913 Abbot Peter brought from Bavaria 24 nuns of the Third Order of St. Francis (which had an American convent in Hankinson, North Dakota) to take over food management. They stayed until 1958.

[9] *Catalogue*, 16 (1912); *Record*, June, July, 1910 (quotations).

[10] Barry, *Worship and Work*, 229, 230 (quotation); *Catalogue*, 20 (1916). The church was redecorated and campus roads improved during Abbot Peter's term in office.

[11] *Catalogue*, 32–34, 36–40 (1900), 13 (1903), 52–62 (1912), 60–77 (1919); Barry, *Worship and Work*, 231 (quotation). The department of drawing by the end of World War I offered courses in such subjects as architectural drafting, elementary machine design, surveying, and show-card writing.

[12] *Catalogue*, 20 (1900), 93 (1913), 34 (1920); Colman Barry to the author, February 23, 1968. In 1913 St. John's began awarding certificates to men who had completed two years of college work. More than 60 were given out by the summer of 1920.

[13] *Catalogue*, 20–31 (1900), 21–37 (1910), 88 (1912), 34–43 (1917). The B.S. degree was not mentioned in the 1918 catalogue or in those for a number of years thereafter.

[14] *Catalogue*, 21 (quotation), 35 (1900), 41 (1910), 28–31, 87 (1912), 39 (quotation) (1920). After six years of the classical course, priesthood candidates entered the philosophy course in the seminary.

[15] *Catalogue*, 39 (1912), 2–4 (1914), 32–36, 43, 48 (1918), 40 (1919). Two-year premedical and prelaw courses were outlined for the first time in the 1918 catalog.

[16] *Catalogue*, 11–16 (1900), 20–28 (1920). To remove seminarians "from the subtle influence of the spirit of the world," they were not permitted to associate with other students. A good survey of life at St. John's is found in *Record*, May, 1921.

[17] *Record*, November, 1911. The Very Reverend Alcuin Deutsch, future abbot, became vice president and rector in 1909; the Very Reverend Kilian Heid succeeded to the post in 1913. See *Catalogue*, 3 (1910), 5 (1914).

[18] Barry, *Worship and Work*, 251–253, 257. For half of his long term as abbot of St. John's, Peter was also president of the American Cassinese Congregation of Benedictines.

[19] *Catalogue*, 44, 78–88 (1918), 44, 89–98 (1919); *Record*, May, October, 1917, March, May, 1918; Reverend Christopher Bayer, archivist at St. John's Abbey, to the author, undated.

[20] Barry, *Worship and Work*, 253–262. According to Barry, 304, Alcuin liked Italian cigars, wines, and travel, although to save money he often passed up meals and rode in day coaches. Among his taboos were "golf, radios, cameras, cigarettes, and especially vacations for Benedictines." He "never tired of recommending fear of God, reverence, humility, patience, and self-control."

[21] Barry, *Worship and Work*, 282; *Catalogue*, 21 (1906), 11 (1918), 22 (1922). Charges had long been modest at St. John's. In 1901 board, room, tuition, and laundry had amounted to $200 a year, by 1918 the figure was $300. In 1920, by insuring two priests for $25,000 each and enlisting alumni to pay the 20-year installments, the university hoped to create an endowment fund. By 1931 alumni payments covered only three-eighths of the premiums and St. John's had to pay the rest. See *Record*, October 27, 1932.

[22] *Catalogue*, 90, 92–96 (1923), 107 (1925); *Record*, October, 1921. Of the 99 college students in 1922–23, Minnesota contributed 67, Wisconsin 13, and North Dakota seven.

[23] *Catalogue*, 107 (1931), 97 (1933), 125 (1940); *Record*, May 3, 1934, September 15, 1938; *St. Cloud Daily Times*, May 20, 1935. In the fall of 1933 St. John's purchased a bus to transport the growing number of day students (about 40) mainly from St. Cloud, whose college costs came to $200 a year.

[24] *Catalogue*, 11, 13 (1922), 9 (1923), 9 (1926). In 1921–22 a new athletic field for the younger students and an addition to the college field were constructed.

[25] *Catalogue*, 10 (1928); *Record*, November 25, 1926, March 29, 1928.

[26] Barry, *Worship and Work*, 263, 275, 286, 298; *Catalogue*, 77 (1917), 5 (1925), 5 (1928), 5 (1929), 5 (1933), 5 (1934). Except for one year, Father Mark Braun (class of 1917) was dean of the college from 1925 until he was appointed abbot of St. Gregory late in 1932. He led "the effort to establish the college on a sound basis," says Barry, 298. Father Walter H. Reger (class of 1917) served as dean the second semester of 1933. From then until his death in November, 1938, famed liturgist Father Virgil Michel was dean.

[27] Barry, *Worship and Work*, 285 (quotation); Hurley, *On Good Ground*, 261 (quotation). In a letter to Alcuin in May, 1937, his good friend President Lars W. Boe of St. Olaf College expressed pleasure "that some colleges were growing restive under agency controls." Any group which added "to the quietness of the spirit" the way St. John's did was, in Boe's opinion, "making a real contribution," records Barry.

[28] Barry, *Worship and Work*, 263, 268, 284 (quotations); *Catalogue*, 32–33 (1922), 36 (1925), 36 (1927), 50–53 (1940). The 1922 catalogue for the first time listed college faculty separately; it numbered 24. By 1940 the total had risen to 56, including 10 laymen, one of whom was Eugene J. McCarthy, a 1935 graduate.

[29] Barry, *Worship and Work*, 263–279, 428n. The revival emphasized a return to the original sources of Christian life and worship, increased lay participation in the Mass and other forms of official public worship, and the use of the vernacular in the ritual. Sister Antonia of St. Catherine's thought the movement "was doubtless of German origin, reminiscent of Cahenslyism" — the movement of the Catholic German immigrants for exclusively German religious institutions. She had little time for the Gregorian chant either, "no matter what Pius X had to say." See Hurley, *On Good Ground*, 208, 261.

[30] Barry, *Worship and Work*, 291, 293.

[31] Barry, *Worship and Work*, 283; *Catalogue*, 33 (quotation), 56 (1922), 33–56 (1923), 35–72 (1924). Schedules of study in business and in music leading to the B.A. and in general engineering and in architecture leading to the B.S. were published in the 1924 catalog, which urged preprofessional students to spend four college years at St. John's.

[32] St. John's registrar's files; *Catalogue*, 29, 99 (1934). Symbolic of the college's emergence as a major entity was the separation of its graduation ceremony in 1934 from that of the preparatory school.

[33] Barry, *Worship and Work*, 290.

[34] *Catalogue*, 54 (1934), 53–56 (1935), 51, 68, 85–94 (1936), 34, 56 (1937), 34, 56–83 (1938), 86 (1939). In the spring of 1935 St. John's began a program in adult education in cooperation with the Minnesota branch of the Central Verein. Known as the Institute for Social Study, it consisted of four week ends a semester for four semesters. Subject matter dealt with social problems of the 1930s, social movements, and communal projects, such as credit unions and the rural life movement.

[35] *Catalogue*, 24–26 (1920), 14, 20–24 (1921), 15, 17 (1922), 13 (1932), 13 (1933), 25 (1940). Tuition remained at $100 a year throughout the 1920s and 1930s; board and room rose from $280 to $336.

[36] *Catalogue*, 51 (1910), 16 (1922), 89–94 (1925), 18–22 (1940); *Record*, November, 1910, October, 1921, January 14, April 22, 1937. Football was played against high schools in 1920 "in an effort to come back gradually." Not until the 1930s under Coach Joe Benda did the Johnnies become a football power in the MIAC.

14. GUSTAVUS ADOLPHUS COLLEGE, PART II
Pages 67 to 71

[1] Lund, *Gustavus Adolphus College*, 81–85; Peterson, *Remember Thy Past*, 64–75.

[2] Lund, *Gustavus Adolphus College*, 88–93.

[3] Lund, *Gustavus Adolphus College*, 85–88. In the fall of 1906 the president of the board, calling for co-operation and harmony, said to the president and faculty: "You are no doubt aware of the disharmony, which has existed especially during the last two years, and of the great harm such disharmony and lack of cooperation are causing our institution." Lund, 87.

[4] Lund, *Gustavus Adolphus College*, 92 (quotation), 103–105.

[5] Lund, *Gustavus Adolphus College*, 94, 101; Blegen, *Minnesota*, 457. The Mattson era also witnessed a steady decline in the use of the Swedish language at Gustavus. The minutes of the board of trustees were kept in English from 1903 on.

[6] Lund, *Gustavus Adolphus College*, 98. Johnson, though born in the humblest of circumstances, was elected governor as a Democrat for three terms in a traditionally Republican state. He might have been a serious contender for the presidency of the United States had not his death in 1909 cut short his brilliant career.

[7] Lund, *Gustavus Adolphus College*, 99–101.

[8] Lund, *Gustavus Adolphus College*, 106; *Gustavian Weekly*, June 9, 1925 (quotation), January 12, 1926; Benson, in Nystrom, ed., *My Church*, 23:104, gives the endowment in May, 1914, as $250,000.

[9] Lund, *Gustavus Adolphus College*, 106.

¹⁰ Lund, *Gustavus Adolphus College*, 107–110, 114–116 (quotation); Peterson, *Remember Thy Past*, 76–78.

¹¹ Lund, *Gustavus Adolphus College*, 110–113 (quotation), 146; Peterson, *Remember Thy Past*, 83. Academic majors and minors and practice teaching were introduced in 1914.

¹² Lund, *Gustavus Adolphus College*, 121–123.

¹³ Lund, *Gustavus Adolphus College*, 135–138.

¹⁴ Lund, *Gustavus Adolphus College*, 145–147.

¹⁵ Lund, *Gustavus Adolphus College*, 113, 148; Peterson, *Remember Thy Past*, 79.

¹⁶ Lund, *Gustavus Adolphus College*, 116, 119; General Education Board, *Annual Report, 1920–1921*, 78 (New York, 1921).

¹⁷ Lund, *Gustavus Adolphus College*, 117–119; *Gustavian Weekly*, January 12, 1926 (quotations); Benson, in Nystrom, ed., *My Church*, 23:104.

¹⁸ Lund, *Gustavus Adolphus College*, 119–121, 124, 131, 144; Peterson, *Remember Thy Past*, 90–101. In 1922 B.A.s were conferred on 52 seniors, in 1929 on 108.

¹⁹ Lund, *Gustavus Adolphus College*, 123–131.

²⁰ Lund, *Gustavus Adolphus College*, 139–144.

²¹ Lund, *Gustavus Adolphus College*, 136–139, 144–147. In 1930 and 1934 Gustavus debating teams won national championships.

²² Lund, *Gustavus Adolphus College*, 131–135, 146; Peterson, *Remember Thy Past*, 102–109. Whereas the church contributed $40,000 a year to the college in the late 1920s, the amount given at the depth of the depression fell to one-fourth of that sum. The academy was abolished in 1931. For a brief but delightful glimpse of life at Gustavus in depression days, see Phyllis Stark, *I Chose A Parson* (New York, 1956).

²³ Lund, *Gustavus Adolphus College*, 148–151. Like President Strong at Carleton 40 years earlier, President Johnson continued to live in the same town with his successor.

²⁴ Lund, *Gustavus Adolphus College*, 151–153.

²⁵ Lund, *Gustavus Adolphus College*, 153–155.

²⁶ Lund, *Gustavus Adolphus College*, 155–158.

²⁷ Lund, *Gustavus Adolphus Coleege*, 158–165.

15. CARLETON COLLEGE, PART II
Pages 72 to 76

¹ Headley and Jarchow, *Carleton*, 96, 114–116, 120; Leonard, *Carleton College*, 291–294. A bachelor when elected president, Sallmon was married six months before his inauguration. His New England bride, who captivated everyone, was a definite asset. In 1903 the faculty numbered 20 and the student body 300 in the college and the academy.

² Headley and Jarchow, *Carleton*, 97, 98.

³ Headley and Jarchow, *Carleton*, 98 (quotation), 276. Sallmon determined how roll should be taken in faculty meetings, never allowed the student paper to use the term "school" in referring to the college, and formulated standardized classroom procedures regarding such matters as ventilation and roll calling. He also spent much time visiting high schools.

⁴ Headley and Jarchow, *Carleton*, 60, 148, 157, 214, 219 (quotation), 314.

⁵ Headley and Jarchow, *Carleton*, 44, 87, 99, 397. Laird became a trustee in 1883 and was president of the college board from 1901 until his death in 1910. His son-in-law, Frederic S. Bell, and his grandson, Laird Bell, later also served in that capacity. His great-granddaughter, Margaret Bell Cameron, became a trustee in 1955. Their contributions to Carleton, material and otherwise, have been monumental.

⁶ Headley and Jarchow, *Carleton*, 99–104 (quotation), 115, 120–122; Robert K. Greenleaf, *Life Style of Greatness: A Personal Appreciation of Donald John Cowling, Third President of Carleton College* (Northfield, 1966).

⁷ Headley and Jarchow, *Carleton*, 100, 104.

⁸ Headley and Jarchow, *Carleton*, 45–47. Cowling favored the traditional English Gothic style of architecture, red brick with Bedford stone trim, and red tile roof. Some college buildings erected in these years have been described as "railroad depot and firehouse style, French-and-Indian renaissance, and Custer's last stand." See Schmidt, *The Liberal Arts College*, 185.

⁹ Headley and Jarchow, *Carleton*, 277 (quotation); Rudolph, *American College and University*, 430; General Education Board, *Annual Report, 1915–1916*, 7 (New York, 1916).

¹⁰ Headley and Jarchow, *Carleton*, 343, 411.

¹¹ Headley and Jarchow, *Carleton*, 324, 469.

¹² Headley and Jarchow, *Carleton*, 337–344 (quotation), 375, 410. After Coach Hunt's arrival, 24 successive football victories followed in the ensuing four years, climaxed on October 7, 1916, with a defeat of Amos Alonzo Stagg's University of Chicago team, 7 to 0. Basketball and track also flourished, and from 1913 to 1923 a state high school basketball tournament, forerunner of the present state event, was held annually in Sayles-Hill gym.

¹³ Headley and Jarchow, *Carleton*, 234, 358.

¹⁴ Headley and Jarchow, *Carleton*, 332, 346 (quotation). Students from Illinois began to appear in sizable numbers from 1929 on.

¹⁵ Headley and Jarchow, *Carleton*, 238, 329, 344–346.

¹⁶ Headley and Jarchow, *Carleton*, 359–367, 376.

¹⁷ Headley and Jarchow, *Carleton*, 30, 35, 37, 47–49.

¹⁸ Headley and Jarchow, *Carleton*, 26, 47–50, 151.

¹⁹ Headley and Jarchow, *Carleton*, 84, 277; General Education Board, *Annual Report, 1919–1920*, 16 (New York, 1920). From 1916 until 1950 the Carleton Corporation handled many business ventures for the college. In 1925 the latter sold a number of properties — the farm, the dormitories, the bookstore, the hospital, the heating system — to the corporation, which thereafter operated them. When the corporation was dissolved, its properties were returned to the college.

²⁰ Headley and Jarchow, *Carleton*, 278; General Education Board, *Annual Report, 1922–1923*, 5, *1930–1931*, 4 (New York, 1923, 1931).

²¹ Headley and Jarchow, *Carleton*, 279; General Education Board, *Annual Report, 1933–1934*, 45 (New York, 1934). With the 1936 payment the General Education Board had contributed a total of $1,225,000 to the college's major fund drives, plus a number of smaller gifts for current expenses.

²² Headley and Jarchow, *Carleton*, 166, 169, 177, 185, 192, 199, 203, 207, 214, 220; Rudolph, *American College and University*, 452–456 (quotation). The department of international relations was underwritten by a gift of $500,000 — the largest Carleton had received up to that time — from Senator and Mrs. Frank B. Kellogg in June, 1937, to establish the Frank B. Kellogg Foundation in International Relations.

²³ Headley and Jarchow, *Carleton*, 224 (quotations), 234; Rudolph, *American College and University*, 456–458.

²⁴ Headley and Jarchow, *Carleton*, 234, 330, 469. Before 1935 only three colleges — Swarthmore, Wesleyan of Connecticut, and Smith — had been granted chapters of Sigma Xi.

²⁵ Headley and Jarchow, *Carleton*, 146, 148–150, 158, 161–210, 456. From 1911 to 1933, with the exception of 1932, a distinguished Harvard professor taught part of each year at Carleton under the Harvard Exchange Plan.

²⁶ Headley and Jarchow, *Carleton*, 157 (quotation). See also Ferenc M. Szasz, "William B. Riley and the Fight Against Teaching Evolution in Minnesota," in *Minnesota History*, 41:201–216 (Spring, 1969).

16. Augsburg College, Part II
Pages 77 to 82

[1] Chrislock, *Fjord to Freeway*, 82–85.

[2] Chrislock, *Fjord to Freeway*, 85–87.

[3] Chrislock, *Fjord to Freeway*, 87, 121–134. Regarded in the 1870s and 1880s as something of a cultural center appealing to all Minneapolitans, Augsburg after 1900 tended to be more isolated. Among the reasons for this alienation were the decision to keep the institution essentially a *Presteskole* serving the limited membership of the Lutheran Free Church, the differential in status between the Yankees and the Scandinavians, and "obsession with prohibition." Dancing, playing cards, and attending the theater fell in the same category with drinking.

[4] Chrislock, *Fjord to Freeway*, 88, 116; *Minneapolis Tribune*, February 22, 1970.

[5] Chrislock, *Fjord to Freeway*, 90, 116; Helland, *Georg Sverdrup*, 265–284. All six recipients of the B.A. degree in 1910 were American-born.

[6] Chrislock, *Fjord to Freeway*, 90–92.

[7] Chrislock, *Fjord to Freeway*, 92–95 (quotation), 138. Elected president of the board to succeed Oftedal was a former pastor, Knute B. Birkeland.

[8] Chrislock, *Fjord to Freeway*, 94, 135–138.

[9] Chrislock, *Fjord to Freeway*, 139.

[10] Chrislock, *Fjord to Freeway*, 140, 142, 151.

[11] Chrislock, *Fjord to Freeway*, 142.

[12] Chrislock, *Fjord to Freeway*, 143.

[13] Quoted in Chrislock, *Fjord to Freeway*, 144.

[14] Chrislock, *Fjord to Freeway*, 145–148, 151–155. To assist in effecting the transition to a coeducational student body, Gerda Mortensen, daughter of a Free Church pastor who had been on the Augsburg staff, was appointed in 1923 as the college's first dean of women. Knowledgeable, able, enthusiastic, she met the challenge of male skepticism and remained a buoyant asset to Augsburg during 41 years on the faculty. Similarly influential was John S. Melby (class of 1914), who joined the staff in 1920 as academy instructor and "Head Master of the Academy Dormitory." In a variety of roles — dean of men, basketball coach, professor of Christianity — "Si" Melby won a lasting place in the minds and hearts of Augsburg people. He died in 1944.

[15] Chrislock, *Fjord to Freeway*, 149; Haynes, in *Minnesota History*, 40:375–383 (Winter, 1967). The "possibility of moving to Richfield" existed until 1946, says Chrislock.

[16] Chrislock, *Fjord to Freeway*, 148, 151, 159.

[17] Chrislock, *Fjord to Freeway*, 151, 155–159, 177. From 1899 to 1920 and from 1936 to 1966, Augsburg was on the two-semester system. During the interval after 1920, the three-quarter calendar was in effect. In 1920 the Minnesota Department of Education recognized the college's secondary teacher training program.

[18] Chrislock, *Fjord to Freeway*, 152, 161–164 (quotation), 166. Along with its problems, Augsburg enjoyed a brief period of fame in intercollegiate athletics in the late 1920s. In 1926–27 its basketball team took the MIAC title; in 1928 both its football and hockey teams won the same distinction.

[19] Chrislock, *Fjord to Freeway*, 161, 165–167.

[20] Chrislock, *Fjord to Freeway*, 162–167. The Free Church operated Oak Grove parochial high school in Fargo.

[21] Chrislock, *Fjord to Freeway*, 165, 168 (quotation).

[22] Chrislock, *Fjord to Freeway*, 168–170, 172.

[23] Chrislock, *Fjord to Freeway*, 177 (quotation), 205.

[24] Chrislock, *Fjord to Freeway*, 172, 176–180. Rules regarding dancing, drinking, and frequenting pool halls were still strict, but good judgment and mature understanding tempered letter-of-the-law enforcement of these regulations.

[25] Chrislock, *Fjord to Freeway*, 180–182, 193.

[26] Chrislock, *Fjord to Freeway*, 88, 158, 183 (quotation).

[27] Chrislock, *Fjord to Freeway*, 184.

[28] Chrislock, *Fjord to Freeway*, 184–188. Denied a part in the presidential selection process, some undergraduates appeared at the Thief River Falls meeting and gave enthusiastic vocal support to their choice. They were reminded that denominational gatherings and athletic contests were dissimilar events.

[29] Chrislock, *Fjord to Freeway*, 173–176 (quotations), 188.

[30] Chrislock, *Fjord to Freeway*, 188–190, 193.

[31] Chrislock, *Fjord to Freeway*, 191–193.

17. St. Olaf College, Part II
Pages 83 to 88

[1] Benson, *High on Manitou*, 93, 100–103; 186, Mellby, *St. Olaf College*, 33–35; *Manitou Messenger*, January 5, 12, 1945. In the *Messenger* of December 13, 1927, Professor Ole E. Rölvaag (class of 1905) recalled the simple and patriarchal life at the college during his student days when the most common complaints concerned the food and the professors.

[2] Benson, *High on Manitou*, 103, 106.

[3] Benson, *High on Manitou*, 111, 114 (quotations); *Manitou Messenger*, June 6, 1925, March 19, 1954.

[4] Benson, *High on Manitou*, 114–119.

[5] Benson, *High on Manitou*, 119–122; Dieson-Hegland, *As It Was in the Beginning*, 69, 88–93, 154–160. A delightful picture of life in Mohn Hall is found in Hilleboe, *Manitou Analecta*, 51–64. The president's home, later known as Manitou Cottage, and the hospital were also erected in this period.

[6] Benson, *High on Manitou*, 123–126; *Manitou Messenger*, January 5, 1945. Students were paid $.15 an hour for part-time work early in the century. Three meals a day in a boarding club cost $1.75 a week in 1904–05.

[7] Benson, *High on Manitou*, 127–136. An article in *Manitou Messenger*, October 3, 1916, was critical of what was regarded as the "practical" trend of the curriculum. It was felt that the result would be "no end of fads." The author contended that the study of philosophy, Greek, and Latin would not only give one culture and mental discipline, but also help him rise above his environment to create a new and better one.

[8] Benson, *High on Manitou*, 139, 174–183; William Seabrook, "Imported Americans," in *American Magazine*, 94 (March, 1937); Dieson-Hegland, *As It Was in the Beginning*, 148–153 (quotation); Simpson, *St. Olaf Choir*, 57–179; Paul G. Schmidt, *My Years at St. Olaf*, 55–63, 115–125 (Northfield, 1968).

[9] Benson, *High on Manitou*, 286, 336; Theodore Jorgenson and Nora O. Solum, *Ole Edvart Rölvaag: A Biography* (New York, 1939); interview with Dr. Jorgenson, January 3, 1970.

[10] Benson, *High on Manitou*, 136–139, 141–143.

[11] Benson, *High on Manitou*, 140, 144–146, 185; Dieson-Hegland, *As It Was in the Beginning*, 98, 100–103.

[12] Benson, *High on Manitou*, 146–167; *Manitou Messenger*, March, 1911 (quotation). Dean Hilleboe has an interesting article on the extracurriculum in the years following 1900 in *Manitou Messenger*, May 9, 1934. See also her *Manitou Analecta*, 19–25.

[13] Benson, *High on Manitou*, 184–188 (quotation); *Manitou Messenger*, February 13, 1917; Erik Hetle, *Lars Wilhelm Boe: A Biography*, 49–53 (Minneapolis, 1949). Vigness favored a strong program of intercollegiate athletics, finding nothing intrinsic in sports which opposed Christianity.

¹⁴ Benson, *High on Manitou*, 189–191.

¹⁵ Benson, *High on Manitou*, 191–193, 200, 276. St. Olaf lost 75 students when its academy was transferred to Red Wing. Its former principal, J. Jörgen Thompson, remained at St. Olaf as dean of men. The *Manitou Messenger*, January 23, 1917, feared that the loss of the academy would create a problem for St. Olaf students in the college's secondary school department. Numbers of academy students had also been registered in the college music department. Neither point proved serious.

¹⁶ Benson, *High on Manitou*, 203–207; Paul G. Vigness, "St. Olaf Fifty Years Ago," in *St. Olaf Alumnus*, 4–6 (quotation) (June, 1966). By the spring of 1918, 40 of the 51 men in the senior class were in some branch of military service, and so were some 100 other undergraduates.

¹⁷ Benson, *High on Manitou*, 207–209 (quotation); Hetle, *Lars Wilhelm Boe*, 23–31, 35–58.

¹⁸ Benson, *High on Manitou*, 210–212. Hilleboe, in *Manitou Analecta*, 31–39, gives a vivid account of wartime life at the college and of the flu epidemic.

¹⁹ Benson, *High on Manitou*, 212–219. An item in *Manitou Messenger*, September 30, 1919, gives the enrollment as 738. Many servicemen had returned, and the freshman class was quite large. St. Olaf's total assets in 1918 were $584,000. See *Manitou Messenger*, May 16, 1934.

²⁰ Benson, *High on Manitou*, 220–223, 227; Hilleboe, *Manitou Analecta*, 41–43. Benson notes that the Norman Gothic style of the famed fortress-monastery Merveille of Mont Saint-Michel in Normandy was selected because the latter was "the home of ideas and ideals similar to those of the modern Christian college. It was the center of inspiration for the thinker and scholar, the poet and missionary, the prophet and reformer, and of those who had a vision of a better world."

²¹ Benson, *High on Manitou*, 225–227, 250–252, 268, 287, 336. The beauty and symbolism of Holland Hall formed the subject of a vignette by Dean Hilleboe, which she was called upon to deliver on a number of occasions. Peter O. Holland came to St. Olaf in 1907 to teach in the academy. A major figure in the college's business and financial affairs, he remained on the staff until his death in 1939. See Hilleboe, *Manitou Analecta*, 45–49.

²² Benson, *High on Manitou*, 262, 270, 279–281; Hilleboe, *Manitou Analecta*, 58, 65–70. Some of the names of the off-campus homes used by women students were Blue Goose, Lazy Manshun, and Wayside Inn.

²³ Benson, *High on Manitou*, 300–305.

²⁴ Benson, *High on Manitou*, 228, 231, 241; *Manitou Messenger*, September 30, 1919, September 26, 1922, September 24, 1929. St. Olaf was the largest private college in the state in 1922.

²⁵ Benson, *High on Manitou*, 228 (quotation), 232–234, 256, 260, 293; Hilleboe, *Manitou Analecta*, 101–107. St. Olaf was placed on the approved list of the American Association of University Women in 1927 and of the Association of American Universities in 1930.

²⁶ Benson, *High on Manitou*, 235–239; Hilleboe, *Manitou Analecta*, 119; *Manitou Messenger*, December 9, 1930. On February 4, 1926, the Norwegian-American Historical Association was incorporated. Its executive office and archives are located at St. Olaf, its museum at Luther College. It has published over 40 bound volumes by and about Norwegians.

²⁷ Benson, *High on Manitou*, 229, 239, 268 (quotation). Tuition in 1929 was $150 a year. Room rent came to $60 a year and board to $4.00 a week.

²⁸ Benson, *High on Manitou*, 269–279 (quotation); *Manitou Messenger*, May 16, 1934. By the mid-1930s the college owned 170 acres, and its endowment exceeded $900,000.

²⁹ Benson, *High on Manitou*, 279, 284–288; *Manitou Messenger*, May 16, 1934. The college had 3,296 graduates by May, 1934. Seventy-five per cent of them had graduated since 1916.

³⁰ Benson, *High on Manitou*, 253, 264–266; *Manitou Messenger*, May 9, 1934; Schmidt, *My Years at St. Olaf*, 79–98.

³¹ Benson, *High on Manitou*, 240, 243, 248–250, 259, 263, 270, 282. In 1922 St. Olaf tied St. Thomas for the MIAC championship in football; the next year St. Olaf had sole possession of the title. The college's basketball team won the MIAC championship in 1929.

³² Benson, *High on Manitou*, 234, 283, 298.

³³ Benson, *High on Manitou*, 308–311; Hetle, *Lars Wilhelm Boe*, 187–203.

18. MACALESTER COLLEGE, PART II
Pages 89 to 94

¹ Funk, *Macalester College*, 231–235, 273; Kagin, *James Wallace*, 187; *St. Paul Pioneer Press*, June 16, 1904. Enrollment in the college and the Baldwin School totaled 136 in 1900.

² Funk, *Macalester College*, 231; Kagin, *James Wallace*, 189–192.

³ Funk, *Macalester College*, 251; Kagin, *James Wallace*, 193 (quotation).

⁴ Funk, *Macalester College*, 252–262.

⁵ Funk, *Macalester College*, 262, 264; Kagin, *James Wallace*, 195–198; Macalester College, *Bulletin*, 5 (October, 1907). Wallace spent a happy vacation in Greece in the summer of 1907 and was accompanied back to the United States by his son Ben, who had just completed his studies at Oxford as Macalester's first Rhodes Scholar. Another son, Robert, graduated from the college in 1908. A third son, DeWitt, was the founder of the *Reader's Digest*.

⁶ Kagin, *James Wallace*, 200–204 (quotation); *Bulletin*, 2 (November, 1910). Hodgman reported in the 1910 *Bulletin*, 3, that "the Christian life of the college is sane, voluntary, devoid of cant, genuine and, therefore, enduring."

⁷ Funk, *Macalester College*, 226–229, 232, 244, 264; Kagin, *James Wallace*, 193, 199; *Bulletin*, 4 (October, 1907), 1 (December, 1910), 1, 4 (June, 1913). There were 105 students in the college and 105 in the academy in the fall of 1907. Wallace Hall in 1969–70 became the college's first coed dormitory. See *Minneapolis Tribune*, *Picture Magazine*, April 12, 1970.

⁸ Funk, *Macalester College*, 241–246; *Bulletin*, 1 (November, 1911), 1, 4 (June, 1913); Hodgman to the Board of Trustees, July 14, September 29, 1913 (quotations here and below), in Davidson Papers. Macalester's budget for 1911–12 was $43,000.

⁹ Hodgman to the Board of Trustees, March 1, 1913, Davidson Papers. Of the 118 Macalester freshmen in the fall of 1912, only a dozen came from the Baldwin School.

¹⁰ "Report of the Committee on the Baldwin School," June, 1912, Davidson Papers.

¹¹ Hodgman to the Board of Trustees, March 1, 1913, Davidson Papers; *Bulletin*, 2 (quotation) (June, 1913). Macalester was on the North Central Association's list of accredited institutions in 1913, but it was dropped from the 1914 list. The college was accredited again in 1915. See Joseph J. Semrow to James F. Holly (Macalester librarian), November 21, 1968, in college files.

¹² Macalester College, *Catalogue*, 5–8 (1910–11); here and below, see Glenn Clark, *A Man's Reach: The Autobiography of Glenn Clark*, 135–146 (New York, 1949).

¹³ *Catalogue*, 30–32 (1910–11); Funk, *Macalester College*, 277; *Bulletin*, 1 (October, 1915).

¹⁴ *Bulletin*, 2 (October, 1918); Kagin, *James Wallace*, 213.

[15] Kagin, *James Wallace*, 214, 219; *Bulletin*, 1 (October, 1918); *Mac Weekly* (student newspaper), October 24, December 4, 1918, May 21, 1919. Wallace, who was a fervent supporter of the League of Nations and greatly upset by its foes in Washington, proclaimed to a Macalester chapel audience in November, 1919: "If I had my way I would put the United States senators in cages and send them around the country with Ringling Brothers circus as the greatest exhibition of political incompetence the world has ever seen." See Kagin, 219.

[16] Kagin, *James Wallace*, 219; *Bulletin*, 2 (October, 1918), 6 (October, 1919); *Mac Weekly*, October 15, 1919. At commencement on June 12, 1918, degrees were awarded to 12 men and 17 women.

[17] *Bulletin*, 8 (June, 1918), 1–4 (June, 1919).

[18] *Bulletin*, 2 (October, 1919), 2 (June, 1921); *Mac Weekly*, October 22, 1919. The Ancient Order of Caluthumpian, an initiation organization started in 1895, was unsuccessfully disbanded by administrative fiat early in 1921 because its existence was regarded as a hindrance to the endowment drive. See *Mac Weekly*, January 12, 1921.

[19] *Bulletin*, 1 (April, 1922), 97–123 (April, 1927), 6–9 (April, 1930). The senior class of 1922 had 48 members. The class of 1926 had 73 graduates.

[20] *Mac Weekly*, October 6, 1922; *Bulletin*, 26 (April, 1922). There was a student council of sorts up to 1916. Its last official act, "so flagrantly violated at present [1920]," provided that freshmen should wear green caps, according to the *Mac Weekly*, November 17, 1920.

[21] Private source; *Mac Weekly*, March 23, 30, 1923, May 27, 1926; *Bulletin*, 6 (April, 1923). Bess died after a long illness in 1926.

[22] *Mac Weekly*, December 19, 1923, January 25, 1924; *Bulletin*, 16 (April, 1924).

[23] *Mac Weekly*, May 9, 1924, January 21, October 6, 13, 27, 1926; *Bulletin*, 6 (April, 1924). In 1924 Macalester Presbyterian Church was built across from Old Main on property donated by the college's trustees. Professors Wallace and Funk worked hard to raise money for the edifice. As a result the congregation permitted Macalester to conduct its daily chapel service in the church auditorium. See *Mac Weekly*, April 11, 1924.

[24] *Bulletin*, 7 (quotation) (October, 1924), 14 (April, 1928); *Mac Weekly*, April 27, September 21, 1927.

[25] *Bulletin*, 10, 107 (April, 1928); *Mac Weekly*, May 16, 1924, April 22, 29, 1926, October 12, 1927, May 2, 1929.

[26] *Bulletin*, 35, 68, 118–132 (April, 1924), 38, 67–69, 78 (April, 1926), 73–75, 80–83 (April, 1929), 47 (April, 1930), 51–53, 82–84 (April, 1940).

[27] *Bulletin*, 25 (April, 1932), 24–26, 98–107 (April, 1933), 114 (April, 1934); interview with Otto T. Walter, October 8, 1968; taped interview of the author, November 12, 1968, with Edwin Kagin, in the collections of the Minnesota Historical Society.

[28] Walter and Kagin interviews; Kagin, *James Wallace*, 240; *Bulletin*, 14 (March, 1938), 6 (April, 1939).

[29] Kagin interview; Kagin, *James Wallace*, 247; *Bulletin*, 11 (April, 1931), 17, 119 (April, 1940); *Mac Weekly*, October 14, 1937. James Wallace, then past 90 years of age, died on August 23, 1939. Since Turck had already been elected president, Wallace in his last days felt more at ease, knowing that his beloved college once more had a permanent head.

[30] *Bulletin*, 6–9, 11, 31–97 (April, 1931), 10, 31, 65 (April, 1934), 87–89 (April, 1935), 7–12, 17, 39–102, 105–119 (April, 1940). The part-time debate coach in 1939–40 was Karl Harold Levander. Minus his first name, he was to be elected governor of Minnesota in 1966.

[31] *Bulletin*, 6, 15–17, 30, 104 (April, 1940), 107 (April, 1941). There were 96 graduates in the class of 1940.

[32] *Bulletin*, 36, 78 (April, 1928), 36 (April, 1937), 51–53, 64, 82–84 (April, 1940), 40, 44 (April, 1941), 45–52 (quotation) (April, 1942).

[33] *Mac Weekly*, March 13, 1936, February 9, October 26, 1939; *Bulletin*, 33 (April, 1939), 21 (April, 1942); Kagin, *James Wallace*, 243; Macalester Board of Trustees, "Minutes," January 30, 1947, in the office of the president, hereafter cited as "Trustee Minutes." The permanent record of board of trustees minutes up to July 7, 1949, was destroyed by fire. Those cited here and in Chapter 33, below, are in the form of drafts circulated to board members before final approval. For 1938–39 tuition and fees were raised from $87.50 to $100 a semester. Board was $90 a semester and rooms about $45.

[34] *Bulletin*, 15, 52–54, 115 (April, 1942), 16, 96–99, 121 (April, 1943). The conservatory of music after a long life passed out of existence in 1942. Henceforth all work in music was concentrated in the regular collegiate department.

19. College of St. Thomas, Part II

Pages 95 to 100

[1] Schauinger, "St. Thomas," 70–76, 86–89.

[2] Schauinger, "St. Thomas," 76–79, 82–86. In 1901–02 Ignatius A. O'Shaughnessy transferred to St. Thomas from St. John's. He was a star football player at both colleges. His later interest in and benefactions to St. Thomas loom large in its development.

[3] Schauinger, "St. Thomas," 90; Keenan, in *Aquin Papers*, 4.

[4] Schauinger, "St. Thomas," 95–97.

[5] Schauinger, "St. Thomas," 132, 136.

[6] Schauinger, "St. Thomas," 135, 143, 145–147, 149, 158, 160–163 (quotation). Final major addition to the plant in the Moynihan period was the athletic field, begun as a project of the alumni association (founded in 1903) in 1906. In 1911 a surrounding eight-foot wall, a grandstand, and a quarter-mile track were added.

[7] Schauinger, "St. Thomas," 97–100; Keenan, in *Aquin Papers*, 10.

[8] Schauinger, "St. Thomas," 113–122. On May 7 and 8, 1908, St. Thomas cadets participated with the Minnesota National Guard in a "Grand Military Tournament," a "blaze of glory" thrilled to by a crowd of 15,000 in the St. Paul Auditorium. Schauinger, 117.

[9] Schauinger, "St. Thomas," 122–129. Alfred M. Gruenther, future general and commander of NATO, was one of the 52 young men to receive their high school diplomas at St. Thomas in June, 1916. He then transferred to the U.S. Military Academy at West Point.

[10] Schauinger, "St. Thomas," 143, 160. Of the first four college graduates, three went to law school and the fourth returned to St. Thomas to teach Latin. Twelve men received bachelor's degrees in 1916.

[11] Schauinger, "St. Thomas," 161, 165, 168.

[12] Schauinger, "St. Thomas," 127–131, 172. To care for the additional men the SATC unit was expected to attract, a long barracks type of building was hastily erected alongside the armory. When the unit was demobilized, the government paid the college $20,000 for the training corps structure.

[13] Schauinger, "St. Thomas," 174, 191.

[14] Schauinger, "St. Thomas," 176–181. On October 20, 1919, the college community happily played host to the president of the Irish Republic, Eamon De Valera.

[15] Schauinger, "St. Thomas," 184–187, 194.

[16] Schauinger, "St. Thomas," 194–202. Father Moynihan was rector of the seminary for 12 years and a Minneapolis pastor from 1933 until his death a decade later. Father Dunphy served as a pastor for more than 30 years after leaving St. Thomas.

[17] Schauinger, "St. Thomas," 190–194, 210.

[18] Schauinger, "St. Thomas," 209, 212–214, 223.

[19] Schauinger, "St. Thomas," 209–212, 230, 233. The department of engineering was discontinued in 1923, a year after its chairman resigned. In 1927 an archdiocesan normal school under the direction of St. Thomas was established in the James J. Hill residence on Summit Avenue, St. Paul, which had been acquired by Archbishop Dowling.

[20] Schauinger, "St. Thomas," 231–235. The beloved Father Cullen died in 1940.

[21] Schauinger, "St. Thomas," 232, 242–246. Despite the college's shortcomings, one instructor pointed out that 41 of his students had earned doctor's degrees — 29 in medicine, 11 in dentistry, and one in philosophy.

[22] Schauinger, "St. Thomas," 248.

[23] Schauinger, "St. Thomas," 249–257, 259. Of all the fetes welcoming the Holy Cross group, that of September 10, 1928, was the high light for the public. At it appeared famed Notre Dame coach Knute Rockne in his role as athletic supervisor of St. Thomas.

[24] Schauinger, "St. Thomas," 257–259 (quotation), 267, 314. In April, 1931, St. Thomas was informed that members of the top one-third of its graduating class of 1931 with majors in classical languages, English, history, philosophy, and psychology and education would be admitted directly into the university's graduate school.

[25] Schauinger, "St. Thomas," 273, 275, 281, 318, 324, 344. St. Thomas' law school did a good job, but the University of Minnesota seemingly was not pleased with the school's existence.

[26] Schauinger, "St. Thomas," 269, 272, 298–301, 307, 312–314, 324.

[27] Schauinger, "St. Thomas," 274–278, 290.

[28] Schauinger, "St. Thomas," 311, 315–317, 325–340. "Such things as renovating old buildings," wrote Father Schumacher, "enlarging and equipping a library and laboratories, creating a campus in harmony with the ideals of a college, and assuming the worries and distractions incident to the erecting of a new building, particularly in a time of great depression — these things are not born of hirelings, but come from the free sons of God." Holy Cross referred the case to Rome, but the latter did not intervene. See Schauinger, 337.

[29] Schauinger, "St. Thomas," 341, 350.

[30] Schauinger, "St. Thomas," 342, 346–352.

[31] Schauinger, "St. Thomas," 356–360.

[32] Schauinger, "St. Thomas," 101, 107, 134, 139, 141, 147, 151, 155, 163, 169; Keenan, in *Aquin Papers*, 9, 12. In 1916 one of three plays presented, *Ready Money*, had in its cast the young Vincent Flynn, who would one day head the college.

[33] Schauinger, "St. Thomas," 182, 188, 212, 215–218, 220, 224, 239, 262. About 1924 automobiles began to appear on campus in growing numbers with attendant noise, confusion, and parking problems. Most common was the black Model T Ford, but others long since largely forgotten included Jewetts, Grays, Nashes, and Columbias.

[34] Schauinger, "St. Thomas," 261, 272, 302, 352 (quotation), 355, 363, 372–374, 377, 386. Typical of similar complaints in institutions of higher learning was this one in the *Aquin*, the student yearbook in 1940: "If we aren't going to get student government, why aren't we? If we are, when are we?"

[35] Schauinger, "St. Thomas," 378.

20. Concordia College in Moorhead, Part II

Pages 101 to 105

[1] Rolfsrud, *Cobber Chronicle*, 43; *Concordian*, October 9, 1941. Bogstad had been at the school since its first day. He taught religion and Norse and served as the first dean of men.

[2] Rolfsrud, *Cobber Chronicle*, 44–47. Drinking water at the time was brought over from Fargo, North Dakota, and placed in tanks on the first floor of each building.

[3] Rolfsrud, *Cobber Chronicle*, 47–52.

[4] Rolfsrud, *Cobber Chronicle*, 50, 53.

[5] Rolfsrud, *Cobber Chronicle*, 54.

[6] Rolfsrud, *Cobber Chronicle*, 54, 60. From 1917 until 1951 Shurson served as financial secretary of the Norwegian (later Evangelical) Lutheran Church.

[7] Rolfsrud, *Cobber Chronicle*, 56–59.

[8] Rolfsrud, *Cobber Chronicle*, 59–64 (quotation); *Moorhead Daily News*, October 10, 1941. Many parents had been loath to send their children to Concordia because of the 48 saloons in Moorhead in 1910.

[9] Rolfsrud, *Cobber Chronicle*, 65–68. Students who waited on table in this pre-World War I era were paid $.75 a week.

[10] Rolfsrud, *Cobber Chronicle*, 68, 72–79.

[11] Rolfsrud, *Cobber Chronicle*, 69.

[12] Rolfsrud, *Cobber Chronicle*, 71, 80–82; *Concordia College Record*, 151 (October, 1966). Nine men and one woman received B.A.s in 1918.

[13] Rolfsrud, *Cobber Chronicle*, 86, 93.

[14] Rolfsrud, *Cobber Chronicle*, 89, 92; *Moorhead Daily News*, October 26, 1923; *College Record*, 16 (February, 1941). By 1941 Concordia's immediate constituency consisted of 1,391 congregations and 261,000 members of the denomination in Montana, North Dakota, and the northern half of Minnesota.

[15] Rolfsrud, *Cobber Chronicle*, 93; *College Record*, 9 (February, 1941). According to Clemens M. Granskou, Aasgaard's election as head of the church was fortunate for its affiliated colleges. He possessed a wholesome attitude toward education, and his influence kept the colleges largely free of ecclesiastical interference. Aasgaard and Lars W. Boe had been classmates at St. Olaf and were close friends. Interview with Mr. Granskou, March 14, 1969.

[16] Rolfsrud, *Cobber Chronicle*, 86, 88.

[17] Rolfsrud, *Cobber Chronicle*, 86–90. A football game with St. Olaf in 1922 provided the excuse for 14 intrepid Concordians to initiate excursions in two Model Ts and a Reo to out-of-town athletic contests. Each car apparently demanded regular radiator refills.

[18] Rolfsrud, *Cobber Chronicle*, 86, 91, 94.

[19] Rolfsrud, *Cobber Chronicle*, 95.

[20] Rolfsrud, *Cobber Chronicle*, 95–97, 99; *College Record*, 151 (October, 1966). Three of the new faculty were Konrad O. Lee (class of 1919), chemistry and physics, Thomas O. Burgess, education and psychology, and Frank Cleve, physical education. Cleve's basketball and football teams won the MIAC title in 1931.

[21] Rolfsrud, *Cobber Chronicle*, 98, 104–106.

[22] Rolfsurd, *Cobber Chronicle*, 98–100; *Concordian*, March 18, 1932. In the fall of 1934 federal assistance became available to students. As late as 1938, 98 students were getting help through the National Youth Administration program.

[23] Rolfsrud, *Cobber Chronicle*, 106–110, 224–226.

[24] Rolfsrud, *Cobber Chronicle*, 87, 90, 92, 144 (quotation), 148, 163–165, 167–170. Concordia's women first participated in an intercollegiate debate tournament in 1927. Sidney A. Rand (class of 1938), who became president of St. Olaf College in 1963, was a prominent debater while a Concordia student.

[25] Rolfsrud, *Cobber Chronicle*, 175–194 (quotation); *Concordian*, June 3, 1935.

[26] Rolfsrud, *Cobber Chronicle*, 102–104, 111. After Fjelstad Hall was completed, North Hall was remodeled to serve the music department and the new art department. Bogstad House was transformed into faculty apartments, and a new frame building was erected to make space for the bookstore, post office, and a lunch room.

[27] Rolfsrud, *Cobber Chronicle*, 111; *Concordian*, March 18, 1932; *College Record*, 45–99, 107 (February, 1941). Through 1940 (including 28 degree holders from Park Region College prior to 1918), Concordia had conferred baccalaureates on 1,493 students, of whom 758 were men and 735 women. Of the total 707 were from Minnesota, 358 from North Dakota, and 56 from South Dakota. Of these alumni 690 were in educational work — 445 as high school teachers and 84 as high school superintendents. Homemaking occupied 289 of the women, and 109 of the men were either ministers or theology students.

21. College of St. Catherine, Part II
Pages 106 to 112

[1] Hurley, *On Good Ground*, 227 (quotation); Sister Clara Graham, *Works to the King: Reminiscences of Mother Seraphine Ireland*, 69 (St. Paul, 1950).

[2] Hurley, *On Good Ground*, 5–13 (quotation), 19–29, 113; Sister Dolorita Marie Dougherty, *et al.*, *Sisters of St. Joseph of Carondelet*, 140–144 (St. Louis, 1966); Sister Helen Angela Hurley, "The Sisters of St. Joseph and the Minnesota Frontier," in *Minnesota History*, 30:1–13 (March, 1949). Rising costs forced the closing of St. Joseph Academy in 1971.

[3] Hurley, *On Good Ground*, 164–193, 228 (quotation); Dougherty, *Sisters of St. Joseph*, 144–151, 163; Graham, *Works to the King*, 32–55, 70.

[4] Hurley, *On Good Ground*, 229, 237; Graham, *Works to the King*, 55; Dougherty, *Sisters of St. Joseph*, 166. The *St. Paul Daily Pioneer Press*, December 21, 1904, described Derham Hall: "There are two large dormitories and 60 private rooms besides a chapel, a study hall, a gymnasium, laboratories and conservatories. There are a number of reception rooms and a roomy library."

[5] Graham, *Works to the King*, 56; Dougherty, *Sisters of St. Joseph*, 161. Born in Omaha in 1873, Sister Antonia received the habit of the Sisters of St. Joseph in 1891. From 1893 until moving to Derham Hall with the first group of sisters, she had taught at St. Joseph Academy. Her drive for educational excellence had the strong support of the archbishop and Mother Seraphine. See Hurley, *On Good Ground*, 228–237.

[6] Hurley, *On Good Ground*, 237–239 (quotation); College of St. Catherine, *Announcement, 1904* (quotation); St. Catherine's catalog, known as *Year Book*, 7, 9, 58 (1906); Graham, *Works to the King*, 57; Sister Teresa Toomey, "Chapters for a History of the College of St. Catherine, Saint Paul, Minnesota," 1–6, an undated hectographed paper in St. Catherine's library. None of the Sisters of St. Joseph possessed a bachelor's degree in 1904, but those who taught were well-read and full of enthusiasm for learning.

[7] Hurley, *On Good Ground*, 241–243; Graham, *Works to the King*, 57; Toomey, "Chapters for a History," 9; *Year Book*, 10 (quotation), 15–33 (1906), 5, 14 (1907), unpaged (1910), 35–37 (1911–12). A commercial course of two years was announced in 1906–07; another of the same duration in "Household Economy and Cooking" followed in 1910–11. The college received its articles of incorporation just before commencement in 1913.

[8] Hurley, *On Good Ground*, 237–244 (quotations), 246; Graham, *Works to the King*, 58; Toomey, "Chapters for a History," 6–8, 10, 14; *Bulletin*, 7 (1914–15). (Starting in 1914, the *Year Books* were replaced by *Bulletins*.) Sister Ste Hélène Guthrie, the first sister to hold a bachelor's degree before entering the congregation, started teaching at St. Catherine's in 1911. She was dean of the college from 1929 to 1937. For 25 years she and Sister Antonia "controlled the whole policy of the college," says Hurley, 242.

[9] Hurley, *On Good Ground*, 245; Toomey, "Chapters for a History," 11; *Bulletin*, 6, 25–100 (1916–17). Some of the sisters attended St. Catherine's college classes, especially from the novitiate which was moved in 1913 to a building situated on college grounds adjoining the campus.

[10] Hurley, *On Good Ground*, 244; Graham, *Works to the King*, 60; Toomey, "Chapters for a History," 14; quotations below in *Bulletin*, back of title page, 86–88, 92–99 (1916–17). Sister Antonia's reminiscences of early days of the college are found in the *Catherine Wheel*, May 17, 1940.

[11] Hurley, *On Good Ground*, 247, 263; General Education Board, *Annual Report, 1918–19*, 6 (New York, 1919); *Bulletin*, inside cover (1922–23).

[12] Hurley, *On Good Ground*, 248; *Bulletin*, 106 (1920–21), inside cover, 120 (1922–23); Toomey, "Chapters for a History," 15 (quotation).

[13] Hurley, *On Good Ground*, 264–266, 281–283; Graham, *Works to the King*, 59 (quotation), 88–101. "Only God knows," wrote Sister Clara, "the hours of prayer she [Mother Seraphine] sent heavenward for the College." Graham, 58.

[14] Mary Ellen Chase, *A Goodly Fellowship*, 229–241 (New York, 1939).

[15] *Bulletin*, 5–7 (1920–21), 2–5 (1922–23); Toomey, "Chapters for a History," 13. To Sister Teresa, Mother Antonia "gave the impression of living in a world of wide horizons and high resolve." People at the General Education Board had suggested to her that the college should have a board of trustees. Toomey, 15.

[16] Toomey, "Chapters for a History," 12–14; "Administrative Reports for the Year 1930–1931," p. 3–5. The annual reports of the president, dean, registrar, and treasurer from June, 1931, onward are bound in these volumes in St. Catherine's archives. The office of the registrar dates from 1917.

[17] Toomey, "Chapters for a History," 16; *Bulletin*, 13 (quotation) (1922–23); *La Concha* (student yearbook), 4 (1922).

[18] *Bulletin*, 7–10 (1924–25); Sally Michener, "The College of St. Catherine," in *Golfer and Sportsman*, 19 (quotation) (January, 1940).

[19] Chase, *A Goodly Fellowship*, 234 (quotation); *Bulletin*, 16 (1924–25), 12–16 (1926–27), 18 (1931–32); Hurley, *On Good Ground*, 250. When the chapel was being built, Mother Antonia persuaded the workmen to work on Thanksgiving by providing an excellent dinner. To those laboring on a Saturday afternoon, she gave cigars.

[20] *Bulletin*, 17 (1927–28), inside cover, 19 (1929–30); Toomey, "Chapters for a History," 17; Hurley, *On Good Ground*, 249; *La Concha*, 12 (1927), 158 (1928). The grant for Mendel Hall required the raising of a matching sum of $200,000.

[21] *Bulletin*, 23 (1931–32), 87 (1938); *St. Paul Pioneer Press*, February 7, 1932 (quotation); Michener, in *Golfer and Sportsman*, 21 (January, 1940); Hurley, *On Good Ground*, 258; "Administrative Reports, 1930–31," p. 5.

[22] *Bulletin*, 28–99 (1919–20), 3, 29 (1920–21), inside cover (1922–23), 112 (1929–30); *La Concha*, 20–25 (1921). Of the lay members of the class of 1921, 13 had concentrated in English, five in chemistry, and two each in Latin, French, and history.

[23] *Bulletin*, 18 (1924–25), 103 (1926–27), 124–126 (1927–28), 125–135 (1929–30), 42 (1931–32); *La Concha*, 9 (1926), 21 (1929).

[24] *Bulletin*, inside cover, 42 (1931–32); "Administrative Reports, 1931–32," p. 5, 81, 134; Hurley, *On Good Ground*, 249, 254.

[25] "Administrative Reports, 1930–31," p. 30, 84, "1931–32," p. 100, "1932–33," p. 219, "1936–37," p. 200; Hurley, *On Good Ground*, 253. The state normal schools opposed the expansion of the curriculum to include elementary education, but both the Minnesota Department of Education and the North Central Association approved St. Catherine's work in this field in 1931.

[26] "Administrative Reports, 1934–35," p. 32, 40.

[27] Taped interview of the author, July 10, 1968, with Sister Eucharista Galvin, in the collections of the Minnesota Historical Society; "The General Report of the College of St. Catherine, St. Paul, Minnesota, to the Committee on Qualifications, United Chapters of Phi Beta Kappa," October 15, 1935, in college files; "Administrative Reports, 1937–38," p. 5; *Catherine Wheel*, May 20, 1938.

[28] Dougherty, *Sisters of St. Joseph*, 155, 161, 376; Toomey, "Chapters for a History," 24; Hurley, *On Good Ground*, 260; "Administrative Reports, 1931–32," p. 89. In October, 1931, Pope Pius XI awarded Mother Antonia the decoration *Pro Ecclesia et Pontifice*. She was also given an honorary LL.D. in June, 1936, by the University of Minnesota.

[29] Interview with Sister Eucharista, July 10, 1968; "Administrative Reports, 1937–38," p. 8, 58.

[30] "Administrative Reports, 1937–38," p. 5–7, "1938–39," p. 73–83, "1939–40," p. 203–206. The typewritten reports of the general education study are bound in three volumes, "Studies in General Education," and those for teacher education in two volumes, "Report on the Study of Teacher Education, Senior Year, 1940–42," and "Final Report on the Study of Teacher Education at the College of St. Catherine," June 1, 1942 — all in college archives. In the fall of 1938 all juniors and seniors entering a vocational field were required also to carry one "in a purely academic subject."

[31] "General Report to Phi Beta Kappa," 35; "Administrative Reports, 1934–35," p. 35, "1935–36," p. 118, 149. Of the 179 freshmen who matriculated in the fall of 1932, about 20 entered the novitiate during their first year at college. Totally, freshman attrition numbered 37.

[32] *La Concha*, 18–31 (1924); "Administrative Reports, 1931–32," p. 150, "1939–40," p. 256, 258.

[33] "Administrative Reports, 1931–32," p. 44, 46, 177, "1935–36," p. 163, "1936–37," p. 197, "1938–39," p. 162, "1939–40," p. 298; "General Report to Phi Beta Kappa," 21. Of the 935 college alumnae by 1935, 118 had entered religious life. See Sister Mary Lucida Savage, *The Century's Harvest, Gathered by the Sisters of St. Joseph of Carondelet in the United States, 1836–1936*, 170 (St. Louis, 1936).

[34] *Bulletin*, 21 (1920), 22 (1929–30).

[35] Toomey, "Chapters for a History," 20; *Bulletin*, 25, 45, 67 (1922–23), 100 (1927–28); Michener, in *Golfer and Sportsman*, 24 (January, 1940).

[36] Interview with Sister Eucharista, July 10, 1968; Toomey, "Chapters for a History," 18; "General Report to Phi Beta Kappa," 120; *La Concha*, 34 (1919), 98–100, 173 (1929).

[37] Michener, in *Golfer and Sportsman*, 46 (quotation) (January, 1940); *St. Paul Daily News*, rotogravure section, May 27, 1928; "General Report to Phi Beta Kappa," 122; Toomey, "Chapters for a History," 18, 22; *La Concha*, 64, 83 (1922), 33, 127–133 (1925), 62, 159 (1928). The yearbook name, *La Concha*, meaning "the shell," seemed fitting since each year it re-echoed the past.

22. COLLEGE OF SAINT TERESA, PART II
Pages 113 to 118

[1] Sister Mary Francis Ann Hayes, "Years of Beginning, A History of the Sisters of the Third Order Regular of St. Francis of the Congregation of Our Lady of Lourdes, Rochester, Minnesota, 1877–1902," p. 1–23, Master's thesis, Catholic University of America, 1956.

[2] Hayes, "Years of Beginning," 24–47 (quotation). After the Illinois bishop's death in 1879, the members of the communities at Joliet and Rochester were again on friendly terms. The Rochester sisters founded world-famous St. Mary's Hospital and worked closely with Dr. W. W. Mayo and his sons, Drs. William J. Mayo and Charles H. Mayo.

[3] Hayes, "Years of Beginning," 2, 44–62, 76–80; Sister M. Bernetta Quinn, *Design in Gold: A History of the College of Saint Teresa, Winona, Minnesota, 1907–1957*, 7–14 (Winona, 1957); "Cornerstone Connotations," 7–11 (1950), a paper prepared by students of Sister Mary David Homan, in college files; *Winona Daily Herald*, August 27, 1894. Mother Alfred, writes Hayes, was "a pioneer of the nineteenth century, building great things for the future." She died in St. Paul in December, 1899. By 1902, 223 sisters had joined the congregation; St. Mary's Hospital had been opened in Rochester and two additions to it had been built; 28 parochial schools with 6,000 pupils enrolled had been staffed by Sisters of St. Francis.

[4] Sister Mary Caedmon Homan, "Years of Vision, 1903–1928: A History of the Sisters of the Third Order Regular of St. Francis of the Congregation of Our Lady of Lourdes, Rochester, Minnesota," 1–5, 67–72 (quotation), Master's thesis, Catholic University of America, 1956; Quinn, *Design in Gold*, 15. In 1903 the seminary had six departments: academic, conservatory, art, expression, physical culture, and household economy.

[5] Homan, "Years of Vision," 36–38; Quinn, *Design in Gold*, 16. Sister Leo was born in New York, but her Irish immigrant parents thereafter migrated to Minnesota and settled near Eyota. She entered the Franciscan order in 1882 when she was 22 years of age.

[6] Homan, "Years of Vision," 73; Quinn, *Design in Gold*, 16.

[7] Homan, "Years of Vision," 85; Quinn, *Design in Gold*, 17.

[8] Homan, "Years of Vision," 9, 75; Quinn, *Design in Gold*, 19–21; *Aldine* (yearbook), 113 (1967). With Dr. Molloy's help, the first yearbook appeared in 1911. It was named the *Aldine* for a Renaissance printer widely known for his craftsmanship. The school also had a literary magazine, the *Tatler*.

[9] Homan, "Years of Vision," 75–77; Quinn, *Design in Gold*, 19, 21.

[10] Homan, "Years of Vision," 78–80 (quotation); Quinn, *Design in Gold*, 23 (quotation); *Winona Daily Republican-Herald*, August 30, 1913. The cornerstone laying occurred on the same day as a similar ceremony for St. Mary's College on Terrace Heights in Winona; see chapter 24, below.

[11] Homan, "Years of Vision," 25, 77, 80; *The Five-Year Book of the College of Saint Teresa, 1919–1924*, vol. 2, unpaged (Winona, 1924); Quinn, *Design in Gold*, 22, 27 (quotation). In 1915 four women received bachelor's degrees. The speaker at the 1916 ceremony was the celebrated poet Joyce Kilmer; most of the young ladies were "awed by the presence of so famous a man." See Quinn, 31.

[12] Homan, "Years of Vision," 14–35, 76–78, 80; Quinn, *Design in Gold*, 30. Confusion over the power of Bishop Heffron to appoint a superior general stemmed from the hazy status of the sisterhood in relation to Rome and to the local diocese. The

congregation received papal approbation of its constitutions on a temporary basis in 1931 and on a definite basis in 1945.

[13] Homan, "Years of Vision," 36–45, 48.

[14] Homan, "Years of Vision," 46–48 (quotation), 81. Approximately 150 sisters attended the college division of the summer session of 1917 at Saint Teresa's, and nearly 125 enrolled in the certificate and normal section.

[15] Homan, "Years of Vision," 45–51 (quotation); *Teresan News Letter*, 1 (September, 1918). At the close of summer classes in 1919, 450 state certification examinations were written on the campus.

[16] Homan, "Years of Vision," 53–56; Selden, *Accreditation*, 51–53; *Teresan News Letter*, 1 (September, 1918).

[17] Homan, "Years of Vision," 27, 49, 86–88; Quinn, *Design in Gold*, 30. The U.S. commissioner of education visited Saint Teresa in the spring of 1916. In December, 1919, the congregation established an endowment fund by borrowing. It was $500,000 in 1924. Since 1925 the income from it has been paid annually to the college.

[18] Homan, "Years of Vision," 81, 85–87 (quotation); Quinn, *Design in Gold*, 34. For "distinguished service to the church," Dr. Molloy in 1918 was recognized by Pope Benedict XV with the decoration *Pro Ecclesia et Pontifice*, the first time this honor was conferred on an educator.

[19] Quinn, *Design in Gold*, 32–38 (quotation); *The Five-Year Book*, vol. 2. Quinn reports that intercollegiate dancing had its inception on November 25, 1919. The affair, restricted to juniors and seniors, started with a formal dinner at the Winona Hotel. Later Teresans and lads from St. Mary's waltzed or fox-trotted "to the latest Irving Berlin tunes . . . until the all-too-early closing hour arrived."

[20] Homan, "Years of Vision," 78, 82; Quinn, *Design in Gold*, 38, 40; College of Saint Teresa, *Bulletin*, 83–94 (1920); *Winona Herald-Tribune*, March 13, 1922; *Teresan News Letter*, 1 (March 12, 1922); *The Five-Year Book*, vol. 2. Board and room in 1920 cost $300 a school year; tuition was $150, plus fees of from $20 to $60 for students taking laboratory science courses, cooking, sewing, and secretarial work.

[21] Homan, "Years of Vision," 82; Quinn, *Design in Gold*, 37, 42, 45 (quotation).

[22] Homan, "Years of Vision," 84; Quinn, *Design in Gold*, 48, 51 (quotation); *Aldine*, 113 (1967). Mother Leo was criticized for building so giant a structure, but developments after World War II testified to the wisdom of her planning.

[23] Homan, "Years of Vision," 88 (quotation); Quinn, *Design in Gold*, 50, 54, 59; *Bulletin*, 26–65 (1920), 31–82 (1932), 7–12 (1940); Sister Mary Paul Norman, "A History of the Home Economics Department of the College of Saint Teresa, 1913–1959," p. 3 (November 30, 1959), a history term paper; *Combined Course in Nursing and Liberal Arts, 1927–1928*, a folder issued by the college; and Sister Ancina Adams, "Historical Development of the Department of Nursing," (1960), a typed paper — all three in the files of the Minnesota Historical Society. See also Sister Mary David Homan to the author, October 7, 1968. A separate department of nursing was organized in the fall of 1935 geared to professional nurses, most of whom were sisters; it provided majors in teaching, supervision, and administration.

[24] Quinn, *Design in Gold*, 52; *Bulletin*, 123–125 (quotation) (1940); *Bulletin*, Alumnae Edition, 5 (March, 1944). Of the slightly over 400 resident students enrolled in 1939–40, 172 were from Minnesota. The four states of Wisconsin, Iowa, Illinois, and Ohio contributed 59, 43, 38, and 22 students, respectively. A total of 12 Teresans were from seven foreign countries. The freshman class numbered 159, the senior class 83.

[25] Quinn, *Design in Gold*, 43 (quotation), 47, 54, 60; maxims from signs on classrooms walls, preserved in Saint Teresa's ar-

chives. Starting with the House of Gold and the Tower of Ivory in 1926, a number of honor societies were formed. By 1940 five more — Rainbow, Burning Bush, Morning Star, Blossoming Rod, and Seven Fair Pillars — had been added. Membership was based on academic achievement.

[26] Quinn, *Design in Gold*, 43, 48–52, 57–59.

[27] Homan, "Years of Vision," 90–93; *Winona Republican-Herald*, May 4, 1951. Mother Leo had arrived in Winona with $3.53 in her pocket. Chosen to succeed her as general superior in 1933 was Sister M. Aquinas, who as Anastasia Norton had been one of the three graduates of the college department in 1914. For a decade and a half before 1933, she had been a member of the history department at Saint Teresa's.

[28] Homan, "Years of Vision," 88; Quinn, *Design in Gold*, 42, 57, 67, 75 (quotation). In 1922 Dr. Molloy was appointed to the executive committee of the college and university section of the National Catholic Education Association; a quarter of a century later she was elected president of the section. In both cases she was the first woman to be so honored.

[29] Quinn, *Design in Gold*, 29, 45, 49–51, 53, 55, 57–60; Homan, "Years of Vision," 35, 57–60; *Bulletin*, 7–10 (1920), 7–12 (1940). Bishop Heffron died in November, 1927. He was succeeded by Auxiliary Bishop Francis M. Kelly, who had served Saint Teresa's as chaplain from 1914 until 1922 and as professor of philosophy until 1926. Part of his education had been obtained at St. Thomas Academy in St. Paul.

23. COLLEGE OF ST. BENEDICT, PART II
Pages 119 to 124

[1] Sister M. Grace McDonald, *With Lamps Burning*, 7–54 (quotation) (St. Joseph, 1957); Barry, *Worship and Work*, 52–54.

[2] McDonald, *With Lamps Burning*, 55–79; Barry, *Worship and Work*, 75.

[3] McDonald, *With Lamps Burning*, 99–108, 156, 178, 188; Sister M. Grace McDonald, "A Finishing School of the 1880s: St. Benedict's Academy," in *Minnesota History*, 27:96–106 (June, 1946). The academy has survived to the present day; it is now known as St. Benedict's High School. In 1938 it changed from a boarding to a day school, but in 1956 it returned to its former status as a residential institution for girls of high school age. Its first directress was Sister Alexia Kerst, a sister of Mother Scholastica.

[4] McDonald, *With Lamps Burning*, 162, 167, 190. Catholic University did not open its doors to women religious until 1911. It established an extension division of its Sisters' College in Dubuque, Iowa, in 1914, and Benedictines enrolled there also.

[5] McDonald, *With Lamps Burning*, 167–170.

[6] McDonald, *With Lamps Burning*, 190 (quotation); St. Benedict's Academy, *Annual Catalogue*, 15 (quotation) (1904–05); *Benet* (February, 1955), St. Benedict's student and alumnae magazine started in 1941 as a continuation of the five-year-old *Handshake*. The second dean, Sister Jeanette Roesch, a native of Austria, was the first sister at St. Benedict to earn a Minnesota teacher's certificate, and the first to receive a master's and a doctor's degree from Catholic University in 1913 and 1918, respectively.

[7] McDonald, *With Lamps Burning*, 172, 191, 313; *St. Cloud Daily Times*, May 20, 1935; St. Benedict's College and Academy, *Annual Year-Book*, 5, 42 (1915–16), 15 (1918–19); College of St. Benedict registrar's files. The latter show that a two-year business course was also offered to prepare young women "for securing positions which will enable them to be self-supporting." There were 22 women in the college section in 1917–18 — one senior, one junior, two sophomores, and 18 freshmen.

[8] Lindbergh's speech of July 5, 1916, entitled "Invisible Government and the Consequence of It," in *Congressional Record*, 64 Congress, 1 session, *Appendix*, 1837–1845 (quotation); *St. Cloud Times*, June 7, 1918, quoted in McDonald, *With Lamps Burning*, 192.

[9] McDonald, *With Lamps Burning*, 179; *Annual Year-Book*, 19 (1914–15).

[10] McDonald, *With Lamps Burning*, 179–189 (quotation). Benedictines taught in parochial schools from the Mississippi River to the Pacific Coast.

[11] McDonald, *With Lamps Burning*, 194 (quotation); *Annual Year-Book*, 9 (1913–14), 21 (1932–33); *College Bulletin*, 18–23 (quotation) (1934–35). An alumnae association was formed as early as 1914. It started a scholarship its first year and in other ways promoted the interests of St. Benedict's.

[12] McDonald, *With Lamps Burning*, 191; *Annual Year-Book*, 37 (1915–16).

[13] McDonald, *With Lamps Burning*, 170, 193, 201 (quotation). During World War I, sisters and students knitted and made dressings for men in the service.

[14] McDonald, *With Lamps Burning*, 171; *College Bulletin*, 14 (quotation) (1927–28).

[15] *Annual Year-Book*, 12–15 (1922–23).

[16] *Annual Year-Book*, 14 (1924–25).

[17] Robert L. Kelly, "The Minnesota Colleges: Their Contribution to Society," in *Association of American Colleges Bulletin*, 14:264 (May, 1928); registrar's files.

[18] Kelly, in *Association of American Colleges Bulletin*, 14:259, 272, 277 (May, 1928); *College Bulletin*, 47 (1926–27), 12–14, 20 (1927–28). According to Kelly, the educational budget for the college in 1926–27, not including expenses for service properties, was $139,200; total faculty salaries, including those of the religious computed at the same rate as those of lay teachers, that year amounted to $43,600. For purposes of perspective the comparable sums for St. Catherine's were $307,700 and $118,000. At Carleton the salary outlay in 1926–27 was $211,800; at Gustavus Adolphus, $49,400; at Hamline, $98,200; at Augsburg, $21,500; at Concordia in Moorhead, $57,100.

[19] McDonald, *With Lamps Burning*, 172; *Benet* (October, 1941); "Report of the Dean, 1930–31," p. 8, and Sister Mariella Gable, "In League with the Future: The First Fifty Years History of the College of Saint Benedict: A Homecoming Address, Spring 1964," p. 7 (quotation) — both in college files.

[20] McDonald, *With Lamps Burning*, 196; Gable, "In League with the Future," 7 (quotation); "Introductory Statement Concerning the Finances of the College of St. Benedict," December 13, 1931; "Report of the Committee on Review of the Commission of Institutions of Higher Education, North Central Association of Colleges and Secondary Schools" (quotation), February, 1932, in college files.

[21] "Report of the Committee on Review," February, 1932.

[22] Gable, "In League with the Future," 7; George A. Works, "Report of the Inspection of the College of St. Benedict," February 27, 1933, in college files.

[23] Works, "Report of the Inspection," February 27, 1933; John G. Fawlkes, "Report of the Inspection of the College of St. Benedict" (quotation), March 22, 1935, in college files.

[24] Gable, "In League with the Future," 7; *Benet* (October, 1941); "Report of the Registrar, 1935–36," p. 1, "1936–37," p. 6, "1941–42," p. 9; "Report of the Dean of Women, 1936–37," p. 1; "Report of the Dean of the College, 1935–36," p. 4 — all in president's files, where all internal reports on St. Benedict cited hereafter may also be found.

[25] Gable, "In League with the Future," 7; *Benet* (June, 1941); *College Bulletin*, 24 (1936–37), 21 (1948–49); "Report of the Dean of the College, 1937–38," p. 5; *St. Cloud Daily Times*, May 20, 1935; *Handshake* (student newspaper), June, 1937.

Delta Epsilon Sigma was founded in Washington, D.C., in April, 1939. The number of graduates from the college in 1934, 1937, and 1941 was 23, 28, and 43, respectively.

[26] Gable, "In League with the Future," 7; Fawlkes, "Report on the Inspection," 3, March 22, 1935; *College Bulletin*, 8 (quotation) (1934–35), 10, 28 (1948–49); *Benet* (October, 1941).

[27] Gable, "In League with the Future," 8 (quotation); *Harvest, 1857–1957*, 58–62 (quotation), a centennial booklet published in 1957; *College Bulletin*, 18 (1939–40); Angeline Dufner, "The Pageant," 25–30, in *Saint Benedict's Quarterly* (June, 1957).

[28] McDonald, *With Lamps Burning*, 172, 210–220; *College Bulletin*, 14, 33, 35, 43 (1940–41).

[29] McDonald, *With Lamps Burning*, 202–205 (quotation); *College Bulletin*, 17–24 (quotation) (1939–40). In the democratic tradition, no undergraduate was permitted to hold all the important student responsibilities. Under a point system, the maximum was 14 points. The presidency of Sodality was equal to 12 points.

24. St. Mary's College, Part II
Pages 125 to 131

[1] *Winona Courier*, November, 1910 (quotation); *Rochester Post and Record*, December 9, 10, 1910; *Owatonna Daily Journal-Chronicle*, November 29, 1910; *Winona Independent*, December 9, 1910; *Winona Daily Republican Herald*, December 5, 1910, May 31, 1912. In a talk to priests on retreat in 1911 or 1912, Heffron said of the college: "This will be my life work. . . . I feel that such a work is better than the building of a Cathedral. . . ." See Scrapbook, vol. 1, in St. Mary's College archives. The *Winona Courier* is the official publication of the Winona diocese.

[2] *Winona Courier*, January (quotation), February (quotation), March, May, 1911; *Winona Daily Republican Herald*, December 5, 1910 (quotation); *St. Paul Pioneer Press*, December 12, 1910, June 11, 1922.

[3] *Winona Courier*, June (quotation), July, September, 1911 (quotation), January (quotation), August (quotation), 1912.

[4] *Winona Daily Republican Herald*, May 31, 1912 (quotation); *Winona Courier*, May, August, September, November, 1912, June (quotation), November, 1913. The prospectus was published in the *Courier* of July, 1913. Of 172 individuals who made pledges by late 1912, 122 were Irish. The generosity of the priests was notable despite their meager pay.

[5] *Winona Courier*, September, 1911, August (quotation), November, December, 1913, January, 1914; *St. Paul Pioneer Press*, June 11, 1922.

[6] *Winona Courier*, September, 1913, May, 1914 (quotation); *Winona Daily Republican Herald*, September 6, 1913, December 14, 1938; St. Mary's, *Annual Catalogue*, 4, 16 (1915–16).

[7] *Winona Courier*, September, November, 1913, May, 1914.

[8] *Winona Courier*, May, 1914, January, 1915; *Annual Catalogue*, 16 (quotation), 55 (1914), 33 (1915), 43–45 (1917), 45–47 (1918). To aid in keeping living expenses at a minimum, St. Mary's produced meat, milk, eggs, and other food on its farm. The Smith-Hughes Act promoted vocational education by paying subsidies to co-operating states on a matching basis. Funds were provided to pay salaries of persons teaching subjects in agriculture, trade and industry, and home economics. The Minnesota Board for Vocational Education, established in 1918, set criteria for personnel, plant, and equipment and made suggestions for curriculum content. Along with such subjects as crops, soils, nutrition, and cooking, the board recommended classes in English, civics and citizenship, history, and science. See

United States, *Statutes at Large*, 39:929–936; Minnesota Board for Vocational Education, *Plans for Vocational Education in Minnesota*, 5–9, 19, 29 ([St. Paul], 1918).

[9] *Annual Catalogue*, 33–38 (1914), 9, 19 (1917), 21 (1919), 41 (1920).

[10] *Winona Courier*, October, 1912, September, 1916, February, 1920; *St. Mary's College*, an undated brochure probably published about 1920, in college archives. Sister Mary Aquinas was not the only Franciscan to help St. Mary's. From 1915 to 1944 members of the Rochester Congregation of the Sisters of St. Francis staffed the domestic department of the college. See Homan, "Years of Vision," 26.

[11] *Winona Courier*, March, May, July, October, November, 1918.

[12] *Winona Daily Republican Herald*, May 14, 1925, March 23, 1926, May 8, 1930 (quotation), December 12, 14, 1938; *Our Sunday Visitor* (Winona Edition), November 5, 1926. The *Winona Courier* was succeeded by *Our Sunday Visitor* as the diocesan paper from 1943 to 1953, when it again became the *Winona Courier*.

[13] *Winona Courier*, November, 1918; *St. Mary's — $1,000,000 Building and Endowment Fund Campaign of 1919*, a four-page publicity pamphlet, in college archives.

[14] *Winona Courier*, April, (quotation), June, August, September, 1919.

[15] Community Counseling Service, Inc., "Fund-Raising Analysis and Projection for the Future," 1963, and interview by Brother Robert Lane of St. Mary's with Bishop Peter Bartholome, August 8, 1962 — both in college archives; *Alumni Bulletin*, June 30, 1923; *St. Paul Pioneer Press*, June 11, 1922; *Winona Courier*, May, 1920, April, 1921, August, 1922; *Winona Daily Republican Herald*, February 5, 1921, August 22, 1922, September 11, 1929.

[16] *Winona Courier*, May, 1920; "Fund Raising Analysis," 1963; Bishop Bartholome interview, August 8, 1962; *Annual Catalogue*, 16 (quotation) (1914); "Rules for the Good Government of the Student Body," 1923; *Nexus*, February 18, 1928. (In October, 1925, the name of the *Alumni Bulletin* was changed to *Nexus*.) Lack of money was Father Peschges' big problem. Many student accounts were delinquent and companies extended credit to the college.

[17] An Austin priest to Father Peschges, February 8, 1924 (quotation), in college archives. The future Bishop Bartholome did recruiting in Wisconsin after World War I; see his interview of August 8, 1962.

[18] Secretary's recruitment letters, September 1, 1923, July 17, 1924, and to "boys of Winona," May 14, 1929, in college archives; *Daily Winona Tribune*, September 5, 1924. The *Winona Daily Republican Herald* of August 7, 1926, headed a story on St. Mary's "A College for Real Men." Thomas H. (Tom) Skemp was the football coach from 1919 to 1932. His teams of 1924, 1925, and 1927 were undefeated in college competition. See *Minneapolis Tribune*, October 14, 1928; *St. Paul Pioneer Press*, November 30, 1924; Brother Robert Lane's interview with Skemp, March 13, 1962, in college archives.

[19] Secretary's recruitment letters, June 13, August 6, 1923, July 11, 1924, June 30, 1925, October 29, 1929; *Winona Daily Republican Herald*, September 8, 1925, September 13, 1926, September 17, 1927; "Fund Raising Analysis," 1963.

[20] *Alumni Bulletin*, December 20, 1923 (quotation), April 30, October 15, 1924. At Christmas, 1925, the college was placed on the fully accredited list of the Catholic Educational Association by unanimous vote of the committee on standardization. *Nexus*, January 15, 1926.

[21] *Alumni Bulletin*, December 20, 1923; *Our Sunday Visitor*, May 20, 1945; *Winona Courier*, May 14, 1959 (quotation); *Minneapolis Journal*, September 12, 1926.

[22] *Winona Daily Republican Herald*, June 1, 1925, June 3, September 8, December 18, 31 (quotation), 1926, May 20, 1927, June 7, 1928. One of the graduates of the college in 1926 was from Wisconsin, the others from small Minnesota towns. Thirteen degrees were conferred in both 1927 and 1928.

[23] *Catalogue*, 45 (1928–29); *Winona Daily Republican Herald*, September 17, 1927, February 10, 1928, June 1, 1929. The catalog for 1924–25 for the first time separated college and academy costs.

[24] Kelly, in *Association of American Colleges Bulletin*, 14:247–306 (May, 1928); St. Mary's secretary to priests, June 7, 1928, in college archives.

[25] Bishop Bartholome interview, August 8, 1962; *Winona Daily Republican Herald*, March 23, November 10, 1926, November 23, 28, 1927, February 13, 1928; *Nexus*, December 15, 1927; *Our Sunday Visitor*, July 2, 1950.

[26] *Nexus*, February 22, 1929; *Winona Daily Republican Herald*, November 10, 1926; rector to faculty, September 15, 1930 (quotation); form letter to parents, October 25, 1928; "Notice Regarding the Library Fund," June 19, 1928 — all in college archives.

[27] Hubert Gerard, F.S.C., ed., *Mississippi Vista: The Brothers of the Christian Schools in the Mid-West, 1849–1949*, 30–35, 61–75, 82, 101–112, 231–234 (Winona, 1948). Scholastics are brothers who have advanced from novices and are engaged in studying for higher education degrees.

[28] Interview of Brother Robert Lane with Brother Leopold Julian Dodd, July 18, 1964, in college archives; Gerard, ed., *Mississippi Vista*, 242.

[29] Brother Leopold interview, July 18, 1964; *Winona Daily Republican Herald*, December 14, 1938.

[30] Brother Leopold interview, July 18, 1964; Gerard, ed., *Mississippi Vista*, 58, 238, 243.

[31] Brother Leopold interview, July 18, 1964; Gerard, ed., *Mississippi Vista*, 245.

[32] Brother Leopold interview, July 18, 1964.

[33] Brother Leopold interview, July 18, 1964 (quotation); Gerard, ed., *Mississippi Vista*, 84.

[34] Brother Leopold interview, July 18, 1964; Gerard, ed., *Mississippi Vista*, 243.

[35] Brother Leopold interview, July 18, 1964; *Winona Daily Republican Herald*, February 5, 12, March 23 (quotation), April 24, 30, 1937, November 12, December 12, 1938, September 30, October 5, 1939.

[36] Brother Leopold interview, July 18, 1964; *Winona Daily Republican Herald*, September 11, 15, 1934, June 7, September 11, December 15, 1937, February 14, May 23, September 26 (quotation), October 3, 17, December 14, 1938; *Annual Catalogue*, 7–9, 69, 71–75, 76 (1938–39); "Fund Raising Analysis," 1963. In the fall of 1937 about 60 freshmen came to St. Mary's from Chicago, a clear reflection of the Christian Brothers' influence. Summer school was inaugurated in the second half of the 1930s.

[37] *Winona Daily Republican Herald*, April 20, 1934, April 9, May 29, 1937, March 4, May 28, 1938, April 24, 1940; commencement programs in college archives; *Nexus*, May 7, October 16, 1937, March 4, 1938. Attrition remained a problem even after accreditation; in the fall of 1938 there were 146 freshmen, 74 sophomores, 59 juniors, and 37 seniors. See *Terrace Heights News*, October 1, 1938, a publication founded in 1938 to foster closer relations between the college and the alumni.

[38] *Winona Daily Republican Herald*, January 26, February 26, March 1, 23, 1937, April 12, 1938, September 30, 1940.

[39] *Winona Daily Republican Herald*, May 1, 1930, February 28, 1931, February 10, 1934, October 9, 12, December 18, 1936, February 12, October 16, November 30, 1937, May 20,

31, December 12, 1938, September 25, October 9, 17, 24, 1939, October 29, 1940. The student dramatic organization was known as the Burbage Players.

[40] *Winona Daily Republican Herald*, December 16, 1938.

25. COLLEGE OF ST. SCHOLASTICA, PART II
Pages 132 to 137

[1] Barry, *Worship and Work*, 161.

[2] Barry, *Worship and Work*, 125, 160–162; McDonald, *With Lamps Burning*, 93–95, 99; *Duluth Register*, April 15, 1960.

[3] McDonald, *With Lamps Burning*, 144–147, 159; *In Memoriam: Right Reverend James McGolrick, First Bishop of Duluth*, 10 [1918?]; *Villa Sancta Scholastica Quarterly*, 6 (Fall, 1911), the college magazine, hereafter cited as *Villa Quarterly*. The last two sources are in St. Scholastica's library.

[4] Sister M. Agnes Somers, "All Her Ways: A short account of the founding, development, and artistic acquirements of the College of St. Scholastica," 4–8 (quotation), a mimeographed undated paper in college files; *Villa Quarterly*, 4, 6, 52 (Fall, 1911); *Duluth Register*, April 15, 1960; Sacred Heart Institute, *Bulletin* (1892–93). The first graduation ceremony at the institute occurred in 1897.

[5] Somers, "All Her Ways," 8–15.

[6] Somers, "All Her Ways," 16, 50; *Duluth News-Tribune*, October 23, 1938; *Duluth Register*, April 15, 1960; *Institute Echoes* (student newspaper), June, September, October, 1908, June, 1909.

[7] [Sister Noemi Weygant], *Swinger of Birches*, 7–11 (Duluth, 1967); *Villa Quarterly*, 2, 7, 38 (Fall, 1911), 486, 489 (March, 1912), 297 (March, 1916); *Duluth Register*, April 15, 1960.

[8] Somers, "All Her Ways," 16; *Villa Quarterly*, 39 (quotation) (October, 1911), 145 (June, 1913).

[9] Somers, "All Her Ways," 17, 18 (quotations); *Scriptorium* (student newspaper), June 5, 1935.

[10] Somers, "All Her Ways," 19 (quotation); *Duluth News-Tribune*, October 23, 1938; *Villa Quarterly*, 80 (quotation) (December, 1914), 148 (June, 1915).

[11] Somers, "All Her Ways," 20; *Villa Quarterly*, 80 (December, 1914).

[12] Somers, "All Her Ways," 21, 24 (quotations); *Villa Quarterly*, 123–135 (June, 1915), unpaged insert (June, 1916), 38 (December, 1916), 122 (June, 1917). One rule stated: "Newspapers sent from home are not delivered, as magazines and periodicals suitable for young ladies are furnished by the Institution." See Somers, 18.

[13] Somers, "All Her Ways," 12, 23; *Duluth News-Tribune*, October 23, 1938; *Villa Quarterly*, 144 (June, 1913), 222 (September, 1913), 49 (October, 1918), 207 (March, 1921); St. Scholastica, *College Bulletin*, 7 (1924). According to Somers, 50, people seeing the gymnasium from the outside often remarked, "What a charming English chapel!"

[14] *Villa Quarterly*, 399 (June, 1914), 362 (June, 1916), 400 (September, 1916), 219 (March, 1918), 34 (October, 1918); Somers, "All Her Ways," 22; Weygant, *Swinger of Birches*, 9. Mother Celestine was a shrewd financier, but she is best remembered as a stimulating and beloved teacher. Mother Chrysostom brought monks from St. John's Abbey to teach the sisters the proper way to recite the Divine Office.

[15] Somers, "All Her Ways," 20–22, 24; *Bulletin*, 8, 32 (1921); *Villa Quarterly*, 79 (December, 1924).

[16] Somers, "All Her Ways," 24 (quotation); *Scriptorium*, May 27, 1942. "It is hoped that the class entering in September will be carried through the entire four years course . . . to the Degree of Bachelor of Arts," reported the *Bulletin*, 12 (1924).

[17] Weygant, *Swinger of Birches*, 13 (quotation); *Villa Quarterly*, 77 (March, 1917), 28 (September, 1924), 271 (December, 1925); Somers, "All Her Ways," 25. "Akin in spirit and vision," Bishop Welch and Mother Agnes were an effective team in furthering the cause of St. Scholastica's; Weygant, 14.

[18] *Bulletin*, 3–5 (1924); College of St. Scholastica, "Reports of the President Read Each Year at Commencement, June, 1926–June, 1940," p. 62. These reports in president's office files are bound together and paged consecutively in backward order from 1940 to 1926.

[19] "Reports of the President, 1926–40," p. 65; Somers, "All Her Ways," 25, 26 (quotation).

[20] Somers, "All Her Ways," 27, 51; *Scriptorium*, May 27, 1942; *Duluth Register*, April 15, 1960. In March, 1928, the college students moved into the new section of Tower Hall.

[21] *Bulletin*, 25–75, 81 (1928–29), 29–71 (1930–31), 71 (1933–34); *Scriptorium*, May 12, 1937, April 27, 1938; Somers, "All Her Ways," 39; *Duluth News-Tribune*, January 10, 1937, October 23, 1938; "Reports of the President, 1926–40," p. 36, 51, 58, 62. Before 1936 most nursing students took the three-year diploma course instead of the five-year degree course which was also available. Sister Olivia Gowan founded the school of nursing and served as its dean for 25 years.

[22] "Reports of the President, 1926–40," p. 53 (quotation); *Bulletin*, 6, 9 (1930–31); *Scriptorium*, January 13, 1932. Dean of the college from 1929 to 1943 was Sister Alice Lamb. She earned her B.S. and M.S. degrees at the University of Chicago, and her Ph.D. at the University of Minnesota. A distinguished scientist, she did a great deal to shape the curriculum and to gain recognition for the college. See Weygant, *Swinger of Birches*, 14.

[23] Somers, "All Her Ways," 34, 35; "Reports of the President, 1926–40," p. 29, 52; *Duluth News-Tribune*, October 23, 1938.

[24] Somers, "All Her Ways," 31, 34–36, 52–61; *Bulletin*, 19 (1937–38); *Duluth News-Tribune*, January 10, 1937, October 23, December 31, 1938; *Scriptorium*, May 27, 1942; "Reports of the President, 1926–40," p. 13.

[25] Somers, "All Her Ways," 39; [Sister Digna Birmingham], *The First Fifteen Years of the College of St. Scholastica*, 15, 109–112 (New York, 1947); *Bulletin*, 72 (1932–33), 34 (1934–35); *Scriptorium*, May 25, 1932, November 22, 1933, January 16, 1935, May 27, 1936, January 28, 1948. Sister Patricia Thibadeau, one of the order's outstanding women, became administrator of St. Mary's Hospital, Duluth, in 1926. Mainly through her efforts the professional courses in nursing, medical record science, and medical technology were integrated with the collegiate curriculum leading to degrees in these departments. See Weygant, *Swinger of Birches*, 14.

[26] Somers, "All Her Ways," 39, 84–89; "Reports of the President, 1926–40," p. 27, 32; *Scriptorium*, March 25, December 9, 1936; *Bulletin*, 51 (1941–42). On the Smith-Hughes Act, see Chapter 24, note 8, above.

[27] Somers, "All Her Ways," 31; Birmingham, *First Fifteen Years*, 118–121.

[28] Somers, "All Her Ways," 36, 37 (quotation). The college's department of education, dating from 1922, was the project of Sister Rose O'Donnell, who was also dean of the college from 1943 to 1952. She held a B.A. and an M.A. from Catholic University, as well as an M.A. from Columbia. She conducted workshops at many colleges and universities. See also p. 120, above; *Scriptorium*, November 13, 1957; Weygant, *Swinger of Birches*, 14.

[29] *Bulletin*, 22, 24 (1932–33), 24 (1941–42); Somers, "All Her Ways," 31, 33, 34, 36 (quotations); *Scriptorium*, October 12, 1932, November 25, 1936, February 9, 1938, June 11, 1941, January 14, 1942; "Reports of the President, 1926–40," p. 29,

43. Rules were still restrictive; smoking was taboo, according to the *Bulletin*, 24 (1933–34), and students were expected to maintain silence when "in the reading rooms, on the stairs and in the corridors during school hours." The main student gripes were the few contacts with men, the isolation of Duluth, too many rules, and too much religion. See Birmingham, *First Fifteen Years*, 124.

[30] Birmingham, *First Fifteen Years*, v, vi, 17–19. The study was a pioneer effort; in the absence of norms for all colleges, it is difficult to evaluate its findings. Alumnae seem to have been fairly well prepared for homemaking, but on such matters as participation in organized civic, educational, and cultural groups, reading habits, and artistic tastes, the record of the respondents was disappointing.

[31] Birmingham, *First Fifteen Years*, 19–21, 24, 42–45.

[32] Birmingham, *First Fifteen Years*, xi, 22, 25–30 (quotation), 40, 53–55, 66, 68–70, 75, 98–107 (quotation), 128–130.

26. INTRODUCTION, PART III
Pages 141 to 153

[1] Carleton College, *Reports of the President and Treasurer, 1969–70*, 4 (October, 1970).

[2] U.S. Office of Education, *Higher Education*, 8:91 (December 15, 1951); University of Minnesota Committee on Educational Research, "Effect of the War on Minnesota Colleges and the Present Enrollment Outlook," 6, 8, 11, 13 (Report no. 4 — [Minneapolis], 1946), copy in University of Minnesota Archives. In 1940, 4.2 per cent of Minnesota's population 25 years of age and older had completed four or more years of college. In this respect Minnesota ranked 29th among the states; California with 6.7 per cent was first. See *School and Society*, 60:191 (September 16, 1944), a weekly issued by the Society for the Advancement of Education.

[3] *North Central Association Quarterly*, 272, 277 (April, 1946), 220 (October, 1946); *School and Society*, 60:277 (October 28, 1944). The tests given draftees during the war uncovered a host of physical and mental health problems and illiteracy, which focused attention on education at all levels.

[4] *School and Society*, 60:123, 187, 227, 235–237 (August 19, September 16, October 7, 1944); *North Central Quarterly*, 274, 321 (April, 1946), 184, 222 (October, 1946), 172 (October, 1948). The Fulbright scholarship program was created in 1946. It became operative in 1948 with 22 nations and 84 grantees. In 1966, 136 nations and 5,100 grantees were involved. Between the two dates 48,000 American and foreign students, 16,000 teachers, 7,500 lecturers, and 10,500 research scholars received Fulbright grants, according to James Cass, "Anniversary of the Fulbright Act," in *Saturday Review*, 47 (August 20, 1966).

[5] *School and Society*, 64:337–340, 342 (November 16, 1946); *North Central Quarterly*, 162 (October, 1945), 274 (April, 1946), 171, 177 (October, 1946); Report of the Harvard Committee, *General Education in a Free Society*, 4 (quotation) (Cambridge, 1945).

[6] Louis G. Geiger, *Voluntary Accreditation: A History of the North Central Association, 1945–1970*, xviii, 15–17, 21, 88 (Menasha, Wis., 1970); *North Central Quarterly*, 4 (July, 1940), 396–400 (April, 1942), 162–169 (October, 1945), 387 (April, 1947), 230 (January, 1949), 251–255, 284–288 (January, 1950), 361–372 (quotation) (April, 1951), 167 (October, 1953); Russell M. Cooper, *Better Colleges — Better Teachers* (New York, 1944). In 1945 Augsburg, Gustavus, Macalester, St. Benedict's, St. Mary's, and St. Scholastica's joined the North Central study. Other private colleges in Minnesota followed later.

[7] United States, *Statutes at Large*, 57:43–45, 58:284–301; University of Minnesota, "Effect of the War on Minnesota

Colleges," 20; *School and Society*, 60:164, 353–355, 65:185–190, 194 (September 9, December 2, 1944, March 15, 1947); *North Central Quarterly*, 5, 16 (July, 1945), 301 (April, 1946). The federal government in 1946 alone paid out $1,100,000,000 in subsistence checks. In 1943 and 1945 Minnesota's legislature authorized the granting of financial aid to a state veteran whose eligibility under the GI bill had expired to help complete his or her schooling. Minnesota, *Statutes*, 1945, p. 1650, 1651.

[8] In 1945 President James L. Morrill of the University of Minnesota urged the creation of a committee to study the state's needs in higher education. The Statewide Committee on Higher Education, which included Martin A. H. Graebner of St. Paul's Concordia College and President Charles J. Turck of Macalester, issued a small report, *Unfinished Business: Minnesota's Needs in Higher Education* (n.p., [1947?]).

[9] Geiger, *Voluntary Accreditation*, 2–8; *School and Society*, 59:433 (June 24, 1944), 61:20 (January 13, 1945), 65:84–86 (February 1, 1947); *North Central Quarterly*, 4 (July, 1945), 323 (April, 1946), 297–302 (January, 1947), 385 (April, 1947), 333 (April, 1955). The American Council on Education published *A Guide to the Evaluation of Educational Experiences in the Armed Services* (Washington, D.C., 1946).

[10] Geiger, *Voluntary Accreditation*, 8; *Higher Education*, 9:85 (December 15, 1952); Minnesota Commission, *Higher Education in Minnesota*, 57; *School and Society*, 64:360 (November 23, 1946). About 1,180,000 ex-GIs also received collegiate training under 81 Congress, 2 session, Public Law 894, and 82 Congress, 2 session, Public Law 550, enacted to benefit veterans of the Korean conflict; United States, *Statutes at Large*, 64:1121, 66:663–691.

[11] For the Mead Bill, see United States, *Statutes at Large*, 60:958; *School and Society*, 61:158 (March 10, 1945), 64:44–46, 182, 204–206, 337 (quotation) (July 20, September 14, 21, November 16, 1946), 65:65, 136, 153–158 (January 25, February 22, March 1, 1947); *North Central Quarterly*, 168 (October, 1946), 165–170 (October, 1948), 350–353, 359–365 (April, 1949). In July, 1946, President Truman appointed a National Commission on Higher Education to draw up guidelines for the future. Its findings and recommendations were presented in six small volumes which provoked much debate among educators. See President's Commission on Higher Education, *Higher Education for American Democracy* (6 vols., Washington, D.C., 1947).

[12] On the Minnesota Private College Council, see Chapter 11, note 16, above; Minnesota Private College Council, "Minutes," May 21, November 22, 1946, February 8, April 18, 1947, December 18, 1948, November 7, 1949, in council offices, St. Paul; *North Central Quarterly*, 377 (April, 1951); Minnesota, *Laws*, 1949, p. 1065; Minnesota Board for Vocational Education, "Minutes," 8 (May 26, 1949), mimeographed copies in the Minnesota Historical Society. Minnesota Commission, *Higher Education in Minnesota*, 248, 282–300, notes that there were about 2,000 fewer elementary school teachers in the state in 1947–48 than there had been 10 years earlier despite increasing enrollments.

[13] National Education Association, *College and University Bulletin*, 1–4 (September, 1949); *St. Paul Pioneer Press*, November 25, 1951; *New York Times*, December 14, 1952, p. 1; Minnesota Commission on Vocational and Higher Education, *Higher Education Looks Ahead: Minnesota Colleges: Their Functions, Their Problems, and Their Goals* (St. Paul, 1953); American Council on Education, *Higher Education and National Affairs*, 3 (January 6, 1958); "Crisis in the Colleges: Can They Pay Their Way?" in *Time*, 28 (June 19, 1950); "Why Korea Is Called 'Poor Man's War': Charge College Deferments Given Too Freely," in *U.S. News and World*

Report, 18–20 (February 20, 1953); *Higher Education*, 13:12, 21–23 (September, October, 1956), 15:77–82 (January, 1959). According to the latter, in 1939, 14.3 per cent of the nation's 18- to 21-year-olds were in college; in 1958 the proportion was 35.6 per cent.

[14] National Science Foundation, *Guide to Programs* (Washington, D.C., 1970); "NSF Enters Its Third Decade," in *Science Teacher*, 33–37 (November, 1970); Louis W. and Maud Hill Family Foundation, *A Report, 1935–1953*, 5–7 (St. Paul, 1953). Hill Foundation reports were issued annually after 1953. William H. Whyte, Jr., "What Are the Foundations Up To?" in *Fortune*, 110–113, 254, 256, 258, 260 (October, 1955), and "Where the Foundations Fall Down," in *Fortune*, 140, 211, 214, 216, 219 (November, 1955).

[15] Hill Foundation, *Report*, 9 (1953), 13 (1954), 15, 20 (1955), 11 (1956), 14–16, 32 (1957), 20, 24, 37 (1958), 23, 27, 45 (1959), 24, 36, 38 (1960); Private College Council, "Minutes," May 3, July 10, 1957. Between 1954 and 1958 the Hill Foundation gave $100,000 for the establishment of KTCA-TV, to which the Ford Foundation earlier had made a matching grant of $100,000. The station went on the air in September, 1957.

[16] A. P. Smith Mfg. Co. *v.* Barlow, 346 *United States* 861; Minnesota College Fund Association, *Reports* [Minneapolis, 1954], in the fund's office, Minneapolis; L. L. L. Golden, "The Case That Cleared the Way," in *Saturday Review*, 59 (September 12, 1964); Joe Alex Morris, "The Small Colleges Fight for Their Lives," in *Saturday Evening Post*, 42, 104, 107, 110, 114 (May 15, 1954). In 1953 a national Council for Financial Aid to Education, Inc., was created "to promote a better understanding between American business and institutions of higher education," according to the *Post*.

[17] Minnesota, *Laws*, 1949, p. 322; B. J. Kemper, executive director, Minnesota Private College Fund, to the author, December 7, 1970; Private College Council, "Minutes," November 7, 1949, June 24, 1950, March 10, April 19, June 22, 1951, July 10, 1957; *St. John's Record*, February 15, 1952, March 27, 1953. The Hill Foundation underwrote the fund association's administrative costs during its early years. At that time federal law permitted corporations to use tax free up to 5 per cent of their income for charitable purposes; none was coming close to doing so.

[18] St. Mary's College, *Terrace Heights News*, April, 1956; John M. Stalnaker, "The Nation's Greatest Talent Hunt," in *Saturday Review*, 60 (December 16, 1961); Governor's Committee on Higher Education, *Minnesota's Stake in the Future: Higher Education, 1956–1970*, 51 (Minneapolis, 1956); Carleton College, *Voice*, 4 (September, 1967), an alumni publication; *Higher Education*, 10:9, 13 (September, 1953). In 1957 to fight the growing shortage of college teachers, the Ford Foundation appropriated $25,000,000 to extend the Woodrow Wilson Fellowship Program. In Minnesota from 1945 to 1968 state university students won 112 of the fellowships, Carleton 101, and St. Olaf 34.

[19] "The Big Wave," in *Time*, 56, 58 (February 21, 1955); "President's Committee Issues Second Report on Education Beyond the High School," in *Phi Beta Kappa Key Reporter*, 1 (quotation) (October, 1957); Private College Council, "Minutes," January 26, April 29, November 4, 1955, April 27, September 5, November 2, 1956; Dwight D. Eisenhower, *Economic Report of the President Transmitted to the Congress January 28, 1954*, 105 (Washington, D.C., 1954).

[20] Frank G. Jennings, "The Revolution in Education: It Didn't Start With Sputnik," in *Saturday Review*, 77–79, 95–97 (September 16, 1967); Arthur E. Bestor, *Educational Wastelands* (Urbana, Ill., 1953) and *The Restoration of Learning* (New York, 1955) were critical studies of current education.

[21] Howard Mumford Jones, "Campus: Echo or Criticism?" in *Harvard Alumni Bulletin*, 161–164 (quotation) (November 5, 1955); Louis T. Benezet, "The Trouble with Excellence," in *Saturday Review*, 44, 63 (October 21, 1961); Paul Goodman, "The Editor's Bookshelf," a column in *Saturday Review*, 68 (October 17, 1964). "Only if we value intellectual excellence shall we have it," proclaimed the Rockefeller Brothers Fund in *The Pursuit of Excellence: Education and the Future of America*, 46 (Garden City, N.Y., 1958).

[22] For a balanced reply to one writer's claim that the "liberal arts tradition is dead or dying," see Paul Woodring's editorial in *Saturday Review*, 53 (April 18, 1964).

[23] *Higher Education*, 19 (December, 1960); Sidney G. Tickton, "A Third Force in College Enrollments," in *Saturday Review*, 70 (March 21, 1964); Fred Johnson, in *Minneapolis Tribune*, October 31, 1966, p. 1, 6; *Minneapolis Star*, August 8, p. 1A, 14A; August 9, p. 1B; August 12, p. 9A; August 13, p. 15A — all 1966; and October 9, p. 1A, 4A; October 11, p. 7C — both 1967. Total enrollment of private colleges treated in this book in 1972 was 25,372. Gains in full-time enrollment from 1968 to 1972 were recorded by 12 of the 16 schools. The largest percentage increases registered were St. Benedict (94.3 per cent) and St. Scholastica (86.6 per cent). Four school enrollments declined in the same period: Saint Teresa by 22.7 per cent, Concordia of St. Paul by 12.2 per cent, Augsburg by 6.6 per cent, and St. Thomas by 1.7 per cent. See Minnesota Higher Education Coordinating Commission, *Public College Enrollment in Minnesota's Changing Population Pattern, 1970–85*, 17 (Minneapolis, 1973), and "Five Years of Full-time Equivalent Enrollments in Minnesota Post-secondary Educational Institutions, 1968–72," p. 8, 9 (January, 1973); Kenneth A. Simon and W. Vance Grant, *Digest of Educational Statistics, 1970 Edition*, published by U.S. Office of Education (Washington, D.C., 1970).

[24] Minnesota Commission, *Minnesota Private Higher Education*, 56–61, 113 (St. Paul, 1970). In 1969–70, $9,895,000 was secured from private and $7,550,000 from public sources to finance building construction in Minnesota's private colleges; the comparable amounts 10 years earlier had been $6,800,000 and $2,360,000, respectively.

[25] See, for example, Christian K. Arnold, "Higher Education: Fourth Branch of Government," in *Saturday Review*, 60, 75 (January 18, 1964); Humphrey Doermann, "Financing Higher Education," in *Saturday Review*, 80, 90 (November 20, 1965).

[26] *Fact Book: Office of Education Programs*, 28 (Washington, D.C., 1968); Minnesota Commission, *Minnesota Private Higher Education*, 114; Rexford G. Moon, Jr., "More Students Are Studying Now, Paying Later," in *Saturday Review*, 74, 83 (June 15, 1963); James Cass, "While School Keeps," a column in *Saturday Review*, 75 (November 16, 1963); Tom Kaser, "The Loyalty Oath: 1964–65," in *Saturday Review*, 60, 79 (November 21, 1964); Hugo A. Bedau, "Loyalty Oath Amended," in *Saturday Review*, 46 (January 16, 1965). A communist disclaimer oath was included in the 1958 act; the disclaimer was deleted in October, 1962, but an oath of allegiance to the United States and the criminal penalties of the original act were retained. See United States, *Statutes at Large*, 72:1580–1605, 76:1070.

[27] United States, *Statutes at Large*, 77:363–379, 78:508–534; *Fact Book*, 25–27 (1968); Cass, in *Saturday Review*, 68 (January 18, 1964); Vernon R. Alden, "Education and Poverty: Planning for Education's Forgotten Men," in *Saturday Review*, 68 (May 15, 1965); Oria A. Brinkmeier, director, Educational Resource Planning, Minnesota Higher Education Coordinating Commission, to the author, April 2, 1971. Grants in Minnesota under the 1963 act had been dispensed by a Liaison and Facilities Commission, which in 1967 was given broader responsibilities

and renamed the Minnesota Higher Education Coordinating Commission. See Private College Council, "Minutes," April 29, November 18, 1965, June 13, December 12, 1967.

[28] United States, *Statutes at Large*, 79:1219–1270, 80:12–28; *Fact Book*, 18–24 (1968); *Minneapolis Tribune*, September 7, 1967, August 12, 1968, August 16, 1970; American Council on Education, *Higher Education and National Affairs*, 1 (August 25, 1967). In 1969–70 Minnesota led the nation in the volume of federally guaranteed student loans per capita. Many banks, however, found such loans too expensive to handle. For a sharp criticism of the 1965 program, see William F. Buckley's column in the editorial section of the *Minneapolis Tribune*, February 15, 1970, p. 3C.

[29] Minnesota, *Laws*, 1967, p. 1823–1826, 1969, p. 2627, 1971, p. 1664–1666; Governor's Committee, *Minnesota's Stake in the Future*, 45–50, 91–97; Private College Council, "Minutes," September 5, November 2, 1956, January 24, February 3, 1957, April 18, May 12, November 7, 1958, February 21, May 1, November 9, December 15, 1959, November 4, 1963, April 30, November 19, 1964, February 8, May 5, 1966, April 25, 1968; interview with George B. Risty, assistant executive director, Minnesota Higher Education Coordinating Commission, March 24, 1971; *Minneapolis Tribune*, November 21, 1970, p. 5. By early 1966 public scholarship programs had been set up by 39 states.

[30] Minnesota Commission, *Minnesota Private Higher Education*, 67–70, 87–90. In 1969–70 tuition and fees for one quarter in the University of Minnesota College of Liberal Arts were $105 for state residents.

[31] Gene R. Hawes, "Academic Philanthropy: The Art of Getting," in *Saturday Review*, 65, 77 (December 16, 1967); Burt Wallace, "Struck by Ford Lightning," in *Saturday Review*, 86, 102 (April 16, 1966); McGeorge Bundy quoted in Duncan Norton-Taylor, "Private Colleges: A Question of Survival," in *Fortune*, 152–154, 180, 185 (October, 1967). Between 1961 and 1966 giving by individuals to higher education went up by over 50 per cent.

[32] Hawes, in *Saturday Review*, 78 (December 16, 1967); Norton-Taylor, in *Fortune*, 185 (October, 1967); Private College Fund, *Annual Report*, 7 (1969); Minnesota Commission, *Minnesota Private Higher Education*, 78, 82. An overwhelming majority of the endowment funds in Minnesota's private colleges were held by fewer than a half dozen of the institutions.

[33] Minnesota Commission, *Minnesota Private Higher Education*, 67, 70–78. Education and general funds expenditures per full-time student in the state's private colleges increased between 1960 and 1968 from an average of $1,073 to $2,067. Speaking at the 1972 St. Thomas commencement, Humphrey Doermann, executive director of the Bush Foundation, St. Paul, outlined three related problems afflicting higher education: the need for greater access to college education for low-income students, the financial crises of private colleges, and the rapidly rising cost to taxpayers of public higher education. Doermann recommended that the charges of public colleges for tuition and fees should more nearly cover the cost of instruction. Much of this additional money should then be plowed back into scholarships and loans to low- and middle-income students. More low- and middle-income students could then attend public colleges without undue financial sacrifices or work burdens; upper-income families would then pay more for public college instruction; and more of the additional college enrollment would attend private colleges. See *Minneapolis Tribune*, June 8, 1972, p. 10A.

[34] Minnesota Commission, *Minnesota Private Higher Education*, 21–31.

[35] Carleton College, *Reports*, 3 (October, 1970); "The Cynical Idealists of '68," in *Time*, 78–83 (June 7, 1968); A. Lament,

pseud., "The Groves of Academe," in *Saturday Review*, 54 (June 16, 1962); Kenneth Keniston, *The Uncommitted* (New York, 1970); Samuel B. Gould, "September Undergraduate: Hope vs. Exasperation," in *Saturday Review*, 53, 70 (September 15, 1962); Bonnie B. Stretch, "Classroom Learning Is Not Enough," in *Saturday Review*, 62, 73 (June 19, 1965); Joseph Katz and Nevitt Sanford, "Causes of the Student Revolution," in *Saturday Review*, 65, 76, 79 (December 18, 1965); *Minneapolis Tribune*, November 27, 1967, p. 17. For caustic but valid criticisms of higher education, see Kenneth E. Eble, *The Profane Comedy: American Higher Education in the Sixties* (New York, 1962); John Keats, *The Sheepskin Psychosis* (New York, 1965); and Paul Goodman, *Compulsory Miseducation* (New York, 1964). More objective is Nevitt Sanford, *Where Colleges Fail: A Study of the Student as a Person* (San Francisco, 1967). For a later glimpse of changing attitudes in the 1970s, see Edmund Faltermayer, "Youth After the Revolution," in *Fortune*, 145–148, 150, 152, 154, 156, 158 (March, 1973).

[36] Katz and Sanford, in *Saturday Review*, 64, 65 (quotations) (December 18, 1965); Benezet, in *Saturday Review*, 44, 45 (quotation), 63 (October 21, 1961); Goodman, in *Saturday Review*, 68 (October 17, 1964).

[37] Katz and Sanford, in *Saturday Review*, 64–66, 76, 79 (December 18, 1965); Gene R. Hawes, "Civil Liberties for College Students," in *Saturday Review*, 61 (June 18, 1966).

[38] Katz and Sanford, in *Saturday Review*, 66, 70 (quotations) (December 18, 1965).

[39] Minnesota Commission, *Minnesota Private Higher Education*, 21–39. According to the commission, 39, "A large number of major fields of study had less than five graduates annually" in the private colleges, a matter of concern in this period of financial stringency.

[40] Edward H. Litchfield, "The Trimester System," Weimar Hicks, "The Kalamazoo Plan," and Marjorie Freed, "The Antioch Plan," all in *Saturday Review*, 50–54 (December 15, 1962); Minnesota Commission, *Minnesota Private Higher Education*, 37. According to the *Minneapolis Tribune*, January 31, 1968, about 8,000 students from Gustavus, Macalester, St. Benedict, St. Olaf, and St. John's were studying a variety of courses on campus and elsewhere during the interim term of 1968.

[41] Cass, in *Saturday Review*, 57 (August 18, 1962), 75 (May 18, 1963), 56 (July 18, 1964), 64 (August 15, 1964); James F. Fixx, "Go to College and See the World," in *Saturday Review*, 75, 79 (February 17, 1962); Richard T. Stavig, "Why Study Abroad Pays Off," in *Saturday Review*, 86, 90 (February 19, 1966); John Brademas, "As Nations Become Neighbors: A New Federal Role," in *Saturday Review*, 52 (August 20, 1966). In 1962–63 over 17,000 American students studied at more than 400 institutions in 64 foreign countries.

[42] Minnesota Commission, *Minnesota Private Higher Education*, 32–39.

[43] Benezet, in *Saturday Review*, 63 (October 21, 1961); Catherine Watson, in *Minneapolis Tribune*, May 12, 1968, p. 1W; Minnesota Commission, *Minnesota Private Higher Education*, 24. According to *Higher Education and National Affairs*, 1, 5, 11 (March 19, 1971), between 1965 and 1970 Black enrollment in American colleges rose 91 per cent, from 274,000 to 522,000.

[44] *Minneapolis Tribune*, November 13, p. 4; November 14, p. 4; November 15, p. 6; November 16, p. 6 — all 1967; September 7, 1969, p. 6B; December 17, 1970, p. 26. The Hill Foundation in 1970 made a contingent gift of $145,000 to the state's private colleges to assist in the enrollment of American Indian students.

[45] Peter Schrag, "Joint Action in Ivied Halls," in *Saturday Review*, 54, 65 (October 21, 1961); George H. Hanford, "The

Consortium Plan: New Hope for Weak Colleges," in *Saturday Review*, 52 (January 16, 1965); Cass, in *Saturday Review*, 74 (April 20, 1963); Minnesota Commission, *Minnesota Private Higher Education*, 32, 62–66; *ACM: The Associated Colleges of the Midwest, Programs 1970–71*, a pamphlet in Minnesota Historical Society and files of participating colleges.

[46] Richard G. Fowler, "Who Should Pay for the Ph.D.?" in *Saturday Review*, 56 (June 16, 1962); Everett Walters, "The Ph.D.: New Demands, Same Old Response — The Immutable Ph.D.," in *Saturday Review*, 62–65, 75–77 (January 15, 1966); Leigh C. Rhett, "Shaking Up College Teaching: Independent Study and the Campus Crisis," in *Saturday Review*, 62–65 (July 16, 1966). Through its agencies, the federal government in 1962 alone spent $129,838,000 to assist 40,000 students in the country's graduate schools.

[47] Minnesota Commission, *Minnesota Private Higher Education*, 40–49.

[48] Minnesota Commission, *Minnesota Private Higher Education*, 40–49, 110.

[49] Greeley, *The Changing Catholic College*, 29; Edward Wakin, "How Catholic Is the Catholic College," in *Saturday Review*, 105 (April 16, 1966). Minnesota had just under 1,000,000 Catholics in 1968; its seven Catholic colleges enrolled 8,800 students that year, according to the *Minneapolis Tribune*, April 25, 1968, p. 11.

[50] The Second Vatican Ecumenical Council was called by Pope John XXIII, who addressed the first session on October 11, 1962. He died in 1963, and the second session's inaugural address was given by Pope Paul VI, on September 29, 1963. The aim of the council was reform and renewal within the Catholic church, with the reunion of all Christian bodies as its ultimate goal. Francis X. Murphy, "The First Historians of the Second Vatican Council," in *Catholic Historical Review*, 49:540 (January, 1964); Andrew M. Greeley, *From Backwater to Mainstream: A Profile of Catholic Higher Education* (New York, 1969); Robert Hassenger, *The Shape of Catholic Higher Education* (Chicago, 1967); James Kavanaugh, *A Modern Priest Looks at His Outdated Church* (New York, 1967).

[51] Hawes, in *Saturday Review*, 61 (quotation) (June 18, 1966).

[52] Hawes, in *Saturday Review*, 77 (quotation) (June 18, 1966).

[53] *Minneapolis Tribune*, November 19, 1967, p. 1W, 2W; June 10, 1968, p. 1; David Kuhn, in *Minneapolis Tribune*, March 23, 1969, p. 1W; Hawes, in *Saturday Review*, 61, 77 (June 18, 1966); Paul Woodring, "Who Makes University Policy," in *Saturday Review*, 65 (April 17, 1965); "Schools Make News," a column in *Saturday Review*, 67 (December 18, 1965); *Higher Education and National Affairs*, 4 (October 6, 1967).

27. HAMLINE UNIVERSITY, PART III
Pages 154 to 160

[1] Nute, "Hamline Halls," 322–329; catalog issue of Hamline University, *Bulletin*, 60 (1941–42). The service flag had 338 stars by the spring of 1943. Lieut. Robert M. Page (class of 1927) became famous for his radar inventions. Lieut. Robert M. Hanson (1944), who was killed after shooting down 25 Japanese planes, was posthumously awarded the Congressional Medal of Honor, and a superdestroyer was named for him.

[2] Nute, "Hamline Halls," 326; Dorothy B. A. Rood, "We Gratefully Remember Charles M. Drew," in *Hamline Alumni Bulletin*, 5 (Winter, 1960).

[3] Nute, "Hamline Halls," 327, 338; *Bulletin*, 64–66 (1956–58). Macalester College sent roses in 1947 when the Little Theatre moved into its new quarters.

[4] Nute, "Hamline Halls," 329, 336.

[5] Nute, "Hamline Halls," 329–331. Hamline was awarded a Phi Beta Kappa chapter in 1973.

[6] Nute, "Hamline Halls," 331–336. Starting in 1942 an annual institute in foreign affairs was started by Professor Charles B. Kuhlmann. Since 1950 it has been called the Institute of World Affairs.

[7] Nute, "Hamline Halls," 337 (quotation). Miss Nute notes that in his report to the board of trustees in June, 1952, Anderson spoke of Hamline's strength "in its passion for liberal learning, for sound scholarship within a framework of Christian devotion. Through the ups and downs of the economic cycle, this has been the constant factor. This has been the spark which when properly kindled accounts for that which has been achieved at Hamline University."

[8] Nute, "Hamline Halls," 338–342.

[9] Taped interview of the author, May 10, 1968, with Paul H. Giddens (quotation), in the collections of the Minnesota Historical Society; *Bulletin*, 11 (March, 1958); "President's Report to the Board of Trustees," April 10, 1968, a mimeographed report in the president's files at Hamline. The college's salary budget went up over 35 per cent between 1952 and 1956.

[10] Giddens interview, May 10, 1968.

[11] "President's Report," April 10, 1968; Giddens interview, May 10, 1968. Hamline won three National Association of Intercollegiate Athletics (NAIA) basketball championships — in 1942, 1949, and 1951. It won or tied 19 similar MIAC titles prior to 1953. Other sports had been subordinated to basketball. From 1955 to 1961 Hamline played 46 conference football games and won only two — one by a forfeit. In 1966 it won the football crown, the first in 45 years. See Paul H. Giddens, "The Anatomy of a Football Team," in *Minnesota Journal of Education*, 12–14 (September, 1967).

[12] Minnesota, *Laws*, 1854, p. 105; 1871, p. 337; Giddens, "The President's Report: Trustees Propose Enlargement of the Board," in *Hamline Alumni Bulletin*, 2, 14 (quotation) (Summer, 1963).

[13] Giddens interview, May 10, 1968; Minnesota Methodist Conference, *Official Journal and Yearbook*, 30 (1963), 26, 29 (1964); Giddens, in *Hamline Alumni Bulletin*, 2 (Summer, 1963). Hamline's 21-member board was small compared with those of some other Minnesota colleges; Macalester's board had 37 members and Carleton's 32.

[14] Giddens interview, May 10, 1968; *Bulletin*, 2 (Winter, 1964).

[15] Giddens interview, May 10, 1968; "President's Report," April 10, 1968; Giddens, "Faculty Salary Increases Bring AAUP Rating to B," in *Bulletin*, 2 (January, 1966). Salaries were increased dramatically in 1965. According to "AAUP Faculty Salary Report, 1966–67," a mimeographed report in the president's office, by 1967 Hamline was one of five Minnesota private colleges with an AAUP rating of B or better in average compensation for all faculty ranks.

[16] Giddens interview, May 10, 1968; "President's Report," April 10, 1968; Giddens, "Progress Through Grants," in *Bulletin*, 9–12 (April, 1967).

[17] Giddens interview, May 10, 1968; "President's Report," April 10, 1968; Minnesota Committee on High School-College Relations, *High School-College Relations Newsletter* (Spring, 1967). By the fall of 1967 all but two of the 18 academic departments had at least three full-time staff members. Over 44 per cent of the upperclassmen were majoring in the social sciences, 25 per cent in the humanities, slightly over 19 per cent in the natural sciences, and 12.3 per cent in the fine arts. Nearly one-third of the total were in teacher education. See *Campus Talk from Hamline University* (December, 1967), a newsletter.

[18] "President's Report," April 10, 1968; *Bulletin*, 23–26 (July, 1967); *Campus Talk* (November, 1967). Hamline was a charter member of the KTCA-TV network.

[19] *Bulletin*, 6 (January, 1967). The non-Western institutes have been continued. Similar programs for high school teachers of biology, physics, history, and English have been held, starting in the summer of 1964.

[20] Giddens interview, May 10, 1968; "President's Report," April 10, 1968. Hamline became a member of the College Scholarship Service and of the College Entrance Examination Board in 1961–62.

[21] "President's Report," April 10, 1968; Fred Johnson, in *Minneapolis Tribune*, November 9, 1966; *Bulletin*, 9–15, 38, 55, 59 (February, 1966).

[22] "President's Report," April 10, 1968; *Minneapolis Tribune*, September 5, 1968, May 3, 1969; according to Hamline, *Bulletin*, 2 (April, 1966), Bush, who was born in Granite Falls, Minnesota, in the late 1880s, had a career reminiscent of those portrayed by Horatio Alger. From a bookkeeper in the Minnesota Mining and Manufacturing Company, he rose to become chairman of its executive committee and a very wealthy man. In the mid-1950s he accepted an invitation to become a Hamline trustee. Up to 1972 through their various gifts, Mr. and Mrs. Bush had given Hamline about $5,500,000 and contributions from the Bush Foundation were continuing, according to information from Wallace S. Wikoff, Hamline vice president for institutional relations.

[23] *St. Paul Pioneer Press*, August 20, 1967 (quotation); "President's Report," April 10, 1968.

[24] Giddens interview, May 10, 1968; "President's Report," April 10, 1968; Giddens, "An Alumni Success Story," in *American Alumni Council News*, 7–9, 28 (March, 1959); *Minneapolis Star*, March 21, 1955.

[25] *Bulletin*, inside front cover (quotation) (September, 1967); 10, 12 (April, 1968). A 64-page report by Kenneth R. Doane, "Our Alumni: A Century of Achievements and Activities," was published in the *Bulletin* of June, 1956. In December, 1966, a comprehensive *Alumni Directory*, compiled by Arther S. Williamson, long-time faculty member, was published. Hamline alumni achievements support the generalization that a liberal arts education is an excellent preparation for a career and for life.

[26] "President's Report," April 10, 1968.

[27] Giddens interview, May 10, 1968; *Oracle* (May 3, 1968); "President's Report," April 10, 1968 (quotation).

[28] *Minneapolis Tribune*, June 29, September 18, November 2, December 12, 1968; *St. Paul Pioneer Press*, July 2, 1968; *Campus Talk*, December, 1968. The *Bulletin*, 14–17 (January, 1969), contains Bailey's inaugural address on November 1, 1968. He holds a B.A. degree from North Central College, Naperville, Illinois, and an M.A. and a Ph.D. from the University of Wisconsin.

[29] *Bulletin*, 2–7 (January, 1969); *Campus Talk*, February, August, September, 1969; *Minneapolis Tribune*, May 29, 1969, May 6, 1970. Construction of a new heating plant also began in 1969.

[30] *Campus Talk*, December, 1968, February, 1969, June, 1970; *Minneapolis Tribune*, December 5, 1969, May 6, 1970, June 15, 1970 (quotation). Hamline's old library, built in 1907 and enlarged in 1927, had shelving for only 90,000 volumes and reading space for 225 students.

[31] *Campus Talk*, August, 1970; "Report from the President," June 15, June 22, 1970. In the first two years of Bailey's administration, Hamline closed and added four blocks of city streets to the campus, purchased most of three other blocks, and demolished or moved away 23 houses.

[32] "Report from the President," June 22, 1970 (quotations).

[33] *Campus Talk*, September, 1969, August, 1970; *Bulletin*, 59–123 (July, 1970). Hamline's summer institutes dealing with non-European areas and supported by the Hill Foundation continued to flourish in these years. The four-week session on South and Southeast Asia in 1969, for example, enrolled faculty from colleges in 15 states. The following summer, Hamline and the Minnesota State Department of Education cosponsored on campus a seven-week institute in remedial reading for elementary school teachers and teacher aides.

[34] *Bulletin*, 17 (quotation) (January, 1969); "Report from the President," June 1, 8 (quotation), 29 (quotation), 1970; *Campus Talk*, June, 1970; *Minneapolis Tribune*, November 17, 1968, June 8, 1970; *St. Paul Pioneer Press*, July 2, 1968.

28. ST. JOHN'S UNIVERSITY, PART III
Pages 161 to 168

[1] St. John's, *Catalogue*, 110–112 (1941), 107 (1942); Barry, *Worship and Work*, 333. In 1941, 52 B.A., 2 B.S., and 2 degrees in architecture were given. Father Gilbert Winkelmann for 30 years was the prime mover behind St. John's offerings in church architecture. After World War II he was assigned to a parish and the department of architecture was dropped.

[2] Historical Section, A-2 Division Headquarters, "History of 87th College Training Detachment, St. John's University, Collegeville, Minnesota," 1–89, appendix (February–March, 1944), a manuscript in St. John's Abbey archives; Barry, *Worship and Work*, 294; *St. John's Record*, February 11, May 20, September 30, 1943, March 8, 1945. The government paid St. John's $25,200 for remodeling and the purchase of equipment and provided additional sums for such services as instruction, medical and dental care, subsistence, and living quarters.

[3] *Catalogue*, 104, 110 (1945), 129 (1947); St. John's, *Annual Bulletin*, 105, 109 (1948); *Record*, July 10, 1945, September 25, 1947. More than 1,625 Johnnies were in uniform in World War II and 64 lost their lives. Twenty-nine alumni, 14 of them Benedictines, served as chaplains.

[4] *Catalogue*, 15 (1947); *Bulletin*, 15 (1948); "Report to the Board of Review of the Commission on Colleges and Universities, North Central Association of Colleges and Secondary Schools, 1949–1950," (October, 1949), in president's files. The college ran a bus to transport off-campus students during this period.

[5] "Report to the Board of Review," 1949; *Catalogue*, 6–10 (1944); *Bulletin*, 8–13 (1952). Barry, *Worship and Work*, 310–312, notes that while St. John's was growing so rapidly, the abbey was also setting up foundations in Mexico, Puerto Rico, Kentucky, and Japan. Over 40 Benedictines were sent from Collegeville to teach in these new schools. From them in turn came students to St. John's, adding to its cosmopolitan character.

[6] *Catalogue*, 48, 54–58, 68, 71 (1942), 46 (1942), 51 (1946), 55–57 (1947); "Report to the Board of Review," 1949; *Bulletin*, 48, 54, 57, 59 (1948); Barry, *Worship and Work*, 291, 292 (quotation). Economics with 44 majors led the list in the class of 1949; philosophy was second with 37.

[7] "Report to the Board of Review," 1949; *Record*, April 13, 1950; *Catalogue*, 27 (1943); *Bulletin*, 28, 31 (1951). The statutes of the American Cassinese Congregation of Benedictine Abbeys set limitations on purchases and expenditures.

[8] Barry, *Worship and Work*, 286; *Bulletin*, 16 (1951); Harold C. Coffman and W. F. Cunningham, "Report to the Board of Review of the Commission on Colleges and Universities, North Central Association of Colleges and Secondary Schools," 1950, in president's files. Rather than dictate to St. John's, the Association urged continued development "along characteristic lines."

[9] Barry, *Worship and Work*, 295 (quotation); *Saint John's* (Summer, 1969), a quarterly alumni publication; *Bulletin*, 6, 17, 104 (1951), 128 (1969–70); "Report to the Board of Review," 1949. Between 1950 and 1970, 217 priests (111 of them Benedictines) were ordained from the seminary.

[10] Barry, *Worship and Work*, 286, 327–329.

[11] Barry, *Worship and Work*, 330.

[12] Barry, *Worship and Work*, 335; *Bulletin*, 17, 22, 121 (1951), 15, 121 (May, 1952), 10 (1965); *Record*, October 20, 1949, February 9 (quotations), July 27, 1950; *Saint John's* (quotation) (Winter, 1969–70); *St. John's University*, a pamphlet published in 1950. St. Joseph House, built in 1902 as a carriage house, was remodeled as a dormitory for 45 men in 1954. Father Walter organized "The St. John's Associates Club" composed of donors who pledged at least $100 a year. It had 1,100 members by late 1969.

[13] Barry, *Worship and Work*, 336, 337 (quotation), 339; *Record*, May 22, 1953; *St. Paul Pioneer Press*, April 22, 1954; "A Benedictine Monastery by Marcel Breuer," in *Architectural Forum*, 148–155 (July, 1954); *Off-Campus Record*, April, 1964. The monastic community in 1954 numbered about 300, of whom 125 were engaged in parochial or mission work.

[14] Barry, *Worship and Work*, 332; president's files; *Bulletin*, 37, 39, 41 (1951), 12, 20, 40, 53 (1953), 110 (1954), 95 (1956); *Record*, March 28, 1952, August 21, 1953; *Off-Campus Record*, November, 1962, November, 1963; "Self-Study of Saint John's University, 1963; A Report Submitted to the Commission on Colleges and Universities of the North Central Association of Colleges and Secondary Schools," 5, 128, in president's files. In the class of 1955 economics and business attracted the largest number of majors (32), social science the second largest (27), and philosophy the third (16). ROTC became voluntary for freshmen in 1965. By 1970 reserve commissions had been earned by 664 Johnnies.

[15] "Self-Study, 1963," p. 27–29; *Record*, July 25, 1952, July 25, 1958; *Off-Campus Record*, Winter, 1967; president's files; *Minneapolis Tribune*, March 20, 1968. Father Dunstan J. Tucker, 1924 graduate, World War II chaplain, and baseball coach who taught English at St. John's for 27 years, was dean from 1958 to 1968. St. John's appointed a director of development in 1962.

[16] *Bulletin*, 10, 105 (1960); *Record*, March 27, 1953, February 28, 1964; memo from Father Gervase J. Soukup to the author, June 15, 1970. The 1952 *Alumni Directory* listed 13,800 alumni of whom 3,600 were deceased. Among these former students were 2 archbishops, 9 bishops, 12 abbots, 40 monsignors, 74 brothers, and 1,244 priests. St. John's returned $280,000 of its loan on Aquinas Hall to the federal government.

[17] *Architectural Forum*, 45 (May, 1968); Barry, *Worship and Work*, 336 (quotation); Wakin, *Catholic Campus*, 130; *Bulletin*, 10 (1962); Soukup memo; *Minneapolis Star*, November 13, 1968. For detailed data on the church building, which received an Honor Award from the American Institute of Architects in 1962, see *Abbey and University Church of Saint John the Baptist*, an illustrated booklet issued by the college. The Minnesota Historical Society library has a copy. The old church was imaginatively remodeled to serve as a reception center and lounge.

[18] *Record*, September 29, 1961, February 28, 1964; *Off-Campus Record*, February, November, 1962, July, 1963, April, 1964; Soukup memo. A new building for the abbey's Liturgical Press was erected just north of the seminary's house of studies in 1962.

[19] "Self-Study, 1963," p. 5, 38–54, 124; *Record*, December 9, 1955, August 30, 1957, May 16, 1958, October 23, 1959, January 22, 1960; *Off-Campus Record*, February, July, 1962; Barry, *Worship and Work*, 332. As it had been 10 years earlier, philosophy was the most popular major among the 205 graduates of 1962.

[20] "Self-Study, 1963," p. 153–166; *Record*, April 17, 1964; *Off-Campus Record*, April, 1964, Summer, 1965; *Saint John's* (Winter, 1969–70); *Bulletin*, 103, 106–109 (1964), 102 (1966). In the summer of 1965, 88 nuns, 62 male members of 18 religious orders, 13 diocesan priests, and 2 lay students were enrolled in the graduate program; 23 students were registered in the regular year course, according to the registrar's files.

[21] Faculty Study Committee, "Minutes," June–July, 1962, in college files; *Off-Campus Record*, November, 1963, February, April, 1964, Winter, 1965; *Saint John's* (Winter, 1968). During the early 1960s, St. John's dominated the state conference in football and won two NAIA national football championships. Its first MIAC basketball title was not won until 1968–69.

[22] "Self-Study, 1963," p. 18–22; *Bulletin*, 21 (1962); *Off-Campus Record*, February, July, November, 1962, July, 1963, Spring, 1966. By 1963, $48,000 was still owed on St. Mary's Hall, and the federal mortgage on St. Thomas Aquinas Hall totaled $1,100,000. Gifts were being used to reduce the former, current funds to meet payments on the latter. Endowment in 1962, including the 1955 Ford Foundation gift of $270,000 for faculty salary improvement, was only $796,500.

[23] *Record*, January 11, 1952, February 8, May 17, 1957; president's files.

[24] *The Library of Saint John's University*, an undated booklet issued by St. John's; *Bulletin*, 10 (1965), 10 (1966); *Record*, June 29, 1964, April 29, 1966; *Off-Campus Record*, April, November, 1964, Summer, Winter, 1965, Spring, 1966; Soukup memo; "Marcel Breuer at St. John's," in *Architectural Forum*, 45–49 (May, 1968). Thirteen honorary degrees were conferred at the library dedication in May, 1966, at which Vice President Hubert H. Humphrey gave the main address.

[25] *Architectural Forum*, 50–53 (May, 1968); *Off-Campus Record*, November, 1964, Summer, 1965, Spring (quotation), Winter, 1967; Soukup memo. In 1966 a $190,000 sewage disposal plant was built.

[26] *Bulletin*, 10 (1965), 124 (1966); *Off-Campus Record*, Spring, 1966; *Architectural Forum*, 55–57 (May, 1968); Soukup memo. In 1964 St. Francis House, the former home of the Franciscan sisters who had conducted the food service until 1958, was remodeled and opened as a residence for 55 men, but this action was only a stopgap.

[27] Barry, *Worship and Work*, 332; *Off-Campus Record*, July, 1962, Summer, 1965, Winter, 1967; *Saint John's* (Summer, 1969); *Christians in Conversation* (Westminster, Md., 1962). Pope Pius XII had called upon the Benedictines to initiate ecumenical work with the Eastern Orthodox Church, but the ecumenical movement did not begin to involve the whole Catholic church until the pontificate of John XXIII (1958–63).

[28] *Minneapolis Star*, May 27, 1968; *Bulletin*, 138 (1969–70); *Off-Campus Record*, July, 1962, Winter, 1967; *Saint John's* (Summer, 1968, Summer, Fall, 1969); *Record*, November 25, 1969; *Minneapolis Tribune*, May 11, 1968. The Ecumenical Institute has its own national board of directors and is administered independently of the monastery and the university. In 1969 the A. G. Bush Foundation gave the institute $75,000 to strengthen library holdings in relevant Protestant and Orthodox works.

[29] *A Message from Abbot Baldwin Dworschak to Alumni and Friends of Saint John's University*, 10 (quotation) (October, 1968); *The Monastic Manuscript Microfilm Library: Its Purpose and Progress*, a booklet issued by St. John's in 1970, copy in Minnesota Historical Society library; *Off-Campus Record*, November, 1964, Winter, 1967; *Saint John's* (Fall, Winter, 1968, Fall, 1969); *Minneapolis Tribune*, January 11, 1969; *Record*, November 12, 1964, May 26, 1967, February 21, 1969.

The library also houses the Kritzeck collection of holograph manuscripts.

[30] "Report and Recommendations of the Joint Summer Study Curriculum Committee, 1965," 2–12, 31; "Co-Institutional Study Report: College of Saint Benedict, Saint John's University, July, 1968," — both in college files. See also Chapter 38, note 20, below; *Off-Campus Record*, April, 1961, Winter, 1967; *Record*, February 8, 1957, October 26, 1962, October 30, 1967, March 28, 1968, September 26, 1969. Sylvester P. Theisen, a sociology professor at St. John's, was appointed co-ordinator in 1969.

[31] "Institutional Profile," 1, 3, 10, 13 (September 1, 1968), in college files; *Off-Campus Record*, Spring, Winter, 1967; *Saint John's* (Fall, 1968); *Bulletin*, 8 (1967–69). St. John's offerings were broadened in 1966–67 by the establishment of a department of psychology. Enrollment in the subject mounted from 135 in the fall of 1966 to 710 in the spring of 1968. Eight part-time people from the St. Cloud Veterans Hospital assisted the full-time staff.

[32] "Institutional Profile," 11 (1968); *Saint John's* (Summer, Fall, 1969); *Record*, March 28, 1968. By the spring of 1969 about 900 students were enrolled in courses on both campuses.

[33] *Record*, August 30, 1957, July 25, 1958; *Off-Campus Record*, Fall, 1966; *Saint John's* (Spring, Fall, 1969); *Minneapolis Tribune*, December 17, 1967; "Institutional Profile," 2 (1968); *Ford Foundation Letter*, 1 (September 1, 1970). In 1967 St. John's received a grant of $182,000 from the Ford Foundation for a microcity study. Directed by Dr. Henry, the study dealt with problems and conditions in 12 Minnesota communities with populations between 10,000 and 50,000. In 1970 the Ford Foundation made a supplementary grant of $118,000 for the project.

[34] *The Central States College Association: What It Is and Does*, a brochure issued by the association; *Bulletin*, 12, 19 (1969–70); "Institutional Profile," 2 (1968); *Off-Campus Record*, Fall, 1966, Spring, 1967; *Saint John's* (Summer, 1968, Fall, 1969). In late 1966 St. John's received federal authorization to construct radio station KSJR-FM, the strongest FM station in Minnesota. In the spring of 1967 KSJN-FM began beaming programs to the Twin Cities. Two years later Minnesota Educational Radio, Inc., a body independent of the abbey and the university, was formed to finance and operate KSJR-KSJN-FM.

[35] *A Report to Investors, 1970*, 15, 17, 51, 54, a six-year report on St. John's issued by the university; *Catalogue*, 30–33 (1969–70); *Record*, September 13, 1967; interview with Father Florian Muggli and James J. Trobec, St. John's business officers, January 5, 1971. St. John's indebtedness in June, 1970, totaled about $4,500,000.

[36] *Saint John's* (Fall, 1968, Summer, Fall, 1969, Winter, 1969–70); *Record*, October 10, 1969, February 13, 1970.

[37] *Off-Campus Record*, Winter, 1967; *Saint John's* (Fall, Winter, 1968, Spring, 1969); *Record*, September 26, November 7, 1969, April 15, May 15, 1970; *Minneapolis Tribune*, November 17, 18, 19, 21, 1970; "Institutional Profile," 42 (1968). Traditional student activities still remained strong. The men's chorus in 1968–69, for example, performed in Europe, as it had in 1960, 1962, and 1965.

[38] *Saint John's* (Spring, 1969); *Report to Investors*, 62. Father Colman resigned as president in August, 1971. His successor was the Reverend Michael P. Blecker, whose special field is medieval history. Father Blecker received his B.A. from Harvard and his Ph.D. from the University of Wisconsin. *Minneapolis Tribune*, July 16, 1971.

[39] *Report to Investors*, 38–45; *Saint John's* (Summer, Fall, 1969, Winter, 1969–70); *Record*, October 10, 1969; *Minneapolis Tribune*, September 27, May 4, 1970; *Minneapolis Star*, September 26, 1970; St. John's, "News Release," November 25, 1969 (quotations), in college files. In September, 1970, St. John's received a grant of $104,000 from the Minnesota State Crime Commission for the establishment of a Criminal Justice Resource Center to engage in research projects aimed at crime prevention and the rehabilitation of offenders.

[40] Greeley, *From Backwater to Mainstream*, 2, 24, 52, 134, 162; Wakin, *Catholic Campus*, 113–132. Edward Wakin and Father Joseph F. Scheuer, in the *De-Romanization of the American Catholic Church*, 255–257 (New York, 1966), refer to Father Greeley as "the Catholic Church's company sociologist. He is also a senior project director at the National Opinion Research Center at the University of Chicago, where he might likewise be designated the company priest." On May 6, 1968, 255 seniors received baccalaureate degrees; 41 per cent of these graduates planned to go on to school. Occupations involving social, civic, and religious service continue to attract many St. John's alumni. *St. John's University Banner* (Summer, 1968), a quarterly newsletter published by the university.

29. GUSTAVUS ADOLPHUS COLLEGE, PART III
Pages 169 to 176

[1] Lund, *Gustavus Adolphus College*, 161–165; Augustana Synod, Lutheran Minnesota Conference, *Minutes of the Annual Convention, April 19–23, 1944*, 69, 72–75, 77–82. "The war crisis was a catalyst that broke the school out of its shell," declared Lunden to Gustavus historian Doniver A. Lund, 163.

[2] Lund, *Gustavus Adolphus College*, 60, 146, 160, 165–172; Augustana Minnesota Conference, *Minutes, 1944*, 76, 93; *Greater Gustavus Quarterly* (October 31, 1944), an alumni association publication, hereafter cited as *Quarterly*.

[3] Augustana Minnesota Conference, *Minutes, 1944*, 77, *1945*, 82–84, *1946*, 81; *Catalogue*, 101 (1943–44); taped interview of the author, June 18, 1968, with Dr. Edgar Carlson, in the collections of the Minnesota Historical Society; *Quarterly* (January, 1945). In May, 1943, 82 students graduated. Dr. Carlson was inaugurated on December 6, 1944.

[4] Augustana Minnesota Conference, *Minutes, 1944*, 85, *1945*, 80, 89, 91, *1946*, 78. The conference gave Gustavus $27,900 for 1943–44 operations; total income was $494,400, of which the V-12 unit provided $274,600.

[5] Augustana Minnesota Conference, *Minutes, 1946*, 77, 79, 81; *Quarterly* (October 31, 1944, June, October, 1945, March, 1946, June, 1957, July, 1968). Some 2,000 former students saw military service in World War II. By mid-1945, 19 of them, including a woman in the Women's Air Force Service Pilots (WASPs), had lost their lives. The commander of the V-12 unit, C. P. McCurdy, Jr., returned to the college to give the commencement address on May 26, 1968.

[6] Augustana Minnesota Conference, *Minutes, 1946*, 79, 84; *Quarterly* (March, June, 1946, December, 1947, March, 1955). The college buildings early in 1946 were valued at $847,000. A librarian was secured immediately after the war.

[7] Augustana Minnesota Conference, *Minutes, 1944*, 84, *1945*, 79, 85, 103, 106, *1946*, 77, 79; *Quarterly* (June, 1946, June, 1947).

[8] Augustana Minnesota Conference, *Minutes, 1946*, 78, *1947*, 73; *Quarterly* (March, June, October, 1946, June, December, 1947); *Gustavian* (yearbook), 85–92 (1948). The value of plant and equipment given Gustavus by the federal government after World War II amounted to at least $200,000.

[9] Augustana Minnesota Conference, *Minutes, 1947*, 77, 80, *1948*, 78, 81; *Quarterly* (October, 1946, March, June, December, 1947). Fall enrollment in 1947 was 1,258, up 30 per cent from the previous year. Veterans numbered 510. The freshman class of 569 was exceeded in size only by that of St. Thomas among the state's private colleges.

¹⁰ Augustana Minnesota Conference, *Minutes, 1945*, 106, *1946*, 88, *1947*, 73, *1948*, 82, *1949*, 77–79; *Catalogue*, 17–23 (March, 1949); *Quarterly* (March (quotation), June, December, 1947, June, October, 1948, March, 1949, October, 1965). In its Pioneer Room the library housed the Almen-Vickner collection of over 4,000 volumes, the gifts of Dr. and Mrs. Edwin J. Vickner, whose generosity to Gustavus provides one of the most inspiring chapters in the college's history. See *The Vickner Story*, published by the Deferred Giving Committee of Gustavus in 1965.

¹¹ Augustana Minnesota Conference, *Minutes, 1946*, 79, 88, *1947*, 81, 83, 89, 92, *1948*, 74, 83, *1949*, 72, 79, *1952*, 82; Lutheran Church in America (LCA), Minnesota Synod, *Convention Minutes, 1965*, 265; Lund, *Gustavus Adolphus College* 175; *Quarterly* (March, June, October, 1946, March, December, 1947, March, 1949). In 1947 Gustavus realized $61,600 from the sale of the last of the C. A. Smith timberlands in Oregon given to the college in 1914. Gustavus' share in the proceeds from the sale of the Minnesota College property in Minneapolis in 1947 was $75,000, which was placed in the library fund.

¹² Augustana Minnesota Conference, *Minutes, 1946*, 90, *1948*, 76, 78, *1949*, 71, 79, *1950*, 70. In 1947–48 the college after three years of annual operating deficits showed a surplus of $36,700. Total capital investment in mid-1949 was $2,840,000.

¹³ *Quarterly* (June, December, 1947); Augustana Minnesota Conference, *Minutes, 1944*, 83, 86, *1949*, 76. Several long-time faculty members such as Ernest C. Carlton and Conrad Peterson reached retirement shortly after World War II. Of the 71 people on the teaching staff in 1949, 45 had been hired in the preceding three years.

¹⁴ Augustana Minnesota Conference, *Minutes, 1944*, 75, 81, *1945*, 87, *1946*, 86, *1947*, 80, *1948*, 80; "Studies in Liberal Arts Education, 1947–1953," in college files; *Quarterly* (October, 1945, March, 1946, June, December, 1947). The department of Christianity with three full-time and four part-time teachers was one of the strongest at the time.

¹⁵ Augustana Minnesota Conference, *Minutes, 1949*, 74, 78, *1951*, 80, 84, 88, 90, 92, *1952*, 79, 82, 85, 93, *1953*, 97–99, 101, 114, *1954*, 78, 81–84, 90, 107, *1955*, 89, *1957*, 93; *Quarterly* (June, 1951, March, September, 1954). The total college debt in May, 1952, was $662,200. The conference's annual gift in 1952–53 represented 13 per cent of Gustavus' cost of operation that year.

¹⁶ Augustana Minnesota Conference, *Minutes, 1951*, 48 (quotation), 76, 84, *1956*, 110, *1959*, 107; *Quarterly* (June, September, 1950, June, 1951, March, December, 1952, March, 1954, 6 (quotation), May, 1957, July, 1960). In the mid-1950s the foundation purchased as income-producing investments the Oakridge Cemetery and Mausoleum Corporations in Chicago.

¹⁷ Augustana Minnesota Conference, *Minutes, 1950*, 76, *1951*, 80, *1952*, 84, *1953*, 104, 107, *1954*, 85–87; *Catalogue*, 62 (February, 1951); *Quarterly* (March, 1951, June, 1952, June, 1953, December, 1954). Library science was dropped in 1951. In 1953–54 Gustavus began offering extension courses in St. Paul and Montevideo. Summer sessions were also held; that of 1952 enrolled 107 students.

¹⁸ Augustana Minnesota Conference, *Minutes, 1951*, 84, 91, *1953*, 96, 102, *1954*, 78, 87, 98–106, *1955*, 107; *Quarterly* (June, 1951, March, September, 1952, May, December, 1954, June, 1956). The conference commission learned that pastors, laity, and alumni regarded a church college as essential; one-third of the alumni said that Gustavus' social life was too conservative. See *Quarterly* (May, 1954).

¹⁹ Augustana Minnesota Conference, *Minutes, 1955*, 91, 98, *1956*, 84, *1962*, 122; *Quarterly* (September, 1955). Of Min-

nesota's high school graduates in 1953, St. Thomas enrolled 318, Gustavus 301, St. Olaf 247, Macalester 227, St. Catherine 225, Hamline 212, St. John's 185, Concordia 178, Augsburg 114, and Carleton 89. See *Quarterly* (March, 1954).

²⁰ Augustana Minnesota Conference, *Minutes, 1950*, 86, *1954*, 79, 89, 109, *1955*, 96, *1956*, 87, *1961*, 106, 119; *Catalogue*, 25 (February, 1956); *Quarterly* (May, September, December, 1954, March, September, 1955, December, 1956, March, 1957, July, 1960). Dr. and Mrs. Edwin J. Vickner built a $25,000 guest house for use of the college and gave it to the Almen-Vickner Foundation in 1956.

²¹ Augustana Minnesota Conference, *Minutes, 1956*, 88, *1957*, 99; *Catalogue*, 131 (1943–44), 27 (March, 1960); *Quarterly* (March, 1949, June, December, 1955, March, 1956, December–March, 1956–57 (quotation), July–November, 1957). The first big event in the union was a banquet on March 22, 1956, at which President Carlson was knighted in Sweden's Royal Order of the North Star.

²² Lund, *Gustavus Adolphus College*, 176; *Catalogue*, 27 (March, 1962); Augustana Minnesota Conference, *Minutes, 1952*, 80, 86, *1954*, 80, *1955*, 98, *1956*, 81, 100, *1957*, 95, 120, *1958*, 101, 110, *1959*, 108, 134, *1960*, 98, *1961*, 120, *1962*, 115, 121, 125; *Quarterly* (March, 1955, May, July–November, 1957, May, December, 1958, June, 1959, February, 1961, March, 1962). By early 1962 the college had received gifts of $143,800 for the chapel; the conference drive raised about $504,000.

²³ Augustana Minnesota Conference, *Minutes, 1958*, 101, *1959*, 108, *1960*, 97, *1961*, 109; *Quarterly* (December, 1958, July, 1960).

²⁴ Augustana Minnesota Conference, *Minutes, 1946*, 77, *1957*, 95, *1958*, 102, 109, *1959*, 109, 115, *1960*, 99; *Quarterly* (June, 1951, December, 1958, June, 1959, July, 1960, March, 1963 (quotation).

²⁵ *The Story of The American Memorial to Alfred Nobel* (quotation), the program of the first symposium in 1965; Lund, *Gustavus Adolphus College*, 176; Augustana Minnesota Conference, *Minutes, 1962*, 116, 121, *1963*, 117, 123, *1964*, 158; *Quarterly* (March, July, 1963, October, 1964, March, 1965).

²⁶ Augustana Minnesota Conference, *Minutes, 1960*, 109, 124, *1961*, 104, 109, *1962*, 115; *Quarterly* (July, 1960, February, July, 1961); Lund, *Gustavus Adolphus College*, 172–174. By early 1960 the gifts of the Vickners to Gustavus totaled over $250,000.

²⁷ Augustana Minnesota Conference, *Minutes, 1961*, 110, *1962*, 114, 116; LCA Minnesota Synod, *Convention Minutes 1963*, 122; *Catalogue*, 9–17 (February, 1964); *Quarterly* (May, 1957, July, 1960, July, 1963, December, 1965). Some of Gustavus' historic buildings — Commerce Hall, old South Hall, the president's home, the Ranch House, old North Hall — fell victim to wrecking crews between 1957 and 1963. The 1962 *Gustavian* includes an excellent report on the centennial.

²⁸ Lund, *Gustavus Adolphus College*, 178; *Catalogue*, 59 (February, 1954); Augustana Minnesota Conference, *Minutes, 1957*, 98, *1958*, 108, *1959*, 113, *1960*, 101, 106–108, 110, *1961*, 118; *Quarterly* (March, 1951, December, 1954, June, 1955, May, 1958, June, 1959, June, July, 1960, July, 1961); "Survey for the North Central Association," December, 1960, in college files. Advanced standing, independent study, and acceleration, especially in mathematics and chemistry, were gaining headway at the college in the late 1950s. A department of political science was established in 1960.

²⁹ Augustana Minnesota Conference, *Minutes, 1951*, 78–80, *1952*, 82, *1953*, 106, *1954*, 83, *1955*, 93, *1956*, 82, 89, *1958*, 103, *1959*, 104, *1960*, 106, *1961*, 119; *Quarterly* (September, 1954, September, December, 1955, March, July–November,

1956, June, November, 1959). Gustavus had a series of stimulating visiting professors between 1953 and 1959 under the five-college program supported by the Hill Family Foundation.

[30] Augustana Minnesota Conference, *Minutes, 1957*, 93, 100, *1958*, 99, 103, 105, 126, 134, *1959*, 105, 109, 114, 117–119 (quotation), 122, *1960*, 99–101, 104, 106, 108, 111, *1961*, 116, 118, 139, *1962*, 120; LCA Minnesota Synod, *Convention Minutes, 1963*, 119, 125, *1966*, 268, 274; *Catalogue*, 32 (March, 1949), 43 (March, 1960). Tuition and fees provided $1,061,000 of Gustavus' income of $1,650,000 in 1961–62; gifts brought in $443,800, and interest on endowment $40,800.

[31] Augustana Minnesota Conference, *Minutes, 1959*, 105, 109, 142, *1960*, 95–97, 110, *1961*, 104, *1962*, 117; LCA Minnesota Synod, *Convention Minutes, 1963*, 116, 145; *Quarterly* (December, 1958); Lund, *Gustavus Adolphus College*, 178.

[32] LCA Minnesota Synod, *Convention Minutes, 1964*, 152, 157, *1965*, 176, *1967*, 215, *1968*, 231, *1969*, 225; *Quarterly* (October, 1963, June, 1964, December, 1965, October, 1967, October, December, 1968, May, 1969); Lund, *Gustavus Adolphus College*, 178; *Catalogue*, 40–44 (February, 1964), 40–44 (June, 1968). A growing number of students since 1963 have studied in various parts of the world during the winter term. A summer study program in Japan and Taiwan had its inception in 1967.

[33] After the formation of the Lutheran Church in America (LCA) in 1962, Gustavus' board was increased to 23 members; in 1966 the number went to 27, four of whom were to come from the Red River Valley Synod, including its president. Augustana Minnesota Conference, *Minutes, 1962*, 127; LCA Minnesota Synod, *Convention Minutes, 1963*, 121, *1964*, 159, *1965*, 175, *1966*, 269, 272, 274, 276, *1967*, 213, *1968*, 230, *1969*, 224; *Quarterly* (October, 1964, October, 1967, October, 1968); "Report of the President of Gustavus Adolphus College," March 1, 1970, in college files. The average request for student aid in 1969–70 was $1,780.

[34] LCA Minnesota Synod, *Convention Minutes, 1964*, 153, *1965*, 170, 177, *1966*, 278, *1967*, 211, *1968*, 227; *Quarterly* (May, December, 1965, October, 1966, October, 1968).

[35] LCA Minnesota Synod, *Convention Minutes, 1965*, 169, *1966*, 265, 278, *1969*, 221, 227; *Quarterly* (June, 1964, March, 1965, October, 1966, July, 1969); "Report of the Chairman of the Board of Trustees," March 1, 1970, in college files. The Liaison Committee on Higher Education was created by the 1959 Minnesota legislature to provide for educational planning and co-ordination of private and publicly supported higher education in the state. See *Report of Liaison Committee on Higher Education in Minnesota, 1959–60*, 1 [St. Paul, 1960].

[36] LCA Minnesota Synod, *Convention Minutes, 1969*, 227; *Quarterly* (March, 1966, December, 1968, March, 1970, October, 1972).

[37] LCA Minnesota Synod, *Convention Minutes, 1965*, 170, 180, *1966*, 266–269, 274, *1968*, 229, *1969*, 221–223, 226; *Quarterly* (December, 1969). In 1950 gifts going into the current budget, other than those of the church, had been $6,400; in 1963–64 the amount was $193,500.

[38] LCA Minnesota Synod, *Convention Minutes, 1966*, 277, *1969*, 222; *Quarterly* (September, 1955, March, October, 1965, October, 1968); *Catalogue*, 10 (June, 1967); Gustavus, "News Release," March 29, 1968, in college files. Dr. Carlson and Sister Antonius Kennelly of St. Catherine's represented the private colleges on the 1947–49 Minnesota Commission on Higher Education and coauthored part of its report published the following year by the University of Minnesota Press under the title *Higher Education in Minnesota*. He also was one of the leaders in the formation of the Central States College Association in 1965.

[39] *The Inauguration of Frank R. Barth as Tenth President of Gustavus Adolphus College* (October 24, 1969); *Minneapolis Star*, June 24, 1969; *Minneapolis Tribune*, June 25, 1969.

[40] Interview with Reynold E. Anderson, vice president for public relations and development, January 25, 1971; *Quarterly* (July, 1970); *Spire* (July, 1970), a newsletter issued irregularly by the Gustavus alumni association; *Minneapolis Tribune*, July 14, 1970. The college was awarded $245,200 by the National Science Foundation in the summer of 1970 for a three-year improvement program involving ten departments to be continued thereafter by Gustavus alone.

[41] LCA Minnesota Synod, *Convention Minutes, 1970*, 261; *St. Paul Dispatch*, January 8, 1970; *Minneapolis Tribune*, January 9, 1970. Substitutes for the administrative offices destroyed in the fire were set up in the union and many of the lost records were reconstructed. Insurance of about $545,000 permitted erection of a new administration building, completed in 1972.

[42] LCA Minnesota Synod, *Convention Minutes, 1970*, 257, 261; *Quarterly* (July, 1970); registrar's records. For an interesting picture of freshman life at Gustavus, see the articles by George Grim in *Minneapolis Tribune*, September 11, 12, 13, 1968.

[43] LCA Minnesota Synod, *Convention Minutes, 1970*, 263 (quotation); *Quarterly* (July, 1970).

30. CARLETON COLLEGE, PART III
Pages 177 to 184

[1] Headley and Jarchow, *Carleton*, 347, 469.

[2] Headley and Jarchow, *Carleton*, 348–350. For the touching story of the parents of Frank M. Shigemura, a Carleton Nisei student who lost his life in World War II, see George Grim in *Minneapolis Tribune*, May 7, 1950.

[3] Headley and Jarchow, *Carleton*, 102–105. In January, 1959, it was announced that $250,000 had been raised toward the endowment of a "Donald J. Cowling Chair of Philosophy" — a fitting memorial for the man who had considered philosophy his lifelong interest.

[4] Headley and Jarchow, *Carleton*, 105, 109, 116–118, 122; Laurence M. Gould, *Cold: The Record of An Antarctic Sledge Journey* (New York, 1931). "Larry," as Dr. Gould was affectionately known, was famed for his collection of red neckties. Students inaugurated a "Red-tie Day" when he was elected president and observed the occasion annually thereafter.

[5] Headley and Jarchow, *Carleton*, 52, 332, 350–352. Freshman traditions were reinstated and a full menu of social activities was sponsored by the Student Social Co-operative. Student rent in Pine Hill Village in 1949 varied from $26.25 to $40.00 a month depending on the dweller's income.

[6] Headley and Jarchow, *Carleton*, 50, 325.

[7] Headley and Jarchow, *Carleton*, 51, 241, 393. In 1948 KARL, a low-power "carrier current" radio station, went on the air from a studio under Scoville Annex. In 1954 it moved to the third floor of remodeled Willis Hall. Scoville was remodeled into offices and classrooms in 1957.

[8] Headley and Jarchow, *Carleton*, 40, 52, 325. Total cost of Musser and Myers halls was $1,350,000. Mr. Musser was a trustee of the college, as were the husband and son of Mrs. Myers.

[9] Headley and Jarchow, *Carleton*, 42, 52–54. Williams Hall was razed in the fall of 1961.

[10] Headley and Jarchow, *Carleton*, 106, 122. In his ability to capture and hold the attention of an audience, President Gould had few peers. He averaged about one speech a week the year round.

[11] Headley and Jarchow, *Carleton*, 107, 146–158. In 1949 the college received two grants for research in the amount of $8,700; a decade later the total was $233,000, a large segment of it for a summer institute in mathematics and general science.

[12] Headley and Jarchow, *Carleton*, 212, 213. Bowles, in *Refounding of the College Board*, 23, notes the hostility to the board in the Midwest in the late 1940s. Much of this feeling disappeared when the National Merit and the General Motors scholarship programs made use of the board tests.

[13] Headley and Jarchow, *Carleton*, 133, 213, 469. Dr. Frank R. Kille, dean of the college from 1945 to 1958, played a major role in the adoption of the board examinations at Carleton. He was active also in the affairs of the board itself.

[14] Headley and Jarchow, *Carleton*, 330.

[15] Headley and Jarchow, *Carleton*, 218, 220.

[16] Headley and Jarchow, *Carleton*, 134, 220 (quotation), 232. During the mid-1950s, as a result of the relatively low interest in secondary schoolteaching exhibited by the college's students, Carleton conducted a study of teacher education. See Ralph S. Fjelstad, "The Carleton Faculty Study of Teacher Education," in *School and Society*, 84:19–22 (July 21, 1956).

[17] Headley and Jarchow, *Carleton*, 221, 223, 225. Some exceptions to the "normal" course of study had been made before 1958. In 1952 Carleton entered into a three-two engineering program with the Massachusetts Institute of Technology and with Columbia University. Four years later the college became a participant in the Washington Semester program at American University, Washington, D.C., and in 1957 curricular and extracurricular offerings in American studies were financed by the Fred C. Andersen Foundation of Bayport, Minnesota.

[18] Headley and Jarchow, *Carleton*, 221.

[19] Headley and Jarchow, *Carleton*, 222.

[20] Headley and Jarchow, *Carleton*, 147, 310.

[21] Headley and Jarchow, *Carleton*, 280, 285.

[22] Headley and Jarchow, *Carleton*, 281, 285; *Ford Foundation Grants in Minnesota* (September, 1963). St. Catherine, St. Thomas, and St. Olaf also received Ford grants in this period.

[23] Headley and Jarchow, *Carleton*, 106, 437. Carleton's record in winning Woodrow Wilson fellowships and Fulbright scholarships has been particularly impressive.

[24] Headley and Jarchow, *Carleton*, 106–109, 437; Robert H. Knapp and Joseph J. Greenbaum, *The Younger American Scholar*, tables 4, 5 (Chicago, 1953). In 1961 the Laurence McKinley Gould Science Fund was established at the college with an initial gift of $670,000, since augmented.

[25] Headley and Jarchow, *Carleton*, 106, 326. See the *Chicago Daily Tribune*, February 25, 1961, for a resumé of Carleton's strengths during the Gould administration.

[26] Headley and Jarchow, *Carleton*, 238, 353, 395–400; *Report of the President and Treasurer, 1963–64*, 5–7. The YMCA and the YWCA were very active for a decade after 1947, as were several denominational clubs and the Sunday Night Club, which met after vespers. From World War II until 1961 a secular college convocation was held on Friday mornings.

[27] Headley and Jarchow, *Carleton*, 109, 113, 118, 123, 157, 285, 380, 437; taped interview of the author, March 11, 1970, with Dr. John W. Nason, in the collections of the Minnesota Historical Society.

[28] Headley and Jarchow, *Carleton*, 110, 348; *Northfield News*, March 13, 1969; *Reports of the President and Treasurer, 1962–1963*, 18, *1963–1964*, 10, *1964–1965*, 14. Just before World War II tuition, board, room, and fees ran to about $875; the comprehensive fee for 1969–70 was $3,200, twice what it had been in 1957–58.

[29] Headley and Jarchow, *Carleton*, 53–55, 110; *Reports of the President and Treasurer, 1962–1963*, 6, *1963–1964*, 11, *1964–1965*, 10.

[30] *Reports of the President and Treasurer, 1964–1965*, 10, 14, *1966–1967*, 7, *1967–1968*, 11; *Northfield News*, February 26, April 17, 1969, April 30, 1970. The center is composed of two separate buildings — a concert hall and a theater — above ground, but it is connected into one large facility below ground. Also in 1970 Carleton was given the historic John C. Nutting residence as a home for its president.

[31] Headley and Jarchow, *Carleton*, 155; *Reports of the President and Treasurer, 1963–1964*, 4.

[32] Headley and Jarchow, *Carleton*, 226; *Reports of the President and Treasurer, 1963–1964*, 4, *1964–1965*, 5. Each year a sizable number of foreign students study on the Carleton campus; in 1968–69 there were 48 such students.

[33] *Reports of the President and Treasurer, 1964–1965*, 3, 9, *1967–1968*, 5.

[34] *Reports of the President and Treasurer, 1965–1966*, 5, *1966–1967*, 3, *1967–1968*, 4 (quotation). Over 25,000 people participated in the various centennial programs.

[35] *Reports of the President and Treasurer, 1966–1967*, 11, *1967–1968*, 4–7, *1968–1969*, 11.

[36] *Reports of the President and Treasurer, 1962–1963*, 14, *1965–1966*, 4, *1966–1967*, 4–6, *1967–1968*, 3. The inauguration of coed dormitory living on eight floors in six of the college's residence halls occurred on February 14, 1970. See *Carletonian*, February 19, April 16, 1970.

[37] Headley and Jarchow, *Carleton*, 256, 398; *Reports of the President and Treasurer, 1967–1968*, 7–10, *1968–1969*, 13; *Minneapolis Tribune*, November 17, 1968.

[38] *Reports of the President and Treasurer, 1966–1967*, 17–21, *1967–1968*, 10, 15, *1968–1969*, 14; *Northfield News*, April 25, 1968. Estimated cash needs of the college from 1968 to 1978 totaled $110,000,000. The Andrew W. Mellon Foundation early in 1970 gave Carleton $500,000 to create a chair in the humanities, the fifth endowed professorship set up since 1968. See *Second Century Report on Growth and Development* (April, 1970), issued by the college.

[39] Taped interview of the author, March 11, 1970, with Dr. John W. Nason (quotations), in the collections of the Minnesota Historical Society. The college's deficit for current operations in 1969–70 was $258,000; long-term indebtedness as of June, 1970, was $2,780,000. Interview with Vice President Frank I. Wright, January 19, 1971.

[40] Interview with Dr. Nason, March 11, 1970 (quotation); *Northfield News*, June 4, 1970. Dr. Nason gave the commencement address at St. Olaf in June, 1970, and was made an honorary alumnus.

[41] *Minneapolis Tribune*, April 26, 1970; *Minneapolis Star*, August 13, 1970; *Northfield News*, February 5, May 7, 1970; *Voice* (March, 1970); *Second Century Report* (February, 1970). In the fall of 1970 Carleton initiated a new method of government under which a council composed of trustees, faculty, students, administrators, and alumni would administer the college.

31. Augsburg College, Part III
Pages 185 to 192

[1] Chrislock, *Fjord to Freeway*, 190, 191 (quotations). In 1935 the Free Church had contributed 55 per cent of Augsburg's operating income; by the 1960s church gifts constituted less than 10 per cent of the college's total income.

[2] Chrislock, *Fjord to Freeway*, 191, 196, 197 (quotations), 232. On the 1920s, see p. 80, above.

[3] Chrislock, *Fjord to Freeway*, 194–196.

[4] Chrislock, *Fjord to Freeway*, 196. Attempts to raise money among Minneapolis business firms met with little success. According to Chrislock, 201, by 1949 only "two $5,000 gifts

and a number of lesser'' donations had come forth, causing Augsburg's board chairman to comment: "It will take time to integrate ourselves more effectively with the Minneapolis community."

[5] Chrislock, *Fjord to Freeway*, 193, 196–198.

[6] Chrislock, *Fjord to Freeway*, 198.

[7] Chrislock, *Fjord to Freeway*, 198–200.

[8] Chrislock, *Fjord to Freeway*, 192, 199. Drama was first offered as a course in 1940. A fourth division, religion and philosophy, was constituted in 1949.

[9] Chrislock, *Fjord to Freeway*, 202. A flurry of interest in the Augsburg Park project revived during the war years, but in July, 1946, the trustees voted unanimously in favor of expansion in the college's present vicinity. Three years later the park area was sold to the village of Richfield for $60,000. See Haynes, in *Minnesota History*, 40:382.

[10] Chrislock, *Fjord to Freeway*, 202.

[11] Chrislock, *Fjord to Freeway*, 203.

[12] Chrislock, *Fjord to Freeway*, 203–205.

[13] Chrislock, *Fjord to Freeway*, 206, 223, 228; *Ford Foundation Grants in Minnesota* (September, 1963).

[14] Chrislock, *Fjord to Freeway*, 206, 208, 218, 224 (quotation), 228. Augsburg won the MIAC championship in basketball in 1963, 1964, and 1965.

[15] Chrislock, *Fjord to Freeway*, 209; *Augsburg College Contact*, Catalog Issue (1964–65), 2 (quotation) (1965–66), 92 (March 1964). After it was decided to keep the college in its urban location, Dr. Christensen declared that "it is among . . . the confining walls and the unprepossessing environment of the cities that human life is largely lived. Here, then, we too are to live and grow and serve Christ." Haynes, in *Minnesota History*, 40:383.

[16] Chrislock, *Fjord to Freeway*, 206–208, 213–215.

[17] Chrislock, *Fjord to Freeway*, 211–213.

[18] Chrislock, *Fjord to Freeway*, 215–221. A Spanish conversation course offered over KTCA-TV by an Augsburg faculty member in 1958–59 attracted favorable comment.

[19] Chrislock, *Fjord to Freeway*, 223–227. In 1953, 35 per cent of the student body came from the Twin Cities; by the early 1960s this proportion had risen to 50 per cent.

[20] Chrislock, *Fjord to Freeway*, 221–223, 229 (quotation). For various reasons, mainly the existence of large measures of academic freedom, a chapter of the AAUP was not organized at the college until 1966.

[21] Chrislock, *Fjord to Freeway*, 227 (quotation), 228; American Lutheran Church (ALC), *Reports and Actions of the Second General Convention*, October 21–27, 1964, p. 78, 286 (Minneapolis, 1964). In 1961 the Free Church contributed $136,200 to Augsburg; in 1963 the ALC allocated $126,750 for current operations and $13,250 for capital funds.

[22] *President's Annual Report, 1963–64*, 3. The board of trustees of the ALC extended a $150,000 line of credit to Augsburg to enable it to buy properties in the campus neighborhood.

[23] Taped interview of the author, July 1, 1969, with President Oscar A. Anderson, in the collections of the Minnesota Historical Society; Chrislock, *Fjord to Freeway*, 228; *Augsburg College Now: Annual Report* (1967–68), (1968–69). By 1969 the support of the ALC for operations was down to $148,320. The quotation is from the periodical *Augsburg College Now* (January, 1970). Titles of Augsburg publications are somewhat confusing. Some designated *Augsburg College Contact* are subtitled *President's Report*. The *Augsburg College Contact* is also a title used for catalogs. Since 1966 the annual reports have carried the title *Augsburg College Now*, a name which also doubles for a publication issued semimonthly in some months and monthly in others. An attempt has been made to differentiate these sources clearly by using subtitles here and below.

[24] Chrislock, *Fjord to Freeway*, 229, 230 (quotation).

[25] Chrislock, *Fjord to Freeway*, 230, 231. Terms of presidents of ALC colleges are six years.

[26] *President's Report, 1963–64*, Foreword, 7, 8 (quotation).

[27] *President's Report, 1963–64*, 3–7 (quotations); "Augsburg College: Basic Institutional Data," March, 1967, in president's files. Notes, mortgages, and bonds payable by June 30, 1964, totaled $2,345,000.

[28] "Academic Blueprint for Augsburg College," February 5, 1970, in president's files; interview with President Anderson, October 15, 1970; *Augsburg College Now: Annual Report* (1968–69).

[29] "Academic Blueprint," 1970; *Augsburg College Now: Annual Report* (1968–69).

[30] *Contact: Annual Report*, 3 (1964–65), 5 (1965–66), 5 (1966–67); "Basic Institutional Data" (1967); Fred Johnson, in *Minneapolis Tribune*, November 8, 1966. When Augsburg's land purchases under these plans are completed, the campus will contain 27.5 acres. In the mid-1950s it owned 8.5 acres; in 1966 the total was 20.5 acres.

[31] *Contact: Annual Report*, 4 (1964–65), 3 (1965–66); *Augsburg College Now: Annual Report* (1966–67); *Augsburg College Now* (January, 1968); interviews with President Anderson, July 1, 1969, October 15, 1970.

[32] *President's Report, 1964–65*, 8, *1965–66*, 4; *Augsburg College Now* (January, 1968).

[33] "Basic Institutional Data" (1967).

[34] *President's Report, 1965–66*, 5; *Augsburg College Now: Annual Report* (1967–68), (1968–69); "Basic Institutional Data" (1967).

[35] *President's Report, 1963–64*, 3, 9, *1964–65*, 3; "Augsburg College Profile," 38–85 (March, 1967), in president's files. The chemistry department conducted five National Science Foundation summer institutes for high school students, but in the late 1960s the department turned from this type of activity to that concerned with student and faculty research.

[36] "Basic Institutional Data" (1967); "Augsburg College Profile," 46 (1967).

[37] *President's Report, 1963–64*, 4, *1964–65*, 3, *1965–66*, 2; *Augsburg College Now: Annual Report* (1966–67), (1968–69) (quotation); *Catalog*, 4, 41–43 (April, 1966).

[38] Chrislock, *Fjord to Freeway*, 234–236 (quotation); *President's Report, 1965–66*, 2; *Augsburg College Now: Annual Report* (1968–69); *Bond*, 4 (June, 1969), a publication of the Lutheran Brotherhood Insurance Company, Minneapolis; *Minneapolis Tribune*, March 27, May 25, July 8, October 12, 1969, September 19, 1970. The college added a summer session in 1968.

[39] *President's Report, 1963–64*, 10, 12, 17–20, *1965–66*, 6, 8–10; *Augsburg College Now: Annual Report* (1966–67), (1968–69); "Basic Institutional Data" (1967); "President's Report to the Regents," October 16, 1969, in president's files; *Catalog*, 12–13 (April, 1966). Annual tuition in 1966 was $1,250, room and board for women at least $511, for men $606.

[40] *President's Report, 1963–64*, 7, 10, *1964–65*, 6; *Augsburg College Now: Annual Report* (1966–67), (1968–69); "Basic Institutional Data" (1967). On June 30, 1964, Augsburg's liabilities included $933,700 in notes and mortgages and $954,000 in dormitory and Si Melby Hall bonds.

[41] *President's Report, 1964–65*, 4, *1965–66*, 5; *Augsburg College Now: Annual Report* (1966–67), (1967–68), (1968–70); "President's Report to the Regents," February 16–17, 1970, June 30, 1970. The ALC's gifts of $152,000 in 1968–69 for current operations, $21,100 for the building fund, and $174,200 from LIFE, while significant, were small in comparison to Augsburg's needs and total budget.

[42] "Academic Blueprint," 1970; "President's Report to the

Regents,'' June 30, 1970; *President's Report, 1966–67*. The college was favorably reviewed by the North Central Association in 1967.

[43] *President's Report, 1964–65*, 2; *Augsburg College Now: Annual Report* (1968–69); *Minneapolis Star*, August 28, October 31, 1970; "Academic Blueprint," 1970; "President's Report to the Regents," May 19, 1969, February 16–17, 1970, June 30, 1970. Four non-Lutherans, all residents of Twin Cities' suburbs, were elected to Augsburg's 23-member board of regents in October, 1970.

32. ST. OLAF COLLEGE, PART III
Pages 193 to 199

[1] Benson, *High on Manitou*, 290–293, 305–314, 317; *Manitou Messenger*, November 4, 1949; Hilleboe, *Manitou Analecta*, 73–86. Government subsidized courses in physics, chemistry, biology, and commercial subjects to train people for war work were conducted in the summer of 1942. Nurses in training in Rochester and Minneapolis took some of their science work at St. Olaf. The first regular summer session was held in 1943.

[2] Benson, *High on Manitou*, 310, 314–317; *President's Annual Report, 1962–1963; The Inauguration of President Granskou*, 15 (quotation), a pamphlet published in 1944; Wilfred Bockelman, "40 Years an Educator," in American Lutheran Church, *Lutheran Standard*, 16 (September 24, 1963). The college records indicate that over 1,500 alumni and students were in military service in World War II and that at least 56 of them gave their lives.

[3] Benson, *High on Manitou*, 326–328; C. M. Granskou, "St. Olaf College," in *American-Scandinavian Review*, 23:205–215 (September, 1944); taped interview of the author, April 5, 1968, with Dr. Granskou, in the collections of the Minnesota Historical Society.

[4] Benson, *High on Manitou*, 318, 322–325; Hilleboe, *Manitou Analecta*, 71, 91–93; *Bulletin*, 10 (August, 1948), 7 (quotation) (July, 1949).

[5] *Bulletin*, 11 (August, 1948), 8 (July, 1949), 6 (August, 1950), 7 (August, 1951); Hilleboe, *Manitou Analecta*, 107–109; "President's Report to the Trustees," November 28, 1960, in college files, where all similar reports cited below may also be found.

[6] Benson, *High on Manitou*, 320; Granskou interview, April 5, 1968; *Bulletin*, 8, 9 (July, 1949); Bockelman, in *Lutheran Standard*, 17 (September 24, 1963). Some of these retiring professors had taught Dr. Granskou in his student days at St. Olaf. By 1950 retiring faculty were allowed to qualify for social security through part-time assignments.

[7] Granskou interview, April 5, 1968 (quotation); *Bulletin*, 8 (August, 1948); President's Scientific Research Board, *Science and Public Policy: Manpower for Research*, 4:20 (Washington, D.C., 1947). The board was chaired by John R. Steelman and the report is often referred to as the Steelman Report.

[8] Carl Billman to Norman Nordstrand, New York, December 30, 1948, September 8, 1949, (quotation), in college files; *Bulletin*, 8 (August, 1949), 4 (August, 1950), 66 (April, 1951); Hilleboe, *Manitou Analecta*, 110. The college also received a chapter of Pi Gamma Mu honorary social science fraternity in May, 1949.

[9] *Bulletin*, 73 (April, 1948), 4–6, 11 (July, 1949), 4 (quotations), 6 (August, 1951), 41, 101–107 (April, 1955); interview with Dean Howard C. Rose, February 12, 1970. The nursing program was fully accredited nationally in 1962; two years later public health courses were added to its curriculum.

[10] *President's Annual Report, 1961–1962*; *Bulletin*, 6 (August, 1951). ROTC was required of freshmen and sophomore men until 1961, when it became voluntary. Including 1970, 296 commissions as second lieutenants in the air force were earned upon completion of the advanced ROTC course, according to information furnished by the St. Olaf registrar's office.

[11] "President's Report to the Trustees," March 31, 1958; *Bulletin*, 3, 7, 10 (August, 1951), 26 (April, 1955); *President's Report, 1961–1962*. First pastor of the student congregation was the Reverend H. B. Hanson, a graduate of the class of 1927 who had taught religion at St. Olaf since 1937.

[12] Granskou interview, April 5, 1968; "Report of Linton, Maupin, Linton, Inc.," 73 typed pages, appendix, charts (March 26, 1951).

[13] "Linton Report," 8; Granskou interview, April 5, 1968 (quotation); *Bulletin*, 6 (August, 1948), 4 (August, 1950); "President's Report to the Trustees," December 7, 1962. Self-studies were being supported in 1953–54 in 21 colleges and universities by the Ford Foundation for the Advancement of Education. Each reflected a concern for better integration in higher education.

[14] "President's Report to the Trustees," August 26, 1957, March 31, November 24, 1958, August 31, 1959, November 28, 1960; *President's Annual Report, 1962–1963*.

[15] "President's Report to the Trustees," November, 1955, November, 1956, March 31, 1958.

[16] "President's Report to the Trustees," November 24, 1958, August 31, 1959, August 29 (quotation), November 28, 1960; *President's Annual Report, 1961–1962*.

[17] *President's Annual Report, 1962–1963*.

[18] Granskou interview, February 19, 1968; "President's Report to the Trustees," November 26, 1956 (quotation), August 31, 1959, November 28, 1960, December 7, 1962; *Manitou Messenger*, May 11, 1956. At the time of his death in December, 1958, Tillman M. Sogge of the St. Olaf faculty was in his third term as chairman of the Joint Union Committee.

[19] "President's Report to the Trustees," November 24, 1958, August 31, 1959. Dr. Granskou's reports to the trustees include clear summaries of current developments in education, as well as cogently reasoned commentaries on Christian higher education in this period. In 1961–62 he served as president of the National Council of Protestant Colleges and Universities.

[20] "President's Report to the Trustees," December 7, 1962; *President's Annual Report, 1962–1963*; interviews with various St. Olaf faculty members. St. Olaf was the sixth college in the nation to adopt four-one-four.

[21] *St. Olaf Alumnus*, 4–17 (quotations) (June, 1963); *A Tribute to President and Mrs. Clemens M. Granskou on Dr. Granskou's Retirement as President of St. Olaf College*, a pamphlet published in 1963; *President's Annual Report, 1962–1963*. Of the roughly 350 graduates in the class of 1963, 114 went into teaching and 105 went on to graduate, professional, or foreign study.

[22] Taped interview of the author, September 10, 1968, with Dr. Sidney A. Rand, in the collections of the Minnesota Historical Society.

[23] *President's Annual Report, 1964–1965, 1965–1966*; *Fram! Fram! the Forward Fund Report* (1967).

[24] *President's Annual Report, 1965–1966*; *Fram! Fram!*; *Northfield News*, January 9, 1969. According to the *Northfield News*, October 10, 1968, more than 1,800 students were enrolled in courses in the natural sciences and about 800 in mathematics in the fall of 1968.

[25] Interviews with Stanley L. Ness, vice president and treasurer, February 24, 1969, January 12, 1971; *President's Annual Report, 1967–1968*; *Saint Olaf*, the successor to the *Alumnus*, 9–11 (Fall, 1970). The college's main long-term indebtedness of $5,570,000 in mid-1970 resulted largely from federal loans on six dormitories and a smaller loan on the athletic

center. Under the Academic Facilities Act of 1963, St. Olaf received government grants of $250,000 and $1,000,000 to help finance the Felland library wing and the Science Center, respectively.

[26] Ness interviews; *President's Annual Report, 1967–1968*; *Saint Olaf*, 9 (Fall, 1970). Alumni gave St. Olaf $274,800 in 1969–70.

[27] *Bulletin*, 76–81 (April, 1967); *President's Annual Report, 1961–1962, 1964–1965*; interviews with Dean Rose, February 26, 1969, February 12, 1970; *Saint Olaf*, 5 (quotation) (Fall, 1970). In 1970 a semester program in minority studies was established, with support from the National Endowment for the Humanities. Dealing with the culture of Blacks, Indians, and Mexican-Americans, the course was interdisciplinary.

[28] Carleton College Curriculum Committee, "Minutes," February 7, 1968, in Carleton files; *Northfield News*, October 10, 1968; *President's Annual Report, 1967–1968*; *Saint Olaf*, 5 (Fall, 1970). Another example of intercollege co-operation was the joint purchase by Carleton and St. Olaf of a $35,000 spectrometer in the fall of 1968. Housed in the St. Olaf Science Center, it is used by the chemistry staffs of both institutions.

[29] *Minneapolis Star*, February 17, 1969; *Minneapolis Tribune*, June 12, 1969, February 24, 1970; *Carletonian*, April 25, 1968; Mellby, *St. Olaf College*, 10; Dean Rose interview, February 12, 1970; *Saint Olaf*, 5, 10 (quotations) (Fall, 1970). In the fall of 1970 there were 130 students and 8 faculty fellows in the paracollege. The Hill Foundation gave an initial two-year grant of $88,500 to help St. Olaf with this experiment. See the foundation's *Report, 1970*, 46.

[30] Fred Johnson, in *Minneapolis Tribune*, November 7, 1966; *Northfield News*, May 2, 1968; Hilleboe, *Manitou Analecta*, 97–100.

[31] *Fram! Fram!*; *President's Annual Report, 1967–1968*; *Saint Olaf*, 6 (Fall, 1970); *Northfield News*, April 25, June 6, 13, 1968, July 10, 1969; *Minneapolis Tribune*, December 30, 1967, July 11, 1969. The retirement of Olaf C. Christiansen in 1968 received wide attention. In the 65 years since his father, F. Melius, had founded the St. Olaf Choir which Olaf directed for 27 years, approximately 1,500 people had sung in the famous organization. See articles by Willmar Thorkelson in the *Minneapolis Star*, April 2, 3, 4, 5, 1968.

[32] *Saint Olaf*, 1–3 (Fall, 1970); Rand interview, September 10, 1968.

[33] *President's Annual Report, 1967–1968* (quotation); *Minneapolis Tribune*, December 4, 7, 1968, April 18, May 2, 6, 1970; *Northfield News*, May 7, 1970; interview with Robert B. Meslow, assistant dean of men, January 13, 1971. In late 1968 about 1,700 St. Olaf students signed a petition asking fewer restrictions on dormitory visits by both men and women. The request was approved by the faculty, and with added stipulations by the regents in March, 1969. The new regulations effective in September, 1969, were liberalized so that open houses in 1970 extended 12 hours a day, seven days a week.

[34] *President's Annual Report, 1967–1968*; *Saint Olaf*, 5, 9 (Fall, 1970); *Bulletin*, 83–86 (August, 1967), 109 (April, 1970); *St. Olaf Alumnus*, 21 (July, 1969); Meslow interview; *Northfield News*, May 28, 1970. Through 1970 over 14,000 men and women had graduated from St. Olaf. Among American colleges and universities not offering doctoral programs, St. Olaf ranked fourteenth in the number of its graduates earning doctorates between 1958 and 1966.

[35] *President's Annual Report, 1966–1967*, (quotation); *Saint Olaf*, 4, 9 (quotations) (Fall, 1970). According to the college's placement office records, of the 565 members of the class of 1970 over 200 went on to graduate and professional schools. Many others entered such service-oriented fields as teaching, nursing, social work, and the Peace Corps.

33. MACALESTER COLLEGE, PART III
Pages 200 to 207

[1] Macalester College, *Bulletin*, 156–174 (April, 1947), 49, 58, 157, 162–164 (April, 1948), 178 (April, 1959); "Trustee Minutes," January 2, March 20, June 2, 1947, June 2, 1949. According to college records, of the 1,313 students enrolled in March, 1947, 593 were veterans of World War II. More than 70 students and alumni lost their lives in that conflict.

[2] "Trustee Minutes," May 5, October 13, 1947, June 3, 1948; *Bulletin*, 171–207 (April, 1949). Enrollment in 1948–49 was up to 1,798, of whom 673 were freshmen and 196 seniors.

[3] "Trustee Minutes," January 2, 30, March 20, September 9, October 13, November 6, 1947, January 8 (quotation), February 5, June 3, September 22, October 7, 1948, June 2, July 7, September 8, 1949. A pageant in the St. Paul Auditorium held as part of the fund drive in 1949 attracted some 2,800 people to each of its three performances.

[4] *Bulletin*, 38–43 (April, 1946), 26, 90 (April, 1951), 196–198 (March, 1953); "Trustee Minutes," June 2, 1947 (quotation), June 3, November 4, 1948. A regular summer session was instituted in 1946. Diplomas in kindergarten-primary education were awarded to 52 students at commencement in 1951. Miss Wood's school was an outgrowth of the Minneapolis Kindergarten Association Normal School, organized in 1892 by a group of women interested in promoting kindergarten training in the public school system. When that objective was attained, the association turned over to Miss Wood the entire charge and maintenance of the school in 1905. See Marguerite N. Bell, *With Banners: A Biography of Stella L. Wood* (St. Paul, 1954); Minneapolis Kindergarten Association Alumnae, *Bulletin, 1892–1917*, 2–6 [Minneapolis, 1917].

[5] "Trustee Minutes," September 22, November 4, 1948; Carl Billman to President Charles J. Turck, July 30, 1948 (quotations), in Phi Beta Kappa correspondence file in the possession of Dr. Hugo Thompson, who kindly permitted the author to use it.

[6] "Trustee Minutes," June 2, July 7, 1949, May 11, 1950, January 4, March 1, April 5, May 3, September 6, October 3, December 6, 1951; *Bulletin*, 219 (April, 1950), 204 (March, 1953). In April, 1951, applications were down 40 per cent from a year earlier; 583 men and 727 women were enrolled that fall. Uncertainty concerning their draft status disturbed many men students during the Korean War period.

[7] "Trustee Minutes," January 4, May 3, October 3, December 6, 1951, January 3, May 29, 1952, January 22, May 21, September 10, October 1, November 5, 1953, January 7, February 4, September 9, 1954, January 6, February 3, June 30, September 14, November 3, 1955, September 6, 1956; *Bulletin*, 187–191 (March, 1953), 217 (April, 1957). The field house cost twice the $200,000 expected.

[8] "Trustee Minutes," September 14, November 3, 1955, January 5, July 12, 1956, June 6, July 13, October 3, 1957; *Bulletin*, 220 (April, 1957), 163–166 (April, 1959); "Profile Presented to the Ford Foundation," table IV, part II, p. 23 (November 1, 1962), in the office of the president.

[9] "Trustee Minutes," February 4, July 7, December 1, 1949, January 4, March 1 (quotation), April 5, 1951; *Bulletin*, 82–97 (April, 1951). In March, 1951, the North Central Association approved the master of education sequence.

[10] "Trustee Minutes," February 1, March 1, May 3, 1951, September 4, 1952, September 10, October 1, 1953, June 3, 1954, September 14, 1955, June 6, 1957; *Bulletin*, 14–26, 136–138 (March, 1953). Additional faculty members, some of them part time, were hired to teach the science courses for nurses, placing a strain on college facilities. The teaching staff numbered

about 130 in 1953, of whom 92 were below the rank of associate professor.

[11] "Trustee Minutes," September 6, 1951, May 29, September 4, 1952; *Bulletin*, 79–85 (March, 1953); Billman to Hugo Thompson, January 28, 1953 (quotation), in Phi Beta Kappa correspondence file.

[12] "Trustee Minutes," October 3, December 6, 1951, May 21, September 10, October 1, 1953, September 9, 1954, September 14, November 3, 1955; *Bulletin*, 68–70 (March, 1953). Macalester also operated evening classes in these years, largely for adults; about 300 were enrolled in them in the fall of 1951.

[13] Billman to Thompson, February 10, 1956, in Phi Beta Kappa correspondence file; "Trustee Minutes," March 1, 1956 (quotation); *Bulletin*, 168–177 (April, 1959). The most frequently conferred degree was the B.A., but after 1950 an increasing number of B.S.s were conferred. In 1957, for example, there were 96 of these in elementary education and 57 in business administration. Thereafter, the number declined.

[14] "Trustee Minutes," January 5, April 12, May 31, November 1, 1956, July 13, 1957. One prominent trustee resigned in 1957, apparently in protest against the policies and practices of the college administration.

[15] "Trustee Minutes," April 16, 1953, October 3, 1957.

[16] "Trustee Minutes," January 21, September 18, 1958; taped interview of the author, April 22, 1968, with President Harvey M. Rice, in the collections of the Minnesota Historical Society.

[17] Interview with Dr. Rice, April 22, 1968; *Bulletin*, 11, 136–139 (April, 1959); "Trustee Minutes," September 18, 1958, November 16, 1961; "Profile Presented to the Ford Foundation," part II, p. 19 (1962). Total gifts and grants in 1952–53 came to $156,880; in 1961–62 the figure was $4,585,000, plus $1,014,000 in deferred gifts. Tuition in 1959 was $685 a year, and board and room came to about $650.

[18] "Trustee Minutes," January 19, February 16, April 20, 1961, October 18, 1962, July 18, September 19, 1963; "Summary of the Actions of the Board of Trustees," September 9, 1961, in the office of the president.

[19] "Trustee Minutes," October 17 (quotation), December 3, 1963; *Bulletin*, Alumni Number (December, 1966), 25–41 (April, 1967); *President's Annual Report to the Shareholders, 1963–64*, [41–44]; *1964–65*, 35–41. By early 1967 the college possessed about 230 endowed scholarships, only 14 of which antedated 1955. As of January, 1972, only $41,457 remained to be pledged to complete the 10-year $32,000,000 Challenge Campaign; United Presbyterian Church in the U.S.A., Minnesota Synod, *Minutes, 1971–72*, 135.

[20] "Trustee Minutes," May 21, October 15, November 19, 1959, January 21, March 17, April 20, 1960, September 9, 1961; *President's Annual Report, 1962–63*, 3; interview with Dr. Rice, April 22, 1968. Contracts for the sale of all college-owned farms were completed early in 1960. The net gain to Macalester was $110,000 over their book value.

[21] *Bulletin*, 22 (December, 1966), 6 (April, 1967); "Trustee Minutes," October 18, November 13, 1962, September 18, 1964, March 25, September 16, December 16, 1965. For an illustrated account of the Janet Wallace Fine Arts Center, see *Planning for the Arts* (1966), a booklet prepared by the Macalester College Fine Arts Commission for submission to the Educational Facilities Laboratories, Inc., New York. The Minnesota Historical Society has a copy. The track on Shaw Field was surfaced with all-weather, nonslip "Tartan," the first one in the nation so surfaced.

[22] "Trustee Minutes," April 14, June 2, 1955, May 31, July 12, September 6, December 6, 1956, January 3, December 5, 1957, December 18, 1958, May 16, 1963.

[23] "Summary of Actions of Trustees," September 9, 1961;

"Trustee Minutes," June 2, 1955, December 6, 1956, January 3, September 5, 1957, May 18, September 9, 1961, May 17, 1962, January 17, 1963, September 15, 1966 (quotation); *President's Annual Report, 1959–60*, 3, *1964–65*, 40. The board late in 1965 adopted a "Statement on Procedural Standards in Faculty Dismissal Proceedings," which had the approval of the Association of American Colleges and the AAUP.

[24] "Trustee Minutes," January 2, 1958, December 17, 1959, September 16, 1965, September 15, 1966; *Bulletin*, 22 (December, 1966); *President's Annual Report, 1962–63*, unpaged insert. About two-thirds of the students lived on campus in the fall of 1965.

[25] Interview with Dr. Rice, April 22, 1968; "Trustee Minutes," March 17, 1960 (quotation), September 9, 1961, September 20, 1962, September 19, 1963, May 20, 1965.

[26] *President's Annual Report, 1959–60*, 2, 31, *1961–62*, 2–4; Lucius Garvin, "Macalester Looks Ahead," in *Bulletin*, 12 (Fall, 1967). A language laboratory was established in the late 1950s.

[27] "Trustee Minutes," September 20, 1962; *Minneapolis Sunday Tribune*, April 7, 1968; *President's Annual Report, 1962–63*, 2.

[28] Garvin, in *Bulletin*, 14–17 (quotation) (Fall, 1967), stated that "no independent liberal arts college can go it alone." At the time Macalester had joined no "full-fledged" association, but it had consorted with other institutions in SPAN, the area studies program, and joint interim term ventures with St. Olaf, Gustavus, and Luther. In 1969, however, Macalester joined the Associated Colleges of the Midwest (ACM). See *Minneapolis Tribune*, April 16, 1969.

[29] Kenneth L. Holmes, *Canadian-American Conference, 1965: 25 Years of Dynamic Friendship*, a booklet issued by Macalester for the 1965 conference; Fred Johnson, in *Minneapolis Tribune*, November 10, 1966; Garvin, in *Bulletin*, 14 (Fall, 1967); *Bulletin*, 14 (April, 1967). A listing of the international programs open to students consumes a page and a half in the 1967 catalog.

[30] Garvin, in *Bulletin*, 17 (quotation) (Fall, 1967); "Trustee Minutes," May 16, 1963 (quotation), April 21, 1966, January 19, September 21, 1967; *Minneapolis Tribune*, February 25, 1970. In 1969–70 about 28 students and a faculty family lived in two houses near the campus as participants in an experimental Inner College. Freed of the usual college requirements, students there attempted to learn in individual ways and to integrate the "academic and non-academic aspects of their lives."

[31] Interview with Dr. Rice, April 22, 1968; "Trustee Minutes," October 20, 1960, May 18, 1961, May 19, 1966 (quotation); Funk, *Macalester College*, 62.

[32] "Trustee Minutes," March 7, 1960, November 19, 1964, April 21, 1966.

[33] *Minneapolis Tribune*, October 11, 17, November 13, 1967, December 7, 1968; Garvin, in *Bulletin*, 17 (Fall, 1967); "Trustee Minutes," September 15, December 15, 1966; *Bulletin*, 23 (December, 1966). In 1966–67, 35 per cent of the student body were from the local commuting area; another 26 per cent came from other parts of Minnesota.

[34] *Minneapolis Tribune*, October 26, 1967 (quotations), November 26, 1968. Dr. Rice went into college fund-raising work in 1968.

[35] *Macalester Report* (June, 1968), a publication issued by the alumni office from 1959 to 1968; *Minneapolis Tribune*, March 29 (quotation), 30, May 6, 1968, May 25, 1969. The Macalester Foundation for the Advancement of Higher Education was established in 1968 with gifts from DeWitt Wallace and others. Its purpose was to make studies dealing with problems in administration and to examine such matters as student

involvement, faculty personnel policies, and the role of institutions of learning in service to society. In May, 1969, Dr. Jarold Kieffer was appointed director.

³⁶ *Macalester Report* (June, 1968); *Minneapolis Tribune*, December 7, 1967, December 14, 16, 1968, January 25, 26, February 23, 1969; "Tartan Topics," February 14, 1969, November 20, 1970, a mimeographed newsletter for Macalester faculty and staff members; *Bulletin*, Alumni Number (September, 1971). On March 13, 1968, Dr. G. Theodore Mitau, of the class of 1940 and chairman of Macalester's political science department, was named chancellor of the Minnesota State College system. In June Trustee C. Gilbert Wrenn became a Distinguished Professor to encourage experiments and innovations.

³⁷ "Tartan Topics," September 6, 1968, August 31, 1969, August 28, 1970; Presbyterian Minnesota Synod, *Minutes, 1968–69*, 104; *1969–70*, 137; *1970–71*, 124. In 1968–69 Macalester had 288 National Merit Scholars enrolled, putting the college fourth in the nation in the number of these students in attendance.

³⁸ Presbyterian Minnesota Synod, *Minutes, 1968–69*, 103, *1969–70*, 136; *1970–71*, 122; "Tartan Topics," January 24, March 7, May 2, June 27, August 31, September 5, 1969, March 13, November 20, 1970; *Bulletin*, 9 (September, 1970). In 1969 the college purchased a nearby building and transferred the business and development offices to it. In 1970 a neighboring filling station was given to Macalester to be transformed into a park area. A number of residences were bought for college use between 1968 and 1970. Macalester was in the vanguard of the coed dormitory movement; six major dormitories were coed in 1969–70. Presbyterian Minnesota Synod, *Minutes, 1969–70*, 136.

³⁹ Presbyterian Minnesota Synod, *Minutes, 1968–69*, 102; *1969–70*, 136 (quotation); "Tartan Topics," March 7, 28, 1969, June 26, August 31, 1970; *Minneapolis Tribune*, March 13, 1970; *Bulletin*, 39–43 (September, 1970). In June, 1968, the college began to phase out its master of education program.

⁴⁰ Presbyterian Minnesota Synod, *Minutes, 1968–69*, 102; *1969–70*, 136; *1970–71*, 123; "Tartan Topics," November 22, 1968, June 27, August 31, October 10, 1969, June 16, September 8, 1970; *Minneapolis Star*, January 25, 1971 (quotation); *Toward a New Pluralism*, [8] (quotation), a brochure describing the EEO program issued by Macalester in 1970. The college had about 40 Blacks enrolled in 1968. In the fall of 1969 a Black House was put into operation and a Black admissions committee was established. Cost of the EEO program for 1969–70 was over $562,000.

⁴¹ Presbyterian Minnesota Synod, *Minutes, 1970–71*, 123; "Tartan Topics," October 25, 1968, December 18, 1969, September 8, December 11, 1970; interviews with John M. Dozier, vice president for financial affairs, February 24, 26, 1971; *Minneapolis Tribune*, September 20, December 5, 1970, January 20, 1971. According to the Synod, *Minutes*, cited above Mr. and Mrs. Wallace's gifts to Macalester totaled over $36,000,000 in the 15 years before 1971. Tuition in 1968–69 was $1,600; for the fall of 1971 it was $2,250; enrollment was 2,190.

⁴² *Minneapolis Tribune*, November 6, 1970, January 5, 21, 26, 1971; *Minneapolis Star*, January 25, 1971 (quotation); "Tartan Topics," September 8, 1970.

⁴³ *President's Annual Report, 1971–72*, 1 (quotation); Presbyterian Minnesota Synod, *Minutes, 1971–72*, 133, 135 (quotations, here and below). Kenneth P. Goodrich replaced retiring Dean Garvin as vice president and provost in August, 1971.

34. COLLEGE OF ST. THOMAS, PART III
Pages 208 to 215

¹ Schauinger, "St. Thomas," 389–395, 412; Marvin O'Connell, *Decoration of the Campus Chapel, College of St. Thomas* (St. Paul, 1960). Capt. Richard Fleming, 1935 graduate of the academy and cadet lieutenant colonel as a freshman at the college, was awarded the Congressional Medal of Honor posthumously for his valor as a Marine aviator at the Battle of Midway, June 5, 1942, in which he lost his life. A naval vessel was named in his honor, and the 1943 *Kaydet*, the yearbook of the St. Thomas Military Academy, was dedicated to his memory. The navy unit left St. Thomas in October, 1945.

² Schauinger, "St. Thomas," 341, 395–398. Father Moynihan after 15 years as a pastor died in February, 1959.

³ Schauinger, "St. Thomas," 399, 414. Almost 4,500 St. Thomas men were in military service by 1945. Of these 176 lost their lives; they are remembered on campus by the Shrine of Our Lady of Peace, a project of the Mothers' Club, dedicated and blessed on October 15, 1950.

⁴ Schauinger, "St. Thomas," 400–404 (quotation), 427–429.

⁵ Schauinger, "St. Thomas," 405, 414, 426.

⁶ Schauinger, "St. Thomas," 406–411, 417, 426. The recently organized St. Thomas chapter of the AAUP in December, 1948, paid tribute to Father Flynn for the wisdom of his policies.

⁷ Schauinger, "St. Thomas," 420–425.

⁸ Schauinger, "St. Thomas," 410, 416, 418, 426, 428, 430, 433.

⁹ Schauinger, "St. Thomas," 435, 438–440.

¹⁰ Schauinger, "St. Thomas," 439, 441–444, 457. One of the college's staunchest friends and generous benefactors was Edward T. Foley, a trustee from 1921 to 1968. He was the contractor for the administration building (Aquinas Hall), and his grant made possible the construction of Foley Little Theater in the armory in 1958.

¹¹ Schauinger, "St. Thomas," 444–455, 475. With foundation support and that of friends, the Vincent J. Flynn Chair of English Literature was set up in 1957 to bring visiting scholars to the campus.

¹² Schauinger, "St. Thomas," 456; *Report of the President to the Alumni*, 11 (October, 1961).

¹³ Schauinger, "St. Thomas," 457; *The O'Shaughnessy Library* and *The Dedication of O'Shaughnessy Library* — two undated pamphlets issued by the college. The dedication was held from October 28 to November 1, 1959. Archbishop Murray died in October, 1956.

¹⁴ *President's Report*, 6 (October, 1958), 8 (October, 1959), 6, 12 (October, 1961). "Tom Town," the post-World War II veterans' village, was razed in 1959 after 13 years of yeoman service to St. Thomas.

¹⁵ Taped interview of the author, June 17, 1968, with Bishop James P. Shannon, in the collections of the Minnesota Historical Society; *President's Report*, 8 (October, 1958), 7 (October, 1961). In December, 1959, Pope John XXIII elevated Father Shannon and Father Nicholas M. Moelter, a veteran history professor, to the rank of domestic prelate with the title of right reverend monsignor.

¹⁶ Shannon interview, June 17, 1968; *President's Report*, 7, 10 (October, 1959), 8, 12 (October, 1961), 10 (October, 1962), 6, 9 (February, 1965). In 1957 the college began offering courses on KTCA-TV.

¹⁷ *President's Report*, 3–5 (quotation) (October, 1962), 13 (October, 1963); *Alumnus* (Spring, 1963), an alumni publication later called *Memorandum*.

[18]*President's Report*, 2 (February, 1965), 3–8 (October, 1966).

[19]*President's Report*, 11, 14 (February, 1965), 6, 9, 10 (October, 1966), 4, 11 (January, 1969).

[20]*President's Report*, 9 (October, 1959), 10 (October, 1961), 15 (October, 1962), 9 (October, 1963), 8 (October, 1966), 10 (January, 1969); *Newsweek*, 68 (August 10, 1964).

[21] Information from Constance Johnson, Management Center staff associate.

[22]*President's Report*, 13 (October, 1962), 5–10 (October, 1963), 6–8, 10 (February, 1965), 4 (October, 1965), 7 (October, 1966); *Alumnus* (Spring, 1965). The library collection of 82,900 volumes in 1962 had grown to 107,200 volumes in 1966.

[23]*President's Report*, 13 (October, 1963), 12 (February, 1965); *Alumnus* (Spring, 1965); St. Thomas Academy, *Headmaster's Report* (1966).

[24] "The Farewell of a College President," in *St. Thomas Bulletin*, 4 (quotation) (July, 1966); *Alumnus* (Spring, 1965). In 1964 *Catholic Digest*, the nation's largest paid-circulation Catholic publication, was acquired as a gift by St. Thomas, and the Catholic Publishing Center was set up as part of the corporate structure of the college. See *President's Report*, 10 (February, 1965). Bishop Shannon withdrew from his functions as a bishop of the church in 1969, married, and became a columnist in the *Minneapolis Sunday Tribune*.

[25]*Bulletin*, inside front cover, 5–7 (quotation) (July, 1966); *Alumnus* (Fall, 1966); Fred Johnson, in *Minneapolis Tribune*, November 12, 1966, quoted President Murphy as saying: "The layman has far more influence here than at any Catholic college I can think of. Our trustees are a governing board . . . and they are predominantly laymen." At the time the board was made up of 14 laymen and 5 clergy.

[26]*Alumnus* (Fall, Winter, 1966, Summer, Fall, Winter, 1967); *Memorandum* (October, 1968). Enrollment in the 1967 summer session was 722, fourth highest in St. Thomas' history. Of these students, 344 (71 laymen, 143 laywomen, 110 nuns, 20 male religious) were in one of the four master's programs offered.

[27]*President's Report*, 7 (October, 1966), 4 (January, 1969). In 1968 St. Thomas received final accreditation from the National Council for Accreditation of Teacher Education.

[28]*President's Report*, 3 (October, 1966); *Alumnus* (Summer, 1967).

[29] St. Catherine and St. Thomas, "Interinstitutional Cooperation: A Year's Report" (March, 1968), in college files, sometimes referred to as the "Barrett Report," for the consultant who had been employed; *President's Report*, 5 (January 1969), 3 (October, 1969); *Memorandum* (April, 1969); *President's Report* (quotation) (November, 1970). The four St. Paul colleges, under a $50,000 grant from the Hill Foundation, in 1969 set up a co-operative Russian major, the first joint one in their history. In the summer of 1970 St. Thomas participated in a field collaboration in Galway with the National University of Ireland.

[30]*President's Report*, 6 (October, 1965), 9 (October, 1966), 8, 10 (January, 1969), 5–9 (October, 1969), (November, 1970). Starting in 1968 the college's fiscal year ran from July 1 through June 30, a change from earlier budget practice.

[31]*President's Report* (November, 1970); St. Thomas business office records. The college's long-term indebtedness by the end of 1970 was about $4,728,000.

[32]*President's Report* (quotation) (November, 1970); *Memorandum* (June, 1969); business office records; *Minneapolis Tribune*, April 29, 1969.

[33]*President's Report*, 10 (October, 1965), (November, 1970); college ROTC records; *Bulletin*, 68 (January, 1963); *Minneapolis Star*, May 6, 1970. ROTC has been voluntary at St.

Thomas since 1963. In 1970, 60 men were enrolled. By that year a total of about 535 Tommies had earned commissions since the program's inception.

[34]*President's Report* (quotation) (November, 1970); *Memorandum* (December, 1970). In November, 1970, the Reverend Monsignor William E. O'Donnell completed his 25th year as academic dean at St. Thomas, where he has been particularly respected for his devotion to high standards of scholarship and for his unflagging good humor.

[35]*Bulletin*, 38–65 (May, 1970); college registrar's files; *the view from the porch*, a brochure issued by the St. Thomas development office in the spring of 1968; *President's Report*, 4 (January, 1969).

[36]*President's Report* (quotation) (November, 1970); *Minneapolis Tribune*, April 2, 1969. By 1970 the graduate school had conferred more than 1,500 master's degrees in education. In that year St. Thomas started a teacher intern program and a Center for Economic Education, both framed to help teachers meet the demands of changing social and educational conditions.

[37] "Interinstitutional Cooperation," 58 (1968); *President's Report*, 4, 7 (quotation) (October, 1959), 5, 9 (October, 1961), 14 (October, 1962), 11, 14 (October, 1963); *Alumnus* (Spring, 1963); *Memorandum* (June, 1969); registrar's files. During the 1969–70 academic year 361 B.A. degrees and 159 M.A.s in education were conferred.

[38]*President's Report* (quotation) (November, 1970); *Minneapolis Tribune*, February 18, 1971. In 1970 and 1971 St. Thomas won the MIAC basketball championship.

35. CONCORDIA COLLEGE IN MOORHEAD, PART III
Pages 216 to 223

[1] Rolfsrud, *Cobber Chronicle*, 111–113; *Concordia College Record*, 151 (October, 1966). More than 30 former students lost their lives in World War II.

[2] Rolfsrud, *Cobber Chronicle*, 113; *College Record*, 51 (April, 1951). A summer session was inaugurated in 1942.

[3] Rolfsrud, *Cobber Chronicle*, 114, 118. In 1945 a residence for the president was purchased, but until 1951 it served as East Hall, a home management house and as a dwelling for a number of women students.

[4] Rolfsrud, *Cobber Chronicle*, 114–116 (quotations); Concordia College, *Annual Report* (1961–62); *College Record*, 151 (October, 1966). Only 5 men and 40 women received B.A.s at commencement in 1945; three years later the number was 75 men and 78 women. The peak came in 1950, when 156 men and 100 women were graduated (six with bachelors of music). Not until 1958 would a larger class receive degrees.

[5] Rolfsrud, *Cobber Chronicle*, 116, 147–149, 153–155, 165, 170, 194–196, 226. In 1958 when Minnesota's centenary as a state was observed, the Concordia choir again performed in Norway and elsewhere in Europe. Governor Orville L. Freeman designated the group as Centennial Ambassadors to Europe.

[6] Rolfsrud, *Cobber Chronicle*, 117–119 (quotation); *College Record*, 151 (October, 1966). Concordia's sponsoring church body, the Norwegian Lutheran Church of America, changed its name to Evangelical Church in June, 1946. The latter, in turn, joined the later merger which produced the American Lutheran Church in 1960. See Chapter 32, above.

[7] Rolfsrud, *Cobber Chronicle*, 117, 120; Bernice White, ed., *Who's Who in Minnesota*, 49 (Waseca, 1958).

[8] Rolfsrud, *Cobber Chronicle*, 116, 120–124; Concordia, *Annual Report* (1961–1962). The old gymnasium, remodeled at a cost of $25,000 in 1953, was turned over to the art department and named the Berg Art Center. That same year a student

lunchroom and lounge, ''The Brown Jug,'' opened in the basement of Brown Hall. A frame post office and bookstore building came along in 1954.

[9] Concordia, *Annual Report* (1961–62), (1963–64); Rolfsrud, *Cobber Chronicle*, 122.

[10] Evangelical Lutheran Church (ELC), *Annual Report*, 1953, p. 116 (quotation) (Minneapolis, 1953).

[11] Rolfsrud, *Cobber Chronicle*, 168; ''Teacher Education at Concordia College,'' 2, 11, 16, 25, 36, 79, 85 (February, 1961), in college library. Of those in the 1960 class who completed teacher training, the largest number majored in elementary education (56), music (27), physical education (22), English (18), and business education (17). Practice teaching had been done in 24 different communities.

[12] ''Teacher Education at Concordia,'' 4, 6, 20, 63, 66, 82; *College Record*, 32, 47, 59–70, 73–139 (April, 1951), 16–20, 38–124 (October, 1966). By the mid-1960s the B.S. degree was given only in elementary education, home economics, rural living, and medical technology.

[13] Concordia, *Annual Report* (1961–62); ELC, *Annual Report*, 1956, p. 152, 1959, p. 153. There were 239 students in the summer session of 1959 and about 570 people taking lessons at Concordia's music branch in Fargo.

[14] Rolfsrud, *Cobber Chronicle*, 122, 124 (quotation); ELC, *Annual Report*, 1955, p. 100, 1956, p. 149, 1957, p. 149. The library in 1957 won an award from the American Institute of Architects.

[15] Rolfsrud, *Cobber Chronicle*, 126–129; *Minneapolis Star*, December 3, 1969; Concordia, *Annual Report* (1965–66), (1969–70). In 1965–66, 325 new members joined C-400; by 1970 membership exceeded 2,000.

[16] *Ford Foundation Grants in Minnesota* (September, 1963); ELC, *Annual Report*, 1955, p. 99–101, 1958, p. 63, 128, 1959, p. 88, 108, 152; Concordia, *Annual Report* (1957–58); Rolfsrud, *Cobber Chronicle*, 124, 130. Concordia's assets in June, 1957, totaled $4,403,000, of which $3,000,000 was in the form of land, buildings, and equipment. Endowment was slightly over $890,000 and loan funds $40,500. Plant fund liabilities were approximately $1,120,000.

[17] Rolfsrud, *Cobber Chronicle*, 124, 129–131; ELC, *Annual Report*, 1959, p. 152, 1960, p. 146; *Call*, 12, 16, a publication of the Concordia office of development.

[18] Rolfsrud, *Cobber Chronicle*, 131; ''Teacher Education at Concordia,'' 57; Concordia, *Annual Report* (1960–61) (quotation), (1961–62); ELC, *Annual Report*, 1960, p. 146–148; American Lutheran Church (ALC), *Reports and Actions of the First General Convention*, October 18–24, 1962, p. 221, 228–230 (Milwaukee, 1962). Total gifts to Concordia in 1960–61 came to $424,500. The ALC gave $190,600, and various of its congregations and organizations $57,200. Individual friends gave nearly $60,000, and alumni almost $50,000. Operating income was $362,000 above that of the previous year, and total indebtedness was under $900,000.

[19] Rolfsrud, *Cobber Chronicle*, 126, 132–135; *Call*, 19; Concordia, *Annual Report* (1960–61), (1961–62), (1962–63) (quotation), (1965–66). Concordia received $324,198 from the Kolbjorn O. Livedalen estate. The C-400 Club gave $75,500 for the music building, and $25,000 came from the Kresge Foundation.

[20] Rolfsrud, *Cobber Chronicle*, 128, 129 (quotation), 135; Concordia, *Annual Report* (1962–63), (1963–64), (1964–65); ALC, *Reports and Actions of the Second General Convention*, 1964, p. 294. In the fall of 1963 an IBM 1620 computer was installed in a room in Old Main; $60,000 of its $100,000 cost was covered by an outside grant.

[21] Rolfsrud, *Cobber Chronicle*, 135, 210–214; Concordia,

Annual Report (1965–66), (1966–67); ALC, *Report to the Third General Convention*, 1966, p. 246. Concordia shared the MIAC football title with Gustavus in 1952 and won it outright in 1957 and 1964. In December, 1964, the team tied a Texas college for the NAIA championship. On the LIFE campaign, see also p. 192, above.

[22] Concordia, *A Blueprint for Concordia College* (November, 1962), in college files; *Annual Report* (1960–61), (1961–62). The college also had a student development commission that trained undergraduates to go out and speak to congregations in Concordia's behalf.

[23] In 1964 a team representing the North Central Association paid a review visit to Concordia. Among the many strengths the outsiders found were high morale, excellent faculty and administration relationships, care in selecting students, and a good physical plant. Special commendation was given for the college's refusal to yield to pressures to add graduate, vocational, and technical programs. See ''Report of a Review Visit to Concordia College, Moorhead, Minnesota, April 26–28, 1964,'' in college files.

[24] Rolfsrud, *Cobber Chronicle*, 135; Concordia, *Annual Report* (1961–62), (1962–63), (1963–64), (1964–65), (1965–66). Among the most frequently selected majors by seniors in 1966 were education 66, English 52, economics 36, and psychology 31.

[25] Concordia, *Annual Report* (1965–66), (1966–67); Curcom, *Curriculum Reform for Concordia College* (1970). The curriculum committee was chaired by Walther G. Prausnitz.

[26] Concordia, *Annual Report* (1967–68), (1968–69), (1969–70).

[27] Concordia, *Annual Report* (1965–66), (1966–67), (1967–68), (1968–69), (1969–70). Cobber Hall was razed in 1968–69 to make room for the library addition. The former occupants then moved into Academy Hall, which had long been a women's dormitory. C-400's fourth project included the library addition gift, $100,000 each for a chapel in Old Main and for scholarships, $50,000 for campus improvement, and $100,000 for Concordia's successful summer language camps for young people nine years of age and over started in leased facilities with 75 youngsters in 1961. Offering instruction in five foreign languages, the camps grew to an enrollment of over 900 in 1969. In 1966 some 800 acres of land on Turtle River Lake near Bemidji were secured as a permanent site; the following year a full-time director was hired. In July, 1970, the first permanent unit called the Norwegian Village was dedicated. Among the other supporters of the camp was the Bush Foundation, which gave $150,000.

[28] Minnesota Committee, *High School-College Relations Newsletter* (Spring, 1967); Concordia, *Annual Report* (1964–65), (1965–66), (1966–67), (1967–68), (1968–69); Fred Johnson, in *Minneapolis Tribune*, November 2, 1966. The $7,500,000 spent on the six major buildings from 1964 to 1969 was twice the amount expended for construction by Concordia during the preceding decade.

[29] Concordia, *Annual Report* (1962–63), (1964–65), (1969–70); *Minneapolis Tribune*, July 23, 1970.

[30] Concordia, *Annual Report* (1963–64) (quotation).

[31] Concordia, *Annual Report* (1962–63), (1967–68), (1968–69), (1969–70). By mid-1969 Concordia had received $576,600 from the ALC LIFE campaign. In 1969–70 government agencies contributed $254,000 to the college for student aid purposes. Like St. Olaf, Concordia has a relatively autonomous administrative structure, and it is not directly controlled by the American Lutheran Church. The congregations of four ALC districts, the Northern Minnesota District, the Eastern and Western North Dakota districts, and the Rocky Mountain District,

form the private Concordia College Corporation. The corporation's members elect the board of regents. Information from head librarian, Verlyn D. Anderson.

[32] Concordia, *Annual Report* (1967–68) (quotation), (1968–69), (1969–70); *Minneapolis Tribune*, July 8, 1969, October 31, 1970. In 1967–68 a nun from the University of North Dakota at Grand Forks taught religion at Concordia, and a Benedictine priest from St. John's at Collegeville and a professor of philosophy at Concordia exchanged teaching posts. In 1970 the Bush Foundation granted $94,000 to the Tri-College University.

[33] Concordia, *Annual Report* (1962–63), (1967–68), (1968–69); *Minneapolis Tribune*, January 23, 1970.

[34] *Minneapolis Tribune*, December 11, 24, 1970, January 28, 1971; Concordia, *Annual Report* (1969–70) (quotation). At this time, President Knutson declared: "When a college newspaper carries defiance of the purposes and goals of the college and the admonitions of staff and students to the point of running a paid ad for an abortion clinic in New York, and when news is put in such perspective as to make drugs and sex seem the predominant theme among Concordia students, I as president have no other recourse than to suspend publication of the paper." See *Minneapolis Tribune*, December 8, 1970.

[35] Concordia, *Annual Report* (1963–64) (quotation), (1969–70).

36. COLLEGE OF ST. CATHERINE, PART III
Pages 224 to 231

[1] "Administrative Reports, 1940–41," p. 24–26, 65, 68, 102; interview with Sister Catherine Ann Taver, registrar, April 16, 1969. Total plant assets by the summer of 1941 were $2,470,000; total college assets were $3,200,000.

[2] "Administrative Reports, 1940–41," p. 2–16, 43, 48–50; [Sister Helen Margaret Peck, ed.], *Teacher Education in a Liberal Arts College*, unpaged (*Bulletin*, series 22, no. 2 — St. Paul, 1941), copy in college library; *Bulletin*, inside front cover (January, 1942).

[3] "Administrative Reports, 1941–42," p. 131–134, 153–156.

[4] "Administrative Reports, 1942–43," p. 236–240, 257, 273, 294; *Bulletin*, 40 (January, 1942). In June, 1943, 15 women received certificates for completing the course in primary-kindergarten education; at the June commencement a class of 111 members received baccalaureate degrees. The most popular majors were English 28, library science 15, foods and nutrition 14, secretarial studies 11, and sociology 11.

[5] Interview with Sister Eucharista, July 10, 1968; "Profile of the College of St. Catherine, St. Paul, Minnesota, 1953 to 1973," appendix (October 26, 1962), in college archives. In March, 1943, the college's articles of incorporation were amended. Henceforth, the institution's official name would be "The College of St. Catherine," not "College of St. Catherine" as before. Real management of the college was vested in an executive board of five sisters.

[6] Taped interview of the author, July 10, 1968, with Sister Antonius Kennelly, in the collections of the Minnesota Historical Society.

[7] "Administrative Reports, 1943–44," p. 3–8, 30–32, 44, "1944–45," p. 135, 153, 183. Graduate Record Examinations for seniors were introduced in 1944–45. Regular enrollment that year reached 706, plus 442 students in nursing.

[8] "Administrative Reports, 1945–46," p. 214 (quotation), 216, 246, 261; *Bulletin*, 55–75 (January, 1945), 67 (January, 1946). Departments in the division of community service at first were education, home economics, library science, nursing, physical education, and secretarial studies. In 1947–48 the college as a special service accepted Ancker Hospital's new class of three-year nursing students for training in certain basic courses.

[9] "Administrative Reports, 1944–45," p. 110, 135, "1945–46," p. 217, "1946–47," p. 4, 18; *Bulletin*, 19 (May, 1944). In 1947 Sister Antonius was appointed to the Minnesota Commission on Higher Education. She was coauthor of the section of the commission's report entitled "Problems Facing Minnesota's Private Colleges." See Minnesota Commission, *Higher Education in Minnesota*, 191–209.

[10] "Administrative Report, 1946–47," p. 5, "1948–49," p. 264.

[11] "Administrative Reports, 1948–49," p. 206 (quotation), 209, 225, 234, 236.

[12] Interview with Sister Antonius, July 10, 1968; "Administrative Reports, 1948–49," p. 254.

[13] Taped interview of the author, July 10, 1968, with Sister Antonine O'Brien, in the collections of the Minnesota Historical Society; interview with Sister Antonine, April 21, 1969; Dougherty, *Sisters of St. Joseph*, 158, 164, 424. From 1945 to 1949 Sister Antonine was provincial assistant to Sister Eucharista, and from 1958 to 1964 she served as superior of the Province of St. Paul.

[14] Interview with Sister Antonine, July 10, 1968; "Administrative Reports, 1949–50," p. 4, 9–11, 32, "1950–51," p. 282. In 1949–50 campus population was composed of about 800 college students, 160 nurses in the three-year course, 140 high school students, and a faculty and maintenance staff of 130.

[15] "Administrative Reports, 1950–51," p. 110, "1952–53," p. 6, 32, "1953–54," p. 113, 189, 218, "1954–55," p. 221–224. The alumnae association in June, 1951, gave $81,500 to the college building fund and added to it subsequently. I. A. O'Shaughnessy also contributed $25,000, but the major cost of St. Joseph Hall was met by a loan of $1,000,000 from a Milwaukee company. The Mankato stone used was given by a friend of the college.

[16] "Administrative Reports, 1949–50," p. 9, "1950–51," p. 108, "1951–52," p. 210, "1957–58," p. 123–126, "1958–59," p. 447; interview with Sister Antonine, July 10, 1968.

[17] "Administrative Reports, 1949–50," p. 8–9, "1950–51," p. 105, "1951–52," p. 240; "Profile of the College of St. Catherine," 9 (1962); St. Catherine's, "Report to the National Council for Accreditation of Colleges for Teacher Education," 57–65 (1960), in college archives. Opportunities were provided for observation and practice teaching in both parochial and public schools, thereby permitting valuable comparisons. Until 1957 some education classes were taught at the archdiocesan campus in downtown St. Paul.

[18] "Administrative Reports, 1950–51," p. 171, "1951–52," p. 209, "1952–53," p. 4–6, 11, "1954–55," p. 226, "1956–57," p. 196. In preparation for its master's program, the college submitted a 61-page brochure on its resources and potential to the board of review of the North Central Association early in 1954. This report, according to the board, was among the three or four best out of some 50 such documents submitted during the previous decade.

[19] "Administrative Reports, 1952–53," p. 4–6, "1953–54," p. 112, "1954–55," p. 227; "Profile of the College of St. Catherine," 3 (1962).

[20] "Administrative Reports, 1949–50," p. 5–7, 18–20, 79, 83, "1950–51," p. 105–107, 120, "1951–52," p. 211, 242, "1952–53," p. 3, 32, "1953–54," p. 110, "1954–55," p. 228. Interest in graduate study, stimulated particularly by a Phi Beta Kappa committee, noticeably increased among senior students. In June, 1951, Sister Antonine expressed the hope that the provincial house "will soon recognize our needs and send generous reenforcements to our staff of Sisters."

21 "Administrative Reports, 1949–50," p. 47, "1952–53," p. 31, "1954–55," p. 224, 229, 233–237, 273. The college's low current radio station KATY went on the air during the 1952–53 academic year.

22 Taped interview of the author, July 24, 1968, with Sister Mary William Brady, in the collections of the Minnesota Historical Society; St. Catherine's, "Self-Survey Report, March, 1964," p. 50 (quotation), in college archives; "Administrative Reports, 1955–56," p. 56. A visiting speaker on campus told Sister Mary William: "You've got a million dollar business on your hands yet you run it like a country store."

23 "Administrative Reports, 1955–56," p. 4, 59, "1956–57," p. 268, 273, "1957–58," p. 277, "1963–64," p. 25. In 1958–59, in keeping with Sister Mary William's policy of looking ahead, St. Catherine's first lay board of advisers composed of 20 men was set up "to supplement the work of the trustees and to relieve them of some of their burden." In 1964 the group's name was changed to the President's Council of the College of St. Catherine, and its composition was broadened.

24 Interview with Sister Mary William, July 24, 1968; *Scan* (Winter, 1956), a quarterly alumnae publication; "Profile of the College of St. Catherine," part II, section C (1962); "Administrative Reports, 1955–56," p. 11–13, "1956–57," p. 202, "1957–58," 10 (quotation), "1958–59," p. 277; *Catherine Wheel*, December 15, 1955. The *Chicago Daily Tribune*, February 25, 1961, carries a picture of Sister Mary William and a highly complimentary description of the college.

25 "Administrative Reports, 1958–59," p. 278, "1959–60," p. 16–18, "1960–61," p. 372–376, 468–476, "1969–70," p. 6; *Scan* (Winter, 1960); *Catherine Wheel*, March 12, 1959. Partial payment for the furnishings in the library was made with $50,000 given by I. A. O'Shaughnessy. By 1969 the library housed 162,500 books and 1,191 different periodicals.

26 Interview with Sister Mary William, July 24, 1968; *Catherine Wheel*, February 2, 1956; "Administrative Reports, 1955–56," p. 6, 9, 12, 76–80, "1956–57," p. 251, 254, 256, 262, "1957–58," p. 4–6, 70, 73–75, "1958–59," p. 271–275, 346, 369–371, "1959–60," p. 5, 96–100, "1964–65," p. 417. An outgrowth of the curricular studies of 1957–58 was St. Catherine's admission in 1958 to the North Central Association's Study on Liberal Arts Education. The humanities course was discontinued in 1964.

27 "Administrative Reports, 1955–56," p. 9, 60, "1956–57," p. 197, "1957–58," p. 9, 79, "1958–59," p. 353–358, "1959–60," p. 8–11, 100–116, "1961–62," p. 344–348, 354, 450–463; *Scan* (Autumn, 1961); "Report to the National Council for Accreditation of Teacher Education," 6–10 (1960). Honors freshmen were admitted in 1956, but their attrition rate was about one-third for the same reasons as that of all students — emotional problems, transfer, and marriage.

28 "Administrative Reports, 1960–61," p. 348–352, 444–468, 523, 528; "Profile of the College of St. Catherine," 9–12 (1962); "Report to the National Council for Accreditation of Teacher Education" (1960). In 1960 a regular academic major was required of students specializing in elementary education.

29 Taped interview of the author, July 24, 1968, with Sister Mary Edward Healy, in the collections of the Minnesota Historical Society; Dougherty, *Sisters of St. Joseph*, 162, 165, 424; *Scan* (Summer, 1961, Summer, 1964); "Administrative Reports, 1961–62," p. 5, 9, 183, 252, 261, "1962–63," p. 393, 397, "1963–64," p. 4–7, 13–16, 163, 166–169, 173, 184, 186, "1968–69," p. 12. The St. Paul Volunteer Bureau cited the college in 1969 for its long record of social service.

30 Interview with Sister Mary Edward, July 24, 1968; "Administrative Reports, 1961–62," p. 9, 12, 19–22, "1962–63," p. 272. Only about 470 students could be provided living quarters on campus.

31 "Administrative Reports, 1961–62," p. 14–18, 21–23, "1962–63," p. 269–271; *Scan* (Summer, 1963, Summer, 1964).

32 Interview with Sister Mary Edward, July 24, 1968; "Administrative Reports, 1963–64," p. 22, 28–31, 39, 132, "1964–65," p. 321–323, 414, "1965–66," p. 13, 14, 99, 103; *Scan* (Winter, 1965). In June, 1964, commencement exercises for the 251 seniors were held in the St. Paul Auditorium because of inadequate space on campus.

33 Taped interview of the author, July 3, 1969, with Sister Alberta Huber, in the collections of the Minnesota Historical Society; *Catherine Wheel*, January 10, 1936; "Administrative Reports, 1964–65," p. 311; *Scan* (Spring, 1963, Summer, 1964); St. Catherine and St. Thomas, "Interinstitutional Cooperation: A Year's Report," 116 (March, 1968), in college archives, sometimes referred to as the "Barrett Report" for the consultant who had been employed. For the first time in 30 years, due to the heavy work load involved, the office of college president and that of local superior were separated in 1964. Sister Antonine became local superior.

34 "Administrative Reports, 1968–69," p. 82–86; *Catalog, 1970–72*, 29–34; *Scan* (Summer, Winter, 1966, Fall, 1967, Winter, 1968). From 1966 on growing emphasis was placed on tailoring programs to student needs and interests.

35 "Administrative Reports, 1968–69," p. 157; interview with Sister Alberta, March 16, 1970; "Interinstitutional Cooperation" (1968). Co-ordinated class schedules for 1969–70 for the two colleges were published in time for student registration the preceding spring. In the spring of 1970, 427 Katies and 585 Tommies were enrolled in various classes on the others' campus. See also Chapter 34, above.

36 "Administrative Reports, 1967–68," p. 10, 11, 99, 113, "1968–69," p. 14; *Catherine Wheel*, September 26, 1969; interview with Sister Miriam Joseph, college treasurer, March 16, 1970; *Minneapolis Tribune*, September 12, 1967.

37 *President's Report, 1969–70*, 10; *The Mother Antonia McHugh Fine Arts Center* (quotation), an unpaged booklet issued by the college in 1970; *Minneapolis Star*, September 23, 1970; *Minneapolis Tribune*, September 27, 1970; Sister Alberta Huber to the author, January 15, 1971. The art department moved from Mendel Hall into its new building in January, 1970, and the music department occupied its recently completed home in the following summer. The education department took over the space released by art, and the nursing department acquired music's former quarters.

38 *President's Report, 1969–70*, 6, 14–52; *Catalog, 1970–72*, 52–60; *Minneapolis Tribune*, July 24, 1968. On June 1, 1968, Dwight W. Culver, chairman of the sociology department at St. Olaf, became the first man and the first person outside the sisterhood to become academic dean at St. Catherine's.

39 *President's Report, 1969–70*, 3, 6, 8–10; *Minneapolis Tribune*, September 8, 1968. Graduates of 1969–70 majored in 28 different fields.

40 *President's Report, 1969–70*, 6; *Catalog, 1970–72*, 21.

41 "Financial Statements as of June 30, 1970, together with Auditor's Report," September 2, 1970, in college files; St. Catherine's, *Bulletin: Development Report, 1969–70*, 5 (September, 1970); Sister Alberta to the author, January 14, 1971. The college's long-term indebtedness in June, 1970, was $1,377,000. The 1970–71 deficit was $344,000 and the 1971–72 deficit dropped to $10,000. Not all colleges use the same accounting methods, and the figures cannot be regarded as comparable. As soon as the fine arts center was completed, depreciation was included in St. Catherine's budget.

42 Hurley, *On Good Ground*, 12; St. Catherine's, *Behold, I Make All Things New*, a booklet commemorating the consecration of Our Lady of Victory Chapel, May 1, 1958; interview with Sister Alberta, January 20, 1971.

37. College of Saint Teresa, Part III
Pages 232 to 238

[1] Quinn, *Design in Gold*, 61; Saint Teresa, *Bulletin*, 5 (March, 1944).

[2] Quinn, *Design in Gold*, 63, 67; *Our Sunday Visitor* (Winona Edition), December 12, 1948, the official newspaper of the Winona diocese; *Campanile* (student newspaper), September 23, 1968 (quotation); Sister Mary David Homan to the author, September 23, 1968. Sister Aloysius in 1947 became the first woman to be elected president of the college and university section of the National Catholic Educational Association. The following year she was elected a Phi Beta Kappa Associate, an honor restricted to 200 persons at any one time.

[3] Quinn, *Design in Gold*, 65–67. The first "strictly informal" dance ever held at the college took place in 1947 with music furnished by an orchestra from St. Mary's College. Enrollment in the fall of 1948 reached 613.

[4] Quinn, *Design in Gold*, 66, 69, 74; "A Report on Teacher Education for the National Council for Accreditation of Teacher Education," 6, 30 (1967), in college archives; Sister Mary David Homan to the author, October 7, 1968; Adams, "Historical Development of the Department of Nursing" (1960). Graduates of the five-year nursing program numbered 169. The first group to graduate under the new program were in the class of 1951. Between then and 1960, 262 women finished the course.

[5] Quinn, *Design in Gold*, 71; Sister Mary David Homan to the author, September 23, 1968; *Bulletin*, 3 (October 3, 1968). Sister Rachel served at Saint Teresa for 46 years. She died suddenly in retirement in Rochester on August 14, 1968.

[6] "Profile: College of Saint Teresa from 1964 to 1976," part 1, section 34 (1964), a self-survey report, in college archives. The dean, Sister Emmanuel, in 1936 had become the first sister to earn a Ph.D. in English at Yale University.

[7] Quinn, *Design in Gold*, 68–71, 80 (quotation); taped interview of the author, September 6, 1968, with Sister Camille Bowe, in the collections of the Minnesota Historical Society.

[8] Quinn, *Design in Gold*, 72; "Profile," part 1, section 44 (1964). The Roger Bacon Center and Loretto and Assisi halls were Phase I of the long-range planning endeavor begun in 1957. At that time a development staff was added to aid in realizing the needs of the college.

[9] *President's Report, 1963–64*; "Profile," part 1, section 44 (1964); "Saint Teresa Basic Institutional Data," 144 (March 7, 1968), part of a study prepared for the North Central Association, in college files; interview with Sister Camille, September 6, 1968.

[10] *College of Saint Teresa Library Learning Center*, a booklet issued by the college about 1968; *Campanile*, March 22, 1967; *Winona Daily News*, October 14, 16, 1970; *Winona Sunday News*, October 11, 1970. One-third of the cost of the library was covered by a federal loan.

[11] *President's Report, Seventeen Years, 1952–69*, unpaged (July 15, 1969); "Profile of the College," part 1, p. 6, 27, 44 (1964); "Saint Teresa Institutional Profile," 3 (March 7, 1968), part of a study prepared for the North Central Association, in college archives.

[12] Quinn, *Design in Gold*, 78; *President's Report, 1964–65*; *President's Report, Seventeen Years*; "Profile," part 2, exhibit D (1964); interview with Sister Camille, September 8, 1968; "Year of Commitment" brochures, in college archives. By 1965 the college had educated 900 religious teachers whose work in 54 parish schools influenced the lives of more than 35,000 children a year.

[13] *President's Report, 1964–65*; *President's Report, Seventeen Years*; "Profile," part 2, exhibit C (1964). Student fees brought in $191,100 in 1954–55; in 1968–69 the sum was $1,338,700.

[14] *President's Report, 1958–59* (quotation); Quinn, *Design in Gold*, 74; "Profile," part 1, p. 2, 14, 33 (1964); "Basic Institutional Data," 121 (1968). In 1962 degrees were awarded to 186 women, 63 of them sisters. Of the 170 degree recipients in 1966, only 15 were members of a sisterhood.

[15] *President's Report, Seventeen Years*; "Profile," part 1, p. 37 (1964); "Basic Institutional Data," 125 (1968). Starting in 1957, the college also held mental health workshops for sister-teachers in elementary and secondary schools.

[16] *President's Report, Seventeen Years*; "Profile," part 1, p. 38 (1964); "Basic Institutional Data," 126 (1968). Starting in 1965, summer institutes were conducted for chemistry teachers in secondary schools.

[17] *President's Report, 1958–59* (quotation); "Profile," part 1, p. 42 (1964); "Basic Institutional Data," 124 (1968); interview with Sister Camille, September 6, 1968.

[18] "Profile," part 1, p. 2, 36, 42 (1964); "Basic Institutional Data," 125 (1968).

[19] *President's Report, 1964–65, 1966–67*, 17, *1969–70*, 11; "Profile," part 1, p. 5 (1964); "Basic Institutional Data," 125 (1968); "Institutional Profile," 30, 46 (1968); Fred Johnson, in *Minneapolis Tribune*, November 5, 1966. One benefit derived from co-operation has been the Tri-College Series of programs under which artists too expensive for the budget of only one college were brought to Winona.

[20] *President's Report, Seventeen Years* (quotation); *1969–70*, 11 (quotation); Johnson, in *Minneapolis Tribune*, November 5, 1966; interview with Sister Lorraine McCarthy, January 29, 1970. The generally favorable reactions of students and faculty from both colleges to the interchange were reported in *Campanile*, March 22, 1967.

[21] *President's Report, Seventeen Years*; "Basic Institutional Data," 5 (1968); *Bulletin*, 7 (June, 1969); interview with Sister Camille, September 6, 1968. Starting in 1961, Teresa of Avila Awards recognizing "distinguished leadership in civic, religious, educational, and cultural affairs" have been conferred on more than two dozen men and women — both laymen and religious.

[22] *President's Report, 1966–67*; *Campanile*, March 22, 1967, September 23, 1968; "Profile," part 1, p. 3, 12, 15, 40 (1964); "Basic Institutional Data," 39, 124 (quotation) (1968). Various calendar modifications were considered by the faculty in the early 1960s, but the semester system was retained. Starting in the fall of 1964, however, the first term ended before Christmas.

[23] *President's Report, Seventeen Years*; "Profile," part 1, p. 12, 15, 36, 39 (1964); "Basic Institutional Data," 126 (1968); interview with Sister Camille, September 6, 1968. The Lee and Rose Warner Foundation underwrote an annual lecture series, which since 1960 has brought a procession of distinguished men and women to the campus. Starting in 1965, mental health institutes for upperclasswomen and faculty — supported by the Hill Foundation — were conducted at the college each January.

[24] "Profile," part 1, p. 13, part 2, exhibit F, G (1964); "Basic Institutional Data," 15, 22–26, 73, 121, 137 (1968); "Institutional Profile," 46 (1968). The fields of business, economics, physics, and political science traditionally have not been well developed at Saint Teresa. Some part-time students do work for college credit at Assisi Heights in Rochester, and sophomores and juniors in the clinical program take courses at St. Mary's Hospital in the same city.

[25] *President's Report, Seventeen Years*; *Aldine*, 26–70 (1970); "Basic Institutional Data," 46, 70, 126 (1960); interview with Sister Camille, September 6, 1968. Extracurricular events peculiar to Saint Teresa's include the celebration of the Feast of Saint Teresa of Avila on October 15, the Christmas party or Night of 1,001 Donuts, and Pledge Day on May 1 to honor the seniors.

[26] *President's Report, 1966–67*; *President's Report, Seventeen Years*; "Profile," part 1, p. 15, 20, part 2, exhibit C, (1964); "Basic Institutional Data," 109, 114 (1968).

[27] *In Recognition of Distinguished Service*, a printed transcript of the program at the dinner honoring Sister Camille, April 25, 1969, copy in the Minnesota Historical Society library; *Minneapolis Tribune*, February 13, 1969; interview with Sister Camille, September 6, 1968. After a leave spent largely in Paris, a city dear to her heart, Sister Camille resumed her teaching career at Saint Teresa's in the fall of 1970.

[28] *Minneapolis Tribune*, August 17, 1967, July 26, 1969; college files. Sister Joyce in 1966–67 had gained valuable experience as a Ford Fellow in Academic Administration at Atlanta University on a program of the American Council on Education.

[29] *President's Report, 1969–70*, 5, 19, 21; *Bulletin*, 98 (June, 1969). Of the 1,148 full-time students enrolled in 1968–69, Minnesota contributed 420, Illinois 319, Wisconsin 143, and Iowa 121. There were 24 undergraduates from 10 foreign countries.

[30] *President's Report, 1969–70*, 12–16; *Bulletin*, 32 (June, 1969). Room, board, and tuition were $2,125 in 1969. In 1969–70 the college retired $215,000 of its debt and made interest payments of $136,000.

[31] *President's Report, 1969–70*, 9–11 (quotation), 16; *Minneapolis Tribune*, January 17, 1971.

[32] *President's Report, 1969–70*, 4, 9 (quotation); *Coming to College*, 19–22, a guidebook for freshmen published by the college in 1970; college "News Release," October 20, 1970. To help students cope with the new system, the college organized a comprehensive advisory system — especially for freshmen — and each department suggested courses for its prospective majors. Freshman symposiums were also organized.

[33] "News Release," October 20, 1970 (quotation); Rose Mary Curtin to the author, February 3, 1971. One immediate effect of the adoption of the three-term calendar was a sharp decline in student exchanges with St. Mary's, which in 1970–71 retained the two-semester system. In the winter term of 1970, only 29 men from St. Mary's were enrolled in classes at Saint Teresa's; less than 20 Teresans were taking work at the men's college.

[34] *The Fifty-fifth Annual Commencement Program* (1968); *President's Report, 1969–70*. Saint Teresa's enrollment declined steadily from 1968 to the fall of 1972, recording the largest drop among the 16 colleges covered by this book — from 1,320 in 1968 to 1,020 in 1972, a drop of 22.7 per cent. See Minnesota Higher Education Coordinating Commission, "Five Years of Full-Time Equivalent Enrollments in Minnesota, 1968–72," p. 9. In the fall of 1973 it rose slightly to 1,065.

[35] "Basic Institutional Data," 124–126 (1968); "Institutional Profile," 1 (quotation) (1968).

38. College of St. Benedict, Part III
Pages 239 to 246

[1] St. Benedict, *College Bulletin*, 35, 43 (1940–41), 10–14 (1942–43); "Report of the Dean, 1941–42," p. 1; *Benet* (October, 1941); Faculty Information Record.

[2] "Report of the Dean, 1941–42," p. 7, 9, "1942–43," p. 1, 7; "Report of the Registrar, 1946–47," p. 1, 7, 9, 14. Resident students for the four years 1942–43 through 1945–46 numbered 143, 134, 164, and 182, respectively.

[3] *Bulletin*, 29 (1942–43); "Report of the Dean, 1941–42," p. 27, "1942–43," p. 5, "1945–46," p. 5.

[4] "Report of the Dean, 1946–47," p. 4; "Report of the Registrar, 1946–47," p. 1.

[5] Faculty Information Record; McDonald, *With Lamps Burning*, 176, 211, 222; *Benet* (October, 1949); *Harvest,*

1857–1957, 26, 138. Notable among Mother Richarda's achievements was a prominent role in the attainment in 1956 of final approval as papal institutes of the priories comprising the Congregation of St. Benedict; these were then located in St. Joseph and St. Paul, Eau Claire, Wisconsin, Nauvoo, Illinois, and Olympia, Washington.

[6] "Report of the Registrar, 1951–52," p. 1, 4, "1954–55," p. 1, "1956–57," p. 1; "Report of the Dean, 1951–52," p. 6.

[7] "Report of the Dean, 1950–51," p. 9, "1952–53," p. 21; *Bulletin*, 45 (1952–53); "Report of the Registrar, 1967–68," p. 100, "1969–70," p. 98. By comparison, English, home economics, and sociology by mid-1970 had accounted for 386, 219, and 159 completed majors, respectively. The first English major graduated in 1924, in home economics in 1921, and in sociology in 1931.

[8] "Report of the Dean, 1953–54," p. 10; "President's Annual Report, 1957–58," p. 3, "1958–59," p. 4; "Report of the Evaluating Committee to the Minnesota State Board of Education on the College of St. Benedict, St. Joseph, Minnesota," November 11, 12, 1958, p. 1–10, filed in the president's office. In preparation for the 1958 visit, the faculty had initiated a thorough self-study.

[9] "Report of the Dean, 1954–55," p. 20, "1955–56," p. 15, "1956–57," p. 6, "1957–58," p. 8, "1958–59," p. 12, "1959–60," p. 10, "1963–64," p. 23, 29, "1964–65," p. 67, "1965–66," p. 62, "1966–67," p. 57. A Benedictine Institute of Sacred Theology for sisters was held at the college each summer starting in 1958. Over 70 sisters from 29 mother houses attended in 1960. In recent years sisters from St. Benedict have also offered extension work for teachers in such nearby towns as St. Cloud, Pierz, and Melrose.

[10] McDonald, *With Lamps Burning*, 176; "Report of the Dean, 1954–55," p. 7; *Benet* (October, 1954).

[11] McDonald, *With Lamps Burning*, 177; "Report of the Dean, 1954–55," p. 8–10, 16, "1956–57," p. 6; "Alumnae Association Report, August, 1958," p. 12. In 1956–57 the college's finances were strengthened, though not for plant expansion, by the receipt of $105,500 as its share of the Ford Foundation grant to improve faculty salaries. See *Ford Foundation Grants in Minnesota* (September, 1963); *Benet* (December, 1955).

[12] McDonald, *With Lamps Burning*, 177; "Report of the Dean, 1954–55," p. 7–9, 19; "President's Annual Report, 1957–58," p. 4; "Report of the Dean of Residence, August, 1955," p. 3, "August, 1957," p. 2.

[13] "Report of the Dean, 1957–58," p. 1; Faculty Information Record; *Benet* (October, 1957); "President's Annual Report, 1957–58," p. 1.

[14] "President's Annual Report, 1960–61," unpaged, "1961–62," p. 4. Sister Firmin Escher became academic dean in 1961.

[15] "President's Annual Report, 1960–61," p. 9, "1961–62," p. 3; "Report of the Registrar, 1959–60," p. 2, 5. For 1960–61 instructional income came to $272,400, of which student fees brought in $222,600. Expenditures totaled $455,800.

[16] "President's Annual Report, 1958–59," p. 5, "1960–61," p. 7, "1961–62," p. 4 (quotation).

[17] "President's Annual Report, 1962–63," p. 5 (quotation), "1964–65," p. 10; *Harvest, 1857–1957*, 21. After suffering many vicissitudes, Sister Benedicta died at the age of 37 in 1862. She lies buried in the convent cemetery at St. Joseph.

[18] "President's Annual Report, 1963–64," p. 4 (quotation), 11, 13, "1964–65," p. 4, 10–15; *Architectural Record*, 116–119 (December, 1964); *Minneapolis Sunday Tribune*, October 11, 1964. Blessing of the center took place July 19, 1964. The

architect was Curtis Green. Impressive dedicatory events began on October 11 with two concerts by the Minneapolis Symphony Orchestra and continued with plays, art exhibits, recitals, lectures, and other cultural activities.

[19] "President's Annual Report, 1957–58," p. 1, 7, "1958–59," p. 1, "1959–60," p. 1, "1960–61," p. 7, "1961–62," p. 6, "1962–63," p. 3, 6, "1963–64," p. 8, "1964–65," p. 4, 28; "Report of the Dean, 1956–57," p. 5, "1959–60," p. 10, "1961–62," p. 24, "1962–63," p. 11, "1963–64," p. 22; *Landmarks* (January, 1969), and *CSB Saint Benedict's* (July, 1972), newsletters issued by the college; Sister Nancy Hynes to the author, May 17, 1972. Other new programs in 1972–73 included family life education, criminal justice, health-related professions, a two-year mental health associate training program in co-operation with the St. Cloud Veterans Administration Hospital, and horsemanship.

[20] "President's Annual Report, 1957–58," p. 2, "1959–60," p. 3, "1960–61," p. 6, "1961–62," p. 6, "1963–64," p. 9, "1964–65," p. 29, "1965–66," p. 20–22; "Report of the Dean, 1958–59," p. 3. See also p. 164, above.

[21] "President's Annual Report, 1966–67," p. 28, "1967–68," p. 16, 21–23; "Report of the Dean, 1969–70," p. 53. In May, 1968, an official of the new Southwest State College at Marshall spoke to St. Benedict's faculty about co-operative sharing of cultural and educational programs. This led in September to the two institutions' first annual joint faculty workshop, which was also attended by students.

[22] "Report of the Dean, 1956–57," p. 1, "1957–58," p. 2, "1962–63," p. 16, "1963–64," p. 23, "1964–65," p. 64–67, "1965–66," p. 59; "President's Annual Report, 1964–65," p. 22. St. Benedict's elementary education major was opened to St. John's students in the fall of 1965.

[23] "President's Annual Report, 1961–62," p. 6, "1962–63," p. 7; "Report of the Dean, 1962–63," p. 11, 14.

[24] Faculty Information Record; "President's Annual Report, 1963–64," p. 2–5, 10, 12. In December, 1963, a department of public relations and development was instituted.

[25] "President's Annual Report, 1964–65," p. 7.

[26] "President's Annual Report, 1964–65," p. 5, 27–29, "1965–66," p. 2–4, 7, "1967–68," p. 2, "1971–72," p. 2, 41, 51; "Report of the Dean, 1965–66," p. 41, 44, 68–70, "1966–67," p. 44, 48, 52, 63; *Bulletin*, 18 (quotation) (1971–72). Amended articles of incorporation were adopted on June 3, 1966, changing the name of the institution from The College of Saint Benedict to College of Saint Benedict, the board of directors to the board of trustees with provision for some lay membership, and the lay advisers board to the associated board of trustees. See "President's Annual Report, 1965–66."

[27] "Report and Recommendations of the Joint Summer Study Curriculum Committee, 1965," p. 2–12 (quotation), 31; "Report of the Dean, 1965–66," p. 60–62, "1967–68," p. 51; "President's Annual Report, 1967–68," p. 2; *College of St. Benedict, St. John's University Combined Course Bulletin*, 8, 15 (1967–69).

[28] "President's Annual Report, 1964–65," p. 6; "Report of the Dean, 1965–66," p. 56–60, 72; "NCATE Visiting Team Report on College of Saint Benedict, November 22–24, 1965," p. 42 (quotation); Rolf Larson to Sister Mary Grell, May 24, 1966. In 1965 the college set up an experimental program in human relations education for prospective teachers, a generally neglected area of their preparation.

[29] "Report on Teacher Education at the College of Saint Benedict, St. Joseph, Minnesota, to the National Council for Accreditation of Teacher Education," September, 1965, p. 3, 7; "President's Annual Report, 1964–65," p. 28, 34; "Report of the Dean, 1967–68," p. 93. As early as the mid-1930s students and alumnae had done volunteer work in such places as

the state school for girls in nearby Sauk Centre and Friendship House in Harlem in New York City. Systematic promotion of graduate study did not begin until 1964–65, when a committee for that purpose was appointed.

[30] "President's Annual Report, 1964–65," p. 2, 177, "1967–68," p. 8, 26; "Report of the Business Manager, 1967–68," p. 35; *Bulletin*, 3 (1967–69); "Report of the Dean, 1967–68," p. 41.

[31] "Report of the Business Manager, 1966–67," p. 41; "President's Annual Report, 1960–61," p. 9, "1966–67," p. 3; *Bulletin*, 51 (1967–69). In 1966 for the first time a layman was appointed business manager, and the college's accounting system was divorced from that of the convent. In 1960–61 before a federal program was involved, the college granted students $45,975 in scholarships and work contracts; in 1966–67 the total was $104,200, of which $32,380 was from federal funds. These figures are from the college business office.

[32] "President's Annual Report, 1965–66," p. 2, 8, 23, 28, "1966–67," p. 8, 33, 36, "1967–68," p. 25; "Report of the Director of Development, 1966–67," p. 147, "1967–68," p. 123. In 1965 the college was given 142 acres of land north of St. Joseph, now called the Linneman Avian and Botanical Sanctuary.

[33] "Co-Institutional Study Report: College of Saint Benedict, Saint John's University," July 1968, p. 3 (quotation). The joint committee held 34 meetings between October, 1967, and June, 1968. That the investigations turned up opposing views regarding greater intercollege co-ordination and some problems in the current interchange was no surprise.

[34] "Co-Institutional Study Report," 8 (quotation); St. John's University and St. Benedict's College, "News Release," August 6, 1969; "Facts About the College of St. Benedict," news release, October, 1971. Dr. Sylvester P. Theisen, a St. John's sociology professor, was appointed co-ordinator for the two institutions in August, 1969. Three months earlier the Benedictine colleges and St. Cloud State had received $60,000 from the federal office of education to stimulate joint endeavors. In 1972–73 about 1,500 out of the 2,700 jointly enrolled students at St. Benedict's and St. John's shared time in a full academic exchange offering 35 majors, seven special programs, and eight preprofessional programs.

[35] "President's Annual Report, 1967–68," p. 2, 8, "1969–70," p. 5; taped interview of the author, July 10, 1969, with President Stanley J. Idzerda, in the collections of the Minnesota Historical Society; *Minneapolis Tribune, Picture Magazine*, October 24, 1971. By 1970 the board was composed of six religious and five laymen. The mother prioress of the community was chairman.

[36] "President's Annual Report, 1969–70," p. 2; "Report of the Registrar, 1969–70," p. 87, 89; "Report of the Dean, 1969–70," p. 140; Sister Nancy Hynes to the author, May 17, 1972. St. Benedict's enrollment continued to increase to 927 in the fall of 1972 and to 1,104 in the fall of 1973; college "News Release," January 12, 1973.

[37] "Report of the Dean, 1969–70," p. 9–14, 58, 61–82. A new faculty handbook was completed in February, 1970. Its section dealing with personnel policies was adopted by the corporate faculty.

[38] "Report of the Dean, 1969–70," p. 9, 25, 30, 36, 43, 49, 54; "Report of the Registrar, 1969–70," p. 88; "President's Annual Report, 1969–70," p. 1, 4. Fifty students from St. Benedict's and St. John's, along with three faculty members, spent two semesters in Luxembourg in 1969–70. Other programs involving study abroad are offered.

[39] "Report of the Registrar, 1969–70," p. 97; "Report of the Director of Placement, 1969–70," p. 120–123. Through 1970 the college had conferred a total of 2,352 degrees.

[40]*Minneapolis Tribune*, September 5, 1971; college "News Release," June 30, 1972. Many of these plans had been implemented by 1973 and the college was launched on a second five-year plan called "Continuing Directions"; Sister Nancy Hynes to Ms. Virginia Rahm, March 19, 1973 in MHS files.

[41]"Report of the Business Manager, 1969–70," p. 131, 137; "Report of the Vice-president of Development and Public Information, 1969–70," p. 124; interview with Terrance McKenna, business manager, January 27, 1971. Gifts and grants to the college in 1969–70 totaled about $277,000; the government provided $86,300 and foundations gave $44,700. The long-term debt in mid-1970 was approximately $3,000,000. The capital fund-raising campaign was launched in June, 1971; see *Landmarks* (June, 1971). About half of the stated goal of $4,785,000 had been pledged by July, 1972; Sister Nancy Hynes to Ms. Rahm, March 19, 1973.

[42]Interview with Dr. Idzerda, July 10, 1969; Sister Nancy Hynes to the author, May 17, 1972; St. Benedict's, "Fact Sheet," February, 1973. The building program included completion in 1972 of two sets of apartments, 23 mobile homes, and a Horsemanship Center with indoor and outdoor arenas and stabling facilities. Additional improvements in the physical education facilities and the renovation of the college dining rooms, the home and community service department, and the Center for Continuing Education were under way in 1972–73.

39. St. Mary's College, Part III
Pages 247 to 254

[1]*Winona Republican Herald*, October 2, 1939, January 9, 16, June 5, July 22, September 19, October 23, 1940, February 17, May 19, 27, 1941; *Catalogue*, 21 (1940), 81 (1941). St. Mary's was one of only a few colleges which were qualified to offer an advanced aviation course.

[2]*Winona Republican Herald*, October 20, December 6, 8, 1941; Gerard, ed., *Mississippi Vista*, 243, 245.

[3]Gerard, ed., *Mississippi Vista*, 59; *Terrace Heights News*, June, 1942; *Catalogue*, 16 (1943). The first increase in board and room since 1926 was made in 1942, from $300 a year to $200 a semester. Tuition was raised from $75 to $80 a term.

[4]*Our Sunday Visitor*, September 5, 19, 26, 1943, February 27, July 16, 30, December 10, 1944, April 15, May 20, June 24, September 9, 30, November 11, 1945, May 2, 1948; *Nexus*, September 29, 1945; *Terrace Heights News*, January, April, 1943. By the middle of 1945 at least 25 Marians had lost their lives in World War II.

[5]Gerard, ed., *Mississippi Vista*, 245; *Our Sunday Visitor*, May 6, September 9, 1945; *Catalogue*, 3 (1944). Two laymen were added to the board of trustees during World War II.

[6]*Our Sunday Visitor*, June 18, 1944, June 24, November 11, 1945, February 3, June 16, 1946, November 7, 1948, June 5, October 2, 1949; *Terrace Heights News*, September, 1947.

[7]*Our Sunday Visitor*, February 17, 1946, March 9, September 28, 1947, September 26, October 3, 1948, January 23, March 20, October 2, 23, 1949; *Terrace Heights News*, February, 1950, October, 1962. The city sewer was extended to the campus late in 1949. After enlargement, the dining hall could serve 400 persons at a time.

[8]*Our Sunday Visitor*, December 11, 16, 23, 1945, March 17, December 15, 22, 1946, May 18, 28, 1947, August 8, September 26, October 10, November 7, 21, 1948, February 27, December 18, 1949, January 22, February 26, 1950. In 1948 Brother Joel brought five foreign students to St. Mary's on scholarships.

[9]*Our Sunday Visitor*, August 1, 1948; *Catalogue*, 25 (1948), 79–83 (1949); "President's Annual Report, 1950–51," p. 3, in college archives. With $100,000 from Bishop Binz, the college offered each year 10 scholarships covering room, board, and tuition to seminarians of the Winona diocese. In the fall of 1950, when seminarians had their own room and board facilities, the scholarships were converted into 20 grants for tuition. In 1971 the provisions of the scholarship fund were changed to state that St. Mary's College "would reimburse Immaculate Heart of Mary Seminary by 25 per cent of the tuition charges of the college for seminarians who are residents of the Diocese of Winona with the annual amount to be not less than $2,000 nor more than $6,000." Thomas J. Ruddy, vice president of college relations, to Mrs. June D. Holmquist, April 6, 1973 in MHS files.

[10]*Our Sunday Visitor*, August 1, October 31, 1948, September 25, 1949, May 14, June 4, 18, July 2, October 1, 1950; *Winona Courier*, May 24, 1953, September 17, 1959, May 25, September 28, 1961; *Terrace Heights News*, April, June, September, 1950, October, 1962; seminary records. Bishop Kelly for whom Kelly Hall was named died in Rochester in June, 1950. Bishop Leo Binz succeeded him. By the fall of that year 91 priests had given or pledged $91,000 toward the cost of the Chapel of Saint John Vianney.

[11]*Terrace Heights News*, February, 1950; *Our Sunday Visitor*, January 28, 1950; *Catalogue*, 7 (March, 1953); "President's Report, 1950–51," p. 1. In mid-1950 an agreement was negotiated between the college and the La Salle Institute, a novitiate in Glencoe, Missouri, whereby the sum of $250,000 owed to the latter by St. Mary's would be transformed into a scholarship fund for the scholasticate on the Winona campus.

[12]"President's Annual Report, 1950–51," p. 5 and appendix, "1951–52," p. 21–23, "1952–53," p. 15–17, "1953–54," p. 16, "1954–55," p. 10–14; *Terrace Heights News*, August, September, 1950, September, 1955, March, 1956); *Our Sunday Visitor*, October 1, 1950. *Terrace Heights News* of October, 1958, gives a graphic representation of St. Mary's college enrollment from 1924 to 1958. Of the 655 students in early 1956, Illinois had contributed 341 and Minnesota 199 — a typical situation.

[13]*Winona Courier*, December 14, 1952; *Terrace Heights News*, November, December, 1952; "President's Report, 1952–53," p. 11. Between November, 1952, and January, 1953, administrators from St. Mary's held seven meetings with Winona leaders in the interest of the college. A professional firm was hired to conduct a fund drive in the local area.

[14]*Winona Republican Herald*, June 15, 1953; "President's Report, 1952–53," p. 11–14; *Terrace Heights News*, January, 1954; *Catalogue*, 18 (March, 1957).

[15]*Winona Courier*, September 23, 1954, May 9, 1957; *Terrace Heights News*, January, 1950, June, 1954, November–December, 1955, July, 1956, March, 1957, May, 1959, June, 1965; "President's Report, 1953–54," p. 6, "1954–55," p. 8, "1955–56," p. 9. A three-story wing to the scholastics' dormitory, St. Joseph's Hall, was built in 1954–55; it was paid for by the St. Louis Province. Alumni and other friends contributed money to build a greenhouse in 1958.

[16]*Terrace Heights News*, November, 1951, November–December, 1955, February, August, 1956, September, 1958; "President's Report, 1950–51," p. 5, "1952–53," p. 3, "1953–54," p. 1, "1955–56," p. 2; *Catalogue*, 41–115 (March, 1957). In 1953 the biology department offered the first of its seminars for nuns. Brother Ambrose helped secure at St. Mary's chapters of seven national honor societies.

[17]*Terrace Heights News*, April, 1950, June, 1955, February, 1956, April, 1960, January, 1965; "President's Report, 1950–51," p. 5, "1951–52," p. 10–12, "1952–53," p. 4, "1954–55," p. 9, "1959–60," p. 117, "1961–62," p. 5. In 1956 and in 1960, master's degrees conferred numbered 6 and 14, respectively; bachelor's degrees awarded in the same years

totaled 103 and 129. St. Mary's gained membership in the American Association for Teacher Education in 1956.

[18] "President's Report, 1950–51," p. 6, "1952–53," p. 2, 12, 21, "1953–54," p. 1, "1954–55," p. 1, "1955–56," p. 2, 11; *Catalogue*, 6–9 (July, 1951), 6–13 (March, 1957); *Terrace Heights News*, April, 1954, August, 1955, February, March, May, 1956. During the early 1950s, Brother Charles Severin, Monsignor Julius W. Haun, Dr. John J. Hoffman, and Robert M. Woods were among St. Mary's most influential and stimulating teachers.

[19] *Terrace Heights News*, November, 1950, October, 1951, August, 1956; *Catalogue*, 7 (March, 1957); "President's Report, 1951–52," p. 5, "1954–55," p. 2, "1955–56," p. 2. Football at St. Mary's fell on sad times in this period. In the autumn of 1951 by defeating Augsburg, St. Mary's achieved its first win in the MIAC since 1946. Finally "after several years of discussion and indecision," the faculty by a vote of 41 to 6 in December, 1954, decided to drop the sport. See *Terrace Heights News*, February, 1955.

[20] *Catalogue*, 123 (March, 1957); *Terrace Heights News*, October, 1959, September, 1960, September, 1961; "President's Report, 1957–58," p. 6, 15–16, "1961–62," p. 5, 8. Seminarians and scholastics were represented in all four college classes. On the novitiate, see p. 251, below.

[21] "President's Report, 1955–56," p. 6, "1956–57," p. 6, 9, "1957–58," p. 6, 8, 13, "1958–1959," p. 8, 11; *Winona Courier*, May 2, 1957, July 2, 1959; *Terrace Heights News*, May, August, 1957, January, April, August, 1958, July, 1959. In the fall of 1957 due to lack of space on campus, 73 freshmen, two student counselors, and one faculty member had to be housed in Winona's Park Hotel, and 37 upperclassmen had to find housing in the city.

[22] "President's Report, 1957–58," p. 7–9, "1958–59," p. 6, 8, 10; *Terrace Heights News*, May, August, November, 1958, June, October, 1959, January, February, 1960, October, 1963, February, 1965. The old chapel in St. Mary's Hall was converted into a library for periodicals. In 1962 it was taken over by the fine arts department, and two years later it became a 175-seat lecture hall.

[23] *President's Report, 1959–60*, 116, 118; *Terrace Heights News*, February, April, 1959, July, November, 1960, January, May, August, September, 1961. Early in December, 1958, a $100,000 fire destroyed the cattle barn and two other buildings on the college's main farm. The trustees then decided to cease farm operations. On March 7, 1959, some 500 people attended the auctioning of St. Mary's 156 registered Holsteins; they brought nearly $78,700. Altogether the farm sale totaled $141,000. The college still owned two farms, one of 725 acres and the other of 200 acres. "President's Report, 1958–59," p. 14.

[24] *President's Report, 1959–60*, 118, *1961–62*, 7, *1962–63*, 8; *Terrace Heights News*, October, November, 1960, January, May, August, 1961, January, 1962, March, 1963, January, 1964. In 1952 St. Mary's spent $23 per student on library expense, in 1961–62, $40.

[25] *President's Report, 1959–60*, 116, *1962–63*, 7, *1968–69*, n.p. (president's reports for the years 1963–64 through 1969–70 are unpaged); *Terrace Height News*, August, 1959, April, May, October, November, 1960, October, 1962, June, 1967; college "News Release," September 28, 1961, in the office of the director of communications. After four years at St. Mary's, the seminarians spent an equal length of time at a major seminary in New Hampshire. The first alumni of Damien Hall were ordained in June, 1967. The building was vacated by the Sacred Heart fathers in the spring of 1972 as part of a consolidation move, and Damien Hall was purchased by St. Mary's College for use as an academic facility.

[26] *President's Report, 1962–63*, 14 (quotation), *1963–64*; *Terrace Heights News*, June, 1958, January, 1961, March, September, October, 1962, July, 1963, Special Issue [September, 1963], January, 1964. Lewis, who died in 1960, had received an honorary degree at St. Mary's in 1958. Thomas P. Coughlan, a member of the college advisory board which had been organized in 1958, gave the stone for the center.

[27] "President's Report, 1957–58," p. 8, 10, 12, 21, "1958–59," p. 6, 12, 21, *1959–60*, 109, 116, *1961–62*, 5, 9, 16, *1962–63*, 4, 12; *Terrace Heights News*, September, 1958, January, 1960, April, June, 1961, July, 1962, January, May, 1963. By 1962 the debt on the Science Building and on De La Salle, St. Edward, and Benilde halls was more than $1,300,000, but this was not a matter of grave concern.

[28] "President's Report, 1956–57," p. 2, "1957–58," p. 4, "1958–59," p. 2–5, *1959–60*, 63, *1960–61*, 6, *1961–62*, 5; *Terrace Heights News*, November–December, 1956, March, 1957, September, October, 1958, February, October, 1960, October, 1961, January, 1965. See also p. 235, above.

[29] St. Mary's, *Revised Self- Study of 1960*, 32–39, 47–49 (Winona, 1961); "President's Report, 1956–57," p. 2, "1957–58," p. 4, "1958–59," p. 4, *1960–61*, 5, *1961–62*, 5, *1962–63*, 6, 9, 12; *Catalogue*, 43–46 (1963–65); *Terrace Heights News*, November, 1966. By the fall of 1966, 90 students were enrolled in the honors program.

[30] "President's Report, 1955–56," p. 7, "1956–57," p. 5, 7, "1957–58," p. 1–3, 8, 13, "1958–59," p. 1, *1959–60*, 99, *1960–61*, 4, *1961–62*, 4, 10; *Terrace Heights News*, August, 1955, February, March, July, September, October, 1956, March, April, October, 1957, May, November, 1958, March, 1959, February, 1961, July, 1962; *Revised Self-Study of 1960*, 41–46.

[31] *Terrace Heights News*, Special Issue, September, 1963. The functions of the president of the college and the religious superior of the community were separated in 1969.

[32] *President's Report, 1963–64*, *1965–66*, *1966–67*, *1967–68* (quotation), *1968–69*; *Terrace Heights News*, January, 1964, March, September, 1965, January, March, 1966, September, 1967, October, December, 1968; *Minneapolis Tribune*, June 13, 1968; *New Heights*, May, 1970, an alumni publication that briefly replaced *Terrace Heights News*. Dining facilities in 1967 were so limited that three shifts were necessary at each meal.

[33] *President's Report, 1967–68*; *Update*, 7 (quotation) (Fall, 1969), an alumni publication; *Saint Mary's College Center*, an undated illustrated brochure. On October 5, 1969, the old College Union was razed.

[34] *President's Report, 1963–64*, *1964–65*, *1966–67*, *1968–69*; *Catalogue*, 88–94 (1968–70); *Terrace Heights News*, February, May, September, 1966, December, 1968, January, 1969. An accounting internship program was introduced in 1965. With federal help a Spanish house was fashioned on the third floor of St. Mary's Hall in 1966, and a master's program for high school teachers of Spanish was instituted.

[35] *President's Report*, *1965–66*, *1966–67*, *1968–69*; registrar's files, copies in college archives; *Terrace Heights News*, October, 1964, August, October, 1966, August, 1967. Through a grant of $52,900 from the Hill Family Foundation in 1966, St. Mary's was able to publish a list of the combined holdings of the city and college libraries in Winona. In the fall of 1967 a jointly financed, tri-college cultural series of lectures, movies, and concerts was inaugurated.

[36] *President's Report, 1968–69*; *Terrace Heights News*, January, 1969; interview with Brother George Pahl, May 27, 1970; "Faculty and Administrative Staff Newsletter," September 8, 1970, in college archives. Both the General Chapter and the United States Regional Chapter of the Christian Brothers endorsed coeducation.

[37] *President's Report, 1963–64, 1965–66, 1966–67, 1968–69*; *Terrace Heights News*, January, April, 1965, March, June, 1966, February, May, August, September, November, 1967, February, December, 1968, May, 1969; *New Heights*, May, 1970. The first layman to serve as academic dean was appointed in 1970.

[38] *Terrace Heights News*, February, May, August, September (quotation), October, November, December, 1967, February, October, December, 1968, May, 1969; *Nexus*, October 17, 1969. Brother Gregory also had to deal with two faculty cases, which brought wide publicity to St. Mary's. The dismissal of an instructor in August, 1967, resulted in the censuring of the college by the American Association of University Professors. In May, 1969, after agreements had been worked out, the AAUP removed the censure. In the fall of 1968 a brother who headed the economics department was one of the 14 individuals who destroyed draft records in Milwaukee. He later received a prison sentence.

[39] *Terrace Heights News*, April, 1954, January, November, 1958, December, 1968, May (quotation), June, 1969; *Minneapolis Tribune*, October 23, 1968. In the summer of 1968 Brother George served as chairman of the first Mississippi River Research Consortium, a group of 65 people from 40 institutions which met at St. Mary's. The next year the college's biology department acquired 252 acres of flood plain across the river in Wisconsin and made it available to the newly incorporated Upper Mississippi River Environmental Studies Corporation.

[40] "Information for Decision-Making," 1–5, 8, 14–17, 25 (June, 1970), 1–3 (1970–71), irregular mimeographed statistical summaries issued by St. Mary's office of institutional research; memo from Brother George Pahl to the author, March 3, 1971. Through 1970 the college conferred 3,792 bachelor's and 412 master's degrees. The B.S. was discontinued after 1965.

[41] "Information for Decision-Making," 40–46 (June, 1970), 9–11 (1970–71).

[42] Memo from Brother George; "Information for Decision-Making," 28–39 (June, 1970), 7–9 (1970–71); St. Mary's, *Alumni Contact*, 2 (Fall, 1970). About 37 per cent of the 1970 class planned to attend graduate school.

[43] Memo from Brother George; "Information for Decision-Making," 47–51 (June, 1970); *Minneapolis Star*, August 24, 1970. The operating deficit in 1970–71 was $563,800; by 1971–72 it was reduced to $14,600, and expenditures were under budgeted allotments for the school year; *President's Report, 1971–72*.

[44] John Geary, "The Four-Year Experience," in *Update*, 15 (Spring, 1970). By 1972–73 women numbered 324 in the 1,135 total college registration; of these 149 were freshmen and 20 were seniors. See "Information for Decision-Making," 1, 2 (1972–73).

40. COLLEGE OF ST. SCHOLASTICA, PART III
Pages 255 to 261

[1] Somers, "All Her Ways," 40, 43, 49; "Reports of the President, 1941–48," p. 7, 14, 22–25, 30, 40, 43; Weygant, *Swinger of Birches*, 33; *Scriptorium*, January 12, October 11, 1944, April 10, 1946.

[2] *Three Year Program of the College of St. Scholastica Department of Nursing, Duluth, Minnesota, 1956–57*, 8; *Scriptorium*, April 26, 1944, May 23, 1945; Somers, "All Her Ways," 33, 42; "Reports of the President, 1941–48," p. 30; St. Scholastica, *College Bulletin*, 73 (1947).

[3] Somers, "All Her Ways," 41 (quotation); Weygant, *Swinger of Birches*, 32. The Duluth Symphony Orchestra in 1941 presented Mother Martina Hughes's symphonic interpretation of *The Highwayman* — a work which gained national attention — and in 1944 her composition *April, 1943*.

[4] Weygant, *Swinger of Birches*, 16, 32; information in priory archives.

[5] Somers, "All Her Ways," 39; "Reports of the President, 1941–48," p. 50, 55; *Scriptorium*, May 13, 27, 1942; *Bulletin*, 20 (1942–43), 24, 54 (1947). In 1940 the old farmhouse, which was located on the property when it was acquired by the sisters, was moved and renamed Tarry Hall to serve as a college store, post office, tearoom, bowling alley, and dormitory.

[6] *Scriptorium*, November 14, 1951, November 13, 1957; Somers, "All Her Ways," 40; Minnesota, *Laws*, 1949, p. 1065.

[7] *Bulletin*, 24, 28 (1950–51), 8, 17, 34, 50, 57 (1955–56), 77 (1959–61); *Three Year Program . . . Department of Nursing, 1956–57*, 8; *Scriptorium*, January 10, 1962.

[8] *Bulletin*, 11–15 (1945); Somers, "All Her Ways," 43, 44 (quotation); Weygant, *Swinger of Birches*, 32. Sister Raymond McLaughlin's study of *Religious Education and the State: Democracy Finds A Way* was published in 1967. On the alumni study, see p. 134, above.

[9] *Towers* (yearbook), 48–79 (1947), 24–38, 52–71 (1952). Oldest of the sororities was the Monocle Club, which had originated as a study group. Commuting students were organized in Alpha Chi, Tri Arts, and Phi Sigma.

[10] Somers, "All Her Ways," 86 (quotations); *Scriptorium*, January 23, 1952; *Bulletin*, 66 (1947); *Towers*, 9–14 (1947), 54, 65–70 (1952). A local unit of the National Federation of Catholic College Students was organized at St. Scholastica in 1947, and in December, 1951, the college became a member of the Confraternity of Christian Doctrine.

[11] Somers, "All Her Ways," 45–47; Birmingham, "A Second Look at the College of St. Scholastica, Duluth, Minnesota: A Report of the Graduates of the College, 1941–1951" (September 1, 1955); *Three Year Program . . . Department of Nursing, 1956–57*, 8.

[12] Birmingham, "A Second Look," 1, 17, 26. There were nearly 2,000 items on the questionnaire answered by 374 graduates, or 61 per cent of the total number between 1942 and 1951.

[13] Birmingham, "A Second Look," 1, 53–57, 92–95.

[14] Birmingham, "A Second Look," 5–13, 15.

[15] Birmingham, "A Second Look," 32, 83, 103–105.

[16] *Ford Foundation Grants in Minnesota* (September, 1963); *Towers*, 10–16 (1954); *Bulletin*, 14 (1955–56), 81 (1957–59); *Scriptorium*, April 25, 1955, November 12, 1958; *Duluth News-Tribune*, March 3, 1970; *Duluth Register*, November 29, 1963; "President's Report, 1962–63," p. 7.

[17] Birmingham, "A Second Look," 86, 106; *Towers*, 88–97, 102–117 (1954).

[18] Somers, "All Her Ways," 42; Weygant, *Swinger of Birches*, 26, 32; McDonald, *With Lamps Burning*, 223.

[19] Information in priory archives; *Duluth Register*, April 15, 1960; *Duluth News-Tribune*, March 27, 1966; Sister Mary Richard Boo to the author, March 9, 1970.

[20] Information in priory archives; Weygant, *Swinger of Birches*, 17.

[21] *Bulletin*, 86 (1959–61), 86 (1961–62), 86 (1962–64); *Duluth News-Tribune*, May 19, 1963, March 27, 1966; *Scriptorium*, January 10, 1962, January 16, May 15, 1963; Somers, "All Her Ways," 39; *Duluth Register*, September 11, 1964; "President's Report, 1962–63," p. 1; *Program: Ground Breaking Ceremony*, May 28, 1963.

[22] Weygant, *Swinger of Birches*, 27; *Duluth News-Tribune*, January 10, 1965, May 29, 1966, December 6, 1966; *Duluth Register*, June 25, 1965; *Duluth Herald*, November 16, 1965; *Bulletin*, 74 (1947), 88 (1966–68). In 1947 the library had 30,000 volumes; in 1966 the total was 56,000.

[23] *Bulletin*, 10, 29–31, 40, 64, 66, 77, 83 (1959–61), 11, 31, 79 (1962–64), 42, 58, 60, 70 (quotation) (1964–66), 10

(1966–68), 14, 20 (1968–69); *Duluth Register*, April 3, 1964, October 8, 1965; *Duluth News-Tribune*, October 2, 1965, January 16, 1966; "President's Report, 1959–60," p. 1. A college honors program was introduced in 1962.

²⁴ *Duluth News-Tribune*, February 19, June 1, July 23, 1967; *Minneapolis Tribune*, July 27, 1967; information in priory archives. In July, 1967, Dr. Gerald J. Kennedy, associate professor of history, succeeded Sister Mary Odile Cahoon as academic dean. He was the first layman to hold a high administrative position at the college. Sister Mary Richard retired from the presidency in 1971. Sister Mary Carol Braun served as acting president until September 1, 1971, when Francis X. Shea, S. J., was appointed, the first man to occupy the post in St. Scholastica's history.

²⁵ *Duluth News-Tribune*, January 16, March 27, May 27, 1966, September 19, October 10, 12, 1967, June 6, 1968, February 5, August 19, 1969; *Duluth Herald*, February 18, 1965, June 18, 1968; *Scriptorium*, October, November, 1967; *College of St. Scholastica: Science Center*, a descriptive brochure. Dedication of the center occurred October 11, 1969.

²⁶ *Duluth News-Tribune*, November 26, 1967, December 1, 1968; undated form letter from Vice President Rex Hudson quoting Dr. James A. Straubel, copy in author's files. A director of the National Laboratory for the Advancement of Education called the Duluth school system "one of the nation's most outstanding examples of innovative educational projects." See Thorwald Esbensen, *The Duluth Experience* (Palo Alto, Calif., 1968).

²⁷ *Duluth News-Tribune*, March 3, 1969; undated form letter from Hudson quoting Dr. Donald R. Stewart.

²⁸ *Bulletin*, 7 (1941–42), 5 (1968–69); registrar's files. In 1969 the number of credits needed for graduation was lowered from 198 to 180.

²⁹ *St. Paul Pioneer Press*, November 10, 1965; *Duluth News-Tribune*, December 17, 1967, June 14, 1970; *Duluth Herald*, February 12, 1968; registrar's files; *Minneapolis Tribune*, February 13, 1968; interview with Sister Mary Richard, February 11, 1971. The college did not plan to drastically alter its curriculum as a result of going coeducational, but it did intend to strengthen economics and library science.

³⁰ *Institute Echoes*, 40 (quotation), May, 1903; *Scriptorium*, 2 (quotation), April 10, 1946; *Duluth News-Tribune*, May 19, 1963, March 27, 1966.

³¹ *Bulletin*, 21 (1962–64), 11 (1968–69); *Duluth News-Tribune*, June 2, September 5, 1965, January 30, 1968; *Duluth Herald*, December 4, 1968.

³² Interview with Sister Mary Richard, February 11, 1971; memorandum from Harold D. Hultberg, college business manager, October 31, 1969; "President's Report, 1969–70," p. 7. In 1969–70 the college received grants and gifts in excess of $100,000 in private funds. By mid-1970, $1,186,000 was owed on Somers Hall and $1,500,000 on the new science hall. In 1972 a modular series of student apartments, known as "The Grove," was completed on campus.

³³ "President's Report, 1969–70," p. 6; *Bulletin*, 8 (1969–71).

³⁴ Interview with Sister Mary Richard, February 11, 1971; "President's Report, 1969–70," p. 1–4 (quotations), 8. The application of the Madrigal Singers for a United Service Organizations (USO) tour overseas in the spring of 1971 was approved in 1970. Two new fraternities were organized on campus in 1969–70.

³⁵ *Bulletin*, 50–54 (1969–71); interview with Sister Mary Richard, February 11, 1971; "President's Report, 1969–70," p. 2–4; *Duluth News-Tribune*, June 6, 1970.

³⁶ *Bulletin*, 12–44, 40–54 (1969–71); "President's Report, 1968–69," p. 14–17, "1969–70," p. 1–33 (quotations); *Duluth*

News-Tribune, June 14, August 5, 1970. In 1969 the college decided to confer only the B.A. degree.

³⁷ Interview with Sister Mary Richard, February 11, 1971. Sister Mary Richard favored renaming St. Scholastica as Greysolon Duluth College, in honor of the French explorer for whom the city of Duluth was named. Although the institution is still officially known as the College of St. Scholastica, it is often referred to simply as Scholastica College in recent publications.

³⁸ Interview with Sister Mary Richard, February 11, 1971; "President's Report, 1968–69," p. 2, "1969–70," p. 2.

³⁹ Interview with Sister Mary Richard, February 11, 1971.

41. CONCORDIA COLLEGE IN ST. PAUL, PART III
Pages 262 to 270

¹ Oswald B. Overn, *A History of Concordia College, St. Paul, Minnesota*, iv, 1 (St. Paul, [1967?]); *Concordia College Catalog*, 5 (1971–72). Concordia is one of 16 colleges and seminaries affiliated with the Lutheran Church — Missouri Synod.

² Overn, *Concordia College*, 1; interview with Harold W. Otte, acting president of Concordia, April 21, 1971. The Missouri Synod in 1969 had 2,875,000 baptized members.

³ Overn, *Concordia College*, 2–4 (quotation).

⁴ Overn, *Concordia College*, 4–6 (quotation).

⁵ Overn, *Concordia College*, 6, 191–193. Buenger died in September, 1943.

⁶ Overn, *Concordia College*, 6, 7, (quotation), 100.

⁷ Overn, *Concordia College*, 7, 116, 117 (quotation).

⁸ Overn, *Concordia College*, 8, 80; *Catalog*, 5 (1917).

⁹ Overn, *Concordia College*, 8, 117–119 (quotations).

¹⁰ Overn, *Concordia College*, 9, 17.

¹¹ Overn, *Concordia College*, 12, 17.

¹² Overn, *Concordia College*, 15.

¹³ Overn, *Concordia College*, 17–19, 82; *Catalog*, 6, 8–12 (1917). The term "junior college," applied here for clarity, was not in general use in the early 1900s.

¹⁴ Overn, *Concordia College*, 20, 83–85; *Twenty-fifth Anniversary of Concordia College, St. Paul, and Dedication of the Recitation Building, June 30, 1918*, in college library.

¹⁵ Overn, *Concordia College*, 22, 101. The *Catalog*, 60 (1920) contains a resumé of Concordia's development to that time.

¹⁶ Overn, *Concordia College*, 23, 109, 111. Professor Overn was the science teacher called in 1920.

¹⁷ Overn, *Concordia College*, 21; University of Minnesota Committee on Educational Research, "The Junior College in Minnesota," 4 (Report no. 6 — August, 1946), copy in the University of Minnesota Archives.

¹⁸ Overn, *Concordia College*, 21, 28–31, 85–88; *Catalog*, 11 (1926), 13 (1931). Between 1919 and 1926, 49 Norwegian students attended Concordia. They belonged to a faction of the old Norwegian Synod which opposed the church merger of 1917 and had thereby been left without a school they could support. In June, 1927, Bethany College of Mankato became this splinter group's official educational institution.

¹⁹ Overn, *Concordia College*, 26–30, 194; *Catalog*, last page (1927), 3 (1928). Graebner had also been admitted to the bar in 1914. Until his assumption of the presidency, Concordia had functioned without an office secretary. At that time the daughter of the steward was hired for $35 a month.

²⁰ Overn, *Concordia College*, 119, 136, 138; *Catalog*, 11 (1928), 14 (1935). In the late 1920s board and room was $100 a year, and tuition for nonministerial candidates was $100. By 1935 college tuition was $80 a year, a result of the depression.

²¹ Overn, *Concordia College*, 122–125, 127–130, 138, 144

(quotation); *Catalog*, 10 (1926). From 1928 to 1948 the June issue of the *Concordia Comet* was enlarged to serve as a yearbook, since the earlier *Concordia Moccasin* had placed too heavy a financial burden on the small student body.

²² Overn, *Concordia College*, 32, 35, 37, 110; *Catalog*, 6 (1931), 14 (1937–38), 14 (1941–42).

²³ Overn, *Concordia College*, 33, 111.

²⁴ Overn, *Concordia College*, 35, 101–103 (quotation); *Catalog*, 11–14 (1939–40).

²⁵ Overn, *Concordia College*, 38; *Catalog*, 14 (1943–44).

²⁶ Overn, *Concordia College*, 38–41.

²⁷ Overn, *Concordia College*, 43–47, 53, 196–198; *Minneapolis Tribune*, May 19, 1946; *Catalog*, 2 (1947–48). In 1947 Graebner represented the Lutheran Church in Europe, advising church groups and assisting in the distribution of relief funds. He died suddenly at his home in St. Paul in November, 1950.

²⁸ Overn, *Concordia College*, 46, 246.

²⁹ Overn, *Concordia College*, 46–50, 112.

³⁰ Overn, *Concordia College*, 112 (quotation), 147; *Catalog*, 8 (1953–54). The three-quarter system replaced the two-semester calendar in 1953 in the college department. The high school retained the semester plan.

³¹ Overn, *Concordia College*, 49, 54, 88–92, 106–108; *Catalog*, 8 (1951–52). Siebert, a former big-league player, has been baseball coach at the University of Minnesota since 1947.

³² Overn, *Concordia College*, 59, 93–95; *Catalog*, 22 (1960–62).

³³ Overn, *Concordia College*, 51; *Catalog*, 11 (1951–52).

³⁴ Overn, *Concordia College*, 52, 55, 62, 246.

³⁵ Overn, *Concordia College*, 104.

³⁶ Overn, *Concordia College*, 67–70.

³⁷ Overn, *Concordia College*, 65, 70–72, 113–115, 187; *Catalog*, 89 (1963–64), 5 (1965–66), 5, 78 (1968–69). During its 74 years, the high school graduated 2,146 students. "President's Annual Report, 1966–67," p. 24; Harold W. Otte, "Report of Concordia College to Milwaukee Convention, July 9–16, 1971," in college files.

³⁸ Overn, *Concordia College*, 65, 186.

³⁹ Overn, *Concordia College*, 81, 95–99, 232–237; *Minneapolis Star*, June 4, 1970; *President's Annual Report, 1968–69*, 6, 10–12; *Catalog*, 7 (1971–72); interview with Acting President Otte, April 21, 1971. The Ebenezer Thankoffering was a synod drive in the mid-1960s which raised $18,000,000 for various church endeavors.

⁴⁰ *Minneapolis Star*, June 2, 1970; *President's Annual Report, 1968–69*, 1, *1969–70*, 1–4 (quotation); *Catalog*, 6 (1971–72); Otte, "Report of Concordia to Milwaukee Convention, 1971"; Overn, *Concordia College*, 96; undated Metropolitan Teacher Education Program brochure (quotation). In 1959 a city block contiguous to the campus was purchased for $400,000. This gain in area was offset two years later when the football field (bought in 1948 for $40,000) was taken over by the state for a highway which opened in 1968–69. The college received $320,000 for the land. That same year a block of property adjacent to the new athletic field was acquired. Dr. Poehler died in December, 1971.

⁴¹ *President's Annual Report, 1968–69*, 16, *1969–70*, 4, 8; *Catalog*, 16, 29, 87–90 (1971–72); *Summer School Bulletin* (1971). The preministerial course is two years in duration; its graduates normally transfer to the senior college in Fort Wayne, but a growing number remain at Concordia to receive a B.A. degree before pursuing seminary studies.

⁴² *President's Annual Report, 1968–69*, 20–22, 26, *1969–70*, 10; Overn, *Concordia College*, 177, 182; Mrs. Omar F. Smith, president's secretary, to the author, April 21, 1971.

⁴³ "Report of Concordia to Milwaukee Convention, 1971"; *Catalog*, 9, 71–74 (1971–72); *President's Annual Report,*

1968–69, 2. Concordia's board of control in 1970 consisted of six men, two of whom were ministers. In 1971 Concordia became a member of the Tri-State Athletic Conference, composed of Bethel, Northwestern, Sioux Falls, Westmar, and Yankton colleges located in Minnesota, Iowa, and South Dakota. See "Athletic Brochure," Spring, 1971.

⁴⁴ *Minneapolis Star*, January 26, March 20, 1971; Concordia College, "News Release," March 15, 1971; Harvey A. Stegemoeller, in an open letter addressed to "Dear Pastor," April 28, 1971 (quotation) — both in college files.

42. BETHEL COLLEGE, PART III
Pages 271 to 279

¹ Adolf Olson, *A Centenary History As Related to the Baptist General Conference of America*, 2, 407 (Chicago, 1952); David Guston and Martin Erikson, eds., *Fifteen Eventful Years: A Survey of the Baptist General Conference, 1945–1960*, 12 (Chicago, 1961); "Report of a Visit to Bethel College for the Commission on Colleges and Universities of the North Central Association," 4, March 10, 11, 1969, in college archives; Bethel Institute, *Bulletin*, 7–9 (October, 1936). Bethel's bimonthly newsletters and catalogs both carry the title of *Bulletin*. The first general gathering of Swedish Baptists in this country was held at Village Creek, Iowa, in 1879. The church adopted a constitution at Moline, Illinois, the following year. In 1945 the word Swedish was deleted from the body's official name, leaving it the Baptist General Conference of America. In 1959 the title was shortened to the Baptist General Conference.

² Olson, *Centenary History*, 1, 6–22, 24, 31, 35, 52, 66, 79, 85, 106, 131, 145. In 1866 of 15 Swedish Baptist churches in the United States, nine were located in Minnesota. By 1950 there were 70,000 Baptists in Sweden.

³ Olson, *Centenary History*, 153–155, 159–162, 165; Adolf Olson and Virgil A. Olson, *Seventy-five Years: A History of Bethel Theological Seminary, St. Paul, Minnesota, 1871–1946*, 8, 21, 25–28 (Chicago, [1946]). During his first seven years with Union Theological Seminary, Edgren had to raise funds for his own salary; even thereafter he was paid less than the American professors. His opposition to divorce and to secret societies created conflicts with some other teachers. A woman was admitted to the seminary in 1879.

⁴ Olson, *Centenary History*, 165, 176, 407, 415, 418; *Bulletin*, 7–9 (October, 1936); Olson and Olson, *Seventy-five Years*, 31–39. In 1892 the Baptist seminary, then called the "Swedish Department of the Baptist Union Theological Seminary," united with the young University of Chicago as part of its divinity school. See Olson and Olson, 36.

⁵ Olson, *Centenary History*, 423, 432, 490; Olson and Olson, *Seventy-five Years*, 43. Bethel Academy opened in Elim Church in Minneapolis in October, 1905. A new building on Como Avenue was provided for the school in the fall of 1907. The institution suffered from a chronic shortage of funds.

⁶ Olson, *Centenary History*, 434, 489, 492; Olson and Olson, *Seventy-five Years*, 37, 44–46. Between 1888 and 1914, 369 students had enrolled in the Swedish seminary at Morgan Park and about 175 of them had graduated.

⁷ Olson, *Centenary History*, 494; Olson and Olson, *Seventy-five Years*, 48, 52; "Self-Survey of Bethel College, 1957–58: A Report Submitted to the Commission on Colleges and Universities of the North Central Association of Colleges and Secondary Schools," 240, June, 1958, in college archives. A power plant costing $8,000 was also constructed in 1914.

⁸ Olson, *Centenary History*, 434, 600; Olson and Olson, *Seventy-five Years*, 49, 53; *Bulletin*, 20 (April, 1930). Graduates of the seminary between 1892 and 1928 numbered 250.

[9] Olson and Olson, *Seventy-five Years*, 55, 57; *Bulletin*, 7 (April, 1931), 22 (April, 1937).

[10] *Bulletin*, 47 (April, 1929), 45–54 (June, 1929), 5–11 (Midwinter Number, 1928–29). The institute also operated a preparatory department for students who needed work of eighth-grade level. There were 16 students registered in it in 1928.

[11] *Bulletin*, 5 (Midwinter Number, 1928–29), 12, 27 (June, 1930).

[12] *Bulletin*, 16–18, 43 (May, 1928).

[13] *Bulletin*, 42–44 (May, 1928), 7 (Midwinter Number, 1928–29).

[14] *Bulletin*, 62 (April, 1934), 11, 53, 57 (April, 1936); Olson and Olson, *Seventy-five Years*, 58. There were 36 students in the seminary in 1935–36.

[15] Olson, *Centenary History*, 497; Olson and Olson, *Seventy-five Years*, 58; *Bulletin*, 7 (April, 1931), 6 (April, 1938).

[16] *Bulletin*, 7, 37 (quotation) (April, 1931).

[17] Olson, *Centenary History*, 498; *Bulletin*, 3–5, 8–12 (August, 1932).

[18] *Bulletin*, 36–41 (April, 1931), 13–15, 36 (April, 1932), 8 (April, 1937), 4 (October, 1937). Walfred Danielson, a 1918 graduate of Macalester College, was the first dean of the junior college. In 1936 he was succeeded by Emory A. Johnson, who had graduated from the University of Minnesota in 1930.

[19] *Bulletin*, 35, 38–43, 72 (April, 1932), 17 (December, 1932), unpaged (June, 1933), 13, 22 (April, 1934), 15, 17, 21 (April, 1937), 4 (March, 1941). A University of Minnesota study covering the period 1939–41 found that religious influences ranked very high in attracting students to Bethel. The same was true in 1952. See "Report of Self-Study Carried Out at Bethel College, St. Paul, Minnesota, 1951–52," p. 7, submitted to the North Central Association of Colleges and Secondary Schools; copy in college archives.

[20] *Bulletin*, [5] (October, 1932), [4] (November, 1933), 15 (April, 1934), [2–4] (January, 1936), 10 (March, 1941), 9 (May, 1941). As late as 1940, it cost only about $370 to attend Bethel for a year — $100 tuition, $235 for board and room, $18 for books, $11 to $25 in fees.

[21] *Bulletin*, 38 (January, 1939), [1] (April 1, 1940), [1] (January, 1941), 12 (May, 1941), [1] (July, 1941), unpaged (November, 1941), [3] (November, 1942). By November, 1942, cash receipts for the dormitory unit totaled $51,800 and unpaid pledges $9,800.

[22] *Bulletin*, 6, 8 (May, 1941), 1, 4 (March, 1943); Olson and Olson, *Seventy-five Years*, 61; Henry C. Wingblade, *Windows of Memory: Memories that Warm the Heart* (Chicago, 1961). President Wingblade's formal inauguration occurred on February 26, 1943.

[23] *Bulletin*, [4] (March, 1942), [1] (July, 1942), [3] (September–October, 1945). The flag is pictured on the cover of the July–August, 1944, *Bulletin*. By 1942 Bethel had sent a total of 83 graduates to foreign lands as missionaries, according to August Berg, "Bethel and Missions," in *Bulletin*, [2] (September, 1942).

[24] *Bulletin*, [2, 5] (November, 1942), [1] (January, 1943), [20] (July–August, 1944), [4] (September–October, 1944), [1, 3] (September–October, 1945), 13 (quotation) (January, 1947); "Self-Survey, 1957–58," p. 240; Wingblade, *Windows of Memory*, 161. According to the *Bulletin* (October, 1946), with veterans back in school, Bethel enrollment was 466. The first Founders' Week was held on campus in February, 1943.

[25] *Bulletin*, [3] (July–August, 1944), [3] (March–April, 1945), 2, 11 (June, 1946); "Report of Self-Study, 1951–52," p. 1; "Self-Survey, 1957–58," p. 3; Guston and Erikson, *Fifteen Eventful Years*, 132. In the fall of 1945, Bethel replaced the semester system with the three-quarter calendar. By 1946 the cost of attending the junior college was about $564 a year, $200 more than in 1940.

[26] Guston and Erikson, *Fifteen Eventful Years*, 140–142; "Report of Self-Study, 1951–52," p. 3; Wingblade, *Windows of Memory*, 146; *Bulletin*, 11–13 (June, 1947), 11 (June, 1948). In 1946–47 the *Bulletin's* name was changed to *Bulletin of Bethel College and Seminary* to reflect the conference's change in the name of the institution. In designing the senior college curriculum, Bethel's Dean C. Emanuel Carlson consulted regularly with University of Minnesota officials. The state institution approved the four-year program at Bethel in February, 1951.

[27] *Bulletin* (August, 1947), 4, 31 (June, 1948); "Self-Survey, 1957–58," p. 239. Bethel initiated collegiate football competition in the fall of 1947, playing various junior colleges at Rochester, Austin, and Estherville, Iowa. Home games were played on the Ramsey High School field.

[28] Guston and Erikson, *Fifteen Eventful Years*, 141, 147; "Report of Self-Study, 1951–52," p. 21–23, 25, 27, 36, 70; "Self-Survey, 1957–58," p. 115, 119, 131, 155, 236–238, 240. In 1953 the old gymnasium in the academy building was converted to a lounge, coffee shop, and bookstore at a cost of $35,000. The library had 42,000 books in 1958.

[29] Wingblade, *Windows of Memory*, 151.

[30] Guston and Erikson, *Fifteen Eventful Years*, 134, 136–138, 143, 151; "Report of Self-Study, 1951–52," p. 38; "Self-Survey, 1957–58," p. 13, 29–57, 67, 72, 75–82, 86, 232, 235, 265; *President's Report, 1955–56*, 2–7, 10, *1956–57*, 7, *1957–58*, 6, *1958–59*, 19. The seminary and the college held separate faculty meetings. Matters of mutual concern were handled by four joint committees. A teacher's tenure was reviewed every five years by the church board of education, but in no case did the latter revoke anyone's tenure.

[31] Guston and Erikson, *Fifteen Eventful Years*, 141; *President's Report, 1957–58*, 12, *1958–59*, 13–15. North Central examiners noted that Bethel's educational task was clearly defined and accepted by the faculty; the strong administration enjoyed a good relationship with the Baptist General Conference.

[32] Wingblade, *Windows of Memory*, 191–195; Guston and Erikson, *Fifteen Eventful Years*, 131–133; "Self-Survey, 1957–58," p. 182. In 1956 the search for a new dean ended when Professor Clifford E. Larson, head of the department of religious education, accepted the position.

[33] Guston and Erikson, *Fifteen Eventful Years*, 131 (quotation); "Self-Survey, 1957–58," p. 14; *President's Report, 1955–56*, 2, 11. Bethel was admitted to the Minnesota Association of Colleges in 1956. By May 1, 1957, Swedish Baptists had 465 churches and 61,700 members.

[34] "Self-Survey, 1957–58," p. 171, 235, 242; David O. Moberg, "Long-Range Planning: A Report of a Faculty Committee to the Board of Education," August 15, 1959, in college archives. The Snelling Avenue campus in 1958 contained 8.3 acres.

[35] Moberg, "Long-Range Planning," 1–4, 17, 167, 217–222, 257 (1959). In 1957–58 the Royal Investment Corporation was formed to secure and hold a site in suburban Arden Hills some five miles north of Bethel's campus.

[36] M. G. Neale, "A Program for the Development of Bethel College [and] Bethel Theological Seminary, 1961–71," April 24, 1961, in college archives; *President's Report, 1959–60*, [21], *1960–61*, [18–22], *1965–66* [2, 3] (quotation). "Decade Ten" refers to Bethel's age.

[37] Neale, "Program for Development," 34; *President's Report, 1961–62*, [18], *1962–63*, [11]; "Self-Survey, 1957–58," p. 148, 160. About 316 students lived on campus and slightly over 240 off campus in 1958. Total enrollment in the fall of 1962 was 850, of whom 126 were in the seminary.

[38] Guston and Erikson, *Fifteen Eventful Years*, 139; *President's Report, 1957–58*, 16, *1958–59*, 3; "Self-Survey, 1957–58," p. 22–24. Bethel stresses preparation for vocations which involve a maximum of human relations.

[39] "Self-Survey, 1957–58," p. 14, 156, 200, 207, 214, 219–222, 224, 227, 230; Guston and Erikson, *Fifteen Eventful Years*, 149; *President's Report, 1956–57*, 3, 15, *1959–60*, [9], *1962–63*, [14], *1963–64*, 11–13, 15, 19. Bethel regarded its federal loans of the mid-1950s for residence construction as banking transactions, not as subsidies. As late as 1957–58 only $18,500 had been allocated in scholarships and grants. "Self-Survey, 1957–58," 156.

[40] "Self-Survey, 1957–58," p. 15, 200, 207, 220; Moberg, "Long-Range Planning," 226 (1959); *President's Report, 1957–58*, 5–7, *1959–60*, [5, 6, 9], *1963–64*, [22]; Guston and Erikson, *Fifteen Eventful Years*, 149–151. The cost of the college's program in 1959–60 was $507,400; that of the seminary was $160,700.

[41] *President's Report, 1961–62*, [4, 23], *1962–63*, [19, 20].

[42] *President's Report, 1964–65*, [5], *1965–66*, [10, 15], *1967–68*, [13]; *The Time Is Always Out of Joint*, 4, 6, 8–10, 16, 18, 22–25 (St. Paul, [1970?]), a booklet published by the college. Enrollment in the seminary in 1968 was 217. Bethel had been fully accredited by the American Association of Theological Schools the previous year.

[43] *President's Report, 1964–65*, [6], *1967–68* [13], *1968–69*, inside back cover; *Catalog*, 3, 12 (April, 1970). Bethel's gross assets between 1961 and 1966 rose from $2,800,000 to $6,000,000. Long-term indebtedness in mid-1970 stood at $2,500,000. Tuition then was $825 a semester; board and room averaged about $375 a semester.

[44] *President's Report, 1967–68*, [26] (quotation); *The Time Is Always Out of Joint*, 10–13, 25.

[45] *President's Report, 1962–63*, [20], *1963–64*, [5, 6], *1967–68*, [7]; "Basic Institutional Data, transmitted to North Central Association, February 14, 1969," p. 56, in college archives; *Bulletin*, 102 (April, 1969). Virgil A. Olson, a graduate of Macalester College in 1938 and of Bethel Seminary in 1941, became vice president and dean of the college in 1968.

[46] *Catalog*, 62 (1970–71); interview with Burton Wessman, vice president for business affairs, February 8, 1971.

[47] "Basic Institutional Data," 12, 21, 25, 28, 39–43, 51, 56, 76, 84, 86 (1969); *Catalog*, 55–59 (1970–71). Of the entire student body in 1968, 43 per cent listed education as their vocational goal and 14 per cent the ministry, according to the *President's Report, 1967–68*, [13].

[48] *President's Report, 1967–68*, [5] (quotation); *The Time Is Always Out of Joint*, 14–17, 24. Bethel is now a member of the Minnesota Private College Fund, but the college and seminary do not participate in gifts from sources "inconsistent with Bethel's emphases," according to *President's Report, 1967–68*, [21]. The institution's current operations have again been in the black in the early 1970s.

[49] *President's Report, 1968–69*, [12, 13] (quotations). About 400 freshmen enrolled in the college in the fall of 1970, the largest number in its history. Bethel's fall 1972 full-time enrollment was 1,163.

[50] *President's Report, 1968–69*, [5] (quotation).

Index

241; St. Mary's, 127, 251, 252; St. Scholastica, 134; Concordia S, 264, 267; Bethel, 275. *See also* Athletics

HADLEY, ARTHUR T., 72
Haggerty, Melvin E., 108
Hagstrom, Rev. G. Arvid, career, 272, 274
Hagstrom (G. A.) Residence, Bethel, 274, 278
Hamline, Bishop Leonidas L., 8
Hamline College of Medicine, 12
Hamline University (St. Paul), 201; origins and name, 2, 7, 8; student activities and organizations, 4–6, 10–12, 52–59, 67, 112, 156, 158–160; church sponsor, 4, 7–10, 12, 55–59, 156, 157, 159; at Red Wing, 7–10; campus and buildings, 7–10, 11, 12, 52, 54–59, 154, 157, 158, 159; tuition and fees, 8, 10, 11, 55–58, 159; closed and proposed relocations, 8–10, 56, 57, 159; curriculum, 8, 10–12, 54, 55, 59, 154–158, 160; preparatory school, 8, 10–12, 54, 90; faculty, 8, 11, 12, 54–59, 144, 155–159; finances, 8–12, 54–59, 154–160, 173; enrollment, 8–12, 55–59, 154, 155, 157, 158; alumni, 9, 10, 12, 55–59, 154–156, 158–160, 173; accreditation, 48, 55, 57, 58; Phi Beta Kappa attempts, 55, 57, 155; trustees, 55–59, 155, 156, 158, 159; intercollege relations, 112, 144, 202, 210, 212, 226, 228, 272; graduate program, 155, 156; centennial, 155, 158
Hamm Foundation, 165
Hansen, Fr. James, author, 61
Harbo, Leif S., career, 189
Harkness, Edward S., 75
Hartford Theological Seminary (Conn.), alumni, 82
Hartke, Sen. Vance, 270
Harvard University (Mass.), 54, 148; curriculum, 3, 142; alumni, 71, 181, 184; faculty, 163
Hauge's Norwegian Evangelical Lutheran Synod, merger, 85, 102, 103
Haun, Fr. Julius W., 127
Hawes, Gene R., quoted, 152
Hazen Foundation, 181
Healy, Sister Mary Edward, career, 228, 229
Heffron, Bishop Patrick R., career, 39, 114–116, 125–129, 233
Heffron Hall, St. Mary's, 127, 247
"Heifer Hall," St. Mary's, 130
Hendrickson, Henrik, career, 81
Henry, Edward L., 167
Higher Education Facilities Acts, *1963, 1965*, 147, 230, 242, 259
Hilger, Sister M. Inez, 242
Hill, James J., 3, 49, 144; college

benefactor, 12, 20, 37, 40, 54, 56, 68, 74, 84, 90, 272
Hill, Louis W., Sr., 144
Hill (Louis W. and Maud) Family Foundation, founded, 144; intercollege grants, 144, 155, 157, 166, 167, 202, 210, 213, 226, 242, 245; Hamline grant, 157; St. John's, 166, 168; Gustavus, 173; Carleton, 182; St. Olaf, 198; Macalester, 201; St. Thomas, 211, 214; Concordia M, 221; St. Catherine, 227; St. Teresa, 234
Hill (James J.) Reference Library, 144, 210
Hilleboe, Gertrude M., 86
Hilleboe Hall, St. Olaf, 194
Held, John, Jr., 51
Hobart, Rev. Chauncey, 7
Hodgman, Thomas M., career, 89–91
Hoffman, Fr. Alexius, author, 61
Hoffman, John J., 128, 249
Hoffman Hall, St. Mary's, 249
Holden, academy, 30
Holland Hall, St. Olaf, 86
Holvik, Johan A., 105
Holy Cross Congregation of Notre Dame, administers St. Thomas, 98, 99
Hong, Howard V., 195
Hope Academy (Moorhead), founded, 41
Houston, Baptist church, 271
Hoyme Memorial Chapel, St. Olaf, 83, 86, 196
Hoyum, Jacob, family, 220
Hoyum Hall, Concordia M, 220
Huber, Sister Alberta (Fides), career, 229, 231
Hughes, Rev. Alfred F., career, 57, 58
Hughes, Mother Martina, career, 255, 258
Humanities Center, Concordia M, 221
Humphrey, Hubert H., 160, 205
Hunt, Claude J., 74
Hunter College (N.Y.), 239
Hutchins, Robert M., 65
Hvidsten Hall, Concordia M, 220

IDZERDA, STANLEY J., career, 245, 246
Illinois, 271, 273; seminaries and colleges, 17, 53, 85, 167, 263, 267; students from, 130, 181, 236, 250, 278
Illinois Institute of Technology (Chicago, Ill.), 201, 249
Immaculate Heart of Mary Seminary, 248, 249, 250, 253
Immigrants and immigration, German, 13, 262; Scandinavian, 17, 25, 30, 31, 271
Incarnation Church (Minneapolis), 208

India, students from, 274
Indiana, 57, 167, 270
Institute Echoes, founded, 132, 133
Institute for Ecumenical and Cultural Research, St. John's, 160
Institute of International Education, scholarships, 111
Institutum Divi Thomae (Cincinnati, Ohio), 255
International Business Machines, Inc., ·Rochester, 251
Iowa, 25, 53, 97, 155, 167, 193, 248; students from, 111, 224, 236, 254, 270, 278
Iowa State College (Ames), 217, 219
Iowa State University, 57, 92, 155
Ireland, Archbishop John, 114; St. Thomas founder, 38–40, 95–97, 99, 100, 209; St. Catherine supporter, 106–109
Ireland, Mother Seraphine, career, 106–109
Ireland Hall, St. Thomas, 96, 99
Irish-Americans, 38, 111

JACKSON, REV. ANDREW, 17, 18
Japan, 182
Jeanne d'Arc Auditorium, St. Catherine, 107
Jerome, Brother Landrick, career, 247
John, Rev. David C., career, 10, 11
Johns Hopkins University (Md.), 3, 16
Johnson, Emory A., 275
Johnson, Gov. John A., 54, 68
Johnson, Julia M., 91
Johnson, Rev. Oscar J., career, 68–71
Johnson Hall, Gustavus, 68, 169, 170, 172
Jones, Howard Mumford, quoted, 145
Jones, Richard Uriah, 91
Junior college movement, in U.S., 146, 264–267, 269, 273–275

KAGIN, EDWIN, quoted, 89
Kalamazoo College (Mich.), calendar, 150
Kaposia, 7
Kappa Beta Kappa, Concordia M, 218
Kappa Gamma Pi, St. Scholastica, 137
Kapsner, Mother Cecilia, 119, 120, 121
Katz, Joseph, quoted, 149
Katzner, Fr. John, 61
Kaydet, founded, 100
Keane, Fr. James J., career, 39, 40
Kellogg, Frank B., 75
Kelly, Bishop Francis M., career, 126, 127, 129, 130, 232
Kelly Hall, St. Mary's, 248